THE SECOND PARTITION OF POLAND

A STUDY IN DIPLOMATIC HISTORY

BY

ROBERT HOWARD LORD

AMS PRESS
NEW YORK

Reprinted from the edition of 1915, Cambridge
First AMS EDITION published 1969
Manufactured in the United States of America

(15-25072)

Library of Congress Catalogue Card Number: 73-101268

AMS PRESS, INC.
New York, N.Y. 10003

TO

MY FATHER

PREFACE

THE diplomatic history of the Second Partition of Poland has never hitherto been made the subject of a monograph. It has by no means escaped attention, but it has always been treated as a matter of secondary or collateral interest: it has been adduced to explain the policy of the great Powers during the Eastern and Northern wars of 1787–92, or in connection with the formation and collapse of the First Coalition against Revolutionary France, or again as a chapter in the long struggle between Poland and Russia; it has not been studied as a whole, by and for itself.

The serious investigation of the diplomatic questions connected with the Second Partition began in the sixth decade of the last century with Häusser's *Deutsche Geschichte* (1854–57), Herrmann's *Geschichte des russischen Staates* (vol. vi, 1860), Zinkeisen's *Geschichte des osmanischen Reiches* (vol. vi, 1859), and Sybel's *Geschichte der Revolutionszeit* (1853 ff.). The first three of these works were based chiefly on the records of the Prussian and Saxon archives and on private papers (particularly Diez's), and, owing to the scantiness of their sources, they went very far astray both in general conceptions and in matters of detail. Greatly superior to all of them was Sybel's masterly work, especially in view of the corrections and additions made in the successive editions through which it passed. In it most of the questions that have since been debated were raised, and many of them were practically settled. The '60s were filled by a rather acrimonious controversy between Herrmann and Sybel with regard to the policy of Leopold II; and a little later Sybel engaged in lively polemics with Vivenot and Hüffer about the falling-out of Austria and Prussia over the Polish Question, and especially about the character and policy of Thugut. Researches on all these problems entered upon a new stage when towards 1870 the Viennese archives were finally thrown open freely to scholars. In the next twenty years investigations and publications of the

Austrian sources followed thick and fast. The predominant interest, however, was usually in the Revolutionary War; and the Polish Question, which had previously been brought forward chiefly in order to cover either Austria or Prussia with ignominy, ceased to attract much attention from German historians when the political rivalry between Berlin and Vienna came to an end. Of late years controversy in this field has centered chiefly about the period of the Oriental crisis, and especially about the policy of Hertzberg, although a few recent monographs (Schrepfer's and Heidrich's, for instance), would seem to indicate a revival of interest in the early Revolutionary period.

In Russia, the first important work on subjects connected with the Second Partition was Blum's biography of Sievers (1853). Some years later Smitt's *Suworow* (1858) and Solov'ev's *History of the Downfall of Poland* (the Russian edition in 1863, the German in 1865) gave the first accounts based on the documents of the Russian archives, and brought to light a multitude of invaluable facts. Since the appearance of Kostomarov's *Last Years of the Polish Republic* and Ilovaïski's *Diet of Grodno* (both in Russian) in 1870, Russian historical writing on this subject has virtually come to a standstill, although the publication of sources in Russia has continued uninterruptedly — and on a scale seldom paralleled.

For Polish historians the period of the downfall of the Republic has always had an intense, if painful, fascination. If the older writers (Lelewel, Schmitt, Bobrzyński, e. g.) intent chiefly upon explaining the catastrophe according to the *a priori* ideas of the ' monarchist ' or the ' republican ' school, had contented themselves with a very inadequate knowledge of facts, Korzon's elaborately documented and admirably scientific *Internal History of Poland in the Reign of Stanislas Augustus* (1887) gave for the first time a secure basis for judging the moral, economic, and political forces of the nation in that crucial period. While Polish scholars have busied themselves preëminently with the study of domestic conditions, Kalinka, Dembiński, and Askenazy have also made important contributions to the diplomatic history of that age by extensive investigations in foreign archives.

At present the literature relating to the Polish crisis of 1788–93 and to the Second Partition is immense.

Of the various collections of printed sources, one of the most important is Vivenot's *Quellen zur Geschichte der deutschen Kaiserpolitik Oesterreichs*, which, for the period from January, 1790 to April, 1793, contains many letters of the Austrian sovereigns; practically all the extant protocols of the *Staatsconferenz;* and the more important ministerial reports (*Vorträge*), dispatches to the Austrian envoys, and reports of diplomats on special missions (notably Spielmann's from Reichenbach and Luxemburg). Vivenot's work has two considerable defects: he refused to print the reports of the Austrian envoys, except in very rare cases; and he gave to the affairs of the Holy Empire a quite disproportionate amount of space — to the detriment of our knowledge of Austrian policy in the Polish Question. Zeissberg, who continued Vivenot's enterprise, has avoided both these faults, and his publication leaves little to be desired in the matter of completeness.

Only second in importance to the Vivenot-Zeissberg compilation are the numerous collections of letters of the Austrian monarchs and ministers of this period, published by Arneth, Beer, Vivenot, Brunner, and Schlitter. Austrian history can boast of nothing in the way of memoirs, except for the somewhat dry reminiscences of Philip Cobenzl and the very amusing ones of the Prince de Ligne.

A publication of much importance for the policy of the Northern Courts is the supplementary volume of Herrmann's *Geschichte des russischen Staates*, which contains a mass of excerpts from the Prussian, Saxon, and English state papers bearing particularly upon the Polish Question. It is a contribution for which one must be grateful; but it is far from affording sufficient evidence on most questions, and the choice of documents in many cases seems arbitrary or even misleading. Fragments from the Prussian archives are also found scattered in Ranke's and Sybel's works, and in Dembiński's first volume to which reference will be made below. The list of Prussian memoirs of interest for this period is also very short: Massenbach's and Schlieffen's are the chief ones that come into account, and, apart from a few valuable

letters, neither offers much that is important, and neither is
thoroughly reliable.

The first volume of Professor Dembiński's *Documents relatifs
à l'histoire du deuxième et troisième partage de la Pologne* deals
with the period from 1788 to May 3, 1791, and contains chiefly:
(1) the correspondence of the Vice-Chancellor Ostermann with
the Russian ministers at Berlin and Vienna; (2) the correspondence of the Prussian government with its envoys at St. Petersburg; (3) the private correspondence between Hertzberg and
Lucchesini. This is a contribution of the first importance, and
the continuation of this work will be awaited with eagerness.

Among the mass of sources printed in Russia the most notable
are: the correspondence and other papers of Catherine II published in the Сборникъ Императорскаго Русскаго Историческаго Общества,
the Русская Старина and the Русскій Архивъ; various papers and
letters of Potemkin in the periodical last mentioned; the invaluable correspondence of the brothers Vorontsov with Bezborodko,
Markov, Zavadovski, and others in the Архивъ Князя Воронцова;
the papers of the Razumovski family published by Wassiltchikow;
and the protocols of the Council of the Empire in the Архивъ
Государственнаго Совѣта. Martens' collection, the *Traités de la Russie*, adduces here and there a document, and meagre as it was,
being in French, it long remained one of the standard source-books
for the Russian policy of this time. The memoirs of Engelhardt,
Deržavin, and Langeron contain some interesting information,
especially with regard to the career of Potemkin; and one cannot
pass over in silence Khrapovitski's diary, which furnishes a
detailed chronicle of Catherine's doings and sayings in the years
1787 to 1789, but becomes somewhat scanty after the latter
date. It contains one story that has been conscientiously retold
by everyone who has written on the Empress' policy towards
Poland.

Of sources relating exclusively to Polish affairs, the most important are: the *Domestic Correspondence* of Stanislas Augustus,
published by Zaleski (i. e., correspondence with Poles pertaining
to the domestic affairs of the country); the documents printed
by Kalinka in the second volume of his *Last Years of the Reign*

of Stanislas Augustus (the correspondence of the King with Catherine, with Bukaty and Kiciński; the diary of Bulgakov, the Russian envoy at Warsaw 1791–92); the curious and not altogether trustworthy book called *The Establishment and Overthrow of the Polish Constitution of the Third of May*, which contains the apologia of the reforming party; and the memoirs of Czartoryski, Ogiński, Koźmian and others.

Of the secondary works that come into account here, Häusser's and Herrmann's are for the most part antiquated, in so far as the Polish Question is concerned. Sybel has the great merit of having first shown the close connection and mutual interaction between the French and the Polish crises, and of having first defined the essential scope and character of the revolutionary policy of Catherine II and the pacific and conservative policy of Leopold. As was to be expected, however, in the case of one who was breaking so much new ground, he fell into numerous errors in matters of detail; he left many questions unexplored; he held obstinately to various untenable views, even after it had been clearly proved that he was in the wrong; and his pronounced Prussian bias too frequently led him to pervert and distort facts in a truly exasperating fashion. Of recent general works, Heigel's *Deutsche Geschichte* is, perhaps, the most notable. It shows a sort of reversion to Herrmann's point of view in its appreciation of Leopold's attitude towards Poland. Heigel has, I think, placed too much faith in the agreeable things that the Austrians saw fit to tell the Prussian envoys.

Among works relating specially to Austria, Beer's study of Leopold's Polish policy (in the volume *Leopold II, Franz II und Catherina. Ihr Briefwechsel*) is the best account of this subject, but, confined as it was to the narrow dimensions of an introductory essay, it was not by any means exhaustive nor altogether accurate. There are no monographs on the era of Spielmann and Cobenzl; and Thugut's storm-encircled figure still awaits a proper biography.

Prussian policy has received much more attention. The period from 1787 to 1790 has been minutely studied by Duncker, Bailleu, Luckwaldt, Andreae, and the brothers Paul and F. C.

Wittichen. The events that led up to the Convention of Reichenbach have been exhaustively investigated — as far as Prussian
policy is concerned — by Sybel, Ranke, and Ritter. The Prussian-Polish alliance of 1790 has lately found a brilliant historian
in Professor Askenazy of Cracow. The policy of Prussia towards
Austria, Poland, and France in 1792 is a subject on which the
conventional account (Sybel's) has long needed revision. This
want has been admirably met by Heidrich's recent book, *Preussen
im Kampfe gegen die französische Revolution.* By a more thorough
exploration of the Prussian archives than had yet been made, and
especially by the use of the rich collection of Lucchesini's papers
(secured by the Berlin Archive some years after Sybel's last
edition appeared), he has reached many new conclusions, and
above all has brought out clearly the essentially aggressive character of Frederick William's policy in that momentous year. I
had already reached views quite similar to his when Heidrich's
book appeared; and, apart from a number of questions of detail,
I have few objections to raise with him.

For Poland Kalinka's great work on the Four Years' Diet
(down to the Third of May) retains a considerable importance,
although his too pessimistic view of internal conditions has been
largely refuted by Korzon, and his fundamental ideas about
foreign policy have been sharply contested by Askenazy. Kalinka's *magnum opus* has found a not unworthy continuation in
Smoleński's *Last Year of the Great Diet,* which is written, however, from a very different point of view. Smoleński's *Confederation of Targowica* is distinctly inferior to his earlier work;
for instance, it leaves the origins of that unhappy movement
almost untouched.

Solov'ev's chapters on the events that led up to the Second
Partition are rich in documentary materials, but for several
reasons they leave very much to be desired. The author wrote
with too strong a nationalist bias (intelligible, perhaps, in a book
published in 1863); he was not always critically minded; he
knew little about the Austrian and Prussian side of the case; and
he often passed over things of the greatest importance with a
few vague sentences. Kostomarov concentrated his attention on

the internal affairs of Poland, and — through a sublime faith in the veracity of Stackelberg's and Bulgakov's dispatches — presented a picture of unrelieved blackness. He dismissed the Partition Treaty with a sentence, and hurried with quite exasperating haste through all the negotiations of Russia with the German Powers. It is interesting to find him asserting that Catherine aimed at a partition from the beginning of her action in Poland in 1792; but he was as little able to offer proof of this as was Solov'ev to establish the contrary.

In general, the mass of secondary works dealing with the Polish crisis of 1788–93 and the Second Partition seemed to have the following defects.

There remained not a few gaps in our knowledge, especially in regard to the policy of Russia and the origin and development of the Austro-Prussian 'indemnity' plan. The period bristled with controverted questions: one has only to recall the widely-divergent or downright contradictory views of Sybel and Vivenot regarding the merits of the dispute between the two German Powers; of Kalinka and Askenazy regarding the Prusso-Polish alliance; of Solov'ev and Kostomarov regarding the aims of Catherine II. It was also to be noted that, with very rare exceptions, the German historians who had dealt with this period, had been unable to use works in the Slavic languages, and Solov'ev, Vasil'čikov (Wassiltchikow), and Kalinka were the only important writers in Russian and Polish whose books had been translated into Western tongues. The greatest part of the rich publications in Russian and Polish had thus remained inaccessible to most Western scholars. On the other hand, Solov'ev and Kostomarov were little acquainted with the German investigations in this field. It seemed necessary, therefore, to collate the materials and the results that were to be obtained from both sides. Furthermore, it appeared that while the Prussian official documents had been very thoroughly studied, the Austrian and still more the Russian archives deserved further exploration.

Above all, there was need of a synthetic presentation of the whole course of events that led up to the Second Partition. Although the Polish crisis of 1788–93 has the same sort of unity as that of 1763–75, no one had attempted to treat the former as a whole, in the way that Beer and Sorel have treated the latter. And yet the Second Partition cannot be properly understood when treated as a mere casual episode in the history of the Revolutionary War, or simply as the result of a political ' deal ' arranged between the great Powers in 1792. In order to understand it, one must follow the whole course of that brave venture to regain national independence which was undertaken by the Four Years' Diet in 1788; one must also study the fundamental aims and ambitions, to which, in spite of many apparent changes of ' system,' each of the neighboring Powers adhered tenaciously throughout this crisis; and finally, one must trace the interaction of these discordant ambitions through the astonishing vicissitudes of five years of very complicated European politics. Hence it appeared that what the existing literature dealing with the Second Partition especially lacked was a comprehensive survey of the development of the Polish Question from the time when that question was re-opened in 1788 by the bold initiative of the Great Diet down to the drastic resettlement of 1793, by which the Poles were punished for their attempt to recover their independence.

To present such a comprehensive survey is the primary aim of the present volume. I have attempted to follow with equal attention the policy of each of the three great neighbors of the Republic, as well as the course of affairs in Poland and such events in the broader theatre of European politics as worked back upon the Polish Question. I have attempted to utilize more fully than has often been done in the past the results gained not only by German and Austrian, but also by Russian and Polish scholarship. For the most part, however, the present work is based on the results of two years of researches in the Austrian, Prussian, and Russian archives, researches which, if not exhaustive, may, perhaps, fairly be termed more extensive than had hitherto been made.

In the *K. u. K. Haus-Hof-und Staatsarchiv* at Vienna I had the opportunity to use:

(1) the correspondence (*Expeditionen* and *Berichte*) of the Austrian government with its envoys at St. Petersburg (1788–93), Warsaw (1790–93), Berlin (1790–93), London (1792–93), Dresden (1791–92), and Munich (1792–93);

(2) the *Vorträge* (reports of the State Chancellery to the monarch and protocols of the *Staatsconferenz*) for the years 1790–93;

(3) Spielmann's reports from his missions to Reichenbach and to the Prussian army headquarters in 1792;

(4) the correspondence relating to Landriani's mission to Dresden, 1791–92;

(5) the private correspondence between Philip and Louis Cobenzl; between Kaunitz, Philip Cobenzl, and Spielmann; between Thugut and Colloredo-Wallsee;

(6) the (unprinted) diary of Count Karl Zinzendorf.

In the *Kgl. Preussisches Geheimes Staatsarchiv* at Berlin I made use of:

(1) the correspondence of the Prussian government with its envoys at St. Petersburg, Vienna, and Warsaw for the years 1792–93, and, in the case of the Warsaw legation, also the acts for the period July, 1788–October, 1789;

(2) the correspondence of the King and Hertzberg with various Polish magnates, 1788–89;

(3) the acts relating to Bischoffwerder's three missions to Vienna in 1791–92;

(4) the reports of the cabinet ministry to the King, 1792–93;

(5) the correspondence of Lucchesini with the cabinet ministry, Bischoffwerder, Schulenburg, Alvensleben, Haugwitz, Manstein, Jacobi, and Caesar;

(6) the correspondence of Schulenburg with Haugwitz and the Duke of Brunswick.

In the Petrograd Archives of the Empire and of the Ministry of Foreign Affairs (Государственный и Петроградскій Архивы Министерства Иностранныхъ Дѣлъ), I had the privilege of using:

(1) a mass of papers of the Empress Catherine II — notes, fragments and comments —, her letters to Potemkin, P. A. Zubov, Bezborodko, Ostermann, and Stackelberg (Rep. V and X);

(2) the papers of Potemkin, preserved in Rep. XI, 950;

(3) the correspondence of A. K. Razumovski with Markov; and various minor series of documents.

In the Imperial Public Library at St. Petersburg, I had the opportunity to go through the papers of the " Archives of V. S. Popov", which contain a large number of letters and notes from

Bezborodko to Potemkin and Popov, and also the reports sent
by Potemkin's and Popov's correspondents at Warsaw from 1790
to July, 1792.

In the Moscow Archives of the Ministry of Foreign Affairs
(Московскій Архивъ Министерства Иностранныхъ Дѣлъ) I made use of:

(1) the correspondence of the Russian government with its envoys at
Vienna and Berlin, 1791–93, and Warsaw, 1791–92 (as also the
rescripts to Sievers for 1793);

(2) the mass of correspondence relating to the Confederation of Targowica
(Сношенія съ Польшею, 1791–93, IX, 1–4), which contains especially
the correspondence of Bühler with the Empress, Zubov, and Ostermann, and that of F. Potocki, Rzewuski, and Branicki with the
Empress, Potemkin, and Zubov;

(3) Bezborodko's reports from Jassy, 1791–92 (Сношенія съ Турціею, 1792,
IX, 60); and some less important collections of papers.

Finally, I had the opportunity of using the correspondence of
Piattoli with Mostowski at Dresden, 1791–92, preserved in the
Archives of Count Zamojski-Ordynat at Warsaw; and the correspondence of Ankwicz, the Polish envoy at Copenhagen, with his
government and with other Polish envoys abroad, 1791–92, from
the Ossoliński Museum at Lemberg (MSS. 516).

From these studies in the archives, I have reached a number
of conclusions with regard not only to questions of detail but to
more fundamental problems, which differ from the views hitherto
generally accepted. The effort is made in the following pages
to show that the Second Partition was not a measure forced upon
Catherine II against her will by the importunities of Prussia, but
rather the consummation of the Empress' secret plans and ambitions. I have endeavored to bring out more clearly than has
yet been done by any writer except Heidrich the aggressive and
acquisitive character of Prussian policy, especially with regard
to the intervention in France. I have tried to correct Sybel's
exaggerated account of Leopold II's efforts on behalf of Poland,
while showing, on the other hand, that the Emperor's advocacy
of the new constitution was far more earnest and active than
Herrmann, Heigel, or Beer admit. In reviewing the long litigation between Austria and Prussia over the indemnity question,
I have advanced the view that Austria was in the right far more

frequently than German historiography, dominated by the writers of the ' Prussian school,' has generally been willing to concede. Finally, the previous accounts of the origin and development of the Polish-Bavarian indemnity plan and of the evolution of Russian policy in the Polish Question are considerably supplemented by new materials in the present volume.

This book was originally prepared in partial fulfilment of the requirements for the degree of Doctor of Philosophy in Harvard University. I wish to acknowledge my indebtedness to the officials of the several archives in which it has been my privilege to work; and to the numerous friends at home and abroad from whom I have received advice and assistance, especially to M. Serge Goriaïnov, Director of the Imperial Archives in Petrograd, Herr Geheimer Archivrat Dr. Paul Bailleu in Berlin, M. Tadeusz Korzon in Warsaw, and Professor Dembiński of Lemberg. I am under many obligations to Mr. G. W. Robinson of Harvard University for assistance in the preparation of the manuscript. Above all, I am indebted to Professor A. C. Coolidge, at whose suggestion this study was first undertaken, and to whose continued encouragement, advice, and criticism I owe more than I can say.

R. H. L.

CAMBRIDGE, MASS.
September, 1915.

LIST OF ABBREVIATIONS

B. A............Kgl. Preussisches Geheimes Staatsarchiv, Berlin.
M. A..........Moscow Archives of the Ministry of Foreign Affairs.
P. A..........Petrograd Archives of the Ministry of Foreign Affairs.
V. A..........K. u. K. Haus-Hof-und Staatsarchiv, Vienna.

F. B. P. G......Forschungen zur brandenburgischen und preussischen Geschichte.
F. R. A........Fontes rerum austriacarum.
F. z. D. G......Forschungen zur deutschen Geschichte.
H. Vjschr.......Historische Vierteljahrschrift.
H. Z..........Historische Zeitschrift.
R. H..........Revue Historique.
R. I. A........Recueil des instructions données aux ambassadeurs et ministres de France. (See Bibliography.)
Vivenot........Vivenot, Alfred von, *Quellen zur Geschichte der deutschen Kaiserpolitik Oesterreichs während der französischen Revolutionskriege.* (See Bibliography.)
Арх. Вор.......Архивъ Князя Воронцова. (See Bibliography.)
Арх. Гос. Сов...Архивъ Государственнаго Совѣта. (See Bibliography.)
Рус. Арх.......Русскій Архивъ.
Рус. Стар. .....Русская Старина.
Сборникъ ......Сборникъ Императорскаго Русскаго Историческаго Общества.

CONTENTS

xix

CHAPTER II

CHAPTER III

CHAPTER IV

CHAPTER V

CHAPTER VI

CHAPTER VII

CHAPTER IX

CHAPTER X

CHAPTER XI

CHAPTER XII

CHAPTER XIII

CHAPTER XIV

CHAPTER XV

CHAPTER XVI

CHAPTER XVII

CHAPTER XVIII

CHAPTER XIX

CHAPTER XX

CHAPTER XXI

APPENDICES

THE SECOND PARTITION OF POLAND

THE SECOND PARTITION OF POLAND

INTRODUCTION

I

SINCE the second half of the seventeenth century Eastern Europe has presented two great international problems of equal interest and equal importance, the Turkish and the Polish Questions. The character and history of the former are familiar to scholars and, indeed, to the general public; but the latter is still, in large part, an unexplored field.

The Polish Question has passed through two very different phases. In the earlier one it resembled the Turkish (or Eastern) Question in not a few respects. In both cases the problem was that of maintaining the existence and integrity of a vast but decrepit state, paralyzed by chronic misgovernment, military inefficiency, racial and religious antagonisms, intellectual stagnation, and economic decline. In both cases the neighboring Powers were constantly tempted to interfere and aggrandize themselves, while religious oppression, the duty of restoring ' order,' and the need of preserving the ' balance of power ' served as ever ready pretexts for aggression. In both cases the chief safeguard of the menaced state was the mutual jealousy of the great Powers. For various reasons the catastrophe which threatened both Turkey and Poland overtook the latter country first. By the Partitions of 1772, 1793, and 1795 the Polish state was annihilated. That drastic attempt at a solution did not end the Polish Question, but it altered its character completely. Thenceforth the problem was that of a conquered and dismembered people attempting to regain its liberty and unity in the face of the three strongest monarchies of Eastern Europe. In this form the Polish Question has been the most difficult and perplexing

3

of the 'national' problems with which the past century has had to deal.

Of the historical importance of the Polish Question numerous illustrations may be given.

No other event in modern times has produced such extensive lasting changes in the map of Europe as did the dismemberment of the Polish Republic, a state which had been the third in size on the Continent, and whose area very considerably surpassed that of France or Germany today. As a result of the Partitions, Russia, previously so remote, and, as long as a strong Poland existed, so largely cut off from communications with the West, extended her frontiers deep into Central Europe, to within two hundred miles of Berlin and Vienna. The territories which she acquired from Poland now support a population almost as large as that of France.[1] They form, indeed, about one-eighth of the area, and they contain nearly one-third of the total population, of European Russia. Through the appropriation of Polish lands the Hohenzollerns were first enabled to unite and round out their scattered possessions into a compact and defensible realm; and if these acquisitions were, as is often maintained, indispensable to the consolidation of Prussia, then the dismemberment of Poland and the unification of Germany appear to stand in very close connection.

The Polish Question has played a large rôle in modern diplomatic history. It is well known that the quarrels over the distribution of spoils in Poland lamed and then disrupted the First Coalition against revolutionary France; that the spectre of a revived Poland chilled the friendship of Tilsit and hastened the great breach of 1812; that the Polish-Saxon question came near to breaking up the Congress of Vienna, and plunging Europe into a new general war; and that the Polish insurrection of 1830 facilitated the triumph of the revolutions of that year in the West, just as the final struggles of the old Republic contributed to the

---

[1] I am referring here to the lands acquired by all four of the partitions of Poland (1772, 1793, 1795, 1815). The present Kingdom of Poland and the ten governments of Western Russia which formerly belonged to the old Polish Republic contained on January 1, 1912, according to the estimates of the Russian Central Statistical Committee, a population of 38,963,000.

victory of France in her first revolution. For a century the Polish Question had an important effect in determining the grouping of the Powers, estranging France and Russia, and binding together Berlin and St. Petersburg through a common interest and a common anxiety. It was by his ineffectual intervention in favor of the Poles in 1863 that Napoleon III completely alienated Russian sympathies, while by his clever complacency towards Russia on that occasion Bismarck secured the benevolent neutrality and moral support of Alexander II during the critical decade when German unity was made. Even down to very recent years, in spite of the new alignment of the Powers, Poland served to ' keep the wire open ' between Berlin and St. Petersburg, while Austria's occasional flirtations with the Poles have furnished one more cause of antagonism between the Dual Monarchy and Russia.

Each of the two states which profited most by the Partitions has acquired an internal problem of the most embarrassing kind. First came the period of insurrections (1830, 1848, 1863), when Poland, like Italy and the Balkan Peninsula, formed one of the permanent danger-zones of Europe. In more recent years the Poles have indeed renounced the method of armed uprisings; but they have maintained and powerfully developed the consciousness of their national unity, their traditions, their strength; they have tenaciously resisted every effort to destroy their national individuality; and they have been struggling hard to gain some recognition of their national rights in each of the empires among which they are divided.

That policy of colonization, expropriation, and persecution, which the Prussian government has been conducting against the Poles for thirty years, has hitherto failed not only to Germanize the Polish districts, but even to prevent the Poles from peacefully conquering new territory, for instance, in East Prussia and Silesia. Prussia is faced by the danger of seeing her eastern provinces slowly but surely Polonized and lost to German nationality. Prince von Bülow has declared that the Polish problem is one of the gravest of those confronting Prussia, and one upon which the future of the Empire and the whole German nation depends.[1]

[1] Cf. Bülow, *Imperial Germany*, pp. 325 f.

The Russians have also met with such difficulties in their
' Kingdom of Poland ' that they have several times considered
abandoning it to Prussia.[1] The forty years of quiet after 1864
did indeed raise hopes that the spirit of the obstinate nation was
broken, but that was only because the nation had no normal and
effective means of manifesting its feelings. Since the Revolution
of 1905–06 has partially removed the obstacles to political discussion and the expression of popular opinion, it has become clear
that the policy of Russification has broken down completely and
that the Poles are more united and determined than ever in the
demand for national autonomy.

At the present moment, a war which has turned Poland into a
second Belgium has once more drawn the horrified attention of
the world to this unhappy country. The belligerents on both
sides have attempted to win Polish support by far-reaching
promises for the future. Whatever the outcome of the struggle
may be, is it too much to hope that this time Poland will not have
suffered in vain; that this time the rights of a nation, which is
after all the sixth or seventh largest in Europe and which has so
many claims upon the respect, the sympathy, and the justice of
the world, will not go unrecognized; that this time the Polish
Question, which has tortured the conscience of Europe for over a
century, will finally be set at rest ?

II

The Polish Question owes its origin to the desperate and wellnigh irremediable decadence which overtook the Polish Republic
about the middle of the seventeenth century, and, continuing
unchecked for a hundred years, brought the country to the verge
of ruin. The causes of this decline and of the ensuing catastrophe have been discussed by numerous historians and publicists
with intense interest, although generally with too little knowledge and too great national or party bias.[2] A final explanation

---

[1] Poschinger, *Also sprach Bismarck*, i, pp. 74 f.; Dmowski, *La Question polonaise*,
pp. 55 f.

[2] A very useful survey of the literature on the downfall of Poland is to be found
in Professor Kareev's book, Паденіе Польши въ исторической Литературѣ.

has not been given, nor can it be given in the present state of investigation. It seems clear, however, that the decline of Poland is to be traced primarily to political causes, to the defects of a wretched system of government. Whatever other cause of weakness one may discover, for instance, the lack of a strong middle class, the oppression of the peasantry, religious intolerance, racial antipathies, intellectual or moral retrogression — these are all of but secondary importance. These evils, or equally grave ones, could be met with in other European states of the old régime, and yet no other great state atoned for them by the loss of its existence. For everywhere else there was a government strong enough to curb or diminish the destructive tendencies and to produce or assist invigorating ones. Poland alone had no such correcting or ameliorating force. Poland had no effective government whatever. The nation lived in an anarchy thinly concealed under the forms of an elaborate republican constitution. It is in the unfortunate historic evolution of that constitution that the explanation of the decline of Poland is to be sought.[1]

The constitution of the Republic in its later years was so nearly unique in Europe that there was — and still is — a widespread tendency to regard it as something quite *sui generis*, as an entirely original creation of a misguided and fantastic people. In reality it was only an exaggerated and one-sided development of a type of political organization once almost universal on the Continent, of what the Germans call the *monarchisch-ständische Staat* or the *Ständestaat*. Nearly all the supposed peculiarities of the Polish constitution can be traced to principles and tendencies inherent in the *Ständestaat:* almost all of them find analogies in other countries in the same stage of development. Even the Liberum Veto, which is often held up as the most unique and most monstrous institution of Old Poland, to be explained only from a national lack of political common sense, or else from a survival of primitive Slavic anarchism — even the Liberum Veto was merely a logical extension of the idea pervading mediaeval parliamentarism, that the vote of a majority cannot bind a minority. In

---

[1] Cf. Bobrzyński, *Dzieje Polski*, ii, pp. 353 ff.

the Aragonese Cortes, for example, a valid decision required the assent of all four *brazos* (orders) and of every member of every *brazo*.[1] In Catalonia a single nobleman by uttering the words ' *Yo dissent* ' could stop the proceedings of the Cortes,[2] much as the Polish deputies did with their famous ' *Nie Pozwalam.* '[3] But when all the parallels have been drawn — and they are very numerous — the fact remains that the *Ständestaat* produced in Poland very different results from those that it brought forth in most other countries.

The main difference is briefly this: that in Poland the struggles of the *Ständestaat* period resulted in the victory, not of the Crown over the Estates (as in most other lands), nor of the Estates collectively over the Crown, but of a single class over the Crown and the other classes alike; this triumphant class then failed to organize its power in such a manner as to give the country an effective government; and finally the ruling class — the *szlachta*[4] — maintained its monopoly of power far too long. A one-sided constitutional development, the failure to create a new political mechanism adapted to the new distribution of power in the state, and then prolonged anarchy and stagnation — these seem to be the essential causes of the decline of Poland.

The *szlachta*, the military land-owning class, began to play a political rôle only in the latter part of the fourteenth century, but thereafter its progress was surprisingly rapid, its triumph only too sudden and complete. Three circumstances especially contributed to its victory over the Crown: these were, the extinction of the ancient dynasty of the Piasts (1370), and the uncertainty as to the succession under the next few kings, which led (by 1434 at the latest) to the recognition of the principle that the Crown was elective; the weakness of character shown by most of the Polish monarchs after the time of Casimir the Great; and finally, the extraordinary military and financial needs of the Crown, resulting from the Hundred Years' War with the Teutonic Order,

---

[1] Marichalar and Manrique, *Historia de la Legislacion y Recitationes del Derecho civil de España*, vi, p. 217.

[2] Pella y Forgas, *Llibertats y antich Govern de Catalunya*, p. 146.

[3] The words mean ' I forbid.'

[4] The gentry.

the struggles against the Muscovites and Tartars, and the efforts of the Polish kings to establish their dynasty on the thrones of Bohemia and Hungary. ' The attempt to play the part of a great power of the modern type with only the resources of a mediaeval feudal state ' [1] inevitably brought to the front the class on which the maintenance of the new position and the success of the new policy of expansion primarily depended. The *szlachta* knew how to improve the opportunity to the utmost. The cornerstone of their power was laid by the Privilege of Kaschau (1374), by which King Louis of Anjou, in order to assure his daughter's succession to the throne, granted the *szlachta* exemption from all taxes (with one rather insignificant exception) and from all duties to the state except unpaid military service. After that, one privilege followed fast upon another. In 1454 Casimir IV was obliged to grant the Statutes of Nieszawa, the Magna Charta of the Polish nobility, by which he promised not to make new laws or to order the *pospolite ruszenie* (the general rising of the nation in arms) without the consent of the *szlachta*. The gentry were thus for the first time legally admitted to a share in legislation, and as they were also free from any military or financial burdens, save those they might voluntarily lay upon themselves, their position in the state was commanding.

These far-reaching concessions required the creation of an organ through which the *szlachta* might regularly exercise their new functions. That need was met by the Diet, which, slowly taking form in the latter half of the fifteenth century, received its definitive organization and legal sanction through the Statute *Nihil Novi* in 1505.

Set over against this vigorous new institution, the Crown steadily lost both prerogatives and prestige, although it retained a considerable measure of independence as long as the Jagellonian dynasty survived. But with the extinction of that family in 1572, the foundations of Polish royalty crumbled. The nine months' interregnum that followed saw a change of really revolutionary

[1] The phrase belongs to Dr. Hötzsch, who has a very suggestive article, " Staatenbildung und Verfassungsentwicklung in der Geschichte des germanisch-slavischen Ostens," in the *Zeitschrift für osteuropäische Geschichte*, i (1911), pp. 363–412.

character. The theory at once spread that, now that the old dynasty had disappeared, the *szlachta* no longer had any master over them and the supreme power had lapsed into their hands. Hence they hastened to take possession of the state, acting by means of armed provincial associations or ' Confederations,' which, replacing the royal courts and officials, undertook to provide for the unity and security of the country and for the establishment of a new government. It was true that the *szlachta* did proceed to the election of another king; but the theory of election had now changed utterly. While the Jagellonian dynasty lasted, the practice of election meant hardly more than the designation of the natural successor by birth and an act of submission to him; the nation had little real freedom of choice, and the Jagellonian princes retained most of the prestige of hereditary monarchs. But from 1572–73 onward, it was understood that the *szlachta* were quite free to choose whom they would, and that the prince whom they chose was only their delegate, entrusted by them with a rigidly limited portion of authority, which might be revoked in case he overstepped his mandate. The *szlachta* had thus anointed themselves with the majesty that had once pertained to the Crown, and henceforth it became their chief concern to see that the sovereignty did not slip away from them. The state had become in fact, as well as in name, a republic.[1]

After this revolution, save for rare instances, the king of Poland was merely the ' painted monarch,' the crowned figurehead, whose impotence could be compared only with that of the conventional doge of Venice. Surrounded by pomp and circumstance, he was yet without any of those effective powers which even in modern constitutional states remain to the monarch. The chief prerogative left to him was the right of appointing to innumerable offices, civil and ecclesiastical; but as appointments were made for life, and the king possessed no means of control over officials once appointed, this prerogative was of little avail. Indeed, it is probable that the jealousies, disappointments, and resentments provoked by the use of the royal patronage quite

---

[1] On the capital importance and the results of the interregnum of 1572–73, cf. Pawiński, *Rządy sejmikowe*, i, pp. 28 ff.; Карѣевъ, Польскій Сеймъ, pp. 45 ff.

outweighed any profit that the Crown may have drawn from it. Certainly nothing contributed more to the suspicion that haunted the *szlachta* in the last centuries of Old Poland, than the fear that the kings were corrupting the nation and endangering liberty by their insidious and unscrupulous use of the appointing power; nothing did more to keep alive that sleepless and ineradicable distrust of the Crown, which proved so formidable an obstacle to every attempt to restore some strength to the executive.

A long series of Polish historians, from Naruszewicz down to Bobrzyński, have deplored the abasement of the royal power as the primary cause of the decline of Poland. It has often been said that so vast, so exposed, and so heterogeneous a realm as this could survive only under a strong monarchy; that Poland needed to go through the wholesome discipline of enlightened despotism like the western nations; that Poland fell because she tried to omit a stage in her evolution. But the more recent historiography tends toward a quite different view. It is urged that Poland might have attained the results that western nations secured through absolutism, by other methods, through the admission of all classes of society to a fair share in the government of the Republic. More serious, more decisive than the victory of the *szlachta* over the Crown, was the victory of the *szlachta* over the non-noble classes. These elements, unfortunately, showed themselves incapable of furnishing support to the falling kingship, or of forcing the *szlachta* to share with them the power wrested from the Crown, or even of defending their own political and economic existence against the attacks of the nobility. If the Polish state fell completely under the control of a single class, with the most disastrous results, it was not so much because in Poland the kings were weaker and the nobility more aggressive than elsewhere, as because the lower classes, and especially the bourgeoisie, exhibited a weakness unparalleled in any western country.[1]

In the fourteenth and early fifteenth centuries an admirable equilibrium existed between the various classes in Poland. Each class enjoyed a fair measure of rights and privileges, and no class was able to encroach seriously upon the others. This equilibrium

---

[1] Cf. Kutrzeba, *Historya ustroju Polski*, pp. 87 f., 162 ff.

was broken down, however, in the later fifteenth and sixteenth
centuries, when the *szlachta* established their complete political
and economic preponderance over townsmen and peasantry alike.

As against the peasantry, the *szlachta* were impelled by the
same imperious economic needs that were about the same period
converting the *Grundherr* into the *Gutsherr* and the free peasant
into the serf in Eastern Germany, Bohemia, Hungary, and
Russia. Into the causes and history of this vast transformation
in the agrarian life of Eastern Europe, it is impossible to enter
here. This economic change coincided in time with the rise of the
szlachta to political power and their conquest of the right of legislation through the Diet. The result was a series of 'constitutions' (the most important of them between 1496 and 1573),
which bound the peasant to the soil, increased his obligations in
rent and labor, deprived him of the protection of the law, and even
subjected his religion to the dictates of his master. Whether or
not the lord was legally vested with the *jus vitae et necis*, it was
assumed that he possessed it, and there are not lacking examples
of its being exercised. The peasant thus sank into the most abject
kind of bondage; the landowner was lord of his land, his property,
his life, and his conscience.[1]

The degradation of the Polish peasantry is not surprising in
view of what was occurring elsewhere in Eastern Europe; but the
abasement of the towns before the *szlachta* is less easy to understand, and in fact an entirely adequate explanation has not yet
been offered. In the fifteenth and early sixteenth centuries the
Polish cities were at the height of their prosperity. Politically,
they were by no means negligible factors. Even earlier than the
szlachta, they had learned to assert their rights by means of Confederations; their approval was frequently sought by the Crown
for important political acts; and all through the fifteenth century
their representatives often appeared at those loosely organized
and little known national assemblies out of which the Diet
developed.[2] But when that body was finally organized through

[1] Cf. Lehtonen, *Die polnischen Provinzen Russlands unter Katharina II*, pp. 38 ff.

[2] The history of the Polish Diet in the fifteenth century is still in very urgent
need of further investigation. Much interesting information as to the participation
of the cities is to be found in Prochaska, " Geneza i rozwój parlamentaryzmu za

the Statute *Nihil Novi*, the cities found themselves virtually excluded. Cracow alone, by special privilege, enjoyed a clear legal right to representation in the Diet; but the exercise of that right encountered such opposition from the *szlachta*, the deputies of the capital were subjected to such humiliations when they ventured to show themselves, that by the end of the sixteenth century they had ceased to appear. It is true that the cities never quite lost their rank as one of the constitutional estates of the realm. Throughout the seventeenth and eighteenth centuries four or five towns continued to participate in elections to the throne, in extraordinary Diets, and in Confederations. The right of the towns to be represented at ordinary Diets was never formally abolished or renounced; but for practical purposes, from the beginning of the sixteenth century on, the cities had lost their place in the national assembly and in the political life of the nation.[1]

This elimination of the bourgeois element from the Diet was a phenomenon not entirely peculiar to Poland. In Hungary, Bohemia, and Moravia — lands whose constitutional development closely resembled that of Poland, and might, perhaps, have paralleled it completely, but for the fortunate advent of the House of Hapsburg — the rôle of the city deputies at the Diets was gradually reduced to little more than the right to be present; in Bohemia that right was restricted to Prague alone, and in Hungary and Moravia in the later years of the old régime all the cities together had only a single vote. But nowhere else did the city estate fall so completely as in Poland, so suddenly, or, what is strangest, with so little apparent effort at self-defence.[2]

The explanation most commonly advanced for this surrender by the cities is the fact that the Polish towns in the Middle Ages

pierwszych Jagiellonów," *Rozpr. Akad. Umiej. w Krakowie, Wyd. Hist.-Fil.*, *Serya*, ii, T. xiii; also Piekosiński, " Wiece, sejmiki, sejmy, przywileje ziemskie w Polsce wieków średnich, *ibid.*, T. xiv.

[1] Cf. Rembowski, *Konfederacya i rokosz*, pp. 274 ff.; also his articles in the *Biblioteka Warszawska*, 1892, iv, and 1893, iii. On the significance of the Statute of 1505 as virtually excluding the townsmen from the Diet, see the article by Balzer, in the *Kwartalnik Historyczny*, xx.

[2] The comparison of the rôle of the cities in the Diets of these four states is made by Kadlec, " Ústavní dějiny Polska podle nových bádání," *Časopis Musea Král. Čes.* 1908.

were peopled chiefly by Germans, living according to German law, separated from the rest of the nation by language, customs, and interests, and neither willing nor able to take an effective and continuous part in the political life of the kingdom. It is true that in the sixteenth century the towns were rapidly being Polonized, but this transformation came too late; the cities then found that their coöperation was not wanted, and that the doors of the Diet were closed against them. They were the less able to defend their political interests, because, despite the external appearance of prosperity, economic decline was setting in. The primary cause was the shifting of the world's trade-centers at the close of the fifteenth century and the ruin of the Black Sea traffic at the hands of the Turks. The Polish towns thus lost that transit-trade on which their prosperity in the Middle Ages had chiefly rested, and henceforth they went steadily down hill. This decline was accelerated by the encroachments of the *szlachta*, who, as soon as they had come into power, rained blow after blow upon the sinking bourgeoisie. The latter were excluded from offices in the state and from the higher places in the Church; they were forbidden to own land outside their walls; their municipal liberties were virtually destroyed in the seigniorial towns, and in the royal cities greatly restricted. Above all, their trade was nearly ruined by the selfish and short-sighted legislation passed by assemblies of country squires, bent only on assuring their own fortunes and ignorant of the first principles of a sound national economy. As typical of this legislation one may cite the law of 1565, which forbade native merchants to export or import any goods whatsoever, or the enactment of 1643 that native merchants were to sell at a profit of no more than seven per cent; foreigners, of five per cent; Jews, of three per cent.[1] The prosperity of the cities might possibly have survived the activity of the Polish Solons; but the terrible devastations suffered during the wars against Swedes, Turks, and Muscovites dealt it the final blow. By the eighteenth century the once brilliant and busy towns presented a perfect picture of desolation: the houses deserted or falling in ruins, the streets grown up to grass, and

---

[1] Kutrzeba, *op. cit.*, pp. 171 f.

business confined to the wretched operations of Jewish money-lenders and petty traders. Poland was thus left destitute of the element most important for a sound political life — a strong, prosperous, and progressive middle class.

Though supported by great wealth and by the prestige naturally attaching to the Church among an ardently Catholic people, the Polish clergy also failed to oppose an effective barrier to the omnipotence of the *szlachta*. It is true that the bishops acquired and maintained a place in the Senate, and that in the fifteenth century the lower clergy were occasionally represented at the Diets.[1] But in Poland, as in England, the clergy preferred to tax themselves and to regulate their relations with the Crown in their separate assemblies; as an estate they soon dropped out of the Diet; and then they too became the object of the attacks of the *szlachta*. Failing in their direct onslaughts, especially in their attempt to oust the bishops from the Senate, the gentry nevertheless succeeded in their essential aim. By securing a monopoly of the higher positions in the Church for members of their own class, they removed the main cause of antagonism, and turned the hierarchy into an aristocratic body, one with themselves in birth, manners, ideas, and interests. With that the victory of the *szlachta* over all opposing elements was complete. They were the State. The struggles of the *Ständestaat* period had led in Poland to a result radically different from that attained in most other states, and to one for which there is nowhere else an exact analogy. The result was the omnipotence of a single caste carried to a point unparalleled in any other European country.

Even this development need not have proved so disastrous, if the *szlachta*, after gaining the supreme power, had only properly organized it. An efficient aristocratic government, awake to national needs and able to concentrate the power and resources of the country for great national tasks, might have provided a tolerable substitute for absolute monarchy. But it was the

---

[1] This representation of the clerical estate in the fifteenth century is one of the most obscure points in Polish constitutional history. Some data may be found in Pawiński, *Sejmiki ziemskie*, pp. 94 f., and in Prochaska, *Geneza i rozwój parlamentaryzmu*, etc., pp. 39 f.

supreme misfortune of Poland that the *szlachta*, after appropriating the sovereignty, seemed bent, not on using it for great national aims, but rather on dividing it equally among all the members of their class, taken as individuals. The authority lost by the Crown passed, not to the Diet, but to the local assemblies (Dietines), and, in the last analysis, to each country gentleman. The supreme power was atomized until it simply vanished, leaving anarchy.

The explanation of this unhappy phenomenon is chiefly to be sought in the geographic and historical conditions under which the *szlachta* had worked their way to power. The Republic embraced an enormous area; it was larger than any of the other states which at that time experimented in popular government. In the German territories, Bohemia, Sweden, or Aragon, for example, all nobles might, without too much difficulty, attend the central parliament; but in Poland, as in Hungary, this proved impossible, and hence the need for the election of representatives, for local assemblies, for local self-government. The mere size of Poland rendered decentralization indispensable.

The particularist spirit had also been fostered by the historic evolution of Poland. After a short period of unity under the Piasts, in the twelfth century the realm had been divided into numerous principalities, which soon possessed no connecting links whatsoever. This period of disintegration, which lasted nearly two hundred years, left very deep and abiding traces. It was then that the various Polish ' lands ' — the principalities of that age, the palatinates of the next — took permanent shape and acquired their marked individuality, their separatist instincts, traditions and prejudices. The reunion of the country effected by Władysław Łokietek at the beginning of the fourteenth century, was only a hasty and mechanical process, each ' land ' retaining its own hierarchy of officials, its own assemblies of dignitaries and magnates, its own law, its own separate life and self-consciousness. Though some progress towards real unity was made under Łokietek and his successor, the speedy extinction of the dynasty and the subsequent weakening of the royal power, which had always been the chief bond of union in Poland, largely arrested this salutary process.

It was at this moment, when the integration of the country was still so incomplete, that the *szlachta* made their entry into political life. Naturally they acted through the agencies with which they were most familiar, namely, the local organizations, and in accordance with those ideas of local independence to which they were accustomed. So it happened that they entrenched themselves first of all, not in a central parliament, but in the local assemblies — the Dietines. About the beginning of the fifteenth century the old provincial councils of dignitaries and magnates were transformed (except for judicial purposes) into assemblies of the whole community of the *szlachta* of each ' land.' These *Sejmiki* or Dietines originally concerned themselves only with modest local affairs; but as the *szlachta* extorted one privilege after another from the Crown, it was through the Dietines as their chief organs that they exercised their new functions. For purposes of taxation, and, after the Statutes of Nieszawa, for calling the *pospolite ruszenie* and for legislation (at least legislation affecting the rights and privileges of the *szlachta*), the King was obliged to consult all the Dietines separately. That procedure was slow and awkward; what was needed was a concentration of the local machinery in a general parliament.

The nucleus of such a body existed in the *Wiec*, the assembly of the chief magnates and dignitaries of the entire kingdom, which, as a royal council, under the first Jagellonians already exerted great influence over the decisions of the Crown in matters of general policy. Throughout the fifteenth century *szlachta* and townsmen and, to some extent, the lower clergy not infrequently attended the meetings of the *Wiec*; but it is still uncertain what form their representation took, and what part they had in the deliberations of the assembly. At any rate, an organic connection between the Dietines and the *Wiec* (or Diet, as it came to be called), was definitely established only at the close of the century. The Dietines slowly formed the habit of sending deputies to the central body; and in 1493, for the first time — as far as we know — deputies from all the Dietines in the kingdom assembled in the general Diet at Piotrków. That was the Polish Model Parliament. The Diet took shape as a bicameral body: the deputies from the Dietines formed the Chamber of Nuncios, from which the city representatives soon disappeared; and the upper house was formed by the Senate, (i. e., the old royal council or *Wiec*, made up of the archbishops, bishops, palatines, castellans, and the great officers of the Crown), which through the Statute *Nihil Novi* was placed on a footing of equality with the Chamber of Nuncios with respect to legislative rights.

The success of Polish parliamentarism now depended on the question of what the relation would be between the newly formed Diet and the older provincial assemblies. The predominance of the former would mean the continuation of the unification of the realm and perhaps the development of a strong central government; the predominance of the Dietines, on the other hand, would involve decentralization, disunion, impotence. At the outset, the decentralizing tendency prevailed. The deputies of the Dietines represented only their respective ' lands '; they were bound by instructions, usually precise and imperative, from their electors; the Diet resembled a congress of ambassadors. Under Sigismund II a determined effort was made by the Protestant *szlachta* to end this state of things and to give the Diet the character of a real parliament by eliminating imperative mandates, establishing the majority rule in voting, and subordinating the Dietines to the Diet. But this effort failed, chiefly owing to the opposition, and later the weakness, of the King himself.[1]

In the next generation the tide set strongly in the opposite direction. The doctrinaire theories of the age about the ' freedom ' and ' equality ' of the *szlachta*, the heightened sense of their own importance produced by the events of 1572 in the minds of the gentry, their natural preference for deciding all matters directly in their local assemblies, rather than through deputies to the Diet, who might be insidiously influenced by the King or the magnates — all these things combined to assure to the Dietines a preponderance such as they had never before enjoyed. Restricted under the later Jagellonians to a very narrow sphere of

---

[1] See Bobrzyński, *Dzieje Polski*, ii, pp. 75 ff., who regarded the proposals of the Protestant party as the most promising reform program ever brought forward in Poland.

activity, these assemblies now extended their encroachments so far and assumed such a plenitude of power and independence, that in the seventeenth century the Republic came to resemble a loose federation of fifty or sixty sovereign states. Not only did the various palatinates develop to the utmost their judicial and administrative autonomy, but decentralization was also carried to dangerous lengths in the financial and military system, on which the strength and security of the Republic primarily depended. The Dietines granted or refused taxes, either through their deputies to the Diet or directly, when the question was referred to them, as frequently happened; they themselves assessed and collected the taxes, turning over to the treasurers of the Crown only so much as they saw fit; and they raised and maintained military forces, which they tended to regard as their own provincial armies.

This excessive decentralization was, indeed, partially overcome during the eighteenth century. The unity of the army was restored; and the Diet of 1717, by establishing permanent taxes levied according to a fixed scale by officials of the central government, put an end to the financial powers of the Dietines, except for the raising of local rates. But by this time it was hard to undo the effects of one hundred years of disorganization and chaos, to curb the deeply rooted particularist spirit, to bring the state back to the path towards unity, on which it had started in the sixteenth century. And above all, even in the mid eighteenth century nothing had been done to remedy the worst evil produced by the long preponderance of the Dietines, namely, the impotence of the Diet.

That impotence was due chiefly to the system of the imperative mandate. Since 1572 the instructions given by the Dietines to their deputies had grown more and more lengthy, detailed, and strict. The deputies might be ordered to put through a project at all costs, or not to allow one to pass under any consideration. Then the custom had grown up of holding so-called ' Dietines of relation ' (*Sejmiki relacyjne*) at the close of each Diet, for the purpose of hearing the reports of the returned deputies. These Dietines of relation not only kept the nuncios in wholesome awe of disobeying their instructions, but also, while they could not *de jure* alter or nullify what the Diet had done, *de facto* they not infrequently did so.

The result of this system was to hamper the action of the Diet to the utmost. Whatever was to come up in the central parliament was discussed and virtually decided in advance by the Dietines, and the latter decided these matters, — questions, it might be, of the most general nature, affecting the whole Republic — on the basis of local interests, local knowledge, local prejudices; decided them prematurely, categorically, in final instance, without regard for what the assembly of the whole nation, after a more comprehensive survey of the situation and more mature deliberation, might be inclined to favor.[1] The fate of every question thus depended not so much upon the debates in the Diet, as upon the referendum taken in fifty or sixty tumultuous gatherings of — for the most part — ignorant and narrow-minded country squires.

The logical development of the system of imperative mandates and the crowning anomaly of the Polish constitution was the famous Liberum Veto: the right of any member of the Diet to interpose a veto, which had the threefold effect of defeating the particular proposition that had aroused opposition, dissolving the Diet, and nullifying all the decisions previously taken by the assembly.

The Liberum Veto was a late constitutional development. In the sixteenth century Diets a determined minority was generally able to check the action of the majority, but if the dissenters were very few, little attention was paid to them. In the seventeenth century, however, with the strong tendency of that age to 'liberty,' and its antipathy to 'tyranny' of any sort, the conception of the rights of the minority developed, until in 1652 for the first time a single deputy, Siciński, by his veto 'exploded' the Diet. After that the use of the Liberum Veto, although it rested on no written law and was in itself a defiance of common sense, became an established constitutional practice, and a chronic evil. The Dietines often expressly ordered its application, taking pleasure in this means of showing their importance. The mass of

---

[1] Cf. the vigorous passage on this subject in Pawiński, *Rządy sejmikowe*, i, p. 409.

the *szlachta* regarded it as a useful safeguard against injustice or tyranny — in fact as the ' palladium of liberty,' the ' jewel of the constitution.' Of the fifty-five Diets held between 1652 and 1764, forty-eight were ' exploded,' almost one-third of them by the veto of a single deputy. During the thirty years' reign of Augustus III not a single Diet lived out its normal time. As the Diet met only once in two years, and then for six weeks only (provided it escaped being 'exploded'), and as each Diet was generally brought to a violent and premature end with nothing accomplished, the result was that the national parliament had virtually ceased to function. And yet, after the collapse of the royal power, the Diet was the one institution that might have given the country a government!

One means of getting around the Liberum Veto existed, but, as has frequently been pointed out, it was a remedy worse than the disease. This was the ' Confederation,' i. e., a voluntary armed association of individuals formed for the purpose of putting through its specified projects in the face of any opposition whatsoever. Confederations — a characteristic mediaeval constitutional device — were much in vogue in Poland in the late fourteenth and fifteenth centuries; they then disappeared for a time, but recurred frequently in the period after 1572, — one symptom more of the reversion in type that marked Polish constitutionalism in that age. Confederations were of three kinds: (1) those formed during interregna, in order to prevent disorders and hold the realm together; (2) those formed during the life-time of a king for the purpose of assisting him in some great emergency; and (3) those formed in opposition to the kings — of which there are only too many examples. Associations of the first two kinds were useful; indeed, a Confederation formed ' at the King's side,' might be merely a technical device for putting through a project in spite of the opposition of a minority, since in a Diet held ' under the seal of a Confederation' the majority ruled. But a Confederation was under any circumstances a hazardous expedient, for it always brought with it the danger of civil war. Nothing reveals in a more glaring light the defects of Polish constitutionalism. Nothing could be more detrimental to stability, legality, and order than a system under which the ordinary authorities might at any moment be violently replaced by a set of ambitious private persons, who usurped control of the administration, the courts, the treasury, and the army, called a Diet, put through what legislation they pleased, and dispersed only when their aims were attained. The right of confederation, as Moltke declared, was revolution legally organized.[1] It gave rise to the epigram that the government of Poland was anarchy tempered by civil war.

Were there any truth in the old Liberal maxim that those states were happiest that were governed least, the Polish Republic must have approached the acme of perfection. The activity of its government had been reduced to the vanishing-point. " No people," said Burke, " have ever taken greater precautions to secure the possession of a sober and well-regulated freedom, than the Poles have to preserve themselves in their present anarchy." [2] In order that the King might not make himself a' tyrant,' he had been stripped of wellnigh every prerogative. In order that the Diet might not endanger ' liberty,' it had been reduced to complete impotence. The Dietines, in which the Liberum Veto also prevailed, were, as organs of government, scarcely more respectable. In Poland, Raynal declared, " everyone has the power to prevent action, and no one the power to act. There the will of any individual may thwart the general will; and there alone a foolish, a wicked, or an insane man is sure to prevail over a whole nation." [3] Montesquieu rightly affirmed that ' the object of the laws of Poland was the independence of every individual,' [4] that is of every nobleman.

The *szlachta* had, in fact, attained the most complete freedom, not only from every kind of oppression, but from any sort of obligation or constraint. From the latter part of the seventeenth century on, they ceased to render military service, since the development of warfare had made the old feudal levies an anachronism; nevertheless they continued to consider themselves

---

[1] Cited in Lehtonen, *Die polnischen Provinzen Russlands*, p. 15.

[2] *Annual Register*, 1763, p. 46.

[3] *Histoire philosophique et politique des Établissemens des Européens dans les deux Indes*, x, p. 52.

[4] *L'Esprit des Lois*, Bk. 11, ch. 5.

the sword and buckler of Poland and to claim all the privileges for which their former service had been the sole justification. They enjoyed a monopoly of land-owning. They exercised sovereign and unlimited power over the serfs on their estates. They could not be taxed without their consent, and in practice they paid none of the usual taxes, not even customs-duties. They could not be arrested or imprisoned or deprived of their property without trial, nor punished for their speeches and opinions. They held a monopoly of the higher positions in the Church, and of political rights and offices. Through their control of the Diet, the Dietines, and the courts of justice, they had in their hands whatever machinery of government existed. Finally, every nobleman, however indigent or insignificant he might be, had the right to attend and to participate in the elections to the throne, as a supreme demonstration of the fact that in Poland the sovereignty belonged to every *szlachcic* individually, as well as to all the *szlachta* collectively. It may be doubted whether any other class has ever obtained such unrestricted independence and such a fullness of power and privilege. The *szlachta* themselves were wont to boast that it was impossible to imagine a happier lot than that of a Polish nobleman, and they looked down upon all the other peoples of Europe as the ' slaves of despots.'

Naturally there grew up in the minds of the ruling class an idealization of this ' golden liberty,' purchased by ' the blood and toil ' of their 'virtuous ancestors,' which became a sort of religion, and a veritable obsession. One hardly knows whether to wonder more at the glorification of the *szlachta* as a caste, or at the panegyrics lavished upon the constitution which the nobility had created. The *szlachta*, it was said, were exalted above all the other classes as the cedars of Lebanon above the common trees. They were the heart and hands of the body politic, as the king was the head and the commoners the feet. As they gave their lives to the defence of the Republic, it was meet that the lower orders should serve them. It was necessary to have in the state one class of people who, disdainful of all gain, sought only the dignity, honor, and advantage of the fatherland. Traders and artisans, absorbed in money-making, were incapable of lofty thought or deeds, just as the *szlachta*, living only for virtue, truth, and right, were incapable of any low action.[1]

As for the constitution, it was defended with a great store of classical erudition, which testifies to the profound influence of Humanism upon Polish thought. With their minds full of political and legal ideas borrowed from antiquity, with the old phrases about ' tyranny,' ' freedom,' and ' equality ' ever upon their lips, the *szlachta* finally came to conceive of themselves as the reincarnation of the Roman Republic. The analogy was useful in a dozen ways. Did not History show that in the ancient republics political rights had also been confined to one class of well-born, wealthy, and leisured citizens, below which stood a servile proletariat ? Was not a deputy exercising the Liberum Veto merely a tribune of the people ? Was not a Confederation simply a new form of the Roman dictatorship ? Nowhere else, perhaps, was the ideal of a democratic republic of the ancient type so popular, or so potent in shaping political theory and practice.[2]

Religion also added its sanction to the apotheosis of the szlachta-state. In order to assure the victory of the Counter-Reformation, the Jesuits had not hesitated to make themselves ardent champions of ' golden liberty,' and to proclaim that the free constitution of the Republic was peculiarly adapted to Catholic principles and teaching. Under the influence of the clergy, the Poles came to regard themselves as under the special protection of Providence, as a chosen people; and confirmation for this belief was found in the many signs and wonders of the seventeenth century, especially in the miraculous deliverance of the country from the Swedes in the time of John Casimir.[3]

Extravagant as such theories were, they took deep root in the minds of the nobility. Combined with material interests, class-egotism, and the instinct of self-preservation, they produced in the *szlachta* a blind conservatism, a horror of all innovations, a fierce determination to maintain the existing state of things, which long rendered reforms almost impossible.

[1] Cf. the interesting essay of Wł. Smoleński, " Szlachta w świetle własnych opinii," in his *Pisma historyczne*, i.

[2] Карѣевъ, Польскій Сеймъ, pp. 42 ff.

[3] Cf. Smoleński, *Przewrót umysłowy w Polsce wieku XVIII*, p. 9.

The constitutional development of Poland from the end of the fourteenth down to the middle of the seventeenth century had been continuous, consistent, and logical. Unfortunate as that evolution had been, there had at least been life and movement. But in the seventeenth century growth ceased. The constitution had taken on fixed forms, and now entered upon a period of petrifaction during which all the disastrous effects of the preceding evolution made themselves increasingly and appallingly felt. The seventeenth century was marked by intellectual and moral retrogression, economic decline, growing political anarchy, and continual, exhausting, and on the whole disastrous conflicts with the neighboring Powers. Then followed the dullest and dreariest period of Polish history, the reigns of the two Saxon Kings (1697–1763), an age in which patriotism, public spirit, energy, and initiative seemed to have deserted Poland. After the incessant wars of the preceding period, amid which the nation could still produce heroes like Czarniecki or Sobieski, the *szlachta* laid aside their swords and abandoned themselves thenceforth to the joys of life on their estates, enhanced by constant and exuberant festivities, and varied by the excitements connected with the Diets, the Dietines, the law-courts, and a sordid and senseless party strife. This age of materialism, selfishness, apathy, and stagnation brought Poland to the depths of degradation. Her impotence was now well known to all the world, her anarchy proverbial, and her complete downfall a matter of common discussion.

III

In the middle of the eighteenth century, just before the period of the great disasters began, Poland was suffering from innumerable maladies. Outwardly, indeed, the Republic might still make a somewhat impressive appearance. With an area of approximately 282,000 square miles, it ranked as the third largest state on the Continent,[1] while in population it stood fourth, with over

[1] Korzon (*Wewnętrzne dzieje Polski za Stanisława Augusta*, i, p. 44) estimates the area in 1772 (after the loss of the Zips, and without counting in Courland) at 13,300 geographical square miles, which would equal 282,382.94 square miles, English. Among European states, only Russia and Sweden were larger.

eleven million souls.[1] But this population was far from homogeneous. The Poles can scarcely have formed more than fifty per cent of it at the most; more than one-third of it was made up of Little and White Russians; while the remainder consisted of Germans, Lithuanians, Jews, Armenians, and Tartars.[2] This lack of national unity was aggravated by the lack of religious unity. The Poles and Lithuanians were, with few exceptions, Roman Catholics; the Germans were mostly Protestants; and the Russians had for many centuries belonged to the Orthodox Eastern Church. It was true that owing to the unceasing efforts of the Polish clergy and the pressure of the landowners, the great majority of the Russian peasantry within the Republic had been brought over to union with Rome; but their conversion had been effected so recently and in part by such unedifying means that their loyalty to the Roman Church was open to grave suspicion. These religious diversities were the more dangerous because, while the Poles had formerly shown themselves the most tolerant nation in Europe, they were now coming to display quite the contrary spirit. During the later seventeenth and early eighteenth centuries the Dissidents (i. e., the non-Catholics) were gradually deprived of political and even civil rights, subjected to many forms of petty persecution, and occasionally exposed to outbursts of violence, such as the so-called Massacre of Thorn in 1724. This unhappy state of affairs contributed not a little to alienating the sympathies of the European public from Poland; it furnished foreign Powers with a welcome pretext for intervention; and it produced among the Russian population a chronic, sullen, and ominous discontent. In the rich palatinates of the southeast, where a small Polish minority of landowners and priests ruled over millions of Russian serfs, the gentry lived in constant fear of a jacquerie, of which the Orthodox popes would be the natural leaders.

[1] After elaborate computations Korzon (*op. cit.*, i, p. 63) concludes that in 1764 the total population was probably about 11–11 1/2 millions. Only France, Russia, and Austria had larger populations at that time.

[2] So much can be gathered from Korzon's statistics with regard to the religious divisions, *op. cit.*, i, pp. 163 ff. Unfortunately he does not attempt to supply any ethnic statistics directly.

If racial and religious divisions sapped the strength of the Republic, the social system of Old Poland was even more ruinous. It has often been pointed out that this state was a paradise for the nobility, but quite the reverse for all the other classes. Now the *szlachta*, although more numerous perhaps than the nobility of any other European country, formed only about eight per cent of the population; the townsmen, Jewish and Christian, about fifteen per cent; and the peasants seventy-two per cent.[1] The interests of all the other classes had been systematically sacrificed in favor of a caste which numbered less than a million.

Five-sixths of the Polish peasantry were serfs on the estates of the Crown, the Church, or the *szlachta*. It seems to be generally admitted that the lot of the serfs in Poland was more cruel than anywhere else, chiefly because the state was here unable to offer any protection to the serf. The many appalling descriptions that have come down to us portray the mass of the peasantry as sunk to a state of misery, apathy, and brutishness that almost defies comparison. One contemporary declares: " These people differ little from cattle, have no property, live from hand to mouth, and rot in filth and poverty; half their offspring die from lack of sunlight and proper nourishment, . . . and they themselves finally perish from hunger, if a year of bad harvest comes. It must be confessed that whatever fate should befall Poland, their condition could not become any worse." [2]

The sad fortunes of the Polish towns have already been described. In the middle of the eighteenth century, the Republic did not contain a single city of 50,000 inhabitants, and only seven with over 10,000; [3] and most of the so-called cities were only " agricultural settlements and collections of straw-covered huts," where a few Jews, artisans, and tinkers dragged out a wretched existence. With their trade and industry ruined, largely by the selfish class-legislation of the Diet, robbed of their municipal

[1] Cf. the table in Korzon, *op. cit.*, i, p. 320. These figures relate to the year 1791; but it may be assumed, I think, that substantially the same ratio between the various classes existed forty years earlier.

[2] Cited in Von der Brüggen, *Polens Auflösung*, p. 54. For general descriptions of the condition of the serfs, see Lehtonen, *Die polnischen Provinzen Russlands*, pp. 32–72, and Korzon, *op. cit.*, i, pp. 350–366.　　[3] Korzon, *op. cit.*, i, pp. 274 ff.

autonomy, exposed to the continual and tyrannous interference of the *szlachta* in their domestic affairs, and excluded from all political rights and offices, the townsmen, like the peasantry, could scarcely be expected to feel any genuine devotion to the Republic.

As the state existed solely for the benefit of the *szlachta*, as everything else had been sacrificed to the interests of the *szlachta*, one might have supposed that this class at least would be in sound and prosperous condition, and able to furnish a great reservoir of strength to the Republic. But even within this exalted caste, poverty and wretchedness were the lot of the great majority. Although in theory all members of this class were equal, and the richest magnate was bound to address the poorest *szlachcic* as 'brother,' in fact this much-vaunted equality was very much a farce. The *szlachta* were divided into several strata sharply differentiated by wealth, education, and social position.

At the top were sixteen or seventeen great families, like the Potockis, the Czartoryskis, or the Radziwiłłs; families who possessed immense wealth and estates which in some cases surpassed in extent many a principality of Germany or Italy. Some of these magnates maintained courts which outshone that of the king in splendor and rigid etiquette; kept up standing armies of their own (their 'house-militia'), a correspondence with foreign monarchs, and a sort of foreign policy; aped the manners of royalty to the best of their ability, and were accustomed to sign themselves, 'We, Palatine (or Castellan), by the grace of God.' In short, they conducted themselves like sovereign princes, and in fact they often had more real power than the king of Poland. Considering themselves born to rule the country and to hold all the most lucrative positions, these families engaged in incessant struggles with one another for power, influence, and plunder. Their rivalry kept the Republic in constant turmoil, and was demoralizing and dangerous, not only because it was so entirely divorced from questions of principle or considerations of patriotism, but also because in order to vanquish its domestic opponents, each faction was generally ready to call in the aid of foreign Powers.

Below the magnates stood the large number of fairly well-to-do *szlachta*, who took but little part in politics, busied themselves chiefly with their estates, and led simple, industrious, God-fearing lives like their ancestors. In spite of their ignorance and prejudices, these middle-class gentry were probably the best element in the nation.

The majority of the *szlachta* belonged to that aristocratic proletariat which was made up of those who had either no land at all or only enough to make a bare living. Poverty-stricken, ragged, and dirty, living like peasants or worse, but still filled with all the pride of their caste, and eager to vent it on all occasions, these people excited the derision of every foreigner, and were, indeed, one of the most unique spectacles to be seen in Poland. Hundreds and thousands of them lived at the courts of the magnates, serving the latter in their militia, in the administration of their estates, or even in menial capacities. It was a point of honor and almost a matter of necessity for every great ' lord ' in Poland to have hosts of such ' clients ' at his disposal, and their services were extremely useful. For it was from this class that the magnates recruited those hordes of tattered and drunken ' citizens,' who swarmed in to every Dietine, ready to acclaim ' whatever the Lord Hetman, (or the Lord Palatine) wishes,' and quick to use their swords in case of opposition. As almost everybody in old Poland, from the Diet down to the humblest law-court, was subject to mob-rule, it was indispensable to have the mob on one's side. It was the magnates who ruined Poland, and the ' barefoot *szlachta*,' who formed their constant and efficacious instrument. And it was a sad commentary upon ' golden liberty ' that more than half of the class which boasted of its republican freedom and equality, had been reduced to pauperism and to lives of groveling servility.

The results of ' golden liberty ' in the political sphere have already in part been described. The administrative system was completely disorganized. The great officials of the central government, the marshals, chancellors, treasurers and hetmans,[1] were irremovable and irresponsible, and each of them did what was

---

[1] These great officials were always in pairs: one for ' the Crown ' (i. e., Poland), and one for Lithuania. The hetmans were the highest military officials.

right in his own eyes. The officials who represented the Crown in the provinces had virtually ceased to discharge their functions. Whatever local administration existed was mainly carried on by the Dietines. It need hardly be remarked that a state in which the executive power was thus atrophied, could undertake none of those tasks of economic and social improvement which were coming to attract the attention of so many governments of that day. At a time when almost every other nation was doing its utmost to foster commerce and industry, Poland did nothing whatever towards that end. And — what was most serious in its immediate consequences — the Poles were blind even to the necessity of having those primary elements of strength, well-ordered finances and a respectable standing army. It has been estimated that about 1750 the annual revenues of the Republic amounted to only one-thirteenth of those of Russia, and one seventy-fifth of those of France.[1] Although the nation was miserably poor, and had neither trade nor industry to be taxed, it could undoubtedly have raised far larger sums with ease, had the *szlachta* been willing to bear their proper share of the burden, had the finances been decently administered, and had the government done anything to develop the great natural wealth of the country. Partly because of the perpetual stringency in the treasury, and partly because the *szlachta* distrusted a large standing army as a potential instrument of ' despotism,' the military forces of the Republic had been reduced to the barest minimum. The Diet of 1717 had fixed the size of the standing army at 24,000 men; but as a matter of fact, hardly half of that number were actually kept on foot. This Lilliputian army was the laughing-stock of the neighbors. There were generally about as many officers as privates in a regiment; the officers' positions were sold, often to mere boys of good family; the troops were chiefly cavalry, since it was beneath the dignity of a Polish gentleman to serve on foot; there was almost no artillery; and there was no discipline at all.[2] The Republic possessed only one fortress, Kamieniec. It had no natural frontier except the Carpathians.

---

[1] Korzon, *op. cit.*, iii, pp. 109 ff.
[2] Bobrzyński, *Dzieje Polski*, ii, p. 274; Von der Brüggen, *op. cit.*, pp. 80 f.

On every other side its vast territories lay open and defenceless, almost seeming to invite the invasion of the three great military monarchies that encircled it.

The *szlachta*, however, refused to recognize the danger. With incredible blindness they even tried to persuade themselves that the very impotence of Poland was the best guarantee of its security. For, as they reasoned, since the Republic had renounced all aggressive enterprises and had voluntarily rendered itself incapable of harming its neighbors, the latter would never think of disturbing a state of things so ideally adapted to their own interests. Each of the neighboring Powers must see the advantage of having a weak state like Poland on its frontiers, rather than another strong military state like itself. And hence there arose among the *szlachta* the insane maxim, ' Poland subsists through its anarchy.'

Without a government worthy of the name, without an army, without trade or manufactures, with misery universal in all classes save a small minority, rotting away under a system of ' liberty ' which a sagacious Englishman described as " merely a system of aristocratic licentiousness, where a few members of the community are above the control of the law, while the majority are excluded from its protection," [1] Poland had become, in the opinion of foreign observers, the weakest and unhappiest of nations.[2] A few among the Poles also recognized it. " Whatever happens," one of them declared, " we cannot be any poorer or weaker or more miserable than we now are, nor less free, nor more oppressed, nor more despised by foreigners." [3]

IV

It was the cataclysm that so suddenly overwhelmed Poland in the reign of John Casimir (1648–1668), the simultaneous and amazingly successful attacks of Swedes, Muscovites, Cossacks, and Tartars, that first revealed to the world the utter weakness of the Republic. Then for the first time Europe saw foreign armies

---

[1] William Coxe, *Travels in Poland, Russia, Sweden and Denmark*, i, p. 15.

[2] *Ibid.*, p. 143; cf. Burke in the *Annual Register*, 1772, p. 6.

[3] Konarski, cited in Zaleski, *Żywot Czartoryskiego*, i, pp. 23 f.

marching from one end of the country to the other, the *szlachta* deserting their own sovereign *en masse* and welcoming an invader as a deliverer, a king of Poland driven a fugitive from his dominions. Then for the first time the idea of a partition of Poland began to be seriously and universally discussed. Charles Gustavus, planning to unite Poland to Sweden, or else to divide up the huge realm with his allies; the Great Elector, stipulating for himself in his numerous negotiations and treaties with the Swedes the acquisition of West Prussia, Samogitia, or Great Poland; Tsar Alexis, seizing Lithuania and looking forward to the day when he should take Poland as well; Austrian diplomats debating the relative advantages for the Hapsburgs of getting the Polish crown or partitioning the Republic — all these actors in that crowded scene were anticipating by a hundred years the things that Catherine and Frederick and Joseph accomplished. So thoroughly had the idea of the imminent disruption of the Republic taken root in men's minds that French diplomats suspected that a partition treaty had already been signed;[1] and the King of Poland, addressing the Diet, solemnly prophesied to the nation its impending fate: Moscow would take Lithuania; the Brandenburger, Great Poland; Austria, Cracow and the neighboring palatinates. In short, the First Great Northern War not only raised the Polish Question, but also marked out the future solution.

It was true that through a belated national uprising and the intervention of the enemies of Sweden, Poland escaped from this first crisis with slighter losses than might have been expected. John Sobieski succeeded in restoring to some degree the prestige of the Polish arms, and in asserting, virtually for the last time, Poland's position as an independent and considerable member of the European political system. But Sobieski's victories brought his country hardly more than an ephemeral glory; the anarchy at home grew constantly worse; while, as a result of that anarchy, the Republic became a prey to foreign intrigues, and in particular a battleground between Hapsburg and Bourbon. It was in this

---

[1] Cf. *R. I. A.*, Pologne, i, p. 81. The best account of the diplomatic history of the First Great Northern War is Haumant, *La Guerre du Nord et la Paix d'Oliva.*

second half of the seventeenth century that there arose among the *szlachta* organized French and Austrian parties, even Brandenburg and Muscovite ones; that the magnates began to treat with foreign sovereigns like independent princes, and to accept bribes and pensions from abroad as a matter of course; that elections to the Polish throne came to be great international events periodically shaking the European political world, inviting and almost compelling the rival Powers to interfere in Polish affairs. As yet, however, this foreign interference was confined to the use of the black arts of diplomacy; except during the Great Northern War, the foreigners had not yet come to dictating to the Republic by force.

With the advent of the Saxon Kings, the Polish Question entered upon a second and more acute phase. Augustus II owed his crown to a more shameful use of bribes and violence and to more undisguised attempts at intimidation on the part of foreign Powers — Russia and Austria — than had been known at any previous election. Once seated on the throne, he found it impossible to maintain himself there without the aid of the foreigners. Having plunged recklessly into the Second Great Northern War, he brought down on the Republic the invasion of Charles XII. The scenes of the time of John Casimir were repeated; a great part of the *szlachta* again deserted their sovereign; the invaders roamed through the country, victorious at all points; Charles set up a rival king; and Augustus saw safety only in throwing himself into the arms of Russia. That was a fateful step. For after Poltava the Swedes disappeared, but the Muscovites remained, nominally as allies and protectors, really as masters. It is a fact not sufficiently recognized that one of the most important results of the Second Great Northern War was to establish the predominant influence of Russia in Poland.

Peter the Great deserves the credit of having inaugurated the policy which aimed at placing the Republic under a Russian protectorate and ended with the three Partitions. He fixed the traditions of Russia's Polish policy for nearly a century. Here, as in so many other cases, Catherine II continued and completed what Peter began. In Peter's time Russian armies first learned to scour Poland from end to end, to make themselves thoroughly at home in the country, and to despise the military power of the Poles. Russian diplomats became familiar with the mysterious, but — to them — highly convenient, devices of the Polish constitution, and with the tangled web of Polish party politics. They learned how to buy up magnates, ministers, and even the court itself; how to manage the Dietines; run a Confederation; cajole, coerce, or 'explode' a Diet. Above all, the Russian government acquired the art of playing off the Polish nation against the king and the king against the nation, and thus holding both in dependence upon itself. Catherine II never displayed greater cleverness in handling the Poles than did Peter when, in 1716–17, he imposed his mediation upon Augustus II and the rebellious *szlachta* alike. And then the world saw for the first time a Russian ambassador dictating a peace between the Polish nation and its king, backing up his terms with a display of bayonets, and placing an important series of political and constitutional arrangements under the guarantee of the Russian sovereign. Prince Dolgoruki, the peace-maker on this occasion, was the worthy forerunner of the Repnins, the Stackelbergs, the Sievers of Catherine's time; and the ' Dumb Diet ' of Warsaw in 1717 foreshadowed the terrorized Polish parliaments of 1773 and 1793. The Republic had now lost its complete independence. It had allowed and invited its most dangerous neighbor to exercise a decisive voice in its internal affairs. It had accepted from the hands of Russia a number of constitutional arrangements, the aim of which was obviously to prevent the King from acquiring effective power in the state, and to prevent the Republic from strengthening or reforming itself.

Significant, also, of the new situation was the fact that by the alliance treaty of 1720 and a long series of subsequent agreements Russia and Prussia bound themselves to watch over the maintenance of the ' liberties ' of Poland. Already two of the neighboring Powers were in formal accord on the principle of perpetuating the anarchy and impotence of the Republic. The protracted negotiations between the cabinets of St. Petersburg, Vienna, and Berlin about the future succession in Poland showed that henceforth the glorified ' freedom of election ' was to be purely illusory. Moreover, the continual disturbances in Poland during the first two decades of the century and the restless ambition of Augustus II brought about a great revival of the talk of a dismemberment. The King of Poland himself repeatedly proposed to Russia and Prussia a partition of the realm whose integrity he had sworn to defend, in order that the fragments of the state left after the avidity of the neighbors had been satisfied, might be handed over to him as an hereditary kingdom. Frederick I of Prussia suggested a partition at least four times to Charles XII, and later tried to press his ' *grand dessein* ' upon Augustus and Peter. The Tsar himself seems to have played for a time with the idea of a dismemberment; but after firmly establishing himself in Poland, he set his face against it, and sternly rebuffed the proposals coming from Berlin and Dresden as impracticable, impolitic, and wicked. Possibly he had arrived at the conclusion that it was useless to divide the realm with others when by influence he could rule it all.[1]

The death of Peter the Great brought some alleviation to Poland, at least in that his immediate successors showed less firmness and consistency in dealing with Polish affairs, while they scarcely attempted to develop to its logical conclusion the policy he had inaugurated toward the Republic. Nevertheless, they adhered in the main to the cardinal principles of keeping Poland weak, maintaining ' golden liberty,' and asserting for Russia a special influence in the distracted state.

On the death of Augustus II in 1733 the question of the Polish succession provoked a general European war. For the first and last time one of the Western Powers drew the sword in order to rescue Poland from the clutches of her neighbors. But neither the capricious and half-hearted efforts of France nor the wishes of the vast majority of the *szlachta* prevented Russia and Austria from establishing by force of arms their protégé, Augustus III of Saxony, upon the Polish throne. Never before had there been

---

[1] On the plans of partition discussed at this time see especially Droysen, *Geschichte der preussischen Politik*, iv[i], pp. 177 f., 188 ff., 197, 217 ff.; iv[ii], pp. 147 f., 317.

such a travesty of a free election, so striking an exhibition of the impotence of the Poles to defend their independence, so clear a demonstration of the fact that the neighboring Powers would tolerate no king in Poland save a creature of their own.

It can hardly be denied that the Court of St. Petersburg failed to exploit properly its triumphs in this war. The Russian statesmen were too much occupied with the ensuing contests with Turkey and Sweden, and then with the great European questions that were being fought out in Germany, to pay much attention to Polish affairs. Under Elizabeth, the close friendship uniting the two Imperial Courts [1] to the Saxon House led the Russian government into acts of complaisance towards the King of Poland which Peter or Catherine II would doubtless have avoided.[2] As Russia had ceased to use other than diplomatic methods in Poland, as she no longer entered actively into the party struggles that rent the Republic, as her whole attention seemed to be concentrated elsewhere, the result was that in Elizabeth's last years the Polish Court paid less and less attention to demands from St. Petersburg; the Diet ventured to assume an independent, and often an unfriendly, attitude; while the ' Russian party ' found itself diminished, discouraged, and almost discredited. Russian policy in Poland seemed to be losing its bearings.

At the moment of the accession of Catherine II (1762), the Polish Question was in a curiously uncertain state, in which, however, several facts stand out clearly. In the first place, Poland was no longer considered an independent member of the European group of states,[3] but rather as what we should call today a Russian ' sphere of influence.' The Russian influence, it is true, had varied greatly in intensity, and it had not yet attained that all-embracing and absolute character which it was to have under Catherine II. The government at St. Petersburg did not yet pretend to control all the actions of the King and Diet; it

---

[1] Austria and Russia.

[2] Such as, for instance, promising the succession in Poland to the Saxon Electoral Prince, or allowing Prince Charles of Saxony to become Duke of Courland. Compare Catherine's remarks on this latter affair, Сборникъ, vii, pp. 91 f.

[3] Cf. Choiseul's instructions to Paulmy, April 7, 1760, *R. I. A.*, Pologne, ii, p. 217.

still paid some regard to the wishes of the court and nation; while aiming to maintain the anarchy in Poland, it did not try to exploit that anarchy in order to gain material advantages for Russia. Finally, while the development of the Polish Question concerned Russia preëminently, it also touched Prussia and Austria very closely, and to a lesser degree France. The ultimate solution must depend on the interaction of the ambitions and interests of three or four great Powers. Hence, before proceeding further, it seems necessary to examine the special interests that guided each of these Powers in its policy toward the Republic.

France was the oldest friend and the most natural ally of Poland. In the classic system of French diplomacy, the Republic occupied a place along with Sweden and Turkey as one of the pivots of French policy in Eastern Europe, as a confederate that might be used either to take the Hapsburgs in the rear or to checkmate Brandenburg-Prussia and Russia. Hence France long endeavored to establish a predominant influence in Poland. The sixteenth century saw two Franco-Polish alliances (1500, 1524) directed against the Hapsburgs, and — for a moment — a Valois installed as King at Cracow. In the seventeenth century Richelieu and Mazarin vainly tried to draw Poland into the Thirty Years' War, and Louis XIV made a supreme effort to turn the Republic into a useful ally. He proposed nothing less than an " eternal league . . . and an indissoluble alliance," by which France and Poland " would hem in the Empire, just as France had formerly been hemmed in between the Empire and Spain," and by which they could raise themselves " to a greater height than ever Austria had attained." [1] But all Louis' efforts to draw Poland into active coöperation proved fruitless, owing to the failure of the *szlachta* to appreciate the advantages of the French alliance, and to the ever-increasing anarchy in the Republic. In the eighteenth century, chiefly, it would seem, out of deference to the classic tradition, French statesmen continued to take a considerable interest in Polish affairs and to lavish money in attempts to build up a party or to place a protégé on the throne. If Poland could no longer be seriously thought of as an ally, France was at

---

[1] Instructions for de Lumbres, December 20, 1660, *R. I. A.*, Pologne, i, pp. 31 f.

least anxious to protect it as a buffer state shutting off the detested Muscovite 'barbarians' from Europe; and she feared, not without reason, the designs the neighboring Powers might form upon the territories of the Republic. But the Polish policy of France was neither well-considered nor well-conducted. With strange blindness, the advisers of Louis XV refused to see that the best means of saving Poland was to assist the nation to reform its government; they rather persuaded themselves that the interests of France demanded the maintenance of anarchy in Poland, in order that Russia might gain no advantage from her influence there; and they contributed not a little to that end. Furthermore, since the keynote of French policy in Poland was opposition to Russia and Austria, the alliance between Louis XV and the Imperial Courts during the Seven Years' War upset that policy completely. The old French party in the Republic was ruined. And then with the advent of Choiseul to power there came a period in which France virtually renounced active participation in Polish affairs and pretended to attach no importance to them. In the critical years that followed the accession of Catherine II, French policy towards the Republic was to vacillate between misdirected and noxious activity and equally disastrous passivity and indifference.

Down to the beginning of the eighteenth century, Austria was the chief rival of France in Poland. Her interest in the Republic was largely of a defensive nature. As long as Poland retained the power to harm, the Hapsburgs had to be on their guard to prevent their neighbor from attaching itself to France or from assisting the frequent rebellions in Hungary and Bohemia. The Polish alliance was frequently sought by Austria against Turkey or Sweden; and at least on one occasion, in the great crisis of 1683, it proved to be of inestimable value. On the whole, Austro-Polish relations were friendly. The two states had no necessarily conflicting interests; they did have many interests in common; and religious affinities and frequent royal marriages cemented a friendship that seemed to lie in the nature of things. Of all the neighboring Powers, Austria had the strongest motives for desiring the preservation of Poland. If the sad condition into which the Republic had fallen in the eighteenth century precluded both the fear of its hostility and the hope of its assistance, the rise of Russia and Prussia supplied new reasons why Austria should support and defend the sinking state; for neither the advance of the Russian colossus into Central Europe nor the further aggrandizement of Prussia could be to the advantage of the Hapsburgs. Austria had nothing to gain and much to lose by the disruption of Poland.

Unfortunately, Austrian statesmen, while realizing this truth in a general way, did not sufficiently act upon it. If the Vienna Alliance of 1719 marked one momentary effort to rescue the Republic from Russian domination, the rivalry with the Bourbons and with Prussia soon led the Hapsburgs to make the Russian alliance the cornerstone of their political system; and the interests of Poland were sacrificed on the altar of the new friendship. Austria allowed and assisted Russia to fasten her grip upon the Republic, while renouncing for herself any active influence in Polish affairs. As long as the Court of St. Petersburg prevented the French party from gaining the upper hand in the Republic and protected the integrity of Poland against Prussia, Austria was willing to tolerate its predominance at Warsaw. For the rest, it had come to be the accepted doctrine at Vienna that the existing anarchy in Poland suited Austrian interests, since it relieved the Hapsburg Monarchy from any danger on its northeastern frontier.

In contrast to Austria, Prussia was of necessity the persistent enemy of Poland. Succeeding to the inheritance of the Teutonic Order, the Hohenzollerns had fallen heirs to the ancient rivalry between that Order and Poland for the possession of the coastland around the mouth of the Vistula, the control of which was of vital importance to both contestants. There was not room enough here for the coexistence of a strong Poland and a strong Prussia: one could rise only at the expense of the other. More than any other neighboring Power, Prussia was interested in promoting the disruption of the Republic, for the scattered territories of the Hohenzollerns could be bound together only by the annexation of Polish lands. Polish Prussia was needed in order to unite East Prussia with Pomerania; a part of Great Poland, in order to connect Silesia with East Prussia.

The Great Elector had already fixed the traditions of the policy towards Poland which his successors followed with remarkable fidelity, perseverance, and consistency. From generation to generation one traces the same persistent effort to safeguard the ' liberties ' of the Republic, to prevent the king of Poland from establishing the hereditary succession or *'den absoluten Dominat,'* to keep the unruly Sarmatians in a state innocuous to their neighbors.[1] The idea of a dismemberment of Poland, hereditary in the House of Hohenzollern from the time of the Great Elector, was brought forward and furbished up anew at each recurring crisis in the North, in the half desperate belief that it was ' *aut nunc aut nunquam.'*[2] Frederick II, while only Crown Prince, declared the acquisition of West Prussia indispensable; he seems to have hoped to get that province during the Seven Years' War; and in his Political Testaments of 1752 and 1768 he designated its acquisition as one of the imperative tasks of the Prussian Monarchy.[3] A third phase of the traditional policy of Prussia was the desire to prevent any hostile Power from gaining control of the Republic. For that reason the Hohenzollerns repeatedly opposed the attempts of France and Austria to establish their protégés on the throne at Warsaw. They viewed with grave misgivings the connection between Poland and Saxony. As long as relations between Berlin and St. Petersburg were intimate, Prussia accepted not unwillingly the Russian influence in the Republic; but during the period of antagonism under the Empress Elizabeth Prussian diplomacy frequently worked hand in hand with the French against the Russian party in Poland, and during the Seven Years' War Frederick learned to his cost the dangers involved in the subservience of the Republic to Russia. That lesson was, later on, not wholly forgotten at Berlin.

[1] Cf. Droysen, *op. cit.*, iii[iii], pp. 120 ff.; iv[i], pp. 111, 177, 260.

[2] Haumant, *La Guerre du Nord*, pp. 46 f., 53, 100 ff., 180 f.; Droysen, iv[i], pp. 177 f., 182, 185 f., 197, 211 ff.; iv[ii], p. 317.

[3] Letter to Natzmer of 1731, *Oeuvres*, xvi, pp. 3 f.; *Politische Correspondenz*, xii, p. 456; xviii, pp. 592, 611 ff.; Lehmann, *Friedrich der Grosse und der Ursprung des siebenjährigen Krieges*, pp. 62, 94.

Finally, to come to the Power most directly concerned in the Polish Question, Russian historians are accustomed to explain their country's encroachments upon Poland by three reasons, which may be called the inheritance, the nationalist, and the religious motives. Poland-Lithuania having once appropriated the western half of Russia, the Muscovite rulers, as heirs of the old Kievan princes and ' gatherers of the Russian lands,' were bound to recover the ancient home of their race, to free their compatriots from a foreign yoke, and to deliver their Orthodox brethren from Roman Catholic oppression. Undoubtedly these motives did actuate the Tsars of the sixteenth and seventeenth centuries in their incessant struggles with Poland. Ivan III, by assuming the title of ' Lord of all Russia,' announced the Muscovite program and hurled a challenge at his western neighbor. He and his successors never tired of complaining of the Polish attempts to force ' *Rus* ' to the ' Roman law '; or of asserting that all the lands where the blood of Rurik had once ruled, were their rightful ' patrimony '; or of striving to make good their claims by force of arms. This policy, pursued by the Muscovite rulers for two centuries with rare perseverance, was temporarily shelved, however, after the Truce of Andrusovo in 1667; and then, as other interests pressed to the front, it was, to all appearances, abandoned.

There is no denying that in the eighteenth century the old traditions about recovering the lost inheritance were very much obscured, if not entirely forgotten. The westernized Russian statesmen of that age were no more likely to take seriously claims that went back to Rurik and Vladimir than French statesmen were to hark back to rights derived from Clovis and Charlemagne. Catherine II might occasionally declare herself determined not to rest until she had recovered the graves of all the old Russian princes, but it would be hard to show that such considerations really affected her policy. The historic rights of Russia to the western lands might be adduced to justify encroachments upon Poland, but they were certainly not the motive that led to those aggressions. Nor were considerations of nationality a serious factor in determining Russian policy towards Poland in the eighteenth century. The western and southern branches of the Russian race had so long lived a separate life under a foreign state, they had developed into types so different from the Muscovites, that the latter hardly considered them Russians at all. In the language of seventeenth century Moscow, the Little Russians (of the south) were the ' Cherkassian nation ' (Черкасскій народъ) and the White Russians (of the west) the ' Lithuanian people' (Литовскіе люди).[1]   In the eighteenth century both the government and the society of Russia proper hardly betrayed a suspicion that the population of the eastern provinces of Poland was not Polish. As for the population in question, it seemed as far removed as possible from any consciousness of its Russian nationality. And even had more exact ethnographic notions prevailed, it would have made little difference. The governments of the eighteenth century were not accustomed to be guided by the wishes of the people; and the ' rights of nationalities ' were not yet recognized. The fact that in the partitions of Poland Russia took only lands in which the bulk of the population was Russian, leaving the purely Polish provinces to the German Powers, is to be explained as a geographic accident. The unification of the Russian race was not, and could not be, the conscious aim of Russian statesmen in that age in their dealings with Poland.

The one part of the old tradition that was not forgotten in the eighteenth century was the religious motive. Their common Orthodoxy was the sole bond that still united the estranged branches of the Russian race. The defence of the faith in Poland was one sure means by which the government at St. Petersburg could always acquire merit in the eyes of society at home. By several treaties, especially by the Eternal Peace of 1686, the Russian rulers had stipulated freedom of worship for their coreligionists in Poland; and on the basis of those treaties they held themselves entitled to interfere in case the rights of the Orthodox were violated. Unfortunately, the religious intolerance which marked the Poles in that decadent age subjected the Dissidents to ever-increasing vexations and even persecutions.

[1] Пыпинъ, Исторія Русской Этнографіи, iv, pp. 12 ff.

The Orthodox clergy in Poland, feeling that they were fighting in the last ditch, assailed St. Petersburg with constant appeals for aid and deliverance. Here was a perpetual, plausible, and indeed quite justifiable pretext for Russian interference in Polish affairs, the first legal basis for intervention that Russia acquired. Down to the time of Catherine II, however, the government at Petersburg did not exert itself sufficiently to procure any permanent relief for the Dissidents; and, when it did interfere on their behalf, its motives were generally political quite as much as religious.

The mainspring of Russian policy towards Poland in the eighteenth century was, in fact, the purely political aim of obtaining a predominant influence over the Republic. That ambition was perfectly natural and not unjustifiable. It was based, in the first place, on the needs of self-defence. Poland had been a dangerous neighbor in the past; it was essential that she should not again become one in the future; hence the need of keeping her in weakness. And, feeble as they were, the Poles might still be capable of making trouble, if they fell under the influence of Russia's enemies. In 1719–20 it was an important part of the plans of George I of England, then in active opposition to Peter the Great, to draw Poland into the proposed coalition against the Tsar. During the wars of 1735–39 and 1741–43 one party in the Republic dreamed of forming an alliance with France, Prussia, Sweden, and Turkey against Russia. It was only through Poland that the Western Powers could strike at Russia by land; and the Russo-Polish frontier was terribly long and unprotected. Thus Russia's own security seemed to demand her control over Poland. Her land communications with the West, and her ability to assert herself in general European affairs, to participate in the wars of Germany, even to strike effectively at the Turks, these also depended on her power to dispose of the vast realm which separated her from the rest of the civilized world.[1] Whether as a

[1] Cf. the view of the French government in 1726 that " if one could make sure of the Poles, all gates would be closed to the Muscovites, and they could no longer safely undertake any outside enterprise," R. I. A., Pologne, i, p. 314. Augustus II thought that if he could make himself absolute master in Poland, he could exclude Russia from all European affairs, Соловьевъ, Исторія Россіи, iv, p. 542.

gateway to the West or as a barrier against the West, Poland was equally important to Russia.

In order to assure their control over the country, Peter the Great and his successors endeavored to keep Poland in a state of weakness, to uphold the existing vicious constitution, to prevent the increase of the army, to preserve the elective kingship, to exclude from the throne any ruler who could not be relied upon to serve Russian interests, to shut out the influence of other foreign Powers, and to maintain a strong Russophile party.

How far territorial aggrandizement at the expense of the Republic entered into the calculations of Russian statesmen from the time of Peter down to the accession of Catherine II is a question not sufficiently cleared up. As was remarked above, Peter seems for a time to have considered seriously plans of partition.[1] During the Seven Years' War it was Russia's declared intention to acquire Courland from Poland, in exchange for the conquered province of East Prussia.[2] Frederick II also claimed to know that the Court of St. Petersburg had designs on the Ukraine.[3] On the whole, however, Russia seems to have shown little desire for Polish territory in that age, and it was chiefly owing to her opposition that the numerous plans for a dismemberment of the Republic collapsed.

At the accession of Catherine II, the Polish Question had been before the Powers for a century. European statesmen had familiarized themselves with all its aspects, and with its possible solutions. The policies of the other states towards the Republic were fixed by long tradition. All the Powers chiefly interested, even France and Austria, were agreed upon upholding the ' liberties ' of Poland. All were accustomed to maintain parties of their own in the country, to distribute bribes and pensions, to ' explode ' Diets when necessary, to interfere at elections to the

---

[1] Herrmann, *Russische Geschichte*, iv, pp. 258 f., especially the note on p. 259, with reference to a plan of partition supposed to have been brought forward by Peter in 1710; see also Förster, *Friedrich Wilhelm I, König von Preussen*, ii, pp. 114–117. In 1705 Patkul came to Berlin as Russian envoy to purchase an alliance against Sweden with the province of Courland and whatever else the King of Prussia might want in Poland, Droysen, *op. cit.*, iv[1], pp. 183 f.

[2] Соловьевъ, *op. cit.*, v, p. 1072.

[3] *Politische Correspondenz*, xviii, p. 613.

throne. The idea of a dismemberment of the moribund state had been common property for a hundred years. At each new crisis in the North that idea was brought forward by someone as the best means of effecting a general pacification by satisfying the appetite of everybody. It is difficult to enumerate all the occasions on which a partition of Poland had been seriously discussed. The remarkable thing is, not that plans of partition had been so frequently brought forward, but that hitherto they had always failed to be realized. This latter fact may have been due in part to some surviving scruples about the morality of robbing a peaceful and harmless neighbor; but chiefly it was occasioned by the practical difficulties in the way of a dismemberment, in view of the mutual jealousy of the great Powers, and by the general concern of that age for the maintenance of the existing equilibrium. After all, a partition of the Republic was possible only under exceptional circumstances.

V

In 1762 an extraordinary revolution placed the crown of the Tsars upon the head of an Empress whom the Rusians revere as the greatest of all their rulers save Peter, and whose name, it has been said, is written in blood in the heart of every Pole.[1] Catherine II is a figure whom it is difficult to approach without admiration or else without a shudder, according as one remembers that she unified Russia or that she dismembered Poland. Of her great ability there can be little question. She undoubtedly possessed masculine will-power and energy, a clear, penetrating intellect, marvelous cleverness and cunning, boundless courage and self-reliance, and an extraordinary talent for managing men. Forced to play the game of high politics against such masters as Frederick II, Joseph II, Kaunitz, Choiseul, and the younger Pitt, invariably she at least held her own, and generally she got the better of her adversaries. She played the game as did most of her contemporaries, with perfect indifference to moral standards. While ' justice,' ' magnanimity,' ' generosity,' and ' disinterested-

---

[1] Kalinka, *Ostatnie lata panowania Stanisława Augusta*, i, p. 96.

ness ' were always on her lips, her policy was one of unscrupulous and relentless selfishness and aggression. The interests of Russia (conceived in the materialistic fashion of that age) and her own ' glory ' were the sole standards of that policy, and these two objects were to her one and inseparable. There was much of Louis XIV about her, especially in her exalted conception of the place her country ought to hold in the world, and in her exaggerated notions of what her own dignity and grandeur required. Like Louis, she was inclined to regard the slightest opposition to her will as a mortal insult; and vanity, pride, and vindictiveness were capable of leading her into acts which a calmer and less self-centered judgment would have avoided. Still, in the main, a remarkably sure instinct kept her in the traditional and natural paths of Russian policy; and she has the glory of having carried through to a successful termination not a few of the tasks pursued by her predecessors for centuries.

Throughout her reign Catherine was largely occupied with Polish affairs, and she, more than any other individual, stands responsible for the violent and, in many ways, unfortunate solution which the Polish Question then received. That dénouement can scarcely have lain within her original intentions. It is highly improbable that in the beginning she desired to annihilate the Polish state or even (as is commonly asserted) to pave the way for the gradual absorption of the whole of Poland into her Empire. At the outset she seems to have had in mind two alternative policies. The one was the policy of governing the Republic by ' influence,' while preserving its integrity; the other the policy of annexing convenient Polish territories from time to time as occasion offered, this latter course involving the necessity of making corresponding concessions to the two German Powers. The former policy was generally safer and easier: the latter was very tempting, and not at all so repugnant to Catherine as it has often been represented. It is, I think, an error to regard the partitions of Poland as measures forced upon the Empress against her will by hard necessity and by the victorious importunities of Prussia. Catherine seems to have kept both courses constantly before her eyes, ready to adopt either as circumstances permitted or suggested. In general, hard and fast programs were not to her taste.

In contrast to her immediate predecessors, Catherine attached extreme importance to Polish affairs. Panin, her mouth-piece in the early years of the reign, declared that without control over the Republic, Russia would lose one-third of her strength, and would be unable either to provide adequately for her own security, or to participate effectively in the affairs of Europe.[1] Catherine felt that Russia had not yet secured a sufficient hold upon Poland, and unless the policy of recent years was altered, was in danger of losing whatever influence she possessed. The Empress therefore began to take steps to gain such an absolute and exclusive control over the Republic that she could not only thwart whatever displeased her, but also positively govern the country in all matters and dispose of it at pleasure. The Poles had never before suffered such a systematic and merciless assault upon their independence. Hitherto Russia had generally posed as their disinterested friend and as the generous protector of their ' liberties.' In such a rôle she could usually count upon the sympathy and support of a great part of the *szlachta*, and she had been able to guard her essential interest — the maintenance of the Republic in a state of weakness — without resorting to much violence or deeply wounding Polish susceptibilities. But Catherine II, by pushing her interference to excess, presently turned almost the entire nation against her. She created an intolerable situation. She precipitated a life and death struggle, which ended in the annihilation of the Polish state. Thus her policy towards the Republic was not a mere continuation of the traditional one: it was in some sense new and revolutionary.

Her first great stroke was to place her candidate and former lover, Stanislas Poniatowski, upon the Polish throne (1764). That enterprise, conducted with masterly prudence and skill, proved unexpectedly easy. The Poles displayed an apathy unparalleled at any previous election, even in 1733; and foreign interference was prevented by Catherine's timely alliance with Frederick II, the complete passivity of Choiseul, and Austria's

---

[1] Чечулинъ, Внҍшняя Политика Россіи, 1762–1774, pp. 208, 226 ff., 231 f.

inability to attempt active opposition. The Empress thus succeeded in setting up a king of Poland selected both because of the known weakness of his character and because, as she herself said, he, being of all the candidates the one who had the least chance of gaining the crown unaided, would owe Russia the greatest debt of gratitude.[1] As the price of his election, Catherine imposed upon him truly terrible conditions. He had to promise always to regard the interests of Russia as his own, to maintain a constant, unfeigned ' devotion ' to the Empress, and never to refuse to support her ' just intentions.' [2] Throughout his reign he was never to escape from the consequences of that Faust-like bargain.

This was the last king of Poland, and the most unfortunate. Stanislas Augustus was a man of keen intellect, broad culture, charming personality, excellent intentions, and enlightened, reforming ideas; but he was also weak of will, morally perverted, incapable of daring, of inspiring others, of making personal sacrifices. He was the last man in the world fitted to lead a nation in its supreme struggle or to save a falling cause. There was not an ounce of heroism about him. He cut a poor figure on horseback: he was not at home in a camp. Throughout the earlier half of his reign, he was detested as no other Polish king had been, both because of his unpopular family connection with the arrogant Czartoryskis, and because of the means by which he had obtained his crown. Unable to count upon his own nation, he was thrown upon the support of Russia, knowing that if the Empress abandoned him, he was lost. Unable to lead his people in opposition to Russia, yet too patriotic to be the docile instrument of Catherine's designs, he remained distrusted, despised, insulted, and buffeted by both sides. Never did a king find himself in a more humiliating position. It was true that Stanislas later succeeded, through tireless efforts and consummate tact, in acquiring a certain measure of popularity which rendered him less dependent on Russian support. But he still remained bound by another shameful chain — his debts. Although the Republic granted him a generous income, and not infrequently extraordinary aid, his extravagance plunged him hopelessly into debt and finally brought him to

---

[1] Русскій Архивъ, 1878[ii], p. 290.   [2] Чечулинъ, *op. cit.*, pp. 228 f.

virtual bankruptcy. One means of financial salvation was ready at hand — the subsidies of Russia — and these Stanislas did not hesitate to accept, even in the greatest crises in Russo-Polish relations. At the time of the First Partition and at the time of the Second, the King was living on money furnished by the Russian ambassadors. How far these shameful transactions influenced his official acts, cannot be definitely ascertained; but probably they did so to no slight degree. It was these wretched debts that kept him on the throne when he could no longer reign without dishonor to himself and disaster to the nation. If he abdicated, who was to save him from his creditors ? It was not the least of the misfortunes of Poland that in the final crisis the nation had at its head a king who was not only a weakling, but the pensioner of his country's worst enemy, and, therefore, a traitor.[1]

The establishment of her protégé on the Polish throne was only the first step in Catherine's aggressive policy. The second was to raise the old question of the Dissidents. Not, of course, merely for love of the abstract principle of religious toleration, however much she desired the western public to think so; but rather in order to please Orthodox opinion at home, and also in the hope that by securing for the Dissidents access to political rights and offices, she could build up a strong party on which Russia could always rely.[2] Another aim of the Empress was to induce the Poles to place their constitution under her formal guarantee. That would assure her a perpetual right of interference in Polish affairs, make a reform of the iniquitous constitution impossible without her consent, and in general place the Russian ascendancy in Poland on a permanent legal basis. Pursuing these demands in her most vigorous and imperious manner, Catherine soon threw Poland into a wild turmoil. She alarmed the King and his uncles, the Czartoryskis, who saw through her plans; she exasperated the mass of the *szlachta* by what seemed an attack upon

[1] The best account of Stanislas' financial affairs is in Korzon, *Wewnętrzne dzieje Polski za Stanisława Augusta*, iii, pp. 4 ff. A brilliant character sketch in Kalinka, *Ostatnie lata*, i, pp. 72 ff.

[2] That this political aim was Russia's chief motive in raising the Dissident question is confessed with perfect frankness by Panin to Repnin in the instruction of August 14/25, 1767, Сборникъ, lxvii, pp. 409 ff.

the Catholic religion. Finding diplomacy useless, she resorted to force. In 1767 Poland was again flooded with Russian troops, and the luckless Confederation of Radom, formed by the *szlachta* chiefly for the purpose of overthrowing the King, served as a pretext for the Russian ambassador to take over the whole government of the country. Then the confederated Diet of 1767–68 was seduced, coerced, and terrorized, by those carefully graded methods of which the Russians were already past masters, into accepting all Catherine's demands: complete religious toleration and full civil and political rights for the Dissidents, and a treaty between the Empress and the Republic, by which the Polish constitution was placed under the guarantee of Russia.

With that Catherine and Panin fancied themselves at the end of their labors. Poland seemed completely crushed, tied, and bound. But one must admit that here the Empress had blundered. She had tried to reach the goal too quickly. She had wounded the Poles too deeply in their strongest feelings, their patriotism and their religious convictions. The shameful Diet of 1767–68 had scarcely dissolved when a Confederation was formed at Bar in the Ukraine for the defence of ' liberty and the faith.' The uprising soon spread over the greater part of the country. Anti-Russian and anti-royalist alike, the Confederation of Bar was a last desperate attempt to save the ideals of the *szlachta-*republic, very typical of Old Poland in its loyalties and its prejudices, its heroism and its follies, its audacity and its ineptitude. It never succeeded in putting an organized army into the field or in conducting a regular campaign; but it subjected Poland to four years of terrible guerilla warfare, during which the country was devastated from end to end, and Russians and Confederates vied with each other in deeds of savagery.

Meanwhile the Porte, stirred up by France, declared war on Russia, taking Catherine's aggressions in Poland as a pretext. The war was marked by brilliant Russian victories on land and sea; but these in turn alarmed the Court of Vienna. Austria armed, concluded an alliance with the Turks, and assumed a very menacing attitude towards Russia, although the will to act was sadly lacking behind these warlike demonstrations. By 1771 the situation appeared to be extremely critical. With her Turkish and Polish wars still on her hands, Catherine was threatened with the armed intervention of Austria, which then might lead to a general European conflagration.

It is well known that out of that crisis grew the First Partition of Poland. That arrangement seemed to have the advantage of reconciling the conflicting interests and satisfying the cupidity of the three great Eastern Powers, while allowing the Turks to escape without too great losses, and ending the long troubles in Poland with a drastic and supposedly salutary lesson to the Poles. Austria unwittingly supplied the pretext for the Partition by occupying the Zips and some neighboring Polish districts; Prussia first openly adopted the plan of a partition and pressed it most vigorously; Russia spoke the decisive word and determined the respective shares.

Into the history of the negotiations it is impossible and unnecessary to enter here; but one point should be noticed, both because it is so generally misunderstood, and because it is important for the comprehension of later events. I refer to the attitude of Russia towards the Partition. In spite of the common opinion that Catherine accepted that arrangement only as a *pis aller*, in order to satisfy her Prussian ally and avoid a war with Austria, I think it may be asserted with confidence that both the Empress and her advisers had long desired a partition, and were well pleased when the opportunity for one at last presented itself. Naturally they did not announce their ambitions prematurely; they found it politic to feign a certain reluctance; they preferred to be begged to take something rather than to beg for it. But all this need not have proved misleading, were it not, unfortunately, the custom of western historians — the Germans particularly — to base their accounts of Russian policy so exclusively on what the Russians saw fit to tell the Prussian or Austrian ministers, while ignoring the documents in which the Russians confidentially expressed their real opinions among themselves.

If one turns to the Russian documents, one finds that very soon after her accession Catherine accepted, sealed up, and kept in the greatest secrecy a memoir (presented by Count Z. G. Černyšev), proposing that at the first convenient moment Russia should annex Polish Livonia, — that is, one of the chief territories which she took at the First Partition. In October, 1763, the Russian Council approved this plan on principle, and, while reserving its execution to a more propitious moment, resolved that it should steadily be kept in view.[1] That it was not lost sight of in the next few years, appears from numerous documents. Thus in the main instructions to Kayserlingk and Repnin before the election of 1764, there is a threat, which has been little noted by historians, that if Russia were drawn into war over Polish affairs, she would not lay down the sword until she had annexed Polish Livonia.[2] At the beginning of the Turkish war in 1768, the Imperial Council, considering what aims were to be kept in view during the war, resolved that there were two great advantages to be sought, one of which was to gain a new frontier on the side of Poland that would assure the permanent security of the Empire.[3] In 1763, 1766, and 1767 Panin hinted significantly to the Prussian envoy that if Poland involved the two allies in great difficulties, they ought to indemnify themselves at the expense of the Republic.[4] Then, when the proper moment had come, at the beginning of 1771, Catherine herself, talking one night at court with Frederick's brother, Prince Henry of Prussia, with smiling lips and jesting tone threw out the idea of a partition of Poland.[5] It is now well established that Frederick took up the plan only after his brother had returned and convinced him that sentiment in St. Petersburg was quite in favor of such an arrangement.[6] It is true that Panin, the leading Russian minister, made a brave parade of being insuperably opposed to so iniquitous a transaction. But his professed scruples — which were exhibited only before the Prussian envoy, and of which there is no trace in his correspondence with Russians — need impress no one who reads how this same Panin, proposing the plan of partition in the Council of the Empire,

---

[1] Сборникъ, li, pp. 8–11.   [2] Ibid., pp. 92 ff.

[3] Архивъ Гос. Совѣта, November 6/17, 1768, i, p. 7.

[4] Сборникъ, xxii, pp. 188 f., 500; xxxvii, pp. 49 f.

[5] Henry to Frederick, January 8, 1771, Politische Correspondenz, xxx, pp. 406 f.

[6] Koser, Friedrich der Grosse, ii, pp. 465 f.; Volz' studies in the Forschungen zur brandenburgischen und preussischen Geschichte, xviii and xxiii.

declared that it offered " just such a chance as we have always thought of, for realizing what we all desire — namely, to make our frontier towards Poland coincide with the rivers." [1] In view of all this, we may well believe in Catherine's sincerity when she declared on ratifying the Partition Treaty that she had never given her sanction to any act with greater satisfaction.[2] The First Partition was not, then, a triumph of the brilliant, all-compelling Frederick over his reluctant and sorely-pressed ally. It was brought about in the first place by the common and equal cupidity of Russia and Prussia; and, in the second place, it was singularly facilitated by the extraordinary situation of Europe at that time, which made a partition a plausible means for averting a general war, forced Austria to become a partner in the nefarious business, and prevented the Western Powers from intervening.

When the three Eastern Powers were once agreed, through the Partition Treaties signed at St. Petersburg on August 5, 1772, it was no great task, though a long and unpleasant one, to compel the victim to assent to his own spoliation. After occupying their respective acquisitions with their troops, the three Courts issued manifestoes announcing their annexations. The Russian and Austrian proclamations were wisely laconic. They simply pointed out that these measures were necessitated by the continual anarchy in Poland and by the obstinacy of the Poles in resisting the well-meant efforts of their neighbors to restore order. Frederick, however, published a ponderous manifesto, establishing his just rights to what he was taking on the basis of all manner of musty documents raked together from the Prussian archives. Frederick for once made himself ridiculous.

The next step was to force the King of Poland to convoke a Diet, in order to get the dismemberment ratified in all form. Stanislas indulged in eloquent tirades of protest — " as good as the best pages in Plutarch," the Russian ambassador attested — and then issued the letters of convocation. The elections were managed

---

[1] Арх. Гос. Сов., May 16/27, 1771, i, pp. 82 ff. Compare also the protocol of the Council of February 7/18, 1771, *ibid.*, p. 74; Panin to Saldern, April 29/May 10, June 11/22, August 28/September 8, 1771, in the Сборникъ, xcvii, pp. 265, 335 ff., 411 ff.

[2] Beer, *Die erste Theilung Polens*, ii, p. 198.

with all the arts known to the Russians; the three allied ministers at Warsaw disposed of a joint *fonds de séduction;* and the presence of their troops sufficed to do what bribes could not effect. The Diet which met at Warsaw in April, 1773, is one of the most melancholy spectacles in Polish history. The deputies, who were for the most part the creatures of the three Powers, were ready enough to strike heroic attitudes in public; but that was merely for the sake of appearances. Behind the scenes they joined in a wild scramble to make their fortunes at the expense of the falling state. It was characteristic of that society that never before had Poland seen such a frenzy for pleasure. At that awful moment, life at Warsaw seemed a long saturnalia.

Effective resistance to the will of the three Powers was virtually out of the question. The nation lay prostrate and exhausted after the late four years' struggle. England and France, absorbed in their mutual rivalry, were perfectly passive in Eastern affairs. There remained no means of opposition except delay, which accomplished nothing except the prolongation of the nation's agony. Finally, on September 18, 1773, King and Diet gave their formal assent to the dismemberment.

By the First Partition Poland lost nearly one-third of her territory and slightly more than a third of her population.[1] The Republic retained an area approximately equal to that of France at that time, while in population it still ranked as the sixth state in Europe, with over seven million people.[2] There was no need to deplore greatly the lands yielded to Russia — the remote, poor, and thinly settled palatinates of Polotsk, Vitebsk, and Mohilev; but the cession of rich and fertile Galicia was a painful sacrifice; and hardest of all was the loss of Warmia and West Prussia, for Poland was thereby cut off from the sea, and her trade down the Vistula placed at the mercy of the enemy at Berlin. As regards the partitioning Powers, Russia, while taking the largest but also the poorest share, had greatly improved her frontier; Austria had gained most in population; Prussia's lot was, from the financial, military, and political standpoints, the most valuable.

However sympathetic the world has since become to the misfortunes of Poland, at the time of the First Partition the con-

---

[1] Cf. Korzon, *op. cit.*, i, pp. 42 ff., 160 f.   [2] *Ibid.*, i, pp. 161 f.

science of Europe does not seem to have been deeply stirred. Voltaire set the tone by sending his praise to Catherine and his congratulations to Frederick. The mass of the public conformed to his opinion. A few there were, however, who sympathized with Poland: Rousseau, Condorcet, Turgot, for instance; and some who condemned the Partition as an international crime. Raynal exposed the moral aspect of the transaction when he wrote: "It is in the security of peace, without rights, without pretexts, without grievances, without a shadow of justice, that this revolution has been effected by the terrible principle of force, which is, unhappily, the best argument of kings."[1] Burke pointed out in the *Annual Register* that the Partition was to be "considered as the first very great breach in the modern political system of Europe," which was thereby threatened with total subversion.[2]

All writers agreed in the gloomiest auguries as to the future of Poland. The Republic had become the reproach and the plaything of nations, said Raynal;[3] it was virtually a province of Russia, added Mably, and ruined beyond recall.[4] "It is hardly possible to suppose," Coxe wrote, "that Poland . . . will ever emerge from her present situation: her misfortunes . . . will gradually increase . . . until by slow progress or some violent revolution, Poland either subsides into an hereditary monarchy, or a well-ordered Republic; or, which is more probable, is totally swallowed up by the neighboring powers."[5] People wondered at the moderation of the three Powers in not appropriating the whole country in 1772, and agreed that, in the natural order of events, a total partition must follow sooner or later.[6]

Thus after a century of waiting, the partition so often prophesied, so often planned, so constantly discussed, had taken place. Now that this precedent had been set, the final solution of the Polish Question seemed to be clearly marked out, and the total ruin of the Republic only a question of time and circumstance.

[1] *Histoire philosophique et politique des Établissemens des Européens dans les deux Indes*, x, pp. 54 f. (1780).

[2] *Annual Register*, 1772, p. 2.

[3] *Op. cit.*, x, p. 54.

[4] *De la Situation de la Pologne en 1776* (*Oeuvres*, Paris, L'an III, xiii), pp. 7 ff.

[5] *Travels in Poland, Russia, Sweden, and Denmark*, 1784, i, pp. 18 f.

[6] Burke, *Annual Register*, 1772, p. 6; Mably, *op. cit., passim*, esp. p. 59.

CHAPTER I

The State of Poland After The First Partition
The Beginning of National Revival

I

BETWEEN the completion of the First Partition and the series of events that led to the Second, lies a period of a dozen years (1775–87), which, while outwardly quiet, was still so full of changes underneath the surface of society that it possesses a deep historical interest. It was then that the Polish people received whatever preparation they were to have for the final struggle, for the great national effort associated with the Four Years' Diet and Kościuszko's rising. On the scope and value of the work done at that time, the judgments of historians vary greatly. Those German and Russian writers who are inclined to deny to the later national movement any genuine vitality or any real possibility of success, commonly see in this period only superficial improvements, half-hearted velleities of reform, continued and ever-increasing demoralization, and opportunities frivolously frittered away.[1] On the other hand, many Polish historians have found in this period the beginnings of a real national regeneration, of a political, economic, and intellectual transformation which, had it not been so soon violently interrupted, would have restored Poland to her proper place among living states.[2] These diversities of opinion are not due simply to partisanship. They reflect the contradictions of a society in a confused state of transition, a society in which the old lawlessness, selfishness, corruption, and prejudices were still terribly deeply inrooted, but which was also, slowly but unmistakably, being leavened by a new reforming and patriotic spirit. In such a situation the amount of progress effected is peculiarly difficult to estimate.

[1] So, for instance, Herrmann, Solov'ev, Kostomarov, and also in much the same sense Bobrzyński among the Poles.

[2] So Lelewel, Szujski, and Korzon; and Brückner among the Germans.

The quiet which Poland enjoyed during this period was due in part to the exhaustion of the nation after the storms of the preceding decade, but also to the constraint imposed by Russia. For after the Partition the Russian yoke was fastened upon the country more firmly than ever. The King and many of the *szlachta*, taught by hard experience, saw safety only in absolute deference to the will of the Empress, in a dependence which, however humiliating and irksome it might be, at least guaranteed the continued existence of the state. During the next years, down to 1788, the Russian ambassador Stackelberg enjoyed a power greater than that of the King himself, so that people jested about his 'coregency' and spoke of him as the Empress' 'Viceroy' at Warsaw.

At all events, the Russian rule in Poland was now very different from what it had been, and in many ways much more tolerable. Having attained her immediate aims in Poland and being absorbed in other matters, Catherine desired to keep the Republic quiet and to maintain the *status quo*. For this purpose, it seemed best to abandon the old policy of playing off the King and the opposition against each other and so holding the balance between equally matched parties. That system was expensive and dangerous; it led to disturbances; it was no longer necessary, now that the King had become the most docile of dependents. Hence Stackelberg adopted the policy of ruling through the King and government of Poland by diplomatic means, avoiding coercion and threats as far as possible, descending into the arena of party politics only when it seemed absolutely necessary. The Russian troops were withdrawn from the country by 1780. Diets and Dietines enjoyed the long-forgotten experience of deliberating without the ' protection ' of foreign bayonets. Even the ambassador's funds for bribery were reduced to a minimum. The new course thus brought a considerable alleviation to the Poles, a diminution at least of the external signs of subjection. The nation began to breathe more freely again, and bolder spirits might dream of ultimate independence.

Another great advantage of the new system from the Polish standpoint was that it allowed — and even brought with it — certain political reforms. The Russians had come to see that complete anarchy in the Republic was not to their interest; and now that they had decided to use the Polish government as their instrument for ruling the country, they were bound to give that government a certain measure of strength and efficiency. Hence among the changes extorted from the Partition Diet of 1773 was the establishment of a new governing body called the Permanent Council. This board of thirty-six members, elected by the Diet every two years, was to advise the Crown in all important matters. As the King was obliged to accept the opinion of the majority, the royal power was virtually put in commission. The Council also served as a supreme administrative board, for which purpose it was divided into the five departments of Foreign Interests, Police, the Army, Justice, and Finance. The new institution was extremely unpopular. It was denounced by conservatives as a menace to 'liberty,' and an engine of 'despotism.' It was detested by patriots as an invention of the Russian ambassador, foisted by him upon the nation as a means of governing the country for Russian interests. This latter charge was quite true, for Stackelberg was the creator of the Council, regularly filled it with his friends, and succeeded in making it the stronghold and organ of Russian influence. But at any rate the Council was a great improvement on anything that had gone before. It gave Poland an executive that could dominate the hitherto independent and lawless great officers of the Crown — the chancellors, treasurers, marshals, and hetmans; it brought all the branches of the public service under a common direction; it gave to the administration for the first time something of unity and vigor.

This was not the only improvement allowed by Russia. The Partition Diet, facing a truly desperate situation, adopted a series of important financial reforms which, under the better fiscal administration of the Permanent Council, assured to the Republic a regular and an annually increasing income. By 1788 the revenues were nearly four times as great as under the last Saxon king, and more than twice what they had been in the early years of Stanislas Augustus.[1] The army, which at the time of the Partition had scarcely existed save on paper, was slowly brought up

---

[1] Korzon, *op. cit.*, iii, pp. 145 ff., 179.

to 18,000 men (in 1786). It was at last regularly paid; it was trained and disciplined according to the Prussian model; it was provided with capable officers from abroad and from the new cadet school. Quite the most important reform undertaken by the government, however, was the effort to found a national system of education. After the suppression of the Jesuit Order in 1773, its property was taken over by the state and entrusted to the new Education Commission. Made up for the most part of men filled with a high appreciation of their task and guided by enlightened and practical ideas, this Commission established a national school system which ranked among the best in Europe at that time and may claim, indeed, an honorable place in the history of pedagogics. This reform in education was of inestimable importance for the transformation of Polish society which was then going on. It created a new liberal and progressive spirit in the younger generation, which then communicated itself to the older one. From the new schools came a great part of the reformers of the Four Years' Diet and the patriots of 1794.

It must be confessed, however, that apart from the work of the Education Commission, the reforms undertaken by the government during this period fell far short of what ought to have been attained. Something was accomplished, but much more could have been done. It was true that no essential changes in the constitution were possible, owing to the Russian guarantee; but neither the revenues nor the army were brought up to the standard which Catherine was willing to allow, and which the country was amply able to support. This failure was due not only to wretched political dissensions and to negligence and lack of energy on the part of those in power, but also in large measure to the general ignorance that then prevailed as to the real resources of the nation. As a result, Poland entered the great crisis that followed ill-prepared from both the military and the financial standpoints.

II

In marked contrast to the unsatisfactory results attained in the political sphere stands the undeniable and striking progress made in matters economic and intellectual. M. Korzon, whose thorough researches have shown us that the Poland of those years has another history besides the conventional *chronique scandaleuse* of the Court, the Diets, and the high society of Warsaw, declares that after the Partition a great and admirable change came over the country. The nation went to work and worked hard. Agriculture, which had reached its lowest level in the Saxon period, experienced a remarkable revival, especially in the Ukraine, whose wealth was again unlocked by the reopening of the Black Sea to European trade. In spite of the merciless transit duties imposed by Prussia and the high protective tariffs of Joseph II, Polish trade developed rapidly. Manufactures, rural and urban, sprang up; there was scarcely a magnate family that did not found a factory of one kind or another; and ephemeral as many of these enterprises were, still the native industries were presently able to supply a great part of the articles needed at home, and even to place Polish manufactured goods — for the first time — in foreign markets. The long decadent and half-deserted towns awoke to new life and animation. Warsaw, which had but 30,000 inhabitants at the accession of Stanislas Augustus, could boast of 100,000 by the time of the Four Years' Diet.[1] It had become a great city, according to the standards of that age, and the center of a commercial, financial, and intellectual activity such as Poland had rarely witnessed. Finally, as a result of these developments, a social class which had long been grievously needed, at last appeared on the scene: a well-to-do, enterprising, and educated middle class, fitted for political life and eager to take its share of duties and privileges in the state; a class which in the final struggle for independence was to equal and perhaps surpass the *szlachta* in patriotism and civic devotion.[2]

When one considers that at the time of the First Partition Poland had been threatened with economic, no less than with political, ruin, the progress made since 1775 appears highly creditable. It shows that the nation was shaking off its lethargy and putting forth new life and energy. It suggests that at bottom the country was far more sound and healthy than the actions of its ruling class would indicate.

[1] Korzon, *op. cit.*, i, pp. 274 f.   [2] Cf. Korzon, ii, p. 411.

Not less important than the economic revival was the intellectual movement that marked this period. After two centuries in
which Poland had dwelt apart in intellectual isolation and almost
in intellectual stagnation, nourishing herself on the dry bones of
scholasticism and an outworn humanism, modern science and the
' philosophy ' of the Enlightenment made their triumphal entry
into the country. The new culture found an ardent champion in
the King, a ready acceptance with the aristocracy and the *bourgeoisie*, an entrance — disputed but soon forced — into the
schools. The familiar phenomena of that age in other countries
were repeated in Poland: the general adoption of the French
language, French fashions, in fact everything that came out of
France; the immense popularity of Voltaire, Rousseau, Condillac,
Locke, and the other prophets of the Enlightenment; the rage for
physics and the other experimental sciences; the spread of free-
masonry, which numbered the King and the leading members of
the aristocracy among its adepts.

In Poland, as elsewhere, the new culture brought with it a
certain deterioration of morals and a wide-spread weakening of
positive religious beliefs; but, on the other hand, it helped to
break down obscurantism, superstition, and prejudice, it aroused
a new critical spirit, it introduced better political, economic,
and social ideas, it promoted the serious discussion of the most
fundamental questions, and it vastly stimulated the demand for
reforms.

III

The demand for reforms was by no means new in Poland.
Ever since the sixteenth century a long line of publicists had
pointed out the evils in the Republic and suggested remedies.
Under the Saxon kings the warning voices grew louder and more
frequent; the question of the increase of the army came to be
discussed at every Diet; and Stanislas Konarski in a masterly
book subjected that ' palladium of liberty,' the Liberum Veto, to
a scathing criticism, which no one in the conservative camp was
able to refute.[1] At the death of Augustus III there appeared a

---

[1] The book *O skutecznym rad sposobie* (" On the Proper Organization of Assemblies "), 1760–63.

reform party, led by the Princes Czartoryski, who hoped, with the aid of Russia and after putting their nephew on the throne, to carry through a comprehensive program of reforms. Unfortunately, the plan which was to have saved the Republic, resulted only in subjecting it entirely to foreign domination. At all events, the tragic experiences of the first decade of the new reign sobered the more intelligent part of the nation. The demand for reforms, raised at the beginning of the century by only a few isolated individuals, and then in 1764 by a small party, now became general. The humiliating dependence upon Russia, the constant danger of a new dismemberment, the unconcealed contempt with which the rest of the world regarded the Poles, the influence of the new ' philosophy ' and of foreign travel, the example of the neighboring states, the general current of reforming ideas in the age of the Enlightenment — all these factors combined to open the eyes of thinking men to the glaring evils in the existing régime and to the fact that without reforms the Republic was hastening to ruin.

The political literature of that age was almost entirely on the side of the reformers. Its greatest representative was Stanislas Staszic, from whose pen appeared in 1785 a remarkable book entitled *Considerations on the Life of Jan Zamoyski*. Staszic demanded the abolition of the Liberum Veto, the establishment of hereditary monarchy, a permanent Diet, an army of 100,000 men, the increase of the taxes, a reform of justice, the systematic development of the national industries, and the emancipation of the serfs. His book had an extraordinary, an unexampled success. Its principles became the fashion in the salons, and penetrated widely in far humbler circles; it furnished an arsenal of arguments to the reforming party; it laid down in outline the program of the Four Years' Diet.[1]

Undoubtedly the nation was coming to a clearer realization of what must be done if ruin were to be avoided, but it remained to be proved that the nation was capable of doing it. The reforms in question demanded the abjuration of the most revered traditions, and almost a complete breach with the past; they de-

[1] Cf. Niewenglowski, *Les Idées politiques en Pologne à la fin du xviiie siècle,* pp. 75 ff.; Korzon, " Początki sejmu wielkiego," in *Ateneum,* 1881, i, pp. 330 f.

manded a sure political instinct, consummate statesmanship, energy, and will-power on the part of the leaders; they demanded unity, discipline, perseverance, and the willingness to make any sacrifice on the part of the nation. Had Poland the moral strength required for so great an effort ? To that question it is peculiarly difficult to give an answer. Diplomats, travellers, and writers of memoirs have left us the blackest pictures of Polish society in that age: of the frivolity and instability of the national character, the corruption of private morals, the general inclination to riotous festivities, drunkenness, gambling, and other forms of dissipation; of the degradation and brutishness of the lower classes, the ignorance, narrow-mindedness, and selfishness of the lesser gentry, the sordid ambitions, the anarchical spirit, the venality, the lack of patriotism of the magnates. Undoubtedly these pictures are often overcharged through personal bias, and often based too exclusively on observation of the small group of people at the top. But in any case enough remains to prove a very deep and dangerous demoralization. The political history of this period shows that too many of the Poles had learned nothing from the Partition, but were still ready to plunge their country into disorder, raise scandals that disgraced the nation in the eyes of Europe, and call in foreigners against their own government, whether for wretched, selfish aims or on account of misguided political ideas or through sheer force of habit. Although the new reforming tendencies were constantly gaining ground, a large part of the *szlachta* still clung blindly to the old prejudices, the old false maxims, the old horror of innovations. In short, while the period from 1775 to 1787 shows a very considerable progress in comparison with what went before, while the worst was over and the nation was undoubtedly on the right course again, still not nearly enough had been accomplished, not as much as could and should have been done. The newer, better tendencies had not yet gained a complete predominance. The nation was not yet ready either materially or morally, when the final crisis came.

CHAPTER II

The Austro-Russian Alliance and the Outbreak of the Russo-Turkish War

I

Of the three Powers who had joined in the First Partition, Russia had perhaps the most reason to rest content with the arrangements then made. After rectifying her hitherto inconvenient western frontier, she had no urgent motives for seeking further Polish territories;[1] and owing to the mutual jealousy of the German Powers, what remained of the Republic had been turned over unrestrictedly to the guardianship of the great Catherine. At Warsaw the King reigned, the Russian ambassador ruled, and the envoys of Austria and Prussia looked on. Under such circumstances it might well appear to be Russia's interest to maintain the *status quo*, rather than to aggrandize her neighbors by new dismemberments. That seems to have been Catherine's view — with certain reservations. Her policy after the First Partition was to protect the Poles in their remaining possessions, as long as they made no effort to escape from her control, and as long as no conjuncture in general European affairs rendered it desirable or necessary to purchase the support of the German Powers with drafts on the usual treasury — Poland. Within these limits, the Empress was committed to maintaining the existing arrangements.

Very different was the position of her chief confederate in depredation, Prussia. If that aspiring young state was to main-

[1] The one further improvement of the Russian frontier on the side of Poland that naturally suggested itself after the Partition, related to that southeastern corner of the Polish Ukraine which projected into Russian territory, and which was of great importance in case of war with the Turks. This acquisition seems to have been discussed at St. Petersburg. Cf. the instructions to the Marquis de Vérac in 1780: " On parle d'un échange qu'elle [Catherine] veut faire des provinces qui lui ont été cédées contre la partie de l'Ukraine que les Polonois ont conservée," *R. I. A.*, Russie, ii, p. 368.

tain the rank Frederick had won for it among the great Powers, it needed above all things to acquire a solid territorial foundation, to unite its scattered members, to secure a defensible frontier. It could not possibly accept as final an arrangement that left a great wedge of Polish territory projecting deep into its side, completely separating East and West Prussia from Silesia, while two highly important towns, Dantzic and Thorn, remained Polish, although surrounded by Prussian territory. For the half-built monarchy of the Hohenzollerns, it was a vital matter that the First Partition of Poland should not be the last. It was true that in his last years Frederick II, grown cautious with age and haunted by the fear of Austria, showed little taste for further adventures in territorial aggrandizement. But the task was only deferred. With the advent of a new king, Prussia's unalterable ambition to obtain Dantzic, Thorn, and part of Great Poland became one of the most constant and important factors in European politics.

Austria's policy towards Poland in these years was determined by opposition to that of Prussia. The fact that Prussia coveted new acquisitions in that quarter sufficed to lead Austrian statesmen to attach the greatest importance to upholding the integrity of the Republic. That any further aggrandizement of the ' natural enemy ' must be prevented at all costs, was one of the cardinal tenets of the faith once for all delivered to Prince Kaunitz. It was held at Vienna that the ' artificial state,' raised to perilous grandeur by Frederick, would, if confined to its existing meagre territories, ultimately collapse of itself. Austria might hope to end successfully the contest for supremacy in Germany, if she could prevent the further dismemberment of Poland. For the rest, she wanted no more Polish territories for herself, and would not have been greatly averse to parting with those she already possessed, if a good exchange could be effected.

Although the policy of the two Imperial Courts thus seemed to afford some security to the Republic, the situation of Poland remained highly precarious. If Russia and Prussia were allied, the latter might at the first emergency extort from the Empress new concessions in Poland as the price of her support. If the Imperial Courts were allied, Prussia might seize the moment when they were engaged in some great enterprise to demand Polish territory as a condition of not opposing them. If all three Powers were united, the combination was almost sure to produce a new partition. In short, any grouping of the three neighbors contained elements of danger to Poland. Similarly, almost any crisis might engender another dismemberment of the Republic. As the system of the balance of power was then practised, any aggrandizement of one of the Eastern Powers was likely to lead the other two to demand equivalent acquisitions; and where were equivalents to be found so conveniently as in the vast, defenceless intermediate realm, in which, as it was said, ' one had only to stoop in order to take ' ? Whenever the equilibrium was threatened, Poland might be' employed to redress the balance. And, unfortunately, the equilibrium was at that time in perpetual danger, owing to the aggressive, the downright revolutionary policy of Catherine, of Joseph II, and, after Frederick's death, of Prussia.

II

The union of the three Eastern Powers at the time of the Partition proved only temporary. The Imperial Courts soon resumed their dissensions over Turkish affairs, while the alliance between Russia and Prussia remained in full force, outwardly at least, down to 1780. The only grave conflict in those years, the War of the Bavarian Succession, did not last long enough to involve Poland seriously; but it did give rise to several projects that were to be of decided importance in the later development of the Polish Question. At the moment when Frederick II was about to draw the sword, his minister Hertzberg came forward with a plan for avoiding war by a bargain, by which part of Bavaria should go to Austria, part of Galicia should be restored to Poland, and the grateful Republic should in its turn cede Dantzic, Thorn, and some districts in Great Poland to Prussia.[1] This was, in embryo, the famous ' Hertzberg plan,' which figured so prominently in the Oriental crisis a decade later. It was also akin to that Austro-Prussian plan of 1792 out of which grew the Second Partition of

[1] Unzer, *Hertzbergs Anteil an den preussisch-österreichischen Verhandlungen, 1778–1779*, pp. 4 f., 122 f.

Poland. Frederick is said to have repudiated the project in 1778 with scant ceremony; [1] nevertheless, after hostilities had begun, Hertzberg returned to the charge with the proposal of conquering Galicia and then trading it off to Poland for the acquisitions desired by Prussia. The King rebuffed him once more, but henceforth the idea of ousting the Austrians from Galicia and acquiring Dantzic, Thorn, and part of Great Poland for Prussia, by exchange if possible, became the favorite project, the ' grand design ' of the persistent, patriotic, and rather pedantic minister.[2] Hertzberg seems to have sounded some of the Poles on the subject of the exchange at the time of the Bavarian war; [3] and his plan may stand in some kind of connection with the project of Stanislas Augustus for recovering Galicia by joining in hostilities against Austria. The King's design, which foreshadows the Polish plans of 1790, was well known at Vienna. It led Austria to take a more active interest in Polish affairs after the war, and it strengthened her desire to keep Poland in a state of impotence.[4]

After the Peace of Teschen, Catherine began to consider a change in her political connections. The alliance with Prussia seemed to have furnished most of the advantages of which it was capable; and for the vast Oriental plans which now filled the Empress' mind, the friendship of Austria was necessary. For a time Catherine may have thought of combining liaisons with both the German Powers by forming that triple alliance which had often been a favorite project at St. Petersburg. What the triple alliance would have led to, is sufficiently indicated in a remarkable conversation that took place between the Empress' favorite Potemkin and the Prussian envoy Görtz in the autumn of 1779. At the order of his master, who was eager to make sure of the favorite, Görtz intimated Frederick's willingness to further Potemkin's supposed plans upon the crown of Poland. There-

---

[1] His reply to Hertzberg was: " Allez vous promener avec vos indignes plans. Vous êtes fait pour être le ministre de gens coujons comme l'électeur de Bavière, mais non pour moi," Bailleu, " Graf Hertzberg," *H. Z.*, xlii, p. 446, and note 1.

[2] Unzer, *op. cit.*, p. 143; Ranke, *Die deutschen Mächte*, i, pp. 22 f.; Krauel, *Graf Hertzberg als Minister Friedrich Wilhelms II*, p. 36.

[3] Cf. his report to the King, September 4, 1778, Unzer, p. 143.

[4] Kalinka, *Ostatnie lata panowania Stanisława Augusta*, i, pp. 300 f.; Herrmann, *Geschichte des russischen Staates*, vi, pp. 481, 483 f., 502, 520 f.

upon the Russian, while roundly denying the ambition ascribed to him, seized the occasion to propose a complete partition of the Republic, as the only means of ending the difficulties to which Poland in its present state must constantly give rise; and he expressly charged the envoy to procure Frederick's views on the subject. For once Frederick professed total lack of appetite. He replied that he thought of nothing except keeping what he had and checking the insatiable ambition of Austria. With that response this highly enigmatic episode ended. Of one thing one may be fairly sure: Potemkin could hardly have been throwing out merely his own ideas, for in that case he could not have insisted upon a reply from Frederick. He must have been acting with a commission from the Empress. But, on the other hand, one cannot be certain whether Catherine was simply trying to probe the secret ambitions of Prussia, or whether she seriously thought of a total partition of Poland as a preliminary to the partition of Turkey, and as a means of bringing the Eastern Powers into complete and durable accord.[1] At any rate, Frederick's answer must have confirmed the idea that the triple alliance was out of the question, and that the Prussian alliance had exhausted its usefulness. With so unambitious and superannuated a partner as Frederick had now become, there was really nothing great to be done.

While the King of Prussia was thus playing the recalcitrant, the Court of Vienna was straining every nerve to supplant his influence at St. Petersburg. And as a result of the indefatigable activity of Prince Kaunitz, the adroit diplomacy of Count Louis Cobenzl, who was sent in 1779 as envoy to Russia, the visit of Joseph II to the Empress in 1780, the influence of Potemkin, and above all Catherine's own clever calculations, Austria in 1781 could boast of a brilliant diplomatic victory. By the letters exchanged between the two sovereigns under the dates of May 21 and 13/24 of that year,[2] the Austro-Russian alliance was consum-

---

[1] For this interesting incident, which deserves a more thorough investigation than it has yet received, cf. Görtz, *Denkwürdigkeiten*, i, pp. 123 ff.; Dohm, *Denkwürdigkeiten*, ii, pp. xlv–xlviii; Reimann, *Neuere Geschichte des preussischen Staates*, ii, pp. 282 ff.; Koser, *Friedrich der Grosse*, ii, p. 606.

[2] Printed in Arneth, *Joseph II und Katharina*, pp. 72–87.

mated: an alliance which in the next few years seemed to dominate Europe, and which was to be portentous both for Turkey and for Poland.

It was the fatal defect of this alliance that the two contracting Powers entered into it with very different aims. For the Austrians the great object was security from Prussia and, if the opportunity occurred, offensive action against that state. For Catherine, however — and circumstances inevitably rendered her the dominant partner — the goal was always the realization of her plans against the Ottoman Empire. For some years after the conclusion of the alliance, the two cabinets were intermittently engaged in the discussion of the grandiose scheme called the ' Greek project,' which aimed at nothing less than the expulsion of the Turks from Europe, suitable aggrandizement for the allies, the restoration of the Byzantine Empire under Catherine's grandson Constantine, and the creation of a ' Kingdom of Dacia,' presumably intended for Potemkin.[1] The Austrians accepted the grand plan in principle, but without enthusiasm and with lively misgivings as to the possibility of its execution.

In Europe at large, enough of the ' Greek project' was known to arouse enthusiasm in the public and consternation in the cabinets. When in 1783 Catherine proceeded to the annexation of the Crimea, the other Powers regarded the step as a preliminary to the final onslaught of both the Imperial Courts upon the Turks; and France and Prussia prepared for the worst emergencies. Both Vergennes, the director of French foreign policy, and Frederick were ready to go to war, rather than to allow the allies to partition the Turkish Empire at pleasure. Vergennes thought of bringing

---

[1] I know of no direct evidence from Russian official documents to prove that Dacia was intended for Potemkin; but such was the general opinion of contemporaries, and that belief has been almost universally accepted by historians. One reservation must be made, however. In case it proved possible to free the Danubian Principalities, but not to restore the Greek Empire, then Catherine would probably have preferred to bestow the crown of Dacia upon Constantine, although doubtless with Potemkin at his side as adviser and mentor. Cf. [Helbig], " Potemkin der Taurier," in *Minerva*, xxiii (1797), pp. 228 f., xxvi, pp. 305 ff., xxxii, pp. 427 ff.; Görtz, *op. cit.*, i, pp. 126 f.; Dohm, *op. cit.*, ii, p. 50; Zinkeisen, *Geschichte des osmanischen Reiches*, vi, p. 351; Jorga, *Geschichte des osmanischen Reiches*, v, p. 91; Брикнеръ, Потемкинъ, pp. 64 ff., 212; Askenazy, *Przymierze polsko-pruskie*, p. 36.

into the field against the Imperial Courts a great coalition con-
sisting of France, Spain, Sardinia, Prussia, Sweden, and perhaps
even Poland.[1] In case Catherine and Joseph were satisfied, however, with wresting a few provinces from the Turks, Vergennes
preferred to avoid a general war by a bargain which would give
France the Austrian Netherlands, and Prussia some Polish territories.[2] Frederick and Hertzberg, discussing the same problems
in 1783, differed in that the King inclined more to war, and the
minister to diplomacy; but the conclusions of both were identical:
that in case Austria made any considerable conquests from the
Turks, Prussia must extort equivalent acquisitions in Poland.[3]
The storm blew over on this occasion, as Catherine contented
herself with the Crimea, the Emperor reserved his claims to a
later time, and the Turks were persuaded not to risk a rupture.
But the execution of the ' Greek project ' was only postponed, not
abandoned; and it was certain that whenever the allies resumed
the plan, they would have to reckon with Prussia, and possibly
even with a great coalition, such as Vergennes had outlined.

The Imperial Courts were by no means ignorant of the opposition to be expected. For a time the Austrians were not unwilling
to bribe Prussia to remain quiet by offering her a bit of Polish
territory, for which the Republic might be compensated out of the
spoils taken from Turkey.[4] Later, however, they talked rather of
coercing the Court of Berlin into passivity by military demonstrations or even active hostilities; and they frequently suggested
that, in general, the indispensable preliminary to the execution of
the 'grand plan' was 'to remove the horns of the King of Prussia.'

---

[1] Flassan, *Histoire de la diplomatie française*, vii, pp. 383 ff.; Zinkeisen, *op. cit.*,
vi, pp. 423 ff.; Tratchevsky, "La France et l'Allemagne sous Louis XVI," in *R. H.*,
xiv; Lucchesini to Frederick William, November 19, 1788: " J'ai vu des lettres
de ce Ministre au Comte de Rzewuski, demeurant alors à Paris, par lesquelles on
voit que le Comte de Vergennes, prévoyant la Guerre actuelle entre la Porte et les
deux Cours Impériales, auroit voulu pouvoir former une Confédération en Pologne,
soutenue par l'argent de la France et de l'Espagne, et y joindre la Puissance de
V. M., avec une diversion que le Roi de Suède auroit dû tenter en Finlande," B. A.,
Pologne, Fasc., 1097.

[2] Flassan, *ibid.*, pp. 391 ff.

[3] Bailleu, "Der Ursprung des deutschen Fürstenbundes," *H. Z.* xli, pp. 424 ff.

[4] *F. R. A.*, II, liii, p. ix; Beer, *Orientalische Politik Oesterreichs*, p. 48.

After the formation of the *Fürstenbund* — a crushing blow to
Catherine's German policy — that view seemed to gain ground
on the Neva.[1] The Empress was, in fact, coming to regard the
Court of Berlin as her most dangerous enemy. The state of
Russo-Prussian relations from 1785 onward ominously recalled
the tension on the eve of the Seven Years' War.[2]

With Poland the Imperial Courts were even less disposed to
share their prospective conquests. They intended that the
Republic should remain as it was — weak and helpless.[3] By the
treaty of 1781 they had pledged themselves to maintain tranquillity in Poland, and had guaranteed the constitution as fixed
by the Diet of 1773; and they were thus committed to upholding
the *status quo.* Practically, the alliance produced a certain improvement in the position of Poland, inasmuch as it set a check
upon the territorial ambition of Prussia, while, by diverting
Catherine's attention to the Eastern Question, it led to a considerable relaxation of the pressure she had hitherto exerted upon
the Republic. On the other hand, the alliance did not in any way
impair Russia's exclusive position in Poland. Austria gained no
additional influence there as a result of her new connection, and the
fear of arousing the suspicions or resentment of Russia deterred
her from any systematic or continued attempt to form a party of
her own. Joseph interfered vigorously in Poland only when the
interests of his Galician subjects were concerned; and if these
interventions occasionally led the Polish opposition (the so-called
'Patriots') to fix their hopes on the Court of Vienna, it was
invariably shown that no permanent support could be expected
from that quarter. At the opening of the Four Years' Diet an
Austrian party in Poland did not exist.

One question frequently discussed between St. Petersburg and
Vienna was that of the future successor to Stanislas Augustus.
Russia consistently declared in favor of a 'Piast' (i. e., a native
Pole); while Austria, from 1782 onward, urged the desirability of

[1] *F. R. A.*, II, liii, pp. xiv ff., 349, 368; liv, pp. 13–21, 78 f., 108, note 1.

[2] Cf. Трачевскій, Союзъ Князей, pp. 384 ff.

[3] Catherine's notes on the " Greek project," written probably about 1782, in
the Русская Старина, lxxvi, pp. 1 ff.

holding out hopes to the Elector of Saxony.[1] Behind this latter
plan lay the wish of the Vienna cabinet not only to lure the
Elector away from the side of Prussia, but also to place upon the
Polish throne a king less dependent on Russia and more amenable
to Austrian influence. Such details were not overlooked at St.
Petersburg. The Polish succession remained an open question
between the two Courts, a germ of future disagreements.

It was not the only rift in the alliance. Indeed the rôle of
' most intimate ally ' to Catherine would have proved a bit trying
to the most patient, the least self-willed of monarchs. Self-
abnegation was not Joseph's forte. Neither he nor Kaunitz had
ever felt any real ardor for the ' Greek project ': both occasionally vented their ill-humor at the frivolity, the megalomania, the
slight regard for her ally, with which the Empress pursued the
scheme. Besides, the advantages of the partnership seemed to
fall out most unequally. The alliance had brought to Catherine
the Crimea — to Joseph, only failure upon failure. The Emperor
began to think about a change of policy.

At the beginning of 1785, after the collapse of his plan for the
Bavarian Exchange, Joseph was reflecting seriously on the desirability of a frank reconciliation with Prussia. United, the two
German Powers could hold all Europe in check, and procure
themselves whatever ' advantages ' they chose.[2] The ' advantage ' the Emperor had in mind for himself was, of course,
Bavaria: what Prussia would have demanded in return, he could
easily have imagined. The point of the alliance, it appears,
would have been directed chiefly against France, while Russia was
to be taken into the partnership. In short, this was the system of
1792, of the First Coalition, of the Second Partition of Poland.
Dropped for a time, the same ideas returned to the Emperor's
mind after the death of Frederick II. Kaunitz dissented vigorously, and Joseph appeared to yield; but behind the Chancellor's
back he continued the discussion with the Vice-Chancellor, Philip

[1] Cobenzl to Joseph, January 18, 1783, and June 3, 1785, Kaunitz to Cobenzl,
February 13, 1787, *F. R. A.*, II, liii, p. 366; liv, pp. 41 f., 108. Also Joseph to
Catherine, November 13, 1782, and her reply of January 4/15, 1783, Arneth,
Joseph II und Katharina, pp. 169–175, 182–188.

[2] Joseph to Louis Cobenzl, January 22, 1785, *F. R. A.*, II, liv, pp. 5–8.

Cobenzl, and Spielmann, the rising man in the *Haus-Hof-und Staatskanzlei*. These two ministers, who were later to reign and fall together, were already very much of one mind, particularly with regard to the policies of their chief, the Chancellor. They agreed that the Emperor's idea of a reconciliation with Prussia pointed to the only course that could lead to great results. Both before and after Joseph's trip to the Crimea, they submitted to him in writing plans for the realization of that project. The exact nature of their program is not quite certain; but there can be little doubt that one feature of it was the exchange of Belgium for Bavaria in the interests of Austria, while it probably included acquisitions in Poland for the Court of Berlin. The combination of those two favorite plans was the natural, the obvious condition of any bargain between the two states for 'reciprocal advantages.' Indeed, towards the end of 1786 an insinuation looking to an understanding on just that basis reached Berlin as coming from Vienna. The whole incident is very obscure, but it is possible that the insinuation had some connection with the projects then under discussion in the Emperor's cabinet. At any rate, those projects came to nothing, at least for the time being. Joseph found the means proposed too adventurous, and the consequences too dangerous.[1]

While these discussions were going on at Vienna, similar desires for a rapprochement were felt in some circles in Berlin. Prince Henry, Frederick's brother, had long advocated an understanding with Austria for reciprocal advantages, and was not averse even to allowing the Bavarian Exchange. The Duke of Brunswick held somewhat similar opinions. Bischoffwerder and Wöllner, the favorites of the new King, Frederick William II, cultivated intimate relations with Prince Reuss, the Austrian envoy, and desired to bring about a meeting between the two monarchs.[2]

---

[1] For the above: Ranke, *Die deutschen Mächte*, ii, pp. 298–308; Ph. Cobenzl to L. Cobenzl, December 21, 1786, *F. R. A.*, II, liv, pp. 93 f.; Brunner, *Correspondances intimes de l'Empereur Joseph II*, pp. 60 f., 66 (Ph. Cobenzl to the Emperor, February 23, 1787; Joseph's reply; also his note to Cobenzl of September 25, 1787); F. K. Wittichen, *Preussen und England in der europäischen Politik, 1785–88*, pp. 118–123, 186 f.

[2] Krauel, *Prinz Heinrich von Preussen als Politiker*, pp. 24, 30, 34 ff., 40 f.; Volz, " Prinz Heinrich von Preussen und die preussische Politik vor der ersten

On both sides there was, then, some desire for better relations, some dawning consciousness that it would be wise to end the long rivalry by a friendly understanding, through which each state would be enabled to make the acquisitions it most needed. But significant as these ideas were for the future, the time for realizing them had not yet come. In the great European crisis of 1787–91, the two German Powers were destined to appear once more as bitter enemies.

III

The prelude to that crisis was the famous voyage of the Empress Catherine down the Dnieper to visit her new Tauric provinces. The King of Poland waited seven weeks at Kanev for a few hours' audience with the Tsarina; the Emperor of the Romans arrived soon afterwards to pay his homage to her. Europe looked on with wonder and uneasiness, and the Turks prepared for war. Joseph had gone to the Crimea much against his will, loaded down with a set of Kaunitz's most masterly and voluminous instructions and determined to do his utmost to dissuade his ally from attempting the execution of the ' grand plan ' just then. The meeting passed off brilliantly and satisfactorily; the Emperor returned to Vienna reassured. Some weeks later (August 16, 1787) the Porte declared war on Russia. Joseph at once acknowledged the *casus foederis*, though his public declaration of war against Turkey was issued only in the following February. After so many years of planning, the allies were now called upon to carry out their projects, and they were caught only half prepared. It remained to be seen whether the despised Turks would prove such easy victims as had been imagined, whether the other Powers would quietly look on, and especially whether the two states that had suffered most from the pressure of the Imperial Courts would not seize the opportunity to make trouble. Those states were Prussia and Poland.

Teilung Polens," *F. B. P. G.*, xviii, pp. 165 ff.; F. K. Wittichen, *Preussen und England*, pp. 18 f.; Koser, " Aus dem ersten Regierungsjahre Friedrich Wilhelms II," *F. B. P. G.*, iv, p. 600; Welschinger, *Mirabeau à Berlin*, pp. 303, 402.

CHAPTER III

THE DESIGNS OF PRUSSIA

I

GREAT was the satisfaction felt at Berlin over the outbreak of the Oriental war. Prussia at once found herself in an extraordinarily favorable situation. With the forces of the Imperial Courts tied up in an arduous and costly enterprise, with the other Powers suing for the friendship of Berlin, with the supposedly invincible army and the well-filled treasury left by the late King, under an ambitious new sovereign and a veteran minister who aspired to surpass all that the great Frederick had done, Prussia seemed to be in a position to make herself the arbiter of the Continent and the foremost Power in Europe. Everyone at Berlin agreed that a unique moment for great enterprises had come; but the question as to just what was to be done was not so simple. One party was for forming an alliance with England, Sweden, and Poland, coming actively to the aid of the Turks, and fighting out the contest with Austria to a finish. If Russia stood by her ally, the Turks, Poles, and Swedes could keep her busy. By fighting two or three campaigns now, it was said, Prussia could realize all her most cherished ambitions, place her position as a great Power upon an indestructible basis, and win peace for the next century.[1] Such plans were bold and alluring, but they were open to grave objections. What reliance could be placed on the Turks, after the figure they had made in their last war, or on such a mad knight-errant as the King of Sweden, or on the feeble and inconstant Poles ? The new Prussian entente with England was still in a very uncertain stage, and Pitt had hitherto manifested no great interest in Eastern affairs. Besides, it ran contrary to Frederician traditions to provoke or even risk a war with Russia. The alliance

[1] Cf. the ideas of Diez in Zinkeisen, *op. cit.*, vi, p. 687; of Goltz, Herrmann, *op. cit.*, vi, pp. 200 ff.; also the plans described by Askenazy, *Przymierze polsko-pruskie*, pp. 19-24.

with the Empress had not yet expired,[1] and there was no wish dearer to most Prussian statesmen than to restore the onetime intimacy of that connection. The indications from St. Petersburg were not unfavorable; for the Russian ministers talked most obligingly, and the Vice-Chancellor Ostermann even spoke of the acquisitions which Prussia might make in the course of this war.[2] Would it not be wiser, therefore, to play the part of the zealous friend, try to draw the Empress away from the Court of Vienna, and in the end be paid for one's services by a handsome acquisition in Poland ? That was, at least, the policy that prevailed at Berlin at the outbreak of the Oriental war; and if it led to a fiasco, one cannot deny that it seemed at the start well adapted to circumstances. Later events were to prove that it was easier to make acquisitions in Poland in alliance with Russia than in opposition to her.

But the particular plan through which Prussia attempted to carry out this policy was in truth the unluckiest that could be imagined. We have seen that Count Hertzberg, now the leading minister of Frederick William II, had, years before, evolved a scheme by which, as he thought, the mistakes of Frederick II at the time of the First Partition could be rectified, the Polish Question settled to perfection, and the whole equilibrium of Europe assured *in saecula saeculorum*. Towards the end of 1787 and at the beginning of 1788, the long-treasured revelation, with some adaptation to present circumstances, was submitted for royal approval, and confided in the greatest secrecy to most of the Prussian representatives abroad, and to a great part of the foreign ministers at Berlin. The plan, now as in 1778, had two chief aims: to secure for Prussia the desired acquisitions in Poland, and to oust the Austrians from Galicia. This was to be effected by purely diplomatic means, and of the most extraordinary sort. Prussia was to induce the belligerent Powers to accept her mediation, and the following terms of peace: (1) the Porte should cede Wallachia and Moldavia to Austria, and Bessarabia and Oczakow to Russia, while renouncing all claims to the Crimea: in return for

---

[1] The alliance lapsed only in April, 1788.
[2] Bailleu, " Graf Hertzberg," *H. Z.*, xlii, p. 468.

this, Prussia and her allies would undertake an eternal guarantee of the Turkish possessions south of the Danube; (2) Austria should restore Galicia to Poland; (3) the Poles, fired with gratitude, should cede Dantzic, Thorn and the palatinates of Posen and Kalisz to Prussia. The monstrous impracticability of this plan has been so often exposed that further criticism seems almost superfluous. Though Hertzberg compared his scheme to the " egg of Columbus " and found that " no reasonable man could resist it," [1] still he was probably the only person at that time who believed in the project, and no plan has ever been more unanimously condemned by historians.[2] The idea that, of five Powers concerned, three would voluntarily submit to be robbed, and the fourth, from sheer gaiety of heart, to accept foreign dictation, for the benefit of the fifth, which had done nothing whatever except to invent this marvelous panacea — this was a thought that could arise only in the mind of an elderly pedant who imagined that his *mémoires* were perfectly irresistible, and who, as Mirabeau said, " saw nothing in this sublunary sphere but Hertzberg and Prussia." [3]

All through the winter of 1787–88 Hertzberg dwelt in a fool's paradise. The King, who in October had indicated his perfect willingness to take the whole left bank of the Vistula, if an opportunity presented itself,[4] was slowly won over to give at least a provisional assent to the ' grand plan.' Diez at Constantinople received copious instructions to prepare the infidels to receive the great light. The Russians were overwhelmed with kindness. After offering the Empress Prussian mediation, subsidies for the war, and a renewal of the alliance treaty, Hertzberg waited only for the expected favorable answer, before laying his plan formally before her. March 12, 1788, the answer was delivered in Berlin: the Prussian proposals were one and all declined or evaded. At

[1] Luckwaldt, in *F. B. P. G.*, xv, p. 97; Zinkeisen, *op. cit.*, vi, p. 676.

[2] From the long list of writers who have condemned it, one might cite Bailleu, Duncker, Treitschke, Koser, Luckwaldt, Krauel, Andreae, Kalinka, and Askenazy. Almost the only defenders have been the brothers Paul and F. K. Wittichen, whose recent attempts at a vindication of Hertzberg are far from convincing.

[3] Welschinger, *Mirabeau à Berlin*, p. 206.

[4] Luckwaldt, in *F. B. P. G.*, xv, p. 97.

the moment when Joseph II was beginning hostilities against the Turks, Catherine was not inclined to compromise herself by a suspicious intimacy with Prussia.

The first onslaught had failed, but Hertzberg was not the man to give up the battle. He concluded only that patience and the support of some other Power were needed. Hence he next started negotiations with England for converting the existing entente into an alliance, while he continued to lavish professions of friendship at St. Petersburg; he refused the proposals of Sweden, which was just then preparing to attack the Empress; and he waited with longing to hear of the expected Russian victories over the Turks. The presence in Berlin during the summer of a Russian secret agent of pronounced Prussian sympathies, Alopeus, was encouraging; and, with the conclusion of the Triple Alliance with England and Holland in August, Hertzberg thought himself on the highroad to success. If his new allies would only properly back him up, if the Turks were once so soundly thrashed that they could seek safety only under the protection of Prussia, if Catherine would only accept the hand of friendship held out to her from Berlin, if the Austrians and Poles could be cajoled or coerced into accepting arrangements so suitable for them and so profitable for Prussia, then the success of the ' grand plan ' was assured.

As a matter of fact, however, not one of these conditions was likely to be fulfilled. Pitt, while glad to coöperate with Prussia in restoring peace in the Orient, was by no means disposed to back up Prussian schemes of aggrandizement.[1] The perverse Turks exasperated their friends at Berlin by not getting beaten. In the summer of 1788 they were holding their own against the Russians, and winning victory after victory over the Austrians. Above all, unknown to Hertzberg, the Imperial Courts had been making new agreements, especially designed to prevent the realization of the ' grand plan.'

[1] Cf. Salomon, *William Pitt*, I[ii], pp. 339 ff., 444 ff.; Rose, *William Pitt and National Revival*, pp. 386, 508 ff.

II

From a very early date (December, 1787), intercepted dispatches had kept the Austrian government constantly informed of the development of Hertzberg's projects. Joseph found the grand plan ' as inadmissible as it was ridiculous ' ; Kaunitz called it a ' chimera ';[1] nevertheless they hastened to raise the alarm at St. Petersburg. It was above all things necessary to make sure that Russia would not succumb to Hertzberg's seductions. The ambassador Cobenzl was ordered to propose that the two Courts should pledge themselves to resist with all their forces any Prussian attempt to make acquisitions in Poland, and that they should at once set to work to conclude an alliance with the Republic.[2] In case of an attack on the part of Prussia, they might even promise the Poles the restoration of the provinces ceded to that Court at the time of the Partition.

On the receipt of these instructions, Cobenzl exerted himself to the utmost to ruin the Hertzberg plan, once and for all. There was no possible case, he declared incessantly, in which his Court could consent to an aggrandizement of Prussia; a gain for themselves, if coupled with advantages for their natural enemy, would be only a loss; the acquisitions contemplated by Prussia in Poland were contrary to the fundamental interests of both the Imperial Courts; and, if necessary, Austria would abandon the Turkish war and sacrifice every other consideration, in order to oppose the Prussian designs with all her might.[3]

This language and these demands did not cause unmixed pleasure at St. Petersburg. Though they were far from captivated by the Hertzberg plan, and were, in general, opposed to Prussian acquisitions in Poland at that time, the Russians disliked binding themselves by too precise engagements, and were even less inclined to take Austria into the alliance then under

---

[1] Joseph to L. Cobenzl, December 11, 1787, *F. R. A.*, II, liv, pp. 229 f.; Kaunitz to L. Cobenzl, December 7, 1787 and February 7, 1788, V. A., *Russland, Expeditionen.*

[2] The project of alliance had been included in the instructions given Cobenzl on his return to Russia in 1786. The orders mentioned in the text are dated December 7, 1787.

[3] Cobenzl's reports of February 3 and March 1, V. A., *Russland, Berichte*, 1788.

discussion between themselves and Poland. They could not, however, rebuff their ally in so serious a matter during the first months of the joint war on the Turks. Hence, after long delays, Cobenzl's importunities were crowned with success. On May 21, 1788, he received from the Russians a formal ministerial declaration, to the effect that if the King of Prussia, under the present circumstances, undertook to acquire any of the possessions of the Republic of Poland, the Empress of Russia bound herself to unite with the Emperor of the Romans in making the most urgent representations to deter the King from such an intention. If these representations proved fruitless, she promised to make common cause with the Emperor in opposing the execution of such a plan with all the forces and means that she could employ compatibly with the security of her Empire and the need of defending herself against the Porte. The Russian ministers announced that this declaration had the force of a formal treaty, and that they held it superfluous to require a similar pledge from Austria.[1]

The Austrians professed themselves completely satisfied. So far as Russia could be considered bound by a solemn engagement, they could rest assured that she would not consent to the Hertzberg plan or to any other Prussian designs upon Poland. But if paper guarantees availed, Poland would never have been partitioned. The declaration remained a secret of the two Imperial cabinets, unknown at Berlin or at Warsaw. In the following years it did not prevent either Austrians or Russians from considering seriously the sacrifice of Polish territory to Prussia, when-

---

[1] The Russian attitude in this matter can be explained from the memoir presented by Bezborodko to the Empress, printed in the Русскій Архивъ, 1875, ii, p. 35; and the protocols of the Council of the Empire for December 23, 1787/January 3, 1788; and April 20/May 1, 1788, in the Арх. Гос. Сов., i, pp. 518 ff., 556 f. Kalinka, the first historian to discover this convention, gave a satisfactory account of its origin, except that he erroneously states that Russia demanded a similar declaration from Austria; he also gives the essence of the text of the agreement, Der polnische Reichstag, i, pp. 52–55. The translator of the German edition of Kalinka's work adds in a note that the text of this Austro-Russian treaty is not to be found among the acts of either the Warsaw or the St. Petersburg mission in the Vienna Haus-Hof-und Staatsarchiv. This is an error. The original of the Russian ' declaration ' is to be found appended to Louis Cobenzl's report of May 24 among the Berichte, Russland, 1788. Since this document has never hitherto been published, I give the text in Appendix I.

ever interest or necessity suggested such a course. Yet if its practical results were small, the declaration still has a certain historical significance as the most explicit expression of the determination of Austria and Russia at that time to maintain the integrity of Poland.

In the same dispatches with which he transmitted the Russian declaration, Cobenzl reported that the alliance of Russia with the Republic was well under way. Not, indeed, that alliance in which Austria also would have participated, as Kaunitz desired, for it did not accord with Russian policy to admit any other Power to so close a connection with Poland. Yet the proposed alliance between the Empress and the Republic had no other object (Ostermann asserted) than that which the Austrians had suggested: namely, to assure the Imperial Courts, of Polish aid in case of a war with Prussia. This was, indeed, the plan Catherine had chosen for thwarting the designs of Hertzberg and for keeping the Republic in order while the Oriental crisis lasted. The plan bore great results. It precipitated precisely the troubles it was intended to avert.

CHAPTER IV

The Plan for a Russo-Polish Alliance

I

STANISLAS AUGUSTUS, with all his weakness of will in emergencies, displayed a remarkable tenacity and perseverance in the pursuit of his fundamental aims. From the beginning of his reign down to its tragic close, he was haunted by the desire to increase his monarchical power, to augment the army and the revenues of the state, and to restore Poland to its place among the active members of the European political system. " Born with a vast and ardent ambition," he said of himself, " the ideas of reform, of glory, of usefulness to my country have become the background of all my plans and of my whole life." [1] Defeated again and again, he invariably returned to his projects, by new detours, timidly, cautiously, but obstinately. The experiences of the first decade of his reign had convinced him that nothing was to be accomplished in opposition to Russia; but he still hoped that much good might be effected with the consent and under the protection of the Empress. The great thing was to persuade her that it was to her interest to make Poland strong enough to render active services, rather than to leave the country a prey to impotence, anarchy, and constant troubles. Especially in case of war between Russia and her neighbors, the King hoped that Catherine would be willing to purchase Polish aid by permitting those military, financial, and political reforms, without which the Republic could not coöperate effectively. It has already been noted that during the War of the Bavarian Succession Stanislas thought of an alliance with Russia; and during the ensuing crisis over the Crimean affair, he offered his alliance at St. Petersburg.[2] Decorously

---

[1] Kalinka, *Ostatnie lata*, i, p. 80.

[2] The date of this offer is given as 1782 by Askenazy, *Przymierze polsko-pruskie*, p. 28; and 1783, by Kalinka, *Der polnische Reichstag*, i, p. 56.

repulsed on this occasion, he returned to the idea some years later.

During his stay at Kanev (March-May, 1787), the King laid before Catherine and her advisers the outlines of a plan for a defensive alliance against the Turks; and this time he received the Empress' assent, at least in principle.[1] In September, after the Porte had begun hostilities, he hastened to send the draft of a formal treaty to St. Petersburg. He proposed that the Republic should join actively in the war, and that he himself should take command of one of the allied armies. In return he begged for some extension of his royal prerogatives, the increase of the army, a large subsidy for the expenses of the war, and, at the peace, the acquisition for Poland of Bessarabia, part of Moldavia, and a port on the Black Sea. The alliance was to be brought about by means of a Confederation, which would also serve to prevent internal disorders in Poland during the crisis.[2] Seldom had this unfortunate King allowed his imagination so bold a flight. Whether the plan in itself was salutary and statesmanlike or quite the reverse, is a disputed question that need not be argued here.[3] The essential fact is that the better parts of the King's project had not the slightest chance of being accepted at St. Petersburg.

Catherine was not in the least disposed either to gratify the personal ambitions which she detected in Stanislas' proposals, or to allow the Republic a greater measure of strength and independence. She attached little importance to the military aid that Poland might render; and while she did desire an alliance, it must be one on her own terms. The primary object of it would be to keep the Poles busy with a harmless enterprise, flattering to their vanity and capable of diverting their attention from more dangerous projects. A Confederation under her auspices would enable her to put down possible outbreaks with firmer hand, while

[1] Cf. the note presented by the King to the Empress May 6, 1787, *Mémoires de Stanislas Auguste*, pp. 95–99; also the very interesting correspondence of the King from Kanev, printed by Kalinka, *Ostatnie lata*, ii, pp. 5–64.

[2] The text of this proposed treaty has not yet been found. The essential features of it can be ascertained, however, from the diplomatic correspondence of the time. Cf. Kalinka, *Der polnische Reichstag*, i, pp. 58 f.

[3] Cf. the qualified approval given the plan by Kalinka, *op. cit.*, i, pp. 56 ff.; and the unmitigated condemnation expressed by Askenazy, *op. cit.*, pp. 30 ff.

various articles might be inserted into the alliance treaty that would extend her legal rights of guardianship over the Republic. As for the means, she would not hear of a Confederation without a Diet, or of the calling of an extraordinary Diet, as the King proposed, for that would arouse the suspicion of the neighbors; she would wait until the next ordinary Diet met, in the autumn of 1788, then put through the alliance as quickly and as quietly as possible, and present the other Powers with a *fait accompli*.[1]

While Catherine was thus deliberately delaying the project, she was being attacked from other quarters on the same subject. Simultaneously with Stanislas' propositions, she received the offers of the most active leader of the anti-royalist opposition in Poland, the Grand Hetman Branicki. He, too, wished a Russian alliance, but one to be put through by a Confederation directed by himself. For that purpose he and his friend Felix Potocki, Palatine of (Little) Russia, offered to put at the Empress' disposal both the troops of the Republic and their own private militia. Catherine, fortunately, rejected this treasonable offer and read the two magnates a lecture on patriotism;[2] but she was soon to hear very similar proposals from a much more exalted personage.

II

Of all the men whose activity was dangerous and baneful to Poland in these years, Prince Potemkin the Taurian stands foremost. Field-Marshal, President of the War College, Commander-in-Chief of the principal army against the Turks, virtual Viceroy of all Southern Russia, the Empress' most intimate friend, her favorite pupil, her " right hand," as she herself said, Potemkin wielded enormous power and influence; and these facilities he employed, not only to render very considerable services to his benefactress, but also to advance his own personal ambitions. His plans, though different in kind, were no less grandiose, revolutionary, and complicated than Hertzberg's; and, like

[1] For some discussion as to Catherine's attitude towards the Russo-Polish alliance project, see Appendix II.

[2] Branicki to the Empress, September 9, 1787, her reply of September 30/October 11, M. A., Польша, II, 6.

Hertzberg's, they related especially to Poland. It is important to bear in mind that during the prolonged Oriental crisis the Republic was equally threatened by the Prussian thirst for aggrandizement on the one side, and by the ambitions of Potemkin on the other.

The Prince's secret designs,[1] once centered upon the Polish crown, were now directed rather upon those rich palatinates of the south that would form so capital an addition to his prospective ' Kingdom of Dacia.' To further his plans, he had long maintained a party of his own in the Republic, a party whose activity conflicted incessantly with the official policy of Russia as represented by the ambassador Stackelberg. To strengthen his position in the south, the Prince was continually making immense purchases of land in the Polish Ukraine. His possessions became so large that he thought for a time of having them erected into a vassal principality, something like Courland. But the outbreak of the Turkish war and Stanislas Augustus' proposals for a Russo-Polish alliance opened the way to even more ambitious projects. What could be more tempting to Potemkin than to draw the Republic into the struggle, get its military forces under his control, occupy the coveted southern provinces with his troops, and then by means of a Confederation under his own direction make himself dictator of Poland and put through what changes he saw fit ?

The Prince was versatile. He knew several routes to the goal. Although at Kanev he had championed Stanislas' alliance project and later continued to negotiate with the King, at the same time he was framing with the leaders of the Opposition very different plans, vast in scope and revolutionary in character. A coup d'état, the overthrow of the royal power, the establishment of an oligarchy, even the transformation of the Republic into a federation of provinces or principalities — such appear to have been some of the objects of these mysterious *pourparlers*. Early in 1788 Potemkin sent to St. Petersburg the plan of action which he had agreed upon with Branicki and Felix Potocki. He proposed to raise quickly and secretly an armed force (' national

---

[1] On Potemkin's schemes with regard to Poland, see Appendix III.

militia ') in the southern palatinates, with the aid of those magnates and *szlachta* who were most devoted to Russia; this 'militia'
would then form a Confederation in the provinces, under the protection of the Russian troops and remote from the malign influence of the King and the agents of foreign Powers; it would
take over the government of the country, overawe or beat down
any opposition that might be attempted, conclude a close alliance
between the Republic and the Empress, and, in general, put
through anything that Russia might desire. Had this plan been
carried out, the result would have been the overthrow of the King
and the lawful government of Poland, a repetition of the disgraceful Confederation of Radom, or a premature mise-en-scène
of the dismal tragedy of 1792.

These projects were the more dangerous because the Polish
malcontents who swarmed in Potemkin's camp, were also in relations with Hertzberg, to whom nothing would have given greater
pleasure than an outbreak of anarchy in the Republic. The
Prussian troops would at once have crossed the frontier ' to
restore order.' And Potemkin himself now inclined towards the
Prussian alliance. He continually urged the Empress to show
more cordiality to Frederick William, and even to win him over
by the gift of Dantzic; and he seems, through his Polish friends, to
have sounded Berlin with reference to his own plans. Obviously
he had more to expect from that quarter than from Vienna.

Even these measures did not exhaust the schemes of the
Tauric Prince. There was still one more plan in reserve — and
this the most audacious of all. Potemkin had an extraordinary
passion for Cossacks. Although it was he who had induced the
Empress to destroy the Zaporozhian *Sěč* [1] in 1775, he had later
made great efforts to create new Cossack armies; and especially
in the winter of 1787–88 he was indefatigable in his exertions to
enlist Cossacks from every quarter. His recruiting officers were
particularly busy in Poland. Doubtless the new Cossack forces,
which were the object of such extraordinary care, were of much
use for the Turkish war; but there is reason to think that they

---

[1] The famous fortified camp of the free Cossacks of the Dnieper, situated on an
island just below the cataracts of the river.

were also raised with a view to one other emergency. If all his other Polish plans failed, if the alliance fell through, if the hostile party gained the upper hand in the Republic, then Potemkin might enter the country at the head of a Cossack army, rouse the Orthodox population of the Ukraine, and repeat the exploits of Bogdan Chmielnicki.

We have dwelt at length on these astonishing projects for several reasons. In the first place, Potemkin's intrigues with Branicki, Potocki, and their associates at the beginning of the new crisis in Polish affairs form the first link in a chain that ends at Targowica. Then it has been so often asserted that the Republic ought to have taken its position firmly and unconditionally on the Russian side in this crisis, that it is of importance to indicate to some extent what advantages Poland might have expected from an alliance which would have handed over her army, her military and financial resources, her strongholds, her southern provinces to so inveterate an enemy, so dangerous a schemer as Potemkin. Finally, the Prince's secret plans form an essential part of the background of Russia's Polish policy in the next few years. Catherine did not, indeed, blindly accept his advice; but, on the other hand, she did not entirely disregard it. She generally tried to satisfy him to some extent; she made many compromises and many concessions. Down to his death in 1791 his opinions and ambitions weighed heavily on the fate of Poland; and then, unfortunately, his plans lived after him.

III

When Catherine was finally ready to declare her precise intentions about the alliance, the plan she adopted differed materially from the proposals both of Stanislas and of Potemkin. While she distrusted the personal ambitions of the King, she also divined to some extent the secret schemes of the favorite, and she was beginning to find them in conflict with her own policies. As early as December Potemkin's growing preference for the Prussian alliance had provoked from her an unusually sharp letter.[1] She

---

[1] November 23/December 4, 1787, Рус. Старина, xvi, pp. 441 ff.

allowed him to take Polish magnates into her service, approved his plans for organizing and employing the Polish armies, and accepted his amendments to the King's plan for the alliance treaty; but, on the other hand, she firmly rejected his plan for an anti-royalist Confederation in the provinces. She was no more inclined to sacrifice the King to the Opposition, than to surrender the opposition to the King; and she could not lend her approval to projects that would almost infallibly provoke a civil war in Poland.

In June, 1788, nine months after Stanislas had sent his propositions to St. Petersburg, the Empress' definite reply at last reached Warsaw. The alliance was to be effected through a confederated Diet under the direction of the King and the ambassador — so much was satisfactory; but the other desires of Stanislas were evaded or refused. The expenses incurred by the Republic through the war were to be repaid only after the conclusion of peace, and then in instalments spread out over six years. The military contingent of the Poles, cut down from 20,000 to 12,000, was to serve under the supreme command of the Russian generals, and immediately under that of Branicki, Felix Potocki, and Stanislas Poniatowski (this was one of the concessions to Potemkin). No territorial acquisitions for Poland were to be thought of. None of the modest constitutional reforms for which the King had hoped, were granted. Finally, an insidious article, the aim of which was to enable Russia to take over the diplomatic representation of Poland abroad, contained a new encroachment upon the independence of the Republic.[1] In short, Stanislas Augustus' original project had been transformed almost beyond recognition. From *this* alliance, Russia alone could have profited: Poland could have gained nothing whatever except a very dubious protection against the designs of Prussia. Nevertheless, though bitterly disappointed, the King accepted the Russian counter-project; perhaps because it was now too late to draw back without offending the Empress.

It was characteristic of Catherine's policy toward her chief ally that the draft of this treaty was communicated at Vienna only

---

[1] For detailed analysis of this Russian counter-project, see Kalinka, *Der polnische Reichstag*, i, pp. 87 ff.

when the Polish Diet was on the point of assembling. Kaunitz fumed and fretted; nevertheless he ordered the Austrian chargé d'affaires at Warsaw (de Caché) to support all the measures of Russia, while he himself administered sage advice to those Polish magnates whom he could influence. Yet just before the Diet assembled, the growing ferment in Poland and the ominous attitude of Prussia so alarmed the Austrian Chancellor that he hastened to urge at Petersburg the danger of even proposing an alliance of this sort at such a time. But this warning came too late.[1]

IV

Towards the end of August Catherine saw fit, as a matter of courtesy, to communicate the alliance project to Prussia. She apparently anticipated no serious opposition;[2] and she was certainly not prepared for the storm that followed.

The communication produced a lively sensation at Berlin; and not unnaturally, for it seemed to mean the shipwreck of the whole policy pursued so patiently for the past year. Hitherto the Prussians had been trying to win back Russia by amicable means, in the fond hope of persuading the Empress to sanction their designs on Poland. Now, as a reward for all their complaisance, they were presented with this treaty, which contained Catherine's guarantee of the integrity of Poland, which was, therefore, designed to close the door in their faces, and to thwart all their plans for aggrandizement. The proposed alliance seemed to be directed entirely against Prussia, and it was the more dangerous because Austria would probably hasten to accede to it. This alliance must be prevented at all costs.[3]

---

[1] For the above: Kaunitz to L. Cobenzl, June 28 and September 20, V. A., *Russland, Exped.*, 1788; Kaunitz to Czartoryski, August 26 and 29, V. A., *Polen, Fasc.* 66; Kaunitz to Rzewuski, September 15 (printed in Beer, *Leopold II, Franz II und Catharina*, pp. 246 f.); Cobenzl's report of October 10, V. A., *Russland, Berichte*, 1788.

[2] See her remarks on Potemkin's plan for the alliance, Русскій Архивъ, 1874, ii, pp. 274 ff.

[3] Hertzberg to the King, September 2, joint report of Hertzberg and Fincken-stein, September 3, rescript to Buchholtz, September 3, B. A., *Fol.* 323 (" Acta betreffend die Allianz welche die Kayserin von Russland der Republick Pohlen ant-ragen lassen . . . hat "). H. to F. W., September 2: "Il ne peut pas être douteux

Moreover, it seemed clear that the time had come for a complete change of policy. Now at last Hertzberg urged acting in open opposition to Russia.[1] At Copenhagen, at Constantinople, at Warsaw, Prussian policy took on a new aggressiveness. At that moment, Gustavus III having attacked Catherine, the Danes, in accordance with the terms of their alliance with Russia, were preparing a counter-attack on Sweden. Berlin immediately served notice that if Denmark did not cease hostilities, 16,000 Prussian troops would invade Holstein. Before this threat and the equally vigorous action of England, the Danes backed down. Hertzberg could hardly have dealt the Empress a severer blow, for at a time when the Turkish war left her but small resources against Sweden, the aid of Denmark would have been of great importance. It was a clear sign of the revolution that had taken place in Prussian policy. The first step had been taken in that uncertain, wavering, ill-starred course which in the next few years led Prussian statesmen further and further into open hostility to the Power whose friendship they most desired, and into unnatural alliances with states whose friendship they despised or whose territories they coveted.[2]

As regards the alliance project, the official Prussian reply delivered at St. Petersburg left no doubt of the King's sentiments.[3] Buchholtz, the Prussian envoy at Warsaw, was ordered to do his utmost to thwart the project by working up public opinion against it and by organizing a strong Prussian party. If possible, he was to prevent the approaching Diet from being confederated; if necessary, he was to form a Counter-confederation, which would then demand the aid of Prussian troops.[4] The cabinet of Berlin was ready, in fact, to proceed to any extremity. If the Empress persisted in her "presumption," Hertzberg

que cette alliance est uniquement dirigée contre V. M., pour lui carrer tout agrandissement, et que l'intérêt de V. M. exige par conséquent de faire tout ce qui sera possible pour la contrecarrer. . . . Je crois qu'en général V. M. sera obligée bientôt de montrer les dents à la cour de Russie."

[1] Report to the King, September 2, and Frederick William's reply, September 3, B. A., *Fol.* 323.

[2] On this abrupt change, see Bailleu, in *H. Z.*, xlii, pp. 484 ff.

[3] Rescript to Keller, September 12, B. A., *Fol.* 323.

[4] Rescripts to Buchholtz, September 3 and 16, *ibid.*

wrote, she would force the King to take sides with Sweden and the Porte.[1]

The Empress, however, was not so rash. Although deeply incensed at the conduct of Prussia, she recognized that the Polish alliance was not worth the risk of a third war in addition to the two she already had on her hands, and so she ordered Stackelberg to suspend negotiations on the subject. But she could not bring herself to renounce entirely a plan she had once taken up: she therefore added that if a more favorable opportunity presented itself in the course of the Diet, the alliance project might be brought forward again.[2]

By this reservation Catherine largely destroyed the value of her concession. The Prussians were not conciliated, but only filled with new suspicions. The Empress, they fancied, was trying to lull them to slumber in order later on to surprise them with a *fait accompli*. Hence they determined to persevere in their policy of stubborn opposition.[3] When the Diet assembled, it was under the shadow of a great impending struggle between Russia and Prussia for control in Poland.

[1] Hertzberg to Buchholtz, September 16. In equally warlike vein Hertzberg to the King, October 2, *Fol.* 323.

[2] Buchholtz's report of September 28, B. A., *ibid.*

[3] Hertzberg and Finckenstein to the King, October 3, rescript to Buchholtz, October 4, *ibid.*

CHAPTER V

THE OVERTHROW OF RUSSIAN RULE IN POLAND

I

' *Jam venit hora!* Now is the time to provide for the needs of the Fatherland.'[1] Such was the general cry in Poland at the outbreak of the Eastern war. The distractions of its neighbors seemed to furnish the country the long-desired opportunity to effect indispensable reforms, and such a chance as might never occur again. "Our sons and grandsons," the Dietine of Samogitia declared, "will not live to see a better occasion than we now have for setting our house in order, increasing the forces of the Republic, assuring our liberties, . . . and reviving the once famous name of Poles."[2] To neglect this opportunity might mean certain ruin. Staszic's words rang in men's ears: "All these reforms must be realized as soon as possible. This matter will brook no delay. The sickness is violent: it demands violent remedies."[3] It appeared, then, that the supreme moment had come.

Almost the whole nation demanded a confederated Diet, the main task of which should be to put through a very substantial increase of the army. The need of other reforms was generally admitted. But precisely what these other reforms should be, how far they should go, whether the nation should keep within the limits imposed by the Russian guarantee of the existing constitution, what attitude the Republic should adopt towards the neighboring Powers — on those questions public opinion was divided. Broadly speaking, there were two programs before the country: that of the King, and that of the loose array of the opposition, which already called itself ' the Patriots.'

[1] Quoted from a letter of M. U. Niemcewicz to the King, in Zaleski, *Korespondencya krajowa Stanisława Augusta*, p. 214.

[2] *Ibid.*, p. 246.

[3] *Uwagi nad życiem Jana Zamojskiego*, p. 144.

The King's hopes and plans have already been described. They were, in substance, that Poland should in this crisis attach herself to Russia more firmly than ever, taking advantage of the opportunity, indeed, to effect certain military and financial reforms, but only such as Catherine in her present conciliatory mood might be found willing to permit. This was the policy of extreme prudence, if not of faint-heartedness and self-distrust. It promised hardly more than a slight increase of the army — perhaps to 30,000 men, the number indicated by Catherine in the guarantee treaty; the honor of sending Polish troops to fight in the Russian ranks in a purely Russian war; and the precarious protection of the Empress against the designs of Prussia. This was very little to offer to a nation which expected so much. Such a program was not fitted to inspire or to arouse to supreme efforts, but rather to disgust and to repel; for it ran counter to the nation's instincts, its sense of dignity, its conviction of what the occasion demanded.

Very different were the ideas that were fermenting in the minds of the Patriots. Vague and inchoate as their program was, it still pointed unmistakably to two goals: the realization of very thoroughgoing reforms, — of the kind sketched by Staszic; and the vindication of Poland's independence. These two ideals were really inseparable. No far-reaching, solid, and decisive political reforms were possible as long as Russia maintained her grip upon the country. The elimination of the Russian ' guarantee ' and the overthrow of the Russian ' influence ' were necessary before the army could be brought up to a really respectable standard or the vicious constitution replaced by something better.

The program of the Patriots was bold and alluring, but was it wise or prudent or practicable ? It appeared that there was a reasonable chance of success only in case Poland could count on the friendship or, if need be, the support of one of the neighboring Powers; and as matters then stood, such support could come only from Prussia. Of the dangers lurking in such a connection, of the natural ambitions and the ill-concealed cupidity of Prussia, the Patriots were by no means ignorant. Their leaders cannot fairly be accused of having thrown themselves blindly into the arms of their worst enemy. From the outset they recognized that Prussia had been, and under certain conditions might again become, the most dangerous foe of Poland. But the existing circumstances gave ground for hope. As long as the close connection between the Imperial Courts lasted — and it seemed very firm at that moment — Prussia must remain in opposition to Russia, and might therefore see in a revived Poland a desirable ally. Moreover, it was supposed that England, Prussia, and Holland were building up a great league of states (the 'Federative System'), into which Sweden, Denmark, Turkey, and the *Fürstenbund* were to be admitted, the object of which was to maintain the balance of power and the existence of the small states against the Imperial Courts. If Poland could gain admission to this league, her future might seem secure. Finally, the character of the new King of Prussia, and especially the generosity and moderation which were supposed to distinguish him so signally from his predecessor, inspired hope and confidence. Might it not be expected that Frederick William, who had so recently intervened to rescue Holland from French influence and had then taken that Republic into his alliance on terms of equality, would be found ready to render equally disinterested services to Poland ?

Long before Prussia made any marked advances to the Poles, the Patriots began to turn their eyes toward Berlin. At the council of war held by their leaders in Paris at the beginning of 1788, plans were discussed for securing the Prussian alliance and even for bringing Poland into the ' Federative System.' [1] In the following summer many of the Patriots openly declared that they meant to stand with Prussia at the approaching Diet,[2] and some of the magnates were already writing Berlin to solicit support against Russia.[3] The situation remained decidedly uncertain,

---

[1] Dembiński, " Piattoli et son rôle pendant la Grande Diète," in *Bulletin de l'Académie de Cracovie, Classe de Philologie*, etc., Juin-Juillet, 1905, pp. 54 f.; Zaleski, *Życie Czartoryskiego*, pp. 225 ff.; Dębicki, *Puławy*, i, pp. 253 ff.

[2] Zaleski, *Korespondencya krajowa*, p. 242; Griesheim to Bischoffwerder, August 23, 1788, rejoices that the Poles are " grösstentheils so gut preussisch gesinnt," B. A., *Fol.* 323.

[3] Letters of Radziwiłł (July 20), Sułkowski (August 6), and Ogiński (September 10) to Hertzberg, B. A., *R.* 9, 27 and *Fol.* 323.

however, down to the opening of the Diet, because the policy of Prussia was still far from clear. A vigorous declaration from Berlin was needed before the Patriots could enter boldly on plans for reform or venture to throw down the gauntlet to Russia.

II

On the 6th of October, 1788, there met at Warsaw the assembly destined to become famous as the Four Years' Diet, or, as patriotic historians prefer to call it, the Great Diet. It opened amid a feverish excitement and a whirl of political and social activity such as Poland had rarely, if ever, witnessed. Warsaw was packed to overflowing. The whole ' political nation ' seemed to have pressed up to the capital: senators and deputies with their families, crowds of simple country gentlemen, the armies of clients and retainers who followed the magnates, and adventurers, sight-seers, and fortune-hunters from every corner of Poland, and indeed from every part of Europe. The lavish and wellnigh fabulous hospitality displayed by the richer noblemen and the constant round of balls, fêtes, dinners, and theatrical performances might suggest a society bent only on holding perpetual saturnalia; and yet amid these carnival scenes the all-pervading interest, the universal topic was politics. People awaited the result of a vote in the Diet with intense anxiety; the galleries of the assembly were constantly filled, especially by the ladies of the high aristocracy, whose interest and influence in politics excited the astonishment of foreigners; in the numerous salons, in clubs like that of the Radziwiłł Palace, in the workshops and in the market-places political discussion ran high; and even coachmen and lackeys divided into ' Patriots ' and ' Parasites,' the latter being the adherents of Russia.[1] This passionate interest in politics is also shown by the immense publicistic activity of the time, by the flood of treatises, open letters, poems, dialogues, ' fables,' and ' catechisms ' evoked by wellnigh every question. In short, never, perhaps, had there been a Diet which had so aroused the country.

[1] Kraszewski, *Polska w czasie trzech rozbiorów*, ii, p. 126.

In the beginning there appeared only one organized and disciplined party, the Royalists. This was a phalanx largely composed of office-hunters, but containing also some few men of
talent who from conviction adhered to the King's policy of friendship with Russia and moderate reforms within the limits that
Catherine prescribed.

The opposition consisted of a loosely-united host of heterogeneous elements, which, after fighting side by side in the early
battles of the Diet, divided into two parties with radically different tendencies, the ' Republicans ' and the ' Patriots.'

The former represented the conservative and reactionary
forces, the partisans of the old institutions, the fanatics of ' golden
liberty,' the bigoted, misguided, or selfish opponents of all change
whatsoever except, perhaps, a change backward — a return to
the undiluted anarchy of the Saxon period. The Republicans
were agreed in opposing the King — the traditional and popular
course in Poland; and as for Russia, the magnates who led the
party were ready to rally to the Empress whenever she showed
herself disposed to throw over the King for their sake; while the
honest, ignorant squires, who made up the rank and file of the
party, detested Russia but still unintentionally served her interests
through their inability to understand the needs of their country
and through their blind hostility to reforms. The Patriots, the
champions of independence and of thoroughgoing reforms, were
undoubtedly the party which appealed most strongly to the heart
and to the enlightened opinion of the nation. To them rallied
spontaneously those who had freed themselves from the ancient
prejudices and desired to reconstruct the state on a new basis in
accordance with the liberal ideas of the age; those who resented
the yoke of Russia as an intolerable degradation; those who had
sufficient faith in the nation to believe that independence, dignity,
and power could be won back by a determined effort. The
strength of the party lay especially in the younger generation, the
men fresh from the new schools, full of the energy, the broader
knowledge, the optimism which the older generation, broken and
disillusioned by the Partition, conspicuously lacked. These
younger men were to play so prominent a rôle in the Four Years'

Diet that critics jested of an assembly of ' Lycurguses and Solons of twenty-five.' The Patriots possessed leaders of high character and reputation: Ignacy Potocki, a man of ardent and noble soul, disinterested, energetic, indefatigable, admired and almost worshipped by his younger compatriots; his brother Stanislas, the most eloquent orator of the party; the Marshal of the Diet,[1] Stanislas Małachowski, ' the Polish Aristides,' a man whose name was synonymous with pure and lofty patriotism; Kołłątaj, the organizer of the party's propaganda, the leader of the more advanced democratic wing, and perhaps the clearest thinker and the best head in Poland; finally, Prince Adam Casimir Czartoryski, the richest and most popular, the most charming and cultivated man of his nation. Unfortunately, not one of these leaders was really a statesman of the first calibre. The party was rich in men of integrity and intellect and fervent patriotism, but it did not contain a single great man of action. Nevertheless, whatever talent Poland at that time possessed was, with few exceptions, gathered within the Patriotic camp.

It was at the outset quite uncertain which of these parties would gain the ascendancy in the Diet. Both Royalists and Opposition could count upon a certain number of reliable supporters, but the majority of the assembly was at first unattached, undecided, and ready to go with the tide.

On October 7th the Diet was, by general agreement, confederated for the specified purpose of increasing the army and the taxes. After the provisional withdrawal of the alliance project, the King and the Russian ambassador had decided that military and financial questions should furnish the chief business of the session; for they hoped that by gratifying the nation's wishes in this respect they could avert a discussion of more fundamental problems and prevent an explosion of popular feeling against Russia. And possibly their hopes might have been realized, possibly Stanislas and Stackelberg might have remained masters of the situation, had it not been for the vigorous intervention of Prussia.

[1] Or more strictly Marshal of the Confederation for the ' Crown ' (Poland), Prince Sapieha being Marshal for Lithuania.

At the first general session of the Confederation (October 13), a note was read from the Prussian envoy Buchholtz, in which, in language very courteous towards the Republic but unfriendly and even menacing towards the Empress, the Prussian government protested against the Russo-Polish alliance project, and announced that if the Poles felt the need of an alliance, Frederick William would offer them his own. This note decided the course of the Four Years' Diet. For the impression produced by it was, as Stackelberg himself reported, indescribable.[1] While the party of the King and the ambassador was seized with consternation, the exultation of the Patriots knew no bounds. For the first time in many years, one of the neighboring Powers had come forward in open opposition to the Russian policy in Poland, had invited the nation to throw off the yoke, and had held out promises of support. For the first time in many years, one of the neighbors had addressed the Republic as if it were an independent and equal Power, and had seemed to seek its friendship. The Poles had the new and delightful experience of being wooed, and above all, they felt the sense of deliverance. It was as if, after a hundred years of servitude, the nation had been in a moment freed from its chains and left master of its own actions. An illustrious Pole, describing many years later that springtime of joy and hope, declared that it was a moment of inexpressible happiness, such as no one could appreciate who had never lived through it, and such as no one who had lived through it could ever again experience in like degree.[2]

The first impulse of the ' liberated ' nation was to give free rein to its strongest passion, hatred towards Russia; a hatred born of the insults and indignities endured for the past thirty years: the brutalities of Repnin and Saldern, the arrogance of Stackelberg, the arrest of the three Polish Senators dragged away from the midst of the Diet of 1767 to imprisonment in Russia, the excesses committed by the Russian troops during the War of the Confederation of Bar, the shame of the servitude that had degraded Poland in the eyes of all Europe. That hatred extended to every person and institution associated with the Russian rule: to the

---

[1] Report of October 15 cited by Smitt, *Suworow*, ii, p. 185.
[2] Ad. J. Czartoryski, *Żywot Niemcewicza*, p. 35.

King, to the Royalist party, to the Permanent Council. The ambassador presently found himself boycotted by Warsaw society. The Royalists were hooted down in the Diet and insulted in the streets. To denounce Russia became the road to popularity, and to attack the Empress personally was held a patriotic deed.[1]

The rising flood of anti-Russian and pro-Prussian feeling swept everything, before it. The Patriots acquired a constantly increasing ascendancy in the Diet, while the King's party melted away. It was in vain that Stanislas Augustus in eloquent and prophetic language warned the assembly that their one chance of safety lay in holding fast to Russia, or at least to the letter of the existing engagements with the Empress, and that Prussians offering friendship were Greeks bearing gifts. The King's not altogether tactful speeches only added to the odium of his past record. Nor was Stackelberg more successful in stemming the tide. The ambassador's one serious effort was the note presented to the Diet on November 5, in which he warned the Poles that the Empress would regard any change in the constitution guaranteed by her as a breach of treaty, which would force her to abandon her friendly attitude towards the Republic. If anything had been needed to complete the ruin of the Russian influence, it would have been supplied by that unlucky note.

Prussia at once seized the opportunity for an effective counterstroke. On November 20 Buchholtz presented to the Diet a new declaration, containing his master's interpretation of the famous guarantee of the constitution by the neighboring Powers. Frederick William, it was said, regarded the guarantee as involving the obligation to defend the independence of the Republic, but not at all as implying a right to limit the freedom of the Poles to change their institutions as they saw fit. This note was couched in even more flattering terms than the last Prussian declaration, and it created scarcely less of a sensation. Its effect was increased by the activity of the Marquis Lucchesini, who had come to Warsaw to assist Buchholtz, and was presently to replace him. This supple Italian displayed an amazing virtuosity in captivating the Poles, maligning Russia, and spreading golden opinions as

---

[1] Cf. especially, Kalinka, *Der polnische Reichstag*, i, pp. 242 ff.

to the beneficent designs of the generous Frederick William. He fairly carried Warsaw by storm. His successes, together with the two declarations from his Court, sufficed to assure the triumph of Prussian influence in Poland, and to drive the Patriots irresistibly forward upon the exhilarating course of revolution.

The first work of the victorious party was one of demolition. Before their onslaughts there went down in rapid succession the War Department, the Department of Foreign Affairs, the Permanent Council — in short the whole edifice of government erected and guaranteed by Russia. There were many reasons to justify so destructive a course: the necessity of clearing the ground before undertaking comprehensive and thorough reforms, the undeniable abuses of which the Council had been guilty, the need of removing control over the government from a king devoted to Russia, whom the nation could not trust; but undoubtedly the primary motive of the Patriots was the desire to assert the nation's independence and to prove that the detested guarantee had become a dead letter. All understood that such changes, made in the face of Stackelberg's solemn warning, constituted a downright challenge to the Empress; and the constant denunciations of Russia in the Diet, the collisions between Russian and Polish troops in the Ukraine, the propaganda of the Patriots in favor of an alliance with Prussia, added to the danger of a rupture. The crowning audacity of the Poles was the formal demand, which, with the encouragement and diplomatic support of Prussia, was repeatedly addressed to Catherine, that all Russian troops should be withdrawn from the territories of the Republic. In view of the exigencies of the Turkish war, which made a free passage through the Polish Ukraine an inestimable and almost indispensable convenience, such a demand was bound to strain Catherine's patience wellnigh to the breaking-point. Great was the surprise, therefore, when at the end of May (1789), for reasons to be explained later, the Empress courteously announced that she would immediately evacuate Polish territory. With that, the emancipation of the Republic seemed complete. Little more than six months had been required to throw off that Russian yoke which had galled the nation for a quarter of a century. The result surpassed all that could have been hoped for at the beginning of the Diet.

But if the Poles had freed themselves, it had been only with the aid of quite exceptional circumstances, which had led Prussia to support, Austria to facilitate, and Russia to tolerate the revolution at Warsaw. It remains to examine the motives underlying the attitude of the three neighboring Powers, in order to understand the reasons which made the liberation of Poland possible and to estimate its prospects of permanence.

III

Prussia had been the chief agent and sponsor of this revolution. Prussia had given the signal for the upheaval, suggested and encouraged each successive move of the Patriots against Russia, and vaguely promised the support of her battalions for the work which the Diet had accomplished. All this was assuredly not done from pure generosity, or from disinterested neighborly friendship. Seldom even in the tortuous diplomacy of the eighteenth century does one find so glaring a contrast as that between the secret aspirations of the cabinet of Berlin and the seductive professions which it lavished at Warsaw. Yet it would be a mistake to regard the Polish policy of Prussia at this time as entirely a tissue of deceptions, as based throughout upon a deep-laid and steadily pursued plan of treachery. To a certain degree the interests of Prussia did coincide with the aims of the Patriots; and a single, definite plan was what the Polish policy of Prussia most signally lacked. That policy was by no means consistent; it varied and shifted; it frequently lost its bearings and miscarried in its reckonings. Prussia might seem to guide events at Warsaw, but she was often hardly less surprised than her neighbors at the results of her work.

The original aim of the Prussian intervention was simply to thwart that Russian alliance project which by its guarantee of the integrity of the Republic [1] had aroused such indignation at

---

[1] This is the aspect of the alliance plan most emphasized by Hertzberg in his report to the King of September 2, 1788, and in the instructions to Buchholtz of the following day.

Berlin. But even before the Diet assembled, Prussian policy had entered upon a new phase. The Court of Berlin was now afraid, not that Catherine would put through her plan, but that she would abandon it. For the antipathy of the Poles to the proposed alliance had become so manifest that in case the Empress had not the good sense to renounce the project, Prussia would have a fine chance for a great stroke. In opposition to the confederated Diet about to be opened by Stanislas and Stackelberg, Frederick William would organize a Counter-confederation, which would then appeal to him for 'protection'; Prussian troops would enter Poland and occupy the long-coveted territories; and the Hertzberg plan, in its most essential part, might be realized immediately. Thus those professions of disinterested friendship, those assurances of armed support, those declarations which so delighted the early sessions of the Diet had for their ultimate aim — civil war, to be followed by the dismemberment of the Republic.[1]

Catherine's withdrawal of the alliance project disconcerted but did not ruin these pious hopes. If one pretext for armed intervention disappeared, others might still be manufactured. Hence Buchholtz and Lucchesini were presently instructed to incite the Patriots to attack the Permanent Council and to protest against the Russian troops taking winter quarters in Poland.[2] One question or the other might, perhaps, produce the desired rupture between the two contending parties at Warsaw. For a moment these hopes seemed near to being realized. The attack on the War

----

[1] Hertzberg to the King, September 21 (B. A., *R.* 9, 27), and October 2, Hertzberg to Buchholtz, September 30, rescript to Buchholtz, October 1 (B. A., *Fol.* 323).

September 21, Hertzberg to the King :

" Si la Cour de Russie insiste sur son projet d'alliance avec la Pologne, V. M. aura le plus beau jeu de lui opposer son alliance et une Réconfédération . . .; mais si la Cour de Russie a le bon esprit de renoncer à cette alliance, comme le C. de Stackelberg le lui a conseillé, notre rôle deviendra plus difficile."

September 30, Hertzberg to Buchholtz :

" Je ne me soucie pas que ces gens-là fassent leur confédération et leur alliance, pourvû que nous puissions parvenir à former un parti à peu près égal, qui nous fournisse le titre de faire une autre confédération au nom de laquelle nous puissions agir."

[2] Rescripts of October 17, 18, 21, B. A., *Fol.* 323.

Department — the prelude to the onslaught on the Permanent Council — led to a decisive trial of strength between the Royalists and the Opposition; party feeling ran high, and Lucchesini, after several nocturnal conclaves with various magnates, reported exultantly that if the royal party triumphed, a large section of the Opposition was ready to resort to a Counter-confederation and to appeal for Prussian aid. The news threw Berlin into excited activity. Lucchesini was at once authorized to promise aid to a Counter-confederation, no matter what the pretext under which it was formed, although he was to avoid committing his Court to too precise engagements. General Usedom was ordered to hold his troops ready to cross the frontier the moment he should receive word from Lucchesini. A manifesto was to be drawn up forthwith to justify the entry of the Prussian army into Poland.[1] But Prussia's plans were crossed by the victory of her own party at Warsaw. The overthrow of the War Department (November 3) ended this crisis.

Whether it was from disappointment at so tame a result, or because the season was growing late for military operations, or because the wind now blew from a more pacific quarter at Berlin, at any rate the Prussians now gave up serious hopes of a Counter-confederation. Instead it became their chief aim to end the Diet as soon as possible. For the great dilemma which had faced the Court of Berlin ever since the beginning of the assembly, was becoming increasingly embarrassing: the dilemma as to how far

[1] Lucchesini's reports of October 29 and November 1, Hertzberg and Finckenstein to Frederick William, November 5, instructions to Lucchesini, November 6, B. A., *Fol.* 323.

This episode furnished Kalinka with material for one of his indictments of the Patriotic party; and indeed, if the leaders of that party were conducting such treasonable negotiations and were ready to call in Prussian troops for so slight a pretext, they might justly be compared with the men of Targowica. It would seem, however, from Lucchesini's very vague reports that the men implicated in this disgraceful and dangerous plan for a Counter-confederation were not the leaders of the party, but men like Sułkowski, Ogiński, and Sapieha — adventurers and broilers of little influence or consideration. The one leader of the Patriotic party who undoubtedly had something to do with these secret conventicles with Lucchesini was Prince Adam Czartoryski, but it is quite uncertain how far he committed himself. I know of no evidence to justify Kalinka's conjecture (*Der polnische Reichstag*, i, p. 218) that Ignacy Potocki took part in these meetings.

Prussia could afford to support a party which, useful as it might be in opposing Russia, was still highly obnoxious in that it aimed at increasing the army, restoring the finances, and reforming the government of Poland. But how break up the Diet with nothing accomplished towards these latter ends, without ruining the popularity and influence which Prussia had just gained at Warsaw ? The plan adopted by the cabinet of Berlin was sufficiently subtle. It was to spur the Patriots on to renewed attacks on Russia, in the hope that Stanislas Augustus would be exasperated or alarmed to the point of dissolving the Diet and taking all the odium of the step upon himself. Such was the real aim of the second Prussian declaration to the Diet — the invitation to repudiate the Russian guarantee.[1] Once more, however, the result fell short of the intention. The Permanent Council was overthrown, but the Diet was not dissolved. The action of Prussia had only sealed the supremacy of the party which now prepared to take up those reforms that Prussia most detested.

In the early months of 1789, when the crisis of the struggle at Warsaw was over, when the Diet had settled down to a quasi-permanent existence under the domination of the Patriotic party, when the Court of Berlin seemed to have definitely replaced Russia as the preponderant Power in Poland, Prussian statesmen surveying the situation hardly knew what to make of their triumph. They might indeed congratulate themselves on a striking diplomatic victory over Russia. It was something to have demonstrated to the Empress how much she had lost when she gave up the Prussian alliance, and how little she could afford to ignore or to slight the Court of Berlin. But what material profit could Prussia expect from her new position in the Republic ? What was mere 'influence' to a Power that wanted territory ? What reliance could be placed upon the friendship or the gratitude of the weak and fickle Poles ? Lucchesini, with natural pride in the work of his hands, discreetly urged the maintenance of the new position won by such labors, pointing to the positive advantages to be expected from a Polish alliance in case of war

---

[1] Hertzberg to Finckenstein and to the King, November 12, rescripts to Buchholtz, November 12, 18, 22, and to Lucchesini, November 21, B. A., *Fol.* 323.

with the Imperial Courts, and the negative advantages of having deprived Catherine of a great kingdom that had been virtually a Russian province.[1] But Hertzberg was much more skeptical about the value of a Polish alliance, and much more impressed with the dangers involved in the obnoxious schemes of the Patriots.[2]

In the final analysis, the future attitude of the Court of Berlin towards Poland depended on whether Prussia was to draw the sword against the Imperial Courts or to satisfy her ambitions by a peaceful bargain with them. This in turn depended on the news expected from Constantinople, from London, and above all from St. Petersburg. The visit of Potemkin to the Russian capital early in 1789 raised hopes of a change of system on the Neva. For months Frederick William and Hertzberg waited with anxiety to see whether the favorite would have the will or the power to effect such a miracle.[3] If he succeeded, then a bargain between Russia and Prussia at the expense of the Republic would be the natural outcome. If he failed, then Prussia might ' break loose ' in the summer, and a Prusso-Polish alliance might yet have its *raison d'être.*[4]

IV

At Vienna the Polish revolution aroused only alarm and evil forebodings. Kaunitz was far from appreciating the strength of the patriotic movement in Poland, or from foreseeing the energy and capacity of which the Four Years' Diet, with all its faults, was to give evidence; but he did judge rightly of the illusion that

[1] Lucchesini to the King, November 5, 1788, B. A., *Fol.* 323; memoir of December 25 and letters to Hertzberg, January 26 and February 18, 1789, B. A., *R.* 9, 27.

[2] Hertzberg to Finckenstein, November 18, to the King, December 7, 1788, H. and F. to the King, March 16, 1789, B. A., *Fol.* 323 and *R.* 9, 27.

[3] See the Prussian correspondence of January–June, 1789 in Dembiński, *Documents relatifs à l'histoire du deuxième et troisième partage de la Pologne,* i.

[4] Hertzberg to Buchholtz, March 3, 1789, B.A., *R.* 9, 27; Hertzberg to Lucchesini, May 30 (Dembiński, *op. cit.,* i, pp. 398 f.).

Hertzberg to Buchholtz, March 3:

Fears that Potemkin will not be able to make the Empress change her policy completely. " Si cela ne peut pas avoir lieu, je crois qu'il vaut mieux que nous entamions les deux Cours Impériales et que nous tachions d'exécuter notre Plan avec la Porte et la Suède et même les Polonois, que nous devons habiliter alors."

the Diet could by mere high-sounding decrees at once restore the
decayed state to life and free it from all foreign influence, and he
saw clearly the danger the Poles would run if they threw themselves into the arms of the one Power that coveted their territory.
Any attempt to reform the constitution, he held, would lead only
to internal disturbances, which would afford Prussia a chance to
carry out her nefarious plans. Hence, as long as it seemed possible to hold back the torrent, he did not spare warnings and exhortations at Warsaw.[1] But by the end of November, after the
second Prussian declaration, the battle was obviously lost. De
Caché, the Austrian chargé d'affaires at Warsaw, was ordered to
suspend further representations and to relapse into the most
cautious reserve.

In his dispatches to Cobenzl at St. Petersburg, Kaunitz now outlined a new policy. The Russian influence in Poland, he declared,
could be restored only by violent means, and that would bring on
a war with Prussia. Austria could not possibly undertake such a
contest while the Turkish war lasted. It was therefore the most
pressing interest of the Imperial Courts to make peace with the
Porte as soon as possible, even on the *uti possidetis* basis, in order
to turn all their attention to Prussia and Poland. In the meantime, as one means of checking the insidious designs of their
enemies, he once more recommended the alliance with the Bourbon Courts, which had already been agitated since 1787, and one
chief point in which would be a guarantee of the integrity of
Poland by France and Spain.[2]

Unfortunately, this plan for a quadruple alliance fell through,
largely owing to the reluctance of the Bourbon states to undertake the defence of Poland; the hope of an immediate peace with
the Turks soon vanished; and almost every dispatch from Berlin

---

[1] Ostensible dispatch to de Caché, November 1, 1788, summarized in Kalinka,
Der polnische Reichstag, i, pp. 376 f.; Kaunitz to Czartoryski, October 29, V. A.,
Polen, Fasc. 66.

[2] Instructions of November 28, V. A., *Russland, Exped.*, 1788. On the protracted negotiations for a quadruple alliance see: Ségur, *Oeuvres*, iii, pp. 266 ff.,
419 ff.; *R. I. A.*, Russie, ii, pp. 441 ff.; Beer, *Die orientalische Politik Oesterreichs*,
pp. 112, 120 f.; Aragon, *Nassau-Siegen*, pp. 176 ff., 274 ff.; Dembiński, *Rosya a
rewolucya francuska*, pp. 33–40; Barral-Montferrat, *Dix ans de paix armée*, i,
pp. 310 ff.

and St. Petersburg announced the growing disposition of those Courts to bring matters to a rupture. Hence it became one chief aim of Austrian diplomacy to remove every pretext for an outbreak on the part of Prussia by preaching at St. Petersburg moderation, patience, and long-suffering, especially with regard to Polish affairs. If the catastrophe that might have been expected did not at once befall the audacious Poles, this was due in large part to the mollifying influence which Austria now brought to bear upon Russian policy.

Count Cobenzl at Petersburg found himself between Scylla and Charybdis. On one side was a party which advocated meeting the high-handed actions of England and Prussia with equally vigorous measures, so that a new war might easily have followed. On the other side there were many who would have gone so far as to sacrifice a part of Poland, in order to conciliate the Court of Berlin. The views of the former party, which was dominant in the Council of the Empire, undoubtedly accorded best with Catherine's own inclinations. Long weaned from any fondness for Prussia, despising Frederick William II almost as much as she did George III, the Empress had felt ever since the beginning of the war a growing and passionate indignation against the two monarchs who had dared to cross her plans and to set themselves up as ' dictators ' in Europe. She approved the bellicose resolutions adopted by the Council in September, 1788, in reply to the first hostile demonstrations of Prussia; and when one of her ministers presented a dissenting opinion, she shed tears of rage.[1] The events in Poland added fuel to the flames. " I swear to Almighty God," she wrote to Potemkin, " that I am doing everything possible to endure all that these Courts, and especially the almighty Prussian one, are doing; but it [the latter] is so puffed up that, if its head does n't burst, I see no possibility of agreeing to its shameful demands. . . . I am not revengeful, but what is opposed to the honor of my Empire and its essential interests is harmful. . . . I will not give province for province, nor have laws prescribed to me. . . . They will come to grief, for nobody

[1] See the protocol of the Council of September 18/29, 1788, Арх. Гос. Сов., i, pp. 606–611, and Храповицкій, Дневникъ, September 29/October 10, p. 95.

ever yet succeeded in such a course. They have forgotten who they are, and with whom they have to deal; and that is why the fools hope we shall yield." [1] " The Empress is entirely ready to strike against the King of Prussia," wrote Cobenzl at the end of November; " the ministers, with the exception of Count Ostermann, are of the opinion that perhaps this is the most favorable moment for the two Imperial Courts, if we can secure, if not the alliance, at least the neutrality of the Bourbon Courts; for it is hard to believe that England will engage to furnish more than indirect aid [to its ally]." [2]

Joseph, however, was furious at the idea. The rôles had changed completely. The Austrians, who for years had been preaching the necessity of ' reducing the Margrave of Brandenburg to his proper place in the world,' were now as disinclined to act against him as the Russians were eager to do so.[3] From December on, Cobenzl counselled nothing but prudence and self-restraint. When at the beginning of 1789 the Russians were much alarmed at the talk of a Prusso-Polish alliance, he urged that such a treaty would be made only to be torn up again, and that protesting about it would be quite useless under the circumstances. In case of war, it might even be better to have Poland on the side of Prussia than neutral; and at any rate, the two Imperial Courts ought to take no open measures to prevent such an alliance.[4] While the Russians refrained from presenting a protest on the subject at Warsaw, while they met even the overthrow of the Permanent Council with studied indifference, there was grave danger that their patience would be strained to the breaking-point by the demand formally made by the Republic, with the diplomatic support of Prussia, for the immediate evacua-

---

[1] Letter of November 27/December 8, 1788, Рус. Стар., xvii, p. 22.

[2] Report of November 28, V. A., *Russland, Berichte,* 1788.

[3] Cf. Joseph's letter to L. Cobenzl of November 24, 1788 as to the Empress' desire to go to war with Prussia, *F. R. A.,* II, liv, pp. 303 f. The view is advanced by P. Wittichen (*Polnische Politik Preussens,* pp. 17 f.), and Beer (*Orientalische Politik Oesterreichs,* p. 112) that if the Russians occasionally talked of war, it was only in order to soothe their allies. A slight study of the Russian documents would show how utterly mistaken is this point of view. Moreover, to talk of going to war with Prussia at that moment was to do anything but to soothe the Austrians.

[4] Cobenzl's reports of January 7 and April 15, 1789, V. A., *Russland, Berichte.*

tion of Polish territory by the Russian troops. But armed with an intercepted letter of Hertzberg, in which that minister declared that his Court hoped to find a pretext for a rupture in the affairs of Poland and expected to be ready to strike in July, Cobenzl was able to argue forcibly that the best way to foil the Prussians was to remove their last remaining excuse for intervention.[1] The Empress was highly exasperated by the constant denunciations to which she was subjected by the Polish Diet, and by the frequent collisions in the Ukraine; she wished nothing so much as to avenge herself in Prussia; but finally prudent counsels prevailed. In May orders were given to withdraw all Russian troops and magazines from the territory of the Republic. Henceforth the Court of Petersburg adopted an attitude of complete indifference to the doings of the Diet of Warsaw. The first period of the Polish crisis thus came to an unexpectedly peaceful close.

While they strove successfully to prevent a rupture with the Court of Berlin over Polish affairs, the Austrians had also to guard against the contrary danger of an agreement between Russia and Prussia at their expense and Poland's. A more conciliatory policy towards Prussia was advocated by the favorite Mamonov; by Ostermann and Šuvalov among the ministers; by the Grand Duke Paul, who had long conducted a secret correspondence with Frederick William; and above all by Potemkin. It seemed only too obvious that Russia could free herself in a moment from all her growing embarrassments by sacrificing the Austrian for the Prussian connection. But there was " the Empress' pretended dignity " (as the heir to the throne expressed it). If any human power could prevail over that, it must be Potemkin's, and after the capture of Oczakow the Prince was coming to Petersburg. The court and the town looked forward to his coming " as to a second Advent," the Prussian and English ministers and their partisans with keen impatience, Cobenzl with natural misgivings. The Prince was coming, people whispered ' to overthrow everything.'[2]

[1] Report of April 15, V. A., *Russland, Berichte,* 1789.
[2] For the above, the letters of Garnovski in the Рус. Стар., xvi; the letters of the Grand Duke Paul and his wife to Nesselrode in the *Lettres et papiers du chan-*

For a time there was, indeed, talk of great changes. Potemkin told the Prussian envoy that the neighboring Powers would have done much better at the time of the Partition to divide up the whole of Poland, and he added that it might still be done if the Prussians would indicate what they wanted.[1] In a slightly different strain he remarked to Cobenzl that he wished the King of Prussia would seize a bit of the Republic; the two Imperial Courts would do the same, the Poles would get their just deserts, and the Court of Berlin would lose all credit in Poland. With equal chagrin the ambassador heard Ostermann declare that a partition of Poland between the three Courts would perhaps be the best way out of the present embarrassing situation.[2]

All this was not merely diplomatic gossip. About this time Bezborodko, the most trusted of the Empress' ministers, laid before her two memorials, in which he advocated using the good offices of Prussia in making peace with Sweden and Turkey, and declared that if in this way Russia could secure the desired terms, there would be no disadvantage in renewing the alliance with the Court of Berlin, or even in allowing the latter some acquisition in Poland. This was to be effected through a secret negotiation with Prussia, into which the Emperor was to be initiated only when it was approaching completion. Had the plan been carried out, Austria might have been confronted by the same situation as in 1793: by a bargain made behind her back between Russia and

celier comte de Nesselrode, i, pp. 126, 130, 133, etc.; the correspondence of the Prussian envoy Keller for January–February, 1789 in Dembiński, op. cit.

[1] Keller's report of February 26, 1789, Dembiński, op. cit., i, p. 180.

[2] Cobenzl's report of April 15, V. A., Russland, Berichte, 1789. The ambassador wrote: " . . . sagte mir Graf Ostermann, dass es ihm lieb seye, dass die Preussen zu ihrem alten Projekt, ein Stück von Pohlen zu erhalten zurückkehrten; dieses würde vielleicht das beste Mittel seyn, sich aus der damaligen verworrenen Lage zu ziehen. Es verstünde sich von selbst dass man dem König in Preussen nicht zulassen würde sich in Pohlen zu vergrössern, ohne dass die beyden Kays. Höfe wenigstens ein gleiches Aequivalent erhielten; der König müsste uns bey solcher Verhältniss der Sachen freye Hände lassen, die Pohlen würden für ihr ausschweifendes Benehmen den verdienten Lohn empfangen, und die beyden Kays. Höfe bald wieder die Oberhand in diesem Königreich gewinnen und den Preussischen Credit vertilgen." Such a transaction would have been a very exact repetition of the Partition of 1772.

Prussia for the partition of Poland.[1] Fortunately, however, the Empress stood firm. The talk of a new partition quickly died out, and the Austrian alliance not only remained unshaken, but was about this- time renewed for another eight years.[2]

Potemkin's stay in St. Petersburg (February-May), while it may have improved his own position, seems to have had no political results, except to confirm the Empress in the resolution to adopt a somewhat more friendly attitude towards Prussia. As an outward sign of a more conciliatory disposition, in the early summer of 1789 Alopeus again appeared in Berlin with a secret commission. Its real object seems to have been merely to lull the Prussian Court with specious hopes, to gain time, and to postpone the outbreak of open hostility in that quarter. It led to a tortuous and futile negotiation, carried on chiefly through the royal favorite Bischoffwerder, which was dragged out for two years and resulted in practically nothing.[3]

---

[1] These memorials are printed in the Рус. Арх., 1875, ii, pp. 36 ff. Cf. also Bezborodko to S. R. Vorontsov, October, 1789, Арх. Вор., xiii, pp. 167 ff.

[2] This time also by the exchange of autograph letters between the two sovereigns under the dates of May 21 and May 24/June 4, 1789.

[3] The character of Alopeus' mission and the credibility of his reports have formed the subject of a lively controversy between Professors Dembiński and Askenazy. See the *Kwartalnik Historyczny*, xvii and xviii. After a study of these reports for the years 1789–93, I find myself quite in agreement with Professor Dembiński. Alopeus was undoubtedly strongly pro-Prussian in his sympathies and extremely eager to effect a reconcilation between the two Courts; but that he was in these years in the pay of Prussia and that his reports were concocted between him and the Prussian ministers, seems to me utterly improbable, M. Askenazy notwithstanding.

Alopeus' mission may probably be regarded as a result of Potemkin's exertions at St. Petersburg. His instructions were drawn up April 28/May 9, i. e., about a week before the Prince set out to return to the army. The mission must also stand in some kind of connection with the proposals of Bezborodko outlined in the two memorials mentioned in the text. In Bezborodko's mind, it was to be something more than a mere 'dilatory negotiation': it was to lead, if possible, to a satisfactory peace with Sweden and the Porte, reconciliation and alliance with Prussia, an agreement with the latter Power for equal 'advantages' to both Courts at the expense of Poland and Turkey (cf. his letter to S. R. Vorontsov of October, 1789, cited above). The mission fell very far short, however, of effecting such important results, owing both to the Empress' " insuperable antipathy to a rapprochement with Prussia " (the phrase is Bezborodko's), and to Hertzberg's obstinate insistence upon his utterly inacceptable ' grand plan.'

CHAPTER VI

The Prusso-Polish Alliance

I

The favoring circumstances of the moment had restored to Poland a precarious independence; but it remained to consolidate the new position, to provide against the dangers of all kinds, external and internal, with which the audacious venture of the Patriots was menaced. On July 1, 1789, at a secret meeting of four leaders of the party,[1] it was decided to direct the future labors of the Diet solely upon three great tasks: the establishment of a new and stronger form of government, the introduction of the hereditary succession to the throne, and the conclusion of an alliance with Prussia. These three projects were inseparable and mutually supplementary. A reformed constitution would be of little avail if at the death of the present elderly and ailing King the state was to be exposed to the anarchy and the foreign intervention that regularly accompanied an interregnum. The Prussian alliance seemed an indispensable guarantee of security at a moment when Poland was engaged in the difficult task of reorganization, and was constantly forced to fear an attack from her powerful and vindictive eastern neighbor.

As we look back upon it now, this Prussian alliance appears to be the supreme and tragic mistake of the Four Years' Diet. Those who in that last hour undertook to save the Republic, pinned their hopes to one Power, and that Power betrayed them. Prussia encouraged the Poles mortally to offend Catherine; she filled them with false hopes, and bound herself to them by the most solemn engagements; she led them on and on from one perilous adventure to another; and then in the end she deserted them and sold them to Russia. That is the history of the Prusso-Polish alliance as viewed from the Polish standpoint. The

[1] The two Marshals of the Confederation, Małachowski and Sapieha, Ignacy Potocki and Bishop Rybiński. (Lucchesini's report of July 4, B. A., *R.* 9, 27.)

Patriots have been overwhelmed with blame for staking their country's fortunes upon so dangerous, so artificial, so unnatural a connection. Unnatural it undoubtedly was, in view of the fundamental contradiction between the aims of the Patriotic party and Prussia's unalterable determination to keep Poland weak and to continue the dismemberment of the Republic. It was an alliance in which there could be little sincerity or confidence on either side, and which could have slight chances of permanence. And, judged by its result, the whole policy of the alliance seems imprudent, false, and wellnigh suicidal.

But if we do not judge merely by the outcome, but attempt to place ourselves in the position of the Polish leaders at that time, we may well ask what else they could have done.

A great and unlooked-for opportunity had presented itself; the nation insisted that that opportunity should not be thrown away; as far as human foresight could predict, it might well be the last chance. National independence and national revival were not to be hoped for, if Poland remained on the side of Russia. Had the Patriotic leaders recommended this latter course, the nation would have repudiated them: they had no choice but to attempt to rid the state of the Muscovite control. But when that had been accomplished, Poland could not relapse into a nerveless neutrality. Forced as she was to guard against the future vengeance of the Empress, too weak, as yet, to defend herself single-handed, obliged also to reckon with the danger that the neighbors would settle their differences, as usual, by a bargain at her expense, Poland was compelled to make sure of the support of one of the great Powers, and as matters then stood, support could be expected only from Prussia.

The Patriots were tolerably well aware of the dangers of the Prussian alliance, although they did not foresee the supreme treachery of 1792, — and how could they, since that desertion is almost without parallel in history? They realized from the outset that the alliance would have to be bought with a heavy price — Dantzic, Thorn, perhaps a part of Great Poland — [1]

---

[1] See the program discussed by the leaders of the party in Paris in January, 1788, Dembiński, "Piattoli et son rôle," *loc. cit.*, pp. 54 ff.; also Lucchesini's report

although later, unfortunately, the leaders were unable to bring the nation to make the sacrifice. They also seem to have recognized that even if this price were paid, no great confidence could under ordinary circumstances be placed in Prussian friendship. But the present situation was of a decidedly extraordinary sort. Prussia had allowed herself to be driven into an antagonism to the Imperial Courts that seemed bound to end in open war. By joining in that struggle, Poland might win solid claims to Prussian gratitude, and also provide handsomely for her own immediate interests. Such a war was likely to spell disaster for the already hard-pressed Imperial Courts; it might put an end to Catherine's power of aggression for good and all; at any rate, it would create such a gulf between Poland's two most dangerous neighbors that a new partition would be out of the question for a long time to come. Under such circumstances the ordinarily 'unnatural' Prussian-Polish alliance might become the most natural thing in the world.

Moreover, there was another contingency in which the Prussian connection might prove useful and salutary. Prussia was a member of the Triple Alliance, which seemed to be more and more the dominant factor in European politics. It was true that that alliance contained divergent tendencies. Prussia was eager to make it the instrument of her own plans of aggrandizement, while Pitt's great aim was to restore peace to Europe, to maintain the balance of power, and to protect the weaker states against such aggressive monarchs as Catherine and Joseph. But whichever tendency prevailed, Poland stood to gain something, providing the Triple Alliance held together and continued its policy of opposition to the Imperial Courts. And if Poland, by means of an alliance with Prussia, could gain admission to this wider union, the advantage would be inestimable. The Republic would not only free itself from too close dependence upon Berlin, but would also gain the security resulting from membership in an imposing league of states — England, Holland, Prussia, Sweden, perhaps also Denmark, Turkey and the German *Fürstenbund* —

of July 4, 1789, as to his first conferences with the Poles on the subject of the alliance.

a league of states banded together for peace and mutual protection. Perhaps it was not too much to hope that the Triple Alliance, which had rescued Holland from France, which had delivered Gustavus III from the direst necessity, which was ready to come to the aid of the struggling Turks, might also undertake to defend Poland against the vengeance of Catherine.

These hopes proved to be fallacious and illusory, but under the circumstances one cannot unreservedly condemn the Polish statesmen for cherishing them. Certainly the Poles were not alone in miscalculating the outcome of the general European crisis: Prussians and Belgians, Swedes and Turks were equally deceived. The difference was only that Poland had infinitely more at stake on the issue. The general situation in 1789 was indeed such as to warrant high hopes, and to make an alliance with Prussia, incongruous as it might be at other times, appear under the given circumstances a matter of sane and practical politics. It seems probable that the alliance would have justified itself, if Prussia had drawn the sword against the Imperial Courts in 1790, or if the Triple Alliance had not executed so inglorious a retreat before Catherine in 1791. Undoubtedly the Poles did not perform all that might have been expected of them to make their alliance with Prussia a success; but the great reasons for the failure of that alliance are to be found, not in anything that they did or left undone, but in the vacillations, contradictions, and fiascos of Prussian policy and in the collapse of Pitt's 'Federative System.'

II

The proposal for a Prusso-Polish alliance came originally from the Poles themselves. The idea, as we have seen, formed part of the program of the Patriots as early as the beginning of 1788. It was strengthened by Frederick William's first declaration to the Diet (October, 1788), in which the King suggested that if the Republic really needed an alliance, he would offer his own. That offer was hardly intended to be taken seriously, for the King was merely trying to checkmate the proposed Russian alliance; but it raised hopes. As soon as the Patriots had gained control of the Diet, they turned their attention to the realization of this favorite project, combining it with the plan of securing admission to the Triple Alliance, and with the establishment of an hereditary monarchy in favor of the Elector of Saxony, who was also to be drawn into the Federative System.

It is significant of the desire of the Polish leaders not to be dependent upon Prussia alone that they at once attempted to open a separate negotiation with England. In January, 1789, and again in June we find them making overtures at London, looking towards closer political and commercial relations between Great Britain and Poland. But Pitt was not yet interested in the Republic. Not long before he had confessed to the Prussian envoy, who wanted to discuss the Polish crisis, that he had not the ghost of an idea about the constitution or the affairs of Poland.[1] His foreign policy had not yet taken on the comprehensive scope and the marked anti-Russian bias that it was soon to have; and moreover, he felt that, as far as Poland was concerned, it behooved Prussia, as the Power chiefly interested, to prescribe the attitude to be adopted by the Triple Alliance. He therefore intimated to the Poles that England could enter into no negotiations, political or commercial, with them apart from Prussia.[2]

The leaders of the Diet had been sounding the ground at Berlin ever since the close of the preceding year; but now, in July, 1789, they came out more openly with their proposals. At a series of secret meetings with Lucchesini and Hailes, the British envoy, they set forth at length their desire for an alliance with Prussia, admission to the Triple Alliance, a new constitution, and the hereditary succession in the House of Saxony.[3]

Hertzberg was fairly aghast at such 'precipitate projects.' The Poles must be bereft of common sense, he wrote, if they imagined that Prussia would aid them to turn their Republic

---

[1] Luckwaldt, *F. B. P. G.*, xv, p. 35.

[2] Salomon, *Das politische System des jüngeren Pitt und die zweite Teilung Polens*, pp. 24 ff.; Lucchesini's reports of June 13 and 17, 1789, B. A., *R.* 9, 27; Kalinka, *Der polnische Reichstag*, ii, pp. 242 ff.

[3] Lucchesini's reports of November 5, 1788, January 26, May 9, 23, 30, July 4, 11, 19, 22, 25, 1789, B. A., *Fol.* 323 and *R.* 9, 27.

into a strong hereditary monarchy in permanent union with Saxony. It might, indeed, be desirable to designate the Elector as the future King, if that prince could thus be won over definitely to ' the Prussian system '; but Prussia could never permit the Polish crown to become hereditary—at least not without obtaining an enormous compensation. It may be that on this point the minister was not in agreement with his master, for in March, through his confidant, Bischoffwerder, Frederick William had assured the Elector of his willingness to allow and support the hereditary succession in the Saxon House;[1] but the King had probably not seen fit to inform either Hertzberg or the Poles of this. As for the project of alliance, Lucchesini was ordered to restrain the ardor of his Polish friends, since only the events of the Eastern war could allow Prussia to make a final decision.[2]

The time for a final decision seemed, indeed, to be close at hand. The general situation in the summer of 1789 was such as to challenge Prussia to action. To all the older sources of embarrassment from which the Imperial Courts had been suffering, there was now added the Revolution at Paris, which robbed them of their one possible new ally, and entirely freed the hands of their enemies; while the growing internal troubles of Austria— the danger of rebellions in Belgium, Galicia, and Hungary — together with the mortal illness of Joseph II, threatened completely to paralyze the energies of the Hapsburg Monarchy. Under such circumstances, what glittering prospects opened up before the King of Prussia, with his untouched resources, his well-filled treasury, his numerous allies, his army of 200,000 of the best troops in Europe! " The events of ten centuries," Lucchesini

[1] Flathe, *Die Verhandlungen über die dem Kurfürsten Friedrich August III von Sachsen angebotene Thronfolge in Polen*, p. 7.

[2] Hertzberg's reflections on the Polish proposals are set forth in his report to the King of July 9, and the rescripts to Lucchesini of July 10 and 20, B. A., *R*. 9, 27. H. to F. W., July 9: " V. M. ne peut jamais permettre selon ses véritables intérêts que le thrône devienne héréditaire en Pologne, à moins que l'Autriche ne sorte entièrement de ce royaume, et que V. M. ne reçoive un tel aggrandissement et accroissement de puissance qui La mette entièrement en sûreté du côté de la Pologne, puisque ce Royaume gouverné par un Roi héréditaire deviendroit trop dangereux pour la Prusse."

declared, " could not bring about a situation more favorable to Prussia for putting the last touch upon her aggrandizement." [1]

Even Hertzberg, whose learned combinations had so long held the Prussian sword in the scabbard, was now — rather suddenly — seized with a fever for action. He proposed that the King, on going to Silesia for the annual reviews, should gather two army corps and then present to the belligerent Powers in the form of an ultimatum a scheme for the general pacification based upon the sacrosanct ' grand plan.' Hertzberg may, not improbably, have thought that a mere military demonstration would suffice to secure the general acceptance of his terms; but if the Imperial Courts refused, then Prussia should strike, at least at Austria; with the aid of the Turks and Poles the business would be finished by winter, and Prussia raised to the pinnacle of earthly grandeur. Seldom had the old minister aroused himself to such a pitch of impetuous energy, and never had he seen success so nearly within his grasp.

But now, for the first time, the King eluded him. At the royal headquarters in Silesia other counsels prevailed. The decision was doubtless due in large part to the influence and intrigues of England, which had never relished Hertzberg's schemes of aggrandizement, and which was now moving heaven and earth to prevent the outbreak of a general European conflagration. Moreover, the Prussian generals declared with one accord that the season was too far, and the military preparations not far enough, advanced to permit of striking a blow that year. Frederick William personally was ready enough to go to war in his own good time, but he did not propose to do so merely in order to obtain an exchange of provinces rather advantageous to Austria. ' He could not bring himself,' he said, 'to do so little harm to his natural enemy.' [2] Never very enthusiastic about the Hertzberg plan, he now seemed to have made up his mind to abandon it for something more practicable.

The plan that the King adopted in its stead was: to await the expected rebellions in Belgium, Hungary, and Galicia; to con-

---

[1] Lucchesini to Hertzberg, August 27, 1789, Dembiński, *op. cit.*, i, p. 405.

[2] Lucchesini to Hertzberg, August 30, 1789, Dembiński, *op. cit.*, i, p. 407.

clude an alliance with the Porte; to keep the Poles ready to act and the Swedes from making peace; to complete Prussia's own hitherto inadequate military preparations, and then in the spring, with the aid of all these allies, to deliver a crushing attack upon the Emperor. Whatever may be thought of the morality of it, this program, compared with the Hertzberg system of 'partitions and exchanges,' 'equivalents' and 'compensations,' seems like a return to sane and practical politics. It had something of the spirit of Frederick the Great. If only the King had the energy and the will-power to conduct the grand venture in Frederick's manner, the "opportunity of ten centuries" would not have come in vain. Hertzberg, however, was inconsolable at the overthrow of his idolized scheme and the loss of the "unique moment" of the summer. Henceforth there appears an ever-growing divergence between the views of the minister, still clinging to his 'grand plan' and perpetually devising new combinations for realizing at least a part of it, and the projects of the King, who was bent not so much on making acquisitions as on settling once for all with Prussia's 'natural enemy.' Henceforth Prussia was to have on more than one occasion two policies, the King's and Hertzberg's, and sometimes even a third, an awkward combination of these two.[1]

At first, however, Prussia started off bravely enough on the new course. Immediately after the King's return from Silesia, orders were sent to Diez at Constantinople to conclude an offensive and defensive alliance with the Porte, and to promise that Prussia would take up arms the following year.[2] Gustavus III was encouraged to persevere in his lonely struggle by a substantial loan, coupled with assurances that Prussia would induce England to send a fleet to the Baltic and might even consent in good time to a Swedish alliance.[3] Negotiations were started for an alliance with Poland; and by underground channels the malcontents of

---

[1] In Appendix IV there will be found an enumeration of the authorities for this episode of the summer of 1789, and some discussion of controversial points.

[2] Zinkeisen, *op. cit.*, vi, p. 740.

[3] Wahrenberg, " Bidrag till historien om K. Gustaf III's sednaste regeringsår," in *Tidskrift för Litteratur*, 1851, pp. 336 ff.

Belgium, Hungary, and Galicia were invited to prepare for Armageddon.[1]

Frederick William's warlike resolutions were only strengthened by the events of the autumn. In October the revolt began in the Austrian Netherlands; by the end of the year the Imperialists had been virtually driven from the country; in January, 1790, the Congress at Brussels proclaimed the independence of ' The United States of Belgium.' On the other hand, the Turks, who had come through the previous campaign tolerably well, now met with a series of crushing reverses: the great defeats of Focşani (August 1) and Rîmnic (September 22), the fall of Bender, Akerman, and Belgrade, and the total loss of the Danubian Principalities. After such disasters it was only too probable that the discouraged Ottomans would make peace at once, unless the King of Prussia speedily came to the rescue.

Driven on by the most imperative and pressing orders from Berlin, Diez at last brought his negotiation to a successful conclusion. On January 31, 1790, the Prusso-Turkish alliance was signed. Prussia pledged herself to declare war on both the Imperial Courts in the coming spring, and not to lay down arms until the Turks had recovered, not only all they had lost during the present war, but also the Crimea. In return the Porte promised to exert itself, at the time when peace should be concluded, to procure the restitution of Galicia to Poland and to obtain substantial advantages for Prussia.[2] This treaty produced a tremendous sensation throughout Europe, and not a little mortification even at Berlin, where it was found that Diez had wildly overstepped his instructions, especially with regard to the Crimea. Nevertheless, the King was well content, for at last he was sure of the Turks, and the cornerstone of his great offensive coalition was laid. Not long afterwards the Prusso-Polish alliance also came into existence.

---

[1] Herrmann, *op. cit.*, vi, p. 282; Van de Spiegel, *Résumé des négociations*, etc., pp. 16 ff. and 61 ff.; Blok, *Geschiedenis van het Nederlandsche Volk*, vi, pp. 513 ff.; Bailleu, " Herzog Karl August, Goethe, und die ungarische Königskrone," in *Goethe-Jahrbuch*, xx (1899), pp. 144–152; Krones, *Ungarn unter Maria Theresa und Joseph II*, pp. 51 f.

[2] This treaty is printed in Martens, *Recueil de Traités des Puissances de l'Europe*,

III

For some months during the autumn Hertzberg had delayed a formal negotiation with the Republic by every device his ingenuity could suggest. If the minister had had his way, the alliance would probably never have been made. But the Poles grew continually more impatient, Lucchesini more insistent, and Frederick William more ardent for " the alliance and war." [1] At last, on December 10, 1789, a letter was communicated to the Diet, in which the King of Prussia formally promised to conclude an alliance as soon as the terms could be agreed upon. The sole condition that he attached to it was that the Poles should put through certain reforms in their constitution, since he saw "more advantage in a well-ordered government in Poland which would assure the political existence of the nation, than in an army of 300,000 men under a state of things that exposed the country to constant revolutions and changes." The Diet, roused to enthusiasm, made haste to act upon this suggestion. A new constitution, avowedly imperfect but designed to meet the emergency and to strengthen the hand of the government, was rushed through in remarkably quick time and with still more remarkable unanimity (December 23). Meanwhile the Deputation of Foreign Interests was authorized to negotiate an alliance, not only with Prussia but also if possible with England.[2]

It was an historic moment, the apogee of the Prusso-Polish honeymoon. Never before nor later were the two sides so nearly at one in purposes, desires, and aspirations. The King of Prussia

iv, pp. 466 ff.; Hertzberg, *Recueil*, iii, pp. 36–43; Angeberg, *Recueil des Traités et Conventions concernant la Pologne*, pp. 216–220.

[1] Hertzberg to Lucchesini, December 1, 1789: " Le roi, qui veut à présent à tout priz alliance et guerre . . . ," Dembiński, *op. cit.*, i, p. 419. Very instructive for Hertzberg's attitude is his " Denkschrift über das zwischen Preussen und Polen im Jahre 1790 geschlossene Bündniss," in Schmidt's *Allgemeine Zeitschrift für Geschichte*, vii, pp. 261–271.

[2] Kalinka, *Der polnische Reichstag*, i, pp. 641 ff.; Askenazy, *op. cit.*, pp. 57 f. The proposal for an alliance subsequently made at London received only an evasive answer, as Pitt was too much occupied with other things and also fearful of Continental connections that involved a danger of war. See Bukaty to Ankwicz, December 18, 1789 and February 16, 1790, Dembiński, *op. cit.*, i, pp. 426 f. (notes).

believed that he had a real need of the Polish alliance in order
to complete his offensive coalition. He was probably sincere in
his professed wish to see a strong government in Poland, in order
that the Republic might prove an efficient confederate. The
mass of the Poles were eager for a treaty that promised security
against Russia, while the leaders of the Patriots, initiated into
the aggressive plans of Prussia, rejoiced in the prospect of a
glorious war, the recovery of Galicia, the restoration of Poland
to an honorable place in the political system of Europe. With
such dispositions on both sides, it might have seemed that the
conclusion of the alliance would be a short and easy matter.

The formal negotiation was begun at Warsaw in the last days
of December; and early in January, the draft of a treaty having
been put on paper, Lucchesini went off to Berlin to procure his
master's final instructions. Then, however, there came a painful
halt, and dangers loomed up that threatened to wreck the project.
The difficulty came, in the first place, from the King of Poland.
Stanislas Augustus was still profoundly convinced that salvation
lay only on the side of Russia, and he was haunted by Stackelberg's frequent warnings that the Empress would pardon anything except an alliance with Prussia. How far he had bound
himself to the Russian ambassador, who had promised him the
payment of his enormous debts if he would thwart the obnoxious project,[1] it is difficult to say; at any rate, it is certain that
the King viewed the alliance with repugnance, and worked
against it as much as he dared.

As one means of checking the project, Stanislas secretly advised
the Imperial Courts to present declarations to the Diet that they
bore no ill will for all that had recently taken place in Poland,
and were themselves willing to conclude treaties of alliance with
the Republic, guaranteeing its independence and integrity.
Possibly such declarations might have had the desired effect;
but nothing could induce the proud lady in Petersburg to such

---

[1] De Caché's report of February 6, 1790, as to Stackelberg's offer, V. A.,
Polen, Berichte. That the King gave the ambassador some kind of a promise to
place obstacles in the way of the alliance appears from the protocol of the Russian
Council of the Empire of January 7/18, 1790, Арх. Гос. Сов., i, p. 758.

an act of condescension. Austria, indeed, took up the King's suggestion. At least, Kaunitz, keenly alarmed at the danger threatening Galicia, approached the Polish minister at Vienna with the rather abrupt offer of an Austro-Polish alliance on the same terms as that which was to be concluded with Prussia. But as this overture was not made public, the leaders at Warsaw, rightly regarding it as a mere snare, returned an evasive answer and avoided bringing the matter before the Diet at all.[1]

While thus disappointed in the hopes he had based upon the Imperial Courts, Stanislas Augustus had been more successful with another device for thwarting the Prussian alliance. From the beginning he had insisted that the alliance must be accompanied by a commercial treaty that would, at least to some extent, free Polish trade from the enormous transit duties and other restrictions imposed by Prussia. This was, indeed, a matter of the utmost importance, in view of the fact that the vast bulk of the foreign trade of the Republic had to pass through Prussian territory, by the Vistula and the Oder or through Silesia; but it involved delicate and complex questions which it would have been wiser not to raise at such a time. The Patriotic leaders fully realized how inopportune the demand for a commercial treaty was; but the demand, which was certain to be popular, became noised abroad, and they did not dare resist. Hence, when the Polish proposals for the alliance went to Berlin, the commercial question had been coupled with the political one.[2]

All this was grist to Hertzberg's mill. He, too, wished to combine the two sets of questions, because, in his pettifogging way, he saw a chance to drive a sharp bargain and to prove once more that for the aggrandizement of Prussia the pen was mightier than the sword. He would sell the Poles the alliance and the commercial treaty in return for the cession of Dantzic and Thorn. Both Hertzberg and his master seem to have believed that the Diet would make the sacrifice without too much

---

[1] Kaunitz to L. Cobenzl, February 10 and 17, V. A., *Russland, Exped.*, 1790; the Deputation of Foreign Interests to Ankwicz, February 24, Museum XX. Ossolińskich, *MS.* 516; Wegner, *Dzieje dnia trzeciego i piątego maja*, pp. 320 f.

[2] Kalinka, *Der polnische Reichstag*, ii, pp. 20 ff.; Askenazy, *op. cit.*, p. 205.

murmuring: an error for which Lucchesini and the Polish envoys at Berlin were probably responsible.[1]

When at the end of February the Prussian minister returned to Warsaw and presented his two treaties, including the demand for Dantzic and Thorn, the impression was staggering. The leaders of the Patriots were, indeed, ready to agree even to these terms, realizing that the natural and inevitable desire of Prussia for two cities enclosed in her own territory could not in the long run be denied; but this mattered little, for no one dared come out openly in defence of so violently unpopular a project. To the rank and file of the so-called ' Prussian party,' it was a terrible disillusionment to find the ' virtuous ' and ' disinterested ' Frederick William a veritable Shylock in disguise. If this was the first sample of his ' generosity,' what might not be expected of him in the future ? To the mass of the nation the idea of the proposed cession was intolerable, because it would have seemed like a new partition, and this time the more shameful because voluntarily accepted.[2] In short, the partisans of the alliance were thrown into consternation, while the ' Russians ' and ' Parasites ' triumphed, declaring that this was what they had always predicted. The Deputation of Foreign Interests did not venture even to lay the Prussian terms before the Diet. Lucchesini did not dare show himself. Sick with fever or chagrin, the envoy shut himself up in his house and wrote home desperately, begging for permission to drop the commercial treaty and the odious conditions attached to it, assuring his Court that the Diet would even rather give up the alliance than consent to sacrifice the two cities.[3]

Hertzberg, much ruffled at the inconceivable blindness of the Poles to their ' true interests,' would probably have renounced

---

[1] Lucchesini to Hertzberg, November 4 and 29, 1789, Dembiński, op. cit., i, pp. 415 and 417; Hertzberg's Memoir in Schmidt's Zeitschrift, vii, p. 267.

[2] Kraszewski, Polska w czasie trzech rozbiorów, ii, p. 287.

[3] For the effect produced by the Prussian demands: Lucchesini to Hertzberg, February 27, in Dembiński, pp. 423, f.; Lucchesini to Jacobi, March 20, B. A., R. 93, 33; de Caché's reports of March 2 and 6, V. A., Polen, Berichte, 1790; Aubert (the French chargé d'affaires) to Montmorin, February 27 and March 3, Dembiński, op. cit., i, pp. 495–498; Engeström, Minnen och Anteckningar, i, pp. 157 f.

the alliance rather than desist from his territorial claims, but the King was not so minded. Through the latter's intervention, Lucchesini was straightway given the orders he had asked for: the commercial question was to be postponed, and the alliance to be concluded at once.[1]

By the time these instructions reached Warsaw, the atmosphere there had already cleared. The evil effects of the Prussian demands had by no means been obliterated; they remained to taint this alliance from its birth; but the news of the Prusso-Turkish treaty, the death of the Emperor Joseph, the exhortations of the English, Dutch, and Swedish ministers, who held out the prospect of admission to the Triple Alliance, and above all the energetic exertions of the Patriotic leaders had combined to produce a marked revulsion of public opinion in favor of the great project.[2]

The demand for Dantzic and Thorn being now laid on the shelf, the final arrangements were quickly pushed through. On March 27 the Diet in secret session approved the proposed draft of the alliance with little opposition. The 29th the instrument was signed.

The treaty contained the usual guarantees of the respective possessions of the contracting parties, although it was stated that this should not exclude a future voluntary agreement about certain territorial questions now unsettled. This referred, of course, to Dantzic and Thorn. In case either side should be attacked, the other was bound to render military assistance: Poland with 8,000 cavalry and 4,000 infantry; Prussia with 14,000 infantry and 4,000 cavalry. In case of extreme necessity either party was bound to aid its ally with all its forces. Article VI, which later acquired a mournful celebrity, ran: " If any foreign Power, by virtue of any previous acts or stipulations or the interpretation thereof, should seek to assert the right to interfere in the internal

---

[1] For Hertzberg's attitude, cf. his above-cited "Denkschrift über das Bündniss," in Schmidt's *Zeitschrift*, vii, p. 267; Kalinka, *Der polnische Reichstag*, ii, pp. 51 ff.

[2] Kalinka, *op. cit.*, ii, pp. 58 f.; Askenazy, *op. cit.*, pp. 59 ff.; de Caché, March 13, 17, 31, V. A., *loc. cit.;* Engeström, *loc. cit.;* Hailes' report of April 29 in Herrmann, *op. cit.*, vi, p. 546; Stanislas Augustus to Bukaty, March 31, in Kalinka, *Ostatnie lata*, ii, pp. 150 f.

affairs of the Republic of Poland, or of its dependencies [i. e. Courland], at any time or in any manner whatsoever, His Majesty the King of Prussia will first endeavor by his good offices to prevent hostilities growing out of such a pretension; but if these good offices should not prove effective and hostilities against Poland result, His Majesty the King of Prussia, recognizing this as a *casus foederis*, will then assist the Republic according to the provisions of Article IV of the present treaty." So much for any future attempt of Catherine II to revive the Russian guarantee. Finally, both sides expressed their desire to conclude a commercial treaty, but that matter was reserved for a future time.[1]

Thus that alliance with Prussia which the Patriot leaders had hoped and worked for ever since the beginning of the Diet; the alliance in which they saw the ' palladium of liberty,' the one guarantee of their new-won independence, their one safeguard against the reprisals and aggressions of Russia; the alliance which was to admit them to the great Federative System and restore them to a secure and honorable place in Europe, had at last come to be. That alliance had not been extorted from Prussia by mere importunities, cajoleries, or ruses. Prussia had entered into it voluntarily, in a spirit of comparative sincerity and amity. However much Hertzberg might writhe and rage, however much Lucchesini might strive to give his reports from Warsaw a fine Machiavellian flavor, the fact remained that at that time Frederick William was really the friend of Poland. The King had ardently desired the alliance; he wished to see the Poles reform their government and strengthen their army; he favored their plan of securing to the Elector of Saxony the succession to the throne; he contemplated admitting the Republic to the Triple Alliance.[2] All this, of course, was not because of any particular

---

[1] The treaty of alliance of March 29, 1790, is printed in Martens, *Recueil*, iv, pp. 471 ff.; Hertzberg, *Recueil*, iii, pp. 1–8; Angeberg, *op. cit.*, pp. 222–226.

[2] Before his return to Warsaw in February, 1790, Lucchesini was sent to Dresden to offer the Elector Prussia's assistance in the matter of the Polish succession (de Caché, February, 13). As to the admission of Poland to the Triple Alliance, see e. g., Hertzberg to Lucchesini, March 6 (Dembiński, *op. cit.*, i, pp. 426 f.) and to Diez, March 9 (Herrmann, *op. cit.*, vi, p. 290).

affection for the Poles, but because the King believed that he needed their alliance for his coalition against Austria.

The alliance was made, then, by both sides in good faith, for precise, practical reasons. It was no mere formality, no hollow form of words. Defensive according to the letter, it was in spirit an offensive alliance, for it was formed with a view to a great joint enterprise. It was an alliance for action, for meeting a great opportunity with a great deed.[1]

[1] Cf. the remarks of Askenazy, *op. cit.*, pp. 60 ff.

CHAPTER VII

REICHENBACH

I

NEVER, perhaps, in the course of its stormy history has the Austrian Monarchy been placed in a more desperate situation than at the moment when Joseph II sank into the grave.[1] With the costly and bloody Turkish war still dragging on, the opulent Netherlands lost, the other provinces apparently ready to revolt, and slight hope of effective aid from an exhausted and unreliable ally, the tottering edifice of the Hapsburg power must have collapsed before a single vigorous blow from without. That the threatening catastrophe was averted is the great merit of Joseph's brother and successor, Leopold II.

The new monarch brought to his colossal task no very brilliant talents; but he possessed a deep understanding of men and affairs, gained during twenty-five years' experience of rule in Tuscany; a clear, dispassionate, and independent judgment; a keen instinct for the practical, coupled with a complete indifference to the ambitious plans and love of glory that had haunted his brother; finally, firmness, prudence, and tact. Having lived in Italy, and not being accustomed to confide his inmost thoughts to all comers, he could scarcely hope to escape the reproach so often cast upon him of being a ' new Machiavelli ' — it comes with such special grace from Lucchesini's lips—but in fact his policy, whenever it was the expression of his own will and not that of Kaunitz, appears straightforward, honest, and surprisingly simple. It seems possible to reduce Leopold's whole political system to a very few principles. He wished to secure and maintain peace at home and abroad; to cultivate the Russian alliance, in so far as it conduced to that end, and no farther; and to effect an understanding with Prussia, as the indispensable condition of per-

---

[1] The Emperor died on February 20, 1790.

manent quiet. Such a policy contains nothing particularly Machiavellian. And it cannot be doubted that his was precisely the kind of policy that Austria most needed at that time.

From the moment of his accession, Leopold's foremost aims were to put an end to the Turkish war, to avert a breach with Prussia and Poland, and to recover the Netherlands. Naturally he wished to save as much as possible of the conquests made during the war, but he was unwilling for their sake to risk the most essential interests of the Monarchy. In general, he was prepared to make any sacrifice compatible with honor, in order to rescue the state from the desperate situation into which his brother had brought it. This pacific policy conflicted from the outset, however, with the ideas of the second power in the Empire, the veteran Chancellor. Hating Prussia with all the accumulated bitterness of a lifetime, viewing the glory of the Monarchy as identical with his own, Kaunitz revolted at the thought of anything resembling a surrender to the rival at Berlin. Rather than endure such shame he would have risked as many wars as might come. The result of these diverging tendencies was, at first, a compromise.

It was decided to keep open both avenues of action. On the one hand, while negotiating with England, whose disinclination to the aggressive plans of Prussia was well known at Vienna, Leopold meant to press operations vigorously against the Turks in the hope of forcing a speedy peace, and to make sure of the assistance of Russia in case of an emergency; on the other hand, he hoped to avert an immediate outbreak of hostilities on the part of Prussia and her satellites by making friendly overtures to the Court of Berlin. Accordingly, immediately after his arrival in Vienna, he wrote Frederick William an eminently amicable letter, expressing his desire for peace and for better relations. With it went a memorial announcing the Austrian terms for a peace with the Turks: the frontier as formerly established by the Peace of Passarowitz.[1]

[1] The letter and the memorial are printed in Van de Spiegel, *op. cit.*, pp. 222–230; the letter also in Hertzberg's *Recueil*, pp. 50 f. In both these texts the date is given as March 25, as also by Duncker, *H. Z.*, xxxvii, p. 14, and Beer,

Even so unexpected and friendly a communication, novelty as it was in the relations between Berlin and Vienna, might of itself have produced little effect upon Frederick William. Since August his heart had been set on war, on fighting out the old rivalry with Austria to a finish. His anti-Hapsburg coalition was formed; his army was mobilizing; it was no time now for turning back from the great enterprise. But just at this moment England intervened and played into the hand of Austria.

It has already been noted that the two leading members of the Triple Alliance pursued very different aims during this protracted European crisis. While Prussia was eager to utilize the situation for her own schemes of aggrandizement, Pitt desired only to restore peace as soon as possible, and in such a manner as would make the least possible change in the existing equilibrium and would ensure the existence of the small states against the aggressive and rapacious Powers. Under such circumstances it had not been easy to maintain even a semblance of harmony between the two allies. Both agreed that the Triple Alliance was called upon to restore the peace of Europe; but when it came to a discussion of ways and means, there were endless bickerings and recriminations. Early in 1790, however, an agreement had apparently been reached. At the close of February, Pitt had brought forward his favorite formula of the *status quo ante bellum* as the basis upon which the allies should attempt to effect a general pacification. Being at that time still ignorant of the real temper of Austria's new ruler, the Prussians readily assented. They reckoned that both the Imperial Courts would reject a principle that involved the sacrifice of practically all their conquests; and in that case, Prussia would have not only a pretext for war, but a right to demand the armed coöperation of England and Holland.[1]

Pitt, who was now determined to take up the great work of pacification in earnest, had meanwhile been vastly encouraged

Leopold II, Franz II und Catharina, p. 16. Ranke (*Die deutschen Mächte*, ii, pp. 174 f., note), Sybel (*Gesch. d. Revolutionszeit*, i, p. 213), and Heigel (*Deutsche Geschichte*, i, p. 250, note 2) give the 26th, which is also the date of the copy of the letter among the *Expeditionen, Preussen*, 1790, in the Vienna Archives.

[1] Salomon, *William Pitt*, i[ii], pp. 465 f.; Rose, *Pitt and National Revival*, pp. 519 ff.

by an event in another quarter. Leopold's first act, on learning of his brother's death, was to summon the British envoy at Florence to a secret interview, at which he expressed in the strongest terms his desire for peace, his willingness to make the sacrifices that might be necessary, and his wish that England should assume the rôle of mediator. It was true that he did not commit himself definitely to the *status quo ante* principle, and that after his arrival in Vienna, under the influence of Kaunitz, his tone altered and stiffened considerably. But Pitt did not wait for further particulars. Delighted by the request for mediation, and convinced that Austria was already converted to his favorite principle, he hastened to send out invitations to all the belligerents for a peace negotiation on the *status quo ante* basis. At the same time he wrote to Berlin that the new King of Hungary seemed sincerely anxious for peace on fair and moderate terms; that he did not share his predecessor's ambition, or his predilection for Russia, or his jealousy of Prussia; and that it was to be presumed that he would accept the *status quo ante* principle, or something approximating it. If Prussia refused that basis, in order to pursue offensive plans of her own, she was warned that she could not count upon the coöperation of England. If she accepted it, on the other hand, the principle need not be interpreted so strictly as to exclude certain reasonable modifications of the old frontiers to the reciprocal advantage of the interested parties; but great changes of territory would be out of the question, and no changes ought to be insisted upon to the point of producing a new war.[1]

This communication from England, following close upon the overture from Austria, placed the Prussians in a highly embarrassing situation. Should they go forward resolutely with their offensive plans, paying no further attention to their inconsiderate ally at London, or should they enter upon the path of negotiation, as Leopold invited, and Pitt exhorted, them to do ? And if they negotiated, could they afford to admit the *status quo* basis ? Undoubtedly that principle now appeared in very different light

---

[1] This dispatch, Leeds to Ewart, March 30, is analyzed in Salomon, *Pitt*, i[ii], p. 470; Rose, *Pitt*, pp. 523 f.; Ranke, *Die deutschen Mächte*, ii, pp. 182 f.

from that in which they had welcomed it only a month before. Then it had meant a device by which they could draw England after them into aggressive action against Austria. Now it meant a formula by which, if they accepted it, Leopold could at any moment strike the arms from their hands. Frederick William was now furious against the English for declaring in favor of so insidious a principle, and he was strongly tempted to ' emancipate ' himself from them entirely. Hertzberg, however, was rather pleased with the course events had taken. Always inclined to prefer diplomacy to arms and increasingly pessimistic about a war with Austria, he now saw a new chance for his old plan, the universal panacea — at least for the old plan in a somewhat reduced and more moderate form. In one report after another he urged upon his master how dangerous it would be to break with England entirely and to risk his fortunes in a war undertaken with no more reliable allies than Turks, Poles, or Hungarian rebels. On the other hand, if he negotiated, he would, indeed, have to admit the *status quo ante* basis, but he could give that principle so loose a meaning as to cover a bargain with Austria for reciprocal advantages. England might be expected to favor certain just and moderate acquisitions for Prussia, since Pitt had himself declared that the *status quo* principle need not be taken too strictly. In this way, perhaps, Dantzic and Thorn might at last be won, without the necessity of striking a blow or risking anything. It would, at least, do no harm to try, and His Majesty could, of course, break off the negotiation whenever he chose. At this point, if ever, it was time to dismiss a minister obsessed by incongruous and impossible schemes. But although Frederick William had long lost faith in the miraculous efficacy of the ' grand plan,' and was still as eager for war as before, he allowed Hertzberg to have his way. The chief reason was that the army was not ready for action, nor likely to be for more than a month. Unfortunately for Prussia, the date for the completion of mobilization had been fixed at May 15.[1] Hence Hertzberg was to have one more chance to exhibit his virtuosity as a diplomat, although, as the King insisted, the military preparations

[1] P. Wittichen, *Die polnische Politik Preussens*, p. 51.

were to continue, and Prussia must be ready to strike within two months.[1]

This was, we think, a disastrous decision. The King committed himself to a formal negotiation in which the only alternatives under discussion were to be: the strict *status quo ante*, which was of all solutions the most repugnant to Prussia, or the *status quo* modified according to Hertzberg's peculiar ideas, which was likely to be repugnant to everybody else. The negotiation was destined to consume many precious weeks, to wear out the patience and arouse the suspicions of Prussia's allies, to involve Prussian policy in a maze of uncertainty, irresolution, and contradictions. Above all, the King was laboring under a delusion as bad as his minister's in imagining that he could keep open at one and the same time the possibility of executing his original offensive plan and that of carrying through the Hertzberg exchange project. The two plans were fundamentally antagonistic and incompatible. The one involved the coöperation of Poland and Turkey and the annihilation of Austria; the other involved the spoliation of Turkey and Poland and advantages for Austria. When both plans became simultaneously known to the world, the result could only be to rob Prussia of the confidence of all parties concerned, and to make the realization of either project almost impossible. Therein lies the cardinal reason for the total fiasco that followed.

II

The Austro-Prussian negotiations were spun out for two months through an interchange of letters between the two sovereigns, and of memorials and 'verbal communications' between the two chancelleries. Hertzberg began by offering the Austrians the choice between two bases for the pacification: either the strict *status quo ante* or an arrangement for reciprocal advantages between the interested Powers. He indicated clearly enough that

---

[1] On this important turning in Prussian policy, see, Duncker, in *H. Z.*, xxxvii, p. 15; Ranke, *op. cit.*, ii, pp. 183 ff.; Ritter, *Die Konvention von Reichenbach*, pp. 3 ff.; Salomon, *Pitt*, I^{ii}, pp. 470 f.; Reede to Van de Spiegel, April 15, Van de Spiegel, *op. cit.*, pp. 196 ff.

Prussia preferred the second alternative. The arrangement he proposed was substantially as follows. The Porte, acting on the benevolent advice of Prussia, should cede to Austria the ' frontiers of Passarowitz '; Austria should restore to Poland the whole of Galicia except the Zips, Pocutia, and Halicz (these last two districts forming the southeast corner of the province, contiguous to the Bukovina); and the Republic should cede Dantzic, Thorn, and some small districts in Great Poland to Prussia.[1] In short, it was the old ' grand plan ' warmed over, very little disguised, abridged, or improved.

These propositions made anything but a favorable impression at Vienna. It was true that the admission of the *status quo* basis by Prussia placed in the hands of the Austrians at least the possibility of avoiding a rupture; but they feared that the Court of Berlin would give that principle a stricter interpretation than England had done, while they found the plan of "exchange, compensation, and depredation" still more inacceptable. At a great ministerial Conference (April 26), it was decided that the negotiation would have to be spun out for a time, because it was impossible to risk a breach with Prussia while the Turkish war lasted, and it was the opinion of the Conference that a double war must be prevented at all costs. If it proved possible by vigorous military operations to extort a speedy peace from the Porte, or if Russia would back up her ally by an imposing parade of force, then Austria might take a bold tone towards the would-be dictator. If not, if it became necessary to accept the mediation of the Triple Alliance, then Austria would prefer the basis of the ' *status quo non matériel* ' (i. e., with certain slight alterations of the old frontier in her favor), or even the *status quo strict*, by which, at least, Prussia would get nothing, rather than to consent to the thoroughly objectionable Hertzberg plan.[2] Steadfastness

[1] The alternative was put to Austria in general terms in Frederick William's letter to Leopold of April 15, 1790, Hertzberg's *Recueil*, iii, pp. 54–58; Van de Spiegel, *op. cit.*, pp. 230–233. The details of the ' arrangement for reciprocal advantages ' were imparted by Hertzberg to Reuss, the Austrian envoy, in an interview of the same date (Reuss' report of April 16, V. A., *Preussen, Berichte*, 1790).

[2] Protocol of the Conference, V. A., *Vorträge*, 1790.

and tenacity in misfortune are virtues that have rarely deserted Austrian statesmen; and, desperate as was the situation in that spring of 1790, these qualities were not lacking on that occasion. However much Leopold might be inclined to concessions, his ministers were resolved to put on a bold face as long as they could, and even, under certain circumstances, to fight rather than surrender their conquests of the past two years or submit tamely to the dictatorship of Prussia.

In accordance with the resolutions of the Conference, Leopold once more wrote Frederick William a friendly yet utterly non-committal letter, announcing that he could give no definite reply to the Prussian propositions until he had consulted his ally, the Empress of Russia.[1] A month earlier such dilatory tactics would scarcely have succeeded in Berlin, but in May the atmosphere at that Court was much more pacific. The trouble once more was with the army. The further the mobilization proceeded, the more the inadequacy of the Prussian military preparations came to light. The services of provisions and transportation were in such woful disorder that the minister responsible for them committed suicide. While it had originally been intended that the army should be ready by the middle of May, it now appeared that at least another month would be required. Meanwhile the Austrians had massed such large forces in Bohemia and Moravia that they had for a time decidedly the superiority. There was a moment when the Prussians feared an invasion of Silesia. Those about the King urged or pleaded with him not to undertake a war. Under the influence of all these deterrents Frederick William's martial ardor was vanishing. His old faith in the absolute military superiority of Prussia was shaken. For nearly a year he had wanted war and nothing but war, but in May of 1790, when the time for action had come, he scarcely knew what he wished.[2]

The natural result of this was that Austria's wholly unsatisfactory reply to the first propositions of Prussia evoked, not a sharp ultimatum, but a mild offer of still a third basis for nego-

---

[1] This letter of April 28 is printed in Hertzberg's *Recueil*, iii, pp. 58 ff., and in Van de Spiegel, *op. cit.*, pp. 235 ff.

[2] For the above see especially Ritter, *op. cit.*, pp. 7 f.; P. Wittichen, *op. cit.*, pp. 50 ff.

tiation. Hertzberg suggested, namely, that Prussia might be
satisfied with a very small cession in Galicia, about one-sixth of
that province, though in that case the Austrian acquisitions from
Turkey would naturally have to be reduced.[1]

Now at last the plans of the Prussian pacificators began to
find an echo at Vienna. Were they not already reducing their
demands ? And this new proposition, it appeared, might not be
their last. Only a little dexterous bargaining, using the *status
quo* to frighten them into concessions, and Austria might get off
with a handsome acquisition from the Turks and an insignificant
cession to Poland. This was, at least, the opinion of the majority
of the ministerial Conference, and especially, it seems, of Spielmann.[2] Kaunitz was not so optimistic about the possibilities of
negotiation. He still pinned his hopes to imposing military
demonstrations to be made in concert with Russia, and would
even yet have trusted, if necessary, to the arbitrament of war.
Leopold was chiefly anxious for peace and the recovery of the
Netherlands. How far he entered into Spielmann's views, it is
difficult to say, but for whatever reason, he still postponed a final
decision. In accordance with the opinion of the Conference, one
more dilatory answer was sent to Berlin, to the effect that Austria
could not declare herself definitely until the arrival of the long-
awaited courier from Petersburg. Provisionally it was stated
that while preferring even the *status quo strict* to the other
propositions as formulated by Prussia, the Court of Vienna was
willing to treat on the basis of the exchange plan, providing it
could be made really fair and reciprocally advantageous.[3]

Such procrastination could not continue much longer without
producing an explosion of wrath at Berlin, as the Austrians were
well aware. In reality, their final decision now depended on the

---

[1] Frederick William to Leopold, May 11, and *note verbale* of the same date,
Hertzberg, *op. cit.*, iii, pp. 60–64; Van de Spiegel, *op. cit.*, pp. 237–243; Reuss'
report of May 12, V. A., *loc. cit.*

[2] Conference protocols of May 21 and June 9, V. A., *Vorträge*, 1790.

[3] Leopold to Frederick William, May 23, with the accompanying *Mémoire*
from the State Chancellery, V. A., *Vorträge*, 1790; printed in Hertzberg, *op. cit.*, iii,
pp. 65–69, and Van de Spiegel, *op. cit.*, pp. 243–248, and in both dated erroneously
May 25.

replies expected from Russia. Had Catherine not failed them, they might, perhaps, have escaped the humiliation of Reichenbach.

III

Ever since the offensive plans of Prussia had come to light in the previous autumn, the ambassador Cobenzl had been straining every nerve to induce the Russians to come to the defence of their sorely-menaced ally. Now, if ever, he incessantly declared, was the time for the Empress to show her gratitude for all the loyal services and sacrifices of Austria in the past ten years. He demanded that Russia should at once send a corps to protect Galicia; that the Empress should issue a declaration that she had guaranteed that province to Austria, and would regard an attack upon it as an attack upon herself; and that a supreme effort should be made that spring to force the Turks to peace. Above all, he wished Russia to make imposing military demonstrations against Prussia and Poland, to indicate precisely what forces she would bring into the field in case of a new war, and to concert with Vienna a plan for joint operations. All these demands and exhortations elicited, however, only unsatisfactory replies.

At times the Russian ministers professed to see no way out of the situation except a new partition of Poland, and they even offered to propose that solution at London and Berlin. As usual, Cobenzl combated this idea with all the arguments at his command, and the Russians did not insist.[1] On the other hand, in May Austria for the first time requested her ally to consent to certain Prussian acquisitions in Poland as a last resource, in case the Court of Berlin insisted absolutely upon the Hertzberg plan. The Russians consented to this without much opposition.[2] Request and assent are equally significant. The Imperial Courts had long made the inadmissibility of further Prussian acquisitions in Poland one of the chief principles of their alliance: now both

---

[1] Cobenzl's report of April 9, V. A., *Russland, Berichte,* 1790.

[2] Kaunitz to L. Cobenzl, May 1, the latter's report of the 18th, V. A., *Russland, Exped.* and *Berichte,* 1790.

of them were willing *in pessimo casu* to allow Prussia such aggrandizement.

In general, the Russians protested warmly their determination to do all that was humanly possible for their ally, but they constantly avoided committing themselves to precise and definite engagements. All the military arrangements, they told Cobenzl, were in the hands of Potemkin, and it was impossible to know what Potemkin would or would not do. These assertions corresponded pretty closely to the facts of the situation. The Empress was really disposed to do what she could for Austria;[1] she was still as bitter against Prussia as ever; but her attention throughout the spring was absorbed in the Swedish war, which was then reaching its climax. At a moment when Gustavus' cannon were thundering almost at the gates of St. Petersburg, or when the Russian and Swedish fleets were breathlessly chasing each other about the Gulf of Finland, the Empress could scarcely venture to commit herself to still a third war, or even give much attention to the course of events in the West. Whatever was to be done for the assistance of Austria depended primarily on Potemkin; and Potemkin had plans of his own.

Throughout the whole first half of 1790 the Tauric Prince was flaunting himself in regal state at Jassy, the capital of his prospective ' Kingdom of Dacia,' already assuming the airs of an Oriental despot,[2] and occupied far less with the Turkish war than with his own schemes for personal aggrandizement. The failure of his project for a Confederation in Poland at the outbreak of the Eastern war, and the new situation created since the opening of the Diet, far from putting an end to his designs upon the Republic, had only led him back to an old plan more dangerous than all the others. He meant to raise a Cossack army, get himself appointed Hetman — a title to conjure with in Little Russia — enter the Republic at the head of his Cossacks, call the whole Orthodox population of the Ukraine to arms against their Polish masters, and then lead a war of national liberation. The

---

[1] Rescript to Potemkin, March 19/30, 1790, M. A., Турція, IX, 15 (copy).

[2] On Potemkin's court and his sovereign airs at Jassy, see Петрушевскій, Суворовъ, pp. 226 f.; Брикнеръ, Потемкинъ, p. 178; Рус. Стар., xiv, p. 226.

result, he believed, would be that the three or four palatinates of the southeast would be wrenched away from the Republic, and annexed either to Russia or, preferably, to the new Kingdom of Dacia.[1] In view of the extreme tension of Russo-Polish relations since 1788 and the probability of war between the two countries, this audacious project, which under ordinary circumstances the Prince would scarcely have dared to acknowledge, could now be urged upon the Empress with some chance of success.

Potemkin seems to have broached the scheme — or part of it — during his stay in St. Petersburg in the spring of 1789;[2] and he then submitted it quite fully in writing the following November. Catherine praised it in general terms, but found various pretexts for not carrying it out immediately. At this time, she wrote, it would be dangerous to stir up the Poles unnecessarily and prematurely; it would be better to wait until after the peace with Sweden and the Porte, and then execute the plan on the occasion of the return of the army from Moldavia through Poland. It was only after long delays that she grudgingly accorded him the coveted title of Hetman of the Ekaterinoslav and Black Sea Cossacks.[3] Undeterred, however, by the obvious coldness at St. Petersburg, Potemkin seemed to center his attention more and more upon his Polish plans. It was to further them, we think, that he steadily increased his Cossack regiments, organized a special corps called the ' Army of the Grand Hetman's Staff,' recommended to the Empress not only peace but an alliance with the Turks, and secured the replacement of Stackelberg at Warsaw by his own creature, Bulgakov.[4] At the same time the

---

[1] Cf. Askenazy, *op. cit.*, pp. 38 f., 199 ff.

[2] Cf. the rescript to Potemkin of July 6/17, 1789, Сборникъ, xlii, p. 17.

[3] Catherine to Potemkin, November 15/26 and December 2/13, 1789, and the rescript of January 10/21, 1790, Сборникъ, xlii, pp. 47, 50 f., 57 f.; see also Bezborodko to S. R. Vorontsov, December 20/31, 1789, Арх. Вор., xiii, p. 173; Garnovski to Popov, March 21/April 1, 1790, Рус. Стар., xvi, p. 426.

[4] Potemkin's correspondence of the early part of 1790 is full of references to the recruiting and organization of the Cossacks: see Сборникъ Военно-историческихъ Матеріаловъ, viii, *passim*. On the ' Army of the G. H.'s Staff,' see Енгельгардтъ, Записки, p. 96, and Langeron's Memoirs, in Hurmuzaki, *Documente privitóre la Istoria Românilor, Suplement* i^iii, pp. 105 f. As to the alliance with the Turks and Bulgakov's appointment, see Catherine to Potemkin, March 19/30 and April 8/19, Сборникъ, xlii, pp. 66 and 62 f.

danger of an attack from Prussia and Poland gave him a very favorable opportunity to press his main project in a somewhat modified form. At the end of March he presented to the Empress a plan, in accordance with which, at the first offensive movement on the part of the Poles, the Russian armies were to occupy the palatinates of Kiev, Podolia, and Bracław, thus establishing communications with the Austrians in Galicia and shortening and improving their own line of defence. And it was not merely a military occupation that the Prince proposed, but the outright annexation of the three palatinates. Russia would thus acquire, he wrote, the most fertile provinces of the Republic and a population of more than a million of her coreligionists. Volhynia also might, perhaps, be annexed; or at least the Russian frontier should be drawn from Choczim to the government of Mohilev.[1] In short, the Prince proposed appropriating substantially the same territories that Russia was to acquire at the time of the Second Partition.

Catherine again both praised and raised objections; but the danger was too pressing to admit of delay. The plan was approved — at least in its military aspects — by the Council April 11/22, and sanctioned by an Imperial rescript of the 19/30.[2]

Soon after, Cobenzl at last received a fairly definite reply to his oft-reiterated questions. By a ministerial note of May 6 he was informed that if the Poles invaded Galicia, Russian forces would then make a diversion by attacking the southeastern provinces of the Republic. This was altogether unsatisfactory to the Austrians, who had constantly demanded that a Russian corps should be sent to Galicia at once, not to avenge but to prevent an attack. But nothing more could be secured from the Russian ministers, who confessed frankly that not even the

[1] This plan is printed in the *Historische Zeitschrift*, xxxix, pp. 238 f., and in the Pyc. Apx., 1865, pp. 401 ff.

[2] Apx. Гос. Сов., i, pp. 775 f. The rescript referred to has not yet been brought to light, but we know of it through the rescript to Potemkin of July 18/29, 1791, published by Liske in the *H. Z.*, xxx, p. 295. Cf. also the letter of Catherine to Potemkin of April 8/19, cited above, and also those of March 30/April 10 and May 13/24, 1790, Сборникъ, xlii, pp. 67, 78 f.; also Bezborodko to S. R. Vorontsov, April 30/May 11, 1790, Apx. Вор., xiii, pp. 182 f.

Empress' commands could make Potemkin do what he did not wish to do; and nothing more could be effected with Potemkin, who left letters from Kaunitz and even from Leopold himself unanswered for months.[1] In this critical moment, when the hopes of Austria so largely depended on him, he was thinking of nothing but a *Kozaczyzna* in the Ukraine. The exasperation in Vienna was increased by the fact that instead of pressing the campaign against the Turks, as the Russian ministers had promised, Potemkin kept his troops idle all the spring, while he pursued a secret and highly suspicious negotiation with the enemy. By the early part of June, then, all hope of getting any effective aid from Russia had practically disappeared.

There was likewise no prospect of driving the Turks to an immediate peace by force of arms, for the bulk of the Austrian troops had been sent off to Bohemia. Little help was to be expected from England, for in view of the danger of war with Spain over the Nootka Sound controversy, Pitt was now less able to act energetically in Continental affairs, and also more anxious than formerly to oblige his ally. Hence even English ministers began to urge the Prussian terms upon the Court of Vienna.[2] In short, the bases of Kaunitz's system were crumbling one after the other. By this time the King of Prussia had gone to his army in Silesia, and was impatiently awaiting Austria's final answer. There was nothing to do but fight or take the best terms one could get from him.

Leopold determined to send Spielmann to Silesia to negotiate a final settlement. The active State Referendary was the man whose views most nearly coincided with those of his sovereign; he did not share the Chancellor's deep-seated hatred of Prussia; and he was, as we have seen, inclined to enter upon the Hertzberg plan. Exchanges, equivalents, compensations, all the beloved political geometry of the time, were almost as much to his taste as to Hertzberg's. His instructions were decided upon at a ministerial Conference of June 15th. As in May, the idea of the

---

[1] L. Cobenzl's report of May 9, Kaunitz to L. Cobenzl, June 19, V. A., *Russland, Berichte* and *Expeditionen*, 1790.

[2] Kaunitz to L. Cobenzl, June 5, V. A., *loc. cit.;* cf. Leopold to Marie Christine, June 23, in Wolf, *Leopold und Marie Christine, Ihr Briefwechsel*, p. 162.

Conference was to pretend to favor the basis of the *status quo non materiel*, in order to drive a better bargain on the other basis — the system of exchanges and equivalents — which they really preferred. So ready, indeed, were the Austrians at this moment to enter into Hertzberg's ideas that they would willingly have accorded Prussia much larger acquisitions in Poland than she had asked for, providing she only showed herself sufficiently generous with the lands of her ally, the Porte. To secure Turkish Croatia, Orsova, and Belgrade, or if possible the frontiers of Passarowitz unmodified; to make the minimum of sacrifices in Galicia; to present a bold front but never to let matters come to a rupture; to bring back peace at any honorable price: such was the substance of the instructions, with which Spielmann set out on his far from promising mission.[1]

IV

At the end of June the eyes of all Europe were fixed upon Silesia in expectation of stirring events. There on opposite sides of the Riesengebirge the hosts of Austria and Prussia once more stood face to face, ready, as soon as the diplomats had had ' their little hour upon the stage,' to renew the ancient struggle.

In Bohemia and Moravia were gathered about 150,000 Austrians [2] under the gallant old Field Marshal Laudon,[3] who had

---

[1] Conference protocol of June 15, and Kaunitz to Leopold, June 16, V. A., *Vorträge*, 1790.

The Conference protocol says: " Vor allem ist die Unterhandlung nach dem Grundsatz des von England vorgeschlagenen nicht materielen *Status quo* zu eröffnen und dem preussischen Ministerio glauben zu machen, dass wir diese Basis der übrigen vorziehen."

Kaunitz to Leopold, June 16: Spielmann had told him that it was the opinion of the Conference: " dass wir absolute und durch alle mögliche Nachgiebigkeits-Mittel den Frieden mit Preussen zu erhalten suchen müssen, weil wir einen Krieg zu führen schlechterdings ausser Stande sind." Mildly protests.

Leopold's reply: " Ich bin Ihnen für ihre Mittheilung ihrer Wohlmeinung sehr verbunden. Unsere innerliche Umstände sind aber leider so beschaffen dass wir alle nur einigermassen anständige Mittel anwenden müssen, um einen Bruch mit Preussen abzuhalten."

[2] 149,000 according to the *Raisonnement* drawn up by Col. Mack at headquarters, June 8, V. A., *F. A. a.* 54.

[3] Laudon fell suddenly ill and died just at the moment of greatest crisis in the negotiations at Reichenbach.

but recently refreshed the laurels of Hochkirch and Kunersdorf by the capture of Belgrade. His troops were posted in such admirable defensive positions that an attack on them would certainly have been far from easy. Austria's weakness in case of war lay not in military unpreparedness, but in the terrible confusion that still reigned in the interior of the Monarchy. The Hungarian Diet was conducting itself in its worst manner and threatening a formal revolt; the Galicians were conspiring with Prussia and Poland; there was dangerous fermentation in the other provinces; the peasantry were in revolt; and everywhere diets, towns, merchants, nobles, and clergy were demanding, as Leopold said, " the privileges of the time of Charlemagne," and clamoring with threats for immediate satisfaction.[1] Under such circumstances, a sustained military effort would have been well-nigh impossible, and a single defeat ruinous.

Brilliant in comparison was the situation of Prussia. Whatever difficulties might have been encountered in the course of the mobilization, the King now stood at the head of 160,000 troops,[2] supposedly without their equals in Europe, the famous veterans of Frederick the Great. Around him was a glittering train of princes, generals, diplomats and visitors: the Duke of Brunswick, reputed the foremost general of that age; Möllendorff, Kalckreuth, and other paladins of the great King; the coryphaei of the *Fürsten-bund*, like Charles Augustus of Saxe-Weimar; the ministers of the allied Powers, England, Holland, and Poland; the agents of those potential allies, the Belgians, Hungarians, and Galicians; and illustrious sightseers like Goethe, who had come to witness the expected triumphs of the Prussian arms.

Apart from the main army in Silesia, two corps were stationed in East and West Prussia to observe the Russians. In case of war, the Poles might also be brought into action; and the army of the Republic, which was mainly concentrated on the Galician frontier, had now been raised to about 56,000 men.[3] Poles,

---

[1] Leopold to Marie Christine, June 31, Wolf, *op. cit.*, pp. 169 f.

[2] 163,000 according to the above cited *Raisonnement* of Mack. Wittichen declares that the Prussian numbers reached 160,000 only after the arrival of Usedom's corps on July 17, *Die polnische Politik Preussens*, p. 68.

[3] Korzon, *Wewnętrzne dzieje*, v, p. 62, correcting Lucchesini's estimate of 43,600.

Turks, and Swedes together might be counted upon to keep the Russians fully employed. That the Sultan's armies were by no means a negligible factor was shown by their valiant repulse of the Austrians at Giurgevo (June 26); while Gustavus III was just then conducting his most glorious campaign, which was soon to be crowned by the splendid naval victory of Svensksund (July 9). On the whole, the chances strongly favored Prussia, if she had the courage to draw the sword.

In such a situation a man of the Bismarck type would probably have forced on a war, regardless of what some timid generals, some lukewarm allies, or some indignant publicists might say. There were difficulties, of course — the defects in the commissariat, the evil impression produced on Prussia's allies by the long delays of the spring and by Hertzberg's diplomacy, the opposition to be expected at London, the ugly appearances inseparable from such a deliberate act of aggression; but such things would scarcely have deterred a statesman of real will-power and determination, possessed by the genuine Prussian *Drang zur Macht*. But Prussian policy was guided at that moment only by a minister who was losing himself further and further in a blind alley, and by a king who, although he was somewhat more self-confident and bellicose, now that he was at the head of his troops, still varied from day to day in accordance with the latest news from abroad or the last conversation he had happened to have.

On June 27, at the village of Reichenbach near the Prussian headquarters at Schönwalde, the negotiation was begun between Hertzberg on the one side, and Spielmann and Reuss on the other. At first things went tolerably well. The conferences were, indeed, not infrequently stormy, but at bottom both sides were agreed in principle, and both dreaded the same things — namely, war or the *status quo ante*. By the 29th a settlement had been outlined, by which Austria should cede to Poland the northern part of Galicia (the circles of Bochnia, Tarnów, Rzeszów and Zamość, and the town of Brody), and should receive from the Porte not only the frontiers of Passarowitz, but also the much-coveted Turkish Croatia (i. e., Bosnia as far as the river Verbas). Although the cessions demanded were unpleasantly large, Spielmann thought them more than outweighed by the glittering acquisitions placed in prospect. He did not feel able to decide without consulting his Court, but his report shows how strongly he was inclined to settle on this basis.[1] At Vienna, however, it was found that the proposed cessions would render Galicia defenceless and useless, and it had just been discovered that Turkish Croatia was a mountainous, turbulent country, extremely difficult to occupy, and not worth any great sacrifices. Hence the envoys at Reichenbach were ordered to save as much of Galicia as possible, to decline some of the Turkish lands so liberally thrust upon them, and — if worst came to worst — in Heaven's name to conclude as well as they could.[2] Probably, after a due amount of haggling and huckstering, an agreement would have been reached on these lines, had there not occurred just then an abrupt revolution in Prussian policy. At the moment when he seemed, so far as Austria was concerned, about to realize his 'grand plan,' Hertzberg had been deserted by his own sovereign.

Frederick William II, with all his faults, and in spite of many sad pages in his history, had a strong sense of honor, a regard for his engagements and his 'glory,' a certain chivalrousness and magnanimity. Hertzberg had never seen anything dishonorable in a scheme which consisted essentially in Prussia's robbing outrageously one or both of the two allies whom she had just pledged herself to defend; but the King had for some time felt growing scruples about it. At the very beginning of the Reichenbach negotiation he informed his minister that unless the Austrians were prepared to cede a large part of Galicia, so that he could offer the Poles a handsome equivalent for Dantzic and Thorn, the exchange plan had better be thrown overboard; for it would only embroil him with the Turks and lose him the confidence of the Poles, and the *status quo strict* would be "*quasi plus honorable.*" [3]

---

[1] Report of Reuss and Spielmann from Reichenbach, June 29, Vivenot, *Quellen*, i, pp. 491–496. In all their joint reports one may regard Spielmann as the man who set the tone.

[2] Kaunitz to Reuss and Spielmann, July 7, Vivenot, *op. cit.*, i, pp. 497 f.; Ph. Cobenzl to Spielmann, July 3, *ibid.*, p. 497.

[3] Note to Hertzberg of June 26, Ranke, *Die deutschen Mächte*, ii, p. 377.

Then a week or so later there happened a number of things in rapid succession, which ended the King's indecision and led him to pronounce definitively against the whole Hertzberg scheme.

In the first place, Jacobi, the Prussian envoy in Vienna, reported that Kaunitz had hastened to inform the Porte of the lavish offers of Turkish lands that Hertzberg was making at Reichenbach. This revelation would probably reach Constantinople at almost the same moment as the Prussian ratification of the Turkish alliance treaty. The consequences were easily to be imagined: at the least, the confidence of the Turks would be alienated forever, and the King would stand convicted before the world of the most flagrant breach of faith.[1]

Almost simultaneously with Jacobi's report (July 6) came a dispatch from Lucchesini repeating in emphatic terms a warning often given before, that the Poles would never voluntarily cede Dantzic, Thorn, and a part of Great Poland in return for a mere fragment of Galicia.[2] Lucchesini's opinion was only too well grounded. The news of Hertzberg's propositions to Austria had created consternation at Warsaw. The Polish envoy to Prussia had straightway been ordered to make earnest remonstrances, and Stanislas Augustus wrote Frederick William a personal letter conjuring him to allow nothing to be decided detrimental to the interests of his ally, the Republic.[3] Soon after, Lucchesini arrived at Schönwalde to enlighten his master still further about the state of public opinion in Poland, and to direct a destructive criticism against Hertzberg's whole political system. To complete the minister's defeat, England, which a few weeks before had seemed to approve the exchange plan, now came out decidedly against it and in favor of the *status quo ante* basis.[4]

Frederick William was now thoroughly convinced that the Hertzberg plan was, as the English envoy declared, " as unsuit-

---

[1] Ritter, *op. cit.*, pp. 18 f.

[2] This dispatch is given at some length in Kalinka, *Der polnische Reichstag*, ii, pp. 157 ff.

[3] Askenazy, *op. cit.*, p. 77; the letter, dated July 3, is cited *ibid.*, p. 210. Deputation of Foreign Interests to Ankwicz, June 26 and July 10, Muzeum XX. Ossolińskich, *MS.* 516.

[4] Ewart to Leeds, July 8, Herrmann, *op. cit.*, vi, pp. 559 ff.; Rose, *William Pitt*, p. 528.

able in itself, as its execution would be difficult and even impracticable." Even if the Austrians accepted it, it would be impossible to induce the Poles and the Turks to do so, voluntarily at least; and to coerce them would be contrary to all honor and decency. Moreover, even to secure an agreement with Austria on this basis would probably require many weeks more of wretched bargaining over the map; and the King was sick of that. He wanted a quick decision. Apart from the cost of keeping his troops on a war footing, it was ridiculous for him to spend his time negotiating, when he stood at the head of an army ready to act. The only sure and honorable course, he now felt, was to abandon the exchange plan entirely, and to fall back on the other alternative, the *status quo strict*, which he had proposed to Leopold at the beginning of the negotiation. If Austria accepted this, he would have the glory of appearing as a disinterested and loyal peacemaker, and the advantage of forcing his ' natural enemy ' to end a long and exhausting war without having gained a single village. If Austria rejected it, he would have a just pretext for beginning hostilities, and a right to count on the assistance of England and his other allies.[1] It has often been said that in going over to the *status quo* basis, the King was trying to make a rupture inevitable; but it would seem that if he had been determined to force on a war, he would have demanded something more than Leopold had already declared himself willing to grant.[2] In general, it was not the way of Frederick William to force or guide events: he waited on them, and allowed them to take their own course. If war had come, he would probably not have been displeased; but he deliberately put the choice of war or peace in his adversary's hands.

It was only after three days of storms, protests, rage, and gloom that Hertzberg consented to accept his defeat and to

[1] See especially the King's note to Hertzberg of July 11, Ranke, *op. cit.*, ii, p. 379.

[2] In the *Mémoire* attached to Leopold's letter of May 23. Sybel takes as proof that Frederick William wished to provoke a war the demand which he at first proposed to make, that Leopold should admit a Prussian guarantee of the Hungarian constitution (*Geschichte der Revolutionszeit*, i, p. 232). But the fact that the King let this demand fall when Hertzberg urged that it would infallibly lead to war, seems to me to point to a conclusion quite the opposite of Sybel's.

execute the new orders given him. On July 15 he presented to the Austrians a note declaring that the King found himself unable to discuss the new propositions of the Court of Vienna, both because he foresaw with certitude that they would be accepted neither by the Porte nor by Poland, and because they were too far removed from the original basis upon which this negotiation had started; that he could therefore only return to the other basis, the *status quo strict;* and that he demanded a precise and immediate answer whether the King of Hungary would consent to that principle.[1] In vain Spielmann and Reuss protested hotly against so abrupt a change of front, and at a demand so derogatory to the honor, so incompatible with the dignity, of their Court. There was nothing to do but to write to Vienna for new instructions. Spielmann's indignation was unfeigned, for his heart was too firmly set on the exchange project, and he revolted at the thought of sacrificing every inch of conquered territory, and at submitting to such arrogant dictatorship.[2] Leopold, however, did not hesitate over his decision. He wanted nothing so much as peace, peace at once, peace on any even half-way honorable terms. The plenipotentiaries might try to secure some slight modifications of the strict *status quo ante bellum* (such as the cession of Orsova to Austria); but that was to him a matter of merely secondary interest. He was quite ready to assent to the main demands of the Prussian declaration.

When these instructions reached Reichenbach (the 24th), the conferences were renewed for the purpose of drawing up a convention; and after frequent violent scenes and more than one moment when a breach seemed imminent over the article of the Netherlands, on July 27 an agreement was finally reached. Austria consented to the principle of the *status quo strict;* to an immediate armistice with the Turks; and to the holding of a Congress, where peace was to be concluded with the Porte under the mediation and guarantee of England, Prussia, and Holland. If at the final settlement the Court of Vienna secured any slight

[1] The note in Hertzberg's *Recueil*, iii, pp. 83–87, and in Van de Spiegel, *op. cit.*, pp. 288 ff.

[2] Reports of the two Austrian envoys of July 13, 16, 18, Vivenot, *op. cit.*, i, pp. 499–503, 506–515.

modifications of the *status quo* in its favor, Prussia reserved the right to claim equivalent advantages. The Powers of the Triple Alliance promised to use their good offices to assist the King of Hungary to recover the Netherlands, whose former constitutions were then to be placed under their guarantee. Finally, Austria agreed not to aid Russia in any way, directly or indirectly, in case the Empress continued the war with the Turks. Such were the chief provisions of the written declarations which constituted the famous Convention of Reichenbach.[1]

V

" Your Grace will see the sad result of the Reichenbach negotiation from the joint report," Spielmann wrote to Kaunitz. " It is, unfortunately, an unavoidable consequence of our internal circumstances and the deplorable aftermath of the late reign." [2] " In sane politics," was Kaunitz's verdict, " we ought never to have consented to this congress. It was an humiliating step. Decided to yield everything, we could have done it at Vienna, and we should thus have avoided insolent and insulting language. . . . The declaration is base, cringing, without a shadow of dignity; besides, it leaves the most essential things undecided." [3] Leopold, however, found the final terms more favorable than Hertzberg's, and believed that of all the bases for peace that were possible at that moment, that of the *status quo* was the least disadvantageous.[4] So diverse were the judgments then passed on the Convention from the standpoint of Austrian interests. The verdict of historians has been rather more unanimous.

To call Reichenbach an Austrian Olmütz [5] is to overstate the case. Doubtless the Convention involved great sacrifices; it represented the total failure of that policy of resistance to Prussia for which Kaunitz had stood; and even Leopold had probably

---

[1] Printed in Neumann, *Recueil des Traités de l'Autriche*, i, pp. 414–420; Hertzberg's *Recueil*, iii, pp. 88–101; Van de Spiegel, *op. cit.*, pp. 297–302, etc.

[2] Letter of July 28, Vivenot, *op. cit.*, i, p. 530.

[3] Note to Ph. Cobenzl, undated, cited by Vivenot, *op. cit.*, preface, i, p. x.

[4] Letters to Marie Christine of July 18 and August 9, in Wolf, *op. cit.*, pp. 181 and 189.

[5] Duncker, in *H. Z.*, xxxvii, pp. 41 f.

hoped for somewhat better conditions.[1]   But the Austrian ruler
had, at any rate, gained the great and essential objects that he
had had in view since the beginning of the negotiation; and such
was emphatically not the case with Frederick William.   In this
sense, the real victor at Reichenbach was not the monarch who
dictated the terms, but the one who submitted to the dictator.

To the King of Prussia the Convention brought a little idle
glamour, purchased at the cost of the hopes, plans, and efforts
of the past three years.   In reality, it marked a dismal fiasco.
After fixing upon that summer for a great offensive action, after
elaborate military and diplomatic preparations, after taking the
field at the head of imposing forces and challenging the attention
of the world to the great deeds that were to follow, Frederick
William returned to his capital wreathed with no laurels, empty-
handed, bringing only the dubious honor of having saved a few
provinces to the Turks and of having paraded himself as the
disinterested peacemaker of Europe.   The pose was awkward,
for all the world knew what chagrin lay behind it, and how involuntary this disinterestedness had been.   For these triumphs
the King had spent half the war-treasure so carefully collected
by his predecessor for an emergency.   What was worse, he had
lost the chance to make those indispensable territorial acquisitions
to which he had looked forward so confidently at the beginning
of the Eastern war.   Worst of all, Prussia had played away the
splendid opportunity to settle once for all with Austria, the finest
opportunity that had presented itself since 1740.   " I cannot
contain myself for shame and grief," Hertzberg wrote to a
friend.[2]

At Warsaw the news of Reichenbach was also a cruel disappointment.   Since the previous autumn the Poles had been
preparing a revolt in Galicia, planning an attack upon that
province, massing their forces on the Austrian frontier, and

---

[1] Sorel's verdict: " Leopold reçut du camp prussien sous forme d'ultimatum ses
propres conditions de paix.   Il lui convînt de se les faire dicter " (*L'Europe et la
Révolution française*, ii, p. 73) is, I think, not quite true.   Leopold's ' own conditions,' it seems, would have been the modified or approximate *status quo*.

[2] Letter of August 1 to Schlieffen, in *Nachricht von einigen Häusern des
Geschlechts der von Schlieffen*, ii, pp. 509 f.

hardly stopping short of deliberately provoking a rupture. By
May relations had become so strained that the Austrian minister
was making ready to leave Warsaw.[1] At that moment the Poles
were honestly and even eagerly intent upon taking their full part
in the great enterprise planned by Prussia. They waited only
for the signal from Berlin. But weeks and weeks passed without
the signal being given, and meanwhile disquieting reports flowed
in about the secret negotiations going on between Leopold and
Frederick William. Irritated and uneasy over the delay, the
Poles became indignant and alarmed on learning how freely
Hertzberg was disposing of their lands and interests without
consulting them. The suspicions bred by the untimely demand
for Dantzic and Thorn some months before, flared up again.
The result was that, on the one hand, the idea of undertaking a
war in conjunction with such an ally began to grow unpopular,[2]
while, on the other hand, the Polish government felt bound, as
we have seen, to register an energetic protest against the Hertzberg plan. Nevertheless, when the news of the dénouement at
Reichenbach arrived, when it became certain that there was to
be no war after all, the first impression at Warsaw was one of
consternation and regret.[3] It was hard now to bid adieu to the
hope of recovering Galicia, and to abandon the dangerously
compromised people of that province to the punishment that
might be awaiting them. There was no denying that by its
warlike gestures and poses of the last few months the Republic
had gone very far in antagonizing the Imperial Courts. Above
all, the leaders of the Patriots could not fail to recognize that the
Prussian alliance itself—the alliance on which their whole political
system rested—was now endangered, both because after all that
had happened the Polish nation could no longer feel the old
confidence in their ally, and because Frederick William, on his
side, had also much ground for complaint. At the eleventh hour,

[1] De Caché's report of May 16, 1790, V. A., *Polen, Berichte.*

[2] De Caché reported, though probably with some exaggeration, that hardly a
dozen members of the Diet would now have voted for war (July 3, V. A., *loc. cit.*).

[3] De Caché's report of July 31 (V. A., *loc. cit.*); Aubert to Montmorin, July
31, Dembiński, *op. cit.*, i, p. 512; Kalinka, *Der polnische Reichstag*, ii, pp. 170 f.;
Askenazy, *op. cit.*, p. 83.

just before the Congress of Reichenbach assembled, the King had learned from Prussian officers sent to inspect it that the Polish army was not yet sufficiently advanced in its reorganization to coöperate effectively.[1] If that discovery was damaging to the credit of the Poles, Frederick William's feelings towards them were not improved by finding his chances for making acquisitions by negotiation thwarted largely by the obstinacy of these same useless allies. After Reichenbach the Prussians made no secret of their irritation. A Polish agent reported that at Berlin the worst opinions prevailed regarding the King of Poland, the Polish army, and the whole Polish nation.[2] Lucchesini, on his return to Warsaw, talked blackly about a complete change of system on the part of his Court.[3] The fact was that the collapse of the proposed attack upon Austria had removed the one cogent motive Frederick William had had for desiring the Polish alliance.

There was, then, dissatisfaction, disillusionment, growing estrangement on both sides. Only four months after its conclusion the alliance seemed on the road to dissolution. One chance remained, however, of saving it, of giving it renewed vitality and real worth in Prussian eyes. If the joint enterprise against Austria could no longer be carried out, the point of the alliance might be turned against Russia. Such a possibility would present itself if the Triple Alliance, having once undertaken to effect a general pacification, attempted to enforce upon Catherine II the same hard terms as had been imposed upon Leopold.

[1] Askenazy, *op. cit.*, p. 72; Kalinka, *op. cit.*, ii, pp. 142 ff.

[2] Kalinka, *op. cit.*, ii, pp. 170, 238 ff.

[3] Herrmann, *op. cit.*, vi, pp. 331 f.

CHAPTER VIII

CATHERINA CONSTANS INVICTA

I

DURING the year after Reichenbach Catherine II was put to the hardest test of her career. She who, like Louis XIV, had long held her neighbors in fear by her continual aggressions, now found a powerful coalition rising up against her; and for a time it seemed probable that her reign would close in humiliation and defeat, as Louis XIV's had ended. In that case, the future of the Polish state would doubtless have been vastly different. For in the duel between Catherine and Pitt, which we are now to follow, it was far less the fate of Turkey than that of Poland that was at stake.[1]

Immediately after Reichenbach the question presented itself, whether Russia, like Austria, could be induced to renounce her conquests, and to make peace on the strict *status quo ante* basis. On that subject Catherine's mind was made up. Nearly two years before, her Council had decided that when the negotiations for peace came, Russia must insist on the cession of the fortress of Oczakow and the territory between the Bug and the Dniester.[2]

Oczakow, which French engineers had long been trying to turn into a sort of Turkish Gibraltar, had a decided strategic importance. It commanded the mouths of the Dnieper and the Bug, and as long as it remained in hostile hands, it formed a constant menace to Russia's newly acquired possessions in the Crimea. The adjacent territory as far as the Dniester was at that time almost an uninhabited desert; but it was of considerable value as affording a broader frontage on the Black Sea and controlling the outlets of several important navigable rivers. On this cession as a *sine qua non* Catherine remained unshakeably firm throughout all the storms that followed.

---

[1] Cf. Rose, *William Pitt*, p. 593.

[2] Sessions of the Council of December 14–16/25–27, 1788, Арх. Гос. Сов., i, pp. 638–655.

As the war turned more and more in her favor, she advanced for a time larger claims. At the close of 1789 Potemkin was secretly instructed to induce the Turks, if possible, to cede all their provinces north of the Danube. The lands as far as the Dniester or even the Pruth were to be annexed to Russia, and the rest was to form the principality of Dacia, the crown of which Catherine at that time destined to her younger grandson Constantine.[1] When in January of 1790 she for the first time announced her terms of peace to the Courts of London and Berlin, she had the courage to include an article providing for the erection of Moldavia and Bessarabia into an independent state under a prince of the Orthodox faith, a demand which the Prussians found as ' arrogant ' and ' extravagant ' as it was ' inadmissible.' [2] It was one of Catherine's better qualities that she generally recognized just how far she could safely go. So on this occasion, after finding how strong an opposition her tentative proposals had aroused, she wisely decided to moderate her claims and then to stand by her guns through thick and thin. In June she announced that her irreducible and ultimate terms of peace were the cession of Oczakow and of its territory as far as the Dniester.[3]

Having chosen the position she meant to defend, Catherine looked on at the proceedings at Reichenbach with indignation but without fear. She could not view that convention without affliction, she wrote, since it was manifestly derogatory to the dignity of her ally. Assuredly she would send no envoy to join the Austrians in making peace under the tutelage of England and Prussia. " No human power shall dictate laws to me. I am delighted," she went on sarcastically, " that the King of Prussia is again demanding Dantzic and Thorn from Poland. I suppose it will be on condition that I cede to Poland White Russia and Kiev, and that is just where His Prussian Majesty will fail." [4]

---

[1] Secret rescripts to Potemkin of November 30/December 11, 1789, and March 19/30, 1790, M. A., Турція, IX, 14, 15.

[2] Ostermann to Nesselrode, December 28, 1789/January 8, 1790, Frederick William to Goltz, January 22, 24, February 5, 22, Dembiński, op. cit., i, pp. 46–53, 277 ff., 282, 285.

[3] Goltz's report of June 18, 1790, Dembiński, op. cit., i, p. 308.

[4] Undated note, perhaps to Bezborodko, P. A., X, 69.

The Empress' courage was increased by the fact that she had just patched up a hasty and very timely peace with Sweden. Gustavus III would probably have preferred to continue the war; but his meagre resources were exhausted, and he despaired of obtaining adequate help from outside. For years he had been storming the Courts of London and Berlin with pleas for military and financial assistance; they had given him a long series of rebuffs; and when at last, after discovering that he was negotiating for peace with the Empress, they came forward with the offer of a subsidy, he found it wretchedly insufficient. Among the mistakes made by Pitt and Frederick William in dealing with the Russian problem, none cost them more, perhaps, than their parsimony and comparative indifference on this occasion. At the moment when they were about to begin their action against Catherine, they found they had lost the most efficient ally they could have secured.[1] On August 14, 1790, Russia and Sweden concluded the Peace of Verelä, by which the territorial *status quo ante bellum* was restored, although vague assurances were given on the Russian side about a future ' rectification ' of the frontier. Catherine's exultation over the peace was equalled only by the discomfiture of the English and Prussians. " We have drawn one foot out of the mire," she wrote to Potemkin; " as soon as we get the other one out, we shall sing Alleluia." [2]

Freed in this manner from her most pressing anxiety, the Empress was ready to show herself perfectly uncompromising on the subject of the peace with the Turks. If aught were lacking to fill her with fiery determination, it would have been supplied by her intense dislike and even contempt for her prospective opponents. Her correspondence of that time is full of satirical thrusts and passionate outbursts against " the new dictators of Europe." Hertzberg is styled " the *enragé*," " the madman," " the puffed-up pedant "; Frederick William is " the universal Protector," " the universal Disposer of other people's property," or " *la Bête* "; and the Kings of England and Prussia are rolled

---

[1] On the relations between Sweden and the Triple Alliance down to this point, see especially Wahrenberg, " Bidrag till historien om Kon. Gustaf IIIe sednaste regeringsår," in *Tidskrift för Litteratur*, 1851, pp. 321–365.

[2] Letter of August 9/20, Сборникъ, xlii, p. 101.

into one as "Gegu,"[1] of whom it is written that 'not all the Gegus possible or imaginable will make her conduct her affairs any differently.' Never would she make her submission to such people. "No human power," she wrote, "will ever make me do that which does not conform to the interests of my Empire or the dignity of the crown I wear."[2] When it appeared that no help was to be expected from outside in case of war, she declared unwaveringly: "Very well, alone, yes, perfectly alone, we shall now conduct our affairs according to our own interests. N. B. I shall not relax a jot from any of the propositions made to the Turks." "Our rôle is to be unchangeable, unmoved by whatever may happen."[3] Such was the attitude and the indomitable temper of the sovereign whom it was now proposed to coerce into surrendering her hard-won conquests.

The application of such rigorous terms to Russia had, assuredly, not lain within the original intentions of the Triple Alliance. When Pitt first suggested a general pacification on the *status quo* basis, in April, 1790, he had not meant, it seems, to interpret that principle so strictly as to exclude moderate acquisitions such as Catherine now demanded. Down to the summer of 1790 both England and Prussia frequently expressed themselves in a sense not unfavorable to the retention of Oczakow and its district by Russia.[4] But Reichenbach had altered the situation. After England had there pronounced so strongly in favor of the *status quo* basis in opposition to the Hertzberg exchange plan, Prussia accepted the principle, but chose to give it the strictest possible interpretation, in order to prevent her rival from gaining even a single village. Having applied the principle to Austria, the allies were then bound to apply it to Russia as well; for without derogating from their professions of high impartiality and disinterestedness, they could not allow the Empress advantages denied to Leopold. Thus England and Prussia were led

---

[1] See the correspondence in the Сборникъ, xlii, *passim*, and especially that with Grimm, xxiii of the same collection. "Gegu" is, of course, a fusion of Georges and Guillaume.

[2] To Zimmermann, January 26/February 6, 1791, Сборникъ, xlii, p. 139.

[3] Undated notes, P. A., X, 69.

[4] Cf. Lecky, *England in the Eighteenth Century*, v, p. 275.

rather involuntarily to raise a demand that was likely to involve them in a war which neither of them had clearly foreseen, and which neither of them had any reason to desire.

Towards the end of August the envoys of the two Courts at St. Petersburg officially communicated the results of the Reichenbach negotiations and invited the Empress to accept peace on the same terms under the mediation of the Triple Alliance. The reply was a courteous but flat refusal, During the autumn the two ministers returned again and again to their demand, but always with the same result. The Vice-Chancellor Ostermann informed them that the Empress was indignant at " the unparalleled conduct " of the allies in attempting " to dictate in so arbitrary a manner to a sovereign perfectly independent and in want of no assistance to procure the conditions which seemed to her best suited to satisfy her honor." [1] At the end of the year the allied Courts made what they considered a great concession. They would no longer insist that the Empress submit to their mediation, if she would only accept their good offices and peace on their terms. But this hardly improved matters, since the Empress still held her to her own terms. Obviously there was no means of dealing with her except by a show of force. The question was how far England and Prussia would go with measures of coercion. Would they risk a war ? That question held Europe in tense anxiety throughout the winter and spring of 1791. The answer to it depended upon many factors: upon the uncertain and incalculable course of Frederick William, the deliberate resolutions of Pitt, the attitude of Austria, Poland, Sweden, Denmark, and various other states.

II

If it is difficult to distinguish with certainty the motives that determined Frederick William's conduct at Reichenbach, the policy of Prussia after that convention presents an almost hopeless maze of perplexities and contradictions. That the King urged England on to the most vigorous measures against Russia, while at the same time he was making overtures to the Empress for an

[1] Lecky, *op. cit.*, v, p. 280.

agreement for mutual advantages between themselves; that he planned with the British cabinet a great Federative System for the preservation of peace and the *status quo* in Europe, while he was simultaneously looking for other connections and for acquisitions wherever they might be found; that he negotiated for an alliance with the Jacobins at Paris while at the same time proposing to Austria a joint crusade against the Revolution — all this, and much more besides, shows a versatility or an incoherence in his plans that almost defies analysis or comparison. The best, though by no means a complete, explanation of his course appears to be as follows.

After Reichenbach Frederick William felt it a point of honor to bring Russia to accept the *status quo;* he soon convinced himself that earnest measures would be required; and he therefore desired to make sure of vigorous support from England and of the neutrality of Austria and France. It was primarily the exigencies of the Russian crisis that determined his conduct, but he also looked beyond. He wished, on the one hand, to gain a more secure basis for his policy than that afforded by his present alliances, and, on the other hand, to effect in one way or another the acquisitions which he considered so necessary to Prussia. Hence he sought to keep all avenues open; to put himself in the strongest position as against Russia, without entirely cutting off the possibility of a friendly agreement with her; to preserve his old connections, while preparing the way for new ones; to be able in the future to choose between England, France, Austria, and Russia, in accordance with the needs of his essentially aggressive policy.[1]

On the King's intrigues with the revolutionists at Paris it is unnecessary to dwell, since they produced no result save to furnish the Imperial Courts with new examples of 'Prussian duplicity.'[2] His advances to Austria, however, deserve attention,

---

[1] Cf. especially, Sevin, *Das System der preussischen Geheimpolitik vom August 1790 bis zum Mai 1791.*

[2] For details on this subject, see Sevin, *op. cit.*, pp. 37 ff.; Sybel, *Geschichte der Revolutionszeit*, i, pp. 348 f.; Sorel, *op. cit.*, ii, pp. 157 ff.; Heidrich, *Preussen im Kampfe gegen die französische Revolution*, pp. 9 ff. That the negotiation was known to the Austrians appears from Mercy's letter to Kaunitz of January 22,

since they mark the beginnings of a change in the grouping of the great Powers, which was to be of great importance in the sequel. Only a few weeks after the Convention of Reichenbach, while Frederick William still remained in Silesia, there first began to be talk of a rapprochement between Austria and Prussia. On innumerable occasions the Austrian envoy, Prince Reuss, was assured by Bischoffwerder, the Duke of Brunswick, and others of the King's desire for a sincere and permanent understanding, and even for an alliance, with Austria. Everyone joined in condemning the old error that the two Powers were 'natural enemies.' These ideas received an additional stimulus from the advent of Baron Roll, an agent of the Count of Artois, come to urge the latter's plans for effecting a counter-revolution in France through a coalition of the neighboring states. Frederick William, who had been sounded by Artois as early as February,[1] was not disinclined to undertake the enterprise as soon as his hands were free. He allowed Bischoffwerder and Prince Hohenlohe-Ingelfingen, the two chief enthusiasts for 'the cause of all sovereigns,' to assail Reuss incessantly with hints on this topic; and these hints were soon followed by the very definite proposals made by Hohenlohe, September 13, looking towards a formal alliance and joint intervention in the affairs of France. The immediate object which Frederick William had in view appears from Hohenlohe's intimation that the proposed alliance was designed ' to free both sovereigns from the need of troubling themselves so much about the friendship of Russia,' and from his statement that the French enterprise could be undertaken only after the final pacification in the East. The King's ultimate aim was shown in the scheme of ' compensations ' for the expenses of the intervention. Austria was to take a part of French Hainault, and Prussia to receive Juliers and Berg in exchange for an equivalent to be carved out in Alsace for the Elector of Bavaria. This was the first communica-

1791, in Feuillet de Conches, *Louis XVI, Marie Antoinette et Madame Elisabeth,* i, pp. 423 ff.

[1] Bailleu, "Zur Vorgeschichte der Revolutionskriege," in *H. Z.,* lxxiv, pp. 259–262. It is not improbable that suggestions on this subject may have been made to him even earlier. Cf. Daudet, *Les Bourbons et la Russie pendant la Révolution française,* p. 18.

tion between the two Courts regarding joint action against the French Revolution; and from the very start the plan was bound up on the Prussian side with projects of aggrandizement that were to be the bane of the First Coalition and the ruin of Poland. Simultaneously with Hohenlohe's overtures to Reuss, the Marquis Lucchesini, passing through Vienna on his road to the peace congress at Sistova, was ordered to sound Leopold about a coalition for the restoration of order in France; and, as a matter of course, the scheme for territorial 'indemnities' was not to be left out of the discussion.

The Austrians replied to these proposals in guarded style, pointing out the difficulties and dangers involved, evading the delicate subject of 'compensations,' urging the need of delay until after the peace with the Turks, but still by no means entirely rejecting the idea of intervention in France.[1]

The friendly exchange of opinions begun on this topic soon extended to other subjects. Kaunitz and Hertzberg might do their utmost to keep their Courts at swords' points in the good old time-honored fashion; but in spite of them the two monarchs, frequently communicating directly with one another, were drawing closer together, and bringing a quite unwonted warmth into Austro-Prussian relations. Both sovereigns had strong reasons for desiring a rapprochement. Leopold had long been resolved not to live in exclusive dependence upon Russia, in servitude to the Tsarina, as he considered that his brother had done. Frederick William, preparing for a possible war with Catherine, was perforce anxious to lure her ally away from her; and this was, indeed, the sole immediate aim of his advances to Leopold. But the old distrust was still very deeply rooted at both Berlin and Vienna. On the one question about which the Prussians were most concerned at that time — namely, whether Austria would remain neutral, in case they went to war with Russia — they

---

[1] For the above: Reuss' reports of August 6 and 31, September 3, 7, 10, 14, 17, 21, 28, Kaunitz to Reuss, September 13 and 19, Ph. Cobenzl to Reuss, October 8, V. A., *Preussen, Correspondenz*, 1790; Brunswick to Schlieffen, June 17, 1792, in Schlieffen, *op. cit.*, ii, p. 565; Sybel, *op. cit.*, i, p. 350; Sorel, *op. cit.*, ii, p. 160; Beer, *Leopold II, Franz II, und Catharina*, pp. 36 f.; F. K. Wittichen, "Zur Vorgeschichte der Revolutionskriege," in *F. B. P. G.*, xvii, pp. 256 ff.

could get no satisfactory answer. Kaunitz replied only with surly bravado, and Leopold with courteous evasions. As long as this situation continued, the reconciliation between the two Courts could be regarded only as a pious wish, rather than an accomplished fact; and so long Frederick William found himself gravely impeded in undertaking to coerce the Empress.

While continually urging the British government to vigorous measures, while talking loudly of war before the Austrians, and massing very considerable forces on the eastern frontier, the Prussians were also ready ' to build a golden bridge ' to Catherine. Every sign of more conciliatory intentions on the Neva was greeted with anxious eagerness at Berlin.[1] Hertzberg assured Alopeus that he cared nothing for the *status quo*, and was convinced that Oczakow was not worth a war.[1] He believed that all might still be arranged satisfactorily to the Empress, if she would offer to assist Prussia to obtain Dantzic and Thorn through a voluntary cession by Poland. He declared that he had not been authorized to make such a suggestion, and that the King had even forbidden him to speak of Dantzic and Thorn. Possibly he was telling the truth in these latter statements, in which case his proposal must be regarded as an amazing bit of insubordination; possibly they were only the white lies of diplomacy. At any rate, a proposition that almost certainly had Frederick William's approval was that made to Alopeus early in February, 1791, by Bischoffwerder, the especial confidant of the Prussian King. Bischoffwerder intimated that the Empress could make sure of her desired acquisitions, if she would by a secret convention pledge herself to renew her old alliance with Prussia at the conclusion of the Turkish war.[2] Catherine doubtless judged the situation at Berlin accurately when she wrote: " Le *Statu quo*, ce trou seroit bouché avec Danzig et Thorn "; but she added, " Ce n'est pas moi qui le proposera." [3]

---

[1] Alopeus' reports of December 6, Dembiński, *op. cit.*, i, pp. 95–104; Reuss' report of January 25, 1791, V. A., *Preussen, Berichte.*

[2] Alopeus' report of February 8/19, Dembiński, i, pp. 116–119, which deserves to be supplemented by the unpublished one of June 11/22, M. A., Пруссія, III, 27.

[3] Undated and unaddressed note, P. A., X, 75.

In truth the Prussians had no stomach for this war. The leading generals were almost unanimously opposed to it, as was the King's uncle, Prince Henry; and Hertzberg mournfully declared that it would be " the greatest disaster, perhaps the grave of the Prussian Monarchy." To invade Russia it was said in military circles, meant to risk a repetition of Poltava.[1] Frederick William was, perhaps, the man in his kingdom who was least averse to war, since he felt that his honor and his engagements required him not to give way; but his moods and projects varied incessantly. He would probably have been relieved, had the Turks succumbed to panic and concluded a precipitate peace on their own initiative; and he would doubtless have abandoned the *status quo* principle entirely, had Austria or Russia proposed to him a bargain for reciprocal advantages. At the end of the year, shaken by the urgent remonstrances of those around him, disgusted with the campaign the Turks were making, and wearied of the endless delays of the British Cabinet in coming to a definite statement of its intentions, the King seems almost to have made up his mind to avoid war, if it could possibly be done.[2] It was high time for Pitt to declare himself, if the Anglo-Prussian league and the Federative System were to be saved from shipwreck.

It has already been noted that Pitt's ideas had been evolving into a comprehensive program, the aim of which was to uphold the existing political and territorial equilibrium, to protect the weaker states against the lusts of the aggressive Powers, and in general to put an end to that system of depredations, conquests, and partitions which Frederick II and Catherine had brought into vogue, and which was threatening to subvert the old political order of Europe. As a means to this end Pitt thought to expand the Triple Alliance through the admission of Sweden, Denmark,

---

[1] Alopeus' reports of December 7/18, 14/25, December 24/January 4, Moustier to Montmorin, March 28, 1791, Hertzberg to Goltz, December 11, 1790, and to Lucchesini, March 3, 26, April 24, 1791, Dembiński, *op. cit.*, i, pp. 107 f., 349–352, 441 ff., 449, 538 (note); Schlieffen, *op. cit.*, ii, pp. 365 f.; notes of Prince Henry to Grimm, Сборникъ, xliv, pp. 436 ff.

[2] I think Alopeus' reports on this subject, (December 14/25, December 24/ January 4, January 25/February 5, Dembiński, *op. cit.*, i, pp. 107 f., 112 ff.), are sufficiently confirmed by Reuss' reports of December and by the overtures made to Austria in January.

Poland, and Turkey, into a great defensive league, extending from the British Isles to Constantinople, covering the North and East of Europe, and strong enough to hold all the unruly Powers in check. The states chiefly threatened at present were Turkey and Poland. Pitt's interest in both countries was of very recent date, but it was steadily growing. It has often been pointed out that he was the first British statesman to view the Eastern Question from that pro-Turkish standpoint which in the nineteenth century became traditional in England. Poland had a special claim to his attention. The Federative System being directed particularly against the ambitions of Russia, it was necessary to provide against the dangers that might result to the extensive trade of Great Britain with that country. From a careful study of the subject Pitt had convinced himself that the articles for which England was chiefly dependent upon Russia — grain, timber, hemp, flax, and hides — could be furnished equally well by Poland, and only by Poland. The preservation and strengthening of the Republic and the establishment of close commercial relations with it thus became indispensable conditions for the success of Pitt's anti-Russian policy. But in order to attain these aims it was, first of all, necessary to free Polish trade from the crushing restrictions imposed by Prussia, and to end the latent antagonism between that Kingdom and its eastern neighbor. Pitt thought to solve both these problems in the following manner. England should mediate a treaty between the two states, by which Poland should cede Dantzic and Thorn to Prussia in return for commercial concessions that would ensure virtual free trade with the outside world; England would guarantee this treaty, in order to relieve the Poles from exclusive dependence on Prussian good faith, and would then effect the admission of the Republic into the Triple Alliance. Such an arrangement would satisfy Prussia's legitimate desires for aggrandizement, and would enable her to adopt permanently a policy of peace, conservatism, and good will towards Poland. It would ensure to England the commercial facilities she required. It would afford Poland the strongest guarantees of security and prosperity that could well be offered to her. So important a place did this Polish plan hold in Pitt's calculations that it has been called, perhaps without very much exaggeration, the keystone of his whole conservative system.[1] Such were the general ideas with which he approached the Russo-Turkish problem.

From April until November, 1790, Pitt's action on the Continent had been fettered by the Nootka Sound controversy and by the resulting danger of war with Spain. When at last, after gaining a signal victory in that affair, he found himself free to concentrate his attention on the Eastern question, he was for a time doubtful whether the situation warranted a resort to extreme measures. There was much to be said for the opinion, if not for the chivalry, of Lord Auckland, who advised strongly against running big risks merely for the sake of " taking a feather out of the cap of an old vixen, or of preserving a desert tract of ground between two rivers to the Turks, whose political existence and safety will probably not be diminished if they are obliged to have their barrier upon the Dniester, or even on the Danube." [2] But about this time Ewart, the immensely active British envoy to the Court of Berlin, came home on leave of absence. He had been the first advocate of the Prussian alliance; he was perhaps the originator, and certainly the most ardent apostle, of the Federative System; he was desperately anxious now to carry his work through. With his usual energy he set himself to convince Pitt and the other ministers that the hour had come for great decisions and bold action. He urged that if the Empress were allowed to keep Oczakow and its district, the security of the Turkish Empire and of Constantinople itself would be perpetually menaced, while Poland, finding the natural outlet for the trade of its richest provinces in Russian hands, would sink back under the Tsarina's influence. But important as the territory in question was, far larger issues were involved. England's whole position as a great Power on the Continent, the alliances she had been building up, the Federative System which she hoped to establish — all this

[1] For the above see especially, Salomon, *Das politische System des jüngeren Pitt und die zweite Teilung Polens*, particularly pp. 35 ff.; also the same author's *William Pitt der Jüngere*, i[ii], pp. 348, 482 ff.; Rose, *Pitt and National Revival*, pp. 385–389, 593, 626 f., 631.

[2] Rose, *ibid*., p. 602.

was really at stake. If England yielded in this crisis, Prussia and the other friendly states would lose all confidence in her; her influence and her political connections would be ruined; she would be left isolated and discredited, as she had been a few years before, and exposed, perhaps, to far greater dangers than were involved in the vigorous measures now proposed. That Ewart badly underestimated Catherine appears from his opinion that while she might, and probably would, make some difficulties at first, there could be little doubt of her accepting the terms offered her before spring, since she could never venture to risk the consequences of a refusal.[1] The Prime Minister and the Foreign Secretary, the Duke of Leeds, allowed themselves to be persuaded by these clear-cut, logical, but too optimistic arguments. About the end of the year Pitt set out on the hardest task he had ever undertaken, that of driving Catherine II to her knees.

The campaign was planned with thoroughness. First of all, there was to be a general diplomatic reconnoissance for the purpose of securing the alliance of as many states as possible, and the neutrality of the rest. Then, if the results were favorable and if Catherine remained obstinate, in the spring the ultimatum would be delivered at St. Petersburg, to be followed by the appearance of British and Dutch fleets in the Baltic, while Prussians, Poles, Swedes, and Turks threatened Russia by sea or land. In January, 1791, the British program was presented at Berlin, while English couriers sped to the four corners of the Continent with orders to every envoy. There followed for some months a diplomatic struggle waged at half the Courts of Europe between the British ministers, more or less supported by their Prussian colleagues, on the one side, and the representatives of Russia on the other.

III

Neither side could expect much aid from the Bourbon Courts. France, which under normal circumstances might have been relied upon to hold England in check, now seemed to be a political zero. The idea of the Quadruple Alliance of the Imperial Courts and

---

[1] Rose, *Pitt*, pp. 598 f.; Salomon, *Pitt*, i[ii], pp. 501 ff.

the Bourbons still lived on, indeed, in the project of the ' Northern League ' (Russia, Sweden, Denmark, Spain, and perhaps France), for which the Spanish ministers professed a certain zeal, and which Genet, the French chargé at St. Petersburg, eagerly urged upon his government. But all Catherine's exhortations that the time had come for France and Spain to set bounds to British arrogance, failed to break down Montmorin's and Florida-blanca's invincible fear of England. The Court of Madrid contented itself with promising England its neutrality and Russia its good offices at Constantinople. And when Catherine, overcoming for the moment her animosity against the National Assembly, that " hydra with twelve hundred heads," attempted to win over the Jacobins, Mirabeau took her money, promised his services, and then, most unseasonably, died.[1]

Count Bernstorff, the prudent and pacific leading minister of Denmark, found himself in a terribly embarrassing position. The Russian government, assuming the imperious tone it was accustomed to take at Copenhagen, insisted that Denmark should arm a fleet, close the Sound to the British, and in general fulfil the obligations resulting from the ' eternal alliance ' of 1773. England, on the other hand, demanded at first a free passage through the straits, and then the use of the Danish ports, and for the rest, strict neutrality. Bernstorff tried to wriggle through by making vague promises to both sides, and begging each not to compromise him with the other, while he also brought forward a plan of conciliation, by which the Empress should be allowed to keep the territories she demanded, on condition of razing the fortresses.[2]

The art of adroit balancing was even better exemplified by the King of Sweden. After fighting, denouncing, and generally

[1] For these little-explored relations of Russia with France and Spain during the crisis of 1790–91, see: Dembiński, *Rosya a rewolucya francuska*, pp. 76–81; S. R. Vorontsov on the Mirabeau episode, Apx. Bop., viii, p. 22; Simolin's reports from Paris of April 1 and 15, 1791, in Feuillet de Conches, *op. cit.*, ii, pp. 24–27, 31 ff.; Apx. Гoc. Coв., i, pp. 849 f., 861 f.; the correspondence of Genet with Montmorin, in *R. I. A.*, Russie, ii, pp. 501–506; Baumgarten, *Geschichte Spaniens zur Zeit der französischen Revolution*, pp. 295 f., 313; Muriel, " Historia de Carlos IV," in the *Memorial Histórico Español*, xxix, pp. 147 ff.

[2] Cf. Holm, *Danmark-Norges Udenrigske Historie . . . fra 1791 till 1807*, i, pp. 2–6; Apx. Гoc. Coв., i, pp. 837, 846, 850.

tormenting her for two long years, since the Peace of Verelä Gustavus III had set himself to woo the friendship of his good cousin Catherine, who met his advances with the coquetry which she so well knew how to combine with her many masculine qualities. During the winter of 1790–91 Gustavus was negotiating at St. Petersburg and Copenhagen with regard to the Triple Alliance of the North, which the Russians were anxious to build up in order to close the Baltic to hostile fleets. Nothing had been concluded, however, when in February England and Prussia approached him with flattering offers, intended to secure at least his neutrality, and if possible his armed assistance. It was of extreme importance for them to win him on account of his fleets, his ports, his strategic position, and his proved efficiency. It was hardly an exaggeration, when his ambassador at St. Petersburg assured him: " All the world recognizes that Your Majesty holds the balance of power in your hands." [1] Keenly conscious of the advantages of his position, Gustavus proceeded with the frankness of an Italian *condottiere* to inform each side of the offers the other was making; he then stated his own price, raised his terms the more the longer the auction continued, and waited to see which competitor would offer him the most in territory and money. In truth, he much preferred to attach himself to Catherine, who treated him as her chosen cavalier, and flattered him in his darling plan for a counter-revolution in France. Still, as Grimm said of him, ' if for heroism he was of the family of the Knight of La Mancha, when it came to the perquisites he agreed entirely with the principles of the good Sancho, who looked out for hard cash.' [2]

Of all the states in question Poland was the one most strongly interested in the success of the Allies. In the previous summer, as soon as the first impression produced by Reichenbach had worn

[1] Stedingk to Gustavus, April 15, 1791, Schinkel, *Bihang*, ii, p. 111.

[2] Сборникъ, xliv, p. 387. For details on Gustavus's policy, see, Odhner, *Gustaf III och Katarina II efter Freden i Wärälä*, pp. 157 ff., especially 168–171; Schinkel-Bergman, *Minnen*, II, pp. 157 ff., and *Bihang*, i, pp. 107–115; Geffroy, *Gustave III et la Cour de France*, ii, pp. 115 ff.; Rose, *Pitt*, pp. 592 f., 600, 609; Salomon, *Pitt*, i^{ii}, p. 508; Hertzberg to Lucchesini, March 3, 12, 26, Dembiński, *op. cit.*, i, pp. 440–443.

off, the Patriot leaders had taken up with ardor the project of a grand concerted attack upon Russia by Prussians, Turks, Poles, English, Dutch, and Swedes. If this coalition could be formed, the Republic would have the best of all conceivable opportunities to settle accounts with its eastern neighbor, to assure permanently its independence, and perhaps even to win back White Russia and Kiev. In the first flush of enthusiasm, the Diet on August 2, 1790 authorized its envoy at Constantinople to negotiate an offensive and defensive alliance with the Porte, although only on condition that the Sultan should grant Poland a favorable treaty of commerce, and should not expect the Republic to declare war on the Empress until after Prussia had done so. Simultaneously the plan for a coalition against Russia was unofficially communicated to Frederick William with an urgent request for his coöperation.[1]

The warlike zeal of the Poles abated considerably, however, in the following months. In the first place, the Peace of Verelä made a sad breach in their calculations. Then the treaties with the Porte, when just on the point of being concluded, were held up by the difficulties unexpectedly raised by the Turks regarding the commercial concessions, on which the Poles insisted as a *sine qua non.* This setback was due to the insidious intervention of Prussia. It was one of Hertzberg's sordid little calculations that if Polish trade were diverted even slightly from the Vistula to the Black Sea, his master would have the less chance to extort the cession of Dantzic and Thorn.[2] The ambiguous attitude and altered tone of Prussia were, indeed, the chief factor in dampening the warlike spirit of the Poles. Lucchesini, who had known so well how to captivate the confidence and play upon the feelings of the nation, had now departed to the Austro-Turkish peace congress at Sistova; and his *locum tenens,* the young Count

---

[1] Askenazy, *op. cit.,* pp. 83 ff., 212–215; Kalinka, *Der polnische Reichstag,* ii, pp. 198 ff.; de Caché's reports of August 4 and 7, V. A., *Polen, Berichte,* 1790.

[2] Details in Kalinka, *op. cit.,* ii, pp. 216–223. A rather ambiguous passage in Smitt's *Suworow und Polens Untergang,* ii, pp. 227 f., has led some historians into the erroneous statement that the Polish-Turkish alliance was actually concluded. See, for example, Zinkeisen, *op. cit.,* vi, pp. 812 f., and Kraszewski, *Polska w czasie trzech rozbiorów,* ii, p. 317.

Goltz, was but little fitted to replace him. In contrast to the astonishing activity of Prussian diplomacy at Warsaw in the past two years, the Court of Berlin now maintained an air of cool, indifferent, and even sulky passivity. The honeymoon was decidedly over. Frederick William had almost abandoned the hope of gaining Dantzic and Thorn by a voluntary cession, since in a moment of irritation against him the Diet had been stampeded into a hasty and ill-considered decree, proclaiming the inalienability of every part of the Republic's territory (September 6, 1790). And the King of Prussia had now formed so low an opinion of the Polish army that in case of war with Russia he hardly cared whether Poland participated or not.[1] On their side, the mass of the Poles regarded their ally with a growing distrust, which was hardly unnatural, perhaps, in view of the now only too well known desire of Prussia for their territories, her utter unwillingness to relax her strangling grip upon their commerce, her perfidious intrigues at Constantinople, and the reigning uncertainty whether the Court of Berlin intended to go to war with Russia or to enter into a bargain with that Power at Poland's expense. Rumors of an impending partition were not infrequent. In March, 1791, a report from Vienna that Prussia had formally proposed such an arrangement to the Emperor created such a panic at Warsaw that Frederick William felt obliged to present a vigorous denial.[2] In general, the Polish public had lost all real

[1] See his communications to Constantinople of early March, 1791, in Zinkeisen, *op. cit.*, vi, pp. 812 f., and his declaration to Jabłonowski in April, in Askenazy, *op. cit.*, p. 224.

[2] It is quite certain that this alarming report of a Prussian proposal to Austria for a new partition of Poland was purely apocryphal. Kalinka (*op. cit.*, ii, p. 282) conjectures that Kaunitz started it in order to undermine Prussian influence at Warsaw and thwart the then pending negotiations for the cession of Dantzic. Jacobi, the Prussian envoy at Vienna, claimed to have found out that the story emanated from Rzewuski, one of the Polish malcontents then stopping in the Austrian capital (Sybel, *op. cit.*, i, p. 366). Golitsyn, the Russian ambassador, reported that he knew on the best of authority that the tale was invented by "some people of the local political [diplomatic ?] corps," and that the Austrian ministry saw fit not to contradict it (for quite intelligible reasons). Cf. Golitsyn to Ostermann, March 12/23, and to Bulgakov, probably of March 15/26, 1791, M. A., Австрія, III, 50. Dembiński has printed these two documents (*op. cit.*, i, pp. 477 f.); but he has mistaken the letter of Golitsyn to Bulgakov for one from

enthusiasm for the Court of Berlin, although the leaders of the dominant party still clung to the alliance, and Stanislas Augustus had at last renounced his Russian affiliations and come over to what was called ' the Prussian system.'

Such was the rather unpromising situation when Pitt intervened in the hope of patching up the differences between Berlin and Warsaw and preparing the Republic to take its place in the Anglo-Prussian league. The Poles themselves had taken the initiative by sending Count Ogiński to London towards the close of 1790 to lay the whole state of their affairs before the English minister. Pitt entered into the matter with much interest and thoroughness. In several interviews with Ogiński he dwelt at length upon the important services that Great Britain and Poland might render each other; upon the flourishing trade and many common interests that had united them in the past and which might now be renewed, if only the Republic would place its commercial relations on a firm basis by treaties with Prussia and England; and upon the necessity, to that end, of making a small, and in the last analysis inevitable, sacrifice through the cession of Dantzic.[1] In January, 1791, Hailes, the British envoy at Warsaw, formally announced the desire of his government to negotiate for closer political and trade relations. The cardinal point was to persuade the Poles to part with Dantzic in return for an advantageous treaty of commerce to be guaranteed by England. There was to be no more question of Thorn, in view of the September decree of the Diet; but it was held that Dantzic might still be ceded, since it was only 'under the protection,' and not an integral part, of the Republic. The Patriot leaders entered into Pitt's plan with much good will, convinced that this sacrifice, hard as it was, was indispensable for saving the Prussian alliance and gaining the greater security and freedom of action that would come from the connection with England. Hailes displayed for some months an amazing, though often a misguided and tactless,

Ostermann to Golitsyn, and is thus led by the phrase " the local political corps " to the conclusion that the story was of St. Petersburg manufacture — a quite erroneous ' discovery.' See his preface, pp. lxix f.

[1] Ogiński, *Mémoires*, i, pp. 92–100.

activity. He negotiated, conferred, promised, apostrophized, and threatened; he resorted to pamphlets and broadsides; in short, he left no stone unturned. But the obstacles were wellnigh insuperable. On the one hand, the Court of Berlin refused to lend any active assistance, holding that Dantzic alone was hardly worth the concessions demanded in return for it; and on the other hand, the majority of the Poles felt an almost invincible repugnance to the abandonment of the last seaport they still possessed. When the question was referred to the Diet at the end of March, there were protracted debates, but the utmost that the Patriot leaders could secure was that the proposed cession was not refused outright. A final decision was postponed for some weeks until the many absent deputies could be brought back to Warsaw, and in the meantime the Deputation of Foreign Interests was authorized to continue the negotiation with Hailes. The action of the Diet on this occasion does more credit to its patriotism than to its judgment; still, if the events of the next few months on the broader stage of Europe had gone according to Pitt's hopes, it is probable that his Dantzic plan would ultimately have succeeded.[1]

Towards Russia, the Poles were now in far less warlike mood than in the preceding summer. Undoubtedly they were eager to see England and Prussia engage the Empress; but as to the advisability of Poland's participation in such a contest, opinion was strongly divided. The King and many others favored strict neutrality.[2] The British and Prussian envoys reported that the nation would gladly take up arms,[3] but the Austrian minister at Warsaw formed quite the contrary impression.[4] At any rate, the warlike feeling flared up again during the exciting days in April, when it was thought that the Allies had crossed the Rubicon.[5] Had there been a war, it is difficult to believe that the

---

[1] Cf. Salomon, *Das politische System des jüngeren Pitt*, pp. 50 f. A more pessimistic view in Kalinka, *Der polnische Reichstag*, ii, pp. 283–297.

[2] Kalinka, *ibid.*, ii, pp. 694 f.; cf. Zaleski, *Korespondencya krajowa*, p. 305.

[3] Salomon, *Pitt*, i[ii], p. 510; Herrmann, *op. cit.*, vi, pp. 342 f., 569.

[4] De Caché's report of April 13, V. A., *Polen, Berichte*, 1791.

[5] Bulgakov's reports of April 2/13, and 5/16, M. A., Польша, III, 63; Goltz's of April 9 and 13, in Herrmann, *op. cit.*, vi, pp. 343, 569.

Poles would not have been drawn into it, whether by their own impulses or by a deliberate aggression of Russia.

The Power whose attitude was of most concern, both to the Allies and to the Empress, was Austria. Since the preceding summer Leopold had been reaping the fruits of his wise moderation at Reichenbach by his election to the Imperial crown (September 30, 1790), the recovery of the Netherlands (November–December), and the gradual pacification of the rest of his dominions. Austria was once more in a position to command respect and to act with vigor. Ever since Reichenbach Leopold had been continuously assailed by demands from St. Petersburg for a promise of aid in case England and Prussia proceeded to extremities. Having sacrificed his own conquests for the sake of peace, he was little inclined to go to war again merely in order to enable his ally to save hers; but it was not the part of prudence to say so flatly. Hence for many months he put off Catherine with vague or evasive replies, with exhortations to prudence, offers of mediation, and promises to assist her as soon as, and so far as, his circumstances permitted.[1] These responses were naturally regarded as far from satisfactory at St. Petersburg. From them one may trace the beginnings of that weakening of the alliance, which later on became so marked.

Meanwhile Leopold was also receiving pressing solicitations from England and Prussia. First, in November, 1790, Pitt dispatched Lord Elgin to Vienna to secure Austria's assistance in persuading Russia to accept the *status quo*. The Emperor amused this raw young envoy with edifying discourses on the horrors of war, the uselessness of conquests, and the need that all conservative Powers should stand together to combat the ravages of the new ' French principles '; he promised to do what he could to bring the Empress to reason; but he avoided binding himself to anything definite.[2] Next arrived the director-general

---

[1] Kaunitz to L. Cobenzl, September 19, 1790, Ph. Cobenzl to L. Cobenzl, October 10, Kaunitz to L. Cobenzl, November 28, January 2, March 28, V. A., *Russland, Expeditionen*, 1790 and 1791.

[2] Herrmann, *op. cit.*, vi, pp. 395–400, and *Ergänzungsband*, pp. 43–48; Leopold to Kaunitz, January 14, Beer, *Joseph II, Leopold II und Kaunitz*, pp. 383 ff.; Kaunitz to Reuss, January 21, V. A., *Preussen, Exped.*, 1791.

of Frederick William's secret diplomacy, the invaluable Colonel Bischoffwerder. His mission, as it was originally planned early in January, 1791, marked an effort of Prussia to ' emancipate herself ' from England. The King was at that time still ignorant of Pitt's resolution to proceed vigorously with the enforcement of the *status quo;* he was decidedly out of humor with his ally, and inclined to seek an understanding with Russia through the good offices of Austria.[1] But during the long delays incidental to a preliminary discussion with Vienna, Frederick William seems considerably to have altered his plans. By the time Bischoffwerder was ready to set out on his mission, the King's aim was no longer to effect a bargain between the three Eastern Courts that should leave England in the lurch, but rather to draw the Emperor over to the camp of the Triple Alliance, so that the King might then dictate his terms to the haughty lady in St. Petersburg. The reasons for the change are probably to be found in the fact that Pitt had meanwhile communicated his new plan of action; that Catherine had made a most unsatisfactory reply to the last Prussian propositions; and that the Turks were pressing for an answer as to whether the King intended to fulfil his engagements with them or not.

In the middle of February it was ostentatiously reported at Berlin that Colonel Bischoffwerder had fallen into disgrace at court, and had retired to his estate in the country. There were not lacking rumors that he had gone instead on a secret mission to London, or, as some indeed surmised, to Vienna; but the real facts were known to very few persons, and least of all to Count Hertzberg. The 18th the ' merchant Buschmann ' arrived in the Austrian capital and took lodgings in an inconspicuous inn. Two days later he was closeted with the Vice-Chancellor, Philip Cobenzl, unfolding in a rambling and incoherent manner that betrayed the novice in diplomacy, propositions as extraordinary as was the secrecy with which his mission was enveloped.

Bischoffwerder proposed an Austro-Prussian alliance, to which England and Holland should be invited to accede—and perhaps

[1] Such seems to be the drift of Bischoffwerder's overtures to Reuss in January, Reuss' reports of January 9 and 29, V. A., *Preussen, Berichte,* 1791.

even the Porte — but from which Catherine was to be excluded. One aim of it should be. to effect such a peace between the Empress and the Turks that the latter " would not be exposed to the danger of being expelled from Europe "; a second aim was to exclude Russia from participation in the affairs of Germany; a third to annul the Russian influence in Poland, " the point from which most of the intrigues of the Court of St. Petersburg have emanated." In other words, the Emperor was invited to desert Russia, join the Anglo-Prussian league, assist the latter to force its plan of pacification upon Catherine, and in general to oppose his late ally at every point. In its strong anti-Russian tendency, its professed aim of freeing Poland from Russian pressure and of setting bounds to the encroachments of a Power " constantly aggressive and avid of universal domination," the alliance proposed by Bischoffwerder might seem merely an extension of Pitt's Federative System; but it differed from that system in so far as it was also intended to serve certain ambitious plans of Prussia for the future. Bischoffwerder suggested, for instance, an agreement with regard to the affairs of France — i. e., a return to the counter-revolutionary projects of the previous summer; and he proposed that the two Courts should come to an agreement respecting the ' peaceable ' territorial acquisitions to which each of them might look forward. With all protestations that his master was not ambitious for new territory, he admitted that Dantzic would be much to Prussia's convenience, and that the King hoped to acquire Ansbach and Baireuth on the death of the present Margrave, and Lusatia in case of the extinction of the male line of Saxony. In return Prussia might be willing to favor Austrian pretensions to some parts of Bavaria on the death of the present Elector. The longer the conferences continued, the more the subject of acquisitions was thrust into the foreground. Presently Bischoffwerder was pressing strongly for a promise that the Emperor would offer no opposition in case Poland could be induced voluntarily to cede Dantzic and Thorn to Prussia. In short, it was clear that the proposed alliance had a double purpose: it was intended not only to extricate the King from his present embarrassing situation, but also — once the Russian crisis was over — to serve as an instrument for his aggressive and acquisitive policy.[1] As was to be expected, Kaunitz found these proposals simply " *incroyables.*" Had it depended only on him, the alliance would assuredly have been rejected entirely. Ever since the first tidings of Bischoffwerder's mission reached him, the old Chancellor had taken feverishly to writing memorials proving in a dozen different ways that " between two Courts whose interests are diametrically opposed, a sincere union . . . is a sheer impossibility, a chimaera, the falsest political project that could ever be adopted." [2] But, as so often, Leopold was of another opinion. It was the Emperor's idea to accept the Prussian alliance, but in a form altered to suit his own interests, stripped — for the most part, at least — of its anti-Russian tendency, capable of being combined with his existing alliance with Catherine. That was a resolution of grave consequence for the future, since in it lay the seeds of the ultimate reunion of all the three great Eastern Powers, a combination fraught with misfortune for Poland. From the standpoint of Polish interests, it would have been far better had the Emperor either accepted the Prussian idea of a league for the protection of Central Europe against the Muscovites, or else rejected the proposed union entirely, thus throwing Frederick William back upon the sole connection with England.

[1] Cf. Cobenzl's report of his conversation with Bischoffwerder on February 20 (V. A., *Vorträge*, 1791). Cobenzl having remarked that in case the proposed alliance were concluded, both Powers would have to renounce all schemes for territorial acquisitions, Bischoffwerder replied: " Oui, sans doute, ou bien s'entendre à l'amiable toutes les fois que les circonstances offriroient à l'une ou à l'autre des deux Cours l'occasion de faire une acquisition, soit par droit de succession, ou par convention volontaire, sans jamais employer des moyens violens." Cobenzl replied that the second alternative was not likely to occur, and put the question bluntly whether the King of Prussia was disposed in good faith to renounce all acquisitions. Bischoffwerder answered, " Oui, très décidément," but then, after a moment, added: " Vous savez sans doute qu'on parle de Danzig, et en effet cette acquisition seroit très-fort de la convenance du Roi, s'il pouvoit la faire tout-à-fait du gré de la Pologne, en faisant à la République d'autres avantages. . . . Le Roi espère que l'Empereur n'y seroit pas contraire, si une fois l'amitié et l'alliance entre eux étoit formée. . . . On s'entendroit facilement sur des acquisitions que vous pourriez faire à votre tour."

[2] This from his " Réflexions relatives à la Cour de Berlin," dated February 2. He proposed rejecting the alliance in a memorial of February 23, immediately after Bischoffwerder had first unfolded his ideas. V. A., *Vorträge*, 1791.

At an audience granted to Bischoffwerder on February 25, Leopold definitively announced his willingness to contract an alliance with Prussia. It remained for the ministers to settle the *quomodo*. In the ensuing conferences it became clear that the affair could not be concluded immediately, chiefly because the Austrians refused absolutely to give up their alliance with Russia, while Bischoffwerder maintained stoutly that that connection was incompatible with the one he was charged to propose. Nor could he obtain the desired promise as to Dantzic and Thorn, although the Austrians covertly hinted at their inclination to see the Oriental crisis ended by a general agreement, by which the Imperial Courts would secure certain acquisitions from the Turks, while Prussia should get the long-coveted cities. Regarding the all-important question of Austria's attitude in case of war between the Triple Alliance and Russia, Bischoffwerder could not extort a binding engagement of any kind from the Imperial ministers; but it is not improbable that he received certain reassuring oral declarations from Leopold himself.[1]

After a last conference with Cobenzl on March 4, at which it was agreed that the negotiations for the alliance should be continued through Prince Reuss at Berlin, and after prodigal assurances on both sides that the grand plan should infallibly go through, Bischoffwerder departed. His mission had been by no means a total failure, but only a half success. He had failed to lure Austria over with bag and baggage into the camp of the Allies, and so to isolate Russia completely; but on the other

---

[1] After his return to Berlin Bischoffwerder repeatedly told Reuss " que l'Empereur lui avoit répondu en propres termes, lorsqu'il avoit demandé si Elle préféroit que l'on s'arrangeât avec la Russie en se désistant du *status quo*, qu'Elle préféroit que la Russie soit contrainte au status quo . . . et que l'Empereur avoit dit qu'il verroit sans peine que la Russie aye du dépit et Lui laisse les mains d'autant plus libres pour s'unir bien étroitement à la Prusse." Reuss to Ph. Cobenzl, April 22, V. A., *Preussen, Berichte*, 1791. It seems hardly probable that Bischoffwerder would have ventured to misquote the Emperor on so weighty a matter in conversations which he knew would be reported to Vienna. Compare also the rescript which Frederick William sent off to his envoy in London immediately after Bischoffwerder's return to Berlin: " Aiant de notions sûres que l'Autriche souhaite de se rapprocher de moi et de mes alliés et de ce que l'Empereur a déclaré à l'Impératrice de Russie de ne pouvoir l'assister dans une guerre qui pourrait naître de son refus d'accepter le Statusquo," etc., Salomon, *Pitt*, i[ii], p. 514, note 3.

hand he brought back the conviction that Leopold strongly desired a rapprochement with Prussia and was not likely to interfere in case the Allies proceeded vigorously with the enforcement of the *status quo*.[1] The envoy did not suspect, perhaps, that Kaunitz would hasten to reveal all his propositions to the Court of St. Petersburg, with the assurance that Austria had not allowed herself to be seduced in any way; or that in the critical months that followed, the Emperor would continue to promise Catherine his aid in case of a rupture, in so far as the condition of his Monarchy would at all permit.[2]

IV

Bischoffwerder returned to Berlin on March 10, in buoyant spirits. He dined alone with the King that afternoon. The result was the ' immediate rescript ' sent off to the Prussian envoy at London the following day. In this dispatch Frederick William announced the favorable dispositions of the Court of Vienna; he declared that the moment for a final decision had come; he suggested that the best course would be to impose the *status quo* upon Russia by a show of superior forces by land and sea; and, at any rate, he must have an immediate "categorical declaration" of what the British government was willing to do.[3]

This challenge produced the desired effect at London. Pitt himself was now ready for action. By this time the preliminary diplomatic campaign begun in January had advanced far enough to enable him to judge the intentions of the various Powers, and on the whole the results were not unsatisfactory. He could count upon the neutrality of most of the states in question, and perhaps upon active assistance from some; while on the other hand, Catherine seemed to be entirely isolated and in a truly desperate position. Misled, perhaps, by the exaggerated reports

[1] Our information as to Bischoffwerder's first mission to Vienna is derived almost entirely from the Austrian side. The chief documents relating to it are printed in Vivenot, *Quellen zur Geschichte der deutschen Kaiserpolitik Oesterreichs*, i, pp. 78–101, and Beer, *Leopold II, Franz II und Catharina*, pp. 230–239.

[2] Dispatches to L. Cobenzl, March 28 and April 27, V. A., *Russland, Expeditionen*, 1791.

[3] Salomon, *Pitt*, i[ii], pp. 514 f.; Rose, *Pitt*, p. 608.

of Whitworth at St. Petersburg, British statesmen were at that moment inclined to believe that Russia was completely exhausted and virtually bankrupt, as a result of four years of continuous warfare, that Catherine had neither generals nor armies nor fleets that were capable of dealing with really formidable opponents, and that her Empire was seething with discontent and even on the verge of revolution. Under such circumstances it seemed impossible that " pride and obstinacy, the only motives which influence the Court of Petersburg," could long hold out. A war would scarcely be necessary: mere military and naval demonstrations would suffice.[1] Acting on these miscalculations, spurred on by the appeal of the Prussian ally, convinced that the time had come for consummating the great work of pacification begun the year before, on March 21 and 22 the British cabinet took its final resolutions, apparently with almost complete unanimity.[2]

On the 27th a courier was sent off to Berlin with momentous dispatches. He bore, in the first place, an ultimatum to be presented by the Allies at St. Petersburg, giving the Empress ten days in which to accept the strict *status quo* principle, and hinting at unpleasant consequences in case of a refusal. This declaration was to be backed up by the most vigorous measures. A British fleet composed of thirty-five ships of the line and a corresponding number of frigates was to be sent to the Baltic, and ten or twelve ships of the line were to be held in readiness to sail for the Black Sea. A Prussian army was to threaten Livonia; the Dutch were to be stirred up to join in the naval demonstration; the King of Sweden was to be brought into action by a subsidy of two or three hundred thousand pounds. Finally, Pitt presented the drafts of two conventions. One was to define more closely the aims of the impending enterprise, which was designed only to force Russia to accept the *status quo*, without thought of conquests or other material advantages for the Allies. The other was a project for a " preliminary commercial arrangement between Great Britain

---

[1] See, for instance, Whitworth's report of January 8, cited by Rose, *Pitt*, p. 598, and Auckland to Grenville, April 30, *Dropmore Papers*, ii, pp. 62 f. Cf. Lecky, *op. cit.*, v, p. 279.

[2] Leeds, *Memoranda*, pp. 150 ff.

and Prussia," by which in return for Dantzic Frederick William was to pledge himself to extensive concessions to British and Polish trade. It was a comprehensive and imposing program.[1]

These communications threw Berlin into a fever of excitement. Two days after their arrival, on April 7, the King held a council at Potsdam, at which Field Marshal Möllendorff, Count Schulenburg, and Hertzberg were present. Of these three, Schulenburg alone seems to have spoken in favor of risking a war; Möllendorff, as always, opposed it from the military standpoint; and Hertzberg, terribly disgruntled at the whole course of affairs, brought forth a variety of objections. But the King's mind was already made up; once more he was aflame for action. Hertzberg's remonstrances only drew down upon his head such a tirade of reproaches for his " wretched political operations " that the old man was stricken with a severe attack of illness on his way back to Berlin.[2] It was decided to conform in everything to the proposals of England. A Prussian army of 88,000 men was to be ready for the invasion of Livonia and the siege of Riga. The King intended to go to the front with his two sons and Möllendorff beside him. The royal equipages were at once sent off to Königsberg. It appeared that the die was cast.

In those April days Europe rang with the news of the King of England's warlike message to Parliament, of the great British fleet fitting out at Portsmouth, of the vast military preparations proceeding in Prussia and Sweden. It seemed as if nothing could now prevent a general war unless the Empress of Russia gave way.

This was the time when Catherine's courage and firmness were put to the severest strain both by dangers from without and by faint-hearted counsels from within. She herself was as determined as ever to brave all the enemies that might come rather than make what she considered an inglorious surrender. The very words *status quo* sufficed to throw her into a passion. " Without Oczakow and its territory as far as the Dniester, peace will

---

[1] Salomon, *Pitt*, i[ii], pp. 515 f.; Rose, *Pitt*, pp. 609 f.; Herrmann, *op. cit.*, vi, p. 591; Leeds, *Memoranda, loc. cit.*

[2] Alopeus' reports of April 9 and 13, Dembiński, *op. cit.*, i, pp. 129, 133; Hertzberg to Lucchesini, April 9, 16, 19, 24, May 14, *ibid.*, pp. 444–452.

not be made," she wrote to Potemkin, "even if the Empress herself consented to the restoration of the *status quo*." [1] " I am now busy preparing to receive the strong English fleet, which has promised to pay us a visit soon," she wrote to Zimmermann early in February: " you will hear of me; but whether they attack me by water or by land, you will never hear that I consented to any of the unworthy conditions which they have the audacity to prescribe to me." [1] But the Empress was wellnigh alone in her obstinacy.   Almost all her advisers were frightened and urged concessions; [2] and their remonstrances were powerfully reën-forced when on March 11 Potemkin arrived in St. Petersburg.

The Prince had come to the capital uncalled and even contrary to Catherine's wishes,[3] partly in the intention of having a reckoning with his enemy, the new favorite Zubov, and partly in order to press his schemes against Poland.   As usual, he had a project for every contingency.   If war came, he proposed to start a Counter-confederation in the Republic, or else to carry out his secret plan of the year before for the Cossack razzia, the revolt of the Ortho-dox peasantry, and the seizure of the Ukraine.[4]   But he much pre-ferred that there should not be a new war; and his scheme for avoiding it was to bring about a new partition of Poland.   As so often in the past, the partition he had in mind was to be on a far larger scale than that of 1772; so ample a one that he might hope, perhaps, to carve out a few territories for himself as well as for his sovereign.[5]

Immediately upon his arrival, Potemkin set himself to pave the way for this plan by effecting a rapprochement with Prussia.   It

[1] Петровъ, Вторая Турецкая Война, ii, pp. 193 f.

[2] See the concurrent testimony of Markov, Zavadovski, and S. R. Vorontsov, Арх. Вор., xx, pp. 19 f.; xii, p. 67; viii, p. 22.

[3] See her letters to him of January 22/February 2, and January 24/February 4, 1791, Сборникъ, xlii, pp. 135 ff.

[4] Before starting for St. Petersburg Potemkin had written to Felix Potocki, who was expected to head a Counter-confederation, inviting him to leave Paris and come to a more accessible place, in anticipation that the Empress would soon be ready to act in Poland (this appears from Potocki's reply of May 14, М. А., Польша, II, 7).   As to the Cossack plan, see the rescript to Potemkin of May 16/27, Рус. Арх., 1874, ii, pp. 246 ff.

[5] Cobenzl's report of April 19, V. A., *Russland, Berichte*, 1791.

will be remembered that just before his departure for Vienna the versatile Bischoffwerder had approached Alopeus with the insidious suggestion that his master might help the Empress to secure Oczakow and its district, if she would at once sign a secret convention pledging herself to renew the alliance with Prussia at the conclusion of the Turkish war. Catherine had received that proposal with indignation: ' she would not sign a pact of servitude,' she wrote on the margin of the dispatch.[1] But Potemkin insisted that she should accept the offer. There followed a severe conflict and not a few lively scenes. From the laconic diary of her secretary we hear of the Empress continually " weeping from rage," — " spasms " — " colic " — " she won't degrade herself and correspond with the King of Prussia " — Potemkin irate and " determined to fight it out with her; " [2] — but in the end, for once, the Prince prevailed. On March 26 very secret instructions were sent to Alopeus, ordering him to announce that the Empress accepted the proposed convention, and would at once send a draft for it and full powers to conclude, as soon as the King of Prussia had confirmed Bischoffwerder's informal overture.[3] But this signal concession came just too late. The warlike proposals of England reached Berlin a few days before; and Alopeus was able to reveal the great secret to Bischoffwerder only on the very afternoon of — perhaps a few hours after — the decisive council held by the King at Potsdam on April 7.[4] The Empress' pride had thus been sacrificed to no purpose.

Potemkin meanwhile continued his efforts for peace and a partition. In a conversation with Goltz, the Prussian envoy, he

[1] Martens, Recueil des Traités et Conventions conclus par la Russie, vi, p. 146.

[2] Храповицкій Дневникъ, March 15/26, 17/28, March 22/April 2, March 23/April 3.

[3] Ostermann's dispatches, dated March 14/25, but obviously sent the following day. The fact that the Empress did consent to this " pact of servitude " is here, I believe, brought to light for the first time. Dembiński, who has published Alopeus' reports on this subject, did not succeed in finding the secret orders of March 14/25, and conjectured that the concession contained in them was the offer to raze the fortress of Oczakow, if Russia were allowed to retain that town and its district (Documents, p. 126, note 1). In order to fill out this important lacuna in the correspondence published by him, I have printed one of the dispatches from Ostermann to Alopeus in Appendix V.

[4] Alopeus' reports of April 6 and 8, Dembiński, op. cit., i, pp. 124–128.

threw out a sufficiently broad hint on the latter topic.[1]   With Cobenzl he discussed his plan for a partition with much frankness, saying that at present it was known only to the Empress, Bezborodko, and himself, that he desired to learn the views of the Court of Vienna on the subject, and that they ought to bring Prussia to make the formal proposal.[2]   But in this last point lay precisely the difficulty.   There are not a few indications to show how seriously a new partition of Poland was then considered at St. Petersburg; it seemed the easiest means of escape from a perilous situation; the Empress herself was ·resigned to it as a last resource; [3] if Prussia had actually proposed it, it seems almost certain that both the Imperial Courts would have agreed; but the trouble was that Frederick William was in no position — and indeed in no mood — to make any such proposition.

The third week of April saw one courier after another dashing into St. Petersburg with the most alarming news from all quarters — from Berlin, London, Warsaw, Stockholm, and the Hague. The worst feature of the situation was the apparent determination of the British government to go to all extremities, a course which the Russian envoy in London had down to the last moment repre-

---

[1] Cobenzl's report of April 7, V. A., *loc. cit.*   Cobenzl claimed to have got the story from a confidant of Goltz.

[2] Cobenzl's report of April 19, V. A., *loc. cit.*

[3] Cobenzl's reports of April (which are full of allusions to the topic); rescript to Potemkin of May 16/27, already cited; instructions to Razumovski, April 30/ May 11, М. А., Австрія, III, 49.

Potemkin told Cobenzl (according to the latter's report of April 19): " Si la guerre avec la Prusse a lieu, il croit qu'Elles [les deux Cours Impériales] devroient s'attacher la Pologne, ou du moins un assez grand parti pour former une Confédération puissante, ... L'autre projet consiste, dans le cas où on parviendroit à un arrangement entre les trois Cours, de faire un nouveau Partage de la Pologne, mais en grand et plus considérable que le premier."

He told Goltz (according to Cobenzl's report of April 7): " Commencez d'abord par finir la guerre actuelle, montrez un changement de conduite à notre égard, que nous puissions voir avec évidence que vous êtes nos amis . . . alors je ferai en sorte que vous ayez Danzig d'une manière très facile que je vous dirai à mon retour et lorsqu'une fois j'aurai terminé avec les Turcs, mais qu'à présent je ne puis pas vous dire."

Rescript of the Empress to Razumovski: " We consider as a measure of extreme necessity our agreement to any acquisitions of the Prussian Court, and in this case, in common with the Court of Vienna, we intend to insist on a complete equality of advantages . . . recognizing this principle as founded on strict justice." (Rus.)

sented as utterly improbable. When this news arrived, Potemkin and Bezborodko united in a supreme effort to break down their sovereign's obstinacy and avert an otherwise inevitable war.[1] But it was all in vain. When the Council met on April 21, at the worst moment of the crisis, the proposals presented to it in the name of the Empress breathed not a word of concessions or surrender; they dealt only with the necessity of taking the most vigorous measures for self-defence.[2] And this tone of uncompromising resolution and grim defiance Catherine maintained unwaveringly through the anxious weeks that followed. Her Baltic fleets were to unite and take up a position in front of Kronstadt to face the English. The Finnish frontier was to be well guarded, while at the same time a special envoy was hurriedly sent to Stockholm to make sure of the slippery Gustavus. While the army on the Danube was to hold the Turks in check, the main forces of Russia were to be kept in readiness to meet the Prussians and Poles: one corps on the Dvina, one near Kiev, and a third near Bender. The moment the Poles began hostilities, or the moment the Prussians entered Polish territory in order to reach Livonia, these three Russian armies were to advance along concentric lines, carrying the war into the heart of the Republic, scattering the Poles, and uniting eventually to fall upon the flank or rear of the Prussians.[3]

Such at least were the plans. How well they could have been carried out, how successfully Catherine could have defended herself against such numerous and powerful enemies, may be a matter for doubt, since there is some evidence that the actual state of the military preparations was very far from corresponding to the sonorous resolutions framed at Petersburg.[4] At any rate, the question was never put to the test.

---

[1] Храповицкій, *op. cit.*, April 7–9/18–20.   [2] Арх. Гос. Сов., i, pp. 843 f.

[3] Арх. Гос. Сов., April 17/28, 19/30, April 24/May 5, April 28/May 9, May 1/12, 3/14, pp. 846–852; Potemkin's plan of operations against the Prussians and Poles, Петровъ, *op. cit.*, ii, pp. 195 ff.; Сборникъ, xlii, pp. 150 ff.; Храповицкій, *op. cit.*, p. 211.

[4] See especially the very pessimistic letter of Bezborodko to S. R. Vorontsov of March 7/18, 1791, in Сборникъ, xxvi, pp. 423–426, and Арх. Вор., xiii, pp. 177–181 (erroneously dated 1790 in this latter collection).

About the end of April a ray of light appeared on the western horizon; early in May there began to be strong hopes at St. Petersburg; and by the last days of the month hope had turned to certitude. The Empress had won, for England had yielded.

V

Pitt can scarcely be acquitted of having gone into the Russian enterprise in too sanguine and rash a spirit, without duly weighing the opposition to be expected in Parliament and the probable temper of the country. He had done little or nothing to prepare public opinion, which was therefore startled and shocked when the crisis arrived. A perhaps exaggerated reluctance to disclose official secrets prevented him from stating his position fully and frankly. This, together with his lack of adequate knowledge about the territory on which the debate was bound to turn, compelled him to rest his case chiefly on generalities about the balance of power, which were hardly likely to satisfy a nation so much more concerned about peace, trade, and taxes.[1]

Anglo-Russian relations had been uncommonly close and friendly throughout most of the eighteenth century. It was true that in recent years there had been some ground for ill-feeling, especially owing to the Armed Neutrality, which was resented in England as a signal display of ingratitude and hostility. But over against this was the great fact that English merchants and manufacturers found Russia one of their very best customers. They furnished that country with the great bulk of its imports, and drew from it large supplies of the most indispensable raw materials. About a thousand English ships went annually to Russian ports.[2] On the other hand, the English trade with the Levant was quite insignificant; commercially as well as politically

---

[1] It is a curious fact that it was apparently not until August, when everything was over, that it was proposed (by Lord Auckland) to send a confidential agent to examine Oczakow and the Dniester country and report on the real political, military, and commercial value of the territory around which so hot a dispute had raged. See Auckland to Grenville, August 19, 1791, *Dropmore Papers*, ii, pp. 169 f.

[2] Cf. Ewart's "Observations on the connection which has hitherto subsisted between Great Britain and Russia," in *Dropmore Papers*, ii, pp. 44–49, and Rose, *Pitt*, p. 590.

Turkey had long been reckoned a client of France; and the conception of the Eastern Question as Pitt now viewed it, as Englishmen generally viewed it in the nineteenth century, had not yet begun to penetrate the consciousness of the British public. Hence the Prime Minister was certain to encounter grave difficulties when he attempted to persuade his countrymen to risk a great war and to sacrifice the lucrative Russian trade for the sake of a nebulous balance of power and for love of the Turks.

On March 28, the day after the ultimatum was dispatched to Berlin, a royal message was sent to Parliament, announcing in rather vague terms that the King felt obliged to augment his naval forces as a means of adding weight to the representations he and his allies were making to the Empress of Russia regarding her peace with the Porte.[1] To the country this was almost like a bolt from the blue; but it was not a total surprise to the Opposition. For some days before, S. R. Vorontsov, the active Russian envoy, had secretly informed Fox and his friends of the plans of the ministry, with details as to the diplomatic situation, the moderate terms the Empress was defending, and, in general, a whole arsenal of arguments to be used against the Government.[2] Hence when on March 29 there took place the first great debate on the ' Russian armament,' the Opposition were armed for the fray.

They protested, in the first place, against the reticence of ministers, who seemed determined to rush the nation into war without giving any explanations whatsoever. They demanded that the country should be informed of the purpose of these armaments. Was it not a case of attacking Russia merely on account of a single town and a few adjacent deserts ? Fox, in an able speech, challenged the Government to show that the balance of power would be fatally upset or any British interest seriously affected, if the Empress were allowed to keep Oczakow. Russia, he said, was the natural ally of England, and the one naval Power that was ever likely to be of assistance to her. To attack such a state for so insignificant an object was as unjust as it was

---

[1] Hansard, *Parliamentary History*, xxix, coll. 31 f.
[2] S. R. Vorontsov to his brother, April 26, Apx. Bop., ix, pp. 193 ff.

impolitic. Pitt replied in not very effective fashion, trying to prove that the existence of Turkey, the independence of Poland and Sweden, and the security of Prussia were British interests, all of which would be imperiled if the Empress were permitted to keep her conquests and continue her aggressive course. Burke followed with a burning tirade against a foreign policy, the object of which was to maintain in Europe " a horde of barbarous Asiatics," " destructive savages " to whom " any Christian Power was to be preferred." In the end Pitt was able to muster a majority in both Houses; but the Opposition had undoubtedly carried off the honors of the debate.[1] The galleries were with them, and it soon appeared that the country was also.

The energetic minister of Russia at this moment began a furious campaign to arouse the British public against its government. Seldom, if ever, has a foreign envoy interfered so actively or so successfully in English politics. Vorontsov relates in his auto-biography that he bought up more than twenty newspapers and a small army of hack-writers; that he scattered pamphlets throughout the provinces; that he and the other members of the embassy worked night and day for months dashing off articles and tracts, carrying them around to the newspaper offices, and rushing about here and there conferring with members of Parlia-ment, merchants, and everyone else whose sympathies or services might be of value. As a result of his exertions, he declares, alarm seized the manufacturing towns; at Norwich, Wakefield, Leeds, and Manchester meetings were held to protest against the policy of the government; letters flowed in in great numbers to members of Parliament begging them to vote against the ministry; and popular feeling in London voiced itself in the inscription which everywhere appeared upon the walls of the houses: " No war with Russia." [2]

Whatever exaggeration there may be in this, it is certain that within a very few weeks the opinion of the country had mani-fested itself as strongly opposed to the warlike plans of the

---

[1] The speeches of Pitt, Fox, and Burke in Hansard's *Parliamentary History*, xxix, coll. 52–79.

[2] Apx. Bop., viii, pp. 19–23; cf. also ix, pp. 191 f., 491 ff., xxxiv, pp. 466–474.

cabinet.[1] The discontent of the merchant and manufacturing classes worked back on Parliament. On successive divisions Pitt did, indeed, manage to keep a majority, but it was much below the normal size. He himself later confessed that from what he knew of the sentiments of the greatest part of his followers and even many of his warmest friends, he was sure that he could not go further with his policy without risking a defeat.[2] On top of all this came differences of opinion in the cabinet. Immediately after the debates of March 29, Lord Grenville and the Duke of Richmond declared that they could no longer approve of coercive measures against Russia, while the Foreign Secretary, the Duke of Leeds, held unswervingly to the line of policy already adopted.[3]

All these things combined to break down Pitt's resolution. The first sign of his weakening came on March 31, when he asked and obtained the cabinet's assent to dispatching a courier to Berlin with the request that the Prussian government should delay forwarding the joint ultimatum to Petersburg until it had received certain new communications presently to be made from London. Then in the next ten or eleven days Pitt slowly and reluctantly made up his mind to yield. His judgment as to the expediency and importance of restoring the strict *status quo* remained unchanged. Many weeks later he wrote that he was still convinced that that would have been the wisest policy, and that " the risk and expense of the struggle with Russia, even if Russia had not submitted without a struggle, would not have been more than the object was worth," if only he could have obtained the support of the nation.[4] But he saw clearly that to persist in so extremely unpopular a course meant to risk the overthrow of the ministry and the ruin of all his other plans. He knew now that he had blundered into the worst predicament in which he had ever yet found himself. With tears in his eyes, he confessed to Ewart that ' this was the greatest mortification he

---

[1] Salomon, *Pitt*, i[ii], pp. 516–520; Stanhope, *Life of Pitt*, ii, p. 115; Auckland, *Correspondence*, ii, pp. 387 f.

[2] Pitt to Ewart, May 24, Stanhope, *Pitt*, ii, p. 116.

[3] For the deliberations of the cabinet during this anxious period, see especially the Leeds *Memoranda*, pp. 152 ff.

[4] To Ewart, May 24, 1791, Stanhope, *Pitt*, ii, pp. 115–118.

had ever experienced '; he had thought of resigning, but could not bring himself to abandon the King and the country to a factious Opposition; he still hoped, however, to find some means of getting out of the scrape without " any serious bad consequences." [1]

On April 10, at Pitt's proposal, the cabinet decided to abandon the demand for the strict *status quo*. There followed the resignation of the Foreign Secretary, the Duke of Leeds, who could not be reconciled to this surrender, and who was succeeded by Grenville, the most pronounced advocate of a pacific policy. Under the new program, a special envoy, Fawkener, was to be sent to St. Petersburg to negotiate an arrangement on a compromise basis, or the so-called *status quo modifié*. Various gradations might be proposed: the land between Bug and Dniester might remain a neutral waste between the two Empires; or it might be ceded to Russia on condition that it was left unfortified and uninhabited; or, at the worst, the Empress might have Oczakow and some adjacent territory without any restrictions, if only both banks of the Dniester remained in Turkish hands. [2] At the same time the indispensable Ewart was to hasten back to Berlin to persuade Frederick William to support these propositions, while Lord Elgin was sent to pursue Leopold, then travelling in Italy, in the hope of winning him over definitively to the side of the Allies. This profusion of diplomatic expeditions pointed to what was the cardinal weakness of the new policy. The ministry soon decided to suspend arming and to abandon all idea of backing up its new propositions with a show of force. [3] Whether a due regard for public sentiment at home rendered so extreme a resolution necessary, may well be doubted. At any rate, this decision proved far more disastrous than the mere abandonment of the strict *status quo* principle. It led England inevitably to a complete diplomatic defeat. It turned what began as a fairly dignified retreat into an humiliating rout.

[1] Ewart to Jackson, April 14, Rose, *Pitt*, p. 617.

[2] Rose, *ibid.*, p. 621; Salomon, *Pitt*, i[ii], pp. 521 f.

[3] Precisely when this resolution was taken it is difficult to say; at the very latest it was by May 6. See the secret instructions to Fawkener of that date, Herrmann, *op. cit.*, vi, p. 410; also Rose, *Pitt*, pp. 617 f.

At first, indeed, matters did not go badly. Frederick William received Ewart and Fawkener with unexpected cordiality, readily accepted the new English propositions, and agreed to support them at St. Petersburg. Just at that time he had made a change in his ministry, which also promised well. Hertzberg, latterly so bitter against ' the British despotism,' had lost all influence and was about to receive his dismissal. Foreign affairs had been entrusted to Counts Schulenburg and Alvensleben, along with the aged Finckenstein, all of whom seemed devoted to ' the English system.' It appeared then that the alliance was not only not shaken but stronger than before.[1] The fact was that Frederick William was not fully informed of the change that had come over English policy. He was not displeased at the more moderate terms now proposed from London, for they would diminish, or at least postpone, the danger of a war which he had, at bottom, always viewed with apprehension. But he expected as a matter of course that the Allies would back up these new terms with a show of force by land and sea, since that was the only means of bringing the Empress to accept an honorable compromise. It was only at the beginning of June, when he learned that England absolutely refused to make any naval demonstrations whatever, that the King at last fully grasped the situation.[2] Then he saw that his ally had abandoned him, that there was nothing to do but to beat a retreat with what grace he could, that all his exertions and expenditures of the past four years had served only to draw down upon him the wrath of the Empress and a series of humiliations before the eyes of all Europe. Naturally he was filled with anger against such a worthless and craven ally. He would still act with England until the wretched Oriental affair was over; but after that he would go his own way and seek other connections.

Under the circumstances Fawkener at St. Petersburg wore very much the air of an ambassador of the vanquished. Catherine treated him with a certain condescending indulgence, but could not refrain occasionally from venting her exultation at his

[1] Cf. Ewart to Pitt, and to Auckland, April 30, *Dropmore Papers*, ii, pp. 61, 68 f.
[2] Cf. Salomon, *Pitt*, i[ii], pp. 524 f.

expense. " How can I be afraid," she once wrote to him, " at the head of a nation which has beaten all its enemies for nearly a hundred years ? Je crains Dieu, cher Fawkener, et n'ai point d'autre crainte." [1] One day in her garden, à propos of a vociferous puppy, she remarked to him, " Dogs that bark do not always bite." [2] Her triumph was increased by the appearance at her court of an ambassador of the English Opposition, Robert Adair, who had been sent by Fox with assurances of his devotion — a pleasant parallel to the embassies which she was accustomed to receive from the ' well-intentioned ' in Poland.[3] As for the negotiation, the English and Prussian envoys simply surrendered on every point. On July 26 they formally gave their consent to the acquisition by Russia of Oczakow and the entire territory between the Bug and the Dniester, subject only to the condition that no restrictions should be placed on the navigation of the latter river. Utterly insignificant as this concession was, the English were vastly surprised to obtain even that, and they were in no position to resent the tone of " impertinence and persiflage " in which Catherine had couched her final declaration.[4]

A few weeks later, the Turks, abandoned by their protectors and beaten by land and sea, gave in and signed the Preliminaries of Galatz (August 11, 1791), by which they too consented to the cession of Oczakow and its district. On this basis peace was concluded between Russia and the Porte at Jassy, January 9, 1792.

Catherine had thus won a complete victory, perhaps the most brilliant of her reign, thanks to her own splendid courage and constancy. In spite of her one false step in March, Grimm could justly acclaim her " Die Mutter der unerschrockenen Standhaftigkeit." But for Poland the outcome of the crisis was unfortunate in the extreme. From the standpoint of Polish interests

[1] Martens, *Traités conclus par la Russie*, ix, pp. 349 f.

[2] Herrmann, *op. cit.*, vi, p. 413.

[3] The very ancient controversy as to whether Adair came to Russia on his own responsibility or with a commission from Fox — a question which so recent a writer as Rose attempts to answer with an exculpation of the great Whig leader — would seem to be settled in a sense extremely damaging to Fox by Vorontsov's letter to his brother of April 26, 1791, Apx. Bop., ix, pp. 196 f.

[4] Whitworth to Grenville, July 21, Auckland to Grenville, August 9, *Dropmore Papers*, ii, pp. 134, 160.

it is probably greatly to be regretted that the threatened general war did not take place. Such a conflict might, indeed, have involved terrible dangers to the Republic — a servile revolt, a deluge of Cossacks, perhaps a repetition of the horrors of 1768. But a struggle for independence against Russia was bound to come sooner or later, and Poland's chances would have been far better in 1791, with the numerous allies which she then had, than they were in the following year, when she was left to fight her battle alone. Moreover, if we may be allowed to speculate so far on what might have been, a general war at that time, if it did not once for all put an end to Catherine's power of aggression, might at least have left such animosities between the three neighbors of Poland that for many years to come they could not have united amicably for a dismemberment of the Republic. As it was, Pitt's defeat on the Eastern Question involved the ruin of all the other plans which he had been pursuing in foreign policy. Deserted by Prussia and discredited with the other states, England for a time withdrew altogether from Continental affairs. Thus perished the Federative System, the one combination of these years that had seemed to promise most for the security of Poland.

The full extent of the loss, however, was not immediately felt at Warsaw, for during the last months of the Oriental crisis two great events had come to renew Polish hopes. The one was the Revolution of the Third of May: the other, the conclusion of the Austro-Prussian alliance.

CHAPTER IX

The Revolution of the Third of May and the Formation of the Austro-Prussian Alliance

I

It is not entirely creditable to the Poles that, granted the opportunity furnished by the Eastern war, they delayed for nearly three years, and only at the eleventh hour nerved themselves to put through — by revolutionary means, as if in desperation — a great and sweeping act of reform. Of the many charges brought against the Great Diet, that of wasting a vast amount of invaluable time is only too well founded. There were many reasons for this procrastination. One must remember the fatal passion for oratory so characteristic of the nation, the prevailing aversion to limiting freedom of speech by any hard-and-fast rules of order, the constant efforts of the reactionaries to hold back the majority by obstructionist tactics, the inexperience of this "body of Solons aged twenty-five," the natural tendency of such an assembly to be swayed by gusts of passion or sentiment, to be easily led aside into digressions or trivialities, to stumble about rather helplessly amid the mass of questions clamoring for solution. One will be inclined to judge such faults less rigorously, if one compares this Diet with the contemporary assembly on the Seine, which was also toiling to regenerate a nation. The *Constituante* suffered from the same *furor loquendi*, the same variability, the same lack of order, foresight, and economy of time; it also was accused of wasting months over syllables, and then in a few hours upsetting the whole ancient order of the kingdom. Such defects are common to all green legislative bodies. Moreover, there was in Poland one special reason for the slow progress of the reformers: the fact that much time was required to educate, solidify, and inflame public opinion as a preliminary to thoroughgoing changes. At the beginning of the Diet the ideas of even the leaders were but vague and half-formed. It was only after three years of intense political discussion, after countless questions had been threshed out by long debates in the Diet and by the flood of books, pamphlets, and counter-pamphlets which poured from the press, that the great and salutary reforms of 1791 became possible.

One chief difficulty lay in the wide diversity of principles and tendencies that had to be faced. At one extreme were the bigoted champions of ' golden liberty,' and *szlachta* omnipotence, who revolted at the thought of sacrificing a particle of the privileges bequeathed to them by their ' virtuous ancestors '; who maintained, with incredible blindness, that the trouble with Poland was an excess, not of anarchy, but of ' despotism '; and who were inclined, many of them, to push their aristocratic republicanism so far as to favor the suppression of the kingship altogether. Then there were the admirers of the English system of government, and those who advocated a constitution similar to the one which was just then being elaborated in France. Finally, there were the advanced reformers, who, attentively following events on the Seine, tended more and more to appropriate the principles, the language, and to some extent the methods of the Parisian radicals. These people took up particularly the slogan of ' equality,' denouncing the privileges and the exclusiveness of the *szlachta*, exalting the Third Estate in the manner of Siéyès, and demanding the political and economic emancipation of the townsmen and peasantry. The growing political activity of the bourgeoisie; the unprecedented episode of November, 1789, when deputies from almost all the cities of Poland came together at Warsaw to discuss their situation, and to petition the King and Diet for the restoration of their ancient rights; the intense and highly organized agitation in favor of democratic principles conducted from the house of Hugo Kołłątaj, the ' smithy ' of the new ideas; the proceedings at the ' Constitutional Club ' in the Radziwiłł Palace — the Warsaw counterpart of the Jacobin Club — whose orators nightly proclaimed ' the Rights of Man,' and whose ringleader closed every speech with the words: " Whatever is exalted shall be abased, and whatever is abased shall be exalted ": all this was calculated to make old-fashioned people stand aghast,

and to lead even enlightened men to fear that the reform movement was getting out of hand.

In the face of such divergent views and such a clash of opinions,
it is not strange that the leaders of the Patriotic party long hesitated.   The wonder is rather that they at last adopted a plan of
constitutional reform which contained so happy a blend of liberal-
ism and conservatism, which ran so contrary to many of their
instincts and prejudices, and which contained so many things of
a kind which it is not easy or popular for statesmen to propose.
Adherents as they were of ' the French principles,' they still
refused to apply them in blind doctrinaire fashion.   Aristocrats,
they demanded heavy sacrifices from their own class, while
championing, as far as was prudent, the interests of the other
classes.   Republicans by inheritance and education, they made
the central point in their program the establishment of a
strong royal power.   In an age marked by its passion for ' freedom ' and hatred of ' despots,' they undertook a reform quite
opposite in character to the one then proceeding in France — a
monarchical revolution.   To a nation extraordinarily attached to
its ' liberties,' they preached ' national existence first, and liberties afterwards.' [1]

It has already been noted that as soon as the struggle to cast
off Russian control was over, in July, 1789, the leaders of the
dominant party resolved to bring to the front the question of a
new form of government and the hereditary succession.   On
September 7 the Diet appointed a commission to draw up a
constitution.   The affair progressed slowly, however, since in
the following months military and financial questions and then
matters of foreign policy absorbed the attention of the reformers.
In December the Diet did, indeed, adopt a first instalment of
the new constitution, as a preliminary to the Prussian alliance;
but this was hardly more than an enunciation of the general
principles on which the future form of government was to be
based.   Then public interest seized upon one particular consti-

---

[1] The classic study of the evolution of ideas in Poland at this time is Roman
Pilat, *O literaturze politycznej sejmu czteroletniego.*   See also, Niewenglowski, *Les
Idées politiques et l'esprit public en Pologne à la fin du XVIIIe siècle;* Smoleński,

tutional question to the exclusion of all others: the question of hereditary monarchy versus the elective kingship. The battle over that issue filled the year 1790; it led both reformers and reactionaries to bring their heaviest controversial artillery into the field; it helped powerfully to spread sound political ideas and to clear up the mind of the nation.

Soon after Reichenbach the leaders of the Diet determined to force on a decision at once, at least with regard to the immediate choice of a successor to the throne, and also, if possible, with regard to the hereditary principle. A considerable number of candidates for the crown came under discussion. Supporters were found for the claims of the brother or the nephew of Stanislas Augustus, for the Duke of York, the Duke of Brunswick, and various minor German princes. Gustavus III, whose head swarmed with fantastic schemes, was suddenly smitten with the ambition to become king of Poland, and long persecuted his reluctant envoy at Warsaw with orders to work for that chimerical project.[1] The Marshal Ignacy Potocki for a time seemed to favor the choice of a Hohenzollern, and at one moment talked even of a personal union between Poland and Prussia. In August, 1790, he sent his confidant, the Italian Piattoli, to Berlin to offer the succession to a Prussian prince, preferably to the King's second son, Prince Louis. Possibly this was done chiefly with the aim of restoring the already shaken alliance by flattering Frederick William, for it is certain that the King had long caressed the idea of placing his son upon the Polish throne. At any rate, the Prussian ministers, now for the first time consulted about this project, protested strongly against it; and the negotiation produced no result except to frighten the Courts of Vienna and St. Petersburg, and to drive the 'Republican' party in Poland, from fear of the Hohenzollern candidacy, to rally to the

Kuźnica Kołłątajowska, and his *Przewrót umysłowy w Polsce XVIII w.;* Kalinka, *Der polnische Reichstag*, ii, pp. 410–511; Kraszewski, *op. cit.*, ii, *passim.*

[1] For details as to this Polish project, which haunted Gustavus from the autumn of 1790 until the 3d of May (1791), see, Odhner, *Gustaf III och Katarina*, pp. 163 ff.; Gustavus' letters to Armfelt, in *Historiska Handlingar*, xii, pp. 172–177; Engeström, *Minnen och Anteckningar*, i, pp. 169 f., 290–304; Schinkel-Bergman, *Minnen*, ii, pp. 175 ff., 309–312.

cause of the Elector of Saxony, whom the great majority of the nation already favored.[1]

At the end of September the Diet decided to refer to the country (i. e., to the Dietines) the question whether a successor to the throne should be designated in the lifetime of the present King, and to recommend the choice of the Elector of Saxony. In November the Dietines almost unanimously answered the question in the affirmative, and also declared in favor of the Saxon candidacy. Only a small number, however, pronounced decidedly for the hereditary succession. At any rate, the Patriots might well be satisfied with this result; and the more so because in the partially renewed Diet (made up of the members of the old one together with an equal number of new deputies chosen at the same November Dietines), the reactionaries were now reduced to a very small minority. In December the long-desired rapprochement between the King and the Patriot leaders was effected. The reformers were now in a position to proceed boldly with their projects.

Early in 1791 there began to be held regular secret meetings, in which the King, Piattoli, Potocki, the Marshal Małachowski, and a few others participated, at which the plan for a new constitution was worked out. Stanislas himself seems to have drawn up the project which served as the basis for discussion, taking the English system as his model. So radical were the changes proposed in this sketch, so far did they go beyond what past experience gave reason to hope for, that the King presented his draft to his fellow-conspirators with the apology that ' these were only the dreams of a good citizen '; but his friends replied unanimously and enthusiastically that this was not a dream, but an excellent constitution, which with energy and good will could easily be put

---

[1] On this affair of the Hohenzollern candidacy, see Askenazy, *op. cit.*, pp. 86–89, 216; Kalinka, *Der polnische Reichstag*, ii, p. 540; Dembiński, *Documents*, i, p. 415, and his monograph on Piattoli, *Bulletin de l'Académie de Cracovie*, Juin–Juillet, 1905; F. K. Wittichen, in *F. B. P. G.*, xvii, pp. 253–262, and *Preussen und die Revolutionen in Belgien und Lüttich*, p. 119; Heigel, *Deutsche Geschichte*, i, pp. 379 ff.; Catherine's " Remarques sur les candidats proposés pour la succession au trône de Pologne," sent to Warsaw for use with the ' well-intentioned,' October 17/28, 1790, P. A., X, 71.

through.[1] The great point was to lose no more time. The Oriental crisis was obviously drawing near its close, and the Patriots were resolved that the end of the war should not find Poland still without a stable and well-organized government. Realizing that at the rate at which the Diet worked it would take years to pass the new constitution in the ordinary way, the reformers undertook to introduce it and have it voted by a *coup de théâtre* in a single session. By the end of April the preparations for the great stroke were completed. About sixty persons had now been initiated into the scheme; a majority in the Diet seemed assured; and the temper of the public appeared to be all that could be desired. In the last days of the month the news arrived that Pitt was beginning to back down on the Eastern Question, and then came the betrayal of the hitherto well-guarded secret to Bulgakov, the Russian minister at Warsaw. That was enough to convince the conspirators that they must strike at once, and that it was now or never.[2]

On the second of May the Diet reassembled after the Easter recess. The Patriots had taken good care to call in their partisans,

---

[1] *Vom Entstehen und Untergange der polnischen Konstitution vom 3. May*, i, pp. 170 f.

[2] Our knowledge of the origin and development of the plan which was crowned with success on the Third of May, is extremely scanty. The chief source is still the book, *The Rise and Fall of the Polish Constitution of the Third of May, 1791* (in German translation, Leipsic, 1793), the apology of the reformers themselves. See also Kalinka, *op. cit.*, iii (a volume which, unfortunately, remained only a torso, owing to the death of the author); the *Memoirs* of Ogiński; Dembiński's monograph on Piattoli, cited above; the account given by the King himself in a long letter to Glayre of June 21, 1791, in Mottaz, *Stanislas Poniatowski et Maurice Glayre*, pp. 250–268; Bartoszewicz, *Księga pamiątkowa konstytucyi 3. Maja*.

It is one of the most curious features of this affair that the secret was kept so long. Since February Bulgakov had had a secret agent in the immediate entourage of Ignacy Potocki (probably the latter's secretary, Parendier, as Kalinka and Smoleński suspect, although Askenazy has doubts of this). From this spy the Russian minister continually received copies of Potocki's confidential papers, and especially of the notes exchanged with Piattoli. Naturally the envoy was led to conclude that some great scheme was under discussion, presumably one for the establishment of a ' dictatorship ' in Poland in case of a general European war; but he was apparently not much alarmed until the last week of April. Then he began to fear a revolution. On the 28th he learned the essence of the whole project through the treachery of the Polish Chancellor, Jacek Małachowski, whom the King

while the Opposition, despite the summons hastily sent out at the last moment by Bulgakov and his friends, had returned only in small numbers. By this time the plan of the conspirators had become an open secret. The English, Dutch, and Prussian ministers were apprised of it, and were already protesting against it. On the evening of the 2nd, at a large gathering in the Radziwiłł Palace, the new constitution was read to all comers, and greeted with shouts of approval. All Warsaw knew that some great event was coming on the morrow.

Early on the morning of the 3rd the streets of the capital and the approaches to the castle were crowded with expectant and agitated throngs. The galleries of the hall of the Diet were packed, and the session began amid tense excitement. First on the order of the day came a report from the Deputation of Foreign Interests. In its name the eloquent Matuszewicz read a number of dispatches from the envoys at Vienna, Paris, Dresden, the Hague, and St. Petersburg, showing various ominous developments in the general situation of Europe, the menacing designs of Russia, and the danger of a new partition unless before the end of the Eastern war Poland had given herself a strong government. The effect was all that could have been hoped for. After some moments of silence, the Marshal Potocki called upon the King to suggest the means of saving the country. Stanislas produced the draft of the new constitution, which was read aloud. Cries of '*zgoda! zgoda!*' (agreed! agreed!) resounded from all sides. But here the handful of reactionaries broke out into wild obstruction. For hours there were storms of eloquence and also tragi-comic scenes — as, for instance, when one republican fanatic raised his young son in his arms and threatened to stab him on the spot, in order that he might not live to see the despotism which this constitution was preparing for Poland. At last a happy interposition of the King saved the situation; the question was put, and with hardly a dozen dissenting voices, amid tumultuous enthusiasm, the great project was passed *en bloc*. Rising on his throne Stanislas at once took the oath to the new

had unwisely acquainted with the plan (Bulgakov's reports of February–April, M. A., Польша, III, 62, 63).

constitution, and then King, senators, deputies, and people went in joyful procession to the nearby Church of St. John, to sing the Te Deum. That night all Warsaw illuminated and celebrated. Thus ended the bloodless ' revolution ' of the Third of May, the one altogether glorious and splendid day in the life of Stanislas Augustus, the last great day of radiant joy and hope that Old Poland was to know.[1]

If there had been some anxiety as to how the country at large would accept the new constitution, these fears were quickly dispelled. In the weeks following the Third of May, letters, addresses, and deputations with warm expressions of approval, praise, and thanks flowed in from all the provinces. The other cities vied with Warsaw in celebrations; the nation seemed intoxicated with joy. From abroad came gratifying tributes. Burke compared the French and the Polish revolutions, greatly to the advantage of the latter, and passed a noble eulogy upon the new constitution. It was difficult, wrote Middleton, to describe the favorable impression created at the Hague. Count Bernstorff declared that no unprejudiced man could fail to view this happy transformation with joy; and Hertzberg, who was not of the unprejudiced class, affirmed gloomily that the Polish revolution was one of the greatest events of the century, and would, in his opinion, have even greater results than the revolution in France.[2]

What then was this much-lauded constitution of the Third of May ? It was essentially an attempt to transform a state of a thoroughly mediaeval and antiquated pattern into a constitutional and parliamentary monarchy of the modern type. It abolished the worst abuses from which Poland had for centuries been sick and dying: the Liberum Veto, the right of Confederation, elections to the throne, the personal responsibility of the King to the Diet,

---

[1] For the events of the Third of May, see the works mentioned in the preceding note; also Wegner, *Dzieje dnia trzeciego i piątego maja;* Herrmann, *op. cit.,* vi, pp. 348–358; Solov'ev, *Geschichte des Falles von Polen,* pp. 246–251; Костомаровъ, Послѣдніе годы Рѣчи-Посполитой, i, pp. 450–493; Smitt, *Suworow,* ii, pp. 234–265. The best appreciation of the constitution is that of Balzer, " Reformy społeczne i polityczne konstytucyi trzeciego maja," *Przegląd Polski,* 1891, ii, and separate.

[2] Smoleński, *Ostatni rok sejmu wielkiego,* pp. 1–21; Hertzberg to Lucchesini, May 28, 1791, in Dembiński, *Documents,* i, p. 453.

and the lack of any effective executive power. The succession was assured to the Elector of Saxony and to his male heirs, or in case he should leave no sons, to his daughter (proclaimed ' the Infanta of Poland ') and her heirs. The prerogatives of the monarch were largely extended. The executive power was lodged in his hands, to be exercised through a council of ministers (the *Straż*), resembling a modern cabinet. If the principle of ministerial responsibility was not clearly asserted, it was approximated by the provisions that every act of the King must be countersigned by a minister, and that ministers were not only criminally but also politically responsible to the Diet, since they might be removed at any time by a two-thirds vote of that body. The administration was to be carried on through four Commissions (Army, Finance, Police, and Education), acting under the direction of the King and Council, but elected by and responsible to the Diet' (a rather unfortunate concession to the old fear of despotism). As regards the legislative power, the chief innovations were these: that the Chamber of Deputies, as the direct representative of the nation, was given a decided preponderance over the Senate, which was confined to the advisory and moderating rôle proper to an appointive Upper House; and, secondly, that the Lower Chamber, which had hitherto been essentially a federal congress of ambassadors from the various provinces, received an entirely new character through the declaration that each deputy was the representative of the whole country and was thus — by implication — not to be bound by imperative mandates from his local constituents. While a thoroughgoing social and economic reform would have been at that moment quite impracticable, the constitution went as far in that direction as was prudent; and it held up a program, an ideal for the future. The economic barriers between nobles and bourgeoisie were broken down; the townsmen recovered their judicial autonomy, and received a number of political rights, especially that of admission to many of the higher offices and magistracies (such as the four great administrative commissions). Above all, the gates to the Diet were once more opened — after two centuries — to the deputies of the Polish cities, although this representation, unfortunately, was still confined within modest limits.[1] Finally, the peasantry, so long left without any recourse against the arbitrary will of their masters, were now taken under the protection of the law.

Through the abolition of the most crying political evils of the old régime, the formation of a strong executive, and the granting of increased freedom of action to the middle and lower classes, this constitution marked a great advance upon all previous attempts at reform in Poland. In its wise conservatism, its adaptation of foreign norms so far as they were applicable, its refusal to follow blindly the abstract political theories of the day, it compares most favorably with the work of the contemporary constitution-makers at Paris. It was not, indeed, free from serious defects; the jurist will find in it much to criticize; but it must be remembered that this was a popular work, framed in a crisis to meet quite peculiar conditions and prejudices, and that on several points its arrangements were never intended to be final. When all is said, this constitution did afford the possibility of a new, sound, and progressive national life. It may have been impolitic to attempt such great changes at that moment, in view of the probable attitude of the neighboring Powers; but at any rate, this heroic breach with the past, this abjuration of the ancient sins, this renunciation of the idolized ' golden liberty ' throws an immortal gleam over the last dark years of the Republic.

II

The revolution of the Third of May essentially altered the views of the outside world upon the Polish Question. Hitherto foreign observers had followed the activity of the Four Years' Diet with skepticism and a certain ironical indifference. The Poles were regarded as noisy, troublesome, and childish people, outlandish in their ideas, fickle in temper, and incapable of great and decisive deeds. The main problem was whether they should

[1] The (royal) cities obtained the right of sending 21 (later 24) representatives to the Diet, as against 204 deputies elected by the *szlachta* in the Dietines. The city-deputies might speak on all matters, but *vote* only on municipal and commercial questions.

live under the tutelage of Russia or Prussia, provided they did not lose their political existence altogether. But after the Third of May the world began to take the Poles more seriously. It was now the general belief that the nation would after all effect its regeneration, if only it were allowed to work out its destinies undisturbed. The great question now was whether the neighboring states would permit a revival, which would in so many ways alter the old balance of power, and which would cut short so many long-cherished ambitions. Would they allow the new constitution to stand ? Of the Powers most concerned Prussia and Austria were the first to express themselves on this question; and for quite diverse reasons both pronounced in a sense unexpectedly favorable to Poland.

The first tidings of the new constitution reached Berlin through a dispatch from Goltz of April 30.[1] The ministers at once drew up a report to the King urging that if Poland were to become an hereditary monarchy, it could not fail to prove extremely dangerous, and perhaps even destructive to Prussia. Goltz must therefore be ordered to do all in his power to dissuade the ' well-intentioned ' party from their plan, if it had not already been carried out.[2] The King approved, but before the appropriate instructions could be sent off there arrived the news of the events of the Third of May, along with a letter from Stanislas Augustus formally announcing the promulgation of the new constitution. It was then a case of making *bonne mine à mauvais jeu*. The cardinal fact in the situation was that at this moment — and until the end of May — Frederick William regarded a war with Russia as quite within the range of possibilities, and hence he desired not to antagonize the Poles and the Elector of Saxony. Perhaps the influence of Ewart and Bischoffwerder, who were

[1] In the early days of the conspiracy, it was the plan of the Polish leaders to send the Marshal Potocki to Berlin to secure the secret approval of Prussia in advance. This plan was not carried out, perhaps because Potocki disliked to absent himself from Warsaw at so critical a moment.

[2] The ministerial proposals of May 6 are given at some length in Häusser, *Deutsche Geschichte*, i, pp. 304 f. It has again and again been stated that these proposals were made after the news of the completed *coup d'état* arrived, but in fact that news reached Berlin only on the 7th.

still preaching the Federative System, counted for something here;[1] perhaps the King's mind was still susceptible to the charms of posing as the patron of revolutions and the liberator of nations; at any rate he now declared himself with a cordiality and effusiveness that surpassed all expectations. In his reply to Jabłonowski, the Polish envoy, in rescripts to his ministers at Warsaw and St. Petersburg, in letters to Stanislas Augustus and the Elector of Saxony, Frederick William expressed his satisfaction, approval, and admiration with regard to the new constitution, which he held to be " indispensable to the happiness of the Polish nation." The conferring of the crown upon the Saxon House would, he wrote, " confirm for ages the close friendship and harmony existing " [between Prussia and Poland].[2] These declarations were within twelve months to receive a bitterly ironical commentary.

Although the statement was made at that time [3] and has since been championed by a great German historian,[4] there is no evidence to prove that the Court of Vienna was informed in advance of the plan which was carried out on the Third of May. Doubtless Austro-Polish relations had improved considerably since the preceding summer. Leopold's separation from Russia by the Convention of Reichenbach, his pacific tendencies, the assurances of his warm goodwill towards the Republic brought back by all the Poles who visited Vienna, the still half-credited tale that he had refused a Prussian proposition for a new partition,

---

[1] Cf. Ewart's account of his intervention here, *Dropmore Papers*, ii, pp. 75 f.

[2] Askenazy, *op. cit.*, pp. 126 f., 224 ff.

[3] Bulgakov's Vienna correspondent, May 16, 1791: " Si je ne juge pas mal des choses, le ministère autrichien s'attendoit, à quelque chose de pareil, et je ne peux même en douter," M. A., Польша, III, 63.

[4] Sybel. There can be no need to enter here into the controversy so warmly conducted between Sybel and Herrmann fifty years ago regarding the Polish policy of Leopold II. The dispute raged chiefly about Sybel's theses: (1) that Leopold had a hand in preparing the *coup d'état* of the third of May; (2) that he then exerted himself actively to secure the general recognition of the new constitution by the Powers; (3) that he originated the plan for the permanent union of Poland and Saxony. It is now clear that Sybel was wrong on the first and third of these points, but quite right regarding the second. Later researches, especially Beer's, have deprived the controversy of practical interest.

all this combined to inspire more confidence in Austria than had previously been felt at Warsaw.[1] Both Republicans and Patriots had begun to form some hopes of gaining the Emperor's patronage. In February, 1791, Rzewuski, one of the leading reactionaries, fruitlessly proposed at Vienna to form a Counter-confederation under Austrian protection [2] very similar to that which was later organized under Catherine's auspices. About the same time one of the most active among the Polish reformers advanced the idea that in view of the untrustworthiness of Prussia the Republic would do well to seek support rather in the friendship of the Court of Vienna. It was undoubtedly proposed to sound Leopold in advance regarding the plan for a new constitution and a *coup d'état;* but apparently the proposal was not carried out.[3] Down to the Third of May no real connection existed between the Warsaw reformers and the Austrian cabinet; and there was still no Austrian party in Poland.

The news of the *coup d'état* was received at Vienna with almost universal approbation. In the salons people lauded ' the Polish revolution ' to the skies, by way of showing their horror for the French one.[4] Kaunitz, too, was extremely well pleased. The new constitution, he was sure, was directly opposed to all the interests, plans, and desires of Prussia: hence he highly approved of it. The old anarchy, the factions, the interregna had offered a fine field to the intrigues of Berlin; and now, it was to be hoped, all that was done away with. Under hereditary monarchs and a

---

[1] Kraszewski, *op. cit.,* ii, pp. 363 f.; Goltz's report of April 13, 1791, in Herrmann, *op. cit.,* vi, pp. 568 f.; Zaleski, *Żywot Czartoryskiego,* pp. 258 f.

[2] Rzewuski's plan is to be found among the *Vorträge* of 1791 in the Vienna Archives, accompanied by an undated note from Leopold to Kaunitz, asking his opinion, and by the Chancellor's reply, dated February 8 — a scathing condemnation of so unholy a project.

[3] The proposal was made by Piattoli in a *Mémoire* of March 4, 1791: see Smolka, " Genezya konstytucyi 3. maja," in *Bulletin International de l'Académie des Sciences de Cracovie, Comptes rendus des séances de l'année 1891,* pp. 350–354. Smolka believed that Leopold was really sounded on the subject before the Third of May, but Dembiński argues convincingly against this view in his above-cited monograph on Piattoli.

[4] Bulgakov's Vienna correspondent, May 14, 18, 28, M. A., Польша, III, 63.

stronger executive, Poland might recover sufficient force to maintain her integrity; that was all he required of her; he reflected
that there would always remain enough of the old republican
leaven to prevent this state from becoming dangerous to its
neighbors, and he believed that in the long run a revived Poland
would see that its true interest lay in cleaving to the Imperial
Courts. For the present, the revolution had come very much
à propos to increase the embarrassments of His Prussian Majesty
over the Eastern Question. If Austria and Russia, by taking
the new constitution under their protection, could win over Poland and Saxony immediately, that would add the crowning blow
to the discomfiture of Berlin.[1] This was, indeed, only a continuation of the Chancellor's previous policy. Of any new departure,
of any independent and specifically Austrian system towards
Poland apart from or in opposition to Russia, there was at that
time no thought.

Leopold at first judged the events at Warsaw less accurately
than Kaunitz had done. He suspected that the King of Prussia
had had a hand in this affair, and that he was scheming to marry
a Hohenzollern to the ' Infanta,' or else to realize his ambitions
upon Dantzic; he also feared that the revolution might lead to
new disturbances in the Republic.[2] But Kaunitz's report of
May 12, together with a reassuring letter from Frederick William,
soon removed these suspicions; and henceforth the Emperor and
his Chancellor were agreed in approving the salutary change in
Poland.[3]

[1] These ideas in Kaunitz's dispatches to Cobenzl of May 25, and his report to
the Emperor of May 12, V. A., *Exped., Russland*, and *Vorträge*, 1791.

[2] Leopold to Kaunitz, May 20, the first expression of the Emperor's opinion
on the Polish revolution that has come to light (printed in Beer, *Joseph II, Leopold
II, und Kaunitz*, pp. 404 f.). This, together with his letters to Marie Christine of
June 2 and 9 (Wolf, *Leopold II und Marie Christine*, pp. 231 ff.) show how unexpected and perplexing the news was to Leopold.

[3] The Emperor's apostil to Kaunitz's report of May 12; Frederick William to
Leopold, May 21, Vivenot, *op. cit.*, i, p. 133; cf. Elgin's reports of May 25 and 26,
F. z. D. G. v, pp. 255 ff.

Sybel's contention that Leopold's suggestion to Elgin on May 9 about a general
guarantee of the Polish constitution related to the new constitution, is quite untenable. The news of the *coup d'état* at Warsaw reached Vienna only on the 10th,
and Leopold was then in Florence.

Meanwhile, even before getting Leopold's orders, Kaunitz had felt sure enough of his sovereign's views to act. Immediately after the news of the revolution arrived, he hastened to order de Caché at Warsaw and Hartig at Dresden to express the Emperor's complete approval of the new constitution and of the succession in the Saxon House.[1] This friendly advance encouraged the Elector Frederick Augustus to turn to Leopold directly for advice as to the acceptance of the proffered crown. He was unable to form a decision, he declared, until the constitution of the Republic and its relations with the neighboring Powers had been arranged in such a way as would enable him to fulfil both the obligations imposed by the crown of Poland and his duties to his hereditary states. The Emperor replied with a very friendly letter, approving the Elector's scruples and assuring him of his own favorable attitude, which he believed he could state was shared by the other Powers. Kaunitz began to make a great show of zeal on behalf of the Court of Dresden, but he did not press it for an immediate decision. It was enough for the moment to bind Saxony to Austria; the final settlement of Polish affairs would have to wait until he had arrived at a thorough understanding with Russia.[2]

In his dispatches to Louis Cobenzl of May 24 and 25, the Austrian Chancellor made the first of what was destined to be a long series of efforts to win Catherine's approval for the new constitution of Poland. With great expenditure of cleverly chosen arguments he labored to prove that the strengthening of the Republic was now as much to the advantage of Russia as its weakening might formerly have been; that the maintenance of the old anarchy could serve only the insidious schemes of the Court of Berlin; that even under the new régime Russia could

[1] Instructions to de Caché of May 14, repeated the 25; instructions to Hartig, May 11, V. A., *Exped.*, *Polen* and *Sachsen*, 1791.

[2] Frederick Augustus to Leopold, May 27, and the Emperor's reply, June 11, Vivenot, *op. cit.*, i, pp. 147, 166 f.; Kaunitz to Hartig, June 4. This seems to have been the first correspondence between the two sovereigns with regard to the Polish crown. The document printed in Vivenot, *op. cit.*, i, p. 106 — ostensibly a letter from Leopold to the Elector of March 24, 1791 — is the draft of a letter which in all probability was never sent.

always exercise as much influence in Poland as she needed; while if she found it necessary to make some small changes in the constitution, means and opportunities would assuredly not be lacking before the new order of things had had time to get thoroughly established. The great thing at present was to outbid Prussia at Warsaw and Dresden. It would be a capital stroke if the Imperial Courts could confront the would-be dictators of Europe with a quadruple alliance of Russia, Austria, Saxony, and Poland.[1] It was a program in Kaunitz's best style, clear, logical, comprehensive, imposing. Nothing could be more adapted to the cardinal principle of the Austrian policy of the past fifty years, for what more formidable barrier could be reared against Prussian ambition than a reinvigorated Poland backed by all the might of Austria and Russia ? It was the last of Kaunitz's great combinations against Prussia, and like so many of his choicest creations it had one very serious defect. He was badly in error regarding the real sentiments that reigned on the Neva.

When the news of the Third of May first reached St. Petersburg, Cobenzl found the Empress, Potemkin, and all the ministers filled with anger and alarm. There was talk of a concert of the three neighboring Powers to undo this work of revolution, of a Counter-confederation, of a new partition.[2] After the first

---

[1] The dispatches of May 24–25 are printed in Vivenot, *op. cit.*, i, pp. 138–145.

[2] Cobenzl's report of May 13, V. A., *Russland, Berichte*, 1791.

Cobenzl wrote: " J'ai trouvé l'Impératrice, le Prince Potemkin et le Comte Ostermann . . . fort affectés de l'Idée que la Pologne pourroit prendre une Consistence réelle, tandis qu'on regarde ici comme l'Intérêt de toutes les Puissances voisines, qu'Elle reste dans son Etat de Nullité. S. M. me fit la grace de me dire, qu'il èst essentiel de se concerter avec Nous à cet égard. J'ai assûré cette Princesse, que Nous étions toujours prêts sur tous les objets possibles. Mais, me dit l'Impératrice, puis-je compter sur vous ? J'ai répondu à S. M. que dès que Nous aurons le moyen, l'Empereur ne connoissoit aucuns bornes à désirer de l'employer pour la cause de la Russie; à quoi S. M. a repondû, il me faut dans ce moment-ci quelque chose de plus positif. . . ." Vorontsov believed " que si la chose s'est faite contre le gré du Cabinet de Potsdam, il en sera d'autant plus disposé à un nouveau Traité de Partage, qui mettroit fin à tout, bien entendû que les deux Cours Impériales agissent en cela comme en tout d'un parfait concert. . . ." " On ne seroit pas fâché s'il resultoit de ce que le Roi de Pologne a entrepris, une scission dans la Nation Polonoise et des Troubles. Le Prince Potemkin est assez porté pour l'idée de former une Confédération dans les Provinces Polonoises, qui avoisinent la Russie, et on m'assure que tout le Monde y est disposé."

flush of anger was over, however, Ostermann began to alter his tone. After all, he declared, the revolution offered many advantages to the Imperial Courts, especially the chance to form an alliance with Poland and Saxony, which would be a stinging blow to Prussia. He was very curious to know what the Court of Vienna thought of this change, and prodigal of assurances that Russia would take no action in the matter except in closest agreement with Austria.[1] When Kaunitz's dispatches arrived, the Vice-Chancellor affirmed that they accorded perfectly with what he himself had already proposed to the Empress; but he could not yet say what Her Majesty's final decision would be. Potemkin also declared that he agreed entirely with Kaunitz.[2] Other questions at this time seemed to absorb the attention of the Russian ministry, which was then in the throes of the final negotiation with England and Prussia. It was only in the middle of July that Cobenzl received a half-way definite answer on Polish affairs, which was to the effect that the Empress would postpone a decision regarding the new constitution until the close of the Turkish war, and would then concert her future course of action with Austria.[3] With that the matter rested. Both Cobenzl and Kaunitz remained for some time in the comfortable conviction that on the Polish question the Russian point of view was not far removed from the Austrian. What the Empress' real intentions were, we shall have occasion to see later. Meanwhile it is necessary to take up the long-dropped thread of the negotiation for the Austro-Prussian alliance.

III

Since Bischoffwerder's return from the Austrian capital in March, the plan which had formed the object of his journey had been at a standstill. The pretence of negotiating about it had been kept up through a fitful exchange of memorials and opinions between Berlin and Vienna; but the great question of the admission of Russia to the proposed union seemed to offer an insur-

---

[1] Cobenzl's reports of May 17 and June 4, V. A., loc. cit.
[2] Cobenzl's report of June 27, ibid.
[3] Cobenzl's report of July 19, ibid.

mountable obstacle, and at least on the Austrian side there was little eagerness to carry the matter further at present. Kaunitz was still eloquently opposed to the project; and the Emperor was well content to delay the affair, as long as there was danger of a war between his present and his prospective allies. What first gave a new impetus to the plan was the mission of Lord Elgin to Leopold, already mentioned in connection with England's back-down on the Eastern Question. During May and June this irrepressible young gentleman pursued the Emperor around Italy, persecuting him with offers for an alliance with England and Prussia, and with appeals for aid in bringing the Tsarina to reason. Leopold was not inclined to exert himself overmuch merely in order to save Pitt's imperiled bark from shipwreck; he made no binding promises; but he did not mind giving pleasant assurances of a general character, which kept Elgin in high hopes and led him to send the most optimistic bulletins to London and Berlin. From one of these reports, communicated by Ewart, the Prussian government was informed of the Emperor's wish to have a confidential agent sent to him by the King, and of his particular desire to see " the excellent Colonel Bischoffwerder " again.[1]

Frederick William at once determined to comply with so flattering a suggestion. At this time — near the end of May — the King still believed in the possibility of war with Russia; and he was encouraged by Elgin's reports to hope that Leopold could be drawn over to the side of the Triple Alliance, or at least induced to promise his neutrality. Besides, he did not mean to let England be the first to conclude an alliance with the Emperor; the principal rôle belonged to himself, since he had originally taken the initiative in this matter. In the lengthy instructions drawn up by the Prussian ministers, Bischoffwerder was ordered first of all to make sure that Leopold would actively support the new terms of peace proposed by the Triple Alliance at St. Petersburg, and also that he would immediately put a stop to the chicaneries by which Kaunitz was insidiously protracting the Austro-Turkish peace congress at Sistova. Once assured on these points, the envoy was authorized to conclude a treaty of

---

[1] See Appendix VI, 1.

alliance, preferably one between Austria and Prussia alone, to which England might later be invited to accede. Under no circumstances was Russia to be admitted to the new union; Leopold must promise to remain neutral in case of war between the King and the Empress; and in fact the whole tenor of the instructions shows clearly that opposition to Russia was intended to be the cardinal principle of the Austro-Prussian alliance. It was quite in accordance with that tendency that Bischoffwerder was ordered to stop en route at Dresden and urge the Elector to accept the Polish crown immediately, contenting himself with the approval of Prussia, England, and Austria, and paying no attention to Russia.[1]

The envoy set out from Berlin May 30, tarried two days in the Saxon capital, where his zealous exhortations failed to shake Frederick Augustus out of his cautious reserve, and arrived on June 9 at Milan, where the Emperor was then staying. Leopold was somewhat glacial at the first meeting, apparently for the purpose of showing that it was not he who was courting allies. But immediately afterwards his tone changed, he became all

[1] Instructions of May 28, 1791, B. A., *R.* 1, *Conv.* 172.

Art. 8 of the instruction: " Il est de la plus grande importance d'écarter toute participation de la Cour de Russie à la Négociation et au Traité à conclure, sur laquelle le Prince Kaunitz et ses Adhérens ne manqueront pas d'insister, mais qui seroit entièrement incompatible avec les intérêts du Roi et la Situation actuelle des choses, et que l'Empereur lui-même, selon les assurances du Lord Elgin, paroît regarder comme telle. . . ."

Art. 7: " Comme la garantie de la Pologne dans ses frontières actuelles et le maintien de la constitution libre et indépendante de la Pologne paroît tenir fort à cœur à ce Monarque [Leopold] et n'est pas moins conforme aux vues et aux intérêts de Sa Majesté, rien n'empêche que le Colonel Bischoffwerder n'y accède tout de suite. . . ."

Art. 2: " Le Colonel de Bischoffwerder étant chargé de prendre sa route par Dresde afin de profiter du séjour qu'il y fera pour fixer les irrésolutions de l'Electeur de Saxe sur l'acceptation du throne de Pologne, il cherchera à se ménager une audience auprès de ce Prince pour rectifier ses idées et celles des personnes les plus influentes de sa Cour sur cette matière. . . . Il semble que la considération qui résultera pour la Saxe même de l'acceptation du throne de Pologne par l'Electeur; les suites fâcheuses qu'un refus ou même la simple vacillation de ce Prince pourroient avoir en Pologne . . .; enfin la sûreté qui résulte pour l'Electeur de l'Amitié et de l'Alliance, s'il en est besoin, de la Prusse et de l'Angleterre, seront les principaux motifs qu'on pourra faire valoir pour inspirer de la fermeté à ce Prince. . . ."

affability, and ' the worthy Colonel ' was soon completely under the spell. The explanation of Leopold's altered attitude is to be found in a startling piece of news which had reached him immediately after Bischoffwerder's arrival. On June 12 came a letter from Marie Antoinette, announcing that the French royal family were about to attempt their escape from Paris; and the Emperor saw before himself the prospect of having to undertake armed intervention on their behalf.[1] In such a case, the assistance of Prussia would be indispensable. The alliance at once became an urgent and pressing matter. Hence he hastened to give Bischoffwerder all the assurances required that peace should promptly be concluded at Sistova; both were agreed in thrusting Elgin aside and negotiating the alliance between themselves alone; and the exact provisions of the treaty furnished no great difficulties. After but slight resistance, Bischoffwerder gave way on the question of inviting the adhesion of Russia, and he entered with the greatest readiness into Leopold's proposals with regard to French affairs. After a few conferences, the two found themselves agreed on the principal points, and it remained only to put their arrangements on paper after the return to Vienna.[2] The conclusion of the formal treaty of alliance was, indeed, to be postponed until after the final pacification in the East; but a preliminary convention containing the essential articles was to be signed at once.

On arriving at Vienna about the middle of July, Bischoffwerder fell into the toils of the Austrians more hopelessly than ever. He was flattered by the Emperor's show of confidence; he was overwhelmed with attentions by Cobenzl and Spielmann, and even by Kaunitz himself; for the old Chancellor, having once made up his mind to what he could no longer prevent, had now developed an astonishing zeal for ' the new system,' and delivered the most edifying disquisitions on this alliance, which would startle the

---

[1] Marie Antoinette to Leopold, June 1, and his reply of June 12, Arneth, *Marie Antoinette, Joseph II und Leopold II*, pp. 166 f., 177 ff.; Feuillet de Conches, *op. cit.*, ii, pp. 72, 78.

[2] The above chiefly from Bischoffwerder's reports of June 14 and 18, B. A., *R.* 1, *Conv.* 172, and from the " Journal über die Verhandlungen mit Bischoffwerder," printed in Vivenot, *op. cit.*, i, pp. 176–181.

world and eclipse even the wondrous Treaty of Versailles.[1]
Never did a negotiation pass off more smoothly; never was diplomat more trustful, more compliant, more facile than 'the
excellent Colonel Bischoffwerder.' Two conferences sufficed for
everything. At the first, the Prussian envoy submitted his propositions, there was general discussion, and Spielmann promised
to draw up the articles of the convention. At the second, Kaunitz presented the completed draft; whereupon Bischoffwerder,
although he had heard it for the first time, and although it
differed greatly from the propositions he had made, signed it at
once, " seeing," as he wrote to his King, " that it was the *ne plus
ultra* of what I could obtain, that there was nothing in it disadvantageous to Your Majesty, and that I should spoil everything
by showing any lack of confidence." [2] In truth, it was a bargain
in which the Austrians had carried every point. Bischoffwerder
agreed to the future admission of Russia to the alliance, and to the
omission from the treaty of every phrase that might wound the
Empress' susceptibilities; he consented to an article providing
for mutual assistance in case of internal disturbances, and to
another which guaranteed the Austrian rights to Lusatia in case of
the extinction of the male line of Saxony; he accepted an article
providing for a concert on the affairs of France.

Particularly important were the stipulations of the convention
regarding Poland. The 'separate article' on that subject ran:
" As the interests and tranquillity of the Powers which are neighbors of Poland render infinitely desirable the establishment of
such a concert between them as will remove all jealousy or apprehension of preponderance, the Courts of Vienna and Berlin will
agree, and will invite the Court of Russia to agree with them, not
to undertake anything contrary to the integrity and to the maintenance of the free constitution of Poland; never to seek to place
a prince of their respective Houses upon the throne of Poland,

---

[1] Bischoffwerder's journal of his negotiation (*passim*), B. A., *R.* 1, *Conv.* 172;
Kaunitz to Leopold, July 26, V. A., *Vorträge*, 1791. The Chancellor wrote that this
alliance " fait à peu près le second Tome du Traité de Versailles, qui a étonné toute
l'Europe dans son temps, et a sauvé alors la Monarchie Autrichienne."

[2] Bischoffwerder's reports of July 22 and 25, B. A., *loc. cit.*; Spielmann to
the Emperor, July 23, V. A., *Vorträge*, 1791.

either by a marriage with the Princess Infanta or in case of a new election; and not to employ their influence in either of these latter cases to determine the choice of the Republic in favor of another prince, save by a common agreement among themselves."

The significance of this article has been much disputed. On the one hand, it has been taken for a guarantee of the Constitution of the Third of May, and a declaration that could only be regarded as an insult at St. Petersburg; [1] and on the other hand, it has been called a virtual surrender of Poland to Russia, the first sign of the abandonment of the Republic by its Prussian ally. [2] Both these interpretations are probably erroneous. This article was a restatement of the one proposed by Bischoffwerder in February, modified in accordance with the circumstances and with certain considerations urged by the Austrians. The original Prussian proposal had had for its chief aim to prevent Russia from recovering her former predominance in Poland; and it had also contained a virtual guarantee of the existing constitution of the Republic. In July the Austrian ministers insisted on toning down this article in such a way as to render it ostensible and fit to be presented for Catherine's acceptance. They fully agreed with Bischoffwerder that the main object was to uphold the new constitution and to prevent Poland from again falling under the control of Russia or any other foreign Power; but Spielmann urged that it was both imprudent and unnecessary to use terms that would lead the Empress to think that ' they were trying to prescribe laws to her,' or meant to extort her consent to the new régime in Poland by force. Moderate language and courteous forms would be far more likely to bring Catherine to accept the Austro-Prussian standpoint. [3] Hence an article the terms of which had been softened down until they had wellnigh lost all clearness and vigor, but the underlying spirit of which was undeniably favorable to Poland.

The provision as to " the free constitution " was indefinite, indeed, but, coupled with that regarding the Infanta, it implied

---

[1] Sybel, *H. Z.*, xxiii, pp. 77 f.

[2] Herrmann, *Ergänzungsband*, p. 40, and *F. z. D. G.*, v, pp. 239 f.; Askenazy, *op. cit.*, pp. 150 ff.

[3] Spielmann's report to the Emperor, July 23, V. A., *loc. cit.;* Bischoffwerder's journal of his negotiation, July 22, B. A., *loc. cit.*

'a recognition of the new constitution, and was so interpreted both at Warsaw and St. Petersburg. There was no guarantee of the new form of government, but the Poles had lately been declaiming a great deal about the irksomeness of such foreign guarantees. The exclusion from the Polish throne of members of the reigning houses of the three neighboring states was in conformity with the interests of the Republic; and — it may be added — it involved the sacrifice of certain plans that Frederick William had long taken very seriously. The fact that Russia was to be invited to join in the concert on Polish affairs did not imply that the other two Courts were at that time ready to concur with Russian plans hostile to Poland. The attitude which the Empress would finally assume towards the new constitution was quite unknown at Berlin and Vienna; indeed Cobenzl's latest reports had led the Austrians to hope that she would adopt their ideas on that subject. The one part of the article that could hardly be reconciled with a strict regard for the independence of Poland was that which suggested the possibility of a future concert of the three Powers with respect to the succession to the throne; for that implied that the contracting parties had not altogether renounced interfering in the internal affairs of the Republic. But taken as a whole these provisions were of a nature to give satisfaction at Warsaw. Their essential significance lay in this: that at a time when the fate of the new Polish constitution hung in the balance, Austria and Prussia had agreed to recognize that constitution, to abstain from all enterprises against it themselves, and to attempt to induce Russia to adopt the same attitude.[1]

The Preliminary Convention of Vienna was signed July 25, and forwarded the next day to Berlin for ratification. The Prussian ministry were filled with indignation when they received this masterpiece of Bischoffwerder's diplomacy. They found that he had been completely the dupe of the Austrians; that he had agreed to articles on which he had never had any instructions (especially that relating to the concert on French affairs); and that he had acted in flat violation of his instructions in signing

---

[1] Some further discussion of this article will be found in Appendix VI, 2.

any convention without first submitting the draft of it to the King. Frederick William, however, was apparently well pleased. He was not averse to the French enterprise, and he was delighted to have secured at last — on whatever terms — an alliance which would free him from the English bondage and furnish the basis for a new forward policy. With scarcely a word of explanation, and without asking for their opinion, he ordered his ministers to send back the act of ratification at once, though under the condition that it should not be presented until peace had been concluded at Sistova.[1] This provision, however, occasioned no delay, for the treaty between Austria and Turkey was signed on August 4. Austria restored her conquests of the late war, but by virtue of certain ancient claims secured the cession of Old Orsova, and thus a partial mitigation of the terms of Reichenbach. Bischoffwerder could then put the crown on his work by proceeding to the exchange of ratifications (August 15). Thus was virtually consummated an alliance which astonished the world as much as did the famous diplomatic revolution of 1756, or as much as would an alliance between France and Germany today.

With the almost simultaneous conclusion of the Vienna Convention, the Peace of Sistova, and the Preliminaries of Galatz, the long Oriental crisis had reached its end. It was an unsatisfactory, a dull and prosaic finale. For four years there had been wars and rumors of wars, mobilizations, coalitions, congresses, negotiations, diplomatic activity almost unparalleled; and the result was that none of the great issues had been settled, none of the great plans had been realized. Out of it all had come only the slightest changes of territory, but a considerable shifting in the positions of the various European Powers. The connection between the Imperial Courts was loosened; the Triple Alliance was practically dissolved; and through the rapprochement sealed by the Vienna Convention Austrian and Prussian policy had received a new basis and struck out into new paths. But the

---

[1] The King to the Ministry of Foreign Affairs, July 31, Schulenburg and Alvensleben to the King on the same date, B. A., *R.* 1, *Conv.* 172; Alvensleben's *Procès-verbal* of August 11 (see Herrmann, *Ergänzungsband,* pp. 40 ff., and *F. z. D. G.,* v, pp. 277 f.). Cf. Appendix VI, 3.

greatest legacy of the Oriental crisis was the reopening of the Polish Question.

It was during those four years of turmoil that the seeds of the Second Partition were sown. The old system, which had seemed to assure the existence of the Republic, had collapsed; the great breach with Russia had taken place, and remained unforgotten and unforgiven at St. Petersburg; and a new spirit had appeared in Poland that made the permanent restoration of Russian domination in the old form impossible. But, on the other hand, the Poles had seized too late the opportunity for internal reforms, they had lost the chance to satisfy the ambitions of Prussia by a peaceful bargain, and they had seen their best chances for securing aid from without vanish one after the other. The three neighboring Powers had at the last moment failed to come to blows, and were now about to unite, and their union had always been fatal to Poland. But if the causes go back to the Oriental crisis, the form which the catastrophe was to take was determined by the struggle in which Austria and Prussia now became involved against the French Revolution.

CHAPTER X

THE DEVELOPMENT OF THE FRENCH AND POLISH QUESTIONS TO THE DEATH OF LEOPOLD II

I

IT is well known that immediately after learning of the flight and recapture of the French royal family, the Emperor Leopold issued the Circular of Padua (July 6, 1791), inviting the chief European Powers to common action for the purpose of ensuring the safety of the King and Queen of France and the maintenance of monarchical government in that country. Of all the sovereigns invited into the concert, the Empress of Russia alone showed an ardent zeal for the cause. Nothing could have suited Catherine better than to see the other Powers embarked in the French enterprise, partly because she detested the Revolution on principle, but even more because she wanted a free hand in her own corner of Europe. As soon as the danger of the Oriental crisis was over, she began the *mise-en-scène* of her next great act on the European stage. Already in May and June she was doing her utmost to persuade her quixotic cousin of Sweden to head a counter-revolution in France, while she also commenced to sound the Austrian cabinet on the same subject.[1] She received Leopold's proposals of July with the warmest approval and regretted only that the measures suggested were not more vigorous. Henceforth the Empress was aflame for ' the cause of all sovereigns.'

Frederick William's attitude was also distinctly favorable, but his ministers succeeded in inserting into his reply certain condi-

[1] Even in February, 1791, Catherine made vague hints about an intervention in France to Austria and Sweden (Cobenzl's report of February 22, V. A., *Russland, Berichte;* Schinkel-Bergman, *Minnen,* ii, pp. 151 ff.) For her later overtures to those Powers: Cobenzl's report of June 11, V. A., *loc. cit.;* Ostermann to Golitsyn, May 30/June 10, 1791, M. A., Австрія, III, 51; Odhner, *Gustaf III och Katarina,* pp. 173 ff.; Geffroy, *Gustave III et la Cour de France,* ii, pp. 110 ff.; Catherine's letters to Stackelberg, in the Русская Старина, iii; Dembiński, *Rosya a rewolucya francuska,* ch. iii.

tions — especially about the coöperation of England — that made it wellnigh declinatory. What was particularly characteristic of the Prussian standpoint was the insistence that any declarations to be addressed to the National Assembly must be backed up by force, and that if military intervention was to be attempted, the Powers must first come to an understanding on the subject of ' conquests.' [1] With all his generous sympathy for a fellow-sovereign in distress, Frederick William saw in the French enterprise first and foremost a chance to make handsome acquisitions.

At Vienna there was little thought of conquests and no real eagerness for action of any kind. Neither a dismemberment of France nor a complete restoration of the old monarchy seemed desirable to the Austrian statesmen. Provided they could secure a decent existence to the French royal family and suitable compensation to the German princes dispossessed in Alsace, they would have been well content to leave France in impotence and anarchy. Universal principles have seldom exercised much influence over the policy of Vienna, and Leopold II, with his constitutional ideas and strong common sense, was the last man to feel any sentimental enthusiasm for ' the cause of all sovereigns.' When the answers received from the various Courts sufficiently indicated that no effective concert of all the Powers could be hoped for, the Austrian cabinet began to think chiefly of retreating from an embarrassing position. This tendency was not arrested by the meeting held by the Emperor and the King of Prussia at Pillnitz as the guests of the Elector of Saxony towards the close of August; for while French affairs were discussed at length on this occasion, Leopold's prudence prevailed over Frederick William's zeal for action and over the importunities of the Count of Artois. The resulting declaration issued in the name of the two monarchs aroused indignation in France, but it bound its authors to nothing whatever. The negotiations for the concert of the Powers continued for a time in a perfunctory way; but when Louis XVI subscribed to the new constitution, Leopold hastened to inform the other Courts that since the King had recovered his

[1] Rescript to Jacobi of July 28, Herrmann, *Ergänzungsband*, pp. 50–58.

freedom and had voluntarily accepted his new position, there was nothing to be done save to await the further course of events in France.[1] The coalition against the Revolution seemed to be definitely abandoned.

II

This lull in French affairs gave the Imperial cabinet the opportunity to take up the hardly less important Polish question. The fate of the Constitution of the Third of May was still undecided; and the longer the suspense lasted, the more the political constellation seemed to change to the detriment of the Poles. Within the Republic, indeed, all was quiet; it was clear that the malcontents were few in numbers and unable to stir without foreign assistance; but the cloud on the eastern horizon grew ever larger and darker. The Court of St. Petersburg maintained an ominous silence, avoided any explanation with Austria on Polish affairs, and hastened forward its peace with the Turks. Kaunitz grew suspicious that the Empress' extraordinary zeal for a crusade against France was based solely on a desire to divert the attention of Austria and Prussia from Poland.[2] There were also disquieting symptoms at Berlin. At Pillnitz Leopold and Frederick William had again agreed to urge upon the Elector the acceptance of the Polish crown;[3] but this was the last occasion when the King showed any real inclination to favor the new order of things in the Republic. Since then Kaunitz had had reason to convince himself that the Prussians were at bottom opposed to the new constitution, embarrassed by the approval which they

[1] Austrian circular of November 12, 1791, Vivenot, i, pp. 270 f.

[2] Kaunitz to the Emperor, November 5, V. A., *Vorträge*, 1791. The Austrians still had no absolute certainty of this. I have been unable to find any authority for the statement made by Sybel, *op. cit.*, i, p. 389, and Heigel, *op. cit.*, i, p. 454, that about this time Golitsyn told Kaunitz that each of the Imperial Courts had its counter-revolution to effect, the one at Paris, the other at Warsaw; and I am strongly inclined to doubt the story. Golitsyn's reports show that he had not the faintest knowledge of his sovereign's intentions about Poland, and he was hardly the man to hazard such statements on his own responsibility. The story is probably a bit of gossip retailed by Jacobi, the Prussian envoy at Vienna.

[3] Spielmann to Kaunitz, August 31, Vivenot, *op. cit.*, i, p. 238; Schlitter, *Marie Christine*, p. lxvi.

had been forced to give to it, and inclined to seize the first opportunity to repair the blunder.

To make the situation even more critical, the Elector was still unable to decide either to accept or to reject the Polish throne. Honorable and well-meaning, but cautious and irresolute in the extreme, Frederick Augustus was torn between his desire for a crown which two of his ancestors had worn and which his mother had always planned to win for him, and his fear that this Polish connection might again bring disaster upon his beloved Saxony. His ambition was spurred on by his wife and by the not inconsiderable ' Polish party ' at his court; but on the other hand his ministers abhorred all political adventures and regarded a system of pure passivity as the Alpha and Omega of Saxon statecraft. Deterrent also were the reports from Warsaw of his resident, the hypochondriac Essen, which contained nothing but the most dismal jeremiads against the depraved Polish nation. So for months the Elector vacillated. He could not bring himself to refuse the honor, as some of his ministers advised him to do; but he was also unwilling to accept without the fulfilment of several conditions. Various changes must be made in the new constitution, extending the royal prerogatives still further; and he would have preferred to see the succession pass to his brother rather than to his daughter, so that Saxony and Poland should be permanently united. Above all, he was determined not to commit himself until assured that there would be no opposition from any one of the great neighboring Powers.

In spite of the warm expressions of friendship and support received from the Emperor and the King of Prussia, Frederick Augustus remained suspicious of both of them, and likewise of the King of Poland. The repeated efforts of the government at Warsaw, the mission of Bischoffwerder to Dresden at the end of May, the interview at Pillnitz did not avail to draw the Elector out of his irresolution. Every day that brought nearer the peace between Russia and the Porte increased the danger to Poland, but that consideration only made Frederick Augustus the more cautious and reserved. By October the Poles had obtained from him nothing more than the consent to open negotiations for the purpose of clearing up the difficulties which he found in the new constitution. At Warsaw this concession was taken for more than it was worth, and it was hoped that a speedy negotiation would end the Elector's scruples and secure an immediate acceptance. In November Prince Adam Czartoryski set out for Dresden to undertake the mission, on which, as the Poles believed, the fate of their constitution depended.

The Austrian cabinet also attached great importance to this negotiation, and they found themselves impelled by several other incidents to undertake immediate action in Polish affairs. In October the government at Warsaw, encouraged by Leopold's friendly attitude to abandon the reserve which it had been accustomed to maintain towards Austria, at last made a formal communication of the new constitution at Vienna, and requested the Emperor's good offices to secure for it the approval of the Court of St. Petersburg. About the same time the Elector turned to Leopold with a new appeal for advice.[1] The Austrians desired nothing so much as to see Frederick Augustus accept without further loss of time; but they hesitated to declare themselves openly at Dresden and Warsaw out of regard for Russia. Cobenzl's reports now left little hope that the Empress would ever give her approval to the work of the Third of May, and they pointed to the grave danger to the alliance, in case she adopted a policy towards Poland which would be accepted by Prussia, but rejected by Austria. And this was not the only peril ahead. The Empress and her ministers were storming for action against France, criticizing Leopold's conduct openly and bitterly, and praising Frederick William's. The spectre of a rapprochement between Prussia and Russia and the shipwreck of the alliance between the Imperial Courts haunted the minds of the ambassador and his superiors.[2]

In this delicate situation, in full realization of the danger of an estrangement from Russia, the cabinet of Vienna still decided to make a new attempt to save the Constitution of the Third of May. To this end they determined to bind the hands of

---

[1] Kaunitz to Leopold, November 25, V. A., *Vorträge*, 1791.
[2] L. Cobenzl's reports of October 4, 7, and 13, V. A., *Russland, Berichte*, 1791.

Prussia by turning the Convention of Vienna into a formal treaty of alliance as soon as possible,[1] to make a last effort to convert Russia to their views on Polish affairs, and to send a secret negotiator to Dresden to persuade the Elector to accept the crown at once.

As far as Prussia was concerned, the plan had somewhat the nature of a stratagem. Kaunitz was quite convinced that the internal consolidation of Poland was directly opposed to Prussian interests and was so regarded at Berlin; but he reckoned that Frederick William had so bound his own hands by his unlucky Polish policy of the past three years, by the assurances given to the Elector, and especially by the Convention of Vienna, that if Frederick Augustus would only accept the crown at once, and if the Convention were turned into a formal treaty, Prussia would not only have to consent, *bon gré mal gré*, to the establishment of the new order in Poland, but would even have to contribute to it.[2] Probably the Chancellor also reflected that it was important to cement the union with the Court of Berlin at once in order to prevent the latter from throwing itself into the arms of Russia and possibly coming to an agreement with Catherine on Polish affairs without the knowledge of Austria. Hence in their discussions with the Prussian·envoy the Imperial ministers emphasized the necessity of settling the Polish question by a concert of the three Courts, and avoided laying too much stress on the solution which they themselves preferred. There was no need to alarm

[1] That this decision to hasten the alliance with Prussia was not due to the exigencies of the French question, as is generally assumed, appears from the fact that the proposal was sent to Berlin along with the circular announcing the suspension of the concert on French affairs. In view of the fact that the new representations in favor of the Polish constitution were dispatched to St. Petersburg the same day (November 12), and that in general throughout November Austrian statesmen were preëminently occupied with this latter question, one may safely assume that it was the Polish crisis that led to the resumption of the negotiation for the alliance. Heidrich is, I think, the only writer who has remarked this (*Preussen im Kampfe gegen die französische Revolution*, pp. 29 f.).

Landriani's mission to Dresden was first formally proposed, it appears, in a report of Kaunitz to the Emperor of November 25, but one would judge from the Chancellor's note to Spielmann of November 2 that it had been practically a settled matter since the beginning of the month (V. A., *Vorträge*, 1791).

[2] Kaunitz's *Vortrag* of November 25, V. A.

the Prussians until the net was firmly fastened around them.[1] In accordance with the proposals made through Reuss, the preliminary discussion of the treaty of alliance was at once begun between Berlin and Vienna;[2] and although the delays inherent in such a method of negotiating and the pressure of other business prevented rapid progress, still Kaunitz could well be satisfied with this part of his program.

The new attack at St. Petersburg was launched through the voluminous instructions sent to Louis Cobenzl on November 12. In these notable dispatches Kaunitz urged that it was imperative for the Imperial Courts to define their attitude towards Poland at once, since in the present critical condition of the Republic further delay must result in the gravest dangers to the general tranquillity. He pointed out with some asperity that the Court of Vienna had communicated its views on Polish affairs as early as May, and had waited vainly for six months for a similar confidence from Russia. In the meantime it had been obliged to express itself in a general way regarding the new constitution to Prussia and to the Elector, and it could only assume that its declarations had not been displeasing to the Court of Petersburg, since otherwise the latter would have remonstrated. If the Empress, however, were now to adopt a policy towards Poland contrary to that to which she had allowed her ally to commit itself, the Court of Vienna would be placed in the most embarrassing position, and the world would draw the most unfortunate inferences as to the lack of harmony between the two allies. But the more he considered the

---

[1] In the face of such decisive documents as Kaunitz's *Vortrag* of November 25, the orders to L. Cobenzl of November 12, and the instructions to Landriani, the casual remarks of the Austrian ministers to Jacobi or the dubious surmises of the Saxon and Polish envoys have no great significance for the interpretation of Austrian policy on this question. Hence I cannot assent to Heigel's view (*op. cit.*, i, p. 490, note 2) that there was no great difference between the attitudes of Austria and Prussia regarding Poland at this time. Both were indeed agreed that a concert of the three neighboring Powers was necessary; but the concert that Prussia had in mind was one in which Russia should speak the decisive word against the new constitution, while that intended by the Austrians was to have no other business than to approve a *fait accompli* — the Elector's acceptance of the crown and the definitive establishment of the new régime in Poland.

[2] Orders to Reuss of November 12, his report of November 19, V. A., *Preussen, Exped.* and *Berichte*, 1791.

situation, Kaunitz continued, the more he was convinced that in this question the interests of both Courts were identical. Both were equally concerned, on the one hand, to shield the Republic from the Prussian lust for aggrandizement, and, on the other, to prevent it from becoming strong enough to endanger its neighbors. Neither Court could desire further acquisitions of territory in this quarter, since their frontiers were already so admirably rounded out. From this it followed that a new partition of Poland would redound only to the advantage of Prussia, and to the positive detriment of the Imperial Courts; that it was, indeed, necessary that the royal power should remain limited, and that the old republican spirit among the *szlachta* should not be allowed to die out; but that it was quite as important that Poland should cease to be the theatre of constant disturbances and a field always open to Prussian schemes of aggrandizement, as it had been under the old constitution. The new constitution was admirable in that it promised to make the Republic just strong enough, and not too strong. The change from an elective to a limited hereditary monarchy was especially commendable, not only because it would put an end to the periodical outbreaks of anarchy inseparable from ' free elections,' but also because from an hereditary sovereign the Imperial Courts could expect a more constant and sincere attachment than from any elected king, who was always sure to be blind to his own interests, or else powerless to follow them. Moreover, if Poland were not allowed a stronger monarchical government and a certain amount of reforms, it was to be feared that the French democratic principles would take root there, and Warsaw become a second Paris. All these considerations led, of course, to the conclusion that the Imperial Courts must at once declare themselves openly and clearly in favor of the Constitution of the Third of May.[1]

From the Austrian point of view, these dispatches were a masterpiece. The appeal to the old principles so long agreed upon between the Imperial Courts — the integrity of Poland, the danger of allowing Prussia further aggrandizement, the desirability

[1] The dispatches to L. Cobenzl of November 12 are printed in part in Vivenot, i, pp. 271–283.

of an Austro-Russo-Polish league; the appeals to the Empress' surviving resentment against Frederick William and to her new hatred for ' the French ideas '; the not unsuccessful attempt to demonstrate the innocuousness of the new constitution — these were the arguments, if any, which might have persuaded Catherine. But with all his belief in the power of his own dispatches, one must doubt whether Kaunitz cherished any great hope that the Empress would allow herself to be persuaded; and the fact that he took this decided step in spite of Louis Cobenzl's warnings shows how strongly he and Leopold desired to uphold the new order of things in Poland.

The third part of the November program, the mission to Dresden, was entrusted to the Chevalier Landriani, a clever Italian, half diplomat and half scientist, a confidant of the Emperor and a man favorably known at both the Saxon and the Polish courts.[1] Taking advantage of these connections, he was ordered to negotiate directly with the Elector or with the favorite Marcolini, avoiding the ill-disposed Saxon ministers as far as possible, and surrounding his actions with the utmost secrecy, so as not to compromise his Court with Russia or Prussia.   The confidential instruction made out for him is a document of much interest; for here, freed from the precautions and reticences necessary in communications to Berlin or St. Petersburg, Kaunitz lays bare the fundamental ideas and inmost wishes that guided the Polish policy of Austria at that time.[2] From it appears the Chancellor's strong conviction that the firm establishment of the new régime in Poland was peculiarly an Austrian interest, and an Austrian interest of the first magnitude.   He desired the consolidation of the new constitution because it would enable the Republic to free itself from all danger from, or dependence upon,

[1] Landriani was an intimate friend of the Elector's favorite Marcolini. He enjoyed the confidence of Stanislas Augustus to such a degree that the King several times tried to get him appointed Austrian minister at Warsaw.

[2] The voluminous *Instruction pour M. le Chevalier de Landriani*, V. A., F. A. 62, dated December 12, and the other papers relating to his mission have hitherto escaped the attention of the numerous investigators who have worked through this period in the Austrian archives.   Very interesting, too, is the *Vortrag* of Kaunitz to the Emperor of November 25, analyzed in Beer, *Leopold II, Franz II, und Catharina*, pp. 114–117.

either Russia or Prussia. He approved of the Saxon succession, because the Court of Dresden was always likely to be more devoted to Austria than to the other Powers.   Best of all, he thought, would be the establishment of a permanent personal union between Saxony and Poland, as Frederick Augustus desired; for there would thus be constituted a fairly strong state which would naturally seek the alliance of Austria, as the one neighbor with whom it had most in common, and from whom it had least to fear.   But Austrian interests also demanded that the revival of Poland should not be carried beyond a certain point; for if the Republic became strong enough to undertake aggressive enterprises, it might cast its eyes on Galicia.   Hence Kaunitz desired that the royal prerogatives should not be extended beyond the limits fixed by the new constitution.

In accordance with these general ideas, the primary object of Landriani's mission was to persuade the Elector to accept the Polish crown immediately.   That would place Russia and Prussia before a *fait accompli*, which they could not with good grace attempt to reverse.   In order to overcome the Elector's irresolution, the envoy was equipped with all manner of arguments, some of which did not bear the stamp of perfect sincerity.   For instance, he was to conceal, as far as possible, the fears entertained at Vienna as to the attitude of Russia, and to insinuate rather that the Empress was really not opposed to the new constitution; if she remained silent, it was only because the Turkish war prevented her from giving serious attention to the subject, or because the conduct of the present Diet towards her must naturally lead her to adopt a certain reserve.   Landriani was also charged to persuade the Elector to abandon his demand for further changes in the Polish constitution, on the ground that such changes would involve an unfortunate delay and could better be effected at some future time.   As for Frederick Augustus' desire to have the succession arranged in such a way as to ensure the permanent union of Poland and Saxony, the envoy was ordered to do what he could secretly to further the project, but without showing his hand openly.   There was a peculiar reason for this caution regarding a plan so warmly approved of at

Vienna. Prince Anton, the Elector's brother and prospective heir in Saxony, was Leopold's son-in-law. To have advocated openly the extension of the Saxon law of succession to Poland would have exposed the Emperor to the suspicion of working for personal and dynastic ends. Hence Leopold felt bound to display a reserve which led many people at that time, and has led many historians since, to conclude that he was averse to the projected union of Saxony and Poland.[1]

On his arrival at Dresden (December 18), Landriani found the negotiations between the Saxon ministers and the Polish commissioners already begun but not progressing. The Elector insisted on constitutional changes which the Poles professed themselves utterly unable to grant; and he was still determined not to accept the crown without the consent of all the neighboring Powers. Under such circumstances Landriani soon convinced himself that no amount of exhortations or arguments could extort the immediate acceptance which he had been sent to obtain. Nevertheless he threw himself with the greatest zeal into the task of smoothing out the difficulties between Frederick Augustus and the Poles over constitutional questions, and here he attained a fair measure of success. Largely through his intervention, it would seem, the Polish commissioners agreed to recommend at Warsaw the alteration of the law of succession, so as to ensure the permanent union of Poland and Saxony; and they were also induced to promise various extensions of the royal prerogatives in accordance with the Elector's wishes.[2] By the end of January matters seemed to be going forward so satisfactorily, the Elector appeared so eager to wear the crown and the Poles so ready to make concessions, that Landriani was at a high pitch of optimism. Given a fair amount of time, he was sure that Frederick Augustus would in the end accept.[3]

Meanwhile, the Austrian diplomat had been displaying a talent scarcely inferior to Lucchesini's for gaining the confidence of the Poles. The circles nearest to Stanislas Augustus came to

[1] See Appendix VII.

[2] Landriani's reports of December 30, January 9 and 14, February 22, V. A., F. A. 62.

[3] Reports of January 20 and February 4, V. A., F. A. 62.

base their hopes of success at Dresden on ' our Landriani,' ' the honest co-worker,' ' the Assisting Angel.' They were encouraged by him to dream of a quadruple alliance between Austria, Prussia, Poland, and Saxony, a league that should relegate Russia to the rank of an Asiatic Power. This glittering project was to be brought to realization by a new mission of Bischoffwerder to Dresden and Vienna and the coming of Landriani to Warsaw.[1] But while the Poles were building these air-castles and the Elector continued his interminable delays, the face of affairs had once more been changed through the revival of the danger from the west.

III

Since the end of November the war fever had been steadily rising at Paris. The exchange of notes then begun with the Austrian government, first on the subject of the *émigrés*, and then regarding Leopold's supposed counter-revolutionary plans, led only to embitterment on both sides. Early in December Louis XVI secretly addressed to the Powers an urgent plea for armed intervention. The danger of a French attack, the spread of ' Jacobin ideas ' in the Belgic provinces, the complaints made by Marie Antoinette at other Courts about her brother's inaction — all this combined to force Leopold and Kaunitz to resume in January, 1792, the plan for a concert of the Powers against the Revolution. They did not intend to venture forward a step without a general concert, and even if the concert came into being,

---

[1] The hold which Landriani soon won over the Poles is shown in the letters of Stanislas' confidant Piattoli at Warsaw to Mostowski at Dresden, in which the Austrian envoy is almost always referred to as *L'Ange Subsidiaire.* For a specimen of the tone of this correspondence one may take the passage in Piattoli's letter of February 3: " Depuis cette époque la condition de l'Ange Subsidiaire devenant celle d'un Esprit lumineux et brillant de toute sa clarté, il n'y a rien que nous ne devions attendre de son heureuse influence." (These curious letters are in the archive of Count Maurice Zamojski-Ordynat at Warsaw.)

As to the idea of the Quadruple Alliance, which aroused great hopes for a time at Warsaw and which was regarded as Leopold's ' own system ': Bulgakov's diary, January–March, *passim*, M. A., Польша, III, 66; Cassini to Popov, February 25 and March 3 (Imperial Public Library, Petrograd, Papers of V. S. Popov); Lucchesini's reports of January 7 and 11, B. A., *R.* 9, 27.

they were not inclined to undertake a complete restoration of the old régime in France, such as was preached so vehemently at Coblenz [1] and St. Petersburg. They hoped rather by mere demonstrations and threats to intimidate the National Assembly and so to procure for Louis XVI the conditions of a tolerable existence; in which event they would have been content to see France remain in a state of " fluctuation, internal weakness, and external nullity." [2]

The whole calculation about the concert was sufficiently erroneous; but it was a yet greater mistake that even before the enterprise was launched Kaunitz saw fit to read biting rebukes to the National Assembly and to admonish the French nation concerning its internal affairs in a manner that could only be taken as an insult at Paris.[3] Whether the great Revolutionary War might have been avoided is a question one need not assume to answer; but beyond a doubt the arrogant and challenging tone adopted by the Austrian government in this crisis greatly facilitated its outbreak. By his failure to understand the character and force of the Revolution, by his unhappy trust in the coercive power of his " strong declarations," Kaunitz was largely responsible for involving Austria in that disastrous struggle, which, apart from its consequences in the west, threw the Court of Vienna into dependence upon its rapacious allies, Russia and Prussia, and forced it to sacrifice Poland.[4]

The first result of the new crisis in Austro-French relations was an effort on the part of the Imperial cabinet to come to a thorough understanding with Prussia on all the pending questions. At the beginning of January, Reuss was sent a draft of the treaty of alliance, with full powers to conclude the matter and instruc-

---

[1] The headquarters of the French émigrés.

[2] From the proposals of the State Chancellery to the ministerial Conference, January 12, 1792, Vivenot, *op. cit.*, i, pp. 330–341.

[3] The Austrian notes of December 21, 1791, and February 17, 1792.

[4] The best characterizations of Austrian policy in this connection are, I think, those of Glagau (*Die französische Legislative und der Ursprung der Revolutionskriege*, ch. vi), and Lenz (" Marie Antoinette im Kampfe mit der Revolution," in *Preussische Jahrbücher*, lxxviii). See also: Ranke, *Ursprung und Beginn der Revolutionskriege*, pp. 128 ff.; Sybel, *op. cit.*, ii, pp. 32 ff.; Sorel, *op. cit.*, ii, pp. 342 ff.; Heigel, *op. cit.*, i, pp. 495 ff.

tions to hasten.[1] Towards the end of the month the proposals
for the concert on French affairs were dispatched to Berlin, with
the categorical inquiry whether the King was ready to accept the
Emperor's views and to offer military coöperation in case the
concert came into existence.[2] Throughout the month constant
discussions also went on between the two Courts regarding the
Polish question. The more pressing grew the danger on the west,
the more necessary Kaunitz found it to settle Polish affairs at
once. The more he became convinced that Russia was invincibly
opposed to the new constitution, the more anxiously he strove
to win Prussia to his principles before the Empress had time to
declare herself.

Prussia, however, regarded both the French and the Polish
questions from a standpoint very different from the Austrian one.
While the Imperial cabinet had only been driven perforce to
resume the plan for a concert of the Powers, and would always
have preferred to get off with mere declarations and demonstrations, Frederick William wanted to bring on a war. He consented readily to the Austrian proposals, but constantly urged
the necessity of agreeing at once on the military measures to be
employed to back up the joint declarations. The Austrian plan
for the concert reached Berlin on January 31, and five days later
the Duke of Brunswick had already been summoned to discuss
plans for a campaign. The only additional diplomatic step that
was suggested by Prussia was one that seemed specially designed
to make war inevitable. It was the demand that the French
government repress by the most vigorous measures the machinations of the society of the *Amis de la Constitution*, and of every
other association tending to propagate in other countries principles subversive of order and tranquillity.[3] When it appeared
that the Austrian ministry inclined more and more to a peaceful
course, Frederick William made one effort after another to spur
them on to action. The extreme importance of not letting ' the
democrats' think the two Courts feared a war, the urgent necessity

[1] Kaunitz to Reuss, January 4, 1792, Vivenot, i, pp. 305 ff.

[2] Kaunitz to Reuss, January 25, *ibid.*, i, pp. 344–350.

[3] The cabinet ministry to the King, February 3, B. A., *R.* 96, 147 *G.;* note
presented to Reuss, February 5, V. A., *Preussen, Berichte,* 1792.

of putting an end to the troubles in France, the dangerous spread of the infectious principles of ' insubordination and license,' the sad plight of the émigrés and the German princes dispossessed in Alsace — one sees that there were arguments enough in the repertory of Berlin.[1] But it was not these edifying reasons nor a purely sentimental zeal for ' the cause of all sovereigns,' that led the King of Prussia to labor so ardently to bring on a war. From the first moment when the enterprise against France appeared possible, Frederick William's dominant aim — the first and last word of his policy — was territorial aggrandizement.

The idea appeared, as we have seen, in September, 1790, and in July, 1791; and from January, 1792 onward it formed the invariable refrain of every Prussian communication on French affairs.[2] The ill-sounding word ' conquests ' was, indeed, avoided as far as possible; the Prussians preferred to speak of ' indemnities ' and ' compensation for the expenses of an intervention,' with the mental reservation that in view of the state of French finances such indemnities could be taken only in land. In response to a note from Berlin of January 13, the Austrian ministry had recognized the justice of the principle that the Powers which took part in an active intervention in France were entitled to compensation for their expenditures; and a confidential communication of the King's views was requested.[3] The Court of Berlin replied that the first step to be taken was to request a secret but formal promise from Louis XVI to repay the costs of the intervention; but that if such an engagement could not be obtained or fulfilled, the conquests which the allied Courts would probably make,

---

[1] Rescripts to Jacobi, February 6 and 9, B. A., *R.* 1, *Conv.* 169; instructions to Bischoffwerder of February 18, B. A., *R.* 1, *Conv.* 172; reports of Reuss, February, *passim.*

[2] One could hardly attempt to point out all the occasions when the claim for ' indemnities ' was brought forward on the Prussian side at this time. It will suffice here to refer to Frederick William's letter to Louis XVI of January 13, 1792; Schulenburg to Breteuil, January 13 and February 13; the notes presented to Reuss, January 13 and February 5; the rescripts to Jacobi of January 14 and to Goltz at St. Petersburg, February 10; Reuss' report of January 14, Alopeus' of January 9/20 and 11/22; the dispatch of Carisien accompanying the letter of Gustavus III to Fersen of February 6, in Klinckowström, *Le Comte de Fersen et la Cour de France*, ii, pp. 164 f.

[3] Kaunitz to Reuss, January 25, P. S. 3, Vivenot, i, p. 353.

would furnish the most natural means of compensation. The Prussians had, indeed, already entered into secret negotiations with Louis' agent Breteuil, who had not hesitated to promise reimbursement in money; but it is uncertain whether his master ever formally consented to the agreement.[1] The Austrians followed this example by making similar proposals to the King of France through Count Mercy; but the matter was so long delayed through the reluctance of the French royal family to commit themselves to a formal engagement, that before anything definite had been arranged, the intervening Powers had agreed upon a very different plan for their ' indemnities.' [2]

With regard to Poland, Frederick William's sentiments had changed greatly since the previous spring. In the early part of May, 1791, he had openly expressed warm approval of the new constitution; at the end of the month he was still not against it; but when, at the beginning of June, he learned that no effective aid was to be expected from England in the Eastern crisis, his attitude towards Poland began to alter immediately. Having now renounced the policy of opposition to Russia, he no longer saw any reason for seeking the friendship of the Republic. One of the first signs of the change was a rescript to Goltz of June 10, 1791, in which the King prophesied that the Empress would never approve the Constitution of the Third of May, and ordered the envoy to take care not to rebuff the Russian ministers if they should make any friendly overtures on that topic.[3] As the Poles saw the storm gathering in the east, they made repeated efforts to induce Frederick William to promise his support in case of a Russian attack. But henceforth the constant tenor of every Prussian declaration at Warsaw was that the King, while remaining loyal to the engagements contained in the alliance treaty, was in no way bound to guarantee or defend a constitution established without his knowledge and subsequent to the conclusion of the alliance. The Poles — to their great misfortune — continued

[1] Details in Flammermont, *Négociations secrètes de Louis XVI et du Baron de Breteuil avec la Cour de Berlin.*

[2] Kaunitz to Mercy, February 19, Mercy to Kaunitz, February 29, March 13, April 17, and 23, V. A., *Frankreich, F.* 261.

[3] Salomon, *Das politische System des jüngeren Pitt*, p. 64.

to cherish some hopes of Prussian support, partly because they imagined that the language of the Berlin ministry did not represent the King's true sentiments, partly because Lucchesini, now returned to Warsaw, exhibited himself as such a Proteus among diplomats that it was difficult to tell exactly what he was charged to say;[1] but these hopes were built on sand. It was now the fixed policy at Berlin to remain entirely passive in Polish affairs until, as was confidently expected, Russia should come out in opposition to the new constitution. The opportunity would then be given to a form a concert of the three neighboring Powers, which would overthrow the hereditary succession and the other dangerous innovations of the Third of May, and would restore the Republic to a becoming state of nullity. Exactly how this beneficent work was to be accomplished was not yet certain; but one may suspect that Schulenburg disclosed his master's *arrière-pensée*, when in August (1791) he prophesied to the English envoy a new partition of Poland.[2]

It was favorable to the success of such plans that the relations between Berlin and St. Petersburg were slowly improving. The estrangement produced by the Eastern crisis lingered, indeed, throughout the summer of 1791. Frederick William was determined not to take the first step towards a reconciliation with the Empress; and as late as September she betrayed her surviving resentment by revelling in sarcasms at his expense.[3] It was French affairs that gave the first impetus to a rapprochement, the earliest sign of which was the letter addressed by Catherine to Frederick William about the middle of October. This encouraged

---

[1] Lucchesini's dispatches are full of solemn assurances that his language conformed exactly to his instructions; but the reports of the Russian, Austrian, and Saxon envoys combine to show that his utterances varied amazingly from day to day. At one moment, he would be insinuating that all the neighbors of the Republic were about to unite against it; at another, he would be firing the Poles with hopes for the formation of a quadruple alliance in their defence. Bulgakov wrote in his diary (December 6/17, 1791): " This Lucchesini in one and the same room tells five people five different tales, and when he is caught contradicting what he has just told someone else, he excuses himself with the plea: ' Qu'il faut parler à chacun selon sa portée, mais le vrai est ce que je vous dis.' " M. A., Польша, III, 66.

[2] Ewart's report of August 4, Herrmann, *Ergänzungsband*, p. 72.

[3] Rescript to Goltz of August 27, in Salomon, *op. cit.*, p. 66, note 1. Cobenzl's reports of September 2, 6, 13, V. A., *Russland, Berichte*, 1791.

the Prussians to make counter-advances. At the end of the month Bischoffwerder suggested to Alopeus that as it might be repugnant to the Empress to accede to the future Austro-Prussian alliance, it would depend only upon her to conclude a separate alliance directly with the King.[1] In December the royal favorite returned to the charge. He regretted, he said, that the alliance with Russia could not precede that with Austria; but, at any rate, it would be better to abandon all idea of a mere accession, and to arrange a treaty directly between their two Courts. He would be delighted to go to St. Petersburg and negotiate it himself, if Alopeus would only propose that to the Prussian ministry as his own idea.[2] These insinuations produced no direct response from St. Petersburg; but still by the close of the year Goltz, the Prussian envoy, began to find himself treated with more consideration: the Empress spoke to him for the first time; the Grand Duke knew him again.[3] As far as the delicate subject of Poland was concerned, Schulenburg did his utmost by hints and sarcastic comments to show Alopeus that the King was hostile to the new constitution, and Bischoffwerder repeatedly asked that envoy directly what his Court thought about Polish affairs.[4] Russia remained absolutely silent on that question, but the Prussians were not discouraged. When the Empress finally got ready to speak, they were sure that an agreement between the two Powers would come of itself.

Under such circumstances, Kaunitz's attempt to win over the Court of Berlin to his Polish policy was doomed to failure. In their note of January 13, the Prussian ministry urged that while the King, like the Emperor, was far from wishing to oppose the new constitution or the succession of the Elector, still it would be a very delicate matter to take any steps in this affair until the sentiments of Russia were known; and that while the Court of Vienna seemed to regard the separate article of the July Conven-

---

[1] Alopeus' report of October 19/30, M. A., Пpycciя, III, 27.

[2] Alopeus to Bezborodko, December 12/23, M. A., Пpycciя, III, 26.

[3] Cf. Heidrich, *Preussen im Kampfe gegen die französische Revolution*, p. 173.

[4] Alopeus' reports of November 15/26, November 22/December 3, December 16/27, January 17/28, February 3/14, and 10/21, M. A., Пpycciя, III, 27 and 29.

tion as referring specifically to the Constitution of the Third of May, they had always understood it to refer only to any free constitution, i. e., one not imposed by any foreign Power. Hence they desired to avoid ambiguities by omitting from the treaty of alliance all mention of the constitution of Poland and promising to maintain only " the liberty and independence of that Kingdom."

The ominous significance of the proposed change was quite appreciated at Vienna. But immediately after the Prussian note there arrived still more exasperating communications from St. Petersburg. The Empress had seen fit to read Leopold a new and impertinent lecture on his slackness in French affairs, and to propose a plan of action which only showed how little she understood the situation or troubled herself about the interests of her ally. The indignation of the Austrians was increased by the fact that these dispatches did not contain the long and anxiously awaited response on Polish affairs, but only a request that the Emperor would take no step regarding them 'which might hinder the freedom of the future joint deliberations.' ' The delay,' it was added, ' was not only without inconvenience, but even necessary in view of the confusion and irresolution still prevailing in the minds of the Poles regarding the delicate and important innovations which had been and were still being introduced.' [1] The inference to be drawn from this was only too obvious. Putting it alongside the answer received from Berlin, the Austrians found themselves in danger of being isolated on the Polish question. What the result of an agreement between Russia and Prussia on that subject would be, seemed equally clear. It would be a new partition. Doubtless under other circumstances the Court of Vienna would have tried to avoid such a disaster by reverting to its old policy of 1781, by giving Russia a free hand in Poland, providing she agreed to keep the Prussians out. But now the danger from France rendered the friendship of Prussia all-important; and moreover, the Austrians were so indignant against their old ally that they began to regard the restoration of Russia's exclusive predominance in Poland as among the worst of evils. Hence they fell back on the concert with Prussia, in the vain hope

[1] Ostermann to Golitsyn, December 25/January 5, M. A., Австрія, III, 51.

that eloquent exhortations and small concessions might induce Frederick William to oppose Catherine's projects and thereby to deprive himself of the chance to gain a long-sought acquisition. In the dispatches of January 25, Reuss was authorized to give way on the article relating to Poland; but at the same time in an ostensible postscript Kaunitz earnestly and forcibly pointed out how dangerous it would be to the new friendship of the two Courts, how inconsistent with the whole spirit of their alliance, if Prussia were now to embark upon schemes for violent aggrandizement at the expense of the Republic.[1] The Chancellor's warnings were only too well grounded. Without throwing the entire blame for what followed upon Prussia, one may still surmise that many later disasters might have been avoided, and especially that the great contest with revolutionary France might have taken a very different turn, if the Court of Berlin could only have brought itself to postpone the realization of its designs on Poland to a more propitious time. But Kaunitz's admonitions fell on deaf ears at Berlin.

At any rate, the difficulty about the treaty of alliance was now removed. It was agreed that the article respecting Poland should pledge the two Courts " to undertake nothing contrary to the maintenance of *a* free constitution " in that country, in place of the old phrase which referred to " *the* free constitution." It was a change of but a single word, but it indicated the momentous alteration that had come about in the Polish policy of Prussia since the previous summer. In other respects the treaty conformed in substance to the Vienna Convention of July 25, while in form it was modeled — significantly enough — after the Treaty of Versailles of 1756. With its signature at Berlin on February 7, 1792, the Austro-Prussian alliance was at last an accomplished fact.[2]

---

[1] These dispatches are printed in Vivenot, i, pp. 353, 358 ff.

[2] The treaty is printed in Neumann, *Recueil*, i, pp. 470–475; Martens, *Recueil de Traités des Puissances de l'Europe*, v, pp. 301–305; the secret articles in Vivenot, i, pp. 370 f.

IV

In accordance with the wish expressed by the Emperor early in January, it had already been agreed that Bischoffwerder should undertake a new mission to Vienna to arrange the measures to be adopted against France. On February 16 a conference was held at Potsdam, at which the King, the Duke of Brunswick, Bischoffwerder, Schulenburg, and Manstein were present, to decide upon a plan of campaign. It appears, however, that other matters were also discussed, and that a new project of the utmost importance was broached here, perhaps for the first time. The day before, a courier had arrived from St. Petersburg with news that must have seemed to the Prussians like the opening of the heavens.

Goltz reported that through a secret channel he had learned the contents of a note from the Empress to her favorite, Zubov, in which she declared: " After all has been arranged with the Turks, I wish Prince Repnin to go to the main army, collect as many troops as he can — which, according to my calculation, will amount to 130,000 men — and with them march by way of the Ukraine into Poland. If Austria and Prussia oppose, as is probable, I shall propose to them either compensation or partition." [1]

This was the first definite information about the Empress' plans that had reached Berlin; and no news could have been more welcome. Immediately the idea was brought forward at the Potsdam conference of combining the settlement of Polish affairs with the French enterprise, in the way that Prussia should take her ' indemnities ' for the expense of the intervention in the west by wrenching territory from her unfortunate eastern neighbor. Nothing final was decided upon; nothing could be until the intentions of Russia were more fully known; but one may safely assert that from the middle of February on, from the moment when the first favorable news arrived from St. Petersburg, the

---

[1] Goltz's report of February 3, printed in Herrmann, *Ergänzungsband*, pp. 231 f. See Appendix VIII.

Prussians were hoping and planning for a new partition of Poland, for which the intervention in France might perhaps furnish the pretext.[1]

The first result of the Potsdam deliberations was that a few days later Bischoffwerder visited Alopeus and, drawing the conversation upon Poland, assured him that the King was not in the least inclined to support the new constitution, but that he regarded any ' explosion ' in the Republic as dangerous, as long as French affairs were not terminated.[2]   Although Bischoffwerder's subtlety was lost on the Russian, the aim of this hint seems clear enough.   If the Empress was ready to propose a partition, in case the other Powers offered opposition to the execution of her plan — very well: the Prussians would offer such an appearance of opposition as would not deter her from her essential aim, but would lead her to take them into partnership.

The effect of the news from St. Petersburg is also seen in the instructions drawn up for Bischoffwerder's mission to Vienna. The article regarding Poland contained first of all the usual protestations that the King's engagements with the Republic were in no sense applicable to the new constitution, and that he intended to act in the most perfect harmony with the Emperor on Polish affairs.   It was denied that there had been any discussions

---

[1] We have very few documents through which to trace these developments of February.   My account is based chiefly on the Duke of Brunswick's letter to Bischoffwerder of February 19: " Die Entschädigungs-Angelegenheit wird grosse Verlegenheit herbeiführen, wenn man den Kaiser nicht vermögen kann, seine Einwilligung zu den Veränderungen in Polen zu geben.   Ich gebe den Erwerbungen, die man in Polen zu machen hofft, den Vorzug vor den Eroberungen in Frankreich. . . . Alles kömmt darauf an, dass man sich mit dem Kaiser erkläre." (Translation from the French in Massenbach, *Memoiren*, i, p. 267.)   Since Goltz's dispatch came February 15, and the Potsdam conference took place the 16th, while the Duke of Brunswick arrived from his capital that morning, departed homeward that evening, and wrote the letter to Bischoffwerder almost immediately after his return, it may safely be presumed that he learned of the " Erwerbungen die man in Polen zu machen hofft " during the discussions at Potsdam.   His championship of the idea of a new partition of Poland is referred to in a letter from the King to Bischoffwerder of March 14: " Il paroit que les vues de l'Impératrice touchant la Pologne pourroit [sic] amener l'évènement que le Duc de Bronsviq souhaite de voir arriver et dont il parle dans la lettre que je Vous envoyé [sic] à Dresde," B. A., *R.* 1, *Conv.* 172.

[2] Alopeus' report of February 10/21, M. A., Пруссія, III, 29.

on the subject between Russia and Prussia, and especially that the Empress had made any overtures about projects of aggrandizement in Poland, " although," it was added, " one doubtless cannot guarantee that this sovereign may not have plans of that kind." If the King received any hints on that topic from Russia, he would not fail to communicate them frankly to the Emperor, in the conviction that in a similar case the Court of Vienna would act in the same way towards him. "These cordial assurances," it was said, " will furnish General Bischoffwerder the most natural occasion to convince the Imperial Court that . . . in order to obtain in full the advantages which the union happily existing [between the two Courts] ought to procure them, it is essential that the most unlimited confidence in one another should animate both in all that concerns their respective interests; and that they should thus from the beginning remove by frank and amicable explanations all that might later sow distrust between them and alter their complete harmony." These words were not merely conventional expressions of loyalty and confidence towards an ally. They were a direct reply to Kaunitz's recent warning that the friendship between the two Courts would be exposed to grave peril, if Prussia entered upon plans for aggrandizement in Poland. They were designed to pave the way for an understanding on the basis of a partition, as soon as Russia had uttered the expected word.

It may at first sight appear a contradiction to that which has just been said, that in the article of the instruction which dealt with the subject of ' indemnities,' the old plan — Alsace and Lorraine for Austria, Juliers and Berg for Prussia — was once more recommended. Probably this was because it seemed necessary to keep up the claim for an acquisition in the West as long as the prospects for making one in the East were still uncertain. Furthermore, the Prussian ministry could hardly have wished to disclose their hand to Austria too fully until Russia had spoken. But, to all appearances, they no longer entertained serious plans for a dismemberment of France. Bischoffwerder seems to have displayed little zeal for that project while in Vienna; and at the end of February Louis XVI's agent at Berlin was joyfully reporting that there was no more talk of demanding a territorial indemnity from his master.[1]

Charged with these equivocal instructions respecting Poland, which showed that Prussia was veering further and further away from the Austrian standpoint on that question, Bischoffwerder was also the bearer of proposals regarding the French problem that were but little in harmony with the Emperor's wishes. The main object of his mission was, indeed, to shake the Imperial cabinet out of its too pacific temper, to inveigle Leopold into armed intervention in France, and to arrange the plan of campaign.[2]

Bischoffwerder arrived in the Austrian capital on February 28; but this time he was not to see that Imperial friend who had so charmingly received him and smilingly outwitted him on his two previous visits. At this crucial moment, when both the long-gathering storms were about to burst in East and West, when an experienced hand was needed more than ever at the helm, Leopold II died suddenly, after an illness of only three days (March 1, 1792). His death was an irremediable loss to Austria, and perhaps to Europe. Whether he could have carried on with success the struggle against revolutionary France must remain uncertain; but he was assuredly the one sovereign of that time least unfitted for that task. Quite certainly he could not have averted the Russian attack on Poland, but he might, not improbably, have prevented a new partition.

It is true that at the close of Leopold's reign his own Polish policy was crumbling. His effort to hold Prussia firm in defence of the new constitution had failed. Fruitless, too, had been his

---

[1] Cf. Fersen to Gustavus III, February 29, and the directly contrary opinion held at the beginning of that month, Gustavus to Fersen, February 6, Klinckowström, *op. cit.*, ii, pp. 182 and 165.

[2] Stripped of its verbiage, the first article of his instruction certainly means this. and nothing else. Compare Carisien's report in Taube, *Svenska Beskickningars Berättelser*, pp. 95 f.; Fersen to Gustavus III, March 4, 1792, Klinckowström, *op. cit.*, ii, p. 193; Alopeus' report of February 10/21, M. A., Пруссія, III, 29. Bichoffwerder himself speaks of " le parti vigoureux que j'ai a proposer " (Report of February 29, B. A., *R.* 1, *Conv.* 172).

Bischoffwerder's instructions are printed in Ranke, *Ursprung und Beginn der Revolutionskriege*, pp. 351–359.

attempt to extort a quick acceptance of the crown from the Elector. At the beginning of March the interminable negotiation at Dresden still dragged on — or rather it was about to be transferred to Warsaw — with no prospects of an immediate decision. War with France was now very nearly inevitable; and in that case Austria would necessarily be quite unable to assert her voice effectively in Polish affairs. Above all, Catherine had at last spoken. At the time of the Emperor's death couriers were speeding westward from St. Petersburg with news that confirmed well-nigh all that was hoped at Berlin and all that was feared at Vienna. That pronouncement from Russia was the ruin of Leopold's Polish system. It may, indeed, be doubted whether his policy in this connection did any good either to Austria or to the Republic. On the one hand, it had deeply offended Catherine, weakened the alliance of the Imperial Courts, and contributed to the rapprochement between Berlin and St. Petersburg; and on the other hand, it had lulled the Poles with false hopes of support from without, which led them sadly to neglect their own preparations for self-defence. It won Leopold golden opinions only at Warsaw.

At the end of his reign the Emperor enjoyed a popularity among the Poles such as the Court of Vienna had not possessed for many years. This was due in part to his mild treatment of his Galician subjects; to the often very exaggerated reports spread at Warsaw about the provisions in favor of Poland contained in the July Convention and the February treaty of alliance; possibly to certain assurances sent from Vienna through secret channels; [1] but above all, to the general confidence felt in the Emperor's love of peace, justice, and moderation, and to the indefatigable activity of Landriani. Leopold had come to occupy much the same position in the minds of the Poles as had once been held by Frederick William.[2] They relied on his beneficent influence at Dresden and

[1] Bulgakov, reporting to the Empress the causes of Leopold's popularity at Warsaw, claimed to know on good authority that a secret correspondence went on between the Emperor and the King of Poland through Corticelli, the former Polish minister at Vienna, Spielmann, and Manfredini (another confidant of Leopold's). Report of March 6/17, M. A., Польша, III, 66.

[2] Lucchesini's report of March 11, 1792: "Léopold II et le Chevalier Lan-

Berlin; and on him many of them based their hopes of security against Russia. It was reported that he intended to build up a quadruple alliance of Austria, Prussia, Poland, and Saxony. " His political system," it was said in the patriotic conventicles at Warsaw " was to establish the general tranquillity on a permanent basis, and to exclude Russia from the circle of European states." Nowhere was his death more regretted than at Warsaw. People declared that the nation had lost its friend, its powerful protector, its support.[1] And in truth the nation had lost the one foreign sovereign who had done his best to uphold the work of the Third of May, and who was sincerely well-disposed towards Poland.

driani avoient hérité de la confiance qu'on avoit cidevant placé en Votre Majesté et moi," B. A., R. 9, 27.

[1] For the above: Bulgakov's report to the Empress of March 6/17, M. A., Польша, III, 66; Lucchesini's reports of January 7 and 11, February 22, March 7, B. A., R. 9, 27; de Caché's of March 10 and 14, V. A., *Polen, Berichte*, 1792.

CHAPTER XI

The Outbreak of War in East and West

I

At the time of Catherine's first Turkish war, Sweden had seized the opportunity to free itself from her grasp by the revolution of 1772, which had reformed a constitution almost as vicious as the Polish one, concentrated the power of the state in the hands of the monarch, and closed the door to further foreign interference. Catherine had not seen fit to go to war about it. During her second conflict with the Turks, Poland had tried to do precisely the same thing as the Swedes had done, by means of a *coup d'état* consciously modeled upon that of Gustavus III. At the close of the Oriental crisis, it was long believed at Warsaw that the Empress would ultimately bow to the accomplished fact, as she had done in the case of Sweden. She might sulk, she might intrigue, she might even make demonstrations on the frontier, but it was not thought probable that she would go further. An attempt to reimpose the Russian yoke by force seemed scarcely likely to be tolerated by the German Powers, one of whom was now the warm friend of Poland, and the other its ally, pledged to defend its independence. Moreover, how could the Empress consistently attack the Poles for having established a monarchical form of government, at a time when she was preaching to all sovereigns the necessity of taking up the sacred cause of monarchy in France ? How could she face the odium of going to war with her neighbors simply because they wished to reform their institutions; of overthrowing by force of arms a constitution which the whole nation, with few exceptions, had gladly accepted, and which had received the applause of all Europe ? Nevertheless, as soon as her peace with the Turks was signed, Catherine proceeded to undertake precisely this graceless task; and one hardly knows whether to wonder the more at the unscrupulousness or at the skill with which the enterprise was carried out.

Although for nearly three years the Empress had maintained an outwardly passive attitude and an ostentatious show of indifference towards Poland, she seems never for a moment to have wavered in the determination not to permit that country to escape permanently from her control. Vindictiveness for the slights and injuries inflicted upon her during the Turkish war may have had some part in influencing her resolution; but she was, undoubtedly, guided chiefly by the firm conviction that the vital interests of her Empire and all the traditions of Russian policy required that Poland should be kept under its old republican constitution and in its old state of perfect impotence. The Poles might fret and strut, they might inveigh against her and intrigue with her enemies, they might make and mar their institutions to suit their fancy for the present; but they should pay for it in the end. Her time for action would come as soon as the Turks were off her hands; and the program, marked out long in advance, was a Confederation under Russian auspices.[1]

All hopes that the nation would of its own accord return to the side of its ancient protector were shattered by the events of the Third of May. Catherine was furious at the news. ' The Poles had outdone all the follies of the Parisian National Assembly,' she wrote to Grimm; ' they must indeed be possessed of devils to act in a manner so contrary to their own interests and to the very conditions of their existence.' The morning after the tidings arrived, she informed Bezborodko: "The question now is whether Poland wishes to be ruled by the mob of Warsaw. If we see the slightest inclination for a Counter-confederation, we must bring one about without further delay. There you have my opinion." [2] The Council of the Empire, when asked for its advice, replied that the new form of government, if once firmly established, could only prove harmful to the neighboring Powers, and especially to Russia; but that as long as it was uncertain whether the King of Prussia had had a hand in the revolution, and as long as the Turkish war lasted, it was impossible to decide upon any

[1] One of her earliest definite utterances on the subject is in the letter to Potemkin of September 30/October 11, 1790: "When God grants peace, then we shall form a Counter-confederation," etc., Сборникъ, xlii, p. 110.

[2] To Grimm, Сборникъ, xxiii, pp. 534 f.; to Bezborodko, ibid., xlii, p. 152.

course of action.[1] After the first flush of anger was over, the Empress too came around to this standpoint. Orders were accordingly sent to Bulgakov, her envoy at Warsaw, to continue the same passive conduct as before, but in private to assure the friends of freedom — if such there still were — that Russia would always be ready to help them recover their liberty, as soon as they showed a desire for it not only by words but by deeds.[2] Henceforth it was the Empress' first and foremost aim to overthrow this thoroughly obnoxious constitution. Henceforth she had a tolerable pretext for action, inasmuch as she had by the treaties of 1768 and 1775 guaranteed to the Republic its old form of government. Henceforth if her aid were invoked, she could color her intervention before the world by the plea that she was legally and morally bound to defend the ' liberty ' of Poland, and that she could not refuse to succor the allied nation now groaning under a ' despotism ' imposed by conspiracy, fraud, and violence.

Determined as the Empress was to act with vigor when the proper time came, it was difficult for her to satisfy Potemkin. It has already been noted that that restless schemer had come to the capital in the spring of 1791 to press his own aggressive projects against the Republic. As usual, he had several irons in the fire. The favorite plan was still that of raising an Orthodox rebellion in the Ukraine and robbing Poland of its richest provinces; but he also talked at times of a new partition on a gigantic scale, and again he urged the immediate formation of a Confederation among the Poles themselves. For this last plan he hoped to find a ready instrument in his friend Felix Potocki, and a pretext in the revolution of the Third of May. These projects did not entirely square with those of his sovereign. Catherine had always regarded the Ukraine scheme with misgivings; if she approved of the idea of a Counter-confederation, she did not mean to be rushed into the enterprise precipitately; and she apparently felt at this time a growing distrust regarding Potemkin's dreams of personal aggrandizement. Moreover, she was vexed with him because of his hostility to the reigning favorite Zubov, and be-

[1] Protocol of May 12/23, Apx. Гос. Сов., i, p. 853.
[2] Rescript to Bulgakov, May 25/June 5, M. A., Польша, III, 63.

cause of his interminable delay about returning to the army.   It was probably mainly in order to get rid of him that at the end of May she gave him a secret rescript once more approving in general terms his plan of the preceding year for the seizure of the Ukraine, but limiting its execution by so many conditions as to render the concession quite illusory.   On the other hand, the project of forming a Confederation was sanctioned, and the Prince was directed to work out the scheme in detail.

Shortly afterwards Potemkin received a letter from Felix Potocki containing quite definite proposals for a Confederation to be formed in the southeastern palatinates under Russian protection for the overthrow of the new constitution.[1]   Armed with this, the Prince returned to the charge; and after long delays he secured one more ' most secret rescript,' this time of a less fictitious and more satisfactory character than the preceding one. It was true that the execution of the Ukraine project was again relegated to the dim future; but the plan for a Confederation was approved in terms that showed the Empress resolved to proceed with that in earnest.   Potemkin was authorized to invite Potocki and the other leading Polish malcontents to his headquarters; to assure them of Russia's most efficacious aid and protection; and to settle with them the details of the future undertaking, subject to the Empress' approval.   If they insisted on forming their Confederation at once, Catherine was willing to begin action immediately; but she preferred to postpone her intervention until after the peace with the Turks, which at that time — the end of July, after the complete backdown of the Triple Alliance and Repnin's brilliant victory at Mačin — seemed to be very close at hand.   The return of the Russian armies from Moldavia through Poland would then afford the best opportunity to strike the great blow.   While outlining with remarkable foresight the means and methods to be employed, Catherine also showed herself fully conscious of the momentous consequences of the enterprise on which she was embarking.   " It is difficult now," she

---

[1] Potocki to Potemkin, May 14, 1791, M. A., Польша, II, 7.   Appendix IX contains the text of this letter, of which only the existence has hitherto been known, and to which may be traced the origins of the Confederation of Targowica.

wrote, " to predict the end to which this policy will lead; but if with the aid of the Almighty it is crowned with success, two advantages may result for us. In the one case, we shall be able to overthrow the present constitution and to restore the old Polish liberty; and thereby we shall gain complete security for our Empire for all time. Or in case the King of Prussia should display an invincible covetousness, we shall find ourselves obliged, in order to put an end to these troubles and disturbances once for all, to agree to a new partition of Poland in favor of the three allied Powers. From this there will result the advantage that we shall extend the boundaries of our Empire, augment by so much its security, and win new subjects of the same faith and blood as ourselves. Poland, on the other hand, will be reduced to such limits that whatever be the strength of its government, it can offer no dangers to the neighboring Powers, and will form only a sort of barrier between them." [1]

Potemkin, however, was not to reap the fruits of all these years of planning and intriguing. He left St. Petersburg at the beginning of August sullen and depressed, and died in Moldavia two months later — the victim of a fever, due to the effects of an ill-regulated life, and perhaps to the chagrins occasioned by his last stay at court. Unfortunately, his death was not to be the end of his oft-confirmed and much delayed plans.

II

Deprived of a helper who towards the last had become a trifle burdensome, the Empress now took Polish affairs more directly

---

[1] The two famous rescripts to Potemkin of May 16/27 and July 18/29, 1791, are printed in the Рус. Арх., 1874, ii, pp. 246–258, 281–289; also by Kalinka in Polish translation in his " Polityka dworu austryackiego," in *Przegląd Polski*, 1873, pp. 82–85, 88–92; and by Liske in German in *H. Z.*, xxx, pp. 286–301. On Potemkin's shaken position at court at the time of his last visit to St. Petersburg, see: Русская Старина, xiv, pp. 241 ff.; Державинъ, Записки, pp. 304–308; Брикнеръ, Потемкинъ, pp. 194 ff. In view of the rather strained relations then existing between the Empress and the Prince, Askenazy seems inclined to deny to both rescripts any importance as an expression of Catherine's real intentions (*Przymierze polsko-pruskie*, pp. 162 f.). I should agree that the first rescript was very much of a sham; but that the second was not appears — best of all — from the fact that almost every plan there announced was duly carried out the next year.

into her own hands, with her usual vigor and with a sureness in the choice of persons, means, and occasions that has rarely been surpassed. The fiery ardor with which she preached the counter-revolution in France to Austria, Prussia, and Sweden, her well-calculated and nicely measured rapprochement to the Court of Berlin, her masterly silence towards Vienna on the Polish ques-tion — all this was designed only to secure her a free hand in the Republic. If she had originally planned to take the Emperor into her confidence,[1] she soon abandoned the idea. Kaunitz's efforts on behalf of the new Polish constitution threw her into transports of rage, while the Emperor's slackness in French affairs aroused her far from disinterested indignation. By the end of the year she and all the Russians in chorus after her were coming to declaim on every occasion that Leopold II was a timid, nay a craven, prince, whose soul knew naught of honor or dignity or magnanimity or any other of the virtues that were supposed to characterize peculiarly the Court of Petersburg. That meant that the Emperor had presumed to have an opinion of his own on both the French and the Polish questions — an unpardonable offence in an ally of the great Catherine. She was coming to see in him the main obstacle to the realization of her plans. But, far from being daunted, she insisted all the more vigorously on going ahead with the Polish project, regardless of the wishes of Austria and Prussia. " I inform the members of the College of Foreign Affairs," she wrote in December, " that we can do everything that we please in Poland, and the contradictory *demi-volontés* of the Courts of Vienna and Berlin will oppose us only with a stack of paper objections, and we shall settle our affairs in Poland ourselves. I am hostile only to those who try to intimidate me. Catherine II has often made her enemies tremble, but I have not heard that Leopold's foes have ever feared him." [2] When one of her ministers objected that nothing should be done until they had built up a party in Poland and made at least some overtures to the German Powers, she wrote: " But I say that we

---

[1] See the above-cited rescripts to Potemkin, especially that of July 18/29.

[2] Notes written à propos of Kaunitz's dispatches to Cobenzl of November 12, 1791, P. A., X, 75.

do not have to utter a word to the other Courts; and a party will always be found when it is needed. It is impossible that there should not be people who prefer the old order. Volhynia and Podolia offer many different pretexts; one has only to choose." [1]

The party, or the nucleus of one, had, indeed, already been found. The two most prominent of the Polish malcontents, Felix Potocki and Seweryn Rzewuski, had come to Jassy at Potemkin's invitation in the middle of October, precisely at the moment of the Prince's death; and they were followed shortly after by another promising recruit, the Crown Hetman Branicki. These three men, under Catherine, were to be the main authors of the Confederation of Targowica. In them the worst vices of Old Poland stand incorporated. Enormously rich, able to count his villages by the score and his ' subjects ' by the thousand, accustomed to live in truly royal magnificence, Potocki represents the typical provincial kinglet, who could brook no superior, no restriction, no abridgment of golden liberty. Honest and well-meaning, perhaps, and virtuous according to his lights, he was also narrow-minded and obstinate, and consumed by pride and vanity. Capable of seeing but one idea at a time, he was now obsessed by the thought that the glorified Republic of his ancestors was doomed to perish, overthrown by ' despotism,' unless he, the one blameless man, could save it — with the aid of foreign bayonets. Rzewuski, Field-Hetman of the Crown, was the best head in this group of reactionaries. He had always posed as the argus-eyed guardian of liberty, the model of republican virtue, the Cato of Poland; and of a Cato he had at least all the unlovely qualities. Branicki was simply the dashing adventurer, a rioter and a brawler, gifted indeed with many of the arts that command popularity, but guided solely by private interest, regardless of loyalty, patriotism or duty — a man whose life was a succession

---

[1] Catherine to Bezborodko, December 4/15, printed in the Сборникъ, xxix, pp. 176 f., and Solov'ev, *Geschichte des Falles von Polen*, p. 265. The German translator of Solov'ev has erroneously, I think, rendered the first part of the last sentence: " Volhynien und Podolien zu nehmen, sind Vorwände genug vorhanden." If this version were correct, it would indicate that the Empress had already decided upon a partition. But the Russian text printed in the Сборникъ gives little warrant for such a translation.

of treasons. Doubtless these magnates had no conception of the ruin they were bringing upon their country. Morally they were no worse than those princes and gentlemen of France who at this same time were inviting all Europe to arms against their fatherland. But never did traitors leave behind them so terrible a monument as did the men of Targowica. In Polish history their names are branded with infamy.

Count Bezborodko, sent down by Catherine after Potemkin's death to conduct the peace negotiations with the Turks, was also authorized to assure the Polish leaders of the Empress' favor and protection, and to receive their plans and proposals. In the conferences held at Jassy from November to February, the main points of the enterprise were discussed at length, although the final decisions were left to be made at St. Petersburg. After the usual fashion of émigrés, the Polish magnates were lavish with assurances that the great mass of their countrymen were on their side; it was only the terrorism of the dominant ' faction ' at Warsaw that prevented the nation from manifesting its true sentiments. " A single spark would suffice to set the whole country ablaze; thousands and thousands of adherents would rally to the good cause at the first opportunity." Still, when they were called upon to name men of prominence whose support might be relied upon, the magnates could scarcely indicate a dozen; and they had to confess that it would require at least 100,000 Russian troops to enable the country to express its real opinions. They proposed, however, to form a Confederation as soon as the Empress' forces had crossed the frontier; the ' royalist ' army, they affirmed, could be easily surrounded and captured, if it did not voluntarily come over to the side of the republicans; the Confederates would then take possession of the whole government of the country, and effect a radical resettlement in accordance with principles to be fixed in agreement with the Empress. The new constitution and all the illegal works of the present Diet were to be summarily annulled; but what was to be put in their place was a question on which the magnates could not agree even among themselves. Rzewuski wished to restore the constitution of 1773, with certain modifications designed especially to place the real control of the state in the hands of the four hetmans, of whom he happened to be one. Potocki, on the other hand, proposed a scheme no less revolutionary in character than were the changes introduced on the Third of May. The country should be reorganized as a federal republic under the name of " The Independent and United Provinces of Poland," on the Swiss or the Dutch model; each province was to possess its own army, treasury, administration, and judiciary; the King was to be deposed and replaced by a President elected for two years. All the Poles agreed that the first act of the liberated Republic should be to conclude an ' eternal alliance ' with Russia; and all of them insisted that the Empress must guarantee in the most solemn manner the territorial integrity of their country.[1]

Bezborodko, while pleased with the eagerness of the Poles to make themselves the tools of Russia, was not strongly enamored of their projects. When early in February he submitted to the Empress a final report on the Jassy conferences, he urged that the first and most essential point in undertaking the settlement of Polish affairs was to attain a confidential understanding with the German Powers, or at least with the Court of Berlin. From Austria no serious opposition was to be expected, since the Emperor could not afford to throw away the friendship of Russia for love of the Poles. But with Prussia the case was different. Frederick William's engagements with the Republic were so clear and unequivocal that unless he were won over in advance, he might feel bound to come to the aid of his assailed ally. Besides, the liberation of Poland had been so largely his work that he might be inclined to defend it out of sheer *amour-propre*. Hence it was advisable to enter into a concert with the King on Polish affairs, and even into an alliance. Otherwise, an intervention in Poland would probably lead to a war with Prussia, a danger which Russia, exhausted by five years of constant fighting, could not afford to risk. An alliance with Frederick William, on the

---

[1] For the above: F. Potocki to Potemkin, May 14, 1791; Rzewuski to Bezborodko, December 7; *plan général* submitted by Potocki and Rzewuski early in December; memorial of Branicki; Potocki to Bezborodko, December 17; plan submitted by Potocki and Rzewuski early in 1792, M. A., Архивъ Варшавской Миссіи.

other hand, would really bind the Empress to nothing; it would be of great assistance in the settlement of the Polish question; later on it would make Russia the arbiter between Austria and Prussia, so that after a period of rest and recuperation she could safely take up any aggressive enterprises that seemed useful and advantageous. A danger might, indeed, arise from the King of Prussia's " thirst for Dantzic and Thorn "; but — Bezborodko concluded — " His Majesty must realize that his ambitions could not be satisfied save by an agreement of the three neighboring Powers for a partition of Poland on the basis of the most complete equality " (of advantages).[1]

Had these counsels been accepted *in toto*, a bargain for a new partition might probably have been the preliminary, rather than the sequel, to the Empress' intervention in Poland. But during Bezborodko's long absence from the capital the management of the Polish enterprise had passed into the hands of a small clique, who, acting of course under the Empress' supervision, conducted it henceforth with few interruptions down to the very end. This inner ' ring ' was made up of Zubov, a very young man, without talent or experience, who was beginning to essay the rôle of Potemkin; Markov, a member of the College of Foreign Affairs, who aspired to rise on the wings of the favorite; and Popov, the former head of Potemkin's chancellery, whose chief political capital was his intimate knowledge of the ideas of the late lamented.[2] With these advisers, the Empress had already decided the most essential questions while Bezborodko was still in the south. They meant to begin the enterprise as soon as possible; they were not at all disposed to hold the troops idle while they were negotiating with Berlin and Vienna; and it was still less to their state to take the other Courts into partnership. Nevertheless, it was impossible to invade Poland without at least some kind

[1] Bezborodko to the Empress, January 25/February 5, 1792, M. A., Турція, IX, 14. This voluminous report, which throws so much light upon the ideas with which the Russians embarked upon their Polish enterprise, and especially upon their attitude towards Austria and Prussia, has hitherto remained unknown to historians. The text of it is printed in part in Appendix X.

[2] As to this clique see the letters of Rostopčin, Bezborodko and Zavadovski to S. R. Vorontsov, Арх. Воп., viii, pp. 52 f.; xiii, pp. 255 f.; xii, pp. 75 f.

of explanation to the German Powers. Whatever Catherine may have intended in December, towards the end of February — perhaps as a result of Bezborodko's exhortations — she decided to make certain preliminary communications to Berlin and Vienna, which, without limiting her own freedom of action, might still prevent opposition on the part of her neighbors.

On the 28th of February, 1792, the first official revelations as to the Empress' momentous projects were made to Cobenzl and to Goltz, the Prussian envoy. To Cobenzl Ostermann read a dispatch addressed to the ambassador Golitsyn in Vienna, which contained the long awaited response on the Polish question. The nine-months' delay was excused with the brazen plea that until the recent peace with the Turks the Court of Petersburg had not had leisure to form an opinion on Polish affairs. The various arguments advanced on the Austrian side on behalf of the new constitution were refuted or ignored in a manner that could only be taken as open scorn at Vienna. The Empress, it was said, was irrevocably determined no longer to allow the Poles to violate arbitrarily their engagements with her; she intended to overthrow the recent innovations in the Republic, so detrimental to all the neighboring Powers; and she invited the Courts of Vienna and Berlin to concur with her in that enterprise, especially by means of vigorous declarations at Warsaw. It was to be expected that in the face of such a manifestation of solidarity the Poles would give way without further difficulty; but should it prove necessary to resort to force, the efforts required could not in any case be considerable enough to prevent the three Courts from pursuing at the same time the concert against France. In the heated discussions that followed the reading of this dispatch, every argument was exhausted on both sides, the Russians laying most stress on the idea that if the new constitution were allowed to subsist, it would infallibly lead either to the establishment of an absolute monarchy or to the rise of a democracy even more dangerous than the French. Cobenzl retorted with some force that he failed to see how the growth of democracy could be checked by destroying the monarchical power and restoring the country to anarchy; but he was given to understand that whatever the Austrians might think, they were bound by the treaty of alliance to uphold the ancient constitution (which was true), and that if they stood out for the new régime they would be alone in their opinion, since Prussia would certainly adopt the Russian standpoint. In vain the ambassador remonstrated that this enterprise would surely end with a new partition. The Russians replied with the most solemn assurances that the Empress would never give her consent to such an arrangement. Nothing was said about a Confederation. The Russian ministers refused to state just what measures their sovereign intended to employ, if it proved necessary to use force against the Poles; but Cobenzl was informed that in such a case the Empress would willingly take the disagreeable work of coercion upon herself, in order that her two allies might be the more free to direct their attention to the other great common enterprise, the counter-revolution in France.[1] The irony of this suggestion lent the crowning touch to a communication than which nothing more inconsiderate, harsh, and dictatorial could well be imagined.

The *insinuation verbale* made the same day to Goltz was friendly enough in tone, but even vaguer than the overtures to Cobenzl. It merely called the attention of the Prussian government to the dangers arising from the new Polish constitution, and suggested a concert to regulate matters in accordance with the common interests of the two Powers. Not a word was said as to the nature or the final aim of the concert; and Goltz, who was not on the same intimate footing with the Russians as Cobenzl, did not dare ask questions. Still, combining his conjectures with the note to Zubov which had so excited his imagination some weeks before, he wrote to his Court that beyond a doubt the Russians would presently come forward with proposals for a new partition.[2]

Thus the sphinx-like silence which the Empress had so long maintained on Polish affairs was at last broken; the veil which had enshrouded her projects was at least partially raised. Her immediate object was clear, although her plan of action and her

[1] Cobenzl's report of February 29, V. A., *Russland, Berichte*, 1792.
[2] Goltz's report of February 29, B. A., *R.* XI, *Russland*, 133.

ultimate goal were still an enigma to the other Courts. It remained to be seen whether the German Powers would raise a hand in defence of Polish independence, whether they would allow the Republic to become once more a Russian province, or whether they would insist on a division of the spoils.

III

The Empress' plans were not a little facilitated by the change of ruler that had taken place at Vienna. The new King of Hungary and Bohemia, soon to be known as the Emperor Francis II, was a sickly young man of twenty-four, sadly lacking in experience, talents, independence, and initiative; fitfully inclined to a bolder policy than that of the late reign; easily tempted by prospects of aggrandizement, but without his uncle's energy, or his father's prudence, or the firmness of will and definiteness of purpose which alone could justify the ventures he undertook: in short, a feeble and colorless personality, a ruler singularly ill-fitted to guide the Monarchy through the stormy age of the French Revolution. Nor was the complexion of the ministry more promising. The octogenarian Kaunitz remained nominally at the helm; but he was losing touch with affairs, and was more and more thrust aside by pupils who fancied themselves cleverer than "the old papa." These ambitious subordinates, Philip Cobenzl and Spielmann, had enjoyed a large measure of the late Emperor's confidence and had identified themselves thoroughly with his policies, especially with the Prussian alliance. Under the new monarch they aspired to play the leading rôles, although neither of them possessed talents rising above a finished mediocrity. To make matters worse, these two ministers, and particularly the parvenu Spielmann, were the object of the special aversion of the members of the State Conference, a body of old grumblers who seemed to find their chief function in criticizing, hampering, and thwarting all the operations of the State Chancellery. The new reign began, therefore, with no happy auguries for vigor and unity in the administration.[1]

[1] The *Staatskonferenz* was at this time made up of Marshal Lacy, Prince Starhemberg, Prince Rosenberg, Count Colloredo-Wallsee, Cobenzl, and Spielmann.

If it had been anticipated that the young sovereign, as the pupil of Joseph II, would lean more towards Russia than towards the Court of Berlin, it soon appeared that the tendency was quite the contrary. While the new King hastened to inform both the Empress and Frederick William of his desire to maintain and strengthen the existing alliances, the Court of Vienna remained silent towards that of St. Petersburg on all important questions for more than a month, while a lively discussion was carried on with Prussia. The Austrian ministers overwhelmed Bischoff-werder and Jacobi with assurances of confidence and friendship; Kaunitz professed to see in the Prussian alliance the greatest achievement of his career; Spielmann called it " the universal panacea." [1] It seemed that the new government would follow strictly in the paths of the late reign and attempt to settle both the French and the Polish questions in closest concert with Prussia.

Quite in accordance with the policy of Leopold, the first effort was to dispose of the latter question before taking up the former. In the early days of March, while still ignorant of the revelation that was coming from St. Petersburg, Spielmann set to work to devise a new scheme for harmonizing the interests of all three of the neighboring Powers with respect to the Republic. The maintenance of the new constitution, though stripped of some of its objectionable features; the establishment of a permanent personal union between Poland and Saxony; the limitation of the Polish army to forty or fifty thousand men; the perpetual neutralization of Polish territory; the incorporation of all these arrangements in a treaty between the three great Powers, Saxony, and the Republic: such were the chief provisions of the plan by which the minister sought to save the essential parts of the late Emperor's system, while making not inconsiderable concessions to Russia

Kaunitz never attended, although of course entitled to do so. Interesting light on the characters of the Austrian ministers is afforded by Arneth's " Graf Philipp Cobenzl und seine Memoiren," in *Archiv für österr. Geschichte*, lxvii, and by his " Relationen der Botschafter Venedigs über Oesterreich im 18. Jht." *F. R. A.*, II, xxii, pp. 349 ff.; also, the anonymous *mémoire* in Vivenot, ii, pp. 467–474, and Zinzendorf's Diary, preserved in manuscript in the Vienna Archives. See also, Schlitter, *Kaunitz, Philipp Cobenzl und Spielmann.*

[1] Bischoffwerder's report of March 13, 1792, B. A., *R.* 1, *Conv.* 172.

and Prussia. The ever-complaisant Bischoffwerder having expressed his perfect approval, it was decided to send the project to Berlin by courier; if Frederick William and the Elector of Saxony agreed to it, the three German Courts would then present it at St. Petersburg with " a very polite but firm declaration " that they insisted on this plan and would accept no other. The poor Empress! She would have to give in, Spielmann reckoned, for she could not refuse without admitting that she had other plans aiming at exclusive domination in the Republic, not to speak of the terror into which she would be thrown by the polite but firm declaration of the high allies.[1]

Unfortunately, however, on the very day when the plan was read to Jacobi and Bischoffwerder in final form, a courier arrived with Ostermann's dispatch to Golitsyn of February 28 — the formal announcement that Russia would never tolerate the Constitution of the Third of May. The effect must have been as painful as possible. After all the confidential communications made by the Austrian cabinet at Dresden and Berlin, it was bitterly humiliating to think of bowing before this imperious fiat. But the strength of the Empress' will was sufficiently known at Vienna. The Austrians can hardly have doubted that their solution of the Polish question had now lost all chance of success. From that moment they must have abandoned the hope of realizing the Polish plan of the late Emperor.

Henceforth the essential thing was to find a basis on which the Courts of Vienna and Berlin could agree, in order to prevent Russia from acquiring a too exclusive control in Poland. If, in accordance with the previous agreement, Spielmann's plan was still sent to Berlin, it was accompanied by the intimation that Austria did not insist on this project, but was willing to accept any other which, in the King of Prussia's opinion, might lead to the desired goal.[2] Doubtless the main object of the ' expedition ' was

[1] Bischoffwerder's reports of March 6, 10, 13, 17–18, the first printed in Ranke, *Ursprung und Beginn der Revolutionskriege*, pp. 360-363; Jacobi's reports of March 3, 6, 14, B. A., *R.* 1, *Conv.* 169; Vivenot, i, p. 417. The plan itself, in the form of seventeen articles, as it was finally sent to Berlin, is printed in Vivenot, i, pp. 418 ff., and by Herrmann, *F. z. D. G.*, iv, pp. 430 ff.

[2] Kaunitz to Reuss, March 17, Vivenot, i, pp. 422 ff.

to induce Prussia to explain her views clearly and, perhaps, to come forward with her own proposals.[1] And even the faintest hope that the Court of Berlin would accept Spielmann's plan must have been dispelled by the orders which reached Bischoffwerder just before the courier left Vienna. Without waiting to get the plan into his hands, Frederick William had decisively, irrevocably rejected it.

On March 11 the King had received a report from Bischoff- werder containing the news that Spielmann was working out a project, the chief features of which were the advocacy of the Saxon-Polish personal union and certain limitations on the mili- tary forces of the Republic. That sufficed not only to make Frederick William reject the scheme in advance, but even to arouse in his mind suspicions as to the secret aims of Austria. A rescript to Bischoffwerder was at once drawn up declaring that the plan appeared infinitely dangerous, since nothing in the world would be more contrary to the major interests of Prussia than the proposed Saxon-Polish union; the King could never acquiesce in it under any conditions whatsoever.[2]

Immediately afterward came Goltz's report of February 29, with the long awaited overtures from Russia. It did not require the unpleasant plan brought forward by Austria to make the King accede with joy to the Empress' proposals. In spite of

[1] Jacobi's dispatch of March 18, B. A., R. 1, *Conv.* 169.

[2] Rescript of March 13:

" Rien au monde ne scauroit [*sic*] etre plus contraire aux interests [*sic*] majeurs de mes Etats et de leurs Souverains futurs, que l'existence d'une Puissance telle qu'on la formeroit par la reunion permanente de la Pologne à la Saxe, qui parta- geant pour ainsi dire en deux le Corps de la Monarchie Prussienne, et s'élevant peutetre de plus en plus par l'influence de sa position locale et de son nouveau Gouvernement, seroit sans contredit le voisin le plus redoutable de mes états. Ajoutés à cela que la Pologne avec sept million [*sic*] d'habitants, réunie à la Saxe qui en a deux, produiroient [*sic*] une masse de population de neuf millions, et qu'une Puissance de cette force dans la position géographique où elle se trouve, exposeroit aux plus grands dangers, soit la Prusse . . . soit mes Etats de Silésie. . . . En vain allegueroit-on les conditions et restrictions, auxquelles on préten- droit assujettir les Polonois, pour leurs troupes et leur commerce. Quelles qu'elles fussent, il me semble impossible que l'on puisse veiller avec assés de soin à leur observation exacte. . . . En un mot, je ne puis, et ne pourrois dans aucun cas acquiescer à un plan de cette nature. . . ."

B. A., R. 1, *Conv.* 172.

much that has been said, the documents at hand afford no traces of any conflict at this moment in Frederick William's breast between the desire for aggrandizement on the one hand, and a sense of loyalty to his engagements with the Republic or regard for Austria on the other. His decision was made in a moment; and it was, as a great historian has declared, the death-sentence of Poland. Immediately upon receiving Goltz's dispatch, without waiting to consult his ministers, the King wrote to 'Schulenburg that Russia was, apparently, not far removed from thinking of a new partition, which would certainly be the surest means of setting " just limits " to the power of a king of Poland, whether elective or hereditary; it might be difficult to find a satisfactory indemnity for the Court of Vienna, but if one could be found, the " Russian project " would be the most advantageous and desirable for Prussia. The most suitable frontier for the acquisitions which he himself might make, would be the left bank of the Vistula. Schulenburg, it is needless to say, was full of admiration for ' the luminous manner in which His Majesty judged the affairs of Poland.' [1]

The Prussians were clear as to the goal they wished to attain, but it was not so easy to lead up to it. They had absolutely no certainty that the Empress was inclined to a partition, since that conjecture rested only on Goltz's surmises and on the possibly apocryphal note to Zubov reported by the envoy in February.

---

[1] Frederick William's note of March 12, Schulenburg's reply of the same date.

The King wrote: " Par la dernière depêche du Ct. de Goltz de Russie il paroit que les vues de l'Impératrice concernant les afaires de Pologne sont fort diferente de ce que le Ct. Rosomowski supose . . . et que la Cour de Russie ne seroit peut etre pas éloignée de penser à un nouveau partage de la Pologne, ce qui seroit certainement le moien le plus sur pour mettre de juste borne au pouvoir dun Roi de Pologne, fut il electif ou hereditaire; mais come un projet pareille renforceroit singulièrement la position des Russes de coté d'Oczakow je doute que l'on put trouver une indemnisation pour la Cour de Vienne dont celle-ci voudroit se contenter. . . . Si lon pouvoit trouver une compensation pour l'Autriche dont elle fut satisfaite le projet Russe seroit le plus favorable pour la Prusse et le plus a desirer bien entendu quelle feroit alors lacquisition de la rive gauche de la Vistule, et que cette longue lisière de frontière actuellement aussi dificile a defendre se trouveroit alors bien couverte. Tel est mon jugement sur les afaires de Pologne." B. A., R. XI, Russland, 133.

(I have tried to reproduce the spelling and punctuation of the original.)

See also Appendix XI.

They were not minded to propose a partition themselves, for they recognized that there was a great difference between making and accepting such propositions. They still had too much regard for Austria and too little confidence in Russia to throw themselves unreservedly into the arms of the Court of Petersburg. Hence the reply delivered to Alopeus on March 13 was friendly but cautious. It stated merely that the King would gladly enter into the concert òn Polish affairs proposed by the Empress, and, confidènt of her approval, was inviting his ally, the King of Hungary, to accede to it as well; that he was ready to come to an understanding with her at once as to the policy to be adopted towards Poland, and the means to be employed; but that it was highly important for him to know her views more in detail.[1]

Having thus gone as far as they dared, the Prussians longingly awaited further communications from the Empress, in the hope that she would presently come forward and offer them Great Poland. It was a bad miscalculation. St. Petersburg once more relapsed into heavy silence. Goltz was put off with demonstrations of friendship and the excuse that no further explanations could be given until an answer had been received from Vienna.[2] On their side, the Prussians lost no opportunity to parade their friendship for the Empress and to offer her occasions for new overtures. Schulenburg declaimed to Alopeus of the common interests of the two Powers in Poland, and the necessity of heading off the strange predilection of Austria for the Saxon-Polish union. If Russia and Prussia, he kept repeating, were once agreed on a program, the Court of Vienna would have to acquiesce. The seat of the concert on Polish affairs, he suggested, might best be fixed at Berlin, as that city was midway between the other two capitals.[3] But such bits of finesse proved quite fruitless. Reports began to flow in that the Russian armies were about to enter Poland. The Prussian ministry were keenly disquieted. Still they continued obstinately to maintain — as if in

---

[1] Alopeus' report of March 3/14, with the accompanying Prussian *insinuation verbale*, M. A., Пруссія, III, 29.

[2] Goltz's report of March 27, B. A., *R.* XI, *Russland*, 133.

[3] Alopeus to Ostermann, March 9/20 and 19/30, to Bezborodko, April 8/19, M. A., Пруссія, III, 29.

a desperate effort to convince themselves of it — that the Empress, after once proposing a concert, would not disavow her own words by undertaking to settle Polish affairs single-handed. And thus the Prussians remained, standing with folded hands and eyes fixed on St. Petersburg, looking for a new dispensation of Imperial grace, waiting for ' the concert,' down to the moment when Catherine was ready to pour her troops into the Republic.

IV

Austrian policy meantime was taking a new direction. Within four days after those first disturbing tidings from St. Petersburg there came the news that Frederick William had vetoed Spielmann's Polish plan and had given a favorable answer to the proposals of Russia.[1] Among the chagrins occasioned by these successive blows, not the least was the suspicion that there was something behind this ready adhesion of the Court of Berlin to the Empress' wishes, that perhaps Austria's two allies had already come to a secret agreement between themselves. The conviction had long existed at Vienna that if the King of Prussia acquiesced in Catherine's designs on Poland, it would be only on condition that he himself might realize his territorial ambitions in that quarter.[2] But if such was his aim, was it possible to oppose it at a moment when his coöperation was imperatively necessary in view of the dangerous trend of French affairs ? Leopold's Polish system had collapsed; a return to Joseph's was wellnigh out of the question, owing to the changed relations between Austria and the other Powers; and the idea was exceedingly obvious that the best way out of the hopelessly confused situation would be to allow Prussia the long-sought acquisitions in Poland, providing Austria could secure a corresponding aggrandizement. That in such a case Austria could not find it profitable to take her share of the spoils in Poland, was recognized from the outset both at Vienna

---

[1] March 14–18.

[2] E. g., the dispatch to Reuss of January 25. This suspicion turns up again in Kaunitz's dispatch to Landriani of March 25, in Jacobi's report of March 21, and in Bischoffwerder's of March 24.

and at Berlin.[1] It was natural that Spielmann turned his thoughts to that favorite project which had haunted the minds of Austrian statesmen for almost a century — the exchange of the Belgian provinces for Bavaria.

As we have already noted, there is some reason to think that as early as 1787 Cobenzl and Spielmann, discussing this plan with Joseph II, hoped to realize it by combining it with a Prussian acquisition in Poland. The next known occasion on which it cropped out was at the meeting of the State Conference on January 17, 1792, when the subject of ' indemnities ' for the expenses of a possible intervention in France was brought under deliberation. It was then proposed, probably by Spielmann, that the Imperial Court should seek its compensation in the exchange of Belgium for Bavaria.[2] The Conference did not formally accept or reject this idea, but held it advisable to let the other Powers be the first to broach the question of indemnities. When that topic was first discussed between Bischoffwerder and Spielmann at the end of February, the Prussian gained the impression that the Austrians intended to revive their old Exchange plan.[3] Then in March, almost simultaneously with the decisive news from Berlin and St. Petersburg, there arrived dispatches from Munich which must have encouraged Spielmann to take up the project. Count Lehrbach, the Austrian envoy to Bavaria, reported that the Elector was once more possessed with his ancient hankering to become a king; that he thought to sell his vote at the coming Imperial election for the price of a crown; and that since Bavaria did not possess all the qualifications of a kingdom, he was willing to consent to an exchange, in order to obtain a " sovereign district." [4] The sovereign district in question could be, of course, only the Austrian Netherlands, the oft-projected ' Kingdom of Burgundy.' At that moment the

[1] Spielmann's discussion with Jacobi of March 21, mentioned below; Frederick William's note to Schulenburg of March 12.

[2] See the *Vorlage* of the State Chancellery, dated January 12, and the protocol of the Conference of January 17, Vivenot, i, pp. 327–341.

[3] Bischoffwerder's report of February 29, 1792, B. A., *R.* 1, *Conv.* 172.

[4] Lehrbach's reports of March 10 and 16, printed in Schrepfer, *Pfalzbayerns Politik im Revolutionszeitalter*, pp. 110–113.

Austrian cabinet could give no definite promises, but it took pains not to cut off the Elector's hopes. Lehrbach was ordered to scatter assurances of his master's desire to oblige His Serene Highness, but to add that the realization of these plans must depend on time and circumstances.[1]

In these eventful March days in Vienna, when all the great questions were clamoring for solution, in innumerable conferences Austrian, Prussian, and Russian diplomats were sounding each other, tentatively throwing out pregnant hints, developing new and far-reaching combinations. Scanty as are the sources of our information, it seems clear that in these ' conversations ' the ideas were broached, discussed, matured, out of which grew the plan for the Second Partition of Poland. For example, Bischoffwerder and Simolin, the former Russian envoy at Paris, fell one day to discussing the Elector of Bavaria's desire to wear a crown; the Russian hazarded the suggestion, " Why not make him King of Burgundy, as it was once proposed to do ? "; and the Prussian replied that he believed his master would consent, if he could obtain in return Dantzic, Thorn, and the adjacent districts.[2] Even more interesting are the discussions of Bischoffwerder with Razumovski, the Russian envoy to the Court of Vienna. The latter had frequently tried to sound the Prussian diplomat on the Polish question, and on one occasion threw out the idea that the best way to keep the Republic in bounds would be to partition it once more. Bischoffwerder was at first cautious and reserved, but soon after getting the orders of March 14 (in which Frederick William indicated very clearly his desire for some such happy consummation), he threw off the mask and told Razumovski frankly that he believed a new dismemberment would be the only means of attaining the common goal of the three Powers with regard to both France and Poland. If the Empress, he added, wished to come to an understanding with his master for

---

[1] Kaunitz to Lehrbach, March 20, V. A., *Bayern, Exped.*, 1792.

[2] L. Cobenzl to Ph. Cobenzl, May 19, 1792, V. A., *Russland, Fasc.* 139, a private letter relating the story as Simolin told it on his return to St. Petersburg; L. Cobenzl's official report of July 21, V. A., *Russland, Berichte*, 1792; Alopeus' report of May 8/19, 1792, giving Bischoffwerder's later allusion to the conversation, M. A., Пpyccia, III, 29.

common aggrandizement in Poland, they could satisfy Austria by reviving the Bavarian Exchange plan in her favor. He denied having any instructions from the King on this subject, but repeated frequently that the proposition would cause his sovereign great satisfaction.[1] Here was already outlined in all definiteness the plan which, it has hitherto been supposed, was conceived only two months later: the plan for combining the French enterprise with the affairs of Poland in such a way that Austria should secure her indemnity for the intervention in the West by means of the Bavarian Exchange, while the other two Powers took theirs at the expense of the unfortunate Republic. Finally, it appears that Bischoffwerder, perhaps as a sequel to his conversation with Razumovski, suggested this same project to Spielmann.[2]

The Bavarian-Polish plan was, then, in the air, when on March 21 Spielmann broached to Jacobi — for the first time in the official intercourse between the two German Powers — the idea of a new partition of Poland. He declared that if the King of Prussia decided that the plan submitted to him by Austria for the settlement of the Polish question did not conform to his interests, it rested with him to propose another plan in its stead, to which the King of Hungary would reply with the same frankness and loyalty as heretofore. If Frederick William desired to profit by circumstances to obtain an acquisition in Poland, the Court of Vienna would never oppose, for it recognized that Prussia could secure a suitable *arrondissement* only in that quarter. What his master would claim in return, Spielmann did not clearly say; but he intimated that Austria could not wish to extend her frontiers on the side of Poland, but could easily find a desirable

---

[1] Razumovski to the Empress, March 11/22, 1792, M. A., Австрія, III, 52. This conversation took place the 21st. It is uncertain whether Razumovski was authorized to make any such insinuation. There are no instructions on the subject in Ostermann's dispatches of this period; but on the other hand, it is perhaps significant that the envoy in his report to the Empress made no apologies for having hazarded a suggestion of such far-reaching importance. It is not improbable that he may have been authorized to make such insinuations through private letters from Zubov or Markov, with whom he maintained a regular correspondence.

[2] Razumovski to Bezborodko, July 4, 1792, from Spielmann's later confidential disclosures, M. A., Австрія, III, 54. A number of documents illustrating these ' conversations ' at Vienna will be found in Appendix XII.

arrondissement elsewhere; and he suggestively declared that there was hardly a plan in the world which the two Courts could not realize, if they were only thoroughly agreed and sincerely resolved upon it. Finally, he did not tire of repeating that the policy to be adopted by the two allies towards Poland was left entirely to Frederick William's decision. That was virtually inviting the King of Prussia to come forward and propose Exchange and Partition.[1] The Court of Berlin, however, was still too cautious to show its hand so openly. It contented itself with expressing its gratitude and pointing to the necessity of awaiting further communications from Russia;[2] and thus the question of indemnities rested for the time being. At any rate, the ground had been prepared for a revolutionary change in the Polish policy of Austria. The seeds had been sown from which sprang the momentous agreements of two months later.

While Spielmann was more or less independently evolving these dangerous and alluring projects, his chief, the Chancellor, was slower to adapt himself to the new situation. Although there could no longer be any expectation of saving the Constitution of the Third of May, Kaunitz did not cease to lavish confidences and good advice upon the Court of Dresden, and he allowed Landriani

---

[1] Jacobi's report of March 21, Bischoffwerder's of March 27, B. A., *R.* 1, 169, and *R.* 1, 172.

Jacobi reported that Spielmann, speaking of Poland, had said:

" . . . que s'il s'agissoit de profiter des Circonstances pour s'arrondir, Votre Majesté pourroit être très sure qu'Elle ne trouveroit jamais le Roi de Hongrie dans son chemin, qu'on reconnoissoit ici que rien que la Pologne pourroit offrir à la Prusse des arrondissements convenables et propres à donner encore plus de solidité et de consistence à la Monarchie Prussienne, que dans le cas que Votre Majesté trouvât ce parti préférable à tout autre, il ne doutoit nullement que les Cours de Vienne et de Berlin étant bien d'accord, et sincèrement résolues de pousser leur pointe, on ne parvient à s'arranger, . . . qu'il s'entendoit que les portions d'aggrandissement devoient être égales pour les deux parties, qu'il ne vouloit pas me cacher que la Cour de Vienne ne pourroit jamais trouver de sa convenance d'étendre ses Etats vers la Pologne, que ce seroit plutôt s'affoiblir, mais qu'il y auroit d'autres moyens pour s'arrondir. . . . Il finit la Conversation sur cette matière par me témoigner son impatience extrême d'apprendre quel seroit le plan que Votre Majesté trouveroit bon de substituer à celui parti dimanche dernier par le Courier du Général de Bischoffswerder."

[2] Rescript to Jacobi of March 24, and in similar tone throughout April, B. A., *R.* 1, *Conv.* 169.

to continue to fire the Poles with hopes that could never be realized. In spite of the pressure from Berlin, in spite of Louis Cobenzl's admonitions, a month went by before a reply was made to Golitsyn's communications. And then what a reply! Cobenzl was instructed, on the one hand, to give the strongest assurances of the devotion of the new King of Hungary to the Russian alliance, and to dispel any feelings of distrust or displeasure that might have arisen at St. Petersburg; but on the other hand, he was ordered to " make the Russian Court ashamed of its unseemly and disloyal conduct," and to intimate that Austria still held — in theory at least — to her former views on the Polish question. Moreover, he was to demand that the Empress should do nothing in Poland until the triple concert came into existence; that she should content herself with such modifications of the new constitution as were absolutely necessary; and that she should avoid recourse to violent measures.[1] Stripped of its verbiage, this answer amounted to a consent to the concert proposed by the Empress, and to a surly admission that the Constitution of the Third of May would have to be sacrificed in whole or in part. Doubtless Kaunitz would have done well to swallow his pride and approve with good grace what he was powerless to prevent. If he flattered himself that by delays and recriminations he could hold back the Empress from carrying out her plans, he was vastly mistaken. That the Court of Vienna should do anything really effective in defence of Poland was almost out of the question, owing to the cardinal necessity of maintaining the Russian alliance, and in view of the equivocal attitude of Prussia. And whatever slight chances of such action there might have been vanished entirely when — only a week after the sending of the reply to St. Petersburg — on April 20 France declared war on Austria.

V

With the outbreak of the Revolutionary War we have no concern here except in so far as it influenced the development of the Polish question. But since the fate of Poland was soon bound up

---

[1] Instructions to L. Cobenzl of April 12, Vivenot, i, pp. 437–448.

with the question of indemnities for this war, and as that question in less than a year became confused by a bitter dispute about the nature of the war, it is necessary to consider briefly the circumstances under which Austria and Prussia entered upon the great struggle.

If it was later maintained that the Court of Vienna went into the war only in order to vindicate ' the cause of all sovereigns,' the statement was, to say the least, hardly a half-truth. Down to the moment when it became convinced that an attack from France was impending — that moment may be fixed about the 10th of April, — the Austrian government had done nothing but temporize, in the hope that there would be no necessity for any serious action. It was only on April 13 that the dispatch of 50,000 troops to the frontier was decided upon, and even this was essentially a defensive measure.[1] It was only on April 21 that the long delayed invitations to the general concert were sent out.[2] It was only on the 28th that, yielding to the pressure from Berlin and to the necessities of self-defence, the State Conference resolved upon aggressive action. And the reasons adduced in the protocol for this last step are highly significant. Since Prussia, it was said, would not send her troops to the front unless assured that Austria agreed to take the offensive with her, since the defence of the Netherlands essentially depended upon the dispatch of those troops, and since little or no aid was to be expected from the other Courts, it seemed necessary that, without waiting for a general concert of the Powers, Austria and Prussia should present the proposed declaration at Paris, and in case of an unsatisfactory answer, proceed immediately to armed intervention.[3] The Court of Vienna thus agreed to aggressive action against France, ostensibly for the common cause of all sovereigns; but its resolution was taken only at the eleventh hour — two days before the French declaration of war was known at the Austrian capital — and it was taken chiefly in order to secure Prussian aid against an attack expected almost with certainty.

[1] Conference protocol of April 13, Vivenot, i, pp. 456 ff.
[2] Vivenot, ii, pp. 1–4.
[3] Conference protocol of April 28, Vivenot, ii, pp. 10 ff.

On the other hand, it may be said that the immediate cause of the war was the refusal of Austria to desist from the concert on French affairs. In this sense, Austria was drawn into the conflict by her adherence to the ' common cause,' and had a right to the help of those Courts which had preached the anti-revolutionary crusade with such ardor.

If there are moral rights in politics, seldom has an attacked Power had stronger claims of that nature to the support of another Power, than Austria had to the support of Prussia. Frederick William had not only approved each of the fateful replies of Kaunitz to the French government, but had constantly urged stronger and more aggressive measures. One need not be deceived by the occasional Prussian declarations that the King was far from wishing to force Austria into a war; and that he sought only to establish the principle that it was necessary either to leave French affairs severely alone, or else to intervene vigorously. Nothing would have grieved him more than to see Austria adopt the former alternative. When at times she seemed likely to do so — especially after Leopold's death — the Court of Berlin took all imaginable pains to prevent the abandonment of the enterprise.[1] From January on, the constant refrain of Prussian communications was the necessity that the two Courts agree at once upon vigorous measures against France.[2] The Prussians attached very little importance to a general concert. They doubted as much as did the Austrians that it would ever come into being. They wanted to interfere in France whether the concert was established or not. If they occasionally pressed for the sending out of the invitations to the other Powers, the reason was simply this: that if Austria and Prussia carried out the French enterprise without any kind of agreement with the other Courts, the latter — especially England and Russia — might try to deprive them of " more or less of their just indem-

[1] Cf. Bischoffwerder's instructions; the rescripts to him of March 6 and 13, and to Jacobi of February 6 and 9 and March 3.

[2] Rescript to Jacobi of January 5; notes to Reuss of January 13 and February 5; rescripts to Bischoffwerder of March 6, 13, 15, 19, 24, to mention only a part of the evidence at hand.

nities." [1] Of the active coöperation of the other Powers there is hardly any serious suggestion in the Prussian dispatches.

How to drive Austria into action without waiting for a chimerical general concert, was for months the problem before Berlin. In March Bischoffwerder reported dismally that nothing short of a French attack would suffice; and he confided to Razumovski his plan for provoking such an aggression on the part of ' the democrats.' [2] It was, therefore, with no little jubilation that the Prussians received the news that the French were planning to invade the Empire. [3] That would end the intolerable delays of the Court of Vienna. Frederick William much preferred to have the enemy assume the rôle of aggressor: ' they would thereby,' as his ministers wrote, ' put the game into the hands of the other Powers, and give the latter a clearer right than ever to demand indemnities at the end of the war.' [4] So great was the King's ardor that his advisers had difficulty in restraining him from going ahead without waiting for the resolutions of Austria. [5] And if any further proof were needed that Prussia did not draw the sword merely in defence of her ally, it could be found in the fact that towards the end of April, when it was thought at Berlin that France was not going to attack after all, the King was still resolved to await only the final decision of Austria before sending his troops to the front and beginning action. [6] He was firmly determined upon a course that could lead only to war, before the news of the French declaration arrived in Berlin.

This declaration did not alter Frederick William's conception of the nature of his participation in the enterprise. As early as the middle of April, Reuss had raised the pregnant question of the

---

[1] Rescripts to Bischoffwerder of April 5 and to Jacobi, April 6, B. A., *R.* 1, 172 and 169.

[2] Bischoffwerder's reports of March 6, 9, 27, B. A., *R.* 1, 172; Razumovski's report of February 28/March 10, M. A., Австрія, III, 53.

[3] Rescripts to Bischoffwerder, April 5, and Jacobi, April 6, B. A.

[4] Rescripts to Jacobi, April 16 and 30, May 9, *ibid.*

[5] Schulenburg to Brunswick, April 20, 22, 24 (P. S.), B. A., *R.* XI, *Frankreich,* 89*b.*

[6] Schulenburg to Brunswick, April 24 (P. S.); the cabinet ministry to the King, April 25, B. A., *R.* 96, 147 *G.*; rescript to Jacobi, April 28, B. A., *R.* 1, 169.

Schulenburg to Brunswick, April 24: the Duke's letter " ne pouvoit arriver plus à propos pour affermir Sa Majesté dans les dispositions où j'avois taché de la

form of the King's coöperation in case of a French attack upon Austria, and had received the answer, ' that it was hardly to be supposed that the Court of Vienna would wish to regard such an attack as a mere *casus foederis*, on the same plane as an aggression of other Powers.' The Prussian ministry ' believed rather that Austria would much prefer to hold to the basis of the broader engagements and stipulations of the concert.' [1] In a rescript to Jacobi a few days later, the King was made to express himself in the same sense. " I persist," he said, " in the most invariable resolution to act in this case [in the event of a French attack] . . . according to the engagements which I have undertaken, on a footing of complete equality with the Court of Vienna." [2] The engagements which the King chose to regard as involved, were not those of the February alliance, but those of the concert agreed upon between the two Courts for an intervention in France. The reason is perfectly obvious. Not by sending the small auxiliary corps stipulated in the alliance treaty, but only by taking part in the war with forces equal to those of Austria, could Prussia claim in the end an indemnity completely equivalent to that of her ally. Furthermore, on receiving the news of the French declaration of war, the King sent to Vienna the significant declaration: " I accept with real satisfaction the assurance that His Apostolic Majesty will act against France in concert with me and with the greatest vigor, even if, contrary to expectation, the other Courts, and especially Russia, should refuse their coöperation." [3] If at the same time he recommended that the Court of Vienna should base its counter-declaration against France on the injustice of the French attack, while he would justify his own intervention by the hostile measures of France against the Germanic Empire,

mettre, d'agir dans cette importante occasion avec la circonspection nécessaire à l'égard des intentions et des vues toujours fort protégées de la Cour de Vienne."

Rescript to Jacobi, April 28: " Je crois que par toutes les circonstances . . . on peut regarder dans ce moment une invasion des François comme de la dernière invraisemblance."

The Cabinet Ministry to the King, April 25: " Il nous paroit donc, qu'il ne s'agit plus que d'attendre l'indication du terme précis où toute l'armée autrichienne sera rendue au lieu de sa destination, et en état de commencer les opérations."

[1] Rescript to Jacobi, April 12, *ibid*.
[2] Rescript of April 16, B. A., *R*. 1, 169.　　[3] Rescript to Jacobi, May 9, *ibid*.

this was only another illustration of the same point of view. It was not in virtue of the treaty of alliance, and not as a member of a nebulous general concert which still remained unformed, that Prussia went into the Revolutionary War. It was rather in accordance with engagements contracted with Austria before the war for a joint intervention by the two German Powers, engagements of which Frederick William himself had been the principal author.

Unfortunately, however, these engagements had never been drawn up in proper form. The communications between the two Courts had been for the most part purely oral. At one moment, indeed, Austria was not far from securing a formal written declaration which might later have served her in good stead. On April 18 the Prussian ministry submitted to the King two alternative drafts for a note to Reuss, in both of which was the stipulation: "*that whether the French attack took place or not, the allied armies should take the offensive as soon as they were assembled, and [the two Powers] should not lay down arms except by common accord, when the aim of the concert had been attained, and the expenses of the intervention had been repaid or at least their repayment assured.*" It was probably due to Schulenburg that a much less definite and significant note was finally drawn up and presented to the Austrian envoy.[1] As matters stood at the outbreak of the war, the chief agreements arrived at were that the two Courts should employ equal forces and act on the offensive. As for the aim of the war, no program existed save that laid down for the general concert; and there was no obligation to adhere to that.[2] The idea that one Power might abandon the struggle without the consent of the other had not even been discussed. Doubtless there was on both sides quite too much optimism about the enterprise; but it was an unpardonable fault in the Austrian ministers that they made no effort to secure any binding engagements on this point from Prussia.

[1] Schulenburg to the King, April 19, B. A., *R.* 96, 147 *G.*; and to Brunswick, April 20, B. A., *R.* XI, *Frankreich*, 89*b*.

[2] Cf. the rescript to Jacobi of May 9: "l'aggression des François . . . nous met dans le cas de n'avoir plus besoin de nous lier les mains en nous en tenant strictement aux réclamations précédement proposées, B. A., *loc. cit.*

Scarcely less unfortunate was the fact that no very definite agreement had been reached on the subject of indemnities. The principle that compensation was to be demanded for the costs of the enterprise had, indeed, been agreed upon; and it was accepted on both sides that the indemnities of both Courts were to be exactly equal.[1] This followed from the principle of parity of efforts, which was the cornerstone of the concert, as well as from that of strict equality in all ' advantages,' which, as Frederick William said, was the basis, and would always be the firmest support, of the alliance.[2] In general, however, the subject of indemnities was little discussed during the critical month preceding the outbreak of the war. At the beginning of May, when Austria found herself attacked and needed to show her ally the utmost complaisance, Spielmann took up the topic again with Jacobi, while Reuss was authorized to say that his Court left it entirely to Prussia to decide whether they should generously renounce all claim to indemnities, or demand reimbursement in money, or seek compensation through conquests.[3] Disinterestedness was no longer Frederick William's rôle. He replied that he could not conceive that the two Courts could afford to go without indemnities; he did not believe that His Apostolic Majesty could make such a sacrifice without detriment to his monarchy.[4] This anxiety for the interests of the Austrian monarchy is almost comic, when one remembers that a year later Prussian statesmen were denying that the Court of Vienna had any rights to an indemnity at all, or at least any rights that could be put on the same plane with those of Prussia. As to what form of compensation he preferred, Frederick William promised to explain later on.

There was one Prussian minister, indeed, who had sought to have the matter definitely settled before embarking upon the war.

---

[1] Instructions to Bischoffwerder, February 18, Art. 4; Kaunitz's declarations to Bischoffwerder reported by the latter March 13, and approved by the King of Prussia March 19; Spielmann's remarks to Jacobi, reported by the latter March 21, etc. (B. A., *R.* 1, 172 and 169).

[2] Rescript to Jacobi, March 26, B. A., *R.* 1, 169.

[3] Jacobi's report of May 3, B. A., *loc. cit.*; Kaunitz to Reuss, May 4, printed in Vivenot, ii, pp. 23 ff.

[4] Rescript to Jacobi, May 9, B. A., *loc. cit.*

Alvensleben repeatedly proposed to Schulenburg that the King should join in the struggle only in case the Imperial Courts allowed him to occupy immediately the coveted territories in Poland.[1] How such a demand could have been reconciled with Prussia's engagements and declarations, it is difficult to see. On the Austrian side, Spielmann later claimed that it was not his fault that his Court had not reached a definite agreement with Prussia regarding the indemnities before the outbreak of the war.[2] That this had not come about was probably due chiefly to Kaunitz, who, disliking the idea of a Prussian acquisition, avoided discussing indemnities as far as he could; and also to the Nestors of the State Conference, who found it the height of wisdom to postpone the topic until Prussia had spoken first.[3] Doubtless in April, in view of Frederick William's burning impatience to begin the enterprise, it would have been easy to secure from him a formal declaration on the subject, or at least a guarantee of the principle of strict parity in future acquisitions. As it was, the two Powers entered upon the war with insufficient agreements, insufficient conceptions of the magnitude of the task, insufficient forces, and — as was soon to be shown — with insufficient confidence in one another.[4]

---

[1] See Alvensleben's well-known *Procès-verbal* of October 1, 1793, in Herrmann, *Ergänzungsband*, pp. 404–409.

[2] See the letter of Thugut to Colloredo-Wallsee of November 1, 1792, in Vivenot, *Vertrauliche Briefe des Freiherrn von Thugut*, i, pp. 4–8.

[3] Cf. the rescript of Kaunitz to Stadion of April 18, 1792, Vivenot, i, pp. 464–467; and the decision of the Conference on January 17, 1792, already mentioned.

[4] On the rôles played by Austria and Prussia in connection with the outbreak of the Revolutionary War, see, Sybel, *op. cit.*, ii, pp. 171 ff., especially pp. 184 f., 192–195; Heigel, *op. cit.*, i, pp. 495 ff.; Häusser, *op. cit.*, i, pp. 327–341; Sorel, *op. cit.*, ii, pp. 351 ff., especially pp. 366–369, 373–376, 424–427, 442–448; Ranke, *Ursprung und Beginn der Revolutionskriege*, pp. 125 ff.; Glagau, *Die französische Legislative und der Ursprung der Revolutionskriege*, pp. 157 ff., especially pp. 174–177, 257–259; Heidrich, *op. cit.*, pp. 31 ff., especially pp. 33–36, 158–162.

Heidrich's account seems to me the most satisfactory, and it is the only one based on a complete study of the Prussian records. It brings out strongly the aggressive character of Prussia's policy, which I have also emphasized in the text. Glagau's attempt to prove a somewhat similar, though a less decidedly aggressive, tendency in Austrian policy seems hardly successful. Doubtless, in his conversations with Jacobi and Bischoffwerder and in some of his numerous memorials Kaunitz occasionally used rather bold language; but from a thorough study

VI

The outbreak of the struggle in the West came marvelously à propos to serve the designs of Catherine II. For many months she had been — according to her well-known confession to her secretary — 'racking her brains to push the Courts of Vienna and Berlin into the French enterprise, so that she might have her elbows free.' [1] Now, through no particular merit of her own but simply through the good luck that so constantly attended her, she saw her neighbors nicely embarked on that tremendous undertaking, just at the moment when she most needed to have them fully occupied. The French declaration of war greatly facilitated, although it did not, as is often said, determine the Empress' onslaught upon Poland.[2]

The Polish malcontents had already presented themselves at St. Petersburg, at Catherine's invitation, in the latter part of March.[3] They numbered hardly more than a dozen. Apart from the three leaders, almost all of them were men without standing or repute at home, mere clients and dependents of Potocki. For this handful of émigrés to set themselves up as the true representatives of the Polish nation, the sole and sufficient embodiment of the Republic, was nothing short of ludicrous; but it was enough for the Empress' purposes to have any sort of a figurehead behind which she might act. Her guests were lodged at her expense, feted, caressed, and overwhelmed with attentions. Their leaders were honored with daily private audiences with Catherine and Zubov, in which the details of the future Confederation were settled.

The Empress presented to the Poles a scheme for the reorganization of their country which she herself had worked out. Drawn

of the Austrian acts one cannot escape the conviction that he was at bottom extremely anxious to avoid a war, and that when he or any of the other Austrian ministers expressed themselves in more or less bellicose terms, it was due either to a momentary outburst of wrath against the National Assembly or to the desire to satisfy the Prussians.

[1] Храповицкій, Дневникъ, December 14/25, 1791.

[2] The news of the French declaration reached St. Petersburg only May 9, long after the final orders for the attack on Poland had been sent off.

[3] Potocki and Rzewuski arrived the 15th, Branicki the 29th.

up in the form of twenty-three articles, which were to be added to the Pacta Conventa, it must have convinced her guests of her sterling republican principles, for she had provided for the annulment of every useful act of the Four Years' Diet and for the restoration of every monstrosity of the old régime.[1] It appears, however, that no definite arrangements were made at that time for the future government of the Republic. The Poles could not agree among themselves; and on one occasion, at the very close of their stay in St. Petersburg, they almost came to blows with one another in Zubov's chamber, when they fell to discussing the delicate subject of the restoration of the power of the hetmans.[2]

The immediate plan of action, however, was fixed with little difficulty. The Act of Confederation was drawn up with Popov's assistance, and apparently in accordance with an old scheme of Potemkin. It was signed and sworn to by the Poles on April 27 at St. Petersburg,[3] but for the sake of appearances was lyingly dated " May 14, Targowica." In other words, it was designed to create the impression that the Confederation had arisen on Polish soil, and on that date when it could first safely begin its activity under cover of the invading Russian troops. The Act itself was worthy of its signatories. It consisted mainly of a prolix, turgid, and muddled indictment of " the usurpers " at Warsaw, who by conspiracy and violence, and especially by " the audacious crime " of the Third of May, had " overthrown all the cardinal laws," abolished the liberty and equality of the nobility, spread " the contagion of democratic ideas," following " the fatal examples set at Paris," imposed " the shackles of slavery " upon the nation — in short, destroyed the Republic and established a " despotism." Wherefore the undersigned " senators, ministers of the Republic, officers of the Crown," etc., etc., united to form a free Confederation in defence of the Roman Catholic religion, the

---

[1] These articles are printed in the instruction for Baron Bühler in the Сборникъ, xlvii, pp. 303 ff. They are also to be found in various slightly divergent drafts among Catherine's papers in the Petrograd Archives, X, 70.

[2] Bühler to Zubov, November 19/30, 1792, M. A., Польша, IX, 3; Rzewuski to Catherine, August 19, 1792 and July 8, 1794, M. A., Польша, II, 7.

[3] As to the place and date, see Smoleński, *Konfederácya targowicka*, pp. 30 f., and the Rescript to Kakhovski of April 16/27, Сборникъ, xlvii, p. 275.

liberty and equality of the *szlachta*, the territorial integrity of the state, and the ancient republican form of government.   They annulled all that had been done at the present Diet contrary to liberty and the laws; they declared that they would pursue all those who in any way sought to defend the Constitution of the Third of May; they ordered all ministers, senators, and deputies to send in within two months a formal disavowal of all adhesion to that illegal constitution; and they invited all ' their brothers in the provinces ' to accede to the present Confederation. Since the faction at Warsaw had usurped control of the armed forces of the state, so that " the subjugated Republic " could not defend its own cause, there remained, it was said, no other course than to appeal for aid to " the great Catherine." " The justice of our prayers," the Act concluded, " the sanctity of the treaties which unite Russia to Poland, and above all the Empress' own grandeur of character give us a well-grounded hope of her disinterestedness and her magnanimity, in a word, of her worthy assistance to our cause." [1]

This masterpiece was supplemented by a formal reclamation for aid, addressed by " the confederated Polish nation " to that " immortal Sovereign," who although " ruling over half the hemisphere " and ' filling the universe with her renown ' was even more fitted by her heroic and godlike qualities to become " the refuge of peoples and of kings " and " the tutelary divinity " of Poland.[2]

In preparation for the glorious rôle thus thrust upon her, the Empress had already made the necessary military arrangements. Early in April full instructions were sent to Generals Kakhovski and Krečetnikov, the former commanding the army still quartered in Moldavia and the other forces in the south, the latter the troops massed on the frontiers of Lithuania. The date for beginning action was fixed at the middle of May, the time set for the evacuation of Turkish territory. According to the elaborate plan of operations drawn up by General Pistor, four Russian corps were to pour suddenly into the Ukraine from three sides; it was

---

[1] The Act of the Confederation is printed in Angeberg, *Recueil*, pp. 262–274.

[2] This document is printed in the Сборникъ, xlvii, pp. 310–316.

expected that the small Polish army, most of which was scattered about in that region, could easily be outflanked, surrounded, dispersed, or captured; and thereupon Kakhovski was to go straight for Warsaw, while Krečetnikov rapidly bore down upon the capital from the northeast. Nearly 100,000 troops were assigned to the enterprise, although the Russians looked forward to a military promenade rather than a serious campaign.[1]

While we are but imperfectly informed of what went on behind the scenes at St. Petersburg during these months, it is clear that there were not a few differences of opinion about the undertaking in Poland. Zubov and Markov, into whose hands the management of the affair had passed, made all their plans with the utmost secrecy and intended to begin action without once consulting the Council of the Empire and without further communications to the other Courts. In this, however, they encountered the lively opposition of Bezborodko, who after being summoned to return to the capital in haste, on his arrival found himself completely thrust aside. Naturally the veteran statesman was full of contempt for the political operations of the twenty-six year old favorite and his clique, and full of indignation that such a coterie should be able to plunge the state into a new war without the knowledge or advice of the Empress' responsible ministers.[2] He insisted that the whole Polish enterprise should be laid before the Council. He was also particularly determined that nothing should be done until an understanding had been reached with the German Power or at least with Prussia.[3] Bezborodko must have recognized that such an understanding would probably lead up to a new partition. His report from Jassy in February had already hinted at such an arrangement; and on his return to St. Peters-

---

[1] See the rescripts to the two commanding generals of March 14/25, April 1/12, etc., in the Сборникъ, xlvii, pp. 241 ff.; also the discussion of the Russian military plans in Soplica, *Wojna polsko-rosyjska*, pp. 9–18.

[2] Cf. Bezborodko to S. R. Vorontsov, May 15/26, 1792, Арх. Вор., xiii, pp. 255 f.

[3] That had been his opinion from the very outset; cf. his letter to Potemkin of August 12/23, 1791, Сборникъ, xxix, p. 124; to A. R. Vorontsov, December 3/14, *ibid.*, p. 174; report of January 25/February 5 to the Empress, M. A., Турція, IX, 14; Cobenzl's reports of March 23 and July 6, 1792, V. A., *Russland, Berichte.*

burg he seems to have urged upon the Empress the necessity of acquiring for Russia the Ukraine and other Polish territories [1] — an acquisition that would inevitably involve equivalent advantages for Austria and Prussia.

It is impossible to say with certainty what was Catherine's attitude towards a new partition at the moment when she began her enterprise in Poland. It is probable, however, that she was by no means averse to the idea. From the rescript to Potemkin of July 18/29, 1791, and from her conduct in the latter part of 1792, it appears that she was not inclined to stand out in opposition, in case the other Powers insisted upon a new dismemberment of the Republic. There is some reason to think that she even tried to hasten such a dénouement by subtle insinuations to Austria and Prussia; although naturally she was not disposed to take upon herself the onus of proposing it formally and openly.[2] That she was quite alive to the advantages to be expected from the annexation of the Ukraine, appears from the oft-cited rescript to Potemkin; and it is perhaps worthy of notice that in 1793 one of her ministers wrote that for " several years " her mind had been filled with the thought of acquiring this territory and of the glory and profit to be gained thereby.[3] Nevertheless, at the time

[1] Cf. Bezborodko's memorial to the Empress, of June 30/July 11, 1793 (Сборникъ, xxix, pp. 236–239), reviewing his past services, and reminding her that he had given this advice about making acquisitions from Poland " at the first moment when an opportunity for making them began to dawn." From the context it would seem that the reference was to the time immediately after his return to St. Petersburg from Jassy. Such is also the opinion advanced by Smoleński, *Ostatni rok sejmu wielkiego*, pp. 313 f.

[2] I am not referring here to the famous note to Zubov reported by Goltz in February, 1792. Although that has been almost universally taken as a hint, or even an invitation, to Prussia to come forward with proposals for a partition, I regard it as quite uncertain whether the note was genuine, and whether Goltz came to be informed of it by Catherine's intention or otherwise. What I have in mind in the statement in the text is: first, the very curious and subtle overtures to Prussia on the subject of indemnities, contained in the instructions to Alopeus of June 10/21, 1792 (to be analyzed later on); and secondly, the pregnant insinuations made by Razumovski to Bischoffwerder, as already noticed, in March, 1792, and repeated in much more definite form to Cobenzl and Spielmann at the end of June. That Razumovski could have ventured so far without being in some manner informed of his sovereign's wishes, seems scarcely conceivable.

[3] Zavadovski to S. R. Vorontsov, July 27/August 7, 1793; Арх. Вор., xii, p. 90.

now under consideration, she seems to have hesitated to disclose her inmost thoughts even to her closest advisers.[1] Officially and before the world she professed to have no object in view in Poland except the overthrow of the new constitution and the vindication of her treaties with the Republic.

Bezborodko's exertions had at least this result, that the Empress was induced to lay the whole plan for the Polish enterprise before the Council of the Empire. While approving it in the main, that body raised objections on some points; and especially they urged the necessity of communicating their projects to Austria and Prussia and securing the consent of those Courts. They were, indeed, little disquieted by the known predilections of Austria, but they feared that without a preliminary understanding Frederick William would not remain a passive spectator. The Empress was indignant at what she considered a criticism of her own policy.[2] Nevertheless, on April 21 new dispatches were sent to Vienna and Berlin, communicating in substantially identical terms the plan for a Confederation and an armed intervention in Poland, and requesting both Courts to support these measures, when the time came, by appropriate and vigorous language at Warsaw. It was a far cry, indeed, from the concert proposed in February to the arbitrary and irrevocable resolutions thus announced; but the slight was glossed over with the excuse that it was absolutely necessary for Russia to act at once, as her troops were bound to return from Moldavia through Poland in May; and it was also alleged that if the Empress had not confided her

---

[1] Cf. the two undated notes to Bezborodko and Zubov, which may not improbably have been written about this period, Сборникъ, xlii, pp. 245 f., 338. To Bezborodko she wrote: ".' La proposition est incongrue; car par cette belle proposition nous attirerions non seulement tout l'odieux de la part des polonais, mais outre cela nous agirions contre nos propres traités et notre garantie en égard à Danzig spécialement. J'opine pour laisser tomber la proposition." To Zubov (in Russian): " Your wish will never succeed with the present Courts of Vienna and Berlin. I remember the partition of Poland with Maria Theresa and Frederick, how it went off as smooth as butter. The comparison is not to the advantage of the former " (the present Courts).

[2] See the protocol of the Council, March 29/April 9, Арх. Гос. Сов., i, pp. 906–910; Catherine's note to Bezborodko, Сборникъ, xlii, p. 224; Храповицкій, *op. cit.*, April 3/14; Bezborodko to S. R. Vorontsov, May 15/26, Арх. Вор., xiii, pp. 255 f.

intentions earlier, it was because she was waiting for the long delayed reply of Austria to her first communications. Some show of regard for the other Courts was made at least; and Bezborodko's intervention may have averted rather embarrassing complications.

Two weeks later the Russian declaration which was to be presented at Warsaw, was also forwarded to Vienna and Berlin, along with some additional explanations. At the same time a pretence was made of replying to the Austrian dispatches of April 12. It could scarcely soothe Kaunitz's irritation that, far from being stricken with shame for its " unseemly and disloyal conduct," the cabinet of Petersburg passed over all his arguments and recriminations without the shadow of a response, and simply reminded its ally of the long-standing engagement between the Imperial Courts to maintain the Polish constitution of 1773. In the dispatch to Berlin, it was emphatically declared that the Empress had no other aim or project in Poland than to restore the old form of government. That was not the declaration the Prussians were hoping for, as the Russians were probably aware.[1]

Having thus set the stage, having organized the Confederation which was to serve as her puppet, having formed her plans without admitting her neighbors to consultation or deliberation — in spite of the proposal for a concert — having then announced to those neighbors what she meant to do at the eleventh hour when they no longer had time for counter-representations, Catherine was ready for action. On May 18 Bulgakov presented at Warsaw the declaration exposing the reasons which impelled his sovereign to intervene on behalf of Polish liberties and in defence of violated treaties against the usurping Diet and the illegal Constitution of the Third of May.[2] On the night of the 18–19, the Russian troops crossed the frontier.

Thus at almost the same moment there burst forth in East and West the two storms which the prudent diplomacy of Leopold II

[1] Dispatches to Razumovski and Alopeus of April 23/May 4, M. A., Австрія, ТII, 52 and Пруссія, III, 28.

[2] The declaration is printed in Angeberg, *Recueil*, pp. 274–281.

had foreseen and vainly striven to avert. The ardor of the Girondists to revolutionize Europe combined with the no less aggressive and revolutionary designs of Catherine II and with the insatiable Prussian thirst for aggrandizement to plunge wellnigh the whole Continent into the vortex of war. France and Poland, the two states which had simultaneously been attempting sweeping reforms and national regeneration, found themselves exposed — each isolated and without connection with the other — to the onslaught of the great military monarchies of Eastern Europe. These two conflicts could not fail to work back upon each other in innumerable ways. Their influence upon each other can hardly be overestimated. Broadly speaking, the results of this interplay may be described as highly favorable to France, and ruinous to Poland. If the struggle brought to the former glory and conquests unparalleled in her history, and to the latter political annihilation, the difference is not altogether due to the genius of the one nation and the weakness of the other.

Without attempting to trace here all the ways in which the conflict in the West affected the fate of Poland, it is incumbent to point out the chief form which that interaction took. Vastly different as were the pretexts for the two wars — since France was being attacked for turning a monarchy into a republic, and Poland for converting a republic into a monarchy — nevertheless, the diplomacy of the predatory Powers succeeded in finding a common formula to justify the two utterly contradictory enterprises, and in establishing a subtle connection between them. Both were ranged in the category of ' counter-revolutions,' benevolently undertaken by the three allied Courts in the interests of order, stability and the general tranquillity of Europe. Both were integral parts of a great common work; although for the sake of an equitable division of labor, the intervention in the West was entrusted to Austria and Prussia alone, while that in the East was reserved for Catherine. Once this insidious theory was established, the deduction was obvious. Pooling the stakes, the three Powers would soon be pooling the profits. What was invested in one quarter could be recouped in the other. Such a combination had already been clearly foreshadowed in the discussions between the diplomats at Vienna in March, at a time when both the French and the Polish enterprises were still only uncertain contingencies of the future. By May both had become realities. It remained only to see whether the two joint ventures would yield results capable of leading up to a gigantic and mutually satisfactory distribution of dividends.

CHAPTER XII

The Russian Reconquest of Poland

I

Catherine's abrupt attack caught the Poles in a state of terrible unreadiness. Down to the eleventh hour they had refused to believe that there was any serious danger. This disastrous optimism was due in part to the Prussian alliance, which, in spite of the unmistakable coldness of Berlin, still seemed to afford a guarantee against a direct aggression from without; in part, it was based upon the friendly attitude of Austria, upon the engagements which the two German Powers were thought to have contracted to defend the independence and the free constitution of the Republic, and upon the hopes aroused by Landriani of a quadruple alliance about to be erected as a barrier against Russia. Hence, although Catherine's opposition to the new constitution grew more and more evident, although since the autumn there had been reports of suspicious movements of her troops along the frontier, although the visit of the malcontents to Jassy was known at Warsaw and its purpose could easily be divined, nevertheless for many months the Poles continued to flatter themselves that the Empress would not venture upon open hostilities.

Confidence was increased by the quiet, unity, and harmony that reigned throughout the country. Patriotic ardor, the enthusiasm for reforms, the progress of enlightened political and social ideas — in short, the hope and promise of a brighter future — had never seemed so great as during the year that followed the inauguration of the new constitution. When at the Dietines, held in February, 1792, for the first time since the revolution the *szlachta* had the opportunity to express their full opinion about what had occurred, the result was a signal triumph for the reforming party. All the provincial assemblies swore loyalty to the constitution, and appointed delegates to thank the King and the Estates. The Diet meanwhile busied itself with completing the reorganization of the government; with questions of finance, the judiciary, a new law-code, the municipalities, religion, Courland — in fact, with all sorts of questions except the most important of all, the military one.

The awakening from this fancied security began towards the close of March, when reports arrived from St. Petersburg and Vienna revealing Catherine's aggressive plans and the communications she had made to Austria. In the next few weeks the news grew steadily more and more alarming. It could no longer be doubted that the Empress meant to attack. Warsaw trembled with excitement, but not with consternation. In the streets, the salons, the clubs there was but one voice: resistance to the last, 100,000 troops to the front, the rising of the whole nation in arms, if need be. Better a new partition, said the Marshal Potocki, than the abandonment of the constitution.[1] On April 16 and 21 the Diet in secret session decided upon the measures necessary to put the country in a state of defence. The army was to be raised at once to 100,000 men. The King was authorized to engage experienced generals, artillery officers, and engineers from abroad, to negotiate a loan for 30,000,000 florins, and to employ 9,000,000 florins then in the treasury for military preparations. These measures were to be communicated to the friendly Powers, especially to the Courts of Berlin, Vienna, and Dresden, along with a declaration that the Republic was determined to defend itself in case of foreign invasion.[2] Energetic and worthy of the moment these decisions were; but they represented a desperate and belated attempt to effect what ought to have been done three years earlier.

In spite of the suddenly darkened horizon, on the 3rd of May the anniversary of the revolution was celebrated with elaborate and splendid fetes. " Warsaw was never more thronged or more brilliant," wrote a contemporary: " that was the last day of Pompeii, dancing over a volcano." [3] Two weeks later (the 18th),

---

[1] Kraszewski, *Polska w czasie trzech rozbiorów*, iii, pp. 124 f.

[2] Smoleński, *Ostatni rok sejmu wielkiego*, pp. 348–354.

[3] Kraszewski, *op. cit.*, iii, p. 127.

Bulgakov presented his declaration, confirming the worst that had been anticipated.

At the next session of the Diet (the 21st), before densely packed galleries, the Russian note was read. Deep silence greeted it; but at the passage which announced that the Empress was sending her troops into the country in order to restore the liberties of the Polish nation, there were groans and laughter. The King spoke with his usual eloquence. He exhorted his people to manly courage and determination, pledging his own best efforts and enumerating the available means of defence. He referred to the Empress in flattering terms, expressing the hope that when better informed, she would decide not to proceed to extremities. He spoke with confidence of the aid to be expected from the King of Prussia, the ally with whose knowledge and approval all the most important acts of the present Diet had been effected. He advised soliciting the good offices of Austria and Saxony; and ' if any other means could be found for settling the issue rather with the pen than with the sword, assuredly none ought to be disdained, none ought to be neglected.' And he ended with the brave declaration: " Believe me, if there be need for sacrificing my own life, assuredly I shall not spare it." [1] It was a moving, an inspiring speech; but behind the phrase " rather with the pen than with the sword," lurked an intimation of where the King's thoughts really lay.

In the following week the final resolutions of the Diet were taken. Stanislas Augustus was appointed commander-in-chief of all the armed forces of the Republic. Save for the right of concluding peace, reserved to the Diet, he was virtually invested with a military dictatorship — a thing unparalleled in Polish history. War taxes were voted; arrangements were made for enlisting regiments of volunteers; and the government was authorized, in case of need, to decree a national *levée en masse*. Finally the Assembly sanctioned a counter-declaration to Russia, which was, unfortunately, too conciliatory and apologetic to be quite effective; a bold and spirited proclamation to the army; and an address of the King and the Estates to the nation.[2] These

[1] Smoleński, *op. cit.*, pp. 398 ff.   [2] Smoleński, *op. cit.*, pp. 408–413.

were the last acts of the Four Years' Diet. Not wishing to hamper the activity of the executive power by continuing its deliberations, on May 29 the assembly adjourned. It had done all that was possible for it to do at that late hour to provide for the needs of the crisis. The rest depended on the King, to whom the whole direction and the whole responsibility for the national defence had been entrusted.

II

If the struggle were not to be utterly unequal, Poland impera-tively needed to secure aid from outside. Naturally she turned first of all to the allied Court of Berlin, to whose assistance she had every right that solemn engagements could give. By the treaty of 1790, the continued validity of which was unquestioned, Frederick William had pledged himself to render military aid ' in case any foreign Power, by virtue of any previous acts or stipula-tions . . . should seek to assert the right to interfere in the inter-nal affairs of the Republic.' No stipulation could more exactly have fitted the situation of 1792. Nevertheless, for many months past the Prussian government had maintained an attitude so cold and forbidding as almost to preclude all hope of its assistance. When the Diet's first resolution to resist a Russian invasion was communicated to Berlin, Lucchesini replied with a stiff note to the effect that his master could not take cognizance of these decisions, since they related to matters utterly foreign to him. Orally the envoy added that as the King of Prussia had had no share in the revolution of the Third of May, he did not consider himself bound to render assistance, in case the Patriotic party wished to defend its work by force of arms.[1]

Ominous as was this reply, it was long before the Poles could convince themselves that the Court of Berlin would be as bad as its word. Of the hostility of the Prussian ministry there could be no doubt; but the world had often been taught that the policy of that ministry did not always coincide with that of its master; and it was reported from many sources that such was the case at

[1] Note of May 4, Lucchesini's report of the 5th, B. A., *R.* 9, 27.

present.[1] At any rate, faint as was the hope, no resource should be left untried. Hence, immediately after the Russian declaration the Polish government formally demanded that Prussia should recognize the *casus foederis*, and furnish the aid provided for in the treaty of alliance. And, as the value of ministerial notes was sufficiently known, it was decided to send a special envoy to Berlin to approach Frederick William personally, to make a supreme appeal to his loyalty and sense of honor, and at least to find out definitely whether he would do anything whatever on behalf of Poland. The painful mission was entrusted to the Marshal Potocki, who had been the author and the foremost supporter of the Prussian alliance.

No visitor could have been more unwelcome at Berlin, and no demands more embarrassing. Frederick William had no time or inclination to consider his engagements with the Republic, for he was already immersed in a negotiation for dismembering that allied state. Potocki was, indeed, favored with two audiences with the King and a conference with Schulenburg; but Frederick William merely stammered out a few platitudes and hastened to make his escape, while his minister took refuge behind such flimsy pretexts as: that the Poles themselves had provoked hostilities by their warlike resolutions of April; that the independence and integrity of the Republic were not endangered by the Russian invasion, and therefore there was no occasion for Prussia to intervene; or that the alliance had been concluded with a republic, Poland was now a monarchy, and therefore the treaty no longer held. Potocki soon had to recognize that there was absolutely no hope. Frederick William's last word was contained in his reply to Stanislas Augustus, in which he flatly refused to render aid, on the ground that the Constitution of the Third of May, which was subsequent to the alliance treaty, had so altered the situation that his engagements were in no way applicable to the present circumstances.[2] That meant definitely that in the moment of Poland's supreme need her ally had left her in the

---

[1] Details as to these reports in Askenazy, *op. cit.*, pp. 175, 233.

[2] The text of this letter (of June 8) is printed in part in Askenazy, *op. cit.*, p. 246. Potocki's detailed account of his audiences with the King and his discussions with Schulenburg, *ibid.*, pp. 237-253.

lurch. Such conduct can be characterized only as a flagrant breach of faith, an act of treachery with few parallels in history.

At Dresden and Vienna the efforts of the Poles were equally fruitless. The Elector would give only vague promises of his good offices; and Austria, while secretly expressing her sympathy, alleged that in the existing situation it was utterly impossible for her to do anything effective in behalf of the Republic. The mission of Prince Czartoryski to Vienna, which was the counterpart of Potocki's to Berlin, proved no more successful.[1] By the middle of June it was evident that no aid whatever was to be expected from any neighboring Power. Poland was thrown entirely upon her own resources.

Those resources were meagre enough. Although the size of the army had been trebled since the beginning of the Four Years' Diet, at the outbreak of the war it amounted to only 57,000 men; and deducting the reserves and the garrisons of various fortresses, there were barely 45,000 men available for field-service.[2] These troops, moreover, were but recently organized, imperfectly trained, and utterly inexperienced; they were inadequately equipped with arms, ammunition, and uniforms; and the commissariat and the field-hospital service left much to be desired.[3] In short, the army lacked almost everything except courage and patriotic enthusiasm. In spite of all deficiencies its spirit was excellent. Granted a little experience and proper leadership, it was capable of giving a good account of itself.

The leadership, however, was also not of the highest order. The command of the forces in the Ukraine, on which the brunt of

[1] Kaunitz to King Francis, June 1, V. A., *Vorträge*, 1792, and to de Caché, June 6, V. A., *Polen, Berichte*, 1792; Haugwitz's report of June 2, B. A., *R.* 1, *Conv.* 170.

[2] Smoleński, *Konfederacya targowicka*, p. 45.

[3] There is some difference of opinion on these points among Polish historians. Korzon (*Wewnętrzne dzieje*, v, pp. 133–137) attempts to prove that in spite of momentary disorders and deficiencies, and in spite of the complaints constantly made by the commanders, the army was adequately supplied and equipped. In a somewhat similar sense, Górski, *Historya piechoty polskiej*, pp. 194 f. On the other hand, the general view advanced in the text is maintained by the most recent historian of the war, Soplica, *Wojna polsko-rosyjska*, pp. 50 f., and by Smoleński, *Konfederacya targowicka*, pp. 46, 167.

the fighting would fall, had been given to the King's nephew, Prince Joseph Poniatowski, an inexperienced young man of twenty-nine, who, with all his gallantry and devotion, had not yet matured those talents that were to win him a great reputation as a marshal of Napoleon. Accepting the command against his will, weighed down by the sense of responsibility and the presentiment of failure, he displayed throughout the campaign a deplorable lack of initiative, an inability to seize what opportunities presented themselves, and an exaggerated unwillingness to take risks. Among the other officers, only one showed signs of real genius. That was Kościuszko; and he, unfortunately, was subordinated to Prince Joseph, and constantly fettered by the latter's excessive caution.

Between the 18th and the 22nd of May, four Russian corps invaded the Ukraine from the east, the south, and the southwest, while four others pressed into Lithuania. In the latter quarter there was no really effective resistance. The Polish forces, numbering 14,500 men, incapably led and faced by 32,000 Russians,[1] could only retreat steadily, fighting occasional unsuccessful rear-guard actions. In the south Prince Joseph and Kościuszko, with about 17,000 men, were pitted against Kakhovski's 64,000.[2] In the face of such an enormous disparity of numbers, the best chance for the Poles would seem to have lain in concentrating all their available forces and hurling them upon one or another of the widely separated Russian corps before the latter had time to unite. That proposal was made by Kościuszko at the very beginning of the campaign, but rejected by Prince Joseph on the ground that with such quite inexperienced troops the issue of a pitched battle would be hazardous, and with no reserves at hand a defeat would be ruinous.[3] The Prince was determined to hold strictly to the defensive, keeping his irreplaceable army intact, and maintaining his communications with the capital. The Russians, on their side, were confident of their ability to cut his line of retreat, surround him, and capture his whole army. As they were constantly able to outflank him, he was obliged to fall

---

[1] Smoleński, *op. cit.*, pp. 45 f.   [2] *Ibid.*
[3] Korzon, *Kościuszko*, p. 227.

back continually before them, abandoning one strong position after another. The campaign turned into a sort of chase, in the course of which Kakhovski more than once allowed the enemy to slip through his fingers, while the Poles displayed a certain dexterity in eluding their pursuers, and occasionally turned and struck back with good effect. Thus on June 18 at Zieleńce, when a Russian corps under General Markov, advancing too ardently and incautiously, suddenly found itself faced by the bulk of Prince Joseph's army, the Russians were rudely repulsed and forced to evacuate the battle-field, although the Polish commander failed to follow up his victory, as he should have done, by crushing Markov completely.

After more than a month of this game of hare and hounds, by early July Prince Joseph had retired behind the line of the Bug, which he hoped to be able to defend. On the 18th all the Polish positions were attacked by the enemy. The hardest fighting came at Dubienka, where Kościuszko with 6,000 Poles and 10 guns held at bay for three or four hours 19,000 Russians with 76 guns.[1] This was the fiercest and bloodiest battle of the war. Under cover of darkness Kościuszko did indeed withdraw, on learning that the passage of the river had been forced at several other points; but at any rate, his men had covered themselves with glory, and he, whose name had hitherto been little known, now became almost in a moment the national hero.

From the Bug the army fell back through Lublin to the Vistula. On July 25 it stood at Kurów on the right bank of that river, some distance to the south of the capital. The army of Lithuania was posted on the lower Bug, almost due east of Warsaw. These were the positions at the moment when hostilities ended.

The situation was not absolutely desperate. In some ways it was even more favorable than in the earlier stages of the campaign. The richest palatinates and the greater part of the territory of the Republic had indeed been overrun by the enemy, and the Russians had penetrated almost to the gates of Warsaw. But the more the scene of operations moved to the west, the farther the invaders were drawn away from their base, and the more

---

[1] Smoleński, *op. cit.*, pp. 177 f.

difficult it became for them to protect a terribly long and exposed line of communications. On the other hand, the various Polish forces were constantly getting closer together and better able to assist one another. The Vistula offered a relatively strong line of defence; and behind it were the still undrained resources of the western palatinates. There were 30,000 regular troops yet available; and volunteers were flocking in daily. The army had not been really defeated once. Only two considerable battles had been fought, the one a Polish victory, the other not a genuine defeat. The troops, green at the start, were getting hardened and experienced and sure of themselves; and in spite of the constant retreats, they were far from discouraged. Officers and men were thirsting for more fighting, eager to repeat the exploits of Zieleńce and Dubienka. Kościuszko later wrote bitterly: " The fighting spirit, ardor, and patriotism were universal. . . . The means of beating the Russian army were still in our hands. . . . But we didn't make use of them." [1] That they were not made use of, that the resistance collapsed at this moment, was not the fault of the army; it was due to the tremors and terrors of the cowardly King.

III

Stanislas Augustus had often sworn that he would never abandon the new constitution while life remained. He had solemnly declared that he would lead his people to battle and, if necessary, die with them. He had promised again and again to go to the field with the army; and indeed he made all the preparations, as if he meant to go. It is doubtful, however, whether he ever had any serious intentions of fighting. It is probable that no cause in the world and no conceivable disgrace could ever have induced this King to sacrifice his life, his crown, or even his personal comfort. When pressed to go to the camp, he inquired anxiously whether he would find there " a proper cuisine." [2]

From the very outset his program was, " rather with the pen than with the sword." The thought of settling everything by

---

[1] Soplica, *op. cit.*, p. 401. On the " comparatively favorable situation " at that time, *ibid.*, pp. 401 ff.

[2] Soplica, *op. cit.*, p. 222.

negotiations was in his mind even before the Russian declaration arrived[1]; and after war had actually begun, he took pains to keep the Russian envoy in Warsaw, and his own in St. Petersburg — anomalous as such a situation was — in order to leave all channels open. The first shot had hardly been fired when through the Chancellor Chreptowicz and the Danish minister Stanislas began to sound Bulgakov about the possibility of entering into negotiations.[2]

The failure of the missions to Berlin and Vienna, the military disasters in Lithuania, and the rapid advance of the Russians everywhere only confirmed the King in the opinion that resistance in arms was hopeless. His sister, his mistress, and others in his entourage continually dinned into his ears that he was on the verge of ruin, and that he must free himself from the perfidious counsels of the Potockis, the hereditary enemies of his family. Apparently he fell into a perfect panic. He saw nothing in the world but his crown. He dreaded nothing so much as to lose that. He was willing to do anything to save it.[3] It can readily be imagined how the defence of the country fared at the hands of a commander-in-chief who shut himself up in his palace in mortal terror, thought of nothing except placating the enemy, and seemed actually displeased at the news of a victory, from fear that it would irritate the Empress.[4]

By the middle of June nothing could hold back the King any longer from starting negotiations. At a session of the Council of War on the 18th, after the reading of various extremely black reports from the front, he succeeded in putting through a decision authorizing Prince Joseph to propose an armistice to Kakhovski, which was to last until the Polish government should have had

---

[1] See his letter to Bukaty of May 9, Kalinka, *Ostatnie lata*, ii, pp. 217 f.

[2] Bulgakov's report of May 22/June 2, M. A., Польша, III, 66. Already on May 12/23 the Russian envoy noted in his diary that the King wanted to negotiate, and was only waiting for the Diet to go home and leave him a free hand. The same opinion was current in the diplomatic corps at Warsaw (Lucchesini's report of June 2, B. A., *R. 9*, 27).

[3] Bulgakov's diary, June 10/21, M. A., *loc. cit.*; Cassini to Popov, June 27, July 4 and 7 (Papers of V. S. Popov, Imperial Public Library, Petrograd).

[4] *Vom Entstehen und Untergange der polnischen Konstitution vom 3. May*, 1791, ii, p. 131; Smoleński, *Konfederacya targowicka*, pp. 140 f.

time to communicate with St. Petersburg. That same day the indispensable Chreptowicz, who had always belonged to the Russian party, hastened to his good friend Bulgakov to disclose the King's propositions. His Majesty meant to beg the Empress to take Poland back into her good graces, give the country her younger grandson Constantine for its future king, and " improve the constitution " according to her superior wisdom, adding or rejecting what she pleased. Bulgakov, somewhat moved by these signs of repentance, suggested the draft of a letter from the King to his sovereign.[1]

The next day all these matters were laid before the cabinet (the *Straż*). Everyone present seems to have recognized the desirability of proposing a truce and of appealing to the Empress to end hostilities. Even the Marshal Potocki, just at that moment returned from Berlin in downcast mood, approved of this; but he strongly opposed the humiliating propositions outlined between Chreptowicz and Bulgakov. The result of the discussion was that a courier was sent to Prince Joseph with orders relating to the armistice (which Kakhovski, however, professed himself unable to grant), while the King's letter to the Empress was to be couched in the bolder and firmer tone recommended by Potocki.[2]

When Chreptowicz presented the document to Bulgakov, however, the Russian envoy declared flatly that this would never do; it did not contain the propositions previously agreed upon between them; the tone was all wrong; the King must simply throw himself on the mercy of the Empress. Thereupon, apparently without consulting his cabinet, and contrary to the sense of that body as manifested at its last session, Stanislas composed a new letter, which Bulgakov was willing to accept. If Potocki had recommended treating as one independent power with another, the King's tone was that of a suppliant. He ' begged and conjured ' the Empress to grant an armistice immediately. He implored her not to carry out in their full rigor the intentions announced in her declaration, while admitting that she had the

---

[1] Bulgakov's report of June 11/22, M. A., Польша, III, 66.

[2] Smoleński, *op. cit.*, p. 134.

material power to do whatever she pleased. The essence of the arrangement that he had to propose was that the succession should be assured to the Grand Duke Constantine, and that Poland should be attached to Russia by an "eternal alliance," while being allowed to enjoy "a better organized government than heretofore," and especially freedom from the perpetual danger of interregna. It will be noticed that the King did not yet offer to renounce the Constitution of the Third of May entirely. Not a word was said about the Confederation of Targowica. Indeed, the letter was essentially an attempt to bribe the Empress, by various advantages to herself, into throwing overboard that Confederation, allowing at least a part of the new constitution to stand, and permitting the King to retain at least a part of the power he had gained by it.[1]

For the next month Stanislas waited in morbid anxiety for a reply from St. Petersburg. As his appeal to the Empress had been kept rigorously secret, he continued to maintain a pretense of zeal for the war. He went on with the old manoeuvre of preparing to go to the army, and never going. He repeated over and over his hypocritical vow to die for his country. On July 4 he at last issued the long delayed summons for a national uprising — an act which might have produced great results, had it come at the beginning, instead of almost at the end, of the war.

The Empress' reply arrived on July 22. It was cold, inflexible, imperious, as only Catherine knew how to write. Every one of the King's proposals was rejected. He was simply advised — or rather ordered — to accede to the Confederation of Targowica without further delay, if he wished to avert the direst consequences to his country, and — it was hinted — to himself.[2] Stanislas was, or pretended to be, overwhelmed with grief and despair at these inexorable terms; nevertheless, before the end of the day he had arranged with Bulgakov the form in which his

---

[1] The King's letter of June 22 is printed in Kalinka, *Ostatnie lata*, ii, pp. 74 ff.; Solov'ev, *Geschichte des Falles von Polen*, pp. 284 f.; Smitt, *Suworow*, ii, pp. 461 ff., and elsewhere.

[2] This letter, dated July 2/13, is printed in Kalinka, *op. cit.*, ii, pp. 76 f., and elsewhere.

accession was to be made. It remained only to save appearances, as far as that could still be done.

For this purpose and no other, it would seem, on the 23rd the King called together an extraordinary council. He had taken pains to supplement the ordinary cabinet, in which he might not have had a clear majority on his side, by the addition of various high officials, on whose subservience he doubtless knew that he could count. Before this carefully picked body he read the Empress' letter, and then proceeded to set forth the situation of the country — naturally in the blackest of terms. There could be no doubt, he said, that the neighboring Powers were leagued together against Poland. Further resistance would lead to the immediate invasion of the Prussian armies already massed on the frontier. · Further resistance was impossible in any case, because of the utter lack of money and the overwhelming superiority of the hostile forces. No one could be more grieved than he at the terms laid down by the Empress; he would willingly give his life for the maintenance of the constitution; but the sense of an obligation higher than self-love, compelled him to consider whether any desperate resolution could now bring the country any real advantage. He therefore put the question whether it would not be better to accede to the Confederation of Targowica in accordance with the wishes of the Court of Petersburg.

The King's brother, the Primate, devoted to Russia from of old, chimed in with the assertion that it was impossible to save the constitution, but imperative to save the country. Others spoke in the same sense, including even Kołłątaj, hitherto always the boldest and most radical of the reformers. Only Małachowski, the Marshal of the Great Diet, Ignacy Potocki, and two others stood out unshakeably for resistance to the bitter end. Potocki denied that the military situation was hopeless. He described the enthusiasm and devotion of the troops. He conjured the King to put himself at the head of the army and thereby set an example that would surely inspire the nation to rise as one man; or if he would not do that, let him at least lay down the crown and leave the country, rather than stoop to associate himself with a band of traitors. Ostrowski pointed to the overwhelming odds in the face of which the Dutch had successfully carried through their struggle for independence against Philip II; and he called upon the King to emulate the bravery and constancy of John Casimir, under whom Poland had been almost miraculously delivered from extremities worse than the present. But all such manly counsels were wasted. Stanislas Augustus leaving his palace, his concerts, his mistresses, his ' proper cuisine,' for the rough life of the camp — that was something inconceivable.

Eight of those present had spoken in favor of submitting to the Empress' demands and four against. After Potocki had made his last appeal, there was a moment's silence. Then the King announced that, having no more hope of saving a constitution dear to him personally, and desiring to spare the country useless bloodshed, complete devastation, and perhaps a new dismemberment, he had decided to conform to the opinion of the majority and accede to the Confederation.[1] The following day (the 24th) his accession was sent to Bulgakov, while the army was ordered to cease hostilities, recognize the Confederation, and leave the road to Warsaw open to the Russians.

The King's shameful desertion produced an indescribable feeling of rage, grief, and consternation in the capital, the army, and the country at large. Nevertheless it immediately ended all resistance to the invaders. For some few days it did indeed appear likely that there would be a general uprising at Warsaw and a repetition of the scenes then familiar at Paris. Crowds gathered in the streets and squares, fiercely denouncing the King, threatening to string up to the lamp-posts the advisers who had misled him, and overwhelming with ovations those who had stood up for the constitution. Inflammatory pamphlets and pasquils were everywhere spread abroad. The police felt obliged to patrol the city in heavy squads with loaded muskets, breaking up gatherings in the streets and suppressing demonstrations. The guard at the castle was doubled; and the King, trembling and quaking, looked forward to the advent of the Russians as to a deliverance. But, whether it was for fear of the oncoming enemy,

[1] Bulgakov's report of July 16/27, M. A., Польша, III, 68; Cassini to Zubov, July 25 (papers of V. S. Popov); Smoleński, *op. cit.*, pp. 210–216.

or because of the lack of leadership, or because the Warsaw mob had not the courage or the violent instincts of the Parisians, at all events no serious outbreak took place.[1]

The Patriotic leaders, unwilling to start a civil war against their King and feeling that for the present their cause was lost, determined to leave the country. The Marshals of the late Diet issued a formal protest against the Confederation of Targowica. Those members of the party who held high offices, resigned. Soon practically all those who were called ' the men of the Third of May ' had departed for Leipsic, Venice, or other havens of refuge. The roads from Warsaw to the frontier were choked with the exodus.

In the army there was some talk of continuing the struggle in spite of everything. Many of the officers, including Kościuszko, urged upon Prince Joseph the bold plan of abducting the King and holding him a prisoner in the camp, while the fight for independence was carried on in his name; but the Prince could not bring himself to such an act of violence against his uncle.[2] Thereupon, rather than betray the cause they had sworn to defend, Prince Joseph, Kościuszko, and several dozen other officers resigned, and many of them retired abroad.

Meanwhile the Russian troops arrived at Warsaw and encamped just outside, to hold down ' the factious city.' Most of the provinces were similarly garrisoned. The Polish army, after being obliged to take the oath to the Confederation, was parcelled out in small detachments about the country, wherever it could do least harm to its new masters. The King, in spite of his submission, was kept almost a state prisoner. The Confederates would have deposed him outright, had the Empress been willing to allow it. Forbidden that satisfaction, they treated him like a convicted criminal, subjecting him to all the humiliations in their power, and denying him any influence whatever in public affairs.

The whole machinery of government was now, nominally at least, in the hands of the men of Targowica. Their rôle had been

---

[1] As to the scenes in the capital in these days, Cassini to Zubov, July 25, and to Popov, July 26; Smoleński, *op. cit.*, pp. 219 ff.

[2] On this plan, see Soplica, *op. cit.*, pp. 419 ff.; Smoleński, *op. cit.*, pp. 226 f.

insignificant enough while the war lasted. Returning to their country under the protection of the invading army, and following at a safe distance in the rear of the Russians, they had done their utmost to produce a popular uprising in their favor, and they had failed utterly. In vain they had attempted to debauch the army that was fighting so valiantly for the nation's independence. In vain they had tried to create an army of their own. Without a strong guard of Cossacks they hardly dared show themselves. Their proclamations, appeals, orders, and menaces produced little or no response from their fellow-countrymen. If they succeeded in forming local confederations here and there in the conquered provinces, it was with the utmost difficulty, and often only by the use of violence and constraint. It was true that after the King's accession the situation was considerably changed in this respect. As the Constitutionalist cause seemed hopelessly lost while the men of Targowica appeared to have the game in their hands, their ranks were soon swollen by the adhesion of all those who, regardless of honor or patriotism, were eager to be on the winning side. The formation of confederations in each palatinate and the union of all these local associations in a ' general Confederation ' then went forward without much trouble. Still it cannot be said that the men of Targowica ever acquired a really considerable popular following. The mass of the nation held aloof, despising and execrating them as a pack of traitors. Even the Russian officers hardly concealed their contempt for their protégés. Without the Empress' support the Confederation could not have held its position a single day. Without her advice and approval its leaders dared not raise a hand. In short, the Confederation remained what it had been from the outset, a mere figurehead behind which Russia could exercise sovereign rights over the Republic.

Thus Poland was once more prostrate before her old oppressors. After enjoying a few brief years of glorious, exhilarating freedom, after attempting to play once more the part of an independent and active power in Europe, after striving so hard to purge itself of the ancient errors and weaknesses and to lay the foundations for a sound and progressive national life, the country suddenly found itself plunged back under the old detested, anarchical régime and into the old servitude to the foreigner. A more bitter history it would be hard to imagine, were it not that the immediate future had even worse disasters in store.

IV

The rapid and complete success of Catherine's Polish enterprise would hardly have been possible but for the strange passivity of the two German Powers. Their inactivity was not due to whole-hearted approval of her conduct. Both Courts had been not a little ruffled when at the beginning of May, instead of forming the proposed concert, she had simply called upon them to acquiesce in her high-handed measures and to give her virtually *carte blanche* in Poland. Although Prussia was anything but displeased at the prospect of seeing the work of the Third of May overthrown, and Austria had at last made up her mind to accept that as inevitable,[1] still neither Court wished to allow Russia to regulate Polish affairs single-handed, or to attain a quite exclusive predominance in the Republic.

In view of the French war, however, downright opposition to the Empress was hardly possible, and in any case both Powers attached too much importance to her good graces to be willing to attempt it. Even to make polite remonstrances was a matter for serious hesitation. It required much ingenuity to devise, and not a little courage to propose, measures that would check the designs, without too much wounding the susceptibilities, of the great lady in St. Petersburg. Neither Court aspired to the honor of being the one to pull the chestnuts out of the fire. For some time each contented itself with begging the other to confide its inmost thoughts about what was to be done.

The Prussians really preferred to do nothing at all for the present. They hoped that if there should be a negotiation between the Empress and the government at Warsaw, they would have a chance to interpose their ' good offices '; and if, on the other

---

[1] As late as May 9, Cobenzl was ordered to urge the Russians to delay resorting to violent measures. It was only on June 9 that the ambassador was instructed that his master agreed entirely with the Empress on the desirability of restoring the old constitution in Poland. Vivenot, *op. cit.*, ii, pp. 31 f., 88 f.

hand, there was a protracted struggle, they might find a pretext for armed intervention. For a time they played with the idea of drawing a cordon across the Polish territory adjacent to their frontier, without, however, finding the courage to take even so half-way energetic a step. Painfully anxious to avoid all that might possibly give umbrage at St. Petersburg, they preferred to stand idle, consoling themselves with the thought that sooner or later — perhaps in the course of the pending negotiation for a Russo-Prussian alliance — the Empress would offer them a partition. Goltz was still strong in the faith that that was her intention. Doubtless there have been happier examples of political sagacity. It is hard to see how the Prussian ministers could have expected Catherine to make so huge a bid for their support, when they were already conceding to her practically all she desired of them. From what we know of the sentiments prevalent at St. Petersburg at this time, it seems almost certain that had Prussia taken a more vigorous tone and insisted on getting the price of her complaisance, she could have secured easily then and there all that she obtained with so much difficulty six or seven months later.

It was from the Austrian side that the first proposals for action were made. Kaunitz had determined to checkmate the Empress by taking up the idea of the triple concert, which she herself had suggested and then apparently abandoned, and making it a reality. He meant to enforce the principle that Polish affairs could not be regulated definitively save by the joint action of all three of the neighboring Powers. In accordance with that principle, the Confederation of Targowica must be induced to request the protection of Austria and Prussia, as it had already invoked that of Russia. The envoys of the three Courts at Warsaw must act together. Above all, the Empress must be invited to sign a convention by which each of the three Powers should bind itself to undertake nothing in Poland without the consent of the other two. By such arrangements Kaunitz hoped to prevent the Republic from becoming once more a mere province of Russia; to win for Austria an influence in Polish affairs such as she had seldom possessed in the past; and also to guard against that danger which had been feared at Vienna ever since the beginning of the crisis — an agreement between Russia and Prussia for a new partition without the knowledge of their common ally.[1]

About the middle of May the Chancellor explained to Jacobi, the Prussian envoy, his ideas about setting bounds, by the means just indicated, to the Empress' activity in Poland. Having reported to his Court, Jacobi received a reply which was, to say the least, far from clear, but from which he concluded that his master fully approved of Kaunitz's suggestions. He could only have been confirmed in this impression by a previous rescript, in which the Prussian ministry had declared that the most essential thing at-present was to prevent Russia from acquiring exclusive control in Poland, and that this aim might be attained by insisting continually on a triple concert.[2] It is not surprising, therefore, that the envoy took up Kaunitz's idea with some energy. Just at this moment Jacobi was performing the last acts of his ministry at Vienna and initiating his successor, Count Haugwitz[3] into current affairs. The latter, inexperienced and zealous, threw himself into the scheme under discussion with a vigor not uncommon with beginners in diplomacy, but at that moment quite inconvenient for his Court.

On getting the ambiguous orders of May 21, the two Prussian envoys began to assail the Austrians with demands for a definite declaration to be presented by the allied Courts at St. Petersburg. Spielmann, who had probably already received a secret proposal from Berlin of a very different sort, met their suggestions rather coolly. He professed himself convinced of the purity of

---

[1] This idea of a quasi-permanent triple concert on Polish affairs was only a development of the principle laid down in the Vienna Convention of July 25, 1791, and in the February alliance treaty. It first appears in fairly definite form in a note of Kaunitz to Ph. Cobenzl of May 4, 1792 (printed in Schlitter, *Kaunitz, Ph. Cobenzl und Spielmann*, p. 59). Cf. the note of Kaunitz of May 18, printed in Vivenot, ii, p. 47.

[2] Jacobi's report of May 16, rescripts to him of May 18 and 21, B. A., R. 1, *Conv.* 169.

[3] Haugwitz, who here began his ill-fated public career, had been destined since October to the post at Vienna, which he owed not only to his personal credit with Frederick William (he was of the Rosicrucian Society), but also to his friendship with the late Emperor, and to his supposed sympathy for the Austrian alliance, to which Jacobi had never been able to adapt himself.

the Empress' intentions, and too busy — on the eve of his departure for the coronation at Buda — to undertake to draw up the desired declarations. Haugwitz and Jacobi, not to be rebuffed, thereupon announced that they would compose the draft themselves, and presently they returned with one at which Spielmann was fairly aghast. It contained, for example, the astonishing demand that the Empress should arrest the advance of her troops until the three Courts had agreed upon the measures to be taken in common. Haugwitz was quite aware that such a demand would have to be backed up by military demonstrations and threats, but he did not shrink from that prospect. Spielmann, however, protested emphatically and outlined a much more moderate declaration, which the Prussians then accepted and at once put upon paper.[1]

Haugwitz next presented this draft to Kaunitz, who, finding in it his own ideas, was highly pleased, declaring that if by this means they could gain their great object, it would be a political stroke of the rarest sort. The court having gone to Buda, it required some time to obtain the royal assent to the project; but this having been secured, the Chancellor proceeded to tone down still more the terms of the declaration, and to add a draft for the proposed convention, by which the three Powers were to bind themselves to do nothing in Poland henceforth except conjointly and by common accord. If the Empress entered upon this agreement, recognized the principle of " a just community of influence," and took steps to induce the Confederation to request the support of Austria and Prussia, the latter were in return to present declarations at Warsaw analogous to Bulgakov's, and also, in case of need, to render active military assistance to the Russians. On June 20 the projects for the joint declaration and the convention were sent to Berlin.[2]

---

[1] Jacobi's report of May 28, B. A., *R.* 1, *Conv.* 169. Haugwitz's readiness to use measures of coercion against the Empress appears again in his report of June 2, B. A., *R.* 1, *Conv.* 170. Spielmann's coldness towards the plan must have been due in great part to the fact that he had probably just received Schulenburg's secret overture regarding a new partition. That proposal was made through a letter of May 22. The post between Berlin and Vienna ordinarily took five days, and Spielmann's conferences with Jacobi and Haugwitz took place the 28th.

[2] For the above: Haugwitz's reports of June 2, 11, 15, B. A., *R.* 1, *Conv.*

The Prussian ministry had been much irritated ever since learning of the independent step of their two envoys. They foresaw that the declaration would not please the Empress, and that the Court of Vienna, or rather its ambassador at St. Petersburg, would probably try to throw the blame upon them. They had been led into sanctioning the plan, however, on the receipt of Jacobi's first dispatches, which made it appear that the declaration proposed by the two envoys awaited only the King of Hungary's approval to be sent off at once to St. Petersburg. When more correctly informed on that point, they did not spare hints to Reuss that they would much prefer not to take this step at present, although constantly repeating that they would abide by the decisions of their ally. They probably breathed a sigh of relief when the draft prepared by Kaunitz reached Berlin; for the Chancellor had moderated the language and eliminated every suggestion of coercion exactly as they would have desired. Frederick William and his ministers approved it therefore, because it ' contained absolutely nothing contrary to their interests and intentions,' without attaching any great hopes to it, as Kaunitz had done. In transmitting it to Goltz, they took care to emphasize that this was really the handiwork of the Viennese cabinet, and not theirs; and the envoy was instructed not to thrust himself unduly forward in conducting this affair.[1]

On receiving their dispatches, neither Cobenzl nor his colleague quite knew what to do with the declaration. It provided for a

170; Kaunitz to the King, May 30, to Reuss and L. Cobenzl, June 21, the Austrian draft of the declaration and convention, and the Jacobi-Haugwitz draft, Vivenot, ii, pp. 67 f., 99–103, 105 ff. In his letter to the King of May 30, Kaunitz vehemently accused Spielmann of advising their sovereign against the plan simply because it was not his own idea. On June 5 the Referendary replied (V. A., *Vorträge*, 1792), calling the King to witness that he had never spoken a word about it to him either *pro* or *contra*, and adding that he had himself dictated the draft of the declaration word for word to Jacobi and Haugwitz, and that in its present form he thoroughly approved of it. It follows from this that Spielmann, although he had received the original propositions of the Prussians rather coldly cannot be said to have opposed the project, as Sybel declares (*op. cit.*, ii, p. 213).

[1] Rescript to Jacobi of June 3, and to Haugwitz, June 7, B. A., *R.* 1, *Conv.* 170; Reuss to Kaunitz and to Spielmann, June 9, V. A., *Preussen, Berichte*, and *Vorträge*, 1792; Schulenburg and Alvensleben to the King, June 27, and Frederick William's reply of the 28th, rescript to Goltz, June 27, B. A., *R.* XI, *Russland*, 133.

formal convention, and yet neither minister had received powers to sign such an act. They agreed to present the declaration jointly, made some half-hearted representations, and went no further. Each regarded the other with dislike and suspicion; neither wished to be the one to bell the cat. Under such circumstances their ' joint action ' could scarcely be very effective.

The Russians were not slow to size up the situation. Markov told Goltz that his Court showed too much deference to that of Vienna. Ostermann remarked to Cobenzl that Austria had just given a very great proof of her intimacy with Prussia.[1] Playing off the one German Power against the other had always been Russia's forte, and nothing could have been more unwelcome at St. Petersburg than to encounter their united and determined opposition. Nothing could have been less to the Empress' taste than a formal, permanent concert on Polish affairs, or the admission of the other Powers to an equal share in guiding and controlling the Republic. She delayed her answer, however, for many weeks, until the complete triumph of her armies had removed the chief pretext for Austro-Prussian intervention. Then in a note (of August 25), which was not without a touch of irony, she thanked the two Courts for their willingness to render assistance that was no longer needed. She promised to employ her good offices to induce the Confederation to invoke the support of Austria and Prussia — as soon as that body had become more firmly established. She politely refused the proposed convention as superfluous, in view of the engagements contained in the treaties of alliance which she had just concluded with both the German Powers. The Russo-Prussian treaty did, in fact, contain a provision for a concert of the three Courts to settle the affairs of Poland; and although the corresponding stipulation in the Austro-Russian one made no mention of Prussia, the cabinet of St. Petersburg professed its willingness to amend that article.[2]

This vague, evasive, and almost sarcastic reply would probably alone have sufficed to put a damper upon Kaunitz's project.

[1] For the above: Goltz's report of July 27, B. A., *R.* XI, *Russland*, 133; Cobenzl's of the 21st, V. A., *Russland*, *Berichte*, 1792.

[2] Cobenzl's and Goltz's reports of August 28, V. A., *Russland*, *Berichte*, 1792 and B. A., *R.* XI, *Russland*, 133.

But by this time the German Powers themselves had lost all real interest in the matter. Another plan of a very different kind relating to Poland was already in full negotiation between them. Hence the proposed convention was relegated to the archives. Nothing more was heard of that triple Areopagus which was to have presided over the destinies of the Republic. Thus ended the one joint effort made by Austria and Prussia to check the Empress' victorious course, and to prevent her from recovering her old exclusive control in Poland. The episode illustrates admirably the difficulties in the way of any effective common action on the part of these Powers in opposition to Catherine. Each Court was far too eager to stand high in her favor to be willing to adopt a really firm attitude. Each was reluctant to take the lead, for fear that it would draw all the blame upon itself. Each hung back, while trying to thrust the other forward. Each was mortally afraid that its ally would outstrip it in Catherine's good graces. Under such circumstances the Empress could go her way unimpeded.

V

How little the two German Powers thought of serious opposition to Russia is shown by the fact that in this summer of 1792 both were engaged in concluding alliances with her. It has already been noted that by the Vienna Convention and the Treaty of Berlin Austria and Prussia had agreed to invite the Court of St. Petersburg to accede to their new union. When in April the two monarchs came to carry out this promise, the forms adopted in both letters suggested not so much a simple accession to the existing treaty, as the establishment of similar engagements between the Empress and the King of Prussia.[1] This latter

---

[1] Francis to Catherine, April 12, 1792 (Beer, *Leopold II, Franz II, und Catharina*, pp. 170 f. In Vivenot, i, p. 409, dated erroneously as " ce (7–8 ?) mars "): " Sa Majesté Prussienne se dispose . . . à L'inviter incessamment à des engagemens analogues à ceux dont Je Lui fais part par la présente " [the Treaty of Berlin]. . . . He wishes to inform her of " les ouvertures que le Roi de Prusse est à la veille de Lui faire," and adds: " je ne saurois me dispenser de Lui témoigner en même tems la satisfaction infinie que je ressentirois en Lui voyant adopter les mêmes principes." This is vague enough, and probably designedly so, as the

method was quite to Catherine's taste. She had never liked triple alliances, for in such associations one might be outvoted. In an *alliance à deux*, on the other hand, she was always sure to be the dominant partner. Hence she replied to the Austrians that certain clauses in the Treaty of Berlin (especially that mentioning the Infanta of Poland, which implied a recognition of the Constitution of the Third of May) prevented her from acceding to it; but that she was confident that she would be conforming to the intentions of His Apostolic Majesty in making a separate treaty with Prussia, which would be based on the same principles as the Austro-Prussian one, and which would be communicated at Vienna immediately after its conclusion.[1] In the meantime, although its term had not expired, she offered to renew her alliance with Austria for another eight years.[2] To the Prussians, on the other hand, the highly welcome reply was given that the Empress was willing to contract directly with the King an alliance based on the former treaties between the two Courts; and that she preferred this procedure as characterizing more perfectly the return of both parties to the old ideas about the utility of a *liaison* between them. Ostermann remarked significantly to Goltz that it would be much better for them to unite " without admitting certain people " (i. e., the Austrians).[3] Doubtless this had been the wish of the Prussians from the outset.[4]

It could hardly give unalloyed pleasure at Vienna to see that Leopold's loyalty to Russia and his steadfast refusal to enter into any connection into which his ancient ally could not be invited,

Austrians were far from eager to have the Empress accede to the alliance. Frederick William to Catherine, April 15, 1792: " Je ne balance donc pas de L'inviter à y concourir en Lui proposant des engagemens defensifs analogues à ceux du susdit Traité," B. A., *R. XI, Russland*, 133.

[1] Catherine to Francis, May 2/13, 1792, Beer, *op. cit.*, pp. 175 f.

[2] Ostermann to Razumovski, May 4/15, M. A., Австрія, III, 52; Cobenzl's report of May 19, V. A., *Russland, Berichte*, 1792. Heidrich is wrong in declaring (*op. cit.*, p. 207) that the proposal for the renewal of the alliance was made from the Austrian side, and that the Russians " wondered at the strange demand."

[3] Catherine to Frederick William, May 3/14, Goltz's report of May 17, B. A., *R. XI, Russland*, 133.

[4] Cf. Bischoffwerder's overtures to Alopeus of the previous autumn. Goltz was highly delighted at the "adroit manner " in which the Empress had avoided acceding directly to the Austro-Prussian treaty.

had resulted only in paving the way for a separate Russo-Prussian alliance. There was a certain irony in the fact that Austria, who for years had made it her business to prevent any connection between St. Petersburg and Berlin, had now become the medium for a reunion of those two Courts. The Viennese statesmen were not a little chagrined at the rôle they had been obliged to play, and not a little disquieted over the possible results of the rapprochement which they had sponsored. At any rate, there was all the more reason to tighten their own connection with Russia. Cobenzl was at once provided with full powers to renew the existing alliance; and he rushed through the treaty with a haste which the jealous Goltz found positively "indecent." There was, indeed, no occasion for delay, since it was merely a question of renewing the engagements of 1781, with a very few slight modifications. The separate article which concerned Poland contained the mutual guarantee of the constitution of 1773, of the 'fundamental laws,' and of the boundaries of the Republic as fixed at the time of the Partition. Austria thereby abandoned the Constitution of the Third of May formally and completely. On July 14, 1792, the Austro-Russian treaty was signed.[1]

The negotiation between Russia and Prussia was not quite so simple a matter. The draft of a treaty, prepared at St. Petersburg on the basis of the treaty of alliance of 1769, encountered some objections at Berlin, especially the clauses relating to Poland. The Russians had proposed a concert of the two Courts

---

[1] The Empress' decision to conclude this treaty was in no way influenced by the Austrian proposal of the Bavarian-Polish plan, as one might judge from Sybel's account (*op. cit.*, iii, p. 163). Razumovski's courier, who brought this proposal, reached St. Petersburg three days after the treaty was signed.

Heidrich says the treaty " kennzeichnet sich gerade durch die Geschwindigkeit seines Abschlusses gelegentlich einer Landpartie von Cobenzl mit Bezborodko als völlig bedeutungslos " (*op. cit.*, p. 207). As to how far it was ' völlig bedeutungslos,' a word will be said in the text; but it deserves to be pointed out here: (1) that the chief reason for haste lay in the necessity of concluding before the Imperial coronation at Frankfort, so as to avoid the usual controversy about precedence between the two Imperial Majesties; (2) The *Landpartie* in question (which took place on the 11th) had nothing in the world to do with it, as the whole affair was previously settled with the exception of a couple of utterly insignificant points — the wording of one phrase and the question of naming France as one of the allies of Austria (Cobenzl's report of July 21, V, A.),

to reëstablish the ancient order of things in the Republic. The Prussian ministry demanded the inclusion of Austria in the concert, and they named as the common aims the reëstablishment *and maintenance* of the Polish government on *approximately* the old bases. The Russians were far from eager to take Austria into the partnership, as they were opposed on principle to threefold ententes; but Goltz stood firm, and after a month of haggling, on August 7, 1792, the treaty was signed at St. Petersburg, substantially in accordance with the modifications proposed at Berlin.[1]

While it has sometimes been asserted, it seems hardly accurate to say that by this treaty Catherine went over from the Austrian to the Prussian system. Undoubtedly the relations between the Imperial Courts were no longer so intimate as in the days of Joseph II; Leopold's independent and pacific policy had aroused dislike and distrust on the Neva; and since his death the reticence, the delays, the reluctant concessions, and "the petty *finasseries*" of the Court of Vienna had often produced no little irritation. But in spite of all, the conviction was deeply rooted in Russian minds that the alliance with Austria was a ' natural ' and a necessary system. Moments of discontent and coolness might occur, but these would be only passing shadows. The renewal of the alliance was by no means a mere hollow formality. Though its immediate object was to allay suspicions at Vienna regarding the Empress' rapprochement with Prussia, it also bore witness to the abiding belief of the Russian statesmen in the permanent utility of the older connection, and to their resolution to wait patiently until the Austrians returned to a sounder appreciation of their true interests.[2]

The Prussian alliance, on the other hand, owed its conclusion chiefly to the exigencies of the moment: the need of conciliating the Court of Berlin until Polish affairs were settled, and the neces-

---

[1] Printed in Martens, *Traités conclus par la Russie*, vi, pp. 148–158.

[2] For the above: Bezborodko to the Empress, January 25/February 5, 1792, M. A., Турцïя, IX, 14; Markov to Razumovski, March 9/20, April 10/21, October 9/15, 1792, October, 1793, P. A., XV, 576. Numerous examples of the same ideas might be cited from the Vorontsov correspondence.

sity of preventing a revival of the Anglo-Prussian league.[1] The conviction of permanent common interests which formed the strength of the Austrian system was lacking here.[2] The best proof of this is the fact that as soon as the Polish question seemed to be settled, the Prussian alliance lost all reality, while the Austrian one continued with growing intimacy down to the time of the Empress' death. But for the present the new *liaison* with the Court of Berlin was of the greatest value. For it gave Catherine a comparatively free hand in Poland, offered her the chance to mediate between Austria and Prussia in the indemnity question, and afforded the desired security against too close a connection between the German Powers.

At the close of the summer the Empress held a truly commanding position. She had brought to a successful conclusion the Polish enterprise which most observers had believed she would never dare risk. Whatever the moral aspects of that affair, she had achieved a spectacular triumph of the rarest sort. With Poland at her feet, with both the German Powers attached to her by alliances and competing for her favor, with her own hands free while her neighbors were just undertaking an enormous, an impossible task, she could well afford to sit back and watch events confidently and serenely. " My part is sung," she wrote to Rumiantsov. " It is an example of how it is not impossible to attain an end and to succeed if one really wills it." [3]

---

[1] Cf. the protocols of the Council of the Empire of April 22/May 3 and May 31/June 11, 1792, Арх. Гос. Сов., i, pp. 912 ff., 920 f.

[2] Cf. Markov to S. R. Vorontsov, January 17/28, and July 27/August 7, 1793, Арх. Вор., xx, pp. 34 ff., 52. Although he was writing to a man of strong pro-Austrian views, Markov's declarations may probably be accepted at their face value, as they were abundantly corroborated by the later course of Russian policy.

[3] Letter of October 29/November 9, 1792, Русская Старина, lxxxi², p. 158.

CHAPTER XIII

Austria and Prussia Agree upon a Partition

I

That the upheaval precipitated by Catherine's violent intervention in Poland would end with a new partition was, in the opinion of many observers, almost a foregone conclusion from the moment the Empress began her enterprise.[1] For such a dénouement the situation was altogether favorable. The close union of the three Eastern Powers, the effacement of England, the assassination of the restless King of Sweden, and the exhaustion of Turkey provided a political constellation of the most auspicious character. Recent events suggested the necessity of taking drastic measures to check the alarming recrudescence of Polish vitality; and no measure could be quite so effective as a repetition of the political-surgical operation performed with such success twenty years before. The appetites of the Eastern Powers, which throughout the protracted Oriental crisis had been constantly whetted but never satisfied, could not much longer be restrained; and the principle that indemnities must be found somewhere for the expenses of the French war supplied a convenient pretext.

It has already been noted that the idea of taking these indemnities in Poland was discussed at Potsdam as early as February of 1792, and that in March at Vienna there was talk of combining this project with that of the Bavarian Exchange. It was not until May, however, that these plans were made the subject of a negotiation. The initiative was taken by Prussia.

From the 12th to the 15th of May conferences were held at Potsdam between the King, the Duke of Brunswick, Schulenburg, Bischoffwerder, and Reuss. In the intimate discussions which

---

[1] Cf. Cobenzl's prophecies to the Russians in January and March, 1792, already cited; the warnings addressed by the British government to Berlin and Vienna in March, Salomon, *Pitt*, i[ii], p. 540; the forecast of Gustavus III, Odhner, *op. cit.*, pp. 204 f.

then took place, the Prussian plan of action was probably decided upon;[1] at any rate, immediately afterward the first fairly definite overtures looking to a partition were made both to Russia and to Austria. It was, of course, an infinitely delicate subject to lead up to; and, as will appear in the sequel, the Prussians went about it with all conceivable caution.

A convenient pretext for sounding the Russians was furnished by a dispatch from Goltz, which arrived in the midst of the discussions at Potsdam. The envoy wrote that he feared the Court of St. Petersburg wished to combine the affairs of France too much with those of Poland. The single word ' *bon* ' scrawled on the dispatch opposite this passage, sufficiently shows that Goltz's superiors were far from sharing his disquietude.[2] Soon after his return to Berlin, Schulenburg hunted up Alopeus and confided to him that he heard from all sides that the Empress wished to combine French and Polish affairs; he personally could not at all understand what this meant, and was curious to be informed. The Russian envoy, unfortunately, could not enlighten him, and Schulenburg did not see fit to speak plainly.[3]

Bischoffwerder, however, was less reserved. Having written from Potsdam to request an interview, he met Alopeus on the 18th at Charlottenburg, guided the conversation to the subject of Poland, and presently threw out the suggestion that in order to remove all occasions for controversy between the three Eastern Powers, it would be best to reduce the Republic to so insignificant a size that it could safely be left free to choose whatever form of government it pleased. If this idea were once adopted, he added, it would be easy enough to come to an understanding; and the principal rôle in directing the affair would naturally be reserved

[1] In a letter to the Duke of Brunswick of May 6, Schulenberg mentioned combining French and Polish affairs, and promised to go into details in case he was summoned to the conference at Potsdam. B. A., *R. XI, Frankreich*, 89 *b*.

[2] Goltz's report of May 1, received the 14th, B. A., *R. XI, Russland*, 133. Cf. Appendix XIII (documents illustrating the earliest discussions between Russia and Prussia regarding a new partition).

[3] Alopeus' report of May 8/19, M. A., Пруссія, III, 29. Goltz was also ordered (May 17) to find out how the Russian Court thought to combine two questions between which the Prussian ministry pretended to see no great connection. B. A., *R. XI, Russland*, 133.

for the Empress. Alopeus reported to his Court that he had merely listened and said nothing.[1] It was apparently the first time that a Prussian had broached the topic of a partition to him.

A week or so later Schulenburg favored the Russian envoy with a long disquisition on the subject of indemnities for the French enterprise, insisting strongly that his master must receive compensation of some sort, and begging for a communication of the Empress' views on that matter.[2] Putting together these various overtures, the Court of Petersburg could hardly be badly at a loss to divine the object of Prussia's aspirations.

While thus paving the way for a future understanding, Frederick William and his advisers did not at that time mean to go further than hints with Russia. Their purpose was, first of all, to make sure of Austria, and then with the suport of their ally to drive the best bargain they could with the Empress.

Schulenburg proceeded to initiate his action at Vienna with one of those little tricks so beloved in eighteenth century diplomacy: a negotiation behind the back of the Austrian Chancellor, quite on a par with Leopold's and Kaunitz's intrigues with Bischoffwerder. As to which of the Viennese ministers to approach first, there could hardly be a question. The one among them who was known to be the most ardent champion of the Prussian connection, was Spielmann. Accordingly, on May 21 Schulenburg confided to Reuss certain ideas on which he desired a very secret and frank exchange of opinions with the State Referendary. In view of the unexpected and high-handed action of Russia in Poland, he declared, it behooved Austria and Prussia to consider measures to safeguard their own interests and prestige. If the Empress continued to conceal her real intentions, while her armies went steadily forward, he would suggest that the two Courts should send corps of observation across the frontier, without declaring themselves for or against anyone, and thus, on the pretext of providing for their own security, establish themselves in Polish territory. Such a demonstration would probably force Russia at last to reveal her true aims. From many indications he

---

[1] Alopeus' report of May 8/19. M. A., Пруссія, III, 29.
[2] Alopeus' report of May 17/28.

thought it likely that the Empress greatly desired to appropriate the Ukraine. If that supposition proved correct, it might facilitate a settlement of the indemnity question: for in that case Prussia, too, might take a part of Poland, while Austria found compensation on the Rhine. In conclusion he begged that this plan should be kept in the utmost secrecy until it had been agreed upon by both Courts, and until the moment for its execution arrived.[1]

On receiving this momentous overture, Spielmann seems to have had little hesitation about entering into the project, which fitted in well, indeed, with ideas that he had had in mind since March or even January. With the approval of King Francis, he replied by a letter to Reuss, in which he declared himself agreed with Schulenburg on the main principle. If Russia, he said, coveted Polish territory, of which, however, he had as yet seen no indication, she could doubtless make no more suitable acquisition than Courland or the Ukraine.[2] He was convinced that the Court of Berlin could nowhere else find more desirable aggrandizement than in Poland; and Austria would assuredly consent to such a Prussian acquisition not only without envy or jealousy, but with a truly friendly readiness to assist in the matter. But it could never suit the Court of Vienna, he protested, to seek its indemnity on the Rhine; for of what value were remote and precarious acquisitions, which could be retained only by immense efforts, and which would expose their possessor to the odium of having been the only Power to take part in a dismemberment of France? Moreover, to seek compensation through conquests in the west would involve prolonging the war beyond the present year — and the allies hoped to finish the struggle within that time — or else altering the whole plan of campaign. He was therefore of the opinion that the only means of realizing Schulenburg's ideas would be a plan based on the

[1] Reuss to Spielmann, May 22, Vivenot, ii, pp. 55 f. This highly important correspondence was first published by Adolf Beer in the *Historische Zeitschrift*, xxvii (1872), and then more fully by Vivenot.

[2] Schulenburg had not mentioned Courland. Probably Spielmann threw out the suggestion in the hope of transferring the Russian acquisition from the south to the north — away from the frontiers of Austria and towards those of Prussia.

exchange of the Austrian Netherlands for Bavaria and the Upper Palatinate. He knew very well, he said, what an anathema had been laid on this project at Berlin during Hertzberg's ministry; but he believed that the circumstances and the relations between the two Courts had now changed so entirely that, with a minister of Schulenburg's insight and high-mindedness, a few hours' conversation would suffice to bring about a perfect agreement. As for the means proposed by Schulenburg for executing his plan, Spielmann objected with much reason that anything which conveyed the least suggestion of coercion produced on the Empress of Russia an effect exactly contrary to that which was desired. Instead of an armed demonstration in Poland, he proposed that after the two Courts had come to an agreement among themselves, they should at once lay their plan frankly before the Empress with the assurance that they were willing to consent to whatever she might demand for herself. The fact that she seemed inclined to coöperate in the French enterprise made it probable that she would readily agree to this method of indemnification.[1]

Schulenburg professed to be, and doubtless was, delighted with this reply. Never, he told Reuss, had ministers of two Courts acted towards each other with such sincerity as he and Baron Spielmann. He readily gave his assent to the modifications of his original proposals which Spielmann had suggested. He agreed as to the inadvisability of a military demonstration in Poland, although he was thereby renouncing for his Court the prospect of taking immediate possession of its proposed acquisition. He not only accepted the Bavarian Exchange plan, but declared that he had all along shared Spielmann's ideas on that subject [2] (although this involved the sacrifice of one of the most sacred of the traditions handed down from Frederick the Great). Invited by Spielmann to indicate the precise acquisition that would suit his Court, Schulenburg could only point to the Polish district that separated Silesia from East Prussia, adding that its size must

[1] Letter of May 29, Vivenot, ii, pp. 63–67.
[2] This was doubtless true, for Schulenburg could hardly have remained ignorant of Bischoffwerder's discussions at Vienna on that topic.

depend on the lot claimed by Russia and could not be definitely fixed in advance.[1]

A few days later, on the King's return from Pomerania, the Prussian minister reported that his sovereign agreed to the Bavarian Exchange and offered to use his good offices with both the Elector and his heir, the Duke of Zweibrücken; that he could not, indeed, think of resorting to coercion in order to secure the assent of those princes, in view of a promise he had once made; but that he flattered himself that the King of Hungary would not expect such extreme measures of him. As both monarchs had now given their consent to the combined Bavarian-Polish plan, Schulenburg requested that the affair should at once be brought into the regular ministerial channel, in order to take advantage of the pending negotiations with Russia.[2]

Spielmann, who received Reuss' last two letters only on June 18 while at Buda, replied with assurances that nothing was more justified than the King's aversion to coercive measures against the Duke of Zweibrücken; he was convinced that there would be no need of them. He was overflowing with joy at the happy course the negotiation had taken, and at the confidence shown by Schulenburg in him personally. He did not doubt, he added, that all the details of the plan could be satisfactorily arranged at the approaching meeting of the two sovereigns.[3]

II

The first step in bringing the affair into the regular ministerial channel was to reveal the secret to Kaunitz. This Spielmann and the King proceeded to do by letters written shortly before their return from Buda. To the old Chancellor, already jealous of his subordinate,[4] this negotiation, carried on with the approval of the monarch behind his back, was a staggering blow. In his reply of June 25 he poured out his wounded feelings in

[1] Reuss to Spielmann, June 4, Vivenot, ii, pp. 80 ff.

[2] Reuss to Spielmann, June 9, *ibid.*, pp. 89 ff.

[3] Spielmann to Reuss, June 22, Vivenot, ii, pp. 110 f.

[4] *Zinzendorf's Diary*, June 6: "Le vieux [Kaunitz] s'est brouillé avec Spielmann. . . . Il a pensé à faire sauter Spielmann." (V. A.)

terms that few ministers would have dared address to their sovereigns. He found the plan which the King had sanctioned, "a chimera," an insult to the Austrian Court, utterly unjustifiable — at least in so far as it concerned Poland, — and contrary to all existing treaties and engagements. He doubted very strongly whether the Bavarian House would ever give its consent; and he was almost sure that the Maritime Powers would oppose; and they would be right in doing so. At any rate, the Austrian indemnity would be left dependent on a long and uncertain negotiation, while Prussia could at any moment take possession of her share. What security was there that the Imperial Court, after being inveigled into assenting to the gains of its allies, would not come forth empty-handed ? What reliance could be placed on the proffered good offices of Prussia with the Elector and his heir ? It was obvious that although the Court of Berlin had no scruples about robbing the allied Republic of Poland, it still objected to using sufficiently earnest language to secure the consent of those princes. " I see then in this whole policy," the Chancellor wrote, " nothing but covetousness, and principles which can inspire little confidence in future times and which therefore promise little good. Such a political morality is not in accordance with my principles, and should . . . never be accepted by a great Power which respects itself, and recognizes the value of its good name. . . . From evil no good can ever result; it is therefore . . . my only wish and my only hope that nothing can and will come of this." [1]

However much personal feelings may have influenced Kaunitz's reply and whatever may be thought of his right to plume himself on his exalted political morality, it must be admitted that his objections and warnings were only too well grounded. On the other hand, it is difficult to blame Spielmann unreservedly. An indemnity had to be found for Prussia somewhere, and in that case Austria could not afford to dispense with an equivalent advantage. To seek compensation at the cost of France involved prolonging the war indefinitely, covering the two Courts with

[1] The King to Kaunitz, June 21, the Chancellor's reply of the 25th, and his appended " Reflections," Vivenot, ii, pp. 107 f., 114 f.

odium, and raising an insurmountable barrier to the restoration of Louis XVI. To refuse Prussia the so ardently desired acquisition in Poland meant to loosen the alliance and to drive the Court of Berlin into the arms of Russia. On the other hand, by consenting, Austria could gain what seemed a unique chance to realize that exchange project which had been pursued with such efforts for almost a century; she might secure what was doubtless the most valuable acquisition the Hapsburg Monarchy could make, while at the same time getting rid of distant possessions which exposed the state to ceaseless trouble and to a galling dependence on foreign Powers. The success of the plan depended, indeed, on the consent of a prince who had hitherto shown himself strongly opposed to the Exchange — the Duke of Zweibrücken; but it may well have seemed that he could no longer refuse when Prussia, hitherto his chief support, urged his acceptance. On the Elector's consent Spielmann might fairly count, both because of his previous attitude and in view of his overtures to Lehrbach in March. Undoubtedly the war introduced a great element of uncertainty into the calculation; but one must remember the exaggerated reports then universally current about the disorganization and impotence of France, and the general belief in the speedy triumph of the allied arms. Spielmann's course is, then, intelligible enough. And yet none of his hopes were to be realized; all of Kaunitz's prophecies were to be fulfilled.

The Chancellor's objections produced no change in the King's resolutions. The only result was a severe tension in the relations between monarch and minister. It was widely noted at Vienna that at his departure for the Imperial coronation at Frankfort, the young King failed to pay Kaunitz the customary visit. Malicious tongues had it that the attention had been omitted for prudential reasons: the old man had proposed to teach his sovereign a salutary lesson.[1] In his note of June 25 the Chancellor had begged the King, if he adhered to the Schulenburg-Spielmann plan, to excuse him from taking part in the affair, ' in order that he might not be obliged, against his own conviction, to end his ministry by such a step.' On this point he was gratified, for not

[1] *Zinzendorf's Diary*, July 6 (V. A.).

only the negotiation over the indemnities, but all important business henceforth passed through other hands. In August the old man insisted on resigning his functions altogether. It was virtually the end of Kaunitz's long and honorable career.

III

Almost immediately after the return of the King and Spielmann from Buda an opportunity presented itself for entering into negotiations with Russia concerning the new plan. Razumovski, the Empress' ambassador, saw fit to force a confidential disclosure of the secret. In a familiar conversation with Cobenzl (June 30), he took occasion to dwell at length on his sovereign's invariable attachment to the alliance and on her great interest in the prosperity of the House of Austria, and thus led up to the suggestion that this might, perhaps, be the most favorable moment to effect the Bavarian Exchange plan, to which the Empress had formerly lent so willing a support. Cobenzl objected that even now the Court of Berlin would not fail to oppose, unless it received a corresponding advantage. Razumovski pointed to Dantzic and Thorn. The Empress, he said, had formerly opposed Prussian aggrandizement in that quarter solely out of regard for Austria. " But do you think," said Cobenzl, " that to-day, if we found such a plan to our advantage, the Empress would consent to it without desiring any acquisition for herself ? " " Oh no! " said the Russian, " I think that in that case she, too, would wish to get something." " But," replied the Austrian, " what is there that would suit her ? She can make acquisitions of value to Russia only in Poland." " Precisely in Poland," said Razumovski; " the acquisition of the Ukraine would be very useful to us." " Yes, the Ukraine or Courland," said Cobenzl, throwing out the same idea that Spielmann had advanced to Schulenburg. The ambassador considered, however, that the annexation of Courland would be of no value to his Court, since that Duchy was already totally dependent on Russia; an advantageous acquisition could be found only in the Ukraine. As for the pretext, he was sure there would be no difficulty; there were plenty of available titles in the archives. Cobenzl then hazarded a suggestion that showed the persistence of the ideas of Leopold. The Poles, he said, were so infatuated with their new constitution that they might, perhaps, consent to territorial sacrifices, in order to obtain its confirmation from the neighboring Powers. Razumovski replied, however, that after restoring the old régime, the Powers could easily obtain the desired cessions from the well-disposed party. That day the conversation went no further. Both diplomats had been profuse in compliments; Razumovski had amused his friend by building air-castles; it was apparently only harmless speculation.

Cobenzl hastened, however, to inform the King and Spielmann. The next day, at the close of the Sunday audience of the ambassadors, he drew Razumovski aside and confided to him that he had penetrated their secret, or rather that there could be no secrets between such allies. With the King's authorization he then set forth the whole plan for the Bavarian Exchange and the Prussian acquisition in Poland, though without mentioning the fact that negotiations on this subject had already been opened with Prussia. It is strange that with all his assurances that the project would be left entirely to the good pleasure of the Empress, he failed to suggest that she, also, should share in the spoils. Razumovski protested profusely about his sovereign's inclination to anything that promised advantages to her allies; but he felt bound to intimate that her interests must also be provided for. Immediately afterward Spielmann confirmed to the ambassador all that Cobenzl had said. It was thereupon agreed that Razumovski should send off a courier to St. Petersburg with a dispatch of his own, and one to Louis Cobenzl.[1]

The instruction drawn up by the Vice-Chancellor for his cousin[2] is interesting, as showing how recent events, especially those of the Oriental crisis, had convinced Austrian statesmen of the impossibility in the long run of defending Poland's integrity against Prussia. It also reveals a curious attitude towards

---

[1] On the above see Appendix XIV, where the text of Razumovski's report of his discussions with Cobenzl is printed.

[2] Dispatch of July 2, Vivenot, ii, pp. 120 ff.

Russia. The Empress, Cobenzl wrote, could not justly demand an acquisition, since the whole burden of the French war was borne by Austria and Prussia, and since all the advantages gained through the alliance of the Imperial Courts had hitherto fallen to Russia. He thought that if the Court of Petersburg consented to the indemnities demanded by the German Powers for themselves, they might in return offer to excuse it from all coöperation in the war with France, and to assist it in the complete restoration of the old régime in Poland. But if, in spite of all, the Russians manifested a very strong desire to make acquisitions, the ambassador was ordered not to contest the claim directly, nor to show any open signs of disinclination to such a demand. The Vice-Chancellor added that the whole plan was only a new idea, about which he desired to learn the Empress' opinion. Much more precise instructions would be sent to St. Petersburg after the meeting of the Emperor-elect and the King of Prussia. Unsettled as the plan might be at that time, one cannot repress a gasp of astonishment that an experienced Austrian statesman could have imagined for a moment that the Empress would renounce a share in the general distribution of indemnities. One sees again that the Viennese ministers were by no means eager to have the Russian eagles approach the frontiers of Galicia.

IV

It is uncertain whether Razumovski, in making his far-reaching suggestions to the Austrians, was acting in accordance with directions from St. Petersburg. There are no instructions on this subject among Ostermann's dispatches to him of this period; and in his report to Bezborodko the ambassador expressed the hope that his step would not be disapproved, since he had sought only to verify a suspicion which he had long felt, that the Court of Vienna desired to revive the Exchange project. The realization of the plan depended solely on the Empress, he added; it could be arrested by a single word from her, in case it did not conform to her views. In spite of this apology, however, it is difficult to suppose that he would have ventured to go so far without at least a hint from some of the persons in power at St. Petersburg, presumably from Zubov or Markov. The suspicion that Russian diplomacy was at work at this moment pulling the most secret wires in order to bring a partition upon the order of the day, is strengthened by the fact that, almost simultaneously with Razumovski's strange performance, his government took the initiative in provoking very similar explanations from the Court of Berlin.

Schulenburg's advances to Alopeus on the subject of indemnities served as the point of departure. The Russians must have been highly gratified by those overtures, both because they thus obtained a chance to take a hand in a matter in which they were keenly interested, and because they probably desired to give the indemnity question a turn adapted to their own special views. As a participant in the French enterprise (by paying subsidies), and still more as being accustomed to take the leading rôle in all great affairs, the Empress could not look on indifferently while her neighbors collected war indemnities or annexed provinces. Nothing could be more vexatious to her than to have Austria and Prussia arranging everything between themselves, instead of referring humbly to the grand court of arbitration at St. Petersburg. She would not have been Catherine II, had she not tried to get the indemnity question into her own hands, so that in the end she might appear on the stage to award the prizes, while incidentally appropriating the largest for herself. Now it was clearly not to her interest that the indemnities should take the form of conquests from France, for in that quarter there were no particularly desirable acquisitions to be found for Russia. It is not improbable that the idea may very early have been adopted at St. Petersburg, as at Berlin, of allowing Poland to pay the costs.[1] That would be far more convenient for Russia and Prussia,

---

[1] In Cobenzl's report of June 11, 1791, relating Ostermann's first overtures to him about an intervention in France, there is an enigmatic but suggestive passage. Ostermann said that the Empress desired an understanding with Austria on the French question " d'autant plus qu'il ne seroit peutêtre pas impossible de lier ces affaires-là avec celles qui occupoient d'ailleurs les deux Cours Impériales." At a time when the Oriental crisis was practically past, and the revolution of the Third of May was very fresh in the minds of the Russians, the " affairs which

and Austria could doubtless be provided for somewhere. By June of 1792, the Empress must have been sufficiently well aware that this idea corresponded to the wishes of the German Powers. Since Razumovski's report of March and Alopeus' of May, she could hardly have been in doubt as to the direction in which the ambitions of Austria and Prussia would turn.[1] In view of all this, Ostermann's reply to the above-mentioned overtures of Schulenburg is highly significant.

In his dispatches to Alopeus of June 10/21, the Vice-Chancellor declared that the Empress entirely approved of Frederick William's claim for compensation, and would hasten to lend her support, if it were needed, as soon as she was informed of the nature and form of the projected indemnities. She expected that a similar demand for compensation would probably be raised by the other Courts coöperating in the French enterprise (i. e., Austria, Sardinia, and Russia). She felt obliged, however, to urge upon the King's consideration that if France, weakened and exhausted by anarchy, were now to be subjected to a dismemberment, as well as burdened with a form of government that would never allow the country to recover its strength (i. e., a constitutional government, instead of the absolute monarchy which she had vainly advised the allies to restore), this state would disappear completely from the political balance of Europe. She left it to the King to decide whether that would be to the general advantage. — The inference from this is obvious. If, as Ostermann plainly hinted, the indemnities were not to be taken in France, there was practically only one other place in which to seek them. There was only one quarter in which the Empress' proffered aid in securing acquisitions for Prussia could be needed or could be of value. Catherine was virtually inviting the King to confide to her how much of Poland she could help him to

occupied the Imperial Courts elsewhere," and which were to be combined with the French enterprise, could hardly have been other than those of Poland (V. A., *Russland, Berichte*, 1791).

[1] Cf. Schulenburg to Frederick William, June 30: "Après les insinuations indirectes qui lui ont été faites, elle [Russia] ne peut ignorer le fonds de Ses [the King's] idées à cet égard " [a partition of Poland], B. A., *R.* XI, *Russland*, 133.

appropriate. Anything less than that these 'ostensible' dispatches could scarcely have meant. This was also the sense in which they were understood by the Prussian ministry, whose joy can easily be imagined.[1]

Only a few days before, in reply to a note in which the King had impatiently inquired what was to be done to bring "the principal aim" (the Polish acquisition) to the front, Schulenburg had urged that it was still advisable to await further advances from Russia, since if they (the Prussians) announced their desires openly, the Court of St. Petersburg might betray everything to the Poles in order to win the whole nation to its side.[2] The furthest he had yet dared to go, was to tell the Prince of Nassau, Catherine's agent in French affairs, who was then in Berlin, that France had no money, and yet that an indemnity in money was the only suitable compensation that Russia and Prussia could find "in that quarter." As usual, the irresponsible Bischoffwerder did not stop there, but proceeded to confide to Nassau the entire plan for the Bavarian Exchange and the Prussian acquisition in Poland — in the certain knowledge that it would be reported straight to the Empress.[3]

A few days later (July 1) Alopeus presented the thrice welcome dispatches of June 21 regarding the indemnities. Soon after the Russian envoy sought out Schulenburg with the direct intention of provoking a confidence, precisely as Razumovski had done.

[1] Ostermann to Alopeus, June 10/21, M.A., Пруссія, III, 28: Schulenburg to the King, July 1, Schulenburg and Alvensleben to the King, July 3, Frederick William's reply of July 4, B.A., R. 96, 147 G. I am strongly tempted to see a connection between these Russian advances to Prussia and Razumovski's simultaneous manoeuvres with the Austrians. Alopeus' reports of May 8/19 and 17/28 must have reached St. Petersburg not later than June 10 or 12. They brought pretty full indications as to the designs of Prussia and provoked the decisive action which Russia then undertook at Berlin. It seems not improbable that the courier who left St. Petersburg for Vienna on June 16, may have carried secret and private directions to Razumovski to draw out the Austrians on the same subject.

[2] Frederick William to Schulenburg, June 28, the minister's reply of the 30th, B.A., R. 96, 147 G.

[3] Alopeus' report of June 19/30, Nassau to the Empress, July 11, both referring to Nassau's conversation of the 29th of June with Schulenburg and Bischoffwerder, M.A., Пруссія, III, 29, and (ibid.) France, IX, Princes et Emigrés, 1792.

Schulenburg resisted temptation no better than the Austrians. Encouraged by Ostermann's so favorable response, he revealed the whole Bavarian-Polish plan, including the acquisition of the Ukraine for Russia, pretending, indeed, not to know his master's views on the subject, but announcing that he meant to ascertain them at once.[1] On July 5 he reported that, as a result of the recent friendly overtures of the Empress, the King would now enter into definite negotiations with the Court of Vienna on the indemnity question, and would inform her of the results with all loyalty and frankness.[2] In order to open the way to negotiations at St. Petersburg, Goltz was next initiated into the secret, and provided with a memorandum, in which the various possible kinds of indemnity were discussed and it was urged that the Bavarian-Polish plan was the only feasible one.[3] This document, however, was represented to be only "first thoughts" on the subject; Goltz was directed not to show it but to advance the ideas contained in it, in case Ostermann brought up the topic. Thus within a surprisingly short time the ice had been broken in every quarter. The Prussian initiative had met with the readiest of responses from Austria; and although the Empress had not yet committed herself, her attitude might seem distinctly encouraging. Frederick William and his advisers, however, were not quite free from fear that she might merely be lulling them with false hopes until such time as she had ended her enterprise in Poland. Decided caution towards Russia was still the watchword at Berlin, and the first article in the Prussian program was to secure a precise and definite agreement with Austria.

That agreement was to be effected, as was confidently reckoned on both sides, at the meeting of the two sovereigns to be held immediately after the Imperial coronation at Frankfort. In the

[1] Alopeus' report of June 22/July 3, M. A., Пруссія, III, 29. From the much more reserved tone of Schulenburg's and Alvensleben's report to the King of July 3, one would judge that the former minister did not see fit to reveal to his colleague how far he had gone with Alopeus. This conversation was on July 2. B. A., R. 96, 147 G.

[2] Alopeus' report of June 26/July 7, M. A., Пруссія, III, 29.

[3] Rescript to Goltz of July 10, B. A., R. XI, *Russland*, 133.

first week of July, from Vienna and Berlin there was a general exodus towards the Rhine. The Emperor-elect, all the Austrian Conference ministers save Kaunitz, the King of Prussia, Bischoffwerder, Schulenburg, Haugwitz, Alopeus, Reuss, Nassau — the whole diplomatic and military world was off to attend either the great spectacle at Frankfort or 'the promenade to Paris.'

CHAPTER XIV

Austria and Prussia Disagree about the Partition

I

On July 14, 1792, at Frankfort, the world saw for the last time the faded splendors of the coronation of a Holy Roman Emperor. Five days later the successor of the Caesars and Frederick William, ' the modern Agamemnon,' held their meeting at Mainz. Amid all the gorgeous festivities, while the public was celebrating the anticipated triumph over the Jacobins, the ministers of the allied Courts were already disputing over the prospective spoils.

Even before the departure from Vienna, clouds had begun to appear on the horizon. When the Bavarian-Polish plan was confided to the Austrian Conference ministers, there were murmurs that this was no time to revive the Exchange project.[1] Probably the cry had already been raised that although by the Exchange Austria would, indeed, round out her territories, she would suffer an actual loss in revenue, while Prussia was to gain in both ways. Much as he clung to his original plan, Spielmann had been obliged to urge upon Haugwitz the necessity of finding some ' supplement,' some additional acquisition that would offset the financial loss in question and establish a perfect equality between the respective indemnities. As one means to that end, he had suggested that in case the two Lusatias should revert to Austria, they might be exchanged for the Franconian Margraviates, Ansbach and Baireuth, which had recently fallen to Prussia.[2]

---

[1] Cf. Rosenberg's *votum* at the Frankfort conference: " Ueber den 2. Punkt des Conferenzialgegenstandes, habe ich meine Meinung in Wien und hier dahin geäussert, dass mir der nun gegenwärtige Zeitpunkt keineswegs der gemessenste scheine, die Negociation des Austausches zu entamiren," Vivenot, ii, p. 142.

[2] Haugwitz to the King, July 26, referring to his conversations with Spielmann before his departure from Vienna, B. A`., R. 96, 155 E. Spielmann had left the door open to such claims for a ' supplement,' when in his first reply to Schulen-

After the coronation, on July 17, the Emperor held a meeting of the State Conference at Frankfort to decide upon the exact propositions to be made to the Prussians at the approaching interviews. Spielmann had presented a memorandum, which set forth the history of the Exchange plan, summed up the advantages of the project, and attempted to refute the objections that were already being raised. Amid all the absurdities that were put on paper by Austrian ministers in those days, it is refreshing to find one statesman who realized that Prussia was sure to insist upon an indemnity; that any attempt to oppose, or even the failure to show real willingness to assist, would not only end all support from that Power against France, but would ruin the friendship built up with such exertions; that the Court of Berlin was in a position to secure its indemnity anyway, through an understanding with Russia or England; and that the only question was whether Austria would seize the opportunity to extract a counter-concession from Prussia, or would bargain and delay until too late. Spielmann admitted that the Bavarian Exchange would involve a temporary loss of from two to three millions in revenue; but he argued that the Monarchy would gain so much in territorial compactness and in freedom of movement, such great improvements might be made in the financial administration of Bavaria, so much could be saved by getting rid of the costly and precarious Belgic possessions, that the loss would be more than made up. The Exchange might possibly be combined with other acquisitions, but he urged that insistence on additional advantages and the resulting delays might involve the failure of the whole plan.[1]

burg he urged the financial loss involved in the Bavarian Exchange, and represented the latter project as only "the chief basis" of the prospective arrangement. Possibly he had already had to face the opposition of some one of his sovereign's confidential advisers, Colloredo, for instance.

[1] This memorandum is printed in Vivenot, ii, pp. 134–141, as of July 18, 1792, i. e., the day after the meeting of the Conference. In the original, which is preserved among the *Vorträge* for 1792 in the Vienna Archives, the date is written in pencil and is not exactly clear; but it is almost certainly the *16th*, rather than the 18th. Besides, the whole context of the memorandum corresponds to the supposition that it was written *before* the meeting of the Conference. Had it been written afterwards, the historic résumé with which it begins could not have failed to mention

Unfortunately these warnings made little impression on most of the members of the Conference. Field Marshal Lacy declared that if the Bavarian Exchange were to be undertaken at all, it must be supplemented by the acquisition of Ansbach and Baireuth from Prussia, the latter Power to be compensated, perhaps, with Juliers and Berg or with additional territory in Poland. He inclined to the opinion that the Exchange plan should not even be discussed at the interview at Mainz, out of regard for the foreign Courts (England), and in view of the internal conditions in the Netherlands. Prince Rosenberg, who was in general bitterly opposed to Spielmann and Cobenzl, joined in the attack. He did not believe the moment fitted for reviving the Bavarian project; but since it had been revived, he opined at least that they should not attempt to execute it without securing the consent of England. He also found it as clear as day that the realization of the Exchange without a ' supplement ' would entail an incalculable loss to Austria. Colloredo agreed entirely with Lacy and Rosenberg. The discussion waxed hot. Overwhelmed with criticisms and accusations, Spielmann was enraged to the point of demanding his own dismissal.[1] Finally the battle ended with a compromise.

It was decided to go on with the plan for the Bavarian Exchange, which the Conference recognized as in itself " the *summum bonum* " of the Austrian Monarchy, but also to make every possible effort to secure such further advantages as would render the Austrian gains absolutely equal to those of Prussia. A graded series of propositions to the Court of Berlin was drawn up, and first on the list stood the demand for the Franconian Margraviates—in return for which Prussia might receive the Duchy of Berg from Bavaria. If none of these supplementary advantages could be obtained, the majority of the Conference agreed to adhere to the Exchange pure and simple. If even that proved impracticable, two contingencies were to be considered: if Prussia secured

the important decisions of the 17th. Beyond a doubt, this is the ' *mémoire* ' which was read at the beginning of the meeting, according to the Conference protocol, and not, as is commonly assumed, an act drawn up by Spielmann after the meeting, as a sort of protest against what had taken place.

[1] Schulenburg to Finckenstein and Alvensleben, July 30, B. A., *R.* XI, *Frankreich*, 89 g.

her acquisition in Poland, Austria must claim an *arrondissement* in French Flanders and Hainault; in the contrary case, both Powers should return to the original plan of demanding a money indemnity from France. The Emperor approved these resolutions, with the reservation that the consent of the other Courts, and especially of England, must be obtained before attempting the realization of the Exchange, and that in case of the slightest opposition, the project was to be abandoned at once.[1]

It has been the general opinion of historians that the conference at Frankfort marked a disastrous turn in Austrian policy. It is true that Lacy and Rosenberg were not far wrong in holding it an unfavorable moment for bringing up the Bavarian Exchange plan, and in declaring the consent of England necessary; there was also some justification for their view that it was not exactly à propos to divide the skin of the bear before he was caught; but they failed utterly to reckon with the main factor in the situation, Prussia. Since that Power insisted on obtaining securities for its indemnity in advance, and since its aid was at that moment indispensable, there was no other sound policy than to accede to its demands and to avoid wounding its susceptibilities. The decisions of Frankfort were so disastrous, not because they put the Exchange plan in danger — for in view of the later turn of the war, it is hardly probable that that project could ever have been carried out — but because they produced the first rift in the coalition and began the alienation of the ally, without whose cordial coöperation a successful prosecution of the war and the acquisition of an indemnity of any kind were wellnigh hopeless.

It was under no favorable auspices that the conferences between the Austrian and Prussian ministers were opened at Mainz. On the one side, Spielmann and Cobenzl found themselves obliged to champion demands of which both at bottom disapproved.[2] On the other side, Schulenburg, who was to conduct the negotiation

---

[1] Conference protocol and the separate *vota* of Lacy and of Rosenberg and Colloredo, Vivenot, ii, pp. 132 ff., 141 f.

[2] Of Spielmann's point of view, it is unnecessary to speak further. For Cobenzl's, see his memorial printed in Vivenot, ii, pp. 142–145 (here erroneously entitled "Beilage zum Protokoll der Frankfurter Conferenz, Juli, 1792." It was in reality presented with a *Vortrag* of August 3, V. A.).

for Prussia, could hardly be in the mood for concessions. His two colleagues, who remained in Berlin, had already fallen to bemoaning the disadvantages of permitting the Bavarian Exchange: the sacrifice of the traditions of the great Frederick, the loss of Prussia's proud position as the protector of the small states of Germany, the immense increase of Austrian power and influence, the violation of the Peace of Teschen, etc., etc. If the hated project must absolutely be allowed, they insisted that their Court must receive a huge aggrandizement, which would enable it henceforth to dispense with the support of the German princes, and would justify its abandonment of a policy that had hitherto formed the glory and the security of Prussia.[1] Furthermore, Haugwitz, who enjoyed great credit with Frederick William, had come to attend the King from Hochheim to Mainz, and had seized the opportunity to combat the system recently adopted, and Schulenburg's policies in particular. If we may believe Haugwitz's later assertion, the King was already discontented with his leading minister, and especially with the too modest indemnity which the latter was disposed to claim.[2] On both sides, then, the personal position of the negotiators rendered concessions to the other party difficult, if not impossible.

The subject of the indemnities was brought up for discussion at the conference of July 21. Schulenburg readily agreed to the principle that the respective acquisitions were to be exactly equal, both with regard to their utility as *arrondissements*, and in 'intrinsic value.' The Austrians then brought forward their claim for a 'supplement' to offset the losses involved in the Bavarian Exchange. Schulenburg seems to have admitted — after not a little argument — that the claim was in itself just; but when informed of the concrete demand based upon it — the cession of the Margraviates, the sacrifice of Prussian territory to satisfy the appetites of this ravenous Court of Vienna — there he

---

[1] These considerations from a letter of Alvensleben and Finckenstein of July 27, i. e., written after they had learned of the propositions made by Austria at Mainz. That they had, however, advanced these same ideas even earlier, appears from their letters to Schulenburg of August 12, B. A., *R.* XI, *Frankreich*, 89 g.

[2] Ranke, *Hardenberg*, ii, p. 277; " Fragment des mémoires inédits du Comte de Haugwitz," in *Minerva*, clxxxiv (1837), p. 4.

balked. His sovereign, he protested, placed a quite peculiar value on these territories, which were the ancient home of his dynasty. Repeatedly he begged the Austrians to devise some other combination. Spielmann insisted that no other plan was possible: if the King's aversion to the proposed cession was insuperable, both Courts would have to renounce their intended acquisitions. From the meagre words of the protocol it is impossible to reconstruct the course of what was undoubtedly a very warm debate; but it appears that at last Schulenburg consented to take the demand for the Margraviates *ad referendum*, and even to indicate the territories that his master would claim in case he agreed to that proposition. They included the palatinates of Posen, Gnesen, Cujavia, and Kalisz, with a part of Sieradz, an allotment considerably smaller than that which fell to Prussia some months later. These claims the Austrians in their turn accepted only *ad referendum*. Finally, Schulenburg agreed without difficulty that his Court should undertake to secure the consent of England and of the Duke of Zweibrücken to the Exchange. The conference ended amicably, but with nothing definite accomplished.[1] The great opportunity for a solid agreement on the original basis had been lost. The full extent of the harm done in the way of disappointing, exasperating, and embittering the Prussians, appeared only a little later.

II

On the homeward journey from Mainz the Emperor stopped several days at Munich, to visit the Elector. It had not been intended, apparently, to broach the great plan of the day on this occasion, but the Elector seems to have outrun the wishes of his guests. In a moment of effusiveness, he assured the Emperor that he entertained for him the same sentiments that he had cherished for Joseph II, and that he did not exclude even his willingness to consent to the Exchange. Encouraging as this was,

---

[1] Protocol of the conference, Vivenot, ii, pp. 146–149; Ph. Cobenzl to Kaunitz, July 31, and to the Emperor, August 3, *ibid.*, pp. 155–158; Schulenburg to Finckenstein and Alvensleben, July 21, printed in Ranke, *Ursprung und Beginn*, pp. 364 f.

the Austrians do not appear to have taken advantage of it. They were not yet ready to begin a formal negotiation at Munich.[1]

At the end of July the court arrived at Prague for the Bohemian coronation. It was only then that the Austrian statesmen began to cast up the situation produced by the conference at Mainz. In the report presented by the Vice-Chancellor to the Emperor on August 3, the tone was sufficiently hopeful. The main thing at present, he declared, was to await the replies of the Courts of Berlin and Petersburg. If the latter answered unfavorably, then the Prussian acquisition in Poland would fall through, as well as the Bavarian Exchange; and in such a case the Emperor could easily console himself. One sees again that the Austrians, unlike their allies, had by no means set their hearts upon aggrandizement;[2] they had virtually been driven into the indemnity project in order to preserve the balance of power. As for the counter-proposals to be expected from Prussia, Cobenzl anticipated that the King would offer not only the Exchange, to which he had irrevocably committed himself, but also some additional advantages — either the Margraviates or acquisitions elsewhere. Evidently the Vice-Chancellor had been encouraged by Schulenberg's acceptance of the abstract principle of 'the supplement,' and did not suspect the indignation and repugnance which the demands made at Mainz had aroused in the Prussian ministry. Still he obviously did not feel the ground quite secure under his feet, for he thought it necessary to add a long memorial rehearsing all the advantages of the Exchange project. The reason may have been that he feared that the Emperor's inclination to the plan had been shaken by the opposition at Frankfort; or possibly that he

---

[1] For the incident at Munich, Razumovski to Bezborodko, September 2/13, on the basis of what Spielmann had told him, M. A., Австрія, III, 54. Cf. Ph. Cobenzl to Mercy, March 26, 1793: " Wie sehnlich der Herr Kurfürst diesen Tausch allezeit gewünscht hat (*und die Fortdauer dieses Wunsches haben noch im Juli v. J. positive Aeusserungen bestätigt*) ist Jedermann bekannt " (Vivenot, ii, p. 532 — the italics are mine). Lehrbach, the Austrian envoy at Munich, was not informed until the spring of 1793 that his Court had revived the Exchange project; and no formal negotiation was ever undertaken on the subject with the Bavarian government in these years.

[2] Spielmann was probably an exception, but the statement applies, I believe, to the other ministers.

was trying to prepare the way for a return to Spielmann's original project, in case the demand for a supplement occasioned too great difficulties or delays. At any rate, the memorial labored to show that the deficit caused by the Exchange would be only temporary, and that the security and freedom of action to be gained by the realization of the plan were far more precious than any acquisitions or any mere increase of revenue.[1]

A few days later a report arrived from Louis Cobenzl that must have afforded considerable satisfaction. Immediately upon receiving the orders of July 2nd, the ambassador had taken up the new project (the Exchange) with his usual zeal, although he had grave doubts about the success of the plan, and was not a little pained at being obliged to champion those ambitions of Prussia which for years he had made it his business to combat.[2] The Russian ministers received his propositions with all graciousness. They could express only their private opinions, since all must be referred to the Empress' decision, but each of them in turn assured Cobenzl that she would surely do everything possible to assist ' her most intimate ally,' just as she had done in 1784. The ambassador was given to understand that the Exchange project would meet with no difficulties whatsoever from Russia, but as to the Prussian acquisition the situation was different. Bezborodko, indeed, thought that in view of the present circumstances the claims of the Court of Berlin would have to be admitted; but the other ministers raised profuse objections and unanimously declared that this was a subject that required the maturest deliberation. Markov asserted that the King of Prussia had no right whatever to demand an indemnity for " the half-campaign " he was making, and ought to be told so plainly. The last-named minister was also the only one who broached the topic of an acquisition for his own Court. If it were a question of gains for Austria alone, he declared, the Empress would act as disinterestedly as Joseph II had done at the time of the Crimean affair; but if Prussia absolutely must get something too, that was quite a different matter: then the balance of power must be pre-

---

[1] *Vortrag* of August 3, V. A. The memorial, in Vivenot, ii, pp. 142–145.

[2] L. Cobenzl to Ph. Cobenzl, July 21 (private letter), V. A., *Russland, Fasc.* 139.

served. Cobenzl's instructions did not allow him to discuss this latter point, but he did not think fit to offer the petty concessions suggested in the orders of July 2 to take the place of a Russian acquisition. It is probable that his failure to propose that the Empress should take her share along with the rest, had something to do with the fact that on this occasion he secured nothing but general assurances of good will. His sovereign would be unable to reply definitely, Ostermann declared, until she learned of the results of the interview between the Emperor and the King of Prussia.[1]

Unsubstantial as was his success, Cobenzl had still progressed much further than his Prussian colleague. The excessively prudent Goltz, bound by extremely cautious instructions, had failed utterly to bring the Russians to speech. Not daring to make his proposals openly, and not being on sufficiently intimate terms with the Russian ministers to draw them out in familiar conversation, the envoy was no nearer to learning the intentions of the Empress now than he had been five months earlier. He and Cobenzl received their orders about the indemnity project at almost the same time; yet so great was their mutual distrust that instead of joining forces in a common effort, each assured the other that he had no definite instructions on this subject.[2]

The news from St. Petersburg — the advance gained by Cobenzl over Goltz, the favorable reception accorded by the Russians to the Exchange project, and their apparent repugnance to the Prussian claims — all this furnished the Austrian ministry with an excellent opportunity to return to the attack on the subject of the Margraviates. Accordingly, on August 8 a dispatch was sent to Reuss ostensibly for the purpose of communicating the results of Cobenzl's overtures. The Prussians were to be given to understand that the obstacles that stood in the way of their demands at St. Petersburg, could probably be removed only

[1] L. Cobenzl to Ph. Cobenzl, July 21 (official report), V. A., *Russland, Berichte*, 1792.

[2] Goltz's report of July 20, B. A., *R*. XI, *Russland*, 133; Cobenzl's of August 24, V. A., *loc. cit.* Cobenzl's ' duplicity ' towards Goltz furnished the Prussian ministry with a theme for frequent jeremiads; but the duplicity was about equal on both sides.

through the earnest intervention of the Emperor; and that this intervention could easily be had — at the price of Ansbach and Baireuth. If the two Courts were once agreed on this latter point, it was said, they could immediately begin a joint negotiation with Russia with good hopes of success.[1]

At the same time Spielmann took up a high tone in his discussions with Haugwitz. Without the cession of the Margraviates, he constantly declared, the whole Bavarian-Polish plan would have to be given up; but, on the other hand, if the King consented to part with those possessions, Prussia might have whatever she might desire in Poland. Haugwitz, however, knew a clever counter-thrust. If the Bavarian-Polish plan were abandoned, he said, the two Courts would have to return to the old idea of seeking their indemnities from France; and in that case his sovereign would claim Juliers and Berg. Spielmann protested vigorously that if the Elector had to part with his possessions on the Lower Rhine the Exchange would be rendered forever impossible; and he added gloomily that in the end the allies would have to fall back on taking their indemnities in French assignats — an idea which filled Haugwitz with horror.[2]

The debate moved around in a vicious circle. Still it appears that Haugwitz did not express himself on the subject of the Margraviates with sufficient firmness to destroy the hopes of the Austrians. It was rather the answer given to Reuss that first enlightened the Imperial ministry on what was to be expected from Prussia.

III

The Ansbach-Baireuth proposition had not appeared to Schulenburg particularly exorbitant and offensive at the moment when it was first brought forward. It was only the day after the conference of July 21, after long rumination, that he convinced himself that the demand was thoroughly unjustifiable and inadmissible. Then the suspicion awoke in him that the Court of Vienna was systematically trying to strew the negotiation with difficulties

[1] Ph. Cobenzl to Reuss, August 8, Vivenot, ii, pp. 159 ff.
[2] Haugwitz to Frederick William, August 16, B. A., *R.* 1, *Conv.* 170.

in order to thwart the whole indemnity project; that it preferred to dispense with compensation for the war altogether, out of a Machiavellian calculation that fifty millions more of debts would not ruin a state with the resources of Austria, while the same loss would be fatal to Prussia.[1] Even the complaisance of the Austrians in other matters filled him with distrust. This proud Court of Vienna was not wont to be so courteous, so pliable: it must certainly have some vast, mysterious, and insidious design on foot.[2]

In this harrowing state of suspicion and uncertainty, Schulenburg clung all the more firmly to one principle and framed one momentous resolution. Whatever might happen, Prussia must obtain an indemnity for the cost of the war; and since Austria had failed him, he decided that the vital point at present was to reach an understanding with Russia. After the Prussian indemnity had thus been ensured, it would be time to consider the demands of the Court of Vienna. Austria might then be allowed to effect the Exchange, and, if it were clearly proved that a deficit would result, she might be permitted to make up the loss by certain acquisitions from France; but the claim for the Margraviates must be categorically, once and finally, rejected. This was a turning-point in Prussian policy. Hitherto Schulenburg's cardinal principle had been the concert with Austria. Now he looked for salvation only to Russia.[3]

If he had found the Ansbach-Baireuth proposition "inadmissible," his colleagues at Berlin declared it " alarming, not to say insolent," and even " revolting." Both of them had long been discontented with the reigning policies; and they now found a chance to give their anti-Austrian proclivities full vent. It was bad enough, they held, to have to consent to the Bavarian Exchange; but to undertake to urge it at London and Zweibrücken was out of the question. It could not be permitted at

---

[1] Schulenburg to Finckenstein and Alvensleben, July 21, B. A., R. XI, *Frankreich*, 89 g.

[2] Alopeus' report of July 13/24, based on Schulenburg's confidences to him, M. A., Пpyccия, III, 30.

[3] Schulenburg to Finckenstein and Alvensleben, July 22, in Ranke, *Ursprung und Beginn der Revolutionskriege*, p. 365.

all, unless Prussia obtained a very handsome acquisition in Poland. Though without great hopes with respect to the Empress' attitude, they agreed entirely with Schulenburg's idea as to the necessity of seeking first of all an understanding with Russia. If that could be attained, the King ought to take possession of his acquisition at once, and then tell the Court of Vienna that he would do what he could for it. That was the only way to deal with Austria, the two ministers declared. In 1771 and 1772 the Court of Vienna had also affected an attitude of disinterestedness; but when it saw Russia and Prussia agreed and determined to have their way, it had hastened to throw off the mask and beg for a share of ' the cake.'

The idea, it must be said, was luminous enough, except that there was this difference between 1772 and 1792: in the latter year Prussia was bound to Austria by an alliance, the basis of which was equality in all advantages; and she was engaged along with that Power in a joint war, the success of which depended upon complete mutual confidence. The alliance and the common enterprise were doomed, the moment Prussia attempted to carry out behind the back of her ally a coup like that proposed by the Berlin ministry. Doubtless the Imperial Court had rendered an agreement difficult by its exorbitant demands, but to seize the coveted lands in Poland without a preliminary understanding and then to present Austria with an insulting *fait accompli* was to turn the alliance to scorn. The project did not, indeed, come to execution at this time, as the sphinx at St. Petersburg could not be brought to speak; but in the ideas here proposed by Finckenstein and Alvensleben, and approved by Schulenburg, one can see the germs of the Note of Merle, the Second Partition Treaty, and the disruption of the First Coalition.[1]

[1] For the above: Alvensleben's and Finckenstein's notes to each other on Schulenburg's letter of July 21/22, their joint reply to him of July 27, his letter to them of August 2, B. A., *R.* XI, *Frankreich*, 89 *g.*

Finckenstein and Alvensleben wrote: " . . . Nous sommes tout à fait du sentiment de V. Exc. que pour nous procurer du côté de la Pologne le dédommagement qui fait notre objet, le consentement de la Russie est un préalable absolument nécessaire avant de pouvoir faire aucune démarche de poids du côté de l'Autriche. . . . L'affaire une fois de règle avec la Russie, nous pensons qu'il faudra la terminer sans perte de tems par nous mettre en possession le plûtôt qu'il se pourroit sans

Unanimous as was the opinion of the cabinet ministry, the King did not at first display the same repugnance to the idea of ceding the Margraviates; and Haugwitz was at bottom inclined to it. In a report to his sovereign of July 26, the envoy urged that the Court of Vienna might, indeed, be induced to content itself with the Exchange alone, but in that case it would probably raise great difficulties about the Polish affair; whereas if it were promised Ansbach and Baireuth, all assistance and good will might be expected from it. Before Schulenburg could intervene, Frederick William replied with a letter in which he showed himself not entirely unwilling to make the proposed cession, if in return he could get for himself the whole left bank of the Vistula.[1] Schulenburg was almost in despair over the royal indiscretion. He did what he could to mend matters by a private letter to Haugwitz, begging him in Heaven's name not to let the faintest suspicion transpire that their master could ever conceive of the possibility of such a cession. In public Haugwitz was to express as his own opinion that the King's aversion to the sacrifice demanded of him was wellnigh invincible. For the envoy's private instruction, Schulenburg added that it was only in the last extremity and only in return for immense acquisitions in Poland, that Prussia could consent to give up the Franconian principalities; and he personally would never lend a hand to such a transaction save with infinite repugnance.[2]

même trop s'apesanter sur un arrangement exact des démarcations . . . et cela fait, dire à la Cour de Vienne que telle est notre indemnité, et que nous sommes prêts à lui en procurer une de la même valeur, en autant que la chose dépendroit de nous. C'est la vraie manière à notre avis de traiter en pareil cas avec l'Autriche. Lors du démembrement de la Pologne en 1771 et 1772 elle suivit à peu près la même marche qu'aujourd'hui, jouant la désintéressée . . . ; mais lorsqu'elle nous vit d'accord avec la Russie et les deux Alliés disposés à aller leur chemin, quelque parti que l'on prit à Vienne, elle revint d'elle même à nous pour avoir sa part au gâteau. . . . Nous . . . avons été vraiment revoltés en apprenant que les Ministres Autrichiens ont osé proposer la cession des Principautés de Franconie. . . . V. Exc. a bien raison de nommer le projet d'une telle cession insoutenable et inadmissible. . . . Nous sommes ainsi bien d'accord tous trois que dans tous les cas il faut rejetter haut à la main une proposition aussi inacceptable sous tous les rapports, et qui ne sauroit même faire un objet de discussion entre les deux Cours."

[1] Frederick William to Haugwitz, July 28, B. A., *R*. 96, 155 *E*.
[2] Schulenburg to Haugwitz, July 30, B. A., *R*. XI, *Frankreich*, 89 *K*.

With that, however, the evil was not quite undone. The King's " indifference " to the " revolting proposition," did not cease to alarm the cabinet ministry. They trembled at the thought that if the Court of Vienna but suspected the weakness of their position, it would, with its usual perseverance, return again and again with offers of advantages and equivalents of all sorts, until finally the King succumbed.[1] The secret of that report of Haugwitz's and the replies made to it, Schulenburg wrote, must be concealed like murder. What if Bischoffwerder should learn of it, with his Austrian propensities![2] It was a trying moment for the Prussian ministers. They feared the weakness of their own sovereign; they had ceased to expect anything good from Austria; they found their hands bound with regard to France by the declaration in which the Duke of Brunswick was made to deny that the allied Powers had any designs upon the territory of that kingdom. Not only the Prussian acquisition in Poland, but a Prussian acquisition anywhere, seemed to be in grave jeopardy.

It was under these circumstances that the Austrian cabinet delivered its new attack through the dispatches to Reuss of August 8. Nevertheless, the communication of Cobenzl's report failed to work the wonders expected. This time Schulenburg was the first to gain the King's ear, and he succeeded in putting through an answer after his own heart. The reply given to Reuss declared clearly and emphatically that Prussia could never think of ceding the Margraviates, except in exchange for Lusatia, if that should ever return to Austrian hands; that whereas Cobenzl reported only the private opinions of the Russian ministers, it was indispensable to learn as soon as possible the sentiments of the Empress; that meantime the King desired to know whether the Emperor would accept the Bavarian Exchange as equivalent to the Prussian acquisition in Poland, and if not, and in case a partition were found impossible, what were his ideas regarding the indemnities that would then have to be sought at the expense

[1] Schulenburg to his colleagues, July 30, their reply of August 4, B. A., R. XI, *Frankreich*, 89 g.

[2] To Finckenstein and Alvensleben, August 11, *ibid*.

of France. To this formal response, Schulenburg added orally that his sovereign fully accepted the principle of a 'supplement' for Austria, and would assuredly be willing to coöperate in procuring one for his ally. His (Schulenburg's) personal opinion was that such an acquisition could best be found in Alsace. The honest Reuss was quite moved by such zeal for the interests of the Imperial Court, and reported with touching simplicity that it was plainly not Schulenburg's fault, if the King refused to cede the Margraviates. The divergence between Schulenburg's 'personal' utterances and his formal, ministerial declarations, Bischoffwerder's profuse sympathy, and the probable ambiguity of Haugwitz's interpretations of orders with which he did not agree, may well have had something to do with the fact that the Austrian ministry still refused for some time to consider the King's decision about the Margraviates as final.[1]

The Prussian ministers, too, were not yet thoroughly assured that the Ansbach-Baireuth question was dead and buried. Haugwitz continued even into September to recommend the cession, in order to secure a very generous acquisition in Poland; and this in spite of Schulenburg's efforts to "indoctrinate him," and in spite of the fulminations of the Berlin ministry against the very idea.[2] The King's mind, however, seemed henceforth fixed.

The Austrian communications through Reuss produced the very reverse of the desired effect on the Prussian ministry. The latter, instead of seeking the proposed concert with the Imperial Court, now hastened their advances to Russia. Goltz, who had hitherto been confined to generalities and hints, was at last ordered to enter into full and frank explanations.[3]

[1] For the above: Reuss' report of August 17, V. A., *Preussen, Berichte*, 1792; Schulenburg to Finckenstein and Alvensleben, August 14, B. A., *R. XI, Frankreich*, 89 *g*. It is to be noted that Schulenburg did not mention to his colleagues his declarations regarding a 'supplement,' and yet Reuss reports them so positively that one can hardly doubt his word, especially in view of the fact that he was admittedly one of the most truthful and honest of diplomats.

[2] Haugwitz to the King, August 16, 20, September 4, B. A., *R.* 1, 170; Schulenburg to Haugwitz, August 15, B. A., *R. XI, Frankreich*, 89 *g*, and September 2, B. A., *R. XI, Frankreich*, 89 *K*; Finckenstein and Alvensleben to Haugwitz, *passim*, August 20 and September 11 especially, B. A., *R.* 1, 170.

[3] Rescripts to Goltz of August 20 and 24, September 1 and 4, B. A., *R. XI, Russland*, 133.

Before these instructions reached St. Petersburg, matters had already begun to progress in that quarter, largely, it would seem, as a result of new communications from Vienna. On August 8 Philip Cobenzl had sent off to his cousin dispatches containing a report of the interviews at Mainz. Until the question of the Margraviates was settled, the Austrians were far from desiring to start a formal negotiation at St. Petersburg; and hence the object of the new communications was only to keep the Russians informed and in good humor. But the dispatches contained one novelty. By this time the Viennese ministers had convinced themselves that it would be impossible to avoid giving the Empress a share of the spoils; and so in order not to be outdone in generosity by the Prussians, and in order to accumulate merits for his own Court, the Vice-Chancellor here mentioned for the first time that, as a matter of course, Russia, too, should get something.[1] When Louis Cobenzl read these dispatches to Ostermann, the latter's face lighted up with pleasure when it came to the passage about an acquisition for Russia. " Well and good, in that case the thing can go through," he declared; " it was impossible that we alone should get nothing." [2] Without yet being in a position to speak ministerially, he gave Cobenzl to understand that the Empress agreed to the principle of the indemnity plan, and that the only question was as to the *quo modo*. Goltz, who arrived for his conference immediately afterward, found that day — for the first time — a ready listener. Ostermann repeated to him the assurance just given to Cobenzl, that his sovereign would certainly not oppose an arrangement for the advantage of all three Courts and wished only to be informed of the plan in more detail.[3]

Now at last the Prussian ministry could, as they expressed it, see a little *couleur de rose* in what had been so black a cloud. In accordance with Goltz's suggestion, they at once begged the King to fix the precise extent of the acquisition to be demanded in

---

[1] Ph. Cobenzl to L. Cobenzl, August 8, Vivenot, ii, pp. 164–169.

[2] " So recht, so kann die Sache gehen, denn es war nicht möglich dass wir die einzigen leer ausgehen."

[3] Cobenzl's and Goltz's reports of August 24, V. A., *Russland, Berichte*, 1792, B. A., *R.* XI, *Russland*, 133.

Poland, so that the envoy might be enabled to bring matters to a definite agreement.[1] Hitherto the Prussians had been by no means clear as to the exact boundaries that they meant to claim. The King had several times spoken longingly of the whole left bank of the Vistula,[2] and he had found Schulenburg's ideas too modest. Haugwitz, on leaving Frankfort, seems to have been charged to go to Silesia and collect topographical information bearing on the problem. In the middle of August, he reported his conclusions. In case of the cession of the Margraviates, he proposed to demand the whole left bank of the Vistula except Mazovia; in the contrary case, a boundary might be drawn from Częstochowa through Piotrków and Rawa to the confluence of the Bug and Vistula, and thence across to the East Prussian frontier at Soldau. This latter proposal is worth noting: it is the first appearance of the line of demarcation adopted in the Second Partition Treaty (with very slight changes).[3] Haugwitz's ideas, however, were apparently too bold to suit his superiors at Berlin, and in the instructions now forwarded to Goltz the size of the acquisition in Poland was cut down to much the same limits as had been proposed by Schulenburg at Mainz.[4] In any case, the road was thus paved for a formal negotiation at St. Petersburg, and the will was not lacking in the Prussian ministry to close with Russia at once, without waiting a moment for Austria. Unless the Court of Vienna hastened to present a really acceptable proposition, it was likely to find itself isolated and ignored. Meantime the Austrian ministers were casting around desperately for their 'supplement,' hopelessly unable to meet the impending danger.

[1] Finckenstein and Alvensleben to Schulenburg, September 10, B. A., *R.* XI, *Frankreich,* 89 g.

[2] In his note to Schulenburg of March 12, and his letter to Haugwitz of July 28.

[3] Haugwitz to the King, August 16, B. A., *R.* 1, 170.

[4] Rescript to Goltz of September 28, B. A., *R.* XI, *Russland,* 133. The line indicated ran from the frontier of East Prussia southward through Lipów and Bołkowa to Płock on the Vistula; thence via Gostyn, Sleszyn and Grzegorzów to the Warta; then up that stream through Uniejów and Sieradz, and across country via Wielkie to the Silesian frontier near Gorzów. It thus included the whole of the palatinates of Gnesen, Posen, Kalisz, and Cujavia, about one-third of that of Sieradz, and also the cities of Dantzic and Thorn.

IV

Apart from its obstinate insistence on the impossible demand for the Margraviates, the Court of Vienna had done nothing throughout the whole month of August, the last month in which by prudent concessions an agreement with Prussia on advantageous terms might still have been reached. The Imperial cabinet presented a sad spectacle of ever-growing feebleness, incoherency, and internal dissensions. Now that Kaunitz had finally retired, the direction of foreign affairs had passed nominally into the hands of Cobenzl, an amiable, easy-going bureaucrat, who scribbled and stuttered placidly through life without displaying an excess of imagination, initiative, or energy. Spielmann was a more vigorous personality, but the ground was already shaking under his feet. If at the beginning of the reign he had passed for the new monarch's most confidential adviser, by this time the hatred of the aristocrats for this parvenu, the discontent of all classes with a war of which he was popularly supposed to be the author, the rankling jealousy of Kaunitz towards his presumptuous pupil, the violent opposition in the Conference — all this had combined to place his position in grave danger. And with him the Bavarian-Polish project stood or fell. In the Conference the parties were equal: Spielmann, Cobenzl, and Starhemberg, the advocates of the Exchange, against Lacy, Rosenberg, and Colloredo. But even Cobenzl, whether from jealousy of his colleague or from a natural inclination to steer with the wind, varied in his attitude towards the project, sometimes apparently going so far as to place the ' supplement ' above the Exchange itself.[1] As for the opponents of the plan, they had nothing to put in its place. To escape from the war as soon as possible; to free themselves from an irritating dependence on Prussia; to avoid compromising the Emperor's good name by complicity in a new dismemberment of Poland: such seems to have been the height of their desires. Without any perception of the real situation, without plan or system, without moderation in their demands or prudence in the

---

[1] Cf. his memorial written in the last days of August, Vivenot, *Zur Genesis der zweiten Theilung Polens*, pp. 43–47.

choice of means, these gentlemen of the Conference found their chief function in criticizing, obstructing, and tearing down; and their activity resulted only in hampering and thwarting the policy of the Emperor's responsible ministers.

The arrival of the reply given to Reuss threw the whole indemnity project into doubt. Spielmann told Haugwitz that ' he was at the end of his Latin '; if the King absolutely refused to cede the Margraviates, there could be no more talk of either Bavaria or Poland.[1] Cobenzl felt bound to advise that the matter should be brought before the Conference.[2] Accordingly, on September 3 another great ministerial field day was held in the Emperor's presence at Schönbrunn.

This time the victory rested with Spielmann. In spite of the renewed efforts of the opposition and especially of Lacy, it was decided to keep on with the Exchange plan, and to make a new attempt to reach an understanding with Prussia about a ' supplement.' In accordance with an idea brought forward by Spielmann, the Conference resolved to propose once more the cession of the Margraviates, this time in return for the promise of an eventual cession of Lusatia whenever that territory should lapse to Austria. But as a new refusal was to be expected here, the State Chancellery had suggested that the ' supplement ' might be found either in Alsace or in Poland. Rosenberg championed the former alternative, but the Emperor decided in favor of the latter; and Lacy was charged to draw up the boundaries of a desirable acquisition in that quarter. It was the first occasion on which the Austrians had seriously taken up the idea of demanding a share in the new dismemberment of Poland. Here, too, they discussed for the first time a possibility that was just beginning to loom up on the horizon. The Bavarian Exchange could hardly be effected until after the peace with France, and in the meantime the definite settlement of Polish affairs could not well be long delayed. What if Russia and Prussia should seize their acquisitions before Austria had gained any securities for hers ? The Conference decided that in such a case the Imperial Court

---

[1] Haugwitz's report to the King of August 25, B. A., *R.* XI, *Frankreich*, 89 g.
[2] *Vortrag* of August 27 (V. A.).

must occupy a district in Poland equivalent to that claimed by Prussia, and retain it as a guarantee until the Bavarian Exchange and the acquisition of the 'supplement' had been effected. Finally, the Emperor announced his intention of sending Spielmann to the King of Prussia's headquarters to present these propositions and to negotiate a definitive agreement. The news from the front was favorable; it seemed probable that the allied armies would soon be in Paris; it was urgently necessary to settle the indemnity question at once.[1]

Though much chagrined by the results of this Conference,[2] the opposition were not yet ready to acknowledge themselves beaten. In the next few days they sent in written *vota* repeating their objections, especially to the idea of joining in the spoliation of Poland, with such force that the Emperor was apparently shaken in his previous resolution. Moreover, on the question of the supplement, Cobenzl now went over to their side, thus giving them the majority in the Conference.[3] One other incident also occurred to render a reconsideration of the recent decisions desirable. Haugwitz, learning of Spielmann's mission, took the occasion to declare that he should regret it, were the Referendary sent in the supposition that the cession of the Margraviates could ever be conceded, since he had recently had cause to doubt more strongly than ever the feasibility of such a project.[4] Hence on the 7th the Conference met again, this time in the absence of the Emperor, who did not enjoy long discussions.

---

[1] Conference protocol of September 3, and the '*separat-vota*,' Vivenot, ii, pp. 180–186. It seems highly probably that Spielmann's remarks on Reuss' reports, which are printed in Vivenot, ii, pp. 172–176, were prepared to serve as the basis of discussion at this conference, and represent the *Vorlage* usually submitted on such occasions by the State Chancellery.

[2] *Zinzendorf's Diary*, September 6: " Rosenberg a honte d'être de la conférence " (V. A.).

[3] Cobenzl's desertion evidently took place after the Conference of September 3. Otherwise the party in favor of taking the supplement in Alsace rather than in Poland would have been in the majority that day, whereas it appears from the protocol of September 7 that it was only the *separat-vota* submitted on the 5th and 6th which showed them to be in a majority.

[4] This from the Conference protocol of September 7, V. A., *Vorträge*, 1792. Haugwitz gives a somewhat more vigorous tone to his declaration in his report of the same day, B. A., *R. 1, Conv.* 170.

Once more the question of Alsace or Poland was hotly fought over. Rosenberg again advocated the former plan, on the ground that it was more honorable to take a just indemnity from a conquered enemy than to join in dismembering a friendly state, and also because of the superior value of this acquisition, which, combined with Bavaria and the Austrian lands in Swabia, would give the Imperial Court a decided preponderance in South Germany. To the difficulties in the way of conquering and defending such a province, Rosenberg seemed completely blind. With less appeal to principle or sentiment, but with far more common sense, Starhemberg argued that the Austrian indemnities must be rendered, as far as possible, independent of the fortunes of war, just as were the Russian and Prussian ones; that an acquisition in Poland would be easy and safe, while one in Alsace would be quite the reverse; and as for the odium of joining in a partition of the Republic, the Imperial Court would only be following the example of its two allies, and even if it did not take an open hand in the affair, the world would never believe that it had not given its consent in order to secure advantages elsewhere. The Conference contented itself that day with elucidating the arguments on both sides, which were to be submitted to the Emperor. Regarding the other great point at issue, the ministers recommended making a final effort to win the Margraviates by offering a special arrangement by which the Bavarian House should cede Juliers and Berg to Prussia.[1]

Two days later the Emperor gave his decision. Characteristically enough, he tore up his own resolution adopted only six days before, and pronounced in favor of just the opposite course: he would take his supplement in Alsace, and not in Poland. One may doubt whether this decision had quite the world-historic importance that has sometimes been given to it;[2] but it would seem to have been a fresh blunder for Austria to renounce the one acquisition that she had any chance of making, in order to launch forth on schemes for impossible conquests from France. It is

[1] Protocol of September 7, in Vivenot, ii, pp. 186–190.
[2] Sybel (*op. cit.*, ii, pp. 355 f.) finds that it changed the whole character of the war by turning the enterprise of the allies into a war for conquests on a grand scale.

more to the credit of the Emperor's judgment that he vetoed the Juliers-Berg project, thus finally consigning the wretched question of the Margraviates to oblivion.[1]

Armed with these new and by no means modest propositions, Spielmann set out on the morning of September 12, accompanied by the high hopes of the Vice-Chancellor that the grand affair would at last be settled to the great advantage of Austria.[2] The wonder and the curiosity of the diplomatic world rose one pitch higher, when on the same day Count Haugwitz also departed in the same direction.[3] All eyes in Vienna were now turned toward the Prussian headquarters. " Judging by what Prince Reuss has just reported," Cobenzl wrote to Spielmann, " your letters will probably soon be dated from Paris." It was the day of Valmy.[4]

---

[1] Cobenzl's *Vertrag* of September 9, and the Imperial apostil, Vivenot, ii, pp. 191 f.

[2] Cobenzl to Spielmann, September 9, V. A., *Mission in das preussische Hauptquartier de 1792, A.*

[3] The reasons for Haugwitz's journey are not quite certain. He had received a letter from the King appointing him cabinet minister and informing him of Schulenburg's impending return to Berlin, but not, apparently, summoning him to the army. He seems to have undertaken on his own initiative to go to Frankfort, in the expectation that he would then be called to the royal headquarters to take Schulenburg's place in conducting the negotiation with Spielmann. The letter to the King (of September 5), in which he explained his reasons for taking this step, is apparently lost. To Schulenburg he excused himself on the plea that he had grounds for suspecting that Spielmann was charged to renew the proposition about the Margraviates, and that hence he had determined to go to Frankfort, in order to be near the King and strengthen the royal resistance to such a demand, supposing that Schulenburg would already have left the army. (Letter of September 30, B. A., *R. XI, Frankreich*, 89 K.) Alopeus reported (doubtless on the basis of what Lucchesini had told him) that Spielmann had asked Haugwitz to accompany him, because he wished to negotiate with a minister in whom he had confidence and with whom he was accustomed to deal. (Report of September 11/22, M. A., Пруссия, III, 30.) This is quite probable, since if Haugwitz had not been present, Spielmann would have had to negotiate with the much distrusted Lucchesini. At any rate, it is clear that Haugwitz's trip was undertaken without orders from anyone.

[4] Vivenot, ii, pp. 211 f.

CHAPTER XV

THE NOTE OF MERLE

I

SPIELMANN reached Frankfort on September 18, closely followed by Haugwitz. As the latter had just received the King's order to come to the army, the two continued on the journey together as far as Luxemburg. On the way Spielmann applied himself with all his skill to win Haugwitz over to his propositions; and he seems to have found a very ready hearer. Haugwitz, it must be remembered, had always been in favor of allowing Austria a ' supplement,' in order to obtain for his own Court a particularly large slice of Poland. He now showed himself so complaisant that Spielmann ventured to claim for his sovereign not only the Bavarian Exchange, but Alsace and Lorraine as far as the Moselle — an acquisition such as the Conference had never dared to demand in even its wildest moments. Haugwitz accepted the proposition, without objections apparently, and, leaving Spielmann at Luxemburg, went on to Verdun (the 26th) to find the King and receive his orders regarding the Austrian demands and the counter-claims to be advanced for Prussia.[1]

But just at this moment there began that rapid series of disasters which ruined the hopes of the invaders of France and gave an entirely new face to the situation. After Valmy (September 20) came Dumouriez's negotiation with Manstein; September 29 the retreat of the allied army was decided upon; October 8 the

---

[1] Haugwitz to Schulenburg, September 30, B. A., *R.* XI, *Frankreich*, 89 *K*; Spielmann to Cobenzl, September 27, V. A., *Mission in das preussische Hauptquartier*, and October 15, Vivenot, ii, pp. 272–277.

Haugwitz wrote: " La Cour de Vienne demandera pour sa part l'échange de la Bavière . . . et ils proposeront d'ajouter au lot de l'Autriche l'Alsace et une partie de la Lorraine jusqu'à la Moselle, ce qui comprend les possessions françoises entre le Rhin et la Moselle depuis les sources de cette dernière jusqu'à Remiez [Remich], tout le long de la rivière en y comprenant les villes et forts situés sur la Moselle " [i. e., Toul, Metz, Thionville, etc.].

Prussians renewed the sham negotiation; on the 12th Verdun was abandoned, on the 22nd Longwy; and in the next few days the last German troops evacuated the soil of France. Meanwhile Custine had made his bold raid down the Rhine, seizing Spires September 30, Mainz October 21, and the next day Frankfort. After the high hopes with which the allies began the ' promenade to Paris,' these unthinkable catastrophes were doubly crushing. Of 42,000 Prussians who had entered France, hardly 20,000 recrossed the frontier, and of these more than half were sick.[1] A soldier who lived through the horrors of 1812, later declared that the Prussians during the retreat from Champagne were perhaps a more terrible sight than even the wrecks of the Grand Army.[2] The effect upon Frederick William's impressionable and glory-loving mind can easily be imagined. He who throughout his reign had had to stand the comparison with his illustrious predecessor, had played away in an expedition as ill-fated as mismanaged the prestige and the nimbus of invincibility which had hitherto clung to the army of the great Frederick. Little wonder that the King was eager to wipe out the shame by a new campaign in the following year, and that he was even more anxious to rehabilitate himself in the eyes of his subjects by securing immediately an acquisition that would balance all his losses.

Under these circumstances, Haugwitz met his sovereign on October 8 at Consenvoye, reported what he supposed to be the aims of Spielmann's mission, and obtained definite instructions as to the share which the King intended to demand in Poland. On the map of the Republic Frederick William traced the line Częstochowa-Rawa-Soldau, which henceforth formed the basis of the Prussian claims. Haugwitz was directed to go back to Verdun, where Spielmann had now arrived, to receive the definite propositions of the Court of Vienna.[3] On his return, however, he found the Austrian minister on the point of retiring to Luxem-

---

[1] Chuquet, *La Campagne de l'Argonne* (1792), pp. 476 f.

[2] *Ibid.*, p. 475.

[3] Haugwitz to Schulenburg, October 15, B. A., *R.* XI, *Frankreich,* 89 *K.* The fact that the King at this time gave definite orders as to his claims in Poland, and traced the line of demarcation on the map with his own hand, appears from Haugwitz's great report of May 6, 1793, B. A., *R.* 96, 147 *H.*

burg, as the evacuation of Verdun had just been decided upon. During the brief conversation that then took place, Spielmann learned only that the King expressed great willingness not only to assist in the realization of the Exchange, but to secure for the Imperial Court a rich 'supplement' in lieu of the Margraviates.[1] On reaching Luxemburg on the 12th, the Referendary fell ill with a fever, so that although Haugwitz arrived the following day, the negotiation had to be still further delayed.

The situation had changed so greatly that Spielmann weighed the question whether he could negotiate at all on the basis of instructions drawn up on quite different presuppositions. Haugwitz urged, indeed, that the King was resolved to make a second campaign, if the Court of Vienna agreed, and was anxious to settle the indemnity question at once. But the Prussian minister also threw out an ominous hint of the kind of settlement his master had in mind, when in a lively discussion (on the 14th) he declared that the King must have his acquisition in Poland, no matter how other affairs turned out, and that he could not leave it dependent on the uncertain course of future events. In other words, the King meant to make sure of his indemnity at once, although, in view of the disastrous turn of the war, the realization of the Exchange seemed still very far in the future. The principle, hitherto accepted on both sides, that the respective indemnities must proceed *pari passu*, was in danger of being repudiated. Spielmann did his best to combat so insidious an idea; but Haugwitz maintained that his own personal standing depended on the realization of his master's wishes.[2] It was the beginning of a decisive turn in Prussian policy.

Nevertheless, after long cogitation, Spielmann determined to go ahead even without instructions, and to make such arrangements as were, on the one hand, required by the dangerous position of affairs, and would, on the other hand, satisfy the desires of Frederick William. He recognized clearly that the continuation of the war was far more indispensable to Austrian than to Prussian interests; the King was eager at present to make a second

---

[1] Spielmann to Cobenzl, October 15, Vivenot, ii, pp. 272–277.

[2] Spielmann to Cobenzl, October 15.

campaign; but if Austria showed any disinclination to it, or to settling the indemnity affair at once, it was only too greatly to be feared that his good dispositions would grow cold, and that he would retire from the war altogether. No doubt the Jacobins would build him 'bridges of gold'; and in the loss of the Austrian Netherlands, Prussian statesmen might find a sufficient gain for themselves, even if they got nothing in Poland.[1] With these reflections in mind, Spielmann drew up a plan for an agreement about the indemnities, in which he advanced for his own Court those none too modest claims to which Haugwitz had already lent so willing an ear, while he added certain stipulations adapted to the altered circumstances and to the wishes of the King of Prussia. Though it was destined to an early grave, this plan is too remarkable to be passed over without some description.

Frederick William desired to make a second campaign; Spielmann had no definite orders on that point, but he knew that the interests of his Court imperatively demanded it: hence the first article of the proposed agreement provided that the two Powers should make a second campaign with forces as large as had been employed in the present; that neither should consent to a truce or a negotiation without the consent of the other; and that both should endeavor to induce England, Russia, and the Germanic Empire to join actively in the war. The struggle was to be continued in common until monarchical government had been restored in France, or until the spread of revolutionary principles had been sufficiently and permanently checked. The King of Prussia would thus find his first wish gratified, and himself nicely bound, too, if he consented to all this. Frederick William also desired to occupy his Polish acquisition at once, without leaving it to the uncertain chances of war. Spielmann was ready to grant this also — on certain conditions. First of all, the Bavarian Exchange must be ensured immediately. If the King would at once send Haugwitz to win the consent of the Duke of Zweibrücken, while Austria simultaneously began negotiations at Munich; if

---

[1] These reflections in Spielmann's letter to Cobenzl cited above. At the end of this report he declared that he would later send in the plan by which he had determined to proceed. The plan followed in his next report of November 6.

a formal treaty was concluded with the Bavarian House (the execution to be deferred till the time of the peace with France); if Prussia would guarantee the Exchange against all obstacles from foreign Powers (England and Holland): then Frederick William might proceed to the occupation of his lot in Poland, the territory bounded by the line Częstochowa-Rawa-Soldau. But the Austrian ' supplement ' must also be brought under cover. Here Spielmann reverted to the idea approved by the Conference on September 3 and discarded four days later. He proposed that simultaneously with the Prussian occupation in Poland the Emperor should also occupy a district there equivalent to the respective acquisitions of his allies, and should retain this as a guarantee until Bavaria and Alsace-Lorraine as far as the Moselle were in his hands. Thus all contingencies would be provided for, every interest of Austria would be ensured, the King of Prussia's chief desires would be complied with: in short, a basis seemed to have been found on which the two Powers could finally agree.

When Spielmann presented this plan to Haugwitz, the latter readily acquiesced, as far as his personal opinion was concerned, in all its points save one. He objected to the proposed Austrian occupation in Poland. If the Court of Vienna must join in that banquet, there would not be enough to go round. He agreed, however, to report all to the King; and one would judge from the tone of a letter of that moment that he was by no means disinclined to the project.[1]

But immediately afterward events began to play havoc with Spielmann's plan. On leaving Verdun he seems to have thought that the allies would retreat only beyond the River Chiers and would still occupy winter quarters in France. But in fact the retreat from Verdun turned into a rout, the combined forces poured over the frontier in the most sorry plight, French soil was

---

[1] Spielmann's plan is printed in Vivenot, ii, pp. 348–354. The other sources relating to it are the Referendary's report of November 6, and Haugwitz's letters to Schulenburg of October 19 and 27, B. A., R. XI, *Frankreich*, 89 K. The account given in the text differs greatly from those of previous writers, owing to the fact that I have placed this plan in the middle of Spielmann's negotiation, while Sybel put it at the very end, and Heidrich at the very beginning. The questions at issue are discussed in Appendix XV.

completely evacuated; and in the meantime the mysterious negotiations of the Prussians with the enemy aroused in Spielmann, as in all the Austrians present, the vehement suspicion that there was treachery afoot. Under these circumstances, the Referendary redoubled his efforts to bring Haugwitz to a categorical declaration as to the King's intentions, but he can scarcely have concealed from himself the fact that the fateful turn of events allowed little chance of success to the plan he had presented only a few days before.[1]

II

Frederick William, for more than one reason, was angry with the Austrians. The common disasters had not failed to bring forth dissensions among the allies; and the refusal of the Imperial general Hohenlohe (Kirchberg) to defend Longwy, followed by his precipitate retreat into Belgium, had capped the climax.[2] The few supporters of the Austrian system had fallen from favor. Schulenburg, who, patriot as he was, had meant to deal loyally with the Court of Vienna, had returned to Berlin discredited and disillusioned. Bischoffwerder was in semi-disgrace and entirely without influence on foreign policy. Of the men who now enjoyed the most credit, the royal adjutant Manstein — the sometime friend and present rival of Bischoffwerder — and Lucchesini, who had been called to the army to direct the anticipated negotiations with France, were united in the desire for peace and for the dissolution of the Austrian alliance. Haugwitz, though unsteady and pliable, had formerly inclined to much the same principles, and now under Lucchesini's influence returned to them. It was Lucchesini who strove most effectually to dampen the King's ardor for the war, persuaded him out of proposing an ' offensive league ' to the Court of Vienna, and continually urged upon him the necessity above all things of

---

[1] Cf. his report of November 6, Vivenot, ii, p. 338.

[2] Cf. Frederick William's outburst to Bischoffwerder after this incident: " Voilà les f—— alliés que vous m'avez donnés; je suis près de rompre avec eux," and his complaints to Nassau, Feuillet de Conches, *Louis XVI, Marie Antoinette et Madame Elisabeth*, vi, pp. 367 f., 372 ff., 392–396.

attending to his indemnity.[1] It was Lucchesini, apparently, who originated the plan embodied in the Note of Merle.

This plan was, substantially, to take advantage of the disastrous campaign, the danger threatening the Austrian Netherlands, the peril menacing the Empire itself, to demand an immediate acquisition in Poland as the price of continuing the war. Austria's necessity must be Prussia's opportunity. The settlement of the indemnity question had been so long delayed and had been so much obstructed by the pretensions of the Imperial Court, that the chance was not to be lost to use the lever thrust into Prussian hands. There could be no doubt that Austria stood greatly in need of further assistance, and that, as far as the French were concerned, Frederick William was free to withdraw from the contest whenever he pleased. It was, indeed, true that according to the spirit of their original engagements, neither of the allied Powers had the right to withdraw without the other. As late as October 15 that principle was plaintively reasserted by the Prussians themselves, when they feared for a moment that Austria might be on the point of backing out of the contest and leaving them in the lurch. On that date the ministers at Berlin wrote to Lucchesini that since the two Powers had undertaken this enterprise at their common expense, in the same spirit and for the same aim, there could be no question of the one abandoning the other; the struggle must necessarily be pursued with united efforts until both Courts could simultaneously make an honorable peace. Neither the ministers at Berlin nor Haugwitz seem at first to have perceived the opportunity created by the new situation. It may be doubted whether even Lucchesini would have ventured to recommend taking so high a tone despite all previous engagements, if he had expected to meet with the united opposition of the Imperial Courts. But just at this moment he felt fairly sure of encountering no obstacles from Russia.

Goltz had recently reported, in a tone of assurance quite uncommon with him, that the Russian ministers showed the best of

---

[1] Lucchesini to Finckenstein, Schulenburg, and Alvensleben, October 15, 23-26, B. A., *R.* 92, *Lucchesinis Nachlass, No.* 14. The papers from this collection are henceforth cited *L. N.*

intentions on the indemnity question, and that he was convinced that the Empress desired a new partition of Poland, provided only that Austria was not allowed to take anything from the Republic.[1] Alopeus had also come to the camp at Consenvoye to present a dispatch from Ostermann, which announced that the Empress was disposed to oblige her allies as soon as she knew their precise plans, and which pressed for a speedy communication of the King's views at St. Petersburg.[2] Such invitations were not to be neglected. They also gave reason to think that the effect of the reply would not be spoiled by a mild threat.

Frederick William made haste, then, to respond with a letter to the Empress (written from Longuyon, October 17), in which he referred to the definite and detailed communications which Goltz was charged to make, and intimated politely but clearly that he could not decide to undertake a second campaign until assured of his indemnities not only for the expenses of the past, but for those to be incurred in the future.

It remained to deal with Austria. From that Power little good will was to be expected, but — thanks to Brunswick's generalship — Prussia was in a position to dictate her terms. To prepare the Austrians for the blow, the King invited the three ministers, Spielmann, Mercy, and Thugut (the latter two had been sent to conduct the expected negotiations with France) to his headquarters near the village of Merle (October 24), and after dinner received them in audience in his tent. Though he treated them graciously enough and spoke warmly of his desire to maintain the alliance, he indicated sufficiently clearly the determination that he had reached. At the close he announced that Haugwitz would present his intentions in writing. Spielmann understood what was coming, and already told his friends that he was a lost man.[3] The following evening the Referendary received the promised ' declaration ' from Haugwitz.

---

[1] Report of September 25, B. A., *R.* XI, *Russland*, 133.

[2] Ostermann to Alopeus, September 3/14, Alopeus' report of October 8/19, M. A., Пруссия, III, 28 and 30.

[3] Lucchesini to the ministers at Berlin, October 26, B. A., *R.* 92, *L. N.* 14; Spielmann's report of November 6. All sources agree in placing this audience on the 24th of October, and not the 25th as in Sybel, *op. cit.*, ii, p. 360.

The famous note, dated from Merle, October 25, is hardly a model of clearness and precision, as neither the King nor Haugwitz, who drew up the document, had at that moment a chancellery at their disposal. Nevertheless, these few paragraphs, so vague in part, were to be the Law and the Prophets for Prussian ministers in the following year; they were to be held up as the complete exposition of the nature of the King's participation in the war, and as the sole basis and measure of his engagements.

The note may be divided into two parts. The first related to the theory of Prussia's further participation in the war. The King was ready, it was said, to continue his exertions either as a member of a concert of all the European Powers, or in case the Diet of Ratisbon declared war on France, as a member of the Empire, i. e., with the small quota due from him as a *Reichsstand*. The first case was obviously unthinkable; and the aid promised in the second would clearly be inacceptable to Austria. These offers were, then, only phrases, intended to lead up to the third case. If the Emperor, the note went on, saw fit to continue the war with all his forces, even if some or all of the other Powers refused to join with him, the King agreed to assist him in the next campaign with the same forces as had been employed in the present one — under one condition. That is to say, all of the previous engagements had been swept out of existence; and if the King went on with the war, it would be only in order to aid Austria, and at the price which he was about to name. It was the beginning of the theory that Austria was *partie principale et attaquée*, and Prussia *partie accessoire et auxiliaire*, a theory which then became the favorite thesis of the statesmen at Berlin, although it stood in glaring contradiction to the agreements with which the two Courts began the war.

But now for the condition of Prussia's further coöperation, which formed the principal part of the note. " Since the present campaign," it was said, " has caused so considerable an expense and so great a loss of life, and the continuation of the war must involve a still greater expenditure, His Prussian Majesty feels himself justified in expecting a complete and speedy compensation and indemnity for the expenses already incurred; and before the King takes further part in the continuation of the war, he considers himself bound by his duty to his realm to demand an indemnity for the expenses of the next campaign. He therefore expects that the *arrondissement* in Poland, with regard to which he has already made overtures to the Emperor, will be assured to him by the Courts of Austria and Russia, and actually taken into his possession."

All this might have been said more precisely, but the drift was clear. The King must have laid his hands upon his indemnities both for the past and for the future, before he could begin a second campaign. And with that, the whole previous plan for the joint indemnification was thrown overboard. Hitherto both Powers had always recognized the principle of complete parity: the respective indemnities were to be equal; they were to be gathered in simultaneously; if the one proved impracticable, the other must also be abandoned. Doubtless the King and some of his advisers were still sincerely willing to help Austria to the acquisition of Bavaria; but the Exchange was obviously impossible at that moment, and not to be realized for a long time to come; and at all events Prussia meant to have her booty at once, whether Austria ever got anything or not. That was the beginning of the thesis that if the Court of Vienna had any titles to an indemnity at all, they were not to be placed on the same line with those of Prussia. The latter were absolutely independent of, and infinitely more valid than, the Austrian claims. That was the crowning blow to the theory of a common enterprise. It was also the ruin of an alliance, the primary basis of which was complete equality in all advantages.

But if the rights were mostly in favor of the Austrians, the facts were all on the side of Prussia. Whatever the aims and nature of the war had been originally, in view of the recent events the allied Powers could no longer have any other object than to repel the victorious Revolutionary armies and to exact such vengeance as they were able. In this the interests of Austria were very much more at stake than were those of Prussia. And if the altered nature of the war lent some color to the new Prussian theory, the King's demand with regard to Poland was also not without justification in the circumstances of the moment. The Empress could not long defer settling Polish affairs in one way or another; she seemed strongly inclined to a partition at present; but it was to be doubted whether her good dispositions would last, if the King long delayed the matter. There was reason for haste then, and an admirable opportunity, if seized in time. To ask the Prussian statesmen to relinquish or to postpone a handsome acquisition that seemed within their reach at that moment, simply out of regard for a jealous ally or out of respect for previous engagements, would be to expect a self-denial and a loyalty not very common in history.[1]

III

Spielmann was filled with indignation and dismay by the Prussian declaration. Taken together with the slack conduct of the recent campaign and the suspicious negotiations with the enemy, it seemed to him to indicate a deep-laid design to " put the knife to the throat of Austria." In two days of heated discussions with Haugwitz, he endeavored to prove that the principles of the note violated all those invariably agreed upon between the two Courts, and ran contrary to all loyalty, fairness, and justice. But irrefutable arguments were powerless against Haugwitz, who had facts on his side. After weighing the situation carefully with Mercy, Spielmann decided to make the best of it, not insisting too strenuously on the old principles, but rather trying to drive a new bargain on the basis of the Prussian note.

The Referendary now directed his main efforts towards making sure of the King's earnest coöperation in effecting the Exchange. On that point Haugwitz was satisfactory enough. He gave the most solemn assurances that his sovereign was, and would remain, sincerely disposed to further the Exchange to the best of his ability; he would gladly employ his good offices with the Duke of Zweibrücken; he would even guarantee the realization of the project against all hindrances whatsoever. But as it was

---

[1] The Note of Merle is printed in Vivenot, ii, pp. 202 f. On it cf. Sybel, *op. cit.*, ii, pp. 359 ff.; Sorel, *op. cit.*, iii, pp. 128 f.; Häusser, *ob. cit.*, i, pp. 398 ff., 435 ff.; Heidrich, *op. cit.* pp. 397–402.

clear that not only the Exchange itself, but even the negotiation with the Bavarian House, must still be postponed for an indefinite period, Spielmann again proposed the plan for an interimistic Austrian occupation in Poland, the district in question to be restored to the Republic in case the acquisition of Bavaria and of a suitable ' supplement ' should later be effected. On this point, too, Haugwitz seems to have shown himself complaisant; at least Spielmann reported that on this occasion the Prussian minister made no objection to the idea, but asked only to know definitely what acquisitions Austria desired to make in that quarter.[1]

The matter seemed so important, however, that in order to get the minister's utterances confirmed, Spielmann sought and obtained through Bischoffwerder an audience with the King (October 27). Frederick William approved all that Haugwitz had said. In a tone which must, as Spielmann reported, inspire nothing but confidence, if such a thing as good faith existed in the world, the King expressed his readiness to guarantee the Exchange and to negotiate at Zweibrücken, and even added the suggestion that in view of the provoking conduct of the Elector of Bavaria, they might in his case adopt a tone other than that of mere persuasion. Spielmann encountered some opposition at first on the subject of the Austrian occupation in Poland, but believed that in the end he had succeeded in winning the King's

---

[1] Spielmann's report of November 6, Vivenot, ii, p. 346. Heidrich holds (*op. cit.*, p. 405, note 2) that Spielmann's statement here is not accurate, and that he was confusing his conversation with Haugwitz with the assurances given him immediately afterward by the King. This view Heidrich bases on Haugwitz's declaration (in a letter to Schulenburg of October 27) that he had rejected the proposition about an Austrian acquisition in Poland. I think it deserves to be pointed out, however, that in the letter to Schulenburg Haugwitz was referring to a previous discussion of this question with Spielmann on the occasion of the ' *mémoire* ' presented to him by the Referendary about a week before the Note of Merle. Spielmann readily admits that on that occasion Haugwitz had opposed the idea, but states positively that he did not raise the slightest objection on the later occasion. It is quite possible that Haugwitz, who was now doing his best to sweeten the bitter taste of the Note of Merle, showed himself this time more compliant on the subject. At any rate, since his statement does not refer to the later conversation, and Spielmann's does, I should prefer to trust the latter, quite apart from the question of the comparative veracity of the two men.

consent. It is not surprising, then, that on leaving Frederick William he declared to Bischoffwerder that the audience had revived all his hopes and cured all his sorrows.[1] The Note of Merle would indeed lose its terrors, if Austria were assured of the Prussian guarantee of the Exchange, the King's good offices at Zweibrücken, and a real security besides in the shape of a Polish province.

It remained to hear the verdict of Vienna. Haugwitz was destined to return temporarily to his old post, in order to receive the reply to the Note of Merle, and to make sure of the Austrian consent to an immediate Prussian occupation in Poland. On October 30 he left Luxemburg on the road to Cologne, and some hours later Spielmann followed.

On arriving in that city the two had further discussions. Spielmann's attention seems to have been called by Reuss to a new plan of a bold and promising character. The King of Prussia and the Duke of Brunswick had suggested that if the Elector of Bavaria continued his more than equivocal relations with the French, the Imperial Court should adopt violent measures against him. The Lower Palatinate and the fortress of Mannheim were too important to be left in danger of falling into hostile hands.[2] Spielmann was favorably impressed with the idea. The Elector's sins and shortcomings might furnish the Emperor with an admirable excuse for putting himself in possession of Bavaria at once.[3] Haugwitz was straightway approached on the subject, and hurried back to Coblenz, where the King had now arrived, to take his orders. Apart from the military grounds, Frederick William

---

[1] Lucchesini to the ministers at Berlin, December 14, B. A., *R.* 96, *L. N.* 14.

[2] Reuss' report of November 6, V. A., *Preussen, Berichte,* 1792. On the Elector's conduct in this connection, see Schrepfer, *Pfalzbayerns Politik im Revolutions-zeitalter,* pp. 50 ff.

[3] Reuss does not expressly say that he suggested the idea to Spielmann, but on the one hand he was very ardent for the project and brings it up continually in his reports of November; and on the other hand Haugwitz refers to it as a proposition brought forward by Reuss (Report of December 1, B. A., *R.* 1, 170). The ministers at Berlin replied (December 6) that they understood that Spielmann originated this idea (and Heidrich, *op. cit.,* p. 407, note 3 accepts their opinion); but it seems that Haugwitz, who was on the spot, was likely to be better informed than they were.

now had another motive for approving the idea. The latest news from St. Petersburg was by no means so favorable as the Prussians had hoped for. It began to appear that Austrian aid might be required in order to induce the Empress to agree to the partition. Hence the King decided to allow the Court of Vienna to occupy Bavaria, but only after the united efforts of the Prussian and Austrian envoys had extorted the Russian consent to the immediate entry of the Prussian troops into Poland.[1] A new demand was thus made upon Austria over and above those contained in the Note of Merle; but this was little compared to the flattering prospect offered to the Imperial Court of taking possession of its indemnity at the same time that the Prussians occupied theirs, of finally getting this long-sought and so elusive Bavaria into its grasp. Spielmann might well congratulate himself upon the last phase of his negotiation. He had almost wrung victory from defeat. But his new plans and expedients had still to be submitted to the timorous, querulous, rancorous, quarrelsome gentlemen of the State Conference. On November 25 he and Haugwitz arrived in Vienna.

[1] Lucchesini's report to the King, November 8, the cabinet ministry to Haugwitz, November 20, and to Goltz, November 17, B. A., *R.* 92, *L. N.* 12; *R.* 1, 170; and *R.* XI, *Russland*, 133.

CHAPTER XVI

HAUGWITZ'S FINAL NEGOTIATION AT VIENNA

I

THE first effect produced at the Austrian capital by the disasters of the campaign had been an outburst of exasperation and indignation against the Prussians. The sober second thought was that the war must be continued with all the strength the Monarchy possessed, and that Frederick William's aid was indispensable. Before the end of October preparations were begun for placing the entire army on a war footing and for hurrying fresh troops to the defence of the Netherlands. At the beginning of November, the Prussian resident, Caesar, was able to give positive assurance that his master was firmly resolved to pursue the common enterprise in complete accord with the Emperor.[1] The battle of Jemappes and the loss of all the Belgian provinces save Luxemburg did not diminish the determination of the Imperial government to continue the war with redoubled vigor.

Another result of the recent calamities was to revive the attacks upon the leading ministers, and especially upon Spielmann.[2] The opposition in the Conference would gladly have seen the whole Bavarian-Polish project at last abandoned. When, in reply to Spielmann's report of October 15, Cobenzl prepared new instructions authorizing the Referendary to continue the indemnity negotiation in spite of the changed circumstances, Lacy, Rosenberg, and Colloredo persuaded the Emperor to have the instructions altered to the effect that for the present the two Powers must occupy themselves with nothing save the vigorous prosecution of the war. One can easily imagine the effect on the Prussians

[1] Caesar's report of November 3. This unconditional declaration was authorized by the ministry at Berlin when they were still ignorant of the Note of Merle and feared that Austria might desert the common cause (rescript of October 26, B. A., R. 1, 170).

[2] *Zinzendorf's Diary*, October 13 and 27 (V. A.); Caesar's reports of October 17, November 7 and 10, B. A., R. 1, 170.

had Spielmann attempted to carry out these orders, had he insisted that the indemnity question should be postponed indefinitely. For once, however, the Emperor's vacillation served to good purpose. When Cobenzl, after sending off the revised instructions, took the liberty to remonstrate against their import, his sovereign protested that neither he nor the Conference ministers had meant that the indemnity negotiation must be abandoned: the Vice-Chancellor was told that he had simply misunderstood. Hence a second courier was sent flying after the first, with dispatches authorizing Spielmann to go on with the negotiation. It was a pitiful spectacle, this comedy between the Emperor and the Vice-Chancellor; but nothing came of it save perhaps a weakening of Cobenzl's personal credit.[1]

The Note of Merle reached Vienna only on November 20, at a moment when the news from Belgium was of the very worst. Serious resistance to the Prussian demands was therefore hardly to be thought of, and, after all, those demands were not so terrify-

---

[1] Cobenzl's first draft of the instructions to Spielmann, October 26, Vivenot, ii, pp. 300–309; the Emperor to Cobenzl and Lacy, October 29, Cobenzl to the Emperor the same day, *Vortrag* of October 30, and the revised instructions, *ibid.*, pp. 313–321; Cobenzl to the Emperor, November 1, the Imperial reply of November 3, Cobenzl's answer of the same day, the new instructions to Spielmann of November 5, *ibid.*, pp. 323, 337 f. There is in the Vienna Archive another note of the Emperor to Cobenzl, of October 29, which is much sharper in tone than those printed in Vivenot (*Vorträge*, 1792). Caesar reported, November 7, that Cobenzl's influence had recently been impaired, and that he had been exposed for a moment to his sovereign's displeasure, B. A., *R. 1, 170*.

I think there can be no question that the Vice-Chancellor had rightly understood the *vota* of the Conference ministers; and the Emperor, in approving the instructions of October 30, had certainly sanctioned the alterations that Cobenzl had accordingly made. The explanation vouchsafed the Vice-Chancellor four days later was, therefore, only an awkward attempt to conceal the Emperor's hopeless vacillation. Cf. Sybel's severe but very fitting judgment, *op. cit.*, ii, pp. 357 f

Sybel is wrong, however, in representing Lacy and associates as putting through their opinion at a meeting of the Conference. Caesar does, indeed, report such a meeting (November 3 and 7), but he was probably mistaken; for the Austrian records speak only of the instructions to Spielmann being put into 'ministerial circulation,' i. e., sent around to the various ministers to receive their written comments. Quite in accordance with this, there is no mention of a protocol, but only of the several 'vota.' Several weeks before, Colloredo had obtained an order from the Emperor that all important correspondence with ministers abroad should regularly be put in circulation in this way. (Colloredo to Cobenzl, October 15, V. A., *Frankreich, F. 261*.)

ing. The Note of Merle was not extremely precise. While the King had demanded to be assured of his indemnity at once, he had not specified the exact form of assurance required. One could distinguish between a mere occupation and a formal annexation. The latter operation could hardly follow immediately upon the former, as it would take some time to prepare the stage in Poland for the last great act. Meanwhile the details of the indemnity arrangements would have to be discussed at length between all three of the participating Powers, and embodied in a formal treaty. It seemed probable, therefore, that the final settlement of the affair would suffer not a little delay, and meanwhile Austria might find means and opportunities to provide for her own interests. The essential thing was to satisfy the King of Prussia at the lowest possible price, to be outwardly all good will, and to make the most of his ardor for the war.

It is probable that Spielmann brought back with him the conviction that however much Frederick William desired his acquisition in Poland, he was even more eager to make a second campaign.[1] The King's conduct lent some color to that idea; for without waiting for the reply to the Note of Merle, he ordered fresh troops to the Rhine, and pressed Reuss for the sending of an Austrian general with full powers to settle the plan for the next campaign — to the lively chagrin of his ministers.[2] The Austrians were tempted to surmise that Frederick William would not stand firmly by the principles of the note, but would allow himself to be put off with half-concessions. Hence the interminable delays of the Imperial cabinet in December, the conditional and ambiguous acquiescence in the Prussian designs on Poland, the show of confidence and complaisance in other matters, and the attempt to inveigle the King into committing himself at once to the continuation of the war.[3] It is highly characteristic of the

[1] Lucchesini wrote to the ministers at Berlin (December 14) that he knew Spielmann had that belief when he left Luxemburg. B. A., *R. 92, L. N.* 14.

[2] The ministers at Berlin to Lucchesini, November 14, the latter's reply, December 14, the King to Haugwitz, December 13, B. A., *R. 92, L. N.* 14 and *R.* 96, 155 *E.* Reuss' dispatches of November and December were full of assurances of the King's lively desire to take the field again in the following year.

[3] Cobenzl to Reuss, December 4, 10, 18, Francis II to Frederick William, December 17, Vivenot, ii, pp. 387 f., 398 ff.

reign of Frederick William II that the Powers who had to deal with him continually reckoned that his generosity, his enthusiasms, or his feebleness would prevail over the less altruistic counsels of his ministers — a calculation that was sometimes justified, but very often proved fallacious.

Another circumstance that essentially influenced Austrian policy at this time was the fact that since the French conquest of Belgium, England suddenly manifested a disposition to take a hand in Continental affairs. Whether the British government wished only to mediate peace or was seriously minded to join in the war, was still uncertain; but in either case its intervention could not be unwelcome to Austria. Towards the end of November, Pitt had addressed inquiries to the Courts of Vienna and Berlin regarding the plans for indemnities which those Powers were known to be pursuing. The question aroused only suspicion and ill humor in the Prussian ministry, who could not doubt Pitt's opposition to a new partition of Poland; but it was favorably received by the Imperial cabinet, which hoped to win the consent of the British government to the Exchange, and regarded that consent as indispensable to the realization of that plan. Possibly, too, they may have counted on England to delay the Prussian occupation in Poland, although there is no clear proof of this in the Austrian records. At any rate, the new activity of England was, from the Austrian standpoint, the most hopeful sign in a generally dismal situation.

II

The policy which the Imperial Court was to pursue for the next few months, was marked out at the meetings of the State Conference on November 29 and 30. It was the unanimous opinion of that body that peace, although desirable, was almost unattainable, and therefore that every effort must be made both to conduct the next campaign with vigor and to gain the assistance of Prussia, Russia, and England. With regard to the indemnity question, it was decided to give the King of Prussia all assurances of the Emperor's willingness to coöperate both at St.

Petersburg and in Poland in order to secure him his acquisition, but to intimate that its size could be fixed only by the concert to be established with Russia. The principle that the respective acquisitions were to be made at the same time could no longer be upheld, for it was clear that not only the Exchange itself, but even the negotiation with the Bavarian House, would have to be postponed for an indefinite period; but meanwhile every precaution must be taken to ensure the ultimate acquisition of an indemnity somewhere. To that end the Conference resolved to demand that the other two Powers should either consent to a temporary Austrian occupation in Poland, or else formally guarantee the realization of the Exchange. In offering these alternatives, the Imperial ministers were well aware of the aversion of their allies to seeing the Austrian troops enter the Republic. If the Court of Vienna occupied a district in Poland, even if only temporarily, the shares of the other Powers would have to be cut down proportionately. The Austrians themselves had no real desire to take such a step, which would involve them in the odium of the partition and would require a considerable military force. They imagined, however, that the threat of such an occupation would render their allies much more willing to accept the second alternative, the formal guarantee of the Exchange. Neither proposal, it must be confessed, does great credit to the insight of the Viennese statesmen. The demand to be allowed to occupy a district in Poland could only irritate both Prussia and Russia. The idea of a guarantee of the realization of the Exchange was not a little difficult to fathom, for how could the other two Powers guarantee an arrangement which admittedly depended on the voluntary consent of the parties directly interested? To find any sense in it at all, one is driven to conjecture that the proposal meant a guarantee of the acquisition either of Bavaria or of an equivalent.

One means there was by which the Imperial Court might have entered into possession of its indemnity at the same time as its allies: this was to adopt Spielmann's and Reuss' plan of seizing Bavaria under pretext of punishing the Elector for his unpatriotic and disloyal conduct. It is impossible to say whether this plan was discussed at the conferences of November 29 and 30, but at any rate there is no mention of it in the protocol. Apparently the Emperor and his advisers could not make up their minds to so drastic and ruthless a measure. The Austrians did not lack appetite, but they had not the bold unscrupulousness that was necessary in order to keep pace with such Powers as Russia and Prussia.

The second main point resolved upon in the Conference was to answer England in a friendly but cautious manner, and especially to confide the plan for the Exchange. It was decided to consult Prussia about this reply and to suggest that she should make a similar communication at London regarding her ambitions in Poland; but even if the Court of Berlin refused to take such a step, the majority of the Conference held that Austria should take England into the secret with respect to her own hopes for an indemnity. Finally, the Court of St. Petersburg was to be fully informed of the negotiations with England and Prussia, and to be begged to do its utmost for the interests of its hard-pressed and ' most intimate ' ally.[1]

After the conferences of November 29 and 30, almost two weeks elapsed before the answer to the Note of Merle was ready. Haugwitz urged and stormed; Razumovski added his exhortations; but the Austrians were not to be hurried. Nothing was effected by this delay except that the Prussians were irritated, and the Empress of Russia lost all patience waiting for the long promised courier from Vienna. The answer, approved by the Conference on December 6, was at last presented to Haugwitz on the 11th. In accordance with the decisions just described, this note recognized the justice of the Prussian demand for an acquisition in Poland, and promised Austrian support for it at St. Petersburg; it referred to the principle invariably agreed upon between the two Courts, of complete equality in the respective indemnities, and expressed the confident hope that the King would coöperate in the realization of the Exchange; finally, it requested either consent to an Austrian occupation in Poland or a guarantee of the Exchange by Prussia and Russia. The most salient feature of the reply was the fact that while the Note of

[1] Conference protocol and *Separat-voten*, Vivenot, ii, pp. 377-382.

Merle was answered article by article, its last clause, which contained the demand that Austria should consent to the King's immediate occupation of his prospective acquisition, was passed over without a word.[1]

The impression produced on the Prussians was unfortunate in the extreme; the more so because Reuss had previously been ordered to announce that the reply would be entirely satisfactory.[2] Lucchesini and the ministers at Berlin vied with each other in expressing their feelings of horror and revolt at such disloyal conduct. Their indignation was especially aroused by " the abominable snare " (*chéville*), that lurked behind the proposition about an Austrian occupation in Poland. That insidious demand, combined with the Court of Vienna's desire to take England into the secret of the indemnity plan, seemed to announce the design of thwarting the partition entirely. Either proposition might furnish the Empress with a sufficient excuse, if she wanted one, for throwing over the whole project. There was only one means of staving off such a disaster: the King must hold inflexibly to the terms of the Note of Merle, and force both Imperial Courts to recognize that not a single Prussian soldier would take the field until the Prussian demands were granted.[3] These conditions and stipulations to safeguard the Austrian indemnities were not to be thought of. The Prussian ministers quite realized the embarrassment of their allies; they observed with grim satisfaction that the recovery of Belgium was hardly probable, and the consent of the Bavarian House to the Exchange still less so; but the Austrians must recognize that their salvation depended on the continuation of aid from Prussia, and must content themselves with such indemnities as " events would permit them to obtain." [4] Doubtless these would not be very extensive, if the Prussian ministers had their way. But whatever hap-

[1] This note is printed in Vivenot, ii, pp. 293 ff. The date should be December 9.
[2] Cobenzl to Reuss, December 4, *ibid.*, ii, pp. 387 f.
[3] The ministers at Berlin to Lucchesini, December 17 and 19, to Haugwitz the 17th, to the King the 19th, Lucchesini to the ministers, December 17, B. A., R. 92, L. N. 14; R. 96, 147 G; R. 1, 170.
[4] The cabinet ministry to Haugwitz, December 17, and to the King, December 19, B. A., R. 1, 170, and R. 96, 147 G.

pened, the Austrians must make no indiscreet pretensions that would interfere with the plans of their allies.

Though apparently not so much incensed as his colleagues, Haugwitz found the Austrian note quite insufficient. He could not be "reassured," he told Cobenzl and Spielmann, until he had seen absolutely satisfactory instructions sent off at once to the Austrian ambassador at St. Petersburg. The Imperial ministers promised and procrastinated. The delay in this case was, indeed, more intelligible, for the ' expeditions ' in preparation for London and St. Petersburg were extremely voluminous, and had, besides, to be sent the rounds of the Conference. Haugwitz, however, grew impatient and suspicious. He later declared that at this time he abandoned the ordinary tone of a diplomat for that of a minister who announces the peremptory will of his master.[1] His reports picture him relentlessly beating down the resistance of the Austrians, ordering and disposing in sovereign fashion; and yet later events were to prove this negotiation such a medley of misunderstandings that one is driven to doubt whether Haugwitz's language was quite so peremptory and unequivocal as he himself made out.

III

The ' expedition ' to London is the first case in point. Cobenzl had drawn up a long ostensible dispatch to Stadion (the Austrian ambassador to the Court of St. James), explaining the aims of the allied Powers in the war against France, and several postscripts in which the Exchange plan was set forth at length with some allusions to the Russian and Prussian designs on Poland.[2] Stadion was expressly ordered, however, to omit all reference to the last-named subject in case his Prussian colleague, Jacobi, was not instructed to make similar communications.[3] Haugwitz's attitude on this occasion is far from clear. In his own dispatches he

---

[1] Report to the King, May 6, 1793, B. A., *R.* 96, 147 *H.*

[2] The dispatches to Stadion of December 22 are printed in Vivenot, ii, pp. 406–425.

[3] Vivenot, ii, p. 423. This fact deserves to be mentioned the more, because the Austrian government has often been charged with insidiously betraying the plans of its allies — a reproach that is hardly justified.

claimed to have protested against making any confidences to England at present with regard to the indemnity plans; but, on the other hand, Cobenzl reported to the Emperor that the Prussian envoy had not only failed to raise the slightest objection to these dispatches, but had declared that his own Court could not do better than to give Jacobi entirely analogous instructions, and that he meant to send off a courier to Berlin to bring this about.[1] The contradiction is flat and glaring.

The same phenomenon appears in the case of the instructions to Louis Cobenzl. The Vice-Chancellor had prepared several ostensible dispatches to his cousin intended to satisfy Haugwitz. In one of these it was said that the Emperor earnestly wished and begged that the Empress of Russia would at once " *enter into a concert* " for arranging and carrying out the proposed partition of Poland and the " *prise de possession éventuelle* " so much desired by the King of Prussia; and hence that she would specify the acquisitions that might be found suitable for her Empire. For the security of the Austrian indemnities the same demands were advanced as in the reply to Prussia: namely, that the Emperor must be allowed to occupy a district in Poland unless before the effectuation of the Prussian acquisition his two allies had found means to assure the realization of the Exchange. He would consider such security as existing if the Empress and the King of Prussia would undertake the guarantee of the Exchange; and in this case he would claim nothing in Poland, even if he found himself unable to obtain a ' supplement ' elsewhere. If the Exchange proved impossible, however, he would have no alternative but to seek his indemnity at the expense of the Republic along with his allies.

With all these conditions, the ostensible dispatches still complied to some extent with the wishes of Prussia. But the Austrian ministry could not resist the temptation to try to diminish the evil by a subterfuge that was neither honorable nor dexterous nor

---

[1] Haugwitz's reports of December 18 and 21, B. A., *R.* 1, 170; Cobenzl to the Emperor, December 21, V. A., *Vorträge*, 1792, and a similar statement in the 2d P. S. to Stadion (Vivenot, ii, p. 423) and in the dispatch to Reuss of December 30 (*ibid.*, ii, p. 448).

effective. It is probable that they did not need to have the idea suggested to them, but they may well have been encouraged in it by one of Louis Cobenzl's recent reports. In the latter part of November, when Frederick William's exploits in Champagne were still exciting lively ill humor at St. Petersburg, the Russian ministers had spoken with irritation of the size of the Prussian demands in Poland, paraded their own devotion to the interests of Austria, and suggested that if the partition took place at all, its execution at least ought to be delayed for some time.[1] This fitted in admirably with the wishes of the Austrian ministry. Accordingly, alongside the dispatches shown to Haugwitz, the Vice-Chancellor prepared a secret instruction for Louis Cobenzl, in which he declared that the Imperial Court had never consented to the present exorbitant territorial demands of Prussia; that it was not, however, in a position to contest them openly; but that it relied upon Russia to cut down the Prussian lot in accordance with the principle proclaimed by Zubov himself,[2] that Poland must remain large enough to form a real buffer state. Doubtless it would be the most desirable solution, the dispatch continued, if the three Powers, while resolving upon the partition now, should postpone its execution. But in view of the impatience and importunities of Prussia, the Court of Vienna felt obliged to propose that the two German Powers should simultaneously occupy equivalent districts in Poland, under the pretext of maintaining order or repressing Counter-confederations. The Empress was begged, however, to assume the responsibility of inducing the Prussians to defer a formal annexation until a more convenient time, when, as it was hoped at Vienna, the Bavarian Exchange might also be effected. Finally, the Vice-Chancellor added the urgent entreaty that Russia should consent to the Prussian aggrandizement only under the double condition that the King should continue the war with all vigor, and that the Exchange should be assured at once and realized as soon as peace was made. The Austrian government thus entrusted its cause entirely to the merciful protection of the Empress. It appealed

---

[1] Cobenzl's reports of November 13, 16, 20, V. A., *Russland, Berichte,* 1792.

[2] Cobenzl's report of November 20, V. A., *loc. cit.*

to her to tame the ally whom it dared not oppose openly. **It** appointed her arbiter of the whole indemnity question.[1]

When the ostensible dispatches to Louis Cobenzl were communicated to Haugwitz, the latter found them somewhat more satisfactory than the note of December 9, but he objected to the term *prise de possession éventuelle*, instead of *actuelle*, and still more to the condition attached to that concession, the Austrian occupation in Poland. In his reports to his government, he claims that he then redoubled his efforts to remove these last difficulties, and that within a few days he had vanquished every obstacle. On December 24 he wrote that he had obtained a formal oral declaration from the Emperor's ministers that their sovereign ' would address the most urgent representations to the Empress of Russia in order to secure her consent to the Prussian *prise de possession actuelle*, without adding any condition relative to an Austrian occupation in Poland, but contenting himself solely with the demand that the Empress and the King should jointly

---

[1] The dispatches to L. Cobenzl are printed in Vivenot, ii, pp. 425–435. Sybel's account of the origin of this ' expedition ' is far from accurate. He conjectured (*op. cit.*, iii, pp. 179 ff.) that the secret instructions were decided upon at the meeting of the Conference on December 19, and that this unfortunate step was forced upon Ph. Cobenzl by the Emperor himself, guided perhaps by Count Colloredo. The basis of this assumption he found in the Emperor's note to the Vice-Chancellor of December 21 (Vivenot, ii, p. 405) in which the Conference of the 19th is mentioned and Cobenzl rebuked for his slowness in getting off the dispatches to London and St. Petersburg. Sybel deplored the fact that Vivenot did not publish the protocol of " this most important session " of the Conference. Vivenot is quite excusable. No protocol of the 19th is to be found in the Vienna Archives. And apparently that is no great loss. From certain other documents not printed in Vivenot, it appears that except for the parts relating to the reply to England, the dispatches to L. Cobenzl were already completed and had received the sanction of the Conference ministers (having been ' circulated ' among them) by December 15. At the session of the 19th only " slight changes and additions " were made, and one further postscript to Stadion was agreed upon (doubtless the 4th, printed in Vivenot, ii, p. 425), as Cobenzl himself relates in a note to the Emperor of December 21 (V. A., *Vorträge*, 1792). If the conference of the 19th had resolved upon anything so important as the secret instructions to L. Cobenzl, it is hardly possible that the Vice-Chancellor would not have mentioned it in this note, in which he sums up the reasons for his previous delays. It appears, then, that this meeting had little or no importance. I do not think there is the slightest evidence to show where the responsibility for the secret instructions rests. Sybel's view may be admitted as a pure hypothesis; but the Vice-Chancellor's delays may equally well be ascribed to his natural slowness, timidity, and indecision.

guarantee their consent to the Bavarian Exchange.'[1] With that he considered his negotiation finished, and prepared to return to Berlin to assume his new post as cabinet minister. At his final audience (December 23), the Emperor assured him that his only fear was that in spite of his own consent and the orders he had sent to St. Petersburg, the Empress of Russia might still refuse to agree to the Prussian demands.[2] Nothing apparently could be more amicable or loyal. Haugwitz left Vienna affirming his conviction that the Imperial Court was acting in good faith and was sincerely disposed to further his master's acquisition.[3]

If he really had secured the oral declaration he reported, he might indeed congratulate himself on a complete diplomatic victory. In that case, Austria had yielded to every Prussian demand, in return for a single concession of the flimsiest and most meaningless sort. For that phrase ' guarantee of consent ' was vagueness itself: anyone could interpret that at his good pleasure. The Berlin ministry hastened to inform Caesar (who had been left as chargé at Vienna) that they accepted the engagement, if it meant ' promise of consent,' but that they would never allow it a broader significance.[4] A promise of consent the King had already given, and as long as its fulfilment was postponed, his ministers were not greatly embarrassed by it. A guarantee of the realization of the Exchange would be quite a different matter.

The question inevitably presents itself: did Haugwitz really secure such complete and momentous concessions? If so, why did he not insist on the alteration of the dispatches to Louis Cobenzl, which were based on quite different principles? Why did he content himself with a mere verbal assurance? How explain the fact that the Austrian records contain not the slightest trace of the promise he claimed to have received, and that the Austrian ministers continued to act as if such a promise had never been given? We find, for instance, that on January 3 the Con-

---

[1] Haugwitz's reports of December 21 and 24, B. A., *R.* 1, 170. See Appendix XI, 1.

[2] Haugwitz's retrospective report of May 6, 1793, B. A., *R.* 96, 147 *H.* See Appendix XVI, 3.

[3] Letter to Lucchesini, December 25, B. A., *R.* 92, *L. N.* 31.

[4] Rescript of December 29, B. A., *R.* 1, 170.

ference met to decide what Polish territories should be occupied
by the Imperial Court, in case the other Powers failed to furnish
a sufficient guarantee of the Exchange.[1] Cobenzl continually
spoke to the astonished Caesar of the alternative — occupation
or guarantee — as quite a matter of course.[2] Such positive
language is unintelligible — assuming Haugwitz's report to be
accurate — except on the hypothesis that Cobenzl and Spielmann
had been driven into concessions which they dared not reveal to
their colleagues, or on the supposition that they did not know the
meaning of the terms in question. Or did Haugwitz misunder-
stand them ? Or did he, in his haste to finish the affair, content
himself with assurances much less positive and satisfactory than
those which he reported ?

In favor of this last hypothesis, we have the testimony of one
witness who was fairly well acquainted with the course of the
negotiation and sufficiently intimate with all the negotiators.
Razumovski had frequently discussed the matters here in question with Haugwitz, Cobenzl, and Spielmann, and he understood
from them that it was entirely settled that Austria should occupy
a district in Poland, unless Russia and Prussia furnished the
desired guarantee of the Exchange. Moreover, when Caesar,
much disturbed over the affair, read to him Haugwitz's final dispatch of December 24, Razumovski wrote to Ostermann that
Haugwitz, in order to facilitate his negotiation, had shown far
more *condescendance* in his conferences with the Austrians than
in his reports.[3]

If the Russian ambassador's view was correct, it would point
to nothing exceptional in Haugwitz's first year of diplomatic
activity. It will be remembered how facile the latter had shown
himself towards the Austrians in May, in the affair of the joint
declaration at St. Petersburg; in July and August, in the affair
of the Margraviates; in October, in connection with Spielmann's
' plan.' If one compares his reports with the Austrian ones

---

[1] Vivenot, ii, p. 457.

[2] Caesar's reports of Jan. 30, Feb. 6 and 25, 1793, B. A., R. 1, 174.

[3] Razumovski's report of January 21/February 1, 1793, Caesar's report of
January 30, M. A., Австрія, III, 54, and B. A., R. 1, 174. Razumovski's report is printed in part in Appendix XVI, 2.

relative to the negotiation at Luxemburg and to the dispatches to Stadion in December, and still more if one studies his long report of May 6, 1793, reviewing the whole course of the indemnity affair, one sees that his conduct as represented to his Court was very much more energetic, decided, ' peremptory,' than it appeared to those with whom he negotiated. It must be remembered that he was only a beginner in diplomacy. He later wrote of this negotiation at Vienna: " These were the preliminaries that were to serve as my schooling." [1] The suspicion lies very near at hand that perhaps the novice did not pass the test so triumphantly as he reported. At any rate, mysterious as is the whole affair, one may perhaps surmise that the Austrian ministers had agreed to acquiesce in all that Prussia demanded for herself, and to renounce their own project of an occupation in Poland, on condition of receiving a guarantee of the Exchange (meaning the *realization* of the Exchange); and that Haugwitz either misunderstood them, or deliberately misrepresented.

The consequences were momentous for the future course of the affair. The Austrian cabinet continued to act on the principles embodied in the dispatches to Louis Cobenzl; continued to regard their assent to the Prussian demands as conditional upon their securing safeguards for the Exchange either through an occupation in Poland or through the guarantee of the other Courts; continued to view the final settlement of the indemnity question as dependent upon a concert of the three Powers, into which England might also possibly be taken.[2] But the Imperial ministry seems to have framed no clear idea as to the form which this concert was to take. Although they knew that Goltz was authorized to conclude a definite treaty with Russia,[3] they took no steps to provide Louis Cobenzl with similar powers. They thus condemned themselves to be excluded from a negotiation

---

[1] Ranke, *Hardenberg*, ii, p. 306.

[2] Cf. Caesar's report of January 23: " Tout se réduit donc à l'idée qu'on paroît toujours avoir ici que l'étendue de l'arrondissement de V. M. en Pologne, ainsi que les formes de l'échange de la Bavière et du nouvel établissement de la maison Palatine, seront définitivement arrangées du concours de toutes les Puissances contractantes par les négociations futures de la paix," B. A., *R.* 1, 174. It was a sort of Congress of Vienna that the Austrians thus prematurely imagined.

[3] L. Cobenzl's report of November 23, 1792, V. A., *Russland, Berichte.*

that concerned their most vital interests, with a lack of foresight, prudence, and consistency that is almost unintelligible.

The Prussians, on their side, viewed the agreements of December only in the light of Haugwitz's final dispatch, and so concluded — quite justifiably — that Austria had given them a perfectly free hand in Poland. The King was satisfied and grateful, but he was almost alone in his opinion. The long delays, the bad grace with which the Imperial Court had yielded, and the snares and subterfuges which they detected in all its utterances, had convinced the Prussian ministers that no confidence was to be placed in the good will of ' their faithful allies ' and ' natural rivals.' " I see more and more clearly," Lucchesini wrote to the ministers at Berlin, " that if we had had to expect our indemnity from the Court of Vienna, we should never have obtained it." [1] At that moment their indemnity no longer depended on Austria. The Empress had spoken at last.

[1] Letter of January 4, 1793, B. A., *R.* 92, *L. N.* 14.

CHAPTER XVII

The Russo-Prussian Partition Treaty

I

It can hardly be doubted that when in July, 1792 Austria and Prussia brought forward the Polish-Bavarian plan at St. Petersburg, they were but anticipating the inmost wishes of the Russians. It was, indeed, in response to Russian hints at Berlin and Vienna that these first overtures were made. Bezborodko confessed to Cobenzl that his Court had expected something of this sort.[1] He himself hastened to lay before the Empress a memorial emphasizing strongly the advantages that would accrue to Russia from a new partition. A. R. Vorontsov likewise championed the project. If Markov at first raised objections, pointing out the inconvenience of granting Prussia so considerable an aggrandizement, he allowed himself to be won over without too much difficulty.[2] As for the Empress, one of her closest advisers observed [3] that the Austro-Prussian plan caused her a secret pleasure, but that she hesitated to express clearly her opinion. At any rate, her sentiments may be inferred from her conduct.

She would not show her hand too early. She would manifest no undue eagerness. Her 'moderation' and 'magnanimity' required that she should make enormous annexations only with an air of reluctance and ostensibly out of sheer deference for her allies. The other Powers must take upon themselves the initiative, and with it the odium, of the transaction. An attitude of reticence was the more advisable because Austria long maintained an ungracious silence regarding any acquisitions for

---

[1] L. Cobenzl's report to Ph. Cobenzl of July 21, V. A., *Russland, Berichte*, 1792.

[2] Cf. his retrospective letter to S. R. Vorontsov of July 27/August 7, 1793, Apx. Bop., xx, p. 48. Markov's statements as to his own attitude and that of his two colleagues receive some confirmation from Cobenzl's reports, especially that of July 21, 1792.

[3] Markov in the letter just cited.

Russia, while Goltz was authorized to present the indemnity plan only in the guise of ' speculations,' avoiding ' all that might give his overtures the appearance or the form of a proposition made officially or according to orders.' [1]

During the month following the initial advances from Berlin and Vienna, the Russian ministers would say no more than that the affair deserved mature deliberation, that the Empress was in general disposed to oblige her allies, but that she could not express herself definitely until the German Courts had composed their differences and communicated their ideas in more detail. But when towards the end of August it became clear that the allies were willing to allow the Court of St. Petersburg an equal share in the spoils, and when appearances had been provided for by a due amount of procrastination, signs multiplied that the Russians were warming to the project. Goltz and Cobenzl were given to understand that the main question was practically decided in their favor, and that it remained only to settle the details and ' the *quo modo*.' Both envoys gained the conviction that in spite of this air of pretended indifference, the Russians eagerly desired the realization of the plan.[2]   How correct this

---

[1] Instructions to Goltz of July 9, B. A., *R.* XI, *Russland*, 133.

[2] Cobenzl's reports of August 24, September 11, 28, V. A., *Russland, Berichte*, 1792; Goltz's reports of August 28, September 25 and 28, B. A., *R.* XI, *Russland*, 133.

Cobenzl reported (September 11): " Le Comte Woronzow . . . m'a temoigné etre tout à fait porté pour ce que j'ai été chargé de proposer en date du 8 Août . . . : il dit qu'il faut seulement observer dans les acquisitions que feroit la Russie d'éviter tout voisinage immediat avec les Puissances copartageantes."

On September 28: " Il me paroit qu'on ne le desire [the realization of the Bavarian-Polish project] pas moins ici, et Marcow me dit à cette occasion, qu'outre l'échange pour égaliser la chose nous devrions prendre un dedommagement du même côté où nous la destinons aux deux autres cours."

Goltz wrote on August 28: " À en juger d'après les vues de ses [Catherine's] Ministres, il ne paroit pas douteux, qu'on entrera avec plaisir aux vues des autres Puissances."

On September 25: " Quoique l'on continue toujours à affecter la plus grande indifférence, je suis cependant sûr que ce n'est que cela et qu'on n'en desire pas moins vivement de réaliser le projet d'un nouveau partage de la Pologne."

On September 28: " Il ne me reste rien à dire sur le plan de dedommagemens, tous les Ministres ici m'assurant que l'Impératrice consentira volontiers à la chose, mais qu'on attend toujours le Courier de Vienne, pour pouvoir s'expliquer sur le comment."

surmise was, is best shown by the fact that when the indemnity project seemed in danger of being held up or even completely frustrated by the dissensions between the German Powers, the Empress intervened to remedy and to expedite matters. In the middle of September, Razumovski and Alopeus were ordered to urge upon the Austrian and Prussian cabinets the need of haste: the final settlement of Polish affairs, it was said, could not be long postponed, and delay was the more embarrassing because the maintenance of the Russian armies in the Republic cost immense sums; the Empress therefore desired that her allies should adjust as soon as possible the questions at issue between them and then provide their envoys at St. Petersburg with the instructions and powers necessary for concluding a formal convention.[1] A three-fold arrangement on the analogy of the treaties of 1772 was then the Russian program. Of the exclusion of Austria there was, and could at that time be, no thought.[2] That the negotiation should be conducted at St. Petersburg, where the Empress could most easily guide and control it, was assumed as a matter of course.

A final explanation from Vienna was expected with the ratification of the Austro-Russian treaty of alliance. Instead, however, the courier brought only the news of Spielmann's mission to the King of Prussia, and the promise that the agreements about to be concluded would be promptly communicated.[3] Hitherto Austria had taken the lead in the negotiations at St. Petersburg: here began that three months' silence on the part of the Court of Vienna, which was to prove so disastrous for it.

Meanwhile Goltz had at last received definite instructions, which allowed him to quit the realm of pure ' speculations,' and to state precisely the acquisitions desired by his Court.[4] From mid-October on, he began to urge that Russia and Prussia should come to an agreement at once without waiting further for the

---

[1] Ostermann's dispatches to Razumovski and Alopeus, September 3/14, 1792, M. A., Австрія, III, 52, and Пруссія, III, 28.

[2] Cf. Markov to Razumovski, October 4/15, Wassiltchikow, *Les Razoumowski*, ii, *4ᵉ partie*, p. 162.

[3] Ph. Cobenzl to L. Cobenzl, September 13, Vivenot, ii, pp. 197–201.

[4] The instructions of September 28, B. A., *R*. XI, *Russland*, 133.

dilatory resolutions of Austria. The Court of Vienna, he declared, was sufficiently informed of his master's views; its allies would not neglect its interests; but they would be in far better position to provide for them after they had duly attended to their own. Towards the end of the month he had even advanced to the point of pressing for consent to the immediate entry of the Prussian troops into Poland.[1]

Although still professing not to know their sovereign's intentions, and protesting that nothing could be decided until the results of Spielmann's negotiation were known, the Russian ministers received these propositions with unmistakable favor. In a highly significant note to a colleague, Bezborodko declared that Ostermann and he were agreed that their Court ought not to oppose the King of Prussia's desire to send his troops into Poland at once, *since that measure fitted exactly into their* [the Russian] *plan*, and would certainly lead to the quickest dénouement of the affair.[2] But just at the moment when matters seemed thus happily started, there came a turn of events which threatened to blast the Prussian hopes.

II

On the 20th of October the news of the retreat of the allied armies reached St. Petersburg. In the next few weeks every courier brought tidings of disaster: the complete evacuation of France, the loss of Belgium, the irruption of " the demons " into the very heart of Germany. The Empress was highly incensed. The " factious," in repelling the invaders, had committed the crime of *lèse Catherine;* the allies had sinned even more atrociously by rejecting all her advice about the enterprise; and worst of all were those mysterious, degrading negotiations of the Prussians with " the rebels." " I confess," she wrote to Grimm, " I feel such ill humor toward certain people that I should like to box their ears." [3] Her letters and conversation

---

[1] Goltz's reports of October 12, 23, 26, B. A., *loc. cit.*

[2] Bezborodko to A. R. Vorontsov, Арх. Воp., xiii, p. 275. This note is undated, but from a comparison with Goltz's dispatches it may be fixed with certainty as of October 26.

[3] Letter of December 7/18, Сборникъ, xxiii, p. 579.

of that time are full of outbreaks and sarcasms against both her high allies.

Under such circumstances, the Empress was for the time being in no mood to listen favorably to the Prussian importunities about a new partition. " After the brilliant campaign the two Courts have made, they still dare to talk of conquests! " she wrote on the margin of a dispatch; [1] and in another place: " It seems to me that in real and strict justice those who have failed in their duties, ought to have no right to compensation." [2] This was no time for starting a new set of troubles, when no one could foresee the end of those already existing, and when she was left in perfect ignorance of the other plans of the high allies, who had hitherto done diametrically the opposite of all that she had proposed to them.[3] After the miserable spectacle they had just made of themselves, their primary concern ought to be to deliver the Germanic Empire out of the hands of the French, and to prepare for a new and more vigorous campaign.[4] In an interesting set of " rules " which she dashed off à propos of the negotiation with Prussia,[5] we find the following:

" To postpone the partition of Poland as long as possible.

" After a wretched campaign, no acquisitions.

" Not to take up this affair without the knowledge of the Court of Vienna.

" [We have] no reason for aggrandizing the King of Prussia.

" To do nothing contrary to honor and promises."

Probably many reasons combined to produce this revulsion in Catherine's attitude towards a project in which she had apparently been keenly interested. The general situation and the presuppositions with which she had entered into the affair had been profoundly altered by the débacle in the West. It was still uncertain how far the successes of the French would go; how far

---

[1] On Alopeus' report of October 8/19.

[2] Letter to Rumiantsov, Рус. Стар., lxxxi[2], p. 161.

[3] Note of the Empress belonging to the papers of the secret Conference of November 4/15, P. A., X, 69.

[4] Note of the Empress belonging to the papers of the secret Conference of October 29/Nov. 9, P. A., *loc. cit.*

[5] Papers belonging to the secret Conference of October 29/November 9. These notes are printed in Appendix XVII.

the Prussians had really been implicated in disloyal intrigues
with the enemy; whether Austria could now be provided for
except by a share in Poland — which would not at all fit in with
the Empress' wishes; or what would be the attitude of England.
The machinations of ' the Jacobins ' at Stockholm and Constantinople were well known at St. Petersburg, and aroused at least a
certain disquietude, as was attested by the rushing of fresh troops
and of no less a commander than Suvorov to the southern frontier. But it may perhaps be doubted whether these considerations contributed as much to delaying the negotiation for the
partition as did the Empress' anger against those allies who had
tarnished her glory by bungling an enterprise to which she had
lent her patronage and her moral and financial support.

It was under no favorable auspices, then, that the Prussians
began their grand assault at St. Petersburg. In the last days of
October, Goltz suddenly found himself the object of a great
coldness. He ceased to be invited to the Hermitage. Ostermann
avoided conversing with him.[1] When the Vice-Chancellor could
be brought to speak at all, he proffered nothing but excuses for
delay: the uncertain state of French affairs; the danger of stirring
up new enemies at such a moment; the alarming attitude of the
Porte; the presence in St. Petersburg of a delegation from the
Confederation of Targowica, come to thank the Empress for
' liberating ' the Republic; the impossibility of deciding on any
course of action until the arrival of news from Austria.[2] The
cabinet of Berlin pressed on the negotiation with restless haste.
Courier after courier was hurried off to Petersburg, bringing to
Goltz orders to present his demands in the most formal ministerial
manner, a royal letter to the Empress, the new and extended
territorial claims which Frederick William had formulated at
Consenvoye, the Note of Merle, full powers to conclude the
treaty, and fresh supplies of arguments with which to beat down
the Russian obduracy. Poland, it was alleged, was seething with
democratic agitation and with plots against Russia and Prussia;
it was superfluous to point out what dangers would threaten all

---

[1] Goltz's report of the 30th, B. A., *R.* XI, *Russland*, 133.

[2] Goltz's reports of October 30, November 2, 6, 13, B. A., *loc. cit.*

the North of Europe if this country were allowed to become " a new theatre of revolution and fanaticism "; the evil must be cut out at the roots, and the most efficacious way of extirpating it was to restrict the tumultuous Republic within such limits as would forever prevent it from menacing its neighbors.[1] If it were merely regard for Austria that held back the Empress, that difficulty, it was said, was now removed, since the King had given his consent to the forcible seizure of Bavaria, which Spielmann had proposed.[2] Even Cobenzl, when informed of the Note of Merle, took it upon himself, without waiting for orders, to press the Prussian claims.[3] But Ostermann remained immovable and generally mute. He could accept Goltz's constantly reiterated demands only *ad referendum;* he was chronically uninformed as to the intentions of his sovereign; he was full of objections and petty fears. So matters continued throughout November. The Court of Berlin had exhausted every device and every attention in order to win over the Russians; its troops stood on the frontier ready to enter Poland at a moment's notice from St. Petersburg; but it seemed as if the word would never come. The Prussian ministry grew quite out of patience. If Ostermann continued his " tergiversations," they wrote, Goltz must declare that the King would no longer think of a second campaign, but would retire from the war altogether.[4]

But just at the moment when Prussian hopes were most depressed, the tide began to turn at St. Petersburg.

III

It is probable that Catherine had never seriously intended to abandon the plan for a partition: she had meant, it would seem, only to postpone its execution. About the beginning of December, however, a number of reasons combined to make further delay inadvisable. The Prussian importunities could not much longer be denied without driving the King to fulfil his threat of

---

[1] Instructions to Goltz of November 3, B. A., *R.* XI, *Russland,* 133.

[2] Rescripts to Goltz of November 17 and 22, B. A., *loc. cit.*

[3] Cobenzl's reports of November 13, 16, 20, V. A., *Russland, Berichte,* 1792.

[4] Rescript of December 1, B. A., *loc. cit.*

withdrawing from an enterprise in which the Empress strongly desired to keep him engaged. Moreover, the rumor of an impending partition was circulating so widely and attracting so much attention that unless the great blow were struck at once, the opposition to be expected from certain quarters would have time to mature, and the difficulty of the task would be very materially increased. England was already making cautious inquiries and remonstrances on the subject at Berlin and Vienna.[1] The French government was trying to stir up the Porte to interfere in Poland.[2] Above all, affairs within the Republic itself seemed to be approaching a new crisis.

The Confederates of Targowica had by this time proved their complete inability either to agree among themselves or to win over their fellow-countrymen to their cause. After a few months of stupefied calm following the collapse of the national defence in the summer, the Polish public had been electrified by the amazing victories of the French. Valmy and Jemappes supplied an inspiring example of a free nation successfully defending itself against a league of despots; they aroused hopes that Poland too might yet be saved by French bayonets. It does not appear that there was at this time any organized plan for a national uprising; of any propaganda in favor of ' Jacobinism,' except in the case of a few insignificant individuals, we find no trace; but there was a wide-spread and enthusiastic sympathy for the French, which could not be prevented from manifesting itself either by the presence of the Russian troops or by the iron-clad censorship and the unprecedented police measures introduced by the champions of liberty who now presided over the government. Every act of the Confederation was greeted with scorn and ridicule. There were manifold demonstrations of devotion to the Constitution of the Third of May. The Empress' officers were almost boycotted by Warsaw society. The English resident reported that the universal hatred of the Russians seemed to increase daily; it

---

[1] The Prussian government hastened to inform the Empress of this step of England and to urge that this made the need of haste all the greater (dispatch to Goltz, November 23, sent by courier, B. A., *R.* XI, *Russland*, 133). Cf. Salomon, *Pitt*, i[ii], p. 580; Lecky, *op. cit.*, vi, pp. 83 f.

[2] Cf. Zinkeisen, *op. cit.*, vi, pp. 848 ff.

was shown on the streets, in the theatres, everywhere to such a degree that he lived in constant fear of an explosion and a great catastrophe.[1] There were rumors of an approaching Sicilian Vespers.[2] Felix Potocki, blind as usual to the effects his words would have, wrote desperately to St. Petersburg that the successes of the French had ' turned the heads of his compatriots '; ' Jacobin principles ' and those of the Third of May were making terrible progress; unless something were done at once to stop the evil, he feared the very worst.[3] The deputation which he had sent to thank the Empress for ' liberating ' their country, had to confess that the moment the Russian troops should be withdrawn, the whole work of the Confederation of Targowica would be overthrown by the nation.[4] In short, it appeared that matters had come to such a pass that the only way out of endless embarrassments was a partition. This nation had shown itself so hopelessly perverse that it must be reduced to a state of perpetual impotence to harm its neighbors. And the sooner the operation was performed, the better.

These considerations, reënforced by the long felt desire for " the finest acquisition the Empire could ever make," [5] proved decisive. It was true that the great excuse for delay which Ostermann had always held up to Goltz, had not been removed, for nothing had yet been heard from Vienna. But it was impossible to defer forever to the incurable slowness of the Austrian cabinet. Besides, it was distinctly to the advantage of Russia to settle the affair with Prussia alone without the participation of the Court of Vienna. From Prussia no opposition was to be expected, no matter how enormous the Empress' claims might be; but it was to be feared that Austria might resist the intended extension of the Russian frontier to the borders of Galicia, and

---

[1] Gardiner's report of November 14, 1792, printed by K. Sienkiewicz, *Skarbiec historyi polskiej*, i, p. 198. Very interesting details as to the expressions of public opinion at this time in Smoleński, *Konfederacya targowicka*, pp. 323 ff.

[2] Cf. Kakhovski's reports to the Empress of October 17/28, November 1/12 and 8/19, Сборникъ, xlvii, pp. 462–465.

[3] Letters to Zubov of November 15 and 24, M.A., Архивъ Варшавской Миссіи.

[4] Instructions to Sievers, December 22/January 2, M. A., Польша, III, 66.

[5] Markov to S. R. Vorontsov, November 8/19, 1792, Арх. Воp., xx, p. 32.

might also try to obtain some portion of Poland for herself in default of the Bavarian Exchange. The Russians were not unwilling to provide for Austrian interests in the course of the negotiation, but in that negotiation they no longer intended to have Austria take part.[1] This exclusion of the Court of Vienna was, furthermore, quite in accordance with the ideas of the Berlin cabinet, as repeatedly expressed at St. Petersburg since October.

In the second week in December, by the 13th at the latest, the Empress' final decision was taken.[2] On the 16th Ostermann announced to Goltz that his sovereign consented to the immediate occupation by Prussia of the entire territory demanded by the King, and that she claimed for herself an acquisition bounded on the west by a line drawn from the easternmost point of Courland due south via Pinsk to the Dniester opposite Choczim, a line which ran for some distance directly along the Galician frontier. The further details of the partition were to be regulated by a secret convention between the two Courts as soon as the King had given his consent to the acquisition demanded by the Empress. Ostermann excused the exclusion of Austria by pointing to the slowness of that Power in communicating its intentions, and the (supposed) fact that Frederick William had already satisfied its chief desire by agreeing to the forcible occupation of Bavaria.

Goltz was naturally astounded at the enormous extent of the Empress' claims, but he did not dare protest. It was agreed that Cobenzl should be told only that the Empress had consented to an immediate Prussian occupation in Poland, and nothing

[1] According to Markov's letter to S. R. Vorontsov of July 27/August 7, 1793, the proposal to exclude Austria from the negotiation was made by Bezborodko, who of all the Russian ministers might pass for the most pro-Austrian (Apx. Bop., xx, p. 49).

Sybel's statement that the Empress' decision was determined by Razumovski's reports of the early stages of Haugwitz's negotiation at Vienna (*op. cit.*, iii, p. 192) is quite erroneous. The first report of the ambassador on that subject was sent by post December 4, and so could not possibly have arrived in time to influence a decision taken by the 13th at the latest.

[2] Cf. the memorandum of Bezborodko of December 2/13, printed in Solov'ev, *Geschichte des Falles von Polen*, p. 305.

more. Goltz congratulated himself that he had avoided, as he thought, all reference to the French war in the future convention.[1] The arrival of the courier caused intense jubilation at Berlin. Although likewise amazed at the Empress' demands, the ministry adjured the King to acquiesce in them rather than lose the chance to secure an acquisition in some respects the most important that the House of Hohenzollern had ever made, an acquisition that would render Prussia for the first time " a coherent kingdom." They suggested, however, that since the Empress seemed determined on a partition on a grand scale, it might not be *mal à propos* to claim something more for themselves — the district of Polangen, for instance, which separated East Prussia from Courland, and which might some day acquire some commercial importance. They also recommended begging the Empress to renounce the strip of territory along the Galician frontier; since that acquisition would irritate Austria — and would deprive Prussia of precious facilities for importing horses from Moldavia for the army! It was not to be expected that the idea of excluding Austria from the negotiation would cause great grief at Berlin. The ministry recognized that the Court of Vienna would probably show some ill humor when the convention was presented to it; but after all it would only be paying the penalty for all its "tergiversations" and "insidious negotiations."[2] They were especially pleased by the prospect of not having to incur any engagements for the continuation of the war. ' Undoubtedly,' they wrote to Goltz, ' their continued coöperation would be a tacit condition of their new acquisition, but there was a great difference between a binding and formal agreement and a voluntary coöperation, which might depend more or less on circumstances and convenience.'[3] The connection between French and Polish affairs had been very useful when it furnished a pretext for acquisitions: when it entailed obligations, that was quite a different matter.

---

[1] Goltz's report of December 16, B. A., *R.* XI, *Russland*, 133.

[2] The cabinet ministry to the King, December 27, B. A., *R.* XI, *Russland*, 133.

[3] Ministerial rescript to Goltz of December 26, B. A., *loc. cit.*

Frederick William's joy was, if possible, even greater than that of his ministers. " Our great aim is, thank God, fulfilled," he wrote to them: " it required efforts to attain it, but he who risks nothing gains nothing. The anxieties that your patriotic apprehensions have given you, are now removed, and succeeded by the satisfaction of seeing your labors crowned with the happiest success." [1] With the King's complete approval of the ministerial propositions, the courier was soon speeding back to St. Petersburg.

The situation on the Neva had meanwhile altered in several respects. The Russian ministers were again showing themselves ominously cold towards Goltz, in order to reduce him to a becoming state of anxiety and humility. This manoeuvre was beautifully calculated to deprive him of the courage to make either new demands or objections. With Goltz the effect was unfailing. A further new element in the situation was the fact that the Austrian dispatches of December 23 had arrived, and the Empress' hand was strengthened in so far as the Court of Vienna had turned over to her the congenial rôle of arbiter in the indemnity question. From the first the Russians gave Cobenzl to understand that it would be impossible to cut down or to postpone the Prussian acquisition. They were lavish in assurances, however, that in the impending negotiation they would take pains to bind the King to the continuation of the war, and would in general provide for Austrian interests as carefully as for their own. This appears to have been the sole effect of the secret instructions sent to Cobenzl. For the rest, the Austrian communications to England regarding the indemnities produced an extremely bad effect at St. Petersburg: from the Empress down, everyone considered those confidences premature, indiscreet, and even insidious. This was one more reason for hastening to settle with Prussia.

The negotiation, which for greater secrecy was conducted between Goltz and Ostermann alone, was rushed through in less than six days. Terrified by reports that a large part of the

[1] Frederick William to the cabinet ministry, December 31, B. A., R. XI, *Russland*, 135.

Russian ministry was opposed to the partition altogether, Goltz feared to ruin all by delaying matters in any way. His proposition about Polangen was curtly refused once for all, on the pretext that the Empress could not acquiesce in Prussian claims more extensive than those already communicated to the Court of Vienna. Goltz dared not make the obvious retort that the size of the Russian acquisition was wholly unknown to that Court. Nor had he better luck with his objections regarding the territory along the Galician frontier. He was obliged to accept an article concerning the French war, which he and his Court would greatly have preferred to see omitted. In short, the Russians simply dictated their own terms. January 23 Ostermann, Bezborodko, and Markov for Russia, and Goltz for Prussia signed the treaty of partition.[1]

IV

The act, which had been drafted by Markov, followed as far as possible the form and phraseology of the treaties of 1772. This time, indeed, there were no 'ancient and legitimate rights' to Polish territory that might be invoked; there was, in fact, no decent pretext of any kind; but the difficulty was met in the preamble by sonorous allusions to " the imminent and universal danger " that threatened Europe as a result of " the fatal revolution in France," and the need that the Powers interested in the maintenance of " order " and " the general tranquillity " should take " the most rigorous and efficacious measures " to arrest the progress of the evil. It required something of a *tour de force* to make Poland an accomplice in the guilt of France, but the formula had long before been discovered. It was said that the contracting parties had ' recognized by sure signs that the same spirit of insurrection and dangerous innovations, which now reigned in France, was ready to break out in the Kingdom of Poland, in the immediate vicinity of their own possessions '; they had therefore ' felt the necessity of redoubling their precautions

[1] For the above: Goltz's reports of January 18, 22, and 24, 1793, B. A., *R.* XI, *Russland*, 135. The text of the treaty is printed in Martens, *Traités conclus par la Russie*, ii, pp. 228–235; Vivenot, ii, p. 516–519.

and efforts in order to guarantee their subjects against the effects of a scandalous and often contagious example '; and they had been obliged to combine those efforts in such a way as to obtain for themselves ' both present and future security and an indemnity for the exorbitant expenses which these exertions must necessarily occasion them.'

The partition being thus represented as part of the wider system of measures for combating the revolutionary plague, and also as an indemnification for such laudable services, it followed that the two Powers could not well avoid committing themselves to some kind of definite obligations regarding the French war. Catherine was, indeed, delighted to seize the chance to bind the hands of the King of Prussia as tightly as possible in this respect; but as for her own coöperation, she preferred that it should remain of the same purely moral and exhortatory sort as heretofore. By Article I of the Convention she generously pledged herself to maintain her military and naval forces " on the same formidable footing as at present," so as to be able at all times to protect her own states against any possible attack, to assist her allies in the cases stipulated by the treaties, and to repress any outbreaks that might occur in Poland. Prussia, on the other hand, was obliged to promise to continue the war in common with the Emperor, and to make no separate peace nor truce until the two sovereigns ' had attained the aim announced by their common declarations,' and forced " the French rebels . . . to renounce their hostile enterprises abroad and their criminal *attentats* in the interior of the Kingdom of France " (Art. IV.). Taken in the strict sense, this article would have bound Frederick William to an interminable war. Here, it must be admitted, the Empress had effectually provided for the interests of Austria — and incidentally for her own.

As an indemnity for the expense of her armaments, and also for the sake of " the general security and tranquillity," Russia was to take possession of the Polish territories east of the line Druja-Pinsk-Choczim: that is to say, of virtually the whole eastern half of the Republic, including the rich palatinates of the Ukraine, the granary of Poland, which had so long formed the object of Potem-

kin's ambition. Prussia's acquisition, bounded by the line
Częstochowa-Rawa-Soldau, embraced the whole of Great Poland,
including the cities of Dantzic, Thorn, Posen, Gnesen, Kalisz and
Sieradz. The yawning gap in the flanks of the Monarchy was
thus filled in more than generous fashion, and the Prussian frontier advanced to within a few miles of Warsaw and Cracow. The
respective shares of the two partitioning Powers were glaringly
unequal. Russia gained over three million new subjects: Prussia
little more than one million. In area the Empress' share was
almost exactly four times as large as the King's. The loss to
Poland was relatively far greater than that in 1772. While the
First Partition had cost the Republic only twenty-nine per cent
of its area and thirty-six per cent of its population, the Second
Partition was to rob it of fifty-four per cent of its remaining
territory and approximately half of its remaining population.
There was left to the ruined state only a long, narrow quadri-
lateral extending from Courland to Cracow and Volhynia.[1]

The formal annexation of the territories in question was fixed
for the period between the 5th and the 21st of April (New Style).
The two Powers agreed to act in the closest concert in effecting
the necessary " definitive arrangement with the Republic of
Poland." Finally, they made certain specious provisions for the
interests of Austria. By Article VII they bound themselves,
when the time should come, and when the request had been made
of them, ' to omit none of their good offices and other efficacious
means in their power to facilitate the Bavarian Exchange, while

---

[1] It is impossible to offer any exact statistical data with regard to the area and
population affected by the Second Partition. According to the calculations presented to the Diet of Grodno on August 21, 1793, the Republic possessed before
the Partition an area of 9,630 (Polish) square miles (= 206,795 square miles, English); the share taken by Russia included 4,157 square miles (= 89,257 square miles,
English); that taken by Prussia 1,062 square miles (= 22,805 square miles, English).
Korzon estimates the area of Poland in 1792 as only 9,438 geographical square
miles = 200,661 square miles, English (i, pp. 160 f.). Sybel puts the Prussian lot as
1,016 square miles (*op. cit.*, iii, pp. 222 f.); Prümers (*Das Jahr 1793*, p. 76) at 1,061.
According to the same statistics presented at the Grodno Diet, the population of
the Republic just before the Partition was 7,660,787 (but Korzon places it as high
as 8,790,000, *ibid.*); that of the lands annexed by Russia 3,055,900; that gained
by Prussia 1,136,389 (see this whole set of calculations in Kraszewski, *op. cit.*, iii,
p. 336). These figures can be regarded as only approximate at the best.

adding to it such other advantages as should be compatible with the general convenience.' This article might mean much or little, according as it was interpreted. The term ' efficacious means ' suggested the idea of coercion to bring about the Exchange, but there followed the limitation to ' means in their power.' The ' other advantages ' sounded well, but were bound up with the elastic phrase about ' the general convenience.' Each concession or promise contained a loophole for escape. Austria was really offered nothing more solid than the eventual good offices of the two Courts in behalf of the Exchange. Article VIII stipulated that after ratification the Convention was to be communicated to the Emperor with the request that he should formally accede to it and guarantee its provisions, the Empress and the King engaging for their part to guarantee the Exchange as soon as it should be effected. Needless to say, this was not the kind of guarantee for which the Austrians had asked.

In general, the treaty was an unsurpassed triumph of Russian policy. The Empress, without having taken any active part in the French enterprise, awarded to herself an enormous ' indemnity '; she accorded Prussia a lot one-fourth as large as her own, under onerous conditions; and she provided chiefly by airy promises for her ' ancient ally,' who bore the main burden of the war.

The Prussian ministry found the terms of the Convention open to more than one objection. They were chagrined at getting no additions to their share and at the obligations imposed upon them, but they were far too clever not to see the various means provided for evading those obligations. The engagement to continue the war was softened by the stipulation ' in common with the Emperor,' for they were confident that they could rely on him to abandon the enterprise at the first good opportunity. The ' efficacious means ' to be employed to further the Exchange could and must be interpreted as referring only to coöperation in the recovery of the Netherlands. At any rate, all such captious considerations were outweighed by the joy of having signed and sealed the treaty which at last " raised the Prussian Monarchy to that degree of material power to which it was destined by the genius of its sovereigns and the vigor of its people." [1] On February 28 the exchange of ratifications took place at St. Petersburg.

V

The execution of the Partition was already well under way. On January 16, 1793, the Prussian envoy Buchholtz presented at Warsaw a note announcing that his master was about to send a corps of troops into Great Poland. As a pretext for this step, it was alleged that " the self-styled Patriotic party " (formerly known as ' the Prussian party,' it may be remarked) was ' continuing its secret machinations, which obviously tended to the total subversion of order and tranquillity,' and which had exposed the neighboring Prussian provinces to " repeated excesses and violations of territory "; that ' the spirit of French democracy was taking deep root in Poland, so that the manoeuvres of Jacobin emissaries were gaining powerful support, and already several revolutionary clubs had been formed, which made open profession of their principles '; that the spread of this " dangerous poison," and the connection of " the zealots" with the French clubs placed the King under the absolute necessity of providing for the safety of his own states, and averting the danger of being attacked in the rear at the moment when he was engaged in war in the west. As the aim of the intended occupation was only to repress those who were fomenting troubles and insurrection, to restore and maintain order, and to assure to honest citizens an efficacious protection, ' the King flattered himself that he could count on the good will of a nation whose well-being could not be a matter of indifference to him, and to which he wished to give substantial proofs of his affection and benevolence.' [2] The sublime irony or the brazen hypocrisy of this declaration will rarely find a parallel. Barring a few eccentric and utterly unimportant individuals, there was at that time in Poland no ' democratic ' propaganda, no ' Jacobin emissaries,' no ' revolutionary clubs.' [3] The King

[1] The cabinet ministry to the King, February 3, Lucchesini to the Ministry, February 7, B. A., *R.* 96, 147 *H*, and *R.* 92, *L. N.* 34.

[2] The declaration is printed in Angeberg, *op. cit.*, pp. 297 ff., and elsewhere.

[3] Cf. Smoleński, *Konfederacya targowicka*, pp. 366 ff. It is pathetic to find an

of Prussia was threatened by no danger on the east — unless he provoked one by undertaking a new partition and thus goading the Polish nation into a supreme act of desperation. And yet the formula, which was henceforth to serve the robber Powers in all their unholy operations against Poland, had been furnished by the Poles themselves; for the men of Targowica, in their blind hatred of their opponents, had long been stigmatizing the adherents of the monarchical constitution of 1791 as 'democrats' and 'Jacobins.'

On January 24 the Prussian troops under General Möllendorff poured over the frontier. The districts to be annexed were occupied without difficulty, almost without resistance. Dantzic alone closed its gates and held out until, threatened with famine and deprived of all hope of succor, the Town Council surrendered the city and begged for its incorporation with Prussia (April 4). Even then on the day of the occupation the mob fired on the incoming Prussian troops.

In the face of this attack, the government of Poland — the 'Generality' of the Confederation, sitting at Grodno — presented the most dismal spectacle of consternation, impotence, and cowardice. That Prussia's action had been taken with the Empress' consent was revealed in Buchholtz's declaration; and that this action was only the preliminary to a new partition, agreed upon between the two Powers, was only too obvious. Deserted by Catherine, upon whose protection alone their power had hitherto rested, the Confederation saw themselves exposed to the execration of a nation, half of which regarded them as dupes, and the other half as traitors. It is characteristic of these men that in such a crisis they thought not so much of their country as of themselves; for it is clear that in what few feeble efforts they made to oppose the Prussians, their main aim was only to save appearances and to vindicate, as far as might be, their own ruined reputations.

The Generality replied to Buchholtz's declaration with a meek protest, denying any need for the entrance of the Prussian troops

historian like Sybel attempting a vindication of the Prussian declaration, and asserting that " the facts " alleged in it were true (*op. cit.*, iii, p. 194).

and requesting their withdrawal. When Felix Potocki, with streaming eyes, announced the news that the invasion had actually begun, the Confederation could think of nothing better to do than to dispatch a pitiful appeal to St. Petersburg, throwing themselves on the mercy of their great Protectress. While awaiting her answer, they made some pretence of activity. They issued a magniloquent proclamation, protesting " in the most solemn manner in the face of the universe against any usurpation of the least part of the Republic's territory," and swearing that ' they were ready to shed the last drop of their blood in defence of the liberty and integrity of the country.' [1] The Hetman Rzewuski bustled about giving orders to the troops to oppose the advance of the Prussians. On February 11 the Generality even mustered up the courage to issue ' universals ' instructing the nation to hold itself in readiness for a *levée en masse* (the so-called *pospolite ruszenie*). How much sincerity there was behind these demonstrations appears from the fact that Potocki and associates hastened to assure the Russians that the universals had been sent out simply because the Confederation had to do something to appease the public, and this had seemed " the most innocent means "·that they could think of.[2]

Any doubts as to Catherine's sentiments and intentions were very soon removed. General Igelström, the new commander of the Empress' forces in Poland, refused to allow a single Polish regiment or a single cannon from the Warsaw arsenal to be sent against the Prussians. Baron Sievers, who had just arrived to replace Bulgakov as Russian ambassador, denied, indeed, any knowledge as to the reasons for the Prussian invasion, but announced that it was the Empress' will that the Generality should attempt no resistance, and should in general avoid all measures that might stir up the nation and disturb " the public tranquillity."[3] Roundly rebuked for their universals of February 11 — so grave a step precipitately taken without consulting him, " the minister of a friendly and allied state " — the Confederation

---

[1] This document, dated February 3, is printed in Angeberg, *Recueil*, pp. 299–304.
[2] Bühler to Zubov, February 1/12, M. A., Польша, IX, 7.
[3] Cf. Smoleński, *op. cit.*, pp. 408 f.

could only issue a new proclamation practically canceling the preceding one and informing the nation that if there were any hope left, it could be only in the magnanimity of the great Catherine.[1] With that it was clear that every thought of national self-defence had been abandoned. Poland lay helpless and passive before her despoilers, while the leaders of the Confederation thought only of making their escape from the scene.

In the middle of March, Potocki went off to St. Petersburg, ostensibly in order to implore the Empress' protection for the Republic. He was to return to the country only after the final partition — a Russian general. Branicki laid down his hetman's staff, retired to the banks of the Neva, and became a Russian subject. His worthy colleague Rzewuski remained for a time nominally in office, busying himself chiefly with attempts to whitewash himself before his fellow-countrymen and with desperate and burning appeals to St. Petersburg. In words that well sum up the tragedy of the Targowicians, he wrote: " Today I am regarded as the opprobrium of my nation, as a man who bargained to lead a people into error and to sacrifice the whole country to the interests of Russia. . . . Woe to the man who has to deal with you Russians. I thought to establish the prosperity of the Republic on eternal foundations: I was wrong. You have wrought the ruin of my country and me." [2]

The King, too, would gladly have joined in the general *débandade*. Foreseeing what was coming, he wrote to the Empress begging to be allowed to abdicate, if only his debts were paid.[3] His prayer was not granted: the Empress still had work for him to do.

On April 7 the two partitioning Powers issued manifestoes announcing the annexation of their respective acquisitions and calling upon the inhabitants to take the oath of allegiance to their new masters. Two days later Sievers and Buchholtz presented to the Generality at Grodno the long-expected formal declarations of " the firm and irrevocable decision" of their Courts

[1] *Konfederacya targowicka*, pp. 413 f.
[2] Letter of March 11, 1793, probably to Zubov, M. A., Польша, IX, 1.
[3] Letter of January 25, Kalinka, *Ostatnie lata*, ii, pp. 80 f.

to execute a new partition. The Polish nation was invited to convoke a Diet " in order to proceed amicably to the arrangements and measures necessary to attain the salutary aim which Their Majesties propose, that of securing to the Republic a firm, durable, and unalterable peace." [1] It then remained only to coerce the Poles into formally surrendering the half of their country, and to provide against whatever opposition to the Partition might be forthcoming from foreign Powers.

[1] See the Russian declaration, Angeberg, *op. cit.*, pp. 306–309.

CHAPTER XVIII

The Attitude of Austria Towards the Partition

I

ALTHOUGH the St. Petersburg Convention seemed to assume that Austria had acquiesced in advance in all the agreements that might be concluded between her two allies, Russia and Prussia saw fit to communicate the treaty at Vienna only after they had virtually completed their arrangements for carrying it out. By the express will of the Empress,[1] the negotiation had been kept strictly secret from Louis Cobenzl, in spite of the latter's reiterated and indignant protests. It was not until March 5 that the ambassador could report that a convention had been signed; and its contents remained unknown to him until after the act had been sent to Vienna.[2] Meanwhile during the three months before the blow fell, the Austrian cabinet presented the spectacle of a ministry vaguely conscious of impending disaster, but helpless to avert it, divided against itself, rejecting or postponing plan after plan, perpetually waiting for a reply from one quarter and a courier from another, incapable of making a vigorous decision of any kind.

In January the main problem was how to gain some real security for the effectuation of the Exchange, in case Russia and Prussia refused to give the precise guarantees demanded. At the ministerial Conference of January 3, the Vice-Chancellor Cobenzl proposed that as the Empress had now given her consent to the entry of Prussian troops into Poland, Austria also should temporarily occupy certain territories in that Republic. As usual, Lacy and his friends interposed a host of objections. It would be imprudent, they urged, to divert any considerable body of troops to the east, when all available forces were needed for the recovery

[1] Goltz's report of January 18, 1793, B. A., R. XI, *Russland*, 135.
[2] Cobenzl's reports of January–February, *passim*, and of March 5, V. A., *Russland, Berichte*, 1793.

of the Netherlands. It would be impossible to decide upon the territory to be occupied until the exact size of the lot claimed by Prussia was known. The Conference finally resolved that if the allied Powers refused to guarantee the realization of the Exchange, the Imperial Court should occupy only the fortresses of Cracow and Kamieniec and the intervening strip of territory along the frontier, although later on, after the precise area of the Prussian acquisition was known, the occupation might be proportionately extended. Owing to Lacy's meticulous anxiety not to get a single village less than the King of Prussia, action was thus indefinitely postponed. The net result of the Conference of January 3 was that no effective measures whatever were taken to obtain a security for the Exchange on the side of Poland.[1]

There was one other means by which Austria might have safeguarded her interests and entered into possession of her indemnity at the same time as did Prussia. The highly suspicious conduct of the Court of Munich still offered abundant excuse for carrying out the plan discussed two months earlier between Spielmann and the Prussians, the plan for the forcible sequestration of Bavaria. If Cobenzl had had his way, it is probable that an attempt would have been made to carry out this project; but once more he encountered the opposition of Lacy and of Prince Colloredo, the Chancellor of the Empire, who urged that such violent measures would alienate all the German princes and compromise the honor of the Imperial Court. If not definitely abandoned, the plan was at least postponed until changes in the military situation and the fall of Philip Cobenzl at last put an end to it.[2]

Hampered and thwarted in both his schemes for obtaining some tangible security for the Exchange, the Vice-Chancellor could only fall back on the uncertain resources of diplomacy; and here,

[1] Cobenzl to Starhemberg, January 1, Lacy's *votum* of January 2 (erroneously given as of January 3 and as written *after* the Conference, in Vivenot, ii, pp. 459 f.), Conference protocol of January 3 and *separat-vota*, Vivenot, ii, pp. 456–461).

[2] For the above: Cobenzl's correspondence with Lehrbach, January–March 1793, *passim*, V. A., *Bayern, Exped.*, and *Berichte*, 1793; Caesar's reports of January 12, 26, February 13, B. A., *R.* 1, 174; *vota* of Lacy, Rosenberg, and Colloredo of January 12, Cobenzl to the Emperor the same day, V. A., *Vorträge*, 1793.

too, fortune was steadily adverse to him. On February 19 Razumovski communicated a dispatch from Ostermann containing a preliminary announcement as to the Partition Treaty. After some explanation of the reasons that had led the Empress to make a decision without a final consultation with Austria, the dispatch stated that she had provided for the Emperor's interests in two equally effective ways, in such a manner that he could not have done better himself, as he would be convinced as soon as the completed act should be presented to him. She had, namely, induced the King of Prussia to bind himself in the most formal and positive manner to make common cause with the Court of Vienna throughout the whole course of the war, and also to assist powerfully and efficaciously both in the matter of the Bavarian Exchange and in procuring "several other advantages" to Austria. For the rest, it was said that it had been impossible to cut down the size of the Prussian acquisition, in view of the consent previously given by the Emperor to all the King's demands; and no direct reply was made to the Austrian request for a guarantee of the Exchange. Immediately after Razumovski, Caesar made an analogous communication in the name of his Court.

Cobenzl took these announcements with good grace. He already knew that Russia and Prussia were negotiating a separate convention, and he does not seem at this time to have felt much uneasiness over the fact. In his reply to Caesar, however, he took pains to indicate once more the provision in its favor to which his Court attached the most importance, and which it confidently expected to find in the treaty: namely, a clear and unequivocal guarantee of the realization of the Exchange.[1] Reporting to the Emperor, the Vice-Chancellor declared that a final judgment could be formed only after the receipt of a detailed report of the Convention from the ambassador in St. Petersburg; but meantime he thought the prospects not unfavorable, although the refusal to reduce the Prussian lot was as unexpected as the reason alleged for not doing so was, according to the records, absolutely untrue.[2]

---

[1] Ostermann's dispatch of January 27/February 7, in Vivenot, ii, pp. 481–484; Razumovski's report of February 9/20, M. A., Австрія, III, 54; Caesar's report of February 25, B. A., R. 1, 174.

[2] P. Cobenzl to the Emperor, February 21, Vivenot, ii, p. 481.

This somewhat optimistic mood must have been disturbed a few days later by the arrival of an ominous report from Louis Cobenzl as to the rigid secrecy with which the Russians concealed from him their negotiation with Prussia.[1] The Austrians now began to discover how completely they had played into the hands of their allies; and in the following weeks their uneasiness and their suspicions were increased by the inexplicable delay in the communication of the Convention.

Almost at the same time with Razumovski's overtures, a courier from London brought the reply of the British government to the Austrian advances of December. The response was favorable enough in so far as England, now committed to the war with France, displayed a strong desire for a close understanding with the Imperial Court; but as to the Bavarian Exchange, Lord Grenville had raised so many objections that there could be little doubt of the decided aversion felt at London towards that project. On the other hand, he had held out hopes that if the Emperor would renounce that plan, England would gladly help him to procure an indemnity at the expense of France.[2]

The British answer made a deep impression at Vienna, the more so in view of the bad news from St. Petersburg. The conviction was gaining ground that Cobenzl and Spielmann had bungled sadly; that they had allowed themselves to be duped by Russia and Prussia; and that by insisting further on their impracticable Exchange project, they would merely be alienating England, the one ally from whom Austria might hope for loyal assistance both in prosecuting the war and in securing a suitable indemnity of some kind. Before the end of February the Emperor was undoubtedly considering a change of ministry and a change of system. A redoubtable competitor for Cobenzl's position was already being brought to the front by the powerful Colloredo family in the person of Baron von Thugut.[3]

[1] Report of February 13, which, being sent by courier, must have reached Vienna about the 25th–27th, V. A., *Russland, Berichte,* 1793.

[2] Stadion's report of February 15, V. A., *England, Berichte,* 1793.

[3] In January Thugut had been appointed political adviser to the commander-in-chief, the Prince of Saxe-Coburg (Vivenot, ii, p. 466), but then the Emperor for some unknown reason authorized him to delay his departure for the army (Thugut

In a memorial which was probably presented to the Emperor early in March, Thugut subjected the Vice-Chancellor's policy to a searching criticism, and outlined a new program. He declared that under the existing circumstances it was impossible to ensure the ultimate realization of the Exchange sufficiently to make that project the basis of a political system. On the most favorable supposition, the Exchange could not be effected for two or three years yet; and during such a period no one could foresee what events would occur to thwart a plan, the execution of which depended on so many contingencies and on so many wills — on the consent of the Elector and of all the members of his House, on that of the Empire, Prussia, Russia, England, and so many others. Austria could not afford to defer her indemnity to so uncertain a future, or to rely on the promises of Prussia, when that Power did not hesitate at present to violate openly the stipulation which formed the cornerstone of the alliance — a perfect equality in all ' advantages.' The Emperor's indemnification must be based on another plan less complicated and better suited to balance the dangerous aggrandizement of the Court of Berlin. The precise nature of this plan Thugut did not attempt to fix at that moment, but he suggested conquests from France. The abandonment of that mirage, the Bavarian Exchange, an effort to free the Imperial Court from too close dependence on a suspected ally, close union with England, and vigorous prosecution of the war with the aim of securing as soon as possible an indemnity completely equal to that of Prussia — such were the chief points in the new program. One can hardly deny that whatever were the later results, it was better adapted to the existing situation than Cobenzl's system.[1]

to Colloredo, January 28, V. A., *F.* 446). In February the Baron began to frequent the State Chancellery daily. On the 24th the Emperor ordered Cobenzl to place all important documents without exception at Thugut's disposal, on the pretext of preparing him for his diplomatic mission (Vivenot, ii, pp. 485 f). In reality Thugut was being prepared to take over Cobenzl's position, as appears from a hitherto unpublished document in the Vienna Archives, written not later than February 27 — a note in Thugut's hand, by which the Vice-Chancellor was to be informed of his dismissal (V. A., *Vorträge*, 1793). Why the note was sent only one month later is not entirely certain.

[1] Thugut's memorial is printed in Vivenot, ii, pp. 498–501.

Provided at last with a program and an able spokesman, the party who had long been opposing the leading ministers redoubled their onslaughts. At the meeting of the Conference on March 11, the Vice-Chancellor found his whole policy violently assailed; and when pressed to explain precisely how matters stood with Russia and Prussia, he was very nearly driven to the wall.[1] His critics affirmed with much justice that he had practically given the other Powers *carte blanche*, without taking any effective steps to prevent a separate negotiation between them or to provide for Austrian interests. Kaunitz is said to have declared to the Emperor that the mere possibility of a Russo-Prussian convention on Polish affairs without the participation of Austria was an unpardonable fault of the Imperial ministers.[2] Overwhelmed with reproaches, Cobenzl nightly poured out his sorrows and anxieties to Razumovski, who could only offer his personal opinion that the Empress would surely guarantee the Exchange and might even admit an Austrian acquisition in Poland, and who assured Caesar that he looked forward to the coming of his courier as to the advent of the Messiah.[3] The town was full of rumors of the impending ministerial revolution, which was, indeed, virtually decided upon. If the Emperor delayed announcing his intentions, it was apparently only because he wished to await the communication of the Russo-Prussian Convention.

On March 23 Razumovski and Caesar successively appeared at the State Chancellery to present that long-expected treaty. The sensation was indescribable. Cobenzl's consternation was such that he could hardly speak. He flew to the map, stammering incoherently: " This changes the whole system of Europe — the French revolution is only child's play, compared with this event — the Emperor must take a great decision — this will break my

---

[1] Conference protocol and *vota*, Vivenot, ii, pp. 489–498. Caesar reported (March 21) that Cobenzl was driven to declare — to the amazement of the Conference — that there was as yet no question of acquisitions on the part of the two Northern Powers, but merely of the military occupation of Polish territory (!), B. A., *R.* 1, 174.

[2] Caesar's report of March 21, B. A., *R.* 1, 174.

[3] Razumovski's reports of March 9/20 and 17/28, M. A., Австрія, III, 55.

neck and my cousin's too." When Razumovski pressed for an answer regarding the Emperor's accession to the treaty, Cobenzl could reply only that he was too much agitated to speak of the affair; he must have time to collect his ideas and to make his report to his sovereign.[1] To Caesar the Vice-Chancellor declared that the Convention was something so great, so decisive, so different from all the preceding agreements that he simply could not grasp it; he had been entirely ignorant of the extent of the King's acquisition; nothing had been definitely arranged, concluded, or signed with Austria, as had now been done between Russia and Prussia; the previous negotiations had been mere trifles compared to this. Spielmann was hardly less confused and dismayed. Razumovski and Caesar could get no further reply that day.[2]

[1] Razumovski's report of March 17/28, M. A., Австрія, III, 55.

Describing the scene when he presented the Convention to Cobenzl, Razumovski wrote: " La sensation inexprimable qu'elle a faite sur lui, me persuade qu'effectivement on ne s'était pas douté le moins du monde de sa teneur. La consternation du comte de Cobenzl fut extrême; il se précipite à la carte géographique, puis me balbutia maintes phrases qui peignaient l'agitation de son ame et la confusion de ses idées ; comme par exemple, ' ceci change tout le système de l'Europe . . . la révolution de. France n'est qu'un enfantillage en comparaison de l'importance de cet évènement . . . il faut que l'Empereur prenne un grand parti . . . voilà qui me cassera le cou et à mon cousin aussi.' Je le laissais revenir à lui; je réclamais son attention sur ce que j'avais à dire touchant l'accession, à laquelle S. M. Impériale m'ordonnait d'inviter l'Empereur. Il me répondit qu'il n'était point en état de me rien dire à cet égard, qu'il était trop agité pour parler de cette grande affaire, qu'il lui fallait du tems pour reprendre ses esprits et faire son rapport à l'Empereur. . . .

Avant-hier je retournai chez le Comte de Cobenzl; je ne le trouvai ni plus rassuré ni mieux préparé à m'entendre. Il me répéta encore qu'il ne pouvait revenir de son étonnement; prenant ensuite le ton de la confiance et de l'amitié, il se plaignit toujours du mystère qu'on leur avait fait, se lamenta sur l'étendue de notre acquisition et surtout sur l'inconvénient de nous rendre limitrophes les uns des autres, mais il se récria encore plus amèrement sur la portion énorme du Roi de Prusse, à laquelle il était bien loin de s'attendre, ayant au contraire esperé, d'après leurs sollicitations à notre Cour, qu'on chercherait à la restreindre plutôt qu'à l'augmenter. . . ." Razumovski replied: " . . . Enfin Mr. le Comte, la chose est faite, pouvez-vous l'empêcher ? Dès lors, je n'ai rien à dire. Mais comme j'en doute fort, ne mettez donc pas de la mauvaise grace à une mesure indispensable, et que des retards inutiles n'augmentent pas le mécontentement que vous nous avez donné plus d'une fois par des lenteurs. . . ."

[2] Caesar's report of March 24, B. A., R. 1, 174.

The communication of the Convention sealed the fate of the two leading ministers. On March 27, while the capital in gala was celebrating the victory of Neerwinden, Cobenzl and Spielmann received notes from the Emperor dismissing them from their posts.

In his memoirs Cobenzl ascribed his fall to a cabal formed against him by Colloredo, Rosenberg, Trautmansdorff, and Thugut.[1] Doubtless personal rancors and intrigues played their part in it, but from the political standpoint the Emperor's decision seems fully justified. In judging the policy of the two ministers one must bear in mind how constantly their better-laid plans were thwarted by their opponents, and how much they had to acquiesce in against their will; but in spite of this one can hardly deny that they had adopted a disastrous political system, and that it had had only too long a trial. Their first great mistake lay in taking up the Exchange project at such a time, and in combining it with the nefarious Partition plan; their second lay in holding to the scheme through thick and thin, after all the sad experiences of the autumn and winter, to the neglect of every other consideration. They had also confided overmuch in Prussia and neglected Russia. Finally, not the least of their faults was the mortal slowness of their conduct of affairs, their months of silence and indecision, the timidity, the lack of energy, the disorganization that crept into the State Chancellery during their year of control. It was time that their outworn system made way for something less visionary, time that a strong and unfettered hand took the helm.

III

Cobenzl's successor was Baron von Thugut, who here began the stormy and tragic ministry which ended at Marengo. Thugut is an enigmatic figure: the "Austrian Pitt" of some historians, the "faunish Mephistopheles" or "the modern Borgia" of others. A parvenu who had risen by immense industry, intelligence, and some less creditable means, he far surpassed his immediate predecessors in knowledge and experience, in the clearness and conse-

[1] Arneth, *Philipp Cobenzl und seine Memoiren*, pp. 154 f.

quence of his views, above all in the strength of his will, his ability to dominate opposition, his justly celebrated courage. It was said of him that he could not have been shaken by an earthquake. But he missed greatness by a considerable margin. In his outlook upon life, his aims and methods, his political morality, he represented only too faithfully the sordid, cynical, unprincipled eighteenth century at its worst. As a diplomat of the old school, familiar with all the tricks of the trade, he believed that territorial aggrandizement was the Alpha and Omega of statecraft, and that all means were hallowed by that end. As a pupil of Kaunitz, he had no stronger passion than hatred of Prussia. He was the last man in the world to be repelled by the moral aspects of the partition of Poland, but no one could be more outraged than he by a transaction which glutted the cupidity of the other Powers while leaving his own Court empty-handed.

The first and the foremost task of the new ' General Director of Foreign Affairs ' was to meet the situation created by the St. Petersburg Convention, to repair — as far as might be — the results of Cobenzl's bungling. And here, whatever might have been his own ideas, he could hardly have ventured to propose an unconditional acceptance of the treaty: the storm of indignation at Vienna was far too strong. Throughout April and long afterwards, the ' political circles ' in the capital alternately abused and execrated the late ministers — Kaunitz referred to Spielmann as " that scourge of Austria " — or raged at the perfidy of the partitioning Powers, who had taken advantage of the confidence of the Imperial Court to put through these vast plans, the full extent of which could not even be conjectured. Poland had been annihilated, it was said; a partition of Austria would be the next project; Russia and Prussia had always been united when it was a case of despoiling the Court of Vienna; the Emperor would probably be reduced to the condition of a mere Elector Palatine.[1]

The causes of this ' indescribable sensation ' are easy to understand. The partitioning Powers had themselves foreseen a

---

[1] *Zinzendorf's Diary*, March 29, April 2, 19, 29, May 3, 19, June 5 (V. A.); Casti, *Lettere politiche*, April 25, June 27, July 4, August 8.

storm.[1] In the first place, the manner in which this affair had been rushed through without the participation of Austria was bad enough, and the mystery so long made of it was flatly insulting. But apart from the form of the transaction, the substance of the treaty did not at all conform to the expectations and desires of the Court of Vienna. The size of the Russian acquisition might well stagger the Austrian ministers: the Empress had never uttered a word to them as to the extent of her claims. It had always been a maxim of the Imperial Courts that Poland was to be maintained as a fair-sized buffer state, but the Republic was now to be reduced to a mere shadow. Another principle equally accepted at all times between the neighboring Powers was violated by the new Russian frontier, which touched directly upon Galicia; and almost as much by the Prussian acquisition of the fortress of Częstochowa, which threatened the adjacent unprotected Austrian province. These grievances were clear and undeniable, but they were not the only ones which the Emperor's advisers felt themselves entitled to raise.

It was here that the fatal misunderstandings of December began to appear in the most unpleasant light. If Haugwitz had really received the declaration announced in his final report from Vienna, the Austrian ministers were now guilty of a gross breach of faith: in the contrary case, they were perfectly justified in taking their stand on the text of the note of December 9 and the instructions to Louis Cobenzl of the 23rd. From those documents it could easily be proved that Austria had consented to an immediate Prussian occupation in Poland only on the understanding that the details of the convention were to be arranged by a concert of the three Courts, and on condition either that the Emperor should be allowed to make a similar occupation temporarily, or else that his allies should guarantee the realization of the Exchange. As has already been stated, it is uncertain whether Haugwitz's assertions are accurate, but at any rate the language of the Austrian cabinet in January accorded perfectly with the view advanced at Vienna in April. If, on receiving the news of

---

[1] The Prussian ministry to Caesar, March 15, 17, 24, B. A., *R.* 1, 174; Markov to Razumovski, February 25/March 8, in Wassiltchikow, *op. cit.*, pp. 167 f.

Catherine's consent to the immediate entry of the Prussians into
Poland, the Emperor wrote to congratulate the King on the fulfilment of his wishes, the letter implied just the converse of the
meaning later ascribed to it on the Prussian side: it meant that
the Emperor considered the King's immediate desires satisfied by
an *occupation de sûreté*, although the partition had not been formally effected.   One would search in vain among the Austrian
utterances of December or January for an admission that the
Imperial Court had given Prussia *carte blanche* to go ahead, conclude a partition treaty, and execute it without a further word
from Vienna.   Haugwitz later maintained, indeed, that he had in
December insisted daily on obtaining Austria's acquiescence in
the immediate formal *prise de possession* of the new Prussian
provinces, and in their immediate and complete incorporation in
the Prussian Monarchy; [1] but his reports of that month speak
only of a *prise de possession effective* or *actuelle*, which is by no
means the same thing and which would certainly not have been
taken as such by the Austrians.   Had Haugwitz really employed
the language which he later claimed to have used, his master
would have been bound not to lift his hand towards the continuation of the war until the formal annexation had actually taken
place.   The fact that Frederick William announced his readiness
to continue his coöperation against France as soon as he was
assured of the entry of his troops into Poland,[2] certainly lent color
to the Austrian theory.

Another objection to the Convention raised at Vienna was that
the new Prussian acquisition went far beyond the limits previously announced to the Imperial Court.   Here, also, one en-
counters an absolute contradiction between the statements
advanced by the two parties regarding their previous negotiations.
In May Haugwitz asserted that soon after the presentation of the
Note of Merle he had shown Spielmann the original map upon
which Frederick William at Consenvoye had traced the frontier of

[1] Report to the King of May 6, 1793, B. A., *R. 96*, 147 *H*. (Printed in Appendix XVI, 3).

[2] Reuss' report of December 28, 1792, V. A., *Preussen, Berichte*; ministerial
rescript to Caesar, January 7, 1793, B. A., *R. 1*, 174.

his desired acquisition.[1] I know of only one previous allusion to this: a somewhat similar but less definite statement in a letter of Haugwitz to Lucchesini of January 21.[2] The Prussian envoy's reports of December contain absolutely no reference to the exact limits of his master's territorial claims. The Austrian records are almost equally blank. Spielmann had, indeed, sent in from Luxemburg a map showing the acquisition desired by Prussia in case of the realization of the plan which he and Haugwitz had agreed upon before the worst disasters of the campaign set in; and from a letter of Haugwitz to Schulenburg [3] it appears that this acquisition was identical with the one assured to Prussia by the Partition Treaty. This plan, however, had been abandoned after the presentation of the Note of Merle. After that note, Spielmann seems to have believed that the King would claim only the *arrondissement* proposed by Schulenburg at Mainz; [4] and that idea is clearly conveyed in whatever allusions we have to the subject in the later Austrian acts — in the secret instructions to Louis Cobenzl and in the Conference protocol of January 3.[5] In view of the meticulous attention with which the Austrians were accustomed to scrutinize the territorial claims of Prussia, it is inconceivable that they would not have noted — and protested about — the difference between the acquisition proposed at Mainz and that bounded by the line Częstochowa-Rawa-Soldau, if they had known of it. The difference was regarded by the Prussians as a sufficient indemnity for a second campaign, and was so great that the Berlin ministry hesitated for a time to propose the second line of demarcation at St. Petersburg. Once

[1] The above-cited retrospective report of May 6.

[2] B. A., *R. 92, N. L.* 31.

In this letter Haugwitz wrote: " Je prie V. Exc. instamment d'assurer à Sa Majesté que le Consentement der Eigenthums-Besitznehmung des Arrondissements Seiner Majestät in Pohlen, tel que je l'ai tracé au Baron de Spielmann à Luxembourg a été formel et donné de façon que la Cour de Vienne ne peut pas se rétracter sans deshonneur."

[3] Letter of October 27, 1792, referring to the earlier negotiation, which, as Haugwitz hastened to add, had had absolutely no consequences, B. A., *R. IX, Frankreich,* 89 *K.*

[4] See the passage in his report of November 6, Vivenot, ii, p. 342.

[5] Vivenot, ii, pp. 429 and 457.

more one is driven to the conclusion that either Haugwitz or Spielmann had failed to inform their Courts correctly of what had passed between them. But if the Emperor and — at least most of — his advisers had supposed that Prussia's claims went no further than the line proposed at Mainz, had found even those demands excessive, and had begged Russia to reduce them, it is easy to understand what must have been their astonishment and indignation to find that the Empress had granted Prussia a vastly larger lot, of which the cabinet of Vienna had hitherto not been informed at all.[1]

Finally, the Convention of St. Petersburg did not accord to Austria either of the two securities which that Court had demanded as the price of its consent to the Prussian occupation in Poland. The promise of good offices and 'other efficacious means' to facilitate the Exchange was very far from being the desired guarantee. The promise of 'other advantages compatible with the general convenience' was as unsubstantial as thin air. The sum of the matter was that the partitioning Powers had made sure of their own acquisitions, assumed the acquiescence of Austria in all that they chose to agree upon in secret, and offered her in return castles in Spain. Little wonder that the Austrians felt themselves in every way injured, deceived, and mocked.

Thugut presented his ideas about the reply to be made to Russia and Prussia in a memorial submitted to his sovereign on April 4.[2] In view of considerations substantially the same as those discussed above, he found that the Emperor's interests and dignity forbade him to accede unconditionally to the Convention, although on the other hand circumstances rendered it inadvisable to refuse accession entirely. He therefore advised demanding a rectification of the proposed boundaries, to the end that neither

---

[1] Sybel declares that in this matter, as in everything else concerning the Prussian claims, the Austrians had been exactly informed in advance by Haugwitz (*op. cit.*, iii, p. 262). Heidrich is of the opinion that no communication of the final Prussian line of demarcation had been made to the Austrians, since — as he, strangely enough, asserts — this line did not differ essentially from that previously announced (*op. cit.*, pp. 445 f.).

[2] This document is printed in Vivenot, *Thugut und sein politisches System*, pp. 378–383.

acquisition should directly touch, or even approach too near, Galicia; and he laid it down as the *conditio sine qua non* of the Emperor's accession that the indemnities of Austria must be determined in advance in a manner that would ensure to the Imperial Court a perfect equality with its allies with regard not only to the intrinsic value of its acquisitions but also to security in obtaining them.

In Thugut's opinion the Partition Treaty had changed the situation so entirely and had gone so far beyond the proportions of the original indemnity project that it was necessary for Austria to base her indemnification on quite a new plan. The Bavarian Exchange, he held, could never be put into the balance against the enormous acquisitions of Prussia and Russia. It would entail a loss of a million in population and four million florins in revenue, while affording no advantage save that of rounding out the Austrian frontier. Prussia's acquisition, on the other hand, combined absolute advantages of every kind. Were the original indemnity plan to be realized, the balance of power between the two German Courts would be shifted by almost three millions in population and eight or nine millions in revenue to the advantage of Prussia. Thugut therefore proposed to abandon the project agreed upon the previous May between Schulenburg and Spielmann, to return to the original principle of the concert — a perfect equality in the respective indemnities — and to build up a new system on that basis. Precisely what the new plan would be, he was not yet in a position to say. It was first of all necessary to know the exact value of the acquisitions of the other Courts. Besides, he hoped that those Courts might be induced to propose acquisitions to Austria. His calculation — which does not do him great credit — was, probably, that it was more advantageous to accept than to make such propositions. He also seems to have feared that if he announced his indemnity plans too early, Prussia would not fail to abuse his confidence and to raise heaven and earth to cut down the Austrian aggrandizement. In this his intuitions did not deceive him. The essential thing at present, he held, was to sound the two allies, whose good intentions were open to some doubts, and to secure, if possible, an agreement on *principles.*

It had been one of the faults of Spielmann and Cobenzl that they had left questions of principle in more or less obscurity. Thugut meant to follow a more systematic course, and to advance surely from step to step by clear and definite agreements. Such a course involved delays, and he recognized it. But he believed that the partitioning Powers would not be able to carry out their plans so speedily; the least sign of opposition from England would probably encourage the Poles to a desperate resistance; in that case the two Powers might find themselves in need of Austria's support, and the Emperor would be in a position to sell his accession to the treaty at a good price.

His sovereign having readily approved this program, Thugut began his campaign with the instructions sent on April 14 to Reuss and Louis Cobenzl.[1] In these dispatches he set forth the reasons which prevented the Emperor from acceding to the St. Petersburg Convention except under conditions that would properly safeguard the interests of Austria; he reviewed the whole history of the negotiation on the indemnity question, and, without stating precisely what acquisition his Court now contemplated, labored to build up his principle of ' equality ' on the basis of the agreements entered into between the allies at the beginning of the war. This historical excursus was not of a nature to please the Prussians: it was to be the beginning of a long litigation fraught with the most unhappy results. In general, however, both replies were couched in moderate terms; there was nothing to suggest threats or open opposition; on the contrary, Austria expressed the willingness to acquiesce in all that had been done, providing her allies showed her an equal regard.[2]

---

[1] Vivenot, iii, pp. 11–23.

[2] I am at a loss to understand where Sybel got the idea that on April 4 Thugut made a declaration to Caesar and Razumovski to the effect that the Emperor refused to accede to the Convention, renounced the Exchange, demanded French territories and a province in Poland, etc. (*op. cit.*, iii, p. 266). As can be proved from the reports of both envoys, no declaration at all was made at this time (it was only on April 16 that Thugut announced to the two envoys the decision conveyed in the dispatches to Reuss and Cobenzl of the 14th); and it is important to notice the fact, since this apocryphal declaration cannot be used to justify certain proceedings which took place on the Prussian side before the Emperor's reply was really first announced by Reuss at the King of Prussia's headquarters on April 21.

Thugut was, of course, well aware that mere arguments, however well grounded, were not particularly effective at Berlin and St. Petersburg. It was necessary to supply the other Powers with more cogent motives for obliging Austria. But here, if ever, thrice-sealed secrecy was indispensable. It was useless to attempt action at Grodno, where the Polish Diet was about to assemble, for a secret negotiation with the Poles was of all things the most impossible. Under the urgent pressure of Razumovski, de Caché was, indeed, instructed to go to Grodno, but he was ordered to maintain an entirely passive conduct — a rôle for which he was eminently fitted, as his Court had never allowed him to play any other.[1] It was England to whom the honor was to be reserved of pulling the chestnuts out of the fire. On April 14 Thugut instructed Mercy to communicate to the British government as much of the Convention as seemed advisable, and to urge that, as the Emperor, although far from wishing a new partition, was unable to oppose one openly, it behooved England to intervene at Berlin and St. Petersburg with representations that might at least lead those Courts to reduce their territorial claims and to postpone the execution of their plans. He also suggested that were England to give some slight signs of sympathy for the Poles, the latter might be encouraged to resist the partition, and thus much valuable time would be gained.[2] In conversation with Sir Morton Eden, the British ambassador, Thugut expressed himself vigorously about the dangers resulting from the enormous aggrandizement and the measureless ambitions of Russia and Prussia; and as a bid for British support against those two Powers, he even declared that the Emperor was ready to desist from the plan for the exchange of the Netherlands out of deference for England.[3]

---

[1] Orders to de Caché of April 3 and 20, V. A., *Polen., Expeditionen*, 1793. Sybel's repeated assertions (*op. cit.*, iii, p. 269; *H. Z.*, xxiii, p. 93) that de Caché was ordered to stir up the Poles secretly to resistance are utterly unfounded.

Thugut to de Caché, April 3: "Uebrigens haben sich Ew. Exc. über die vorliegenden Pohlnischen Umstände aller Aeusserungen gegen wen immer zu enthalten, und alle Anfragen mit gänzlichem Abgang von Instructionen zu beantworten."

Thugut to de Caché, April 20: "Vor der Hand haben Sie sich daselbst [in Grodno] in die Rolle eines aufmerksamen Beobachters und ruhigen Zuschauers lediglich zu beschränken. . . ."   [2] Vivenot, ii, pp. 24 ff.

[3] Eden to Grenville, April 15, Herrmann, *Ergänzungsband*, pp. 386 ff.

The new minister had thus begun his campaign by undertaking two distinct and somewhat contradictory actions. On the one hand, by protests, recriminations, and arguments he attempted to induce Russia and Prussia to modify their agreements in such a way as to provide effectively for the Emperor's interests: on the other hand, by intrigues with England he hoped to raise up such obstacles in the way of the partitioning Powers as would render them more amenable to the demands of Austria. To frustrate entirely the dismemberment of Poland was something which he probably neither expected nor desired to do; but he did intend to impede and delay the consummation of the partition until Russia and Prussia could be brought to pay a sufficient price for Austria's coöperation.

This policy, which was to have such unhappy consequences, has often been severely condemned by historians. It was, indeed, unfortunate that Thugut began at once with a double game. His insinuations to England, although quite in the approved diplomatic style of the period, were to bring him no laurels. They straightway came to the knowledge of Razumovski, and one can imagine the indignation they produced at St. Petersburg. But the refusal to accede unconditionally to the Partition Treaty was not without much justification. It may well be doubted whether any Power not in the last extremities would have submitted without a word of protest to such treatment as Austria had met with from her allies. At that moment, in view of the triumphant recovery of the Netherlands, the Court of Vienna did not feel itself in extremities. Thugut had no intention of breaking with the partitioning Powers. It may well have seemed that with a display of firmness Austria could secure an acceptable price for her accession to the Convention. The conditions proposed by Thugut were, in strict justice, sufficiently well founded. To condemn Austria for a shocking breach of faith in not submitting unconditionally, to represent Prussia as the really aggrieved party in this transaction, seems a singular perversion of the case.[1]

---

[1] I am referring, of course, to the view advanced by Sybel, *op. cit.*, iii, pp. 266 ff., and *H. Z.*, xxiii, pp. 85 ff. For the contrary view, substantially the one I have taken, see Hüffer, *Oestreich und Preussen*, pp. 132 ff., and *Ergänzungsband*, pp. 32–35.

Whether Thugut's policy was politically wise, is, of course, another question. To understand its consequences, one must glance at the temper, plans, and calculations of the cabinet of Berlin.

III

Since the conclusion of the St. Petersburg Convention the Prussian ministry had been largely occupied with devising means for evading as far as possible the obligations imposed by that treaty. How to avoid continuing the war after the close of the present year, how to thwart the Bavarian Exchange — " that fatal project " — while still keeping up the appearance of favoring it, how to reduce to the minimum the ' additional advantages ' stipulated for Austria in the Convention — those were subjects for maturest deliberation. Long before the Court of Vienna had announced its attitude towards the Partition Treaty, the Prussian ministers were agreed that their master could not make a third campaign without being assured of still a further ' indemnity ' in territory or money; [1] they were already sounding the alarm at St. Petersburg with regard to Austria's " insidious designs " on Alsace and Lorraine; [2] and they were secretly laboring to encourage the Duke of Zweibrücken in his opposition to the Exchange, and to bring him into close relations with England, which might be expected to stand forth openly as his protector.[3] This attempt to play off England against the Exchange was quite on a par with

[1] This appears from Haugwitz's retrospective letter to Lucchesini of July 1, 1793, B. A., *R. 92, L. N.* 31.

[2] Lucchesini's letter to the cabinet ministry of April 3, their reply of April 8, B. A., *R. 92, L. N.* 14; rescript to Goltz of the 9th, B. A., *R. XI, Russland,* 135. Cf. Lucchesini's memorial to the King of March 17, printed in [Schladen's] *Mittheilungen aus den nachgelassenen Papieren eines preussischen Diplomaten,* pp. 155–170.

[3] Lucchesini's letters to the cabinet ministers of April 9, 15, 16, 22; their letter to him of the 21st, B. A., *R. 92, L. N.* 14.

Lucchesini wrote (April 15): " Le Duc de Deux-Ponts m'a paru disposé de faire quelques démarches auprès de l'Angleterre pour la déterminer à prendre en considération les dangers qu'elle courroit . . . si elle ne fesoit point tomber le projet du troc. Comme Mylord Elgin va s'établir au Quartier General, et que le Duc de Deux-Ponts est intentionné d'y venir remercier Sa Majesté de la visite qu'Elle lui a faite à Manheim, je n'ai pas cru devoir retenir ce Prince de s'ouvrir confidentiellement à ce Ministre Anglais. . . . J'ai même jugé être de l'intérêt du Roi d'appuyer

Thugut's nearly contemporaneous effort to induce the same Power to oppose the Partition. It is hard to see that either of the high allies yielded to the other in the matter of duplicity. At any rate, there was plenty of material on hand for discussion between the two Courts. To imagine that had the Emperor only acceded unconditionally to the Convention of St. Petersburg, all trouble would have been avoided and the coalition would have advanced in perfect harmony, would be decidedly naïve.

After the communication of that Convention at Vienna, the Prussians awaited the Emperor's reply with a sort of malicious curiosity, but with no trace of anxiety. The ministers at Berlin expected that in spite of her jealousy Austria would end by acceding, but the more far-sighted Lucchesini prophesied conditions and long discussions. The situation was, however, quite to his taste. " If the Emperor accedes," he wrote, " he will subscribe to very considerable acquisitions in favor of other Powers, while obtaining for himself nothing but hopes exposed to the inexhaustible chapter of future accidents. If he refuses us his assent, the two partitioning Courts will keep their acquisitions none the less, and will find themselves freed from all the obligations that they have contracted in favor of the Court of Vienna." The Berlin ministry professed themselves charmed by Lucchesini's exposition of this " admirable dilemma"; they assured him that they meant to improve to the utmost the " beautiful situation " resulting from the expected embroilments between the Imperial Courts.[1]

On April 21 Reuss presented the Emperor's answer at Frederick William's headquarters. The effect was most unpleasant. The

en mon particulier cette idée, sans en laisser cependant aucun témoignage de mon approbation."

April 16, Lucchesini continued: " Je l'ai mis [the Duke] sur les voyes pour qu'il parvienne . . . à avoir un entretien sur cet objet avec Mylord Elgin. . . ."

April 21, the ministers at Berlin replied: " Nous applaudissons . . . aux encouragemens indirects que V. Exc. lui a donnés [the Duke] . . . . Malgré toute notre aversion pour ce funeste projet [the Exchange], nous n'en persistons pas moins à croire que le Roi doit avoir l'air de le favoriser, d'après les engagemens qu'il a contractés. . . . Il suffiroit selon nous de mettre le Duc de Deux-Ponts en relation avec Mylord Elgin, pour être sur que sa proposition sera bien reçue. . . ."

[1] Lucchesini to the cabinet ministry, March 31, their replies of April 4 and 11, B. A., *R.* 92, *L. N.* 14.

Prussians, although prepared for objections, had not expected the Imperial Court to disavow the engagements which, according to Haugwitz, it had contracted in December. From their stand-point, they were quite justified in considering this a gross breach of faith. The ministry at Berlin pronounced Thugut's reply " a veritable labyrinth of false assertions, captious arguments, and insidious propositions," which deserved to be solidly refuted.[1] Haugwitz, as the man whose honor was involved, was called upon to enter the lists. He drew up a memorial [2] recounting his entire negotiation at Vienna and Luxemburg, and proving to the satis-faction of his colleagues that the Austrian ministry had in Decem-ber consented unconditionally to the immediate occupation and annexation of precisely those territories which had been assigned to the King by the Partition Treaty. Lucchesini, thus thrice-armed, then went forth to confound the Austrians.

His *note verbale* to Reuss of May 15 is a document which has hitherto received little notice, but which deserves a prominent place in the history of the disruption of the Austro-Prussian alliance. Thugut had invited a discussion on principles; he had sought especially to reassert that original principle of perfect equality in the respective indemnities, which, as even the Berlin ministry in confidential moments admitted,[3] had been agreed upon between the two Courts at the beginning of the war. The Prussians took up the challenge and replied with the first clear expression since the Note of Merle of their position on the in-demnity question. There were two ways of defending that posi-tion. The one hitherto employed consisted in maintaining that the unexpected turn of the war had completely changed the character of the enterprise, and that the Note of Merle must therefore be regarded as superseding all previous engagements.[4]

[1] Lucchesini to the cabinet ministry, April 22, their reply of the 28th, B. A., *loc. cit.*

[2] Report to the King, May 6, B. A., *R.* 96, 147 *H* (printed in part in Appendix XVI, 3).

[3] E. g., in the ministerial rescript to Caesar of March 8:

" Je suis bien loin de méconnoitre, que dans l'origine les indemnités des deux Cours devoient aller de pair, les miennes devant se trouver en Pologne et celles de la Cour Impériale par le troc de la Bavière ou par d'autres avantages équivalens."

[4] This is the view advanced in the rescript to Caesar cited above.

" Mais depuis que des evenemens imprévus . . . nous ont obligés de songer à

Lucchesini chose, however, the other and bolder course of denying the previous engagements altogether. In his note to Reuss he declared that the principle of parity had never been explicitly recognized by Prussia as applicable to the indemnity question; he asserted — on the strength of Haugwitz's (quite untrue) state-ment — that that envoy had always maintained, from the very beginning of his ministry at Vienna, that if Austria had any rights to an indemnity, they could not be placed in the same category with those of Prussia. The King was merely *partie accessoire et auxiliaire* in the war, and was sacrificing himself for a cause not his own — for the defence of Austria; the Imperial Court ought to be grateful that he did not claim an indemnity at its expense, but was willing to seek one instead in Poland. If that Court had any titles of its own to an indemnity, they could apply only to France, and could never be admitted to be of the same nature or validity as, or to stand in any connection with, the rights of Prussia.[1]

This note was the counterpart of Thugut's recent pronounce-ment. The Austrians denied the concessions relating to Poland which Haugwitz claimed to have received; the Prussians denied the agreements and principles on which the alliance and the con-cert against France had been based. The issue was thus squarely drawn. The two Powers proclaimed quite contradictory views regarding their past and their present relations. While each held to its own standpoint, a reconciliation was impossible.

There were two important omissions in the note of May 15. In the first place, no further attempt was made to persuade Austria to accede to the Partition Treaty. The explanation is obvious. With the probable exception of the King, none of the Prussians really desired the Emperor's accession. They had no fear that Austria would be able to prevent the execution of the partition, and they reflected, as Haugwitz wrote to Lucchesini: " If the

une continuation de la guerre de France, qui ne regarde directement et principale-ment que la Cour de Vienne, j'ai du stipuler les conditions sous lesquelles *seules* je pouvois me preter à y concourir ultérieurement, . . . et il ne dépend plus de la Cour de Vienne . . . de vouloir en revenir à celui [the principle] d'une reciprocité rigoureuse, à laquelle depuis ce changement de circonstances, elle n'a certainement plus les mêmes titres."

[1] This note is printed in Vivenot, iii, pp. 63-67.

Court of Vienna had hastened to accede unconditionally to the Convention of St. Petersburg, the evil would be done, and we could no longer set limits to our coöperation in the war. . . ."
"This refusal, if we are fortunate enough to see it maintained, delivers us from this very onerous obligation . . . and we shall no longer be bound to Austria except by the provisional promise of coöperation contained in the Note of Merle, which relates only to the present campaign."

Secondly, Lucchesini's note contained only the vaguest assurances with respect to the Austrian indemnities. Thugut's demand had put the Prussians in a really embarrassing position, for it was impossible for them to press very far the distinction which they had set up between their own and the Emperor's rights to an acquisition, without also invalidating the claims of Russia. Hence Lucchesini had not dared to deny Austria an indemnity altogether, but had announced that his master would consult with the Empress on that "important subject," and that 'he flattered himself that his past conduct and his known principles would be a sufficient guarantee of his zeal to contribute to the satisfaction and the advantages of his ally.' In reality, the Prussian ministry hoped that 'the Court of Russia, driven out of patience by the tergiversations of Austria, would end by excluding that Power entirely from the advantages stipulated in its favor by the St. Petersburg Convention, this consequence flowing naturally from the [Emperor's] refusal to accede.' Still, as they wrote to Goltz, 'it was not yet time to touch that chord.' They preferred to let the Empress speak first on so delicate a matter.[2]

At the first signs of opposition from Austria, the partitioning Powers had exchanged assurances that they would not allow themselves to be deterred thereby in the execution of their plans.[3] The Russians were irritated enough at the — to them — unexpected stand taken by the Court of Vienna, but they were by no means alarmed. Having just cemented their relations with England by the convention signed March 25 (regarding a com-

[1] Letters of May 5 and 10, B. A., *R*. 92, *L. N*. 31.
[2] Rescript to Goltz of May 6, B. A., *R*. XI, *Russland*, 135.
[3] Rescript to Goltz of April 5, Goltz's report of April 16, B. A., *loc. cit.*

mon policy, if not a common action, against France), they found Austria powerless to harm and themselves in position to wait tranquilly until the Emperor 'returned to reason.'[1] Hence Cobenzl's complaints and recriminations fell upon deaf ears. The Russian ministers always replied that they had consented to a negotiation with Prussia only at the request of Austria; that Goltz had repeatedly assured them that the Court of Vienna had acquiesced in all his master's demands; that once the affair had been begun, it had been necessary to put it through without delay; that it was impossible now to retrace their steps or to alter the terms of the treaty; that Kamieniec and the territory adjacent to Galicia could not be restored to Poland, because the inhabitants had already taken the oath of allegiance to the Empress. Cobenzl soon convinced himself that it would be utterly impossible to secure any changes in the Convention.

On the other hand, the Russian ministers showed a real eagerness to obtain the Emperor's accession to the treaty, and were lavish with assurances that their sovereign would do anything in her power to provide an equal indemnity for Austria. " Flanders, Lorraine, Alsace," said Markov, " offer you a vast field for acquisitions, and you can exchange what is not to your convenience. The King of Prussia offers to consent to the secularization of some bishoprics in Germany; take advantage of that. England will not be at all averse to the acquisitions that you may wish to make at the expense of France; perhaps it will not think the same of the Bavarian Exchange; but by acceding to the Convention you will give us the right to speak firmly and to oblige Prussia to do likewise." The Empress' generosity with other people's property knew but one limit: when Cobenzl suggested that Austria might finally have to take her share in Poland, he was told with some emotion that there would then be nothing left of that unfortunate kingdom, and that it was the more uncalled for to put it out of existence because if the King of Prussia were once " bound," nothing could prevent Austria from finding her indemnity elsewhere. In general, the Russian ministers were over-

[1] Markov to S. R. Vorontsov, April 29/May 10, Арх. Воp., xiv, pp. 253 f.; Ostermann to Razumovski, May 16/27, M. A., Австрія, III, 54.

flowing with friendship, professed to love the Austrian alliance as much as they hated the Prussian one, and dwelt with unction on the approach of the day when the one ' natural system ' could be established — a combination of the Imperial Courts and England.[1] Their final answer was given, however, only after they had learned what reply Prussia had made to Austria. Then through the dispatches to Razumovski of May 16/27 the Empress announced her firm resolution to uphold the St. Petersburg Convention, and pressed vigorously for the Emperor's accession — for the quite disinterested reason that otherwise the Court of Vienna could not obtain from that of Berlin the least favor or even strict justice. In truth, the Empress desired Austria's accession for the same reason for which the Prussians would have preferred to avoid it: without it the Court of Berlin would have an excuse for withdrawing from the war. In the same dispatches the cabinet of St. Petersburg invited the Emperor to choose whatever he found to his convenience in France, with assurances that Russia would not oppose. If the Court of Vienna could be induced to base its hopes on conquests in the West, the war would last all the longer.

Through Alopeus the Prussians were informed of as much of this reply as they were fitted to receive, with the reassuring explanation that the Austrians were never likely to make conquests extensive enough to cause alarm.[2] The Berlin ministry were delighted that the Empress had not revived the Exchange project; they resolved to follow her cue and to divert the Court of Vienna to the path of conquest, with the mental reservation that they would make it their affair to set just limits to the Emperor's aspiring course. Hence they now delivered through Caesar their promised reply on the subject of the indemnities of Austria.[3] This reply was couched in a much friendlier tone than the note of May 15. It expressed the King's continued readiness to do whatever he could to procure for Austria a just indemnity, either by

---

[1] For the above: Cobenzl's reports of April 30, May 10, and 31, V. A., *Russland, Berichte*, 1793.

[2] Ostermann to Alopeus, May 16/27, M. A., Пруссія, III, 31.

[3] The cabinet ministry to Lucchesini, June 11, B. A., *R*. 92, *L. N.* 14; rescript to Caesar, June 10, B. A., *R*. 1, 174.

his good offices in the matter of the Bavarian Exchange, or, if the
Court of Vienna, considering the difficulties in the way of that
project, preferred to take its indemnities at the expense of France,
by coöperation to that end with all means that lay within his
power. His Majesty desired only to be informed of the precise
extent of the acquisitions that the Emperor desired to make in
that quarter, and he flattered himself that these acquisitions
could be secured by the end of the present campaign. This last
phrase was intended at Berlin, and understood at Vienna, as an
intimation that the King did not bind himself to continue the war
beyond the close of that year. This was, indeed, the crux of
Prussia's position. Chiefly out of regard for the Empress,
Frederick William's ministers had not dared refuse Austria an
indemnity altogether; they were mortally anxious to divert the
ambitions of that Power away from Bavaria; but they were no
less anxious that the satisfaction of those ambitions should not
involve a third campaign. How to wriggle out of this embarrassing situation was the problem that occupied the cabinet of Berlin
for the next three months.

England had meanwhile replied to Thugut's overtures in a
manner at least half satisfactory. It was true that the British
ministers could offer little consolation with regard to Poland; for
while expressing freely their regret and disgust at the proceedings
of Russia and Prussia, they admitted that the French war rendered it absolutely impossible for them to oppose the Partition.
On the other hand, however, they showed the utmost willingness
to assist Austria to secure a handsome acquisition at the expense
of France, and they left no doubt that they were eager for a close
alliance with the Imperial Court.[1]

By the middle of June Thugut's first action might be regarded
as at an end. He had failed to secure any modification of the
Partition Treaty, or any postponement of its execution. There
was nothing left to be done except to accede on as favorable conditions as could be obtained with regard to the Austrian indemnities. As far as these indemnities were concerned, the replies from

[1] Stadion's report of May 10, and those of his successor, Starhemberg, of May 24
and 31, V. A., *England, Berichte*, 1793.

Russia and England were not unpromising; and Prussia, although denying the principle of ' parity,' still professed her eagerness to know and to concur in the Emperor's desires. On the basis of these results, Thugut's policy entered upon a new phase.

IV

Since inaugurating his first action, the Director-General had been busy planning a revision of the map of Europe. The more clearly he saw the impossibility of impeding the execution of the Partition Treaty, the more passionately he clung to the idea of procuring for Austria acquisitions that would fully counterbalance those of her allies. Aggrandizement in one quarter or another became his first and last thought, and he turned his eyes in every direction restlessly seeking whom or what he might devour. The problem was not a little difficult.

The Bavarian Exchange being now definitely abandoned as impracticable, the most obvious expedient was conquests from France — a course which all the allied Powers combined to urge upon Austria. Count Mercy had drawn up a plan for an acquisition which even he admitted was " gigantic ": it was to include all the land as far as the Meuse and the Somme, i. e., Alsace, Lorraine, Artois, and half of Picardy. Thugut was not embarrassed by the extent of this claim, but he was none too sanguine about the ease of making conquests in this quarter; and he felt the need of providing himself with an alternative, in case France made too great difficulties about being partitioned.[1] The last resort of disappointed conquest-hunters was Poland; and although Russia and Prussia had shown a vexatious tendency to regard that realm as their exclusive field of exploitation, Thugut had not entirely lost hope of picking up something there. At any rate, Poland was not the only neighboring republic where Jacobins could be discovered at pleasure: one might, perhaps, find a few in Venice. The spoliation of that decayed state seemed both easy and

---

[1] Mercy to Starhemberg, May 31, and to Thugut, June 15, Starhemberg, to Thugut July 12, Thugut to Starhemberg, August 13, Thürheim, *Briefe des Grafen Mercy*, pp. 86 ff. and Vivenot, iii, pp. 112 f., 145–148, 184 f.

profitable.[1]   The new program was, then, to retain Belgium; to
carve out an enormous acquisition in France, if possible; and if
this failed, to fall back on Polish or Venetian territories.   The
realization of this plan was, of course, far in the future, but Thugut aimed to provide for all eventualities immediately by securing
guarantees from the allied Powers.   In the case of Russia and
Prussia, the obvious procedure was to demand such guarantees in
return for Austria's accession to the Partition Treaty.

On the Court of Berlin the Director-General placed, indeed, no
great reliance.   He had begun his ministry with a strong aversion
to Prussia, and everything that had happened since convinced
him that that Power was aiming at the ruin of the House of
Austria.[2]   On receiving Lucchesini's declaration of May 15, he
wrote to the Emperor that if there could have been any doubts
before, this note would have sufficed to reveal the hateful purposes
of Prussia in the fullest light.[3]   He found it a document " truly
remarkable in the history of diplomacy " for " the absurdity of its
principles " and " the alteration of facts in a manner not only
fabulous but incredible "; and its tone was as provoking as its
substance.   As it was not a moment, however, for beginning a
guerre de plume, he decided to leave the Prussians to their own
guilty consciences; and he found that their overtures of June
were only the result of their uncomfortable reflections.   Even
these overtures, although " less revolting " than the first declaration, were far from satisfactory, since they upheld in passing " the
palpable incongruities " of the note of May 15, and because their
tone was anything but frank and loyal.[4]   As long as Prussia
refused to admit the sacred principle of ' parity,' Austria would
arrange her indemnities with the other Powers alone.   These
indemnities could, indeed, scarcely be secured without Frederick
William's coöperation, but Thugut held it dangerous to enlighten
the King in advance about his plans of conquest.   Any project

---

[1] Thugut to Colloredo, June 4, 1794: "Adieu au secret [as to " nos vues sur
Vénise "], qui *depuis un an* a été conservé avec tant de soins! " Vivenot, *Vertrauliche Briefe*, i, p. 107 (the italics are mine).

[2] Cf. his letters to Colloredo of May 4 and 11, *ibid.*, i, pp. 15 f.

[3] *Vortrag* of May 23, V. A.

[4] Thugut to L. Cobenzl, June 30, Vivenot, iii, p. 125.

tending to a considerable aggrandizement of Austria would arouse the Prussian jealousy to the highest pitch, and the Court of Berlin would hasten to raise up difficulties of every sort. Hence the Director-General desired to conceal his game, while binding the King to the war through the intervention of England and Russia, and so leading him on blindly to serve the interests of Austria. It would be best of all, he thought, if the realization of the Prussian acquisitions in Poland could in some way be postponed and made conditional on the vigorous prosecution of the war; for once those acquisitions were finally secured, the King would have no motive and no desire for continuing his exertions in France. Among Thugut's various miscalculations none was more persistent and disastrous than this idea that the true way to render Frederick William active in the coalition was to raise up obstacles in his path in Poland.

It was upon Russia that the Director-General chiefly relied for bridling "the Prussian malevolence" and assuring the indemnities of Austria. Since the middle of May — that is, since learning that England would not oppose the Partition, and since receiving Lucchesini's note—he had begun to show Razumovski all the old-time confidence, to expatiate on his orthodox faith in the alliance of the Imperial Courts, and to sigh for the coming of the Russian courier. On June 10 the ambassador presented Ostermann's dispatch; Thugut professed himself greatly pleased; and the reconciliation was all the more effusive for the recent estrangement. When Razumovski demanded, however, that the Emperor should at once accede to the Convention of St. Petersburg, Thugut replied that there would be no difficulty about that, but that his sovereign must make his accession dependent on more precise and reassuring stipulations regarding his indemnities. The ambassador observed that the real way to captivate the Empress would be to accede unconditionally; after that her generosity and solicitude would know no bounds.[1] But Thugut was not to be paid with such coin. He determined to test the generosity of the Court of St. Petersburg by a few concrete propositions.

---

[1] The above from Razumovski's report of June 6/17, M. A., Австрія, III, 55.

By a dispatch of June 16 he ordered Cobenzl to demand that the Empress should guarantee Austria the right to take her indemnity in Poland, in case it should prove impossible to make any considerable conquests from France. He would not contest the objection already raised by the Russian ministers that in this case the Polish state would be completely annihilated; but he found that since the other Powers had appropriated such enormous acquisitions, the total partition of the Republic would involve no great inconveniences; besides, since the balance of power absolutely required that Austria should gain aggrandizement somewhere, all other considerations must give way before this "peremptory reason." This was, of course, only a guarantee for the future — for an extreme case; but in the meantime the Emperor desired to profit by the present circumstances to improve his Galician frontier by annexing a small strip of territory along the boundary. If the Empress acquiesced, as was to be expected, Thugut suggested that Sievers should receive instructions, so that the Republic might conclude the necessary treaty with Austria at the same time as those with Russia and Prussia. Finally, Cobenzl was informed that in eight or ten days full powers would be sent to him to accede in the Emperor's name to the St. Petersburg Convention.[1]

Thugut's object in making this move was probably to gain a foothold in Poland at once, before the conclusion of the impending treaties at Grodno, which might contain guarantees of the integrity of the remaining possessions of the Republic. If Austria could establish herself immediately on Polish soil, she could rely on future events to furnish opportunities for extending her acquisitions.

As might have been foreseen, however, the demand ran counter to one of the Empress' firmest principles. Regarding Poland as her peculiar property, she had felt her late concession to Prussia as a personal loss, and she was not inclined to make a new sacrifice of this sort in favor of the Court of Vienna. Cobenzl therefore encountered objections and subterfuges of all kinds. He was told that it was impossible to change the whole indemnity plan every

---

[1] Dispatch of June 16, printed in Vivenot, iii, pp. 113–117.

week; that if Austria had demanded a share in Poland in the beginning, she might have obtained it, but that it was too late now; that if the Empress had dreamed that it would be a question of destroying the Republic entirely, she would never have consented to a partition. Above all, the Russian ministers took refuge behind Prussia, affirming that Frederick William would be so enraged by this new demand of Austria that he would probably withdraw at once from the coalition, if he did not proceed to worse extremities. The most that Cobenzl could obtain was a promise that the question should be left in suspense until the arrival of the courier who was to bring the proposals of Austria in full and instructions regarding the promised accession to the Partition Treaty.[1]

That courier was long in coming. The fact was that Thugut was now absorbed in watching the proceedings at Grodno, where the Polish Diet was making an unexpectedly vigorous resistance to the demands of the partitioning Powers. That resistance revived his hope that it might still be possible to delay the consummation of the Partition, and thus ' bind ' the King of Prussia to the common cause. One means of doing so immediately presented itself, when the hard-pressed Diet dispatched a special envoy, Wojna, to Vienna with an urgent appeal for the good offices of the Imperial Court as a guarantor of the integrity of Poland. Thugut refused, however, to allow himself to be seduced into an open intervention. He did not conceal from Wojna his aversion to the Partition, and his conviction that Austrian interests were seriously menaced by it; but he always ended by pointing to the French war, which rendered action against the allied Powers impossible. Wojna's audience with the Emperor was equally fruitless; he received plenty of sympathy, and nothing more.[2] The Austrians were well advised in committing themselves no further with the Poles, for Wojna's first dispatches were read in the open Diet — to the lively chagrin of the Russian and Prussian envoys.[3] But while it is true that Thugut did not

---

[1] Cobenzl's reports of July 2 and 5, Vivenot, iii, pp. 128 ff., 133–137.

[2] Wojna's reports of July 10, 17, August 7, 10, М. А., Архивъ Царства Польскаго. Сношенія съ Австріею, Сб. 8.

[3] De Caché's report of July 28, V. A., *Polen, Berichte*, 1793.

encourage the Diet in its resistance — as he has been accused of doing by Prussian ministers at that time and by Prussian historians since — he did endeavor to delay the Partition by a new action at St. Petersburg.

At the moment when the crisis at Grodno was at its height, the Director-General sent off an appeal to Catherine to postpone the settlement of Polish affairs until after the peace with France. The Poles, he said, would not give in without coercion; and the use of violent means would place the allied Powers in the most unenviable light before the world, it might lead Turkey to declare war, and it might, especially, so arouse public opinion in England that the British government would be compelled to retire from the coalition. And he hinted that this was, indeed, a spectacle to shock all Europe, to see those Courts which were waging war on France for the cause of sovereigns and the sanctity of treaties, simultaneously overwhelming an unfortunate monarch with indignities and tearing up their own solemn guarantees. Some delay in so delicate a matter would involve no real inconveniences, for the Russians would remain complete masters of Poland; it could be cloaked with pretexts that would only lend added glory to the Empress; and it would be the only means of ensuring Prussia's active coöperation in the war.[1]

By the time this dispatch reached St. Petersburg, the Diet had given in to all the demands of Russia, but still remained obdurate towards those of Frederick William. Cobenzl therefore applied himself solely to the task of holding up the conclusion of the Prussian treaty. Ostermann objected, warning him with great good sense that the Court of Vienna deceived itself in imagining that it could ensure the coöperation of the Prussians by keeping them on tenterhooks regarding their acquisition; the King would presently lose patience and proceed to violent measures, which Russia could not prevent and which would furnish him with an excuse for withdrawing from the French war altogether. Markov, however, assumed quite the opposite tone, and assured Cobenzl that the Empress wished nothing better than to delay

---

[1] Thugut to L. Cobenzl, July 12, Vivenot, iii, pp. 141–145.

the Prussian treaty.[1] And this time the deed followed the word. Although it was not entirely a result of Austria's insinuations, Thugut had the satisfaction of seeing the Prussian treaty held up for more than a month, until there came the inevitable catastrophe which Ostermann had prophesied and which Thugut ought to have foreseen. This catastrophe was closely connected with another negotiation to which it is now necessary to turn.

V

Determined as he was to settle all the great questions first of all with Russia, Thugut had long realized that it would be impossible to maintain a total silence towards the Court of Berlin. He therefore resolved to send an experienced diplomat, Count Lehrbach, to Frederick William's headquarters on a mission, the primary aims of which were simply to gain time, to 'amuse' the Prussians, and to sound them on the subject of conquests from France.[2] The instructions which Lehrbach received — after long delays — on the 3rd of August, were based on a rather complicated and perilous plan. Thugut had, since April, repeatedly promised the British government that the Emperor would abandon the Bavarian Exchange in return for guarantees from England of definite acquisitions in France. This promise he had carefully kept secret from the Prussians, for the very good reason that if they learned of it, they would hold themselves absolved from the engagement regarding the Exchange contained in the St. Petersburg Convention and, indeed, from every definite obligation to assist in procuring indemnities for Austria. Furthermore, Thugut was convinced of Prussia's mortal antipathy to the Exchange project, and he knew more or less of Lucchesini's intrigues with the princes of Zweibrücken. He believed that these intrigues had gone further than was really the case, and that the King had made definite

[1] Cobenzl's reports of July 30 and August 2, Vivenot, iii, pp. 156 ff., 160 f.

[2] The earliest mention I have found of Lehrbach's mission is in Thugut's letter to Colloredo of June 4 (Vivenot, *Vertrauliche Briefe*, i, p. 20). As to Thugut's aims in connection with this mission, see his dispatch to L. Cobenzl of June 30 (Vivenot, iii, pp. 125 ff.) and his letter to Colloredo of July 30 (Vivenot, *Vertrauliche Briefe*, i, pp. 25 f.).

promises to those princes contrary to the engagements of the Partition Treaty.[1] Hence he formed the plan of taking the Prussians by their weak side and pressing to know in what manner they intended to fulfil the obligations of the Convention; the King, unable or unwilling to discharge those obligations or to explain the reason why, would be caught in a trap, from which he would be glad to escape by undertaking the desired new engagements respecting Austrian acquisitions in France. The plan was not altogether badly conceived. It was, indeed, indispensable to begin on the basis of the previous negotiations and obligations; and Thugut's suppositions about the Prussian attitude towards the Exchange, although somewhat exaggerated, were in the main correct. As for the principle involved here, one may recall Hüffer's remark that anyone who has pledges from several parties for the same thing, may always release one party from the obligation without absolving another until he has secured a promise of equivalent advantages in return for his renunciation.[2] Thugut's great mistake, however, was that he did not sufficiently reckon with England.

Lehrbach was charged, then, to bring up Bavaria first of all, and thus to prepare the way for the Austrian project for conquests from France, or for an acquisition in Poland in case of necessity. If possible, he was to secure the King's promise to continue the war until the Court of Vienna's indemnities had been assured; but he was not authorized to make definite propositions regarding the extent of those acquisitions until he had received further orders. On the result of his negotiation, it was stated, the Emperor's accession to the Partition Treaty would depend.[3]

A refinement of subtlety, an entire lack of confidence, and the absence of any sincere intention of coming to a definite agreement were the outstanding features of these instructions. Thugut was only too fully persuaded that nothing good was to be expected from Prussia, that concessions were useless, and that confidence

---

[1] Thugut to L. Cobenzl, June 16, to Starhemberg, August 31 (P. S.), Vivenot, iii, pp. 113–117, 234 f.; Razumovski's report of June 22/July 3, M. A., Австрія, III, 55.

[2] Hüffer, *Oestreich und Preussen*, p. 35.

[3] These instructions are printed in Vivenot, iii, pp. 163–169.

would only be abused. A negotiation begun with such presuppositions had little prospect of success.

But even had Lehrbach come in the best of faith, it is scarcely possible that he could have effected an agreement. What decided the course-of events more, perhaps, than all the dissensions between the two allies, was the fact that the limited resources of the Prussian state rendered it infinitely difficult for the King to undertake a third campaign at his own expense. Since the spring this thought had haunted the minds of the Prussian ministers, and had formed the constant burden of their reports to their sovereign. To retire from the war if possible, but if not, to avoid continuing it without further ample indemnities, became their first and last thought. After much discussion they had come to the conclusion that since the territorial market was somewhat depleted, the compensation to be demanded for a third campaign must take the form of subsidies from England, Austria, and the Empire. As usual, the great element of uncertainty lay in the fitful moods of Frederick William himself, who, although decidedly cooled in his zeal for the war since he had got Great Poland into his possession, was still long subject to relapses of military ardor. Before the end of July, however, he had practically succumbed to the importunities of his advisers. A categorical declaration that the King could not consent to make a third campaign without further indemnities was henceforth reserved as the Prussian *pièce de résistance* for the negotiation with Lehrbach.[1]

This resolution about the continuation of the war decided the Prussian attitude towards the two closely related questions, the Austrian indemnities and the Emperor's accession to the Partition Treaty. In June the Court of Berlin would still have preferred to see Austria fasten her ambitions upon France. It was important to ward off the Bavarian Exchange, and at this time it seemed not impossible to make considerable conquests from

[1] Alvensleben and Haugwitz to Lucchesini, July 25, 28, and August 8, B. A., *R.* 92, *L. N.* 14. Frederick William's final assent to the program of his ministers seems to have been contained in a cabinet order of August 12, which I have been unable to find, but the sense of which appears from the report of Alvensleben and Haugwitz of August 19, B. A., *R.* 96, 147 *H.*

France in the course of this campaign. But the more the latter hope diminished, the less the Prussians were inclined to commit themselves to furthering the Emperor's ambitions in this direction. On the other hand, they did not yet see their way clear to avoid assisting Austria to secure acquisitions somewhere. They vacillated between repugnance to the Exchange and the dread of a third campaign. They were also frightened by the rumor that Austria and England were planning to transfer the Elector of Bavaria to Alsace-Lorraine. The situation was the more harrowing because the Court of Vienna maintained a profound silence about its projects. Rescue from these embarrassments came from an unexpected quarter.

On July 10 Lord Yarmouth arrived at the royal headquarters to conclude a convention relating to the war. He soon became confidential with Lucchesini, and began to make revelations about the secret negotiations between London and Vienna. By deftly drawing him out, Lucchesini learned that the Emperor had already promised England to renounce the Bavarian Exchange.[1] This was, indeed, *lux e tenebris*. The chance to utilize this renunciation could not be overlooked. The ministers at Berlin adjured Lucchesini to hold fast to the Exchange project in the approaching negotiation with Lehrbach. " It would be superfluous," they added, " to observe to Your Excellence why we insist on the exchange of the Netherlands. We must hold to it the more strictly because it is to be foreseen that England will persist in thwarting it. If the question were then raised of substituting [for it] a plan for conquests, this would be a new order of things, which would have nothing in common with the agreements decided upon between Prussia and Russia; and in consequence it would be necessary to begin the negotiation all over again, without prejudice to the indemnities that we have already secured in the past." [2] Thugut's previsions on this point were nothing if not accurate.

Lucchesini determined to seal the fate of the Exchange project once for all by still another stroke. As Lord Yarmouth had been

---

[1] Lucchesini to the cabinet ministry, July 14, B. A., *R.* 92, *L. N.* 14.

[2] Letter of August 8. Much the same strain in a letter of July 28, B. A., *R.* 92, *L. N.* 14.

instructed to draw Bavaria into the coalition, the clever Italian proposed to him that England should conclude with the Elector a subsidy treaty, which should contain a mutual guarantee of the present possessions of the contracting parties.[1] He also broached the same scheme to the Duke of Zweibrücken, who then went off to present it to his uncle, the Elector. Presently Lucchesini was able to report to his colleagues glorious news from Munich. " Everything has succeeded wonderfully in that quarter," he wrote; " now I shall see whether Lord Yarmouth is already provided with full powers in order to profit by the Elector's good dispositions. If he is, then all roads to the acquisition of Bavaria are barred to the House of Austria by England. It remains only to ask the opinion of Your Excellencies about the utility of concluding at present a formal alliance between the King [of Prussia] and the Duke of Zweibrücken." [2] Neither this alliance nor the Anglo-Bavarian treaty came into existence; but it must be confessed that Thugut's much-condemned duplicity pales before Lucchesini's sheer breach of faith. It was surely irony of the choicest sort to insist that the Emperor should accede to the St. Petersburg Convention and content himself with the promise of Prussia's good offices in favor of the Bavarian Exchange, when at the same time Prussia was secretly doing everything in her power to make the realization of that Exchange absolutely impossible.

It is true, indeed, that Frederick William's ministers had never really desired Austria's accession. They were seriously disquieted by Razumovski's renewed importunities on that subject in June, for they hardly ' dared flatter themselves that the Emperor would persist in his refusal.' [3] But these fears presently showed themselves groundless. As the moment of Lehrbach's arrival approached, the Prussian ministers began to meditate a new scheme. Lucchesini proposed that in case the Austrian diplomat brought only a conditional accession to the Convention, as was to be expected, they should at once declare that until the Court of Vienna saw fit to keep its engagements (i. e., to acquiesce *sans*

---

[1] Lucchesini to the cabinet ministry, July 17, B. A., *R.* 92, *L. N.* 14.

[2] Letter of September 6, B. A., *loc. cit.*

[3] The cabinet ministry to Lucchesini, June 21 and 22, B. A., *R.* 92, *L. N.* 14.

phrase in the Partition Treaty), the King could enter into no discussion of the Emperor's indemnities.[1] The ministers at Berlin thoroughly approved, and added the suggestion that if by the time of Lehrbach's arrival the treaty was not concluded at Grodno, the King might declare that in view of the resistance of the Poles he felt obliged to cease his operations on the Rhine in order to direct his attention towards securing his acquisitions in Poland. Such a threat seemed the more à propos because it might stop the (supposed) intrigues of the Court of Vienna at the Diet.[2] These ideas rapidly matured until at the moment Lehrbach appeared the Prussians had agreed on the following plan. If events went well at Grodno, the King was to declare that he no longer demanded the Emperor's accession to the Convention, and that he would take part in the next year's campaign only on condition of being assured of a sufficient indemnity. In the contrary case, they would add to the foregoing the declaration that the King was obliged to suspend action against France in order to attend to his interests in Poland arms in hand. This would be killing a great many birds with one stone. It would frustrate for good and all the danger of the Emperor's accession; it would throw the blame for everything upon Austria, who had delayed her adhesion until it could be of no further value; it would furnish the pretext for retiring, or threatening to retire, from the French war. One precaution, however, was still necessary. The ministers at Berlin recommended some delay in presenting the proposed declaration, in the hope of a favorable turn of affairs at the Diet. To reject the Emperor's accession before their treaty had been concluded at Grodno would be to expose themselves to the redoubled intrigues of Austria; and then there was always the danger of compromising themselves with the Empress.[3] Thus everything was prepared in advance to give Lehrbach's negotiation a striking finale. The Prussians had even less desire for a reconciliation and an amicable agreement than had the Austrians:

---

[1] Lucchesini to the cabinet ministry, July 19, B. A., R. 92, L. N. 14.

[2] Alvensleben and Haugwitz to Lucchesini, July 25, B. A., *loc. cit.*

[3] The cabinet ministry to the King, August 20 and 28, to Lucchesini, August 23, B. A., R. 96. 147 H, and R. 92, L. N. 14.

instead they were resolved to force on what was virtually the rupture of the alliance.

Lehrbach arrived at the royal headquarters on August 18, and three days later held his first conference with Lucchesini at the village of Edenkoben. He began with the declaration that the Emperor had always intended to accede to the Convention and stood ready to do so now with pleasure, but on condition that the King should agree to procure for him an indemnity fully equal to the Prussian one. After reviewing the history of the previous negotiations and establishing the principle of parity, he launched into a discussion of the various means of indemnifying Austria. He began with Bavaria, spoke of the antipathy of the members of the House of Zweibrücken to the Exchange, alluded to several indications that these princes supposed themselves to be backed up in their opposition by Prussia, and ended by declaring that unless the King could reassure the Emperor as to the efficacy of the means that he was willing to employ in this connection, the Exchange project must be abandoned. There would then remain no other course than that of seeking conquests from France, as the Court of Berlin had suggested by the dispatch to Caesar of June 10. Alsace and Lorraine seemed the most desirable acquisitions in this quarter. Lehrbach then demanded formally that the King should agree to continue the war until the Emperor was in actual possession of his indemnity.

Lucchesini replied that he would report everything to his sovereign, but that in the meantime he must observe how surprised the King would be that the Emperor had not yet seen fit to accede to the Convention of St. Petersburg, which formed the basis of Prussia's coöperation in the present campaign. Wishing to draw Lehrbach out, he then asked whether the Court of Vienna really foresaw no other obstacles in the way of the Exchange than those which had just been mentioned. Was there nothing to be feared from England ? Caught unprepared by this thrust, Lehrbach hesitated, and finally admitted that some opposition had been raised by the London cabinet, but said that he had not been ordered to speak of it. Lucchesini triumphantly retorted that it would have been unfair then to place at the King's charge the ill success of his good offices, and to compromise His Majesty un-necessarily with the other Powers. With this the conference ended.[1]

All things having fallen out as he had foreseen, Lucchesini found no reason for giving the Austrian a definite reply at once; instead he set out to protract matters until the long hoped-for news should arrive from Grodno. Meantime he amused Lehrbach with long-winded discussions on the origin and nature of the war — a subject which might be argued *in saecula saeculorum* without the slightest results; and he excused his delays on the ground of the necessity of communicating with Berlin and St. Petersburg. During this period of waiting he made a discovery which gave him a final assurance of victory. Lord Yarmouth, probably alarmed by the news that Lehrbach had brought up the subject of the Exchange, saw fit to inform the Prussian minister that in June a secret convention had been signed in London, by which the Emperor formally renounced alienating the Netherlands. It is quite certain that this convention existed only in Yarmouth's imagination, but this fact could hardly be known to Lucchesini. The latter's jubilation knew no bounds. " This transaction," he wrote to the ministers at Berlin, " destroys all the obligations which the Convention of Petersburg imposed on the King with regard to Austria's indemnities; and it serves as the key to Count Lehrbach's negotiation. They [the Austrians] would like to sub-stitute new engagements about conquests in France for those which English policy has forced them to sacrifice. . . . Your Excellencies will know better than I what use can be made of this renunciation at St. Petersburg." [2] Lehrbach thus saw his chief weapon struck from his hands, his whole game exposed, his plan of campaign confounded and upset. One may doubtless believe Lucchesini's statement that the Count was in despair.[3] For some weeks the negotiation was completely at a standstill. Then the turn of events at Grodno precipitated the dénouement.

---

[1] Lucchesini to the cabinet ministry, August 21, B. A., *R.* 92, *L. N.* 14; Lehr-bach's report of the same day, printed in Vivenot, iii, pp. 198 ff.

[2] Letter of August 26, B. A., *R.* 92, *L. N.* 14.

[3] Lucchesini to the cabinet ministry, August 31, B. A., *loc. cit.*

On September 2 the Diet had finally agreed to the Prussian treaty, but only under conditions that strained the patience of Frederick William's advisers to the breaking-point. On the 14th the ministers at Berlin sent in a report urging the most prompt and vigorous measures: they implored the King to suspend all operations against France and return with 50,000 men (out of the 80,000 on the Rhine) to enforce his claims on Poland in person. This step was to be accompanied by a fulminating declaration that should show the Austrians that Prussia was through with them, that she was free of all obligations to them, that for whatever might happen they had no one to blame but themselves. On receiving these proposals, Lucchesini and Manstein set to work energetically to win over the King. It was no easy task, for Frederick William's sensibilities revolted at the thought of deserting the good cause of all sovereigns to seek sorry laurels in chastising a few helpless Poles. He consented, then retracted, and finally gave in under conditions: he would first of all fulfil his promise to turn the lines of Weissenburg; he would then go to the east, but he would leave almost his entire army on the Rhine, under the command of the Duke of Brunswick; and he would return later, if possible, to finish the campaign with a few brilliant feats of arms.[1] Even this concession might not, perhaps, have been wrung from him, had he not been incensed against the Court of Vienna by disputes with General Wurmser, by Lehrbach's 'insidious negotiation,' by the supposed complicity of Austria in the resistance of the Poles, and by the suspicion that the Imperial Courts had secretly agreed to hold up his treaty at Grodno.[2]

Lucchesini was now ready to unchain the lightning. On September 22 he presented to Lehrbach and Reuss a written declaration which announced: (1) that as the King was obliged to go in person to assure his acquisition in Poland, he would leave

[1] Lucchesini to the cabinet ministry, September 19, 22, and 26, B. A., *R.* 92, *L. N.* 14.

[2] Cf. Sybel, *op. cit.*, iii, pp. 433 ff. There is not the slightest evidence that the Austrians had done anything directly to stir up the Poles to resistance; though this is not to deny that the known antipathy of the Imperial Court to the Partition may have encouraged the opposition at Grodno. The Prussians were not far wrong, however, in their suspicions regarding Thugut's intrigues at St. Petersburg.

to the Emperor the care of attending to his own indemnities in France; (2) that, respecting the motives which had hitherto prevented the Court of Vienna from acceding to the St. Petersburg Convention, the King would no longer insist on that formality; (3) that his duty, to his subjects and the need of husbanding the last resources of his Monarchy forbade His Majesty's continuing the war another year, unless the allied Powers provided him with the means of doing so.[1] This declaration brought Lehrbach's mission to a close. It ended the long negotiation between the German Powers on the indemnity question. It terminated the discussion between them with regard to the Emperor's accession to the Partition Treaty. It dealt what was practically the *coup de grâce* to the Austro-Prussian alliance.

VI

In spite of the disastrous outcome of Lehrbach's negotiation, Thugut continued to treat of the Emperor's adhesion to the St. Petersburg Convention with Russia — though henceforth with Russia alone. The wider grew the breach with Frederick William, the more ardently the Austrian minister threw himself into the pursuit of Catherine's wonder-working graces. Time did not count with Thugut: though it took ages, he would end by presenting his sovereign with an acquisition in some quarter that would conform in every respect to the sacrosanct principle of 'perfect parity.' Into the details of this long negotiation it is impossible to enter here.

The failure of his attempt during the summer to secure the Empress' consent to an Austrian acquisition in Poland had for a time embarrassed Thugut. For some months St. Petersburg was studiously silent. In the autumn, however, especially after Frederick William's pronunciamiento, the reconcilation between the Imperial Courts proceeded steadily. By December Thugut was at last ready to declare himself with all precision at St. Petersburg. The Court of Berlin having rejected Austria's accession — a fact over which he was not particularly grieved — he announced that the Emperor desired to accede to the Partition

---

[1] This declaration is printed in Vivenot, iii, pp. 290–295.

Treaty in such a manner that his adhesion would apply to Russia alone. In return for this Thugut demanded the Empress' guarantee for that acquisition in France which Mercy had suggested — namely, the territory as far as the Meuse and the Somme; and in case these conquests could not be effected, a similar guarantee for an indemnity to be taken at the expense of Venice. All claims for a share in Poland were, in deference to the Empress, at last abandoned.[1]

These propositions were sufficiently to Catherine's taste. Markov repeatedly assured Cobenzl that, excluding Poland, the remains of which she desired to keep intact, there was no plan of aggrandizement that Austria might form of which the Empress would not approve. Encouraged by this reply, Thugut proceeded to draft the letters in which — as was usual in treaties between Austria and Russia — the two sovereigns were to embody their agreement.[2] His proposals were about to be formally accepted at St. Petersburg, the ministers were putting the final touches upon the bargain, when the face of things was suddenly changed by the outbreak of the revolution in Poland. The Russians again felt the need of Prussian coöperation; a new partition was soon in prospect; both sides recognized that retroactive arrangements about a now ancient treaty were inappropriate.

The course of the negotiation henceforth belongs to the history of the Third Partition. This time Austria was the preferred suitor. Behind the back of Prussia, the Imperial Courts concluded the secret convention of January 3, 1795, which settled the new partition. By the third article the Emperor acceded to the Second Partition Treaty, but only in so far as it concerned the Court of St. Petersburg. The acquisition secured for Austria, though somewhat larger than that reserved for Prussia, was not sufficient to make up for the defeat of 1793. Nevertheless, the long litigation over the Second Partition Treaty had ended in what may be considered a triumph, though hardly a justification, of Thugut's policy.

---

[1] Thugut to L. Cobenzl, December 18, 1793, Vivenot, *Thugut und sein politisches System*, pp. 382–392.

[2] Thugut to L. Cobenzl, February 27, 1794, *ibid.*, pp. 399–403.

CHAPTER XIX

THE ATTITUDE OF ENGLAND AND FRANCE TOWARD THE PARTITION

I

" THIS, at least, you cannot deny," wrote one of the Russian ministers to a friend on the eve of the Second Partition, "that the moment at which we are making this acquisition is the most opportune that can be imagined, for no one is able to offer opposition; everyone has his hands full." [1] And in fact, Russia and Prussia could never have found a situation more extraordinarily favorable than that of 1793 for perpetrating a great act of international rapine without hindrance from the other Powers. If Austria, bound by her past guilty bargains and by the exigencies of war, was helpless to avert or delay the Partition, England and France were even less in a position to do so.

Pitt had formerly displayed a lively concern for the defence of the weaker states against the great predatory monarchies; he had shown a particular interest in Poland; he had once been willing to risk a war with Russia over so comparatively trifling a question as that of Oczakow and its district. But his experiences in 1791 had taught him that the British public was not prepared to support so active, far-sighted, and altruistic a policy. Henceforth he avoided every enterprise that might lead to war, unless the vital interests of England were directly and palpably at stake. Henceforth he seems to have abandoned the hope of saving Poland. For a year and a half after ' the Russian armament,' he pursued a policy of strict non-intervention in Continental and especially in Polish affairs.

It was true that during the early part of 1792 the London cabinet discreetly warned Prussia of the danger of allowing the

[1] Zavadovski to S. R. Vorontsov, January 27/February 7, 1793, Apx. Bop., xii, pp. 77 f. (here erroneously dated 1792).

Empress to regain her old ' influence ' in Poland. But as these counsels passed unheeded, when the crisis came in the summer of that year, Pitt refused to take any action on behalf of Poland. All appeals from Warsaw were met with the excuse that, in view of the attitude adopted by Prussia, the Maritime Powers alone could not intervene, " at least not without a much greater exertion and expense than the importance to their separate interests could possibly justify." [1] Nor was Pitt moved from his course by the widespread sympathy which the Polish struggle for independence excited in England. The Lord Mayor of London started what was intended to be a national subscription to assist Poland against ' the infamous oppression of Russia.' [2] The Whig newspapers were full of tirades against their former ally, the Empress, and the whole ' nefarious association of monarchs ' to which Poland was falling a victim. Fox and his friends now bitterly confessed how mistaken had been their attitude the year before: if Oczakow had not been abandoned, Catherine would have had neither the power nor the inclination to attempt what she was now doing.[3] In short, such was the storm of indignation that the Russian ambassador reported that if Poland had been nearer to England, the nation would have forced the government to intervene.[4]

In view of Pitt's complete passivity on this occasion, in the face of this popular outcry and at a time when his hands were free, it may well be doubted whether he would later on have done anything effective to prevent the Partition, even had he not become entangled in the conflict with France. At all events, it was only towards the end of November that he learned through indirect channels of the indemnity plans of the Eastern Powers; and in that same month Dumouriez's conquest of Belgium suddenly produced that acute tension in Anglo-French relations which led to the outbreak of the war three months later. Repug-

[1] Lord Auckland to Sir Morton Eden, August 14, 1792, *Auckland Journal*, ii, p. 432. Instructions to Col. Gardiner at Warsaw, August 4, cited by Rose, *Pitt and the Great War*, p. 54.

[2] Apx. Bop., ix, pp. 249, 253 f.; *Parliamentary History*, xxx, col. 171.

[3] Burges to Auckland, July 31, 1792, *Auckland Journal*, ii, pp. 423 f.

[4] Report of S. R. Vorontsov, June 10/21, Apx. Bop., ix, p. 241.

nant as the schemes of the allies might be — and most English-men would doubtless have concurred in Sir Morton Eden's dictum that " such iniquitous projects, in so awful a moment, seem to bid defiance to God and to man," [1] — nevertheless, when it became a question either of saving Belgium and Holland from the French or of attempting to rescue far-off Poland, the choice of the British government could hardly be doubtful. Already in November, Pitt began to seek a rapprochement with the Eastern Powers, and to solicit from them a frank explanation of their aims and ideas with regard to the struggle with France.

In response to this invitation, on January 12, 1793, the Austrian and Prussian ministers at London for the first time officially informed Lord Grenville of the Polish-Bavarian indemnity project. Though not entirely unexpected, the announcement was vexa-tious and unwelcome in the extreme. Grenville made a brave show of virtuous indignation over the impending partition of Poland. ' The King,' he said, ' would never be a party to any concert or plan, one part of which was the gaining a compensa-tion for the expenses of the war from a neutral and unoffending nation.' [2] According to the Austrian ambassador, he even went so far as to declare that the project was " screamingly unjust," and that "England could never consent to it, much less contrib-ute to its execution." [3] This protest was repeated soon after-ward by Sir James Murray, who was then at the King of Prussia's headquarters on a diplomatic mission, with the additional warning that in case the Partition were actually carried out, the British government would feel obliged to issue a public declara-tion that it had had nothing to do with this measure and highly disapproved of it. [4] At St. Petersburg the English envoy Whit-worth, acting on his own initiative and without committing his Court, endeavored for some weeks to avert or at least to postpone the Partition. [5] But these few diplomatic steps practically make up the sum of British effort on behalf of Poland.

---

[1] *Dropmore Papers*, ii, p. 341.　　　　[2] Lecky, *op. cit.*, vi, p. 91.

[3] Stadion's report of January 25, V. A., *England, Berichte*, 1793.

[4] Lucchesini to the King, January 28, 1793, B. A., *R. 92, L. N.* 12.

[5] See his reports of January 25, 27, 29, and February 12, in Herrmann, *Ergänz-ungsband*, pp. 359–364.

Pitt does not appear to have thought seriously at any time of going further than harmless remonstrances. And even these remonstrances soon became singularly mild. As early as January 20, Murray was ordered to declare that England had no intention of interfering by force in the Polish affair or of hindering the execution of the Partition.[1] About the same time Grenville assured the Prussian envoy that the British government would maintain a complete silence and an entirely passive attitude with regard to the dismemberment of Poland; and such a line of conduct, the Berlin ministry declared, was " all that we require from England." [2] If Pitt had thus renounced the idea of intervention in the East even before the French declaration of war reached London (February 8), after that event there could be absolutely no thought of such an action. Henceforth the British cabinet insisted on ignoring everything that happened in Poland. How little it allowed moral scruples to interfere with its political friendships was shown by the fact that at the moment when the Partition was about to be proclaimed to the world, the treaty signed at London on March 25 announced the restoration of the old close liaison between England and Russia.[3]

It has, indeed, been asserted by a distinguished historian that

[1] Salomon, *Das politische System des jüngeren Pitt*, p. 78.

[2] Schulenburg and Alvensleben to Lucchesini, February 4, commenting on Jacobi's report from London of January 22, B. A., R. 92, L. N. 14.

[3] No credence can be given to Sybel's statement that about the middle of February, 1793, Catherine wrote an autograph letter to S. R. Vorontsov, her ambassador in London, authorizing him to declare that if England found means to hinder the Partition of Poland, she would have no objections, since she had been forced into this measure by Prussia (*op. cit.*, iii, p. 202). This astonishing tale rests only upon gossip retailed by Hogguer, the Dutch minister at St. Petersburg; it finds no corroboration in Vorontsov's voluminous published correspondence (which includes many letters written to him by the Empress); and it is in itself highly improbable.

Sybel's dictum, " Der Streich, welcher den Nacken Ludwigs XVI bedrohte, war zugleich auch der tödliche Schlag für das nationale Dasein Polens " (*op. cit.*, iii, p. 196) seems to me misleading, like most historical epigrams. Apart from the question whether the death of Louis XVI had any essential part in bringing on the war between England and France, it may well be doubted whether even without that war Pitt would have acted effectively to save Poland. In 1793, as in the preceding summer, he would probably have found that an isolated intervention would have involved more danger and expense than English interests in Poland would justify.

at one moment Pitt offered Austria his consent to the Exchange, if she would make peace with France under his mediation and then unite with England in opposing the Partition of Poland.[1] In reality, however, his policy seems to have tended in quite the opposite direction. The Bavarian Exchange might be morally less reprehensible than the Partition, but it was, from the standpoint of British interests, by far the more objectionable of the two projects. Hence, while the London cabinet refused from the outset to do anything effective to hinder the Partition, it evinced an ever more and more pronounced opposition to the Belgian-Bavarian plan. Unable to contest the latter project openly in the beginning, at a time when the three Eastern Powers seemed to be united in support of it, England soon found her opportunity when the Emperor fell out with his two allies. Then the British government, taking advantage of Austria's new dependence upon its assistance, succeeded, as has already been seen, in frustrating the Exchange project entirely. But on the other hand, all Thugut's efforts to induce England to oppose the Partition were fruitless. The Austrians were told that the British government abhorred the conduct of Prussia and Russia, but saw no possibility of opposing their plans at a time when it needed their coöperation for the war with France.[2] The moment for protesting against the Partition was past, Grenville declared, and the only thing to be done was to take care that such abuses should not be renewed in the future.[3] A little later, in the midst of the crisis at Grodno, when the Polish Diet was sending out agonizing appeals to the world for aid, a British diplomat was assuring the Prussians that if his government had at one time shown some inclination to protest against the Partition, that was due simply to reasons of domestic politics; and that he was authorized to declare that England no longer took any interest in Poland, and had no intention of embroiling itself with Prussia and Russia on

---

[1] Sybel, *op. cit.*, iii, p. 195. Salomon denies that any traces of such an offer are to be found in the English records (*op. cit.*, p. 76), and I have met with none in the Austrian diplomatic correspondence.

[2] Stadion's report of May 10, V. A., *England, Berichte*, 1793.

[3] Starhemberg (Stadion's successor) to Thugut, May 24, Vivenot, iii, pp. 77 ff.

account of the port of Dantzic and a few Polish articles of mer-
chandise.[1]

Under such circumstances, it mattered little that the decimated
Whig opposition in Parliament indulged in virulent invectives
against the partitioning Powers—those "plunderers," "robbers,"
"murderers," whose hands were "reeking with the blood of
Poland"—branded Frederick William's conduct towards the
Republic as "the most flagrant instance of profligate perfidy
that had ever disgraced the annals of mankind"; denounced the
Partition as "one of the foulest crimes and blackest treacheries of
despotism"; and accused the government of being an accomplice
in "spreading the gloom of tyranny over the Continent."[2] Pitt
in general replied that he had never hesitated to express his dis-
approval of the treatment Poland had suffered; but that ' the
question was whether they should allow one act of injustice to
deprive them of the assistance of the Eastern Powers in resisting
a system of intolerable injustice, not merely existing in France,
but attempted to be introduced in every other country.'[3]   Other
speakers for the government furbished up the well-worn argument that when your own house was on fire, you could not afford
to go to the assistance of your neighbor; "while we lament the
misfortunes of Poland," said Jenkinson, "let us look to ourselves"; and Burke, the one-time eulogist of the Constitution of
the Third of May, had now discovered that, in respect to England,
"Poland might be, in fact, considered as a country *in the moon*."[4]
Such was the pitiable ending of the Federative System.

---

[1] Lord Beauchamp's declaration to Lucchesini on July 11, 1793: "Que si le
Ministère Anglois s'étoit cru obligé, au commencement de l'hyver passé de montrer
des dispositions à protester contre nos acquisitions en Pologne, ç'avoit été une
mesure de politique interne qu'il a abandonné toute suite [*sic*] après que notre
partage a été définitivement arrêté entre les cours intéressées, et qu'il étoit autorisé
à assurer qu'on ne songeoit plus à la Pologne et qu'on se garderoit bien de se brouil-
ler avec la Prusse et la Russie pour le port de Danzig et quelques denrées de Pologne," Lucchesini to the ministers at Berlin, July 11, B. A., *R. 92*, *L. N. 14*.

[2] *Parliamentary History*, xxx, coll. 1108, 1468, 1471, 1477 f., 1485.

[3] This from his speech of March 6, 1794, *ibid.*, xxx, col. 1485.

[4] *Ibid.*, xxx, coll. 1476 and 1009. The italics are mine.

II

A classic tradition, going back at least to Richelieu and Mazarin, ranged Poland, along with Sweden and Turkey, in the group of states, whose protection and preservation were an essential interest of France. It was true that during the last decades of the Bourbon Monarchy, after the Austrian alliance had dislocated French policy in Eastern Europe, this tradition had been very much neglected, if not entirely abandoned; but the memory of the old system was still strong both in France and in Poland, especially among those Revolutionary statesmen who had been bred on the doctrines of Favier and in the hatred of the ' monstrous ' alliance of 1756. And nothing might seem more natural than a return to the classic tradition at a time when France was grappling with a coalition of which Russia and Prussia were members: according to all time-honored precedents, it must then be the aim of French diplomacy to create a diversion in the East by bringing the Turks and Swedes into the field and by succoring hard-pressed Poland. The idea of attempting such a diversion was so obvious that it was taken up with more or less energy by all those who came to the helm at Paris during the first year of the Revolutionary War. Upon the success of these attempts Poland's one real chance of deliverance from without depended. France was, indeed, the one great Power which had neither the need nor the wish to court the good graces of Catherine; the one great Power whose situation not only allowed but seemed to require active intervention on behalf of Poland. The old fixed principles of French foreign policy, the new maxims about championing the cause of oppressed peoples against usurping despots, the exigencies of a war in which the enemies of Poland were also the enemies of France, combined to suggest vigorous opposition to the Second Partition.

Nevertheless, France did nothing effective to save Poland. For this there were many reasons. The failure was not due merely to the tremendous difficulties and dangers that beset the Revolutionary government at home; nor to the instability, the inexperience, or the doctrinairism of those who successively held power at Paris; nor to the remoteness of Poland; nor to the undeniable lack of sympathy with which many Jacobins regarded the ' aristocratic ' and too conservative reformers of the Third of May.[1] One of the most potent factors in the situation was the predilection of the disciples of Favier for Prussia. The idea of detaching Frederick William from Austria and of securing a separate peace, perhaps even an offensive alliance, with him, haunted the minds of French statesmen, generals, and publicists. But reconciliation with Prussia and action on behalf of Poland were two incompatible policies. If Frederick William showed any signs of reciprocating the advances made to him, his would-be allies at Paris were not likely to scrutinize too closely the ' crimes of despotism ' in the East. Prussia was, indeed, the pivot around which the European political system revolved. Just as the fear of losing Frederick William's aid precluded Austria and England from actively opposing the Partition, so the hope of inducing the King to desert the coalition tempted France to acquiesce in that unholy transaction. This inhibitory regard for Prussia crops out continually in the calculations of French diplomacy in 1792 and 1793, strangely intermingled with plans of a rather different character, in which the deliverance of Poland occasionally figures.

At the beginning of the Revolutionary War, it was the favorite project of the dominant Girondist party and of Dumouriez, then Foreign Minister, to win the alliance of Prussia, and, if possible, of England. Failing in this, they fell back on the classic idea of forming a coalition which should include Sweden, Poland, and Turkey. Before anything had been effected towards this end, however, Poland succumbed before the Russian invasion, while the proposed mission of Sémonville to Constantinople came to nothing, because the Porte, yielding to the vehement remonstrances of the three Eastern Powers, refused to receive the ambassador.[2] The only part of Dumouriez's program that bore fruit was the diplomatic campaign begun at Stockholm.

---

[1] As to the indifference or downright contempt felt by a large part of the French public for Poland, see Askenazy, " Upadek Polski a Francya," in *Biblioteka Warszawska*, 1913, i, pp. 16 f.

[2] August 20, 1792. Cf. Sorel, *op. cit.*, ii, pp. 455 f.; Grosjean, " La Mission de Sémonville à Constantinople," in *La Révolution Française*, xii (1887).

There the new French envoy, Verninac, enjoyed the experience, unique in the annals of Revolutionary diplomacy at that time, of finding a court which not only tolerated but welcomed his advances. The foreign policy of Sweden had, indeed, undergone a sort of revolution within a few months after the death of Gustavus III (March 29, 1792). The new Regent, the Duke of Södermanland, was determined to free himself from the alliance with Russia formed by the late King, which he regarded as a galling and dangerous pact of servitude. For this purpose he needed the support of some foreign Power, both as a guarantee against future Russian aggressions, and in order to obtain subsidies that would enable him to dispense with those that Catherine had hitherto paid. Hence during the summer of 1792, while Russo-Swedish relations grew steadily worse, the secret discussions conducted with Verninac progressed so rapidly that by September it was agreed that a formal negotiation for a defensive alliance should be opened at Paris. The French envoy then went home to pave the way for this negotiation, while Baron de Staël-Holstein, the Swedish plenipotentiary, was to follow in good season.

At this moment French foreign policy was very near to losing its bearings altogether, as a result of the astonishing victories of the republican arms during the autumn. Dazzled and blinded by success, the Girondists were now talking of nothing less than a general war on kings, the deliverance of all nations from their ' tyrants,' a universal revolution. Swept along by the reigning enthusiasm, the Convention passed the famous decrees of November 19 and December 15,[1] by which it declared that it would ' accord fraternity and aid to all peoples who should wish to recover their freedom,' and laid down a set of rules for the establishment of liberty and equality in all the lands to which the armies of France might penetrate. Such sonorous resolutions were fitted to arouse the hopes of oppressed nations like the Poles; but they were a reckless and extravagant challenge to all monarchical Europe, widening the breach between France and her enemies and rendering difficult an agreement even with the well-disposed monarchies. At any rate, Lebrun, who had suc-

---

[1] *Moniteur* (réimpression), xiv, pp. 517, 755 f.

ceeded Dumouriez as Minister of Foreign Affairs and who was far from sharing the Utopian illusions of the Girondists, quietly went on with the old plan of seeking friends and building up a counter-coalition in Eastern Europe.

From November to March, the liberation of Poland seems to have been an integral part of Lebrun's political program. The cardinal feature of his plans was an offensive and defensive alliance between France and Turkey, to which Sweden, Poland, and perhaps Prussia, might be admitted. If the Turks could be induced to declare war on the Imperial Courts and to invade the Crimea, the Empress would be obliged to evacuate Poland; the Poles would then fly to arms against their ancient oppressors, while the Swedes were to deliver an attack in the Baltic and in Finland. If the King of Prussia insisted on remaining in the ' despotic ' coalition and carrying out his iniquitous designs on Poland, he might be brought to reason and forced to surrender his usurpations by a French invasion of Westphalia, combined with a Swedish attack on Pomerania. To increase the Empress' embarrassments, Lebrun hoped to provoke a revolt of the Cossacks and Tartars, and even to find a hardy soul " to repeat Puga-čhev's adventure." [1] And at times he talked of supplementing all these measures by sending French fleets to the Black Sea and the Baltic.[2] It was a comprehensive program, quite in the style of the cabinets of the old régime, closely resembling Pitt's plans of 1791 or the projects of French diplomacy during the War of the Polish Succession; it could hardly have appeared chimerical at that time, in view of the amazing military successes of the last few months; and it was infinitely more practical than the contemporary schemes of the Gironde for revolutionizing the universe.

Lebrun's activity reached its height about the end of February and the beginning of March. At that time a new envoy,

---

[1] I. e., to set up as a pretender to the Russian throne and to start a servile insurrection.

[2] For the above, see Lebrun's instructions to Sémonville, probably drawn up in November, 1792, Grosjean, *op. cit.*, p. 896; the instructions given to Descorches in January, 1793, Sorel, *L'Europe et la Révolution française*, iii, pp. 302 ff.; Lebrun to Parendier, February 28, and to Descorches, March 4, *ibid.*, pp. 305 ff.

Descorches, was en route for Constantinople charged to persuade the Turks to draw the sword immediately. Baron de Staël had at last reached Paris (February 25), eager to put through the alliance with Sweden, and fearful only that Dumouriez's victories would render the French indifferent to such connections.[1] Through his agent Parendier, Lebrun had for some time been in touch with the leading Polish Patriots, the ' men of the Third of May,' who gathered at Leipsic; he knew of their plans for a national uprising, encouraged them, and promised them money.[2] At the end of January, Kościuszko had come to Paris to negotiate for French support in a new struggle for Polish independence. He was authorized by the leaders of his party to give assurance that in case the Patriots regained control in Poland, they would abolish royalty, episcopacy, aristocracy, and serfdom, and establish liberty and equality according to the most approved Parisian standards. These promises are significant as showing, not indeed that the conservative reformers of the Third of May were turning into Jacobins, but that they had taken at their face value the recent decrees of the Convention and that they were ready to accept the principles laid down on the 15th of December in order to secure the aid of the triumphant Republic. What Kościuszko chiefly desired was the landing of a French army in the Crimea, which in conjunction with the Turks should assist in the liberation of his country; after this had been accomplished he promised that Poland would unite with France, Sweden, and the Porte in the final struggle against the league of crowned despots.[3] Kościuszko had several conferences with Lebrun, and he also met such prominent personages as Brissot, Vergniaud, Barère, Hérault, and Robespierre.[4] " The French Republic is actively occupied," Lebrun wrote to Parendier on February 28, " with the great measures that may release this interesting nation [Poland] from the odious yoke that oppresses it. . . . Courage, energy, and perseverance, and Poland will be saved." [5]

---

[1] Boethius, "Gustav IV Adolfs förmyndareregering och den Franska Revolutionen," in *Historisk Tidskrift*, xviii, pp. 182 ff.   [2] Sorel, *op. cit.*, iii, p. 305.

[3] On the aims of Kościuszko's mission, cf. Askenazy, "Upadek Polski a Francya," in *Biblioteka Warszawska*, 1913, i, pp. 20 ff.

[4] *Ibid.*, p. 23.   [5] Sorel, *op. cit.*, iii, p. 305.

All these hopes and plans, however, depended primarily upon the continued success of the French arms, and in March a series of terrible reverses began: the failure of the invasion of Holland, the defeat at Neerwinden (March 18), the complete loss of Belgium, the treason of Dumouriez (April 5), the invasion of France from all sides, and the outbreak of civil war at home. This sudden and bewildering change in the situation necessarily produced momentous changes in policy. In the first Committee of Public Safety (appointed April 6), in which Danton was the leading spirit, the tendency was to abandon that system of cosmopolitan idealism, armed propaganda, and universal revolution, by which the Girondists had so aroused the fears of sovereigns and the hopes of peoples, and instead to fall back on a policy based exclusively upon the practical needs and the material interests of France. While determined to prosecute the war with all the vigor necessary to defend the independence and integrity of the Republic, the new government desired to make peace if possible, and at least to diminish the number of its enemies; and for that purpose it was ready to adapt itself to the methods and usages of the older Europe, without allowing Revolutionary principles to stand too much in the way.[1]

Danton and his associates no longer thought seriously of doing anything to liberate Poland. To undertake the defence of that country would mean prolonging the war indefinitely, while the French people obviously wanted peace. Such an attempt might ruin France without saving Poland. Besides, the impending Partition would not be without its advantages for France, since it would almost certainly arouse jealousies among the three Eastern Powers and might greatly facilitate peace between France and some of them. Under the new government the idea of a separate peace and an alliance with Prussia had become the cardinal aim of French policy, and there was no surer way to conciliate Frederick William than to assent to his designs on Poland. It is highly probable that in the secret conferences held

[1] Cf. the admirable characterizations of the foreign policy of the first Committee of Public Safety in Sorel, *op. cit.*, iii, pp. 380 ff.; Aulard, " La Diplomatie du premier Comité de Salut Public," in his *Études et leçons sur la Révolution française, 3ᵉ série.*

about this time with the Prussians, verbal assurances were given that France would not oppose the Partition.[1] At any rate, it seems clear that from the outset the Committee of Public Safety was ready, in case of a formal negotiation with Prussia, to offer, not indeed an open approval, but a tacit recognition of the Partition, and to make capital out of its acquiescence in what it was unable to prevent.[2] Thus France prepared to abandon Poland just at the moment when Russia and Prussia announced to the world the new Partition.

The rest of Lebrun's plans did not long survive the disasters of the spring. When Descorches, after protracted delays, reached Constantinople (June 7), he found that the Turks had lost all stomach for war, and that nothing could tempt them out of a timorous neutrality.[3] With Sweden matters did for a time progress more favorably. On May 17 Lebrun signed the treaty of defensive alliance which he had agreed upon with Baron de Staël, and which the latter then sent home for the approval of his government. Although the Regent was fearful of the consequences of the adventure and by no means inclined to plunge into the general war if he could avoid it, still he was so badly in need of funds and his relations with the Empress had reached so acute a state of tension that he would probably have consented to ratify the treaty, providing a few slight alterations were made in it. But meanwhile Danton and Lebrun had fallen, and the new Committee of Public Safety, appointed July 10 (the second or 'great' one), had no real desire for the Swedish alliance. According to the ideas of Robespierre, who was now the real head of the government, the proposed treaty was dangerous because it might involve France in wars in which she had no concern; whereas once liberty had been consolidated and the Republic recognized,

[1] Aulard, *op. cit.*, p. 205.

[2] The best expressions of the new French attitude towards Poland are to be found in the instructions to Descorches of April 20 (in Sorel, *op. cit.*, iii, pp. 396 ff.) and the 'plan de pacification,' drawn up in the Ministry of Foreign Affairs, probably early in May (cf. Sorel, iii, pp. 394 ff., and Aulard, *op. cit.*, pp. 205 f.).

[3] Zinkeisen's very inaccurate account of Descorches' negotiation contains the statement that the French envoy actually succeeded in concluding a secret treaty of alliance with the Porte (*Gesch. d. osmanischen Reiches*, vi, pp. 872 ff.). The true history of the affair is to be found in Aulard, *op. cit.*, pp. 229–240.

the latter ought never again to draw the sword except to defend itself and other peoples who wished to shake off the yoke of ' tyrants.' Through the fault of France and not of Sweden — and for such doctrinaire reasons — the project of alliance was presently dropped [1] (September). And with it disappeared, at least for the time being, all hope of forming that 'League of the North,' that ' anti-despotic coalition,' which was the one combination that might have done something in 1793 to check the designs of Catherine and Frederick William and to succor prostrate Poland.

Under the second Committee of Public Safety France virtually renounced having a diplomacy or a foreign policy, save that pursued with the sword. If Robespierre desired any foreign connection, it was only one with the Swiss Cantons.[2] Switzerland was said to be a respectable Republic: Poland was not, at least according to Jacobin standards.

[1] By far the best account of this much-misunderstood subject, and especially of the causes for the failure of the Swedish alliance project, is to be found in Boethius, *op. cit.* (which alone is based upon both the French and the Swedish Archives). Cf. also René Pétiet, *Gustave IV Adolphe et la Révolution française*, pp. 51 f.

[2] Sorel, *op. cit.*, iii, p. 436.

CHAPTER XX

The Diet of Grodno and the Consummation of the Partition

I

If no resistance to the Partition was to be expected from foreign Powers, Poland itself was quite without the means of self-defence. No nation threatened with ruin was ever caught in a more helpless and prostrate condition. One hundred thousand of the Empress' troops occupied the entire country, save those western palatinates where the Prussians had marched in and taken possession. Warsaw, the hotbed of ' Jacobinism ' (i. e., patriotic feeling), was heavily garrisoned with Russians and encircled by armed camps. The Confederation of Targowica had done whatever it could to render the national army useless by splitting it up into small detachments, and scattering them about the country in such a way that each detachment was surrounded by superior Russian forces; and the Polish troops had also been deliberately deprived of cannon and ammunition.[1] The best men of the nation, the leaders of the Constitutional party, were in exile. Whatever government existed was in the hands of a rapacious, blind, and cowardly crew, equally despised by the Power whose interests they served, and by the nation upon which they had brought such disasters. When the Partition was announced, the original leaders of Targowica hastened to desert the sinking ship; and those who remained behind at the head of the Confederation were, with few exceptions, only those who had no scruples about exploiting their country's ruin for their private gain, and who were willing to render whatever services the Russian ambassador might require.

In order that no kind of misfortune might be lacking, the political crisis was accompanied by an economic one. The nation was

---

[1] Korzon, *Wewnętrzne dzieje*, v, p. 279.

suffering terribly from the exactions and depredations of the Russian troops, and still more perhaps from the lawless operations of the Targowician brigands, under whom no man's rights or property were safe, and who practised what even a Russian ambassador described as "a truly Asiatic despotism."[1] The crowning blow came in February, 1793, with the failure of almost all the leading banks, which ruined a host of capitalists, reduced the richest families to penury, and completed the economic prostration of the country.[2]

With calamities of all sorts following thick and fast upon each other, it is not strange that while the announcement of the impending Partition aroused vehement indignation and protests, it also produced general consternation and despair. Armed resistance seemed out of the question; the Republic was obviously doomed. Many people were chiefly anxious to end the tragedy as soon as possible by quiet submission to the inevitable; and some regretted that the Powers had not decided to partition the country entirely, and thus spare the moribund state the agonies of a lingering death.[3] It was true that the idea of a national uprising and a final struggle for independence was already fermenting in the minds of the émigrés in Saxony and in certain military and other patriotic circles in Poland.[4] But these projects had assumed no definite form, nothing was yet ready, at the time when Catherine set out to finish her work by extorting the consent of the Republic to its own dismemberment.

The management of this disagreeable business had been entrusted to Baron Sievers, the new Russian ambassador, who arrived in Warsaw in February, 1793; and perhaps the Empress could not have made a happier selection. Sievers was a benevolent, elderly, old-fashioned gentleman, with a dash of sentimentality, pleasant and tactful manners, a perpetual smile, and a

[1] Blum, *Sievers Denkwürdigkeiten*, iii, p. 264.

[2] Cf. Korzon, *op. cit.*, ii, pp. 159 ff.; Ogiński, *Mémoires*, i, pp. 235 ff.

[3] Kraszewski, *Polska w czasie trzech rozbiorów*, iii, 283; Костомаровъ, Послѣдніе годы Рѣчи-Посполитой, ii, p. 276; Ogiński, *op. cit.*, pp. 233 ff.; Buchholtz's reports of March 14, May 5 and 8, 1793, B. A., R. 9, 27, 1; de Caché's reports of January 23 and February 9, V. A., *Polen, Berichte*, 1793.

[4] Korzon, *op. cit.*, ii, p. 176, v, p. 276; Korzon, *Kościuszko*, pp. 266 ff.

face that bespoke only candor and simplicity. Behind this appearance of patriarchal bonhomie there lay a clear, cool head, an inflexible will, an independent and self-reliant judgment, and the readiness to use all means that would serve his purpose. At bottom he seems to have felt not a little disgust at his sordid task, pity for the King whose friend and companion he had been forty years before, and sympathy for the nation which he had been sent to coerce and terrorize. He would have liked to avoid violent measures as much as possible; to ameliorate conditions in Poland, as far as was compatible with Russian interests; to turn the country into a well-ordered Russian satrapy. Throughout his stormy embassy, in the midst of the brutalities which he was obliged to perform " with bleeding heart," as he wrote to his daughters, he consoled himself with the thought that he was doing a service to humanity by transferring millions of men to the benefi-cent sway of the Empress, and by restoring order, justice, and tranquillity in what was left of Poland.[1]

Sievers' first task was to induce the King to go to Grodno, where by the Empress' orders the coming Diet was to be held — far from the tumults and excitement of ' Jacobin ' Warsaw. Although the ambassador at that time professed to know nothing of an impending partition and declared that the chief aim of the Diet was to settle definitively the constitution of the Republic, still Stanislas could hardly be in doubt about what was in the wind. As usual, he sighed, wept, expostulated, ran the gamut of the tragic emotions. " Heavens," he cried out, " will they force me to sign my shame, to subscribe to a new partition ? Let them throw me into prison, let them send me to Siberia, but I will never sign ! "[2] But in spite of these heroics, the King had one — to him — irresistible motive for yielding, a motive that was to make him the pliant tool of Russia throughout the sad events that followed. His debts had now swollen to over thirty million florins;[3] owing to the general failure of the banks he could

---

[1] See, e. g., Blum, *Sievers*, iii, pp. 84, 94, 189, 241, 274.   [2] Blum, *op. cit.*, iii, p. 114.

[3] Sievers reported in February that the royal debts amounted to 30 millions (Blum, *op. cit.*, iii, p. 60); but that figure is almost certainly too low, since the detailed statement drawn up in September, 1793, and signed by the King, gave a total of 33,515,236 fl[s]. See Korzon, *Wewnętrzne dzieje*, iii, pp. 89–92.

borrow no more; the state treasury was almost empty; and he was absolutely at his wit's end to find money. In these straits he was ready to descend once more to the depths of baseness by becoming the pensioner of Russia — at such a moment. Hence in his interviews with Sievers patriotic outbursts alternated with pleas for the Empress' assistance in paying his debts, to which the ambassador replied that the subject of the royal debts might be taken up at the close of the Diet, i. e., after the King had done all that should be required of him. Hence, after a month of evasion and petty subterfuges, Stanislas consented to go to Grodno, and accepted twenty thousand florins from Sievers for the expenses of the journey.[1] And hence he told one of his confidants at this time that he would assuredly sign the partition treaty that was to be presented to him, although in public he continued to declare on every occasion that he would never, never sign.[2]

Having thus entrapped the King, Sievers hastened on ahead to Grodno, where on April 9 he and his Prussian colleague Buchholtz transmitted to the Generality of the Confederation the manifestoes of the allied Courts, announcing the Partition and demanding the convocation of a Diet to settle the affair ' amicably.' The Generality, whose leading members had known very well in advance what was coming, protested *pro forma;* but they had no more desire than the King to court the martyr's crown by indiscreet resistance to Russia. They hesitated, however, to assume the odium of summoning a Diet, the outcome of which was only too clearly to be foreseen. They assured Sievers that they were precluded from sending out the ' universals ' (i. e., the letters of convocation) by the oath of the Confederation, which bound them to defend the integrity of the Republic. Still, as they were men of resource, they found a way around this difficulty by an ingenious device. They restored the Permanent Council (an institution established by Russia in 1775, and abolished by the Four Years' Diet), and entrusted that body with the ignominious

---

[1] Blum, *op. cit.*, iii, pp. 114, 130 f., 186.
[2] Blum, iii, pp. 131 f.; Kraszewski, *op. cit.*, iii, p. 309.

duty in question.[1] The revived Council was packed with Sievers' creatures, whom even the Russian general Igelström described as " men of the worst character, gamblers, crooks, and brigands."[2] Its first act was to issue the universals for the, Diet, which the King was forced to sign — as a gratuitous humiliation — on the 3rd of May.

The elections were planned by the ambassador with great care, and with all the savoir faire which a long experience in Poland had taught the Russians. Sievers gathered around him at Grodno an unofficial committee of his Polish ' friends,' with whom he settled the details of the campaign, the list of the deputies to be elected, and the instructions to be given them. Electioneering agents, mostly Poles, were appointed to manage each Dietine; Russian troops were to be everywhere on hand to overawe opposition; and no means of persuasion, bribery, or coercion were to be neglected. The ever-complaisant Generality assisted as much as it could by issuing a couple of *sancita* (decrees), which excluded from voting or from being elected all those who had not ' renounced ' the Four Years' Diet; those who had participated in the establishment of the Constitution of the Third of May; those who had not joined the Confederation of Targowica; and those who, having joined that Confederation, had presumed to protest against any of its decisions.[3]

After such comprehensive preparations and in view of the utter depression of the nation, it is not surprising that the elections passed off quietly and smoothly. In 1773, at the time of the First Partition, patriots had tried to protest by preventing the election of deputies, and at least half of the Dietines had been ' exploded ';[4] but on this occasion most of the better citizens simply stayed away from assemblies where their presence could do no good, and where they were exposed to every kind of insult and violence. In many cases those from whom opposition was

---

[1] That this solution of the problem emanated from the Poles themselves (Bishop Kossakowski and others) and not from Sievers, appears from Buchholtz's report of April 11, B. A., *R.* 19, 27, 1.

[2] Blum, *op. cit.*, iii, p. 206.

[3] Blum, *op. cit.*, iii, p. 236.

[4] Over thirty Dietines (out of a total of about sixty), Kraszewski, *op. cit.*, i, p. 92.

feared, were driven away from the Dietines by the Russian troops or forcibly confined in their homes. In the assemblies thus effectually ' purified,' the crowds of poor *szlachta*, bought up at ten, twenty, or thirty florins a head, acclaimed without debate the deputies nominated by the Russian agents, and the instructions approved by the Russian ambassador, and then adjourned to the customary Gargantuan banquet, to drink the health of the Empress and the King amid the thunder of Russian cannon.[1]

Sievers was delighted with the outcome. Writing to congratulate the Empress on " the complete success of the Dietines," he assured her: " Never has a Diet cost so little as this one, and there never was one that did so much in fourteen days as I shall do, sick though I am. The one of 1772 lasted three years." [2]

Soon afterward the ambassador received two highly significant rescripts in which Catherine outlined her plans for the Diet. In accordance with the procedure followed at the First Partition, he was ordered to demand at the outset the appointment of a committee or ' delegation,' with full powers both to negotiate with the two allied Courts (with Russia first) on the basis of their declarations of April 9, and to conclude the required treaties of cession. In this negotiation the ambassador was directed to make common cause with his Prussian colleague.[3] But the extortion of the territories in question was only the first part of Catherine's program; the second half of it reveals the fact that her ambition was still unsatisfied, and that she was firmly determined to rivet her chains upon what was left of the unhappy Republic. For, as the rescript proceeds to suggest, Poland, in the condition to which it would be reduced by the Second Partition, could no longer exist as an independent state; the Empress would have

---

[1] For general accounts of the Dietines of 1793, see, Иловайскій, Сеймъ Гродненскій, pp. 59 ff.; Костомаровъ, *op. cit.*, ii, pp. 271 ff.; Blum, *op. cit.*, iii, pp. 232 ff.; Morawski, *Dzieje narodu polskiego*, v, pp. 352 f.; Kraszewski, *op. cit.*, iii, pp. 299 f.

Ilovaĭski gives an interesting description of the Dietine of Lublin and the instructions drawn up for the deputies of the palatinate of Troki; but for the most part we sadly lack detailed knowledge of the course of these last Dietines of the Republic.

[2] Letter to the Empress of May 21/June 1, 1793, Blum, *op. cit.*, iii, pp. 255 f.

[3] Rescript of May 24/June 4, M. A., Польша, III, 70.

been glad to annex the whole country, but felt unable to do so at that moment in view of the jealousy of the neighboring Powers; and she had, therefore, resolved to attain her essential aim by concluding with the Republic an alliance of so close and intimate a nature as to render the two nations henceforth one and inseparable. Sievers was instructed to arrange matters so that the proposal for this alliance should seem to come spontaneously from the Poles. He was also to take pains to secure for himself a decisive influence in the settlement of the Polish constitution, and in general it was made clear that however powerless and innocuous the Republic might have become, the Empress did not intend to allow it a shadow of liberty. But in these ulterior arrangements, the Court of Berlin was to have no voice whatever. Once the treaties of cession had been disposed of, Sievers and Buchholtz were to part company; the Prussians were to be given to understand that their rôle was played out, and they were henceforth to be excluded from all participation in Polish affairs. Luminously summing up her policy of that period in a single sentence, Catherine declared: " We must profit by the preoccupations of our neighbors in order to arrange all our affairs with the Republic on a solid and stable basis." [1]

Thus, according to the Empress' will, the coming Diet was doomed not only to cede away more than half of the national territory, but also to sign a bond of servitude, surrendering what remained of the Republic to the guardianship and the scarcely-disguised domination of Russia.

II

The Diet which met at Grodno on June 17, 1793, was the last and stormiest one in the history of the Republic. The terrible position in which this assembly was placed, the unparalleled acts of violence to which it was subjected, the eloquent and pathetic language in which it poured forth its sufferings to the world almost suffice to invest it with the dignity of tragedy; but when one considers the shameless venality shown by so many of its

---

[1] Rescript of May 26/June 6, M. A., Польша, III, 70 (printed in Appendix XVIII).

members, the contrast between their flaming speeches in public and their private bargains with the Russian ambassador, the frivolity and the passion for amusement that marked the social life at Grodno even at such a moment, one is tempted to regard the whole episode as only an unholy and disgraceful farce.

The great majority of the deputies had been chosen at the dictation of Russian agents and under circumstances that made it very difficult for honest men to be elected. The Austrian chargé d'affaires declared that most of them were " men without property or influence or decent reputations, who could be expected to render blind obedience and to look out only for their personal interests." [1] The public from the first derided them as 'hired land-ceders.' [2] The leaders of the assembly — the Hetman Kossakowski; his brother, the Bishop of Livonia; Pułaski and Zabiełło, the two Marshals of the Confederation; Bieliński, the Marshal of the Diet; Ożarowski and the rest—were the men who had managed the Dietines for Russia, and who throughout the Diet continued to draw the largest sums from the *caisse de séduction* maintained by the Russian and Prussian ministers in common. At least seventeen other deputies enjoyed regular pensions from the same source; while a still larger number of inconspicuous and impecunious members — how many it is difficult to say — appear to have sold themselves for modest sums at the time of their election, and to have received occasional gratuities later on. The ambassador furnished many of them with board, lodging, and carriages, and his own table was constantly thronged by crowds of hungry hirelings. In short, it may safely be asserted that from one half to two thirds of the members of this assembly were under financial obligations to the Powers whose demands it was their bounden duty and their loudly professed intention to resist. One will judge them less harshly, however, if one remembers that the King himself was foremost in setting an evil example; for it is certain that in the course of the Diet Stanislas accepted not less than thirty-five thousand ducats from the Russian ambassador.[3]

---

[1] De Caché's report of June 7, V. A., *Polen, Berichte*, 1793.

[2] De Caché's report of June 23 (" vermiethete Landabgeber "), V. A., *loc. cit.*

[3] On the corruption practised at the Grodno Diet and the preceding Dietines:

In view of these facts, it is all the more surprising that this assembly should have offered so violent and protracted a resistance to the demands of the partitioning Powers; a resistance that astonished Europe, confounded all the prophets, and forced Sievers to take, not two weeks, as he had originally expected, but three months, to put through his treaties. A partial explanation is doubtless to be found in the natural desire of the venal majority to save their faces before their own fellow-countrymen. In order to avoid the appearance of too gross collusion with the foreigners, it was necessary to make a brave show of resistance. Besides, even these men may not have been without some remnant of patriotism; and at least they possessed the national talent for oratory and the sense of what the dramatic proprieties demanded. If they were to consummate the dismemberment of Poland, they would do it in the grand manner: with floods of eloquence, with passionate protests, with sighs and tears, with all the appearances of yielding only to brute force, with appeals to the civilized world and to posterity.

It is also clear that Sievers' plans were often crossed by intrigues emanating, one might say, from those of his own household. Among all the Polish satellites of Russia, none were warmer in their professions of devotion than the Kossakowskis; and doubtless that powerful family was loyal enough as long as Russia allowed them to exercise the monstrous tyranny which they had set up in Lithuania in the name of the Confederation. But when Sievers, indignant at their proceedings, attempted to put a stop to them and also threatened to dissolve the Confederation, the Kossakowskis passed into secret but none the less active and insidious opposition to him. The family was not an enemy to be despised; for they controlled almost all the sixty deputies of Lithuania, and they had powerful Russian backers, notably General Igelström [1] at Warsaw and the favorite Zubov at St. Petersburg. Their great aim, apparently, was to effect the dis-

Blum, *op. cit.*, iii, pp. 102 f., 236 f., 252, 254 ff., iv, pp. 29–35; Buchholtz's reports of February 15, March 6, May 12, 15, 20, July 10, 14, 18, August 3, September 17, B. A., *R.* 9, 27, 1; Костомаровъ, *op. cit.*, ii, pp. 272 ff.; Иловайскій, *op. cit.*, pp. 59 ff.

[1] Commander-in-chief of the Empress' forces in Poland.

ruption of the Diet, in order that the Confederation of Targowica might remain the sole authority in the Republic, and that they themselves might continue to work their evil will in Lithuania. Apart from that, they seem to have tried to create as many difficulties as possible for Sievers, with the aid of their deputies and their Russian friends; and it may be noted in passing that at the close of the Diet, by a particularly subtle stratagem, they succeeded in bringing about his recall in disgrace.[1]

The most determined opposition, however, came from the small group of patriots who were known at Grodno as the party of 'the Zealots.' In spite of all the precautions and rigors employed at the Dietines, a few bold and incorruptible citizens had managed to get elected, chiefly in the palatinates of Mazovia and Płock, and had come to the Diet with the sole purpose of putting up a desperate resistance to the Partition. They numbered only about twenty-five, out of a total of one hundred and forty deputies; but they were to play a rôle quite disproportionate to their numbers. They can hardly have expected to be able to thwart the Partition, and they could offer no concrete plan for doing so; their one hope lay in delaying matters until some lucky accident, some change in the European situation, might intervene to save them. At any rate, they insisted on fighting to the last ditch; they indignantly repudiated the favorite argument of the majority that by consenting to the Partition the integrity and independence of what was left of Poland might at least be assured; their watchword was: 'If we must perish, let us perish with honor, not with shame.' Constantly in the forefront of the battle, inexhaustible in devices for delaying and obstructing, eloquent, indefatigable, and irrepressible, they succeeded in making endless trouble for Sievers and Buchholtz; they staved off the inevitable surrender far longer than anyone had anticipated; and they saved this Diet from complete ignominy by proving that there were still brave men and honest men in Poland.

The turbulent temper and the probable course of this assembly were sufficiently revealed by the opening sessions. First of all,

[1] On the relations between Sievers and the Kossakowski clique and Zubov, cf. Blum, *op. cit.*, iii, pp. 31 ff., 215 ff., 261 ff., 270, 290 ff., 358 ff., 444 ff.; iv, pp. 22, 24 ff., 28, 136.

the ambassador put through, without difficulty, the election of Stanislas Bieliński, a ruined gambler and a notorious hireling of Russia, as Marshal (i. e., president). Immediately afterward, however, the deputies fell to quarreling over the oath to be taken by the Marshal, and two days were spent in tumultuous and fruitless wrangling. It would seem that the Kossakowski party, the Zealots, and the King's friends united in provoking and prolonging this dispute in the hope of disrupting the assembly; for, according to custom, if a Diet were not constituted within three days after meeting, it was considered dissolved. Seeing through this intrigue, Sievers promptly intervened and arrested five of the disturbers. Thereupon the majority calmed down; the Marshal was allowed to take the oath, and the assembly was duly organized as a Confederated Diet (under the ' bond ' of the Confederation of Targowica), with the Senate and Chamber of Deputies sitting together and the operation of the Liberum Veto suspended.

The next day (June 20) Sievers and Buchholtz presented identical notes demanding the appointment of a delegation fully empowered to negotiate and conclude treaties with them on the basis of their declarations of April 9. After the reading of these notes before the Diet, the King arose and made the brave-sounding declaration: " I acceded to the General Confederation guaranteed by the Empress only because its Act assured me of the integrity and independence of the Republic. I cannot free myself from the obligations incurred by my adhesion to the Confederation, and I have resolved under no conditions to sign any treaty whatsoever which has for its aim to deprive the Republic of even the smallest part of its possessions. I hope that the members of the Diet, bound by the same oath, will follow my example." He proposed that the Estates reply to these notes in moderate language requesting that the two Courts should restore to the Republic the lands they had taken, as the Polish nation had given no excuse for their seizure.[1] Although probably no one imagined that the King would stand by the firm resolution thus announced — who could forget how often he had sworn to die for the Con-

---

[1] Костомаровъ, *op. cit.*, ii, p. 281.

stitution of the Third of May ? — still his speech was received with loud applause; the Diet appeared to be entirely a unit, and responses in accordance with his suggestions were sent to the two foreign ministers.

Sievers and Buchholtz at once reiterated their demand in more emphatic form. They had anticipated some initial ebullitions of Polish patriotism, but they were by no means prepared for the storm of violent and impassioned oratory that marked the sessions of the next three days (June 24–26). Unfortunately, it soon became apparent how illusory had been the semblance of unanimity at the outset. Although the Zealots demanded that the Diet should resolve never to consent to a partition or even to appoint a delegation to treat with the two Powers, although the King exhorted the deputies to arm themselves with manly courage, the out-and-out partisans of Russia were already beginning to urge the necessity of giving way in order to save what remained of the fatherland, and the Kossakowskis offered a compromise proposal, which was to negotiate with Russia but not at all with the Court of Berlin. This latter suggestion had much to commend it to the majority. If there was any feeling common to all Poles at that moment, it was bitter hatred towards the perfidious and perjured Frederick William. On the other hand, their sentiments towards Russia were moderated by the reflection that after all Catherine had had some grounds for complaint against them, and that her friendship and protection could best guarantee the Republic a tranquil existence in the future. The Kossakowskis and their partisans talked of establishing some kind of organic connection between Poland and Russia, like the union between Poland and Lithuania, apparently with the idea that by flattering the Empress with such projects they could induce her to renounce the thought of a partition. Or, in case it was necessary to satisfy her demands for territory, might it not be hoped that she would then turn round and protect the Republic against the demands of Prussia ? Acting upon such calculations, on June 26 the Diet voted, on the one hand to appeal to the foreign Powers to use their influence with the Courts of St. Petersburg and Berlin on behalf of Poland — an appeal which proved perfectly fruitless —

and on the other hand to appoint a deputation to negotiate with Russia and with Russia alone.

This attempt to separate the interests of the partitioning Powers and to play off one against the other placed Sievers in a rather embarrassing position. Though alarmed at the unforeseen course that the Diet was taking, convinced that the King was playing him false, and suspicious that the recent decision was only a trick intended to gain time and embroil the situation, still the ambassador could not fail to be gratified by the marked preference shown to his Court, and somewhat tempted by the professed desire of the Kossakowski party for a union with Russia. Reporting to the Empress his conversations with the Bishop of Livonia, he intimated that it would not be difficult to bring about the voluntary submission of Lithuania, or indeed of all Poland. Should he not at least attempt to buy from the Republic the overlordship over Courland ? From many indications it appears that both then and later he inclined to bolder and more ambitious projects than had originally been contemplated, and that he would have preferred not to be satisfied with taking merely the half of Poland when it would be so easy to take the whole of it.[1] Catherine, however, was not to be seduced into so radical and dangerous a change of system. She ordered her ambassador to hold to the plan of action originally prescribed; not to raise the question of the suzerainty of Courland now; to let the Lithuanians alone, and to prevent any premature and indiscreet movement in favor of a union.[2]

Meanwhile the Diet continued its dilatory tactics, amid frequent scenes of uproarious disorder and constant demonstrations of a wayward and refractory temper. The notes sent in by Sievers and Buchholtz on June 28, protesting against the attempt to separate the two Courts and demanding that the Deputation be authorized to treat with Prussia, remained without effect.

---

[1] Regarding Sievers' attitude towards the proposed union, cf. his letter to Zubov of April 17, and his reports to the Empress of June 23, 26, July 4, August 13, Blum, *op. cit.*, iii, pp. 186, 281 ff., 290, 337; as to Courland, his reports of May 14, 25, June 23, *ibid.*, iii, pp. 239 f., 281.

[2] Rescripts to Sievers of June 15/26 and June 23/July 4, M. A., Польша, III, 70. The latter rescript is printed in Appendix XVIII, 2.

Even the preparations for a negotiation with Russia advanced at only a snail's pace. The Diet could not be driven forward a step without continual resorts to coercion. Sievers began by sequestrating the King's revenues — a measure which promptly broke down what slight powers of resistance Stanislas possessed, and made him throughout the rest of the Diet the docile instrument of Russia. Later the ambassador temporarily arrested seven deputies of the opposition by way of making an example;[1] he deported two others from Grodno, heavily reinforced the Russian troops in and about the city, and sequestrated the estates of Count Tyszkiewicz; finally, in one fulminating note after the other he threatened the assembly and the country with the direst disasters, unless his demands were immediately satisfied. Even these severities generally resulted in extorting only half-concessions. The ambassador was unable to procure for the Deputation either the instructions or the full powers he desired, or to get it chosen by the method he preferred, or to fill it entirely with his creatures as he had planned. In fact, in appointing this committee (on July 11), the Poles still pretended that they were consenting to a negotiation, not about cessions of territory, but about a treaty of commerce and the 'perpetual alliance' which the Deputation was authorized to offer to the Empress.[2] At all events, Sievers was satisfied to have secured any deputation at all, and he intended to pay no attention to the limited powers or the futile instructions it might have received.

The 'negotiation' with this committee was a pure farce. At the first meeting (July 13), the ambassador presented the ready-

---

[1] It is characteristic of the diversity of statements in the historical works dealing with the Grodno Diet that the number of deputies arrested on July 2 is given as 5, 7, 9, 12, or 16 by different writers. In fixing the number at 7, I am following Buchholtz's report of July 4, B. A., *R.* 9, 27, 1.

[2] The original draft of the instruction to the Deputation had spoken of proposing to the Empress so close an alliance that " Poland and Russia should in future be considered as one indissoluble body." This draft probably emanated from the Kossakowskis. The Zealots had raised so strong an opposition to this 'incorporation' of Poland with Russia that in the final draft all suggestion of an organic connection between the two states had been abandoned. Possibly the Kossakowskis had also learned from St. Petersburg that the Empress did not approve of their projects for a union. Cf. Костомаровъ, *op. cit.*, ii, pp. 293 ff.

made draft of a treaty by which the Republic was to cede to the Empress the lands she demanded; he added that no changes or additions would be allowed, and begged the Deputation to report at once to the Diet. The Polish counter-proposals were scarcely honored with a moment's consideration.

On July 15 the Deputation reported to the Diet; the draft presented by Sievers was read, and also a note from the ambassador demanding that the Deputation be authorized to conclude the treaty at once as the only means of saving the country. The crisis had now arrived, and it was time for this assembly to show its mettle. That day and the following no decision was reached, but amid the general flood of patriotic declamation one deputy in the pay of Russia, Łobarzewski, had the temerity to present a motion in favor of yielding to the demands of the ambassador. Sievers, growing impatient, sent in a new note (on the 16th), threatening that if by the close of the next day the Diet had not granted the Deputation full powers to sign the treaty, he would regard it as a refusal to treat and as a hostile declaration; and the Russian troops would then do military execution on the estates of those members of the assembly who should be found opposing " the general will of honest people and of the nation." [1] The King, the Kossakowskis, and other dependents of Russia were warned that they would be held responsible for everything that might follow.

The 17th, then, was to be the decisive day. At the opening of the session, the King delivered a moving but rather ambiguous speech,[2] the general tendency of which was to counsel submission to the inevitable. But thereupon the Zealots broke loose, and for hours this handful of strong-lunged patriots over-awed a majority already determined to yield but still afraid to say so. One deputy, Gałęzowski, proposed replying to Sievers that the Polish nation calmly awaited the execution of his threats, as the Roman Senate awaited the Gauls.[3] Karski declared that if there were in the chamber anyone who would sign this treaty,

---

[1] This note is printed in Angeberg, *Recueil des Traités*, pp. 314 ff.
[2] The text in Angeberg, *op. cit.*, pp. 316 f.
[3] Костомаровъ, *op: cit.*, ii, p. 314.

he would be the first to set an example of how to deal with traitors.[1] Mikorski cried out, " Better for us to perish with honor than to crown ourselves with eternal infamy in the lying hope of saving the remainder of the country." [2] Kimbar reproached the King for all his past mistakes and adjured him to efface their memory by giving one immortal example of heroism now. " They threaten us with Siberia," he added. " Let us go to Siberia then! It will not be without charms for us; its deserts will be our Elysian Fields, for everything . . . will remind us of our virtue, our devotion to our country. . . . Yes, let them send us to Siberia. Sire, lead us thither! " [3] The Diet, quick to catch fire, joined in the cry, " Yes, to Siberia! To Siberia! "

As the assembly was reaching a dangerous pitch of exaltation and he himself had been personally attacked, the King spoke again, exerting all his undeniable eloquence to justify himself and to moderate the chamber. He praised the patriotism of those who feared neither prison nor desert nor death, but would such personal self-sacrifice save the country ? Since they could do nothing for those compatriots who had already passed under a foreign domination, their duty was to their remaining country-men whom they still might save. It would be folly to say to Russia: ' Destroy, enslave three and a half million more of Poles, whose representatives we are; we will it, because you have already made yourself master of four millions of our brothers.' He pictured the horrible state of the country in case the am-bassador were driven to fulfil his threats: devastation, famine, pestilence, and universal misery. The Diet had already done all that was possible to save the brothers wrenched away from them, and now it was necessary to renounce further resistance, which would not only be perfectly fruitless but would plunge what was left of the state into the most terrible disasters.[4]

The King's speech made an obvious impression upon the assem-bly. Taking advantage of this, the partisans of Russia came forward more boldly in favor of the Łobarzewski motion of the

---

[1] *Ibid.*   [2] Иловайскій, *op. cit.*, p. 110.
[3] This speech is printed in Angeberg, *op. cit.*, pp. 317 ff.; cf. Иловайскій, p. 111.
[4] This speech is printed in Angeberg, *op. cit.*, pp. 319–322.

preceding day. Bishop Kossakowski assured the Diet that their patriotic declarations alone would suffice to justify them in the eyes of Europe and of posterity; he advised signing the treaty, and added that by yielding to Russia, the Poles might hope that the Empress would protect them against the Court of Berlin.[1]

As midnight approached, the Marshal Bieliński declared that it had been sufficiently shown how indispensable it was to resort to the one means of saving the rest of the country. He directed the secretary to read the Łobarzewski motion, in spite of the desperate efforts of the Zealots to prevent it by cries and protests. The vote was taken, and with only twenty dissenting voices [2] it was resolved to authorize the Deputation to sign the treaty. By way of justification for this surrender, the instruction to the Deputation recited that since the members of the Diet found themselves under threat of violence, left only to their own resources, without any hope of outside aid, with but few troops and the treasury quite empty; as humanity forbade undertaking a war which Poland could not conduct, and the useless shedding of blood: therefore, it remained for them only to call upon a just God to witness their sufferings and their innocence, and to entrust the fate of the country to the magnanimous Catherine.[3]

Five days later, on July 22, the treaty was signed by Sievers and the Deputation. In return for the cession of the lands allotted to her by the St. Petersburg Convention of January 23, 1793, the Empress guaranteed the integrity of the remaining possessions of the Republic (excluding, however, by implication the lands claimed by Prussia); she bound herself not to oppose any changes in the form of government which the King and the present Diet should find it necessary to make, and — as a proof of her friendship! — offered to guarantee the revised constitution, if she were invited to do so. Vague allusions were made to a new commercial treaty and other new stipulations for mutual advantage (i. e., the treaty of alliance), with which the Empress in the near future might reward the Poles for their present sacri-

---

[1] Иловайскій, *op. cit.*, p. 114.

[2] Костомаровъ, *op. cit.*, ii, p. 316.

[3] Blum, *op. cit.*, iii, pp. 311 f.

fices.[1] Sievers had thus brought the first part of his dismal task to a successful conclusion, but the hardest work remained to be done.

III

If the Russian treaty had encountered an unexpectedly protracted resistance, it was universally recognized that the passing of the Prussian one would involve infinitely more trouble, in view of what even Buchholtz described as " the hatred which a combination of events . . . has inspired in the whole Polish nation against the cabinet of Berlin." [2] To the Poles at that time Catherine's aggressions seemed almost innocent compared with the unexampled treachery of Frederick William. Russia had many partisans in the Diet, among them some who served from conviction, not for hire; but Prussia had scarcely a friend in the assembly. It was the Russian ambassador alone who had in his hands the means of coercing the Diet. The success of Buchholtz's negotiation depended therefore chiefly upon Sievers' willingness to employ on behalf of the Court of Berlin the same unswerving firmness and the same violent methods as he had employed in the case of his own treaty; and here some unpleasant surprises were in store for the Prussian minister.

Catherine had long before determined that when the time for the Prussian negotiation came, it would be expedient to take the cause of the Poles in hand. She may have felt a certain impulse to atone for her own indignities to them by protecting them against the ravenous Prussians; perhaps she relished the opportunity to show Frederick William how utterly dependent he was upon her good graces; and possibly she was not unwilling to oblige Austria, who had long been begging her to delay Prussia's treaty at Grodno in order to stimulate that Power to greater activity in the French war. But her chief motive, apparently, was the desire to give the Poles a practical demonstration of the value of her friendship, and to pave the way for that alliance which was to deliver the Republic into her permanent tutelage.

[1] The text of this treaty is printed in Angeberg, *op. cit.*, pp. 322–329.
[2] Buchholtz's report of July 28, B. A., *R.* 9, 27, 1.

Hence Sievers was instructed that while the Prussian treaty must indeed be put through, it would be as well to take one's time about it, and to insist upon certain concessions to the unfortunate Poles. In particular, since Prussia had always evaded her commercial obligations to Poland (while Russia had religiously observed hers), the ambassador was to insert into the treaty substantial provisions in favor of Polish commerce, together with the assurance that Prussia would grant the Republic a thoroughly satisfactory commercial treaty in the near future.[1] As the Prussian general Möllendorff, under the pretence of ' rectifying ' the new frontier, had occupied a very considerable amount of territory not assigned to his Court by the St. Petersburg Convention, Sievers was ordered to sustain the Poles in demanding the restitution of the land thus unjustly seized. With regard to the general attitude which the ambassador was to assume during Buchholtz's negotiation, the Empress wrote: " When the Prussian minister's turn comes, you will naturally establish yourself as arbitrator between him and the Poles. You will employ only the degree of activity and energy analogous to the intention enunciated above,[2] leaving the field open to Polish objections, and supporting them even in so far as reason and justice demand. There will be not only no inconvenience but much advantage in gaining time in this second negotiation." [3] It was a dangerous game which Catherine was thus undertaking, for the Prussians were not inclined to wait for their so ardently desired acquisition, and they were in no mood to be trifled with.

As soon as the passing of the Russian treaty had been assured, Buchholtz lost no time in sending in a note demanding that a deputation should now be authorized to treat with him (July 20). Sievers gave him his word of honor that he would act with the same vigor in this affair as in his own negotiation; Bishop Kossakowski promised his support; and the King also secretly assured the Prussian envoy that he wished to finish the matter

---

[1] Instructions to Sievers of June 15/26, M. A., Польша, III, 70.

[2] This seems to refer to the Empress' desire to put the Prussians into so chastened a mood that they would accept the conditions she proposed to insert in their treaty.

[3] Rescript to Sievers, June 23/July 4. See Appendix XVIII, 2.

speedily.[1] But when the note was read in the Diet (July 23), there burst forth such a storm of opposition as even this assembly had not yet witnessed. All parties joined in burning philippics against Prussia, the Power which had been the cause of all the misfortunes of Poland, which had originally suggested the First Partition, which had perfidiously spurred on the nation against Russia during the Four Years' Diet, the Power " whose business it was to betray and to rob." [2] But as usual with this Diet, after the first flush of patriotic indignation — real or feigned — timid or venal souls began to talk of ineluctable necessity; the King (by prearrangement) proposed an appeal to Sievers for counsel, and the latter responded with a couple of notes urging the assembly to proceed at once to the negotiation with Prussia. As a result of this pressure, coupled with lavish promises of bribes, on July 31 the Diet authorized the same Deputation which had treated with Russia to open conferences with Buchholtz, although with the injunction to take up only commercial questions and to entertain no proposals for any cessions of territory.[3]

On August 5 the Prussian minister began his discussions with the Deputation; but for several weeks scarcely any progress was

[1] Buchholtz's reports of July 17 and 24, B. A., R. 9, 27, 1.

[2] Kraszewski, op. cit., iii, p. 327; Morawski, Dzieje narodu polskiego, v, p. 360.

[3] Buchholtz's report of August 3. The Prussian envoy ascribed this concession on the part of the Diet chiefly to " les soins tout à fait particuliers que nous avons pris de monter les nonces et les chefs de parti." In the same dispatch he furnishes an interesting but unpleasant picture of the operations that went on behind the scenes at Grodno. He writes:

" Les Nonces de la diète engagés pour quinze jours ou trois semaines sont au désespoir. Ils veulent tous partir, et comme la vie est très chère ici, ils sont dans la nécessité de vendre leurs nipes [sic]. . . . En considération de ceci l'Ambassadeur et moi, nous avons fait un plan, qui leur a été communiqué par Pulawski et le Commandeur Mozelewski [sic], qui traitent avec eux. Nous leur promettons de les recompenser et indemniser après la signature du Traité avec Votre Majesté, mais pas plustôt [sic]. Ceci a produit déjà un bon effet et nous nous sommes même assurés d'un grand nombre de Nonces de l'opposition, de façon que ces gens dans l'espérance de pouvoir gagner quelque chose poussent maintenant à la roue. On avoit trop bien recompensé les grands par de belles charges, et trop peu donné aux petits, qui pourtant font le plus de bruit à la Diète. . . . La dépense que ce plan produit, pourra aller à dix-huit ou dix-neuf mille Ducats, pour chaque Cour. Elle est très nécessaire pour nous conserver la pluralité. . . . La plus part [des Nonces] sont arrivés ici sans argent, et même beaucoup sans habits, mais tous ont crû qu'ils s'enrichiroient à cette occasion. Comme cela n'est pas arrivé, ils se sont mis de

made, owing to disputes over small points. Meanwhile the Diet enjoyed a period of rest and relaxation. It was at this time that the gaiety and the mania for amusements, which characterized the social life at Grodno even in the darkest moments, reached their height. Although the town was almost in a state of siege, the streets full of Russian soldiers and Cossacks, and camps, pickets, and patrols everywhere in evidence, in the houses of the citizens there was one continual round of entertainments and celebrations. Throughout the Diet the leaders of the majority dispensed the proverbial Polish hospitality, with Russian money. The deputies flocked from the tragic scenes in the chamber to balls and banquets: their mission was to be alternately dined and imprisoned by the Russian ambassador. The adulation lavished upon Sievers almost passes belief. At the close of July Grodno society celebrated for eight days running the name-day of the man who had just wrenched half its territory away from the Republic. At one evening assembly on this occasion a transparency was lighted with the device: " Vivat Jacob Sievers, who brought peace and order and freedom to the Polish nation." [1] Abject servility could go no further. " They consider here," wrote one disgusted onlooker, " that no nation ever gave away its lands and people so merrily as the Poles. . . ." [2] The Republic was perishing amid fêtes and illuminations.[3]

While Sievers' negotiation with the Deputation had not lasted three days, that of Buchholtz dragged on for three weeks, with results most disheartening for the Prussian envoy. The Russian ambassador, who at the invitation of the Poles had been admitted

mauvaise humeur, et ont voulu à toute force rompre la diète. . . ." B. A., *R.* 9, 27, 1.

That Catherine had an equally low opinion of the assembly appears from a rescript to Sievers (of July 13/24) in which she wrote: " Il n'est pas nécessaire que Je vous observe que de tous ceux qui se sont déterminés à venir comme Nonces à la Diète actuelle, il n'en est peut être aucun qui y soit venu avec un autre but que celui de soigner ses propres intérêts," M. A., Польша, III, 70.

[1] Kraszewski, *op. cit.*, iii, p. 329.

[2] *Ibid.*, p. 337.

[3] Interesting details about the social life at Grodno are to be found in Kraszewski, *op. cit.*, iii, ch. vii, *passim;* Blum, *op. cit.*, iii, pp. 271 ff., 315, 328 ff., 343 ff.; Fr. Schulz, *Reise eines Liefländers*, i, pp. 39 ff.; Иловайскій, *op. cit.*, pp. 146 ff.

to the conferences as mediator, did indeed persuade the Deputation to discuss the question of territorial cessions; but on the other hand, he warmly supported the contentions of the Poles in regard to commercial matters and the exact demarcation of the new frontier, while the unusual mildness of his tone seemed to encourage the Deputation to raise new demands and difficulties of all sorts. Buchholtz was thrown into " the most cruel embarrassment " by the " feebleness," the " capriciousness," the new-found tenderness of his Russian colleague for the Poles; he suspected the Austrian and Swedish ministers of terrible intrigues against him; and he was fairly bewildered by the "perfidy," the " immorality," and the " horrible clamors " of the Deputation. He was " alone in Lithuania," he wrote to his Court, face to face with a nation which showed " an unbelievable hatred " for Prussia, and " absolutely unable to effect anything without the assistance of the Russian ambassador." His one resource would have been to call in General Möllendorff's troops, as the ministry at Berlin had authorized him to do; but to this Sievers strongly objected, declaring that he could not approve of the use of force when everything might be settled amicably in a few weeks, if Prussia would only defer to the just and moderate demands of the Poles. Thus driven from pillar to post, and fearing to see his negotiation collapse altogether, the mortified envoy was finally induced to accept *sub spe rati* the revised draft of the treaty prepared by Sievers and the Deputation. This draft conceded to Prussia the lands assigned to her by the St. Petersburg Convention, but only half of the ' rectified ' frontier established by Möllendorff. It also provided that a commercial treaty should be concluded in the near future under the mediation of the Empress, which should reduce the crushing tariffs hitherto levied by Prussia to the very moderate basis of a two per cent duty on exports, imports, and goods in transit. The present treaty was to be placed under the guarantee of Russia (by way of implying that otherwise the Poles did not expect Frederick William to keep his engagements).[1]

[1] For the above, Buchholtz reports of August 13, 14, 20, 21, 22, 25, B. A., *R.* 9, 27, 1.

Having thus imposed his will on the Prussian minister, Sievers next prepared to force the treaty through the Diet. On August 26 the Deputation reported to the assembly. The debates of the next four days surpassed all previous records for tumultuousness and violence. When Podhorski, a deputy from Volhynia, who later received eight hundred ducats for his shameful services,[1] proposed that the Deputation be authorized to sign the treaty, he was hooted down, threatened with death, and driven from the hall as often as he dared show himself. Szydłowski (of Płock), the most active of the Zealots, demanded the breaking off of the negotiation, on the ground that it was useless to negotiate with a Power which had violated its last two treaties with the Republic (of 1773 and 1790) for no cause whatever. There were wild cries of execration against ' the Brandenburger,' and against that ' Catiline ' Podhorski, and stinging accusations against the King for his past errors and his present slackness. Again and again the whole chamber was on its feet and swarming into the aisles, and it seemed as if it would come to blows. Amid the general uproar speeches could scarcely be heard.[2]

Sievers determined to make an end of the matter. After several vigorous notes had passed unheeded, on September 2 he surrounded the castle where the Diet met with grenadiers and cannon; all exits were closed; the Russian general Rautenfeld and twelve officers took their seats in the chamber, and the assembly was informed that no one would be allowed to leave until the Prussian treaty was passed. As a pretext for such unheard-of indignities, the ambassador alleged the necessity of guarding the King, since a (purely fictitious) plot had been discovered against His Majesty's person. The Diet sat until far into the night, and then, after the usual scenes, decided to yield. But while authorizing the Deputation to sign, they added five new conditions, the most important of which was that the treaty of cession should not be ratified until the promised commercial treaty had been concluded.[3]

---

[1] Blum, *op. cit.*, iv, p. 35.

[2] On the scenes of August 26–30, cf. especially Иловайскій, *op. cit.*, pp. 157 ff., and Костомаровъ, *op. cit.*, ii, pp. 339 ff.

[3] The other conditions were: (1) that the present Primate of Poland, although

Buchholtz, who had fancied himself at the end of his labors, was fairly aghast at these new demands, which threatened to spin out his negotiation for another weary month or two. There followed angry scenes between him and Sievers. The latter refused to employ further violence against the Poles, or to allow the Prussians to do so on their own account. He even went so far as to justify the new pretensions of the Poles and to declare that he would never coerce the Diet into retracting. Quite in despair over Russia's " insidious " policy, Sievers' absurd mania for "making Poland happy," and his own helplessness and isolation, Buchholtz could only beg his government for new instructions, while advising it to acquiesce in even these conditions.[1]

It has already been noted that an explosion of wrath ensued at Berlin. The Prussian ministry felt that they had carried complaisance far enough by agreeing to the revised treaty proposed by Sievers and the Deputation, and that their patience and generosity were being abused. Long indignant at the delays at Grodno, suspicious that the Poles, the Imperial Courts, Sweden, and everyone else were leagued together to rob the King of his indemnity or at least to postpone its realization indefinitely, they concluded that the time had come for bold and decisive action.[2] The great result of this crisis was the memorable declaration already described, by which the King informed Austria that he was obliged to abandon the campaign against France in order to go to the east and assure his acquisition in Poland. How unnecessary this resolution was appears from the fact that the day after it was announced the dénouement took place at Grodno in a manner altogether satisfactory to Prussia.

On September 13 Buchholtz had been ordered to present one more vigorous note demanding the immediate conclusion of the

remaining Archbishop of Gnesen, should be permitted to reside inside the Republic; (2) that in case of the extinction of the family of the Princes Radziwiłł, the House of Brandenburg should raise no claims to its inheritance; (3) that both the treaty of cession and the commercial treaty should receive the guarantee of Russia; (4) that the much-revered statue of the Virgin of Częstochowa should be restored to the Republic.

[1] Buchholtz's report of September 7, B. A., R. 9, 27, 1.

[2] Alvensleben to his colleagues in the ministry, September 12, B. A., R. 9, 27, 1: the cabinet ministry to the King, September 14, B. A., R. 96, 147 H.

treaty as presented to the Diet on August 26, i. e., without any of the conditions or amendments made on September 2; if this step failed he was to break off the negotiation and await further instructions.   Sievers could not afford to risk this latter contingency, for he had always been ordered to see to it that the treaty was passed.   Moreover, recent dispatches from St. Petersburg indicated that the Empress was growing impatient to have the affair terminated, in order to clear the path for the negotiation of her alliance with the Republic.   Hence Buchholtz was delighted to observe a complete change of attitude on the part of his colleague.   Accurately divining his sovereign's wishes, although left without very precise instructions, Sievers now announced that he was ready to use the most efficacious means to put through the Prussian treaty in the exact form desired at Berlin.[1]

The ensuing *journée* of September 23 was very largely a repetition of the scenes of September 2.   As a preliminary step, at dawn of that day the Cossacks dragged from their beds and transported out of Grodno the four leading members of the opposition.   When

---

[1] Buchholtz's reports of September 17 and 24, B. A., *R.* 9, 27, 1. Several writers (e. g., Kostomarov, *op. cit.*, ii, pp. 376 ff., and Sybel, *op. cit.*, iii, p. 439) assume a sudden and complete change of attitude on the part of the Empress with regard to the Prussian negotiation, and urgent instructions to Sievers to finish at once. Kostomarov explains this by the conjecture that Catherine foresaw the danger of Frederick William's abandoning the French war.   It is possible that she had such a presentiment, but there is no proof of it in her rescripts to Sievers of this time; in fact the only motive there given for hastening the affair is the desire to expedite the alliance negotiation.

The rescript to Sievers of September 3 (N. S.) (practically the last instructions he received before the dénouement at Grodno) was not particularly urgent or categorical: the ambassador was directed to "accelerate" the Prussian treaty " par tous les moyens qui sont en votre pouvoir, évitant toujours la violence et conservant autant qu'il vous sera possible le rôle de conciliateur qui vous a si bien réussi jusqu'à présent."

But that Sievers rightly foresaw her intentions appears from the rescript of September 7/18, which could scarcely have reached him before the decisive events at Grodno: for here he was authorized to use " toutes sortes de moyens " (without exception).   " Quelque désir que J'aye de faire empêcher les voyes de violence extrême," the Empress added in another passage, " Je n'en ai pas un moindre de voir enfin terminer cette affaire."   The general sense of this rescript is that as she had now procured for the Poles all the concessions that they could reasonably expect from Prussia, there was no longer any reason for delaying the conclusion of the treaty.   М. А., Польша, III, 70.

towards evening the deputies gathered at the castle, they found it once more encircled by battalions of grenadiers, with cannon trained on the doors, and the artillerymen standing by with lighted matches. General Rautenfeld took his accustomed place in the chamber near the throne, and once more the word was given out that the Diet would be held captive until it had passed the Prussian treaty without any of the conditions prescribed on September 2. The Zealots at once set up the cry that it was useless and shameful to debate under such conditions. For hours the assembly wrangled over the question whether the session should or could not be opened. One deputation after another was sent to Sievers to expostulate — to no purpose. Finally, about midnight, the Diet relapsed into total silence, as the one means left to it of protesting against violence. General Rautenfeld, growing impatient, several times reminded the members of their situation: the King would not be allowed to leave the throne, the Senators might sleep on straw, if they chose, but no one would be permitted to leave the hall until the ambassador's demands had been satisfied. If the assembly remained incorrigibly obstinate, he was ordered to proceed to the most extreme measures. The deputies continued to sit like statues. At last, towards 4 A.M. the Russian general strode to the door, declaring that it only remained for him to call in the grenadiers. The Marshal Bieliński thereupon put the question: " Does the chamber consent that the Deputation should sign the Prussian treaty sent to the Diet by the Russian ambassador ? " No one answered. Twice the question was repeated without response. Bieliński then declared that since silence was a sign of consent, the motion was unanimously carried.[1] Scarcely speaking a word, the King closed the session, and the deputies trooped out in silence and in tears.[2]

Two days later the treaty was signed.[3]

[1] The majority had probably made up their minds in advance to end the affair in this manner. There were precedents for such procedure.

[2] Probably the best and fullest description of this famous ' Dumb Session ' is that in Костомаровъ, *op. cit.*, ii, pp. 385–400.

[3] The text in Angeberg, *op. cit.*, pp. 342–347.

IV

The final labors of the Grodno Diet were devoted to reorganizing the petty state that Poland now was, in accordance with Catherine's plans for its future. Although the work done at this time was to last but a few months, it is not without a certain interest; for it illustrates the consequences which the Empress meant to draw from the recent dismemberment, it completed what may be called the Second Partition resettlement of the Polish Question, and it indicates to some degree what the lot of the Polish nation would have been, had that resettlement proved permanent.

Five days after that 'Dumb Session,' at which the Russian ambassador had subjected the Diet to brutalities unexampled in the history of any other parliamentary body, the deputy Ankwicz of Cracow proposed the conclusion of a perpetual alliance with Russia, on the ground that Poland's only hope of salvation in the future lay in the support of the great neighboring Empire.[1] By an artful bit of comedy, the draft of a treaty of alliance sent down from St. Petersburg was then formally presented to the ambassador by a deputation of the Diet as representing the *summa desideria* of the Polish nation; Sievers was graciously pleased to accept it; and on October 14 it went through the chamber 'unanimously,' the Marshal pretending not to hear the opposing voices.[2] The significance of the vote was well summed up by one of the Zealots the following day with the words, "Poland has now become a province of Russia." [3] It was not without justice that Sievers boasted to his daughter that he had put through a treaty without a parallel in modern history.[4]

By the terms of this remarkable document, both sides promised to aid each other with all their forces in case of war, and the chief command was always to belong to the Power which furnished the greater number of troops. Since the burden of the common defence would fall chiefly on Russia, the King and government of Poland recognized the justice of allowing the Empress that

---

[1] Костомаровъ, *op. cit.*, ii, pp. 406 f.   [3] *Ibid.*

[2] Костомаровъ, *op. cit.*, ii, p. 407.   [4] Blum, *op. cit.*, iii, p. 395.

degree of "influence" in military and political matters that might seem most conducive to the security and tranquillity of the Republic. Under the same pretext, Russia obtained the right of sending troops into Poland "in all cases of necessity," after having amicably notified the Republic; and of keeping them there indefinitely; and of maintaining military magazines on Polish soil. The Republic agreed to enter into no foreign alliances and no important dealings with foreign Powers without the consent of Russia, while the Empress promised to accord her most efficacious support to all diplomatic steps of the Polish government that had been " concerted " with her in ·advance. The ministers of the two states abroad were to act in harmony, and to keep each other informed of all the important business that passed through their hands. Russia received the right of representing Poland at courts where the Republic did not maintain diplomatic agents. Finally, the Empress guaranteed the constitutional and other cardinal laws that the present Diet might enact; and the King and the Republic bound themselves in turn to make no constitutional changes in future without her consent.[1]

The treaty thus gave Russia practically unrestricted control of the army and the foreign relations of the Republic. It deprived the Poles of the right of altering and reforming their fundamental laws and institutions at their discretion. It gave legal sanction and the widest opportunities for Russian interference in almost every branch of Poland's domestic affairs. It was indeed a *pactum subjectionis et incorporationis*, as the Zealots in the Diet ventured to call it.[2] Catherine deserves the credit of having invented, or at least of having first perfected, that system of 'veiled protectorates' which European Powers have applied so frequently in Asia and Africa in recent times; for the position of Poland as fixed by this alliance treaty can be compared only to that of Egypt, Tunis, or the vassal states of India today.

That the Empress did not intend to allow the Republic the slightest vestige of real independence appears from a rescript sent to Sievers immediately after the conclusion of the treaty.

---

[1] The text of this treaty is printed in Angeberg, *op. cit.*, pp. 347–353.

[2] De Caché's report of October 16, V. A., *Polen, Berichte*, 1793.

The alliance, she declared, was only a device for adding what remained of Poland to her Empire without stirring up the opposition of Austria and Prussia. She meant to assert the right to advise the Republic how to act and conduct itself; and it must ask for her advice and follow it. She expected from Poland ' complete submission to her counsels, plans, and views.' Her ambassador at Warsaw was to direct everything that went on in the Republic, and to consider himself " the head of the country." [1] And Sievers, accurately grasping her intentions, assured her: " The future king of Poland will be chosen by Your Imperial Majesty, and will receive a major-domo under the name of the Russian ambassador, who will have infinitely greater power than any Sicilian viceroy or than the governor-general of Your Majesty's province of Tver." [2]

From the standpoint of such principles, Sievers' practice during the last months at Grodno left nothing to be desired. He directed all the operations of the Diet with so high a hand that one of the Zealots declared openly that it was a farce to go on with this assembly: it would be far better for the Marshal simply to invite the ambassador to make whatever arrangements about Poland he chose, and to let the deputies go home.[3] Among the characteristic enactments of that period were the law annulling all the acts of the Four Years' Diet; the decree reducing the army to approximately 18,000 men; and the revised constitution, prepared by the ambassador, and rushed through with scandalous haste during the last hours of the assembly.[4] This set of ' cardinal laws ' sanctioned the traditional rights of the Diet and the traditional impotence of the Crown; the Liberum Veto and the elective kingship; the exclusive rights of the *szlachta* to civil and ecclesiastical honors and dignities; serfdom — and in short all the worst features of the old constitution. In order to perpetuate these abuses, it was decreed that no future Diet could " change, correct, modify . . . or interpret " these cardinal laws, even by a

---

[1] Many excerpts from this remarkable rescript are given in Костомаровъ, *op. cit.*, ii, pp. 411 ff.

[2] *Ibid.*, p. 415.

[3] Wegner, *Sejm grodzieński, ostatni ustęp*, pp. 169 f.

[4] The text is printed in Angeberg, *op. cit.*, pp. 354-357.

unanimous vote; and that they were to remain forever " sacred, stable, and immutable."

After this worthy pronouncement, and after sending an envoy to Catherine to thank her for her benefits to Poland, the assembly dispersed (November 24) in gloom, shame, and humiliation.

" The name of Poland has virtually been erased from the list of states," was the comment of the ' men of the Third of May ' upon the work of the Grodno Diet.[1] The Second Partition had terminated with the loss, not only of more than half the territory of Poland, but of the independence of what was left. It was practically the end of the old Republic.

But the Polish people remained to be heard from. No nation not utterly bereft of a sense of honor, patriotism, and self-respect, could have submitted passively to such disasters, losses, and humiliations. Caught helpless, unprepared, and almost dazed by the action of the partitioning Powers in the spring of 1793, and then goaded to desperation by the shameful scenes at Grodno, the better part of Polish society had been gathering itself and rousing itself for a great effort. Since July of 1793 plans were on foot which were to lead in the following spring to the great national uprising under Kościuszko and to the final struggle for Polish independence. But that story belongs to the history of the Third Partition.

---

[1] *Vom Entstehen und Untergange der polnischen Konstitution vom 3 May*, ii, p. 311. This book, the apologia of the exiled Polish reformers, appeared in Germany about the close of 1793.

CHAPTER XXI

Conclusion

I

THE Second Partition was the death-sentence of the Polish state — of that there can be no question. The First Partition had foreshadowed the ultimate catastrophe, but did not render it inevitable. That initial dismemberment was only an amputation at the extremities; it left a body politic that still contained the elements essential to continued national life; in some respects it was even a salutary operation. The Third Partition, on the other hand, was the necessary and immediate result of the Second: it merely ended an intolerable situation in the only possible way. It was the Russo-Prussian Treaty of 1793, therefore, that decided the solution which the Polish Question was to receive. It was the Second Partition that sealed the fate of the Republic.

While any attempt to analyze the causes of this historic tragedy or to assess responsibilities must be attended by grave and obvious difficulties, the reader may, perhaps, fairly expect the author to state whatever conclusions he has reached, and to explain to what extent the results of the present investigation accord with the views advanced by previous historians.

The favorite thesis of German and Russian writers—that the Poles themselves were primarily responsible for their own downfall—is, of course, true in this sense, that through individual and class egoism, indifference to the common weal, and blindness to the most elementary laws of sound political life, the Poles had reduced their country to a state of weakness without which the Partitions would scarcely have been possible. One can hardly escape the feeling that the First Partition was the just retribution for all the accumulated sins and errors of the two preceding centuries. But with the Second Partition, the case is different. The crime for which the Poles were then punished was that of an attempt at national regeneration. The Second Partition was the reply of the neighboring Powers to the effort made by the Four Years' Diet to reform the constitution, recover the nation's independence, and restore Poland to its proper place among European states. Hence Polish patriotism has been able to find some consolation — or additional motives for embitterment — in the thesis set up by the men of the Third of May in their apologia, that Poland fell " without any fault on her side, without having given the neighbors the slightest cause for revenge or hostility — just at the moment when she had prepared all things necessary for her happiness." [1]

But the question presents itself: was it wise or prudent to make the attempt for independence at that time and under the given circumstances ? It is often said that the Poles made the mistake of seeing the root of their troubles in the Russian domination, whereas the real causes of the evil lay in their own perverted political habits and prejudices, their own moral and intellectual shortcomings, their own military and economic weakness; that a long period of internal transformation was necessary before the nation could safely try to recover its independence; and that in the meantime it was the part of prudence to submit to the Russian protectorate, which at least ensured the continued existence and the territorial integrity of the state, and which was not, in the last analysis, incompatible with gradual and moderate reforms. This was, in essence, the policy of Stanislas Augustus after the First Partition. But, we are told, " fantastic political ideas " and " patriotic impatience " prevailed. Unwilling to content themselves with what might have been attained by protracted hard work, the Poles threw themselves into the pursuit of external political independence, which was at that time unattainable. With no accurate appreciation of their own resources or of the hard realities of the situation, they insisted on hazarding everything upon a single throw, and thus the existence of the Republic was played away.[2]

[1] *Vom Entstehen und Untergange der polnischen Konstitution vom 3. May, 1791,* II, pp. 323 f.

[2] The above represents fairly, I think, the views of Bobrzyński and Kalinka among Polish historians, and Kostomarov and Karěev among the Russians.

However convincing this indictment may seem in view of what actually happened, it is nevertheless open to many objections. If the decline of the Republic is to be ascribed chiefly to the defects of the worst constitution then to be found in Europe, as most historians agree, then the first and most indispensable step in the regeneration of Poland must be to get rid of this constitution, and to establish a government capable of concentrating the strength of the nation for great national tasks, of repressing the evil tendencies, and of creating and fostering the ameliorating forces. The material and moral resources of the country were not altogether inadequate; the worst evil was the lack of a government able to make use of them. In our opinion, the Polish patriots of that time were right in raising the political reform to the first plane. But no such reform was possible as long as Russia retained her control over the country. Moreover, the indictment in question rests upon the utterly unproved and unprovable hypothesis that Poland's integrity was safe as long as the nation submitted passively to the Russian protectorate. It assumes that under the beneficent auspices of Russia the Republic could have looked forward to a long unbroken period of peace, recuperation, and steady progress; and that Poland could have afforded to remain for a generation or two unarmed and defenceless, trusting solely to the protection of her great neighbor. The men of the Four Years' Diet refused to make so naïve an assumption. Since 1772 they had lived in constant fear of a new partition; they knew that every crisis in the North put their political existence in peril; they believed that they could never be safe as long as the country remained in its helpless condition, dependent solely upon the mercy of the foreign Powers. In this case, too, it is difficult to blame them. We do not believe that the Empress was so averse to a new partition as is commonly asserted. At any rate, it is not at all certain that in case of a serious crisis in general European politics she would not have decided to free herself from embarrassments by a new partition, no matter how docile the Poles might have shown themselves. It has already been pointed out that the rest of Europe constantly expected a further dismemberment of the Republic, and that this had become, one might almost say, the accepted formula for settling conflicts between the great Eastern Powers. When one recalls, moreover, how long and assiduously Potemkin pursued his designs against the Republic; how seriously a partition was discussed at St. Petersburg in almost every year of the Oriental crisis, in 1789, 1790, 1791 — and that not so much as a means of punishing Poland as of disarming the hostility of Prussia; and how readily the Empress succumbed to the temptation of a new partition in 1792; one can hardly avoid the conclusion that submission to Russia afforded no guarantee of security to Poland, and that the policy advocated by Stanislas offered no more certainty of salvation than the policy adopted by the Patriots. Indeed, it is probable that had Poland remained submissive and passive, she would have fallen a victim to a new partition and to the loss of her political existence sooner or later — with the sole difference that then she would have perished shamefully, and her ruin would have been infinitely more deserved.

The general European crisis following the outbreak of the Oriental war offered the Poles a great opportunity and forced them to make a great decision. Three courses lay open to them: alliance with Russia, alliance with Prussia, or timorous neutrality. An alliance with Russia could have been purchased by bartering away still more of the sovereignty of the Republic, and by handing over the nation's army, its fortresses, and its richest provinces to Potemkin, whose ambitions to become King of Dacia, Duke of the Ukraine, or liberator of the ' oppressed ' Orthodox people were tolerably well known at Warsaw. It would almost certainly have drawn down upon the country an attack from Prussia, and one may imagine how much protection Poland would have received from Catherine, absorbed, as she was, with the two severe wars she already had on her hands. Neutrality would apparently have been the worst of all courses, for it would have left the Republic exposed unaided to aggressions from both sides. The Four Years' Diet decided in favor of alliance with Prussia; decided to seize what seemed to be a unique and, if lost, irrecoverable opportunity; decided to attempt at once the great venture of throwing off the foreign yoke and putting through the political reforms, without which no solid national revival was possible.

The attempt itself was justifiable enough, but was it well carried out ? On the whole, we think the effort was distinctly creditable. The Diet displayed an energy, a patriotic enthusiasm, a liberal, enlightened spirit, and a high appreciation of its task, such as no Polish parliament had shown for two centuries. It succeeded within three years in doubling the revenues and trebling the military forces of the state; it gave the country an administrative system which, within the short period of its existence, performed an immense work; it made a brave and promising attempt to win for the Republic the sympathies and support of the classes always hitherto neglected — the bourgeoisie, the Dissidents, the Jews, the peasantry — by legislation in their favor; and finally, by establishing the Constitution of the Third of May, it proved that the nation had broken away from its old errors and prejudices and was ready to enter upon a new period of sound and well-ordered political life.[1] But, as against all this, there is much to be put on the debit side. The Diet was guilty of wounding Catherine unnecessarily by tactless oratory and some gratuitous affronts. The refusal to cede Dantzic and Thorn and even a small part of Great Poland to Prussia was probably a mistake, although a very intelligible one, for the Poles thus lost their last chance of satisfying the natural ambitions of Berlin without a new partition, their last chance of giving their alliance with Prussia some prospects of permanence. It would have been wiser, perhaps, had the makers of the new constitution contented themselves with designating the Elector of Saxony as the future king, while postponing the establishment of the hereditary succession until a later period; for they would thus have gained their essential object — to guard against the dangers of a new interregnum — at least for a long time to come, and they would have avoided stirring up that storm of alarm and exasperation which

[1] Cf. the quite contrary opinion about the new constitution of Костомаровъ, *op. cit.*, ii, pp. 115 ff., and Solov'ev, *op. cit.*, pp. 251 f. Most of the Polish historians pass eulogies upon the constitution itself, but some of them (Bobrzyński and Kalinka) doubt the wisdom of introducing such fundamental changes at such a moment.

the idea of an hereditary monarchy in Poland aroused at Berlin and St. Petersburg.[1] But the worst mistake of the Diet lay in not pressing forward sufficiently the military preparations of the Republic. The army of 100,000 men, which was voted at the beginning of the Diet, could and should have been raised; but three and a half years after that memorable vote, at the outbreak of the war with Russia, hardly more than half of the appointed number of troops were actually under arms, and in other respects as well Poland was lamentably unready. This fatal negligence was due in part to the fact that the Diet, which had such a multitude of affairs on its hands, did not find time to attend properly to military matters; in part, to an exaggerated reliance upon the friendship and support of Prussia, and later, of the Emperor Leopold; in part, and chiefly perhaps, to the lack of money and credit. Both might have been procured, if the Polish leaders had known how to set about the task. Hence a distinguished historian has expressed the opinion that the fundamental cause of the disasters of Poland was the amazing ignorance of the Polish statesmen of that time, particularly with regard to economic and financial matters.[2] At all events, the failure of the Poles to arm themselves properly during the three years' respite that was granted to them, avenged itself with ruinous results in the campaign of 1792.

That campaign presents a painful spectacle. What is one to think of a nation which, after boasting of its regeneration, when called upon to fight for its liberty and very existence allows itself to be conquered by a hostile army of only 100,000 men, after a struggle lasting barely two months ? Many historians have drawn the conclusion that the heart of the nation was not in this contest; that the enthusiasm manifested over the work of the Third of May was purely factitious outside the capital; that the mass of the *szlachta* preferred the old constitution and secretly sympathized with the Targowicians; and that the nation as a whole was too far sunk in lethargy and demoralization to be able

---

[1] Cf. Korzon, *Wewnętrzne dzieje, Zamknięcie*, pp. 40 f., Kalinka, *Der polnische Reichstag*, ii, pp. 755-760.

[2] Korzon, *op. cit., Zamknięcie*, pp. 33 f.

to rouse itself to a manly effort even in such a crisis.[1] On the other hand, the historian who has most thoroughly investigated the question, has discovered so many signs of real enthusiasm and self-devotion for the national cause that he arrives at the conviction that "patriotic zeal was universal"; "the government received from all sides encouragement and exhortations to perseverance"; "the nation ardently desired to defend its independence."[2] Why, then, this sudden and shameful collapse? The blame must fall largely upon the King, who, after voluntarily undertaking the direction of the national defence, mismanaged everything, refused to issue the summons for a general rising of the nation in arms until it was too late, and then, while the military situation was still far from desperate, cravenly and traitorously went over to the enemy. But it is unfair to make the King the scapegoat for the whole disaster. What shall one say of the Patriotic leaders who, with unpardonable shortsightedness, entrusted the direction of the defence to a man whose whole past record showed him tragically unfitted for such a responsibility? Or, when the King's intention to surrender had become apparent, why did no one find the courage to thrust him aside and to force on the continuation of the struggle till the bitter end? Or why did the mass of the *szlachta* wait for a summons from Warsaw, instead of rushing spontaneously to their country's defence? The sum of the matter would seem to be that — in spite of warm and widespread patriotic zeal — the nation did not find in itself or in its leaders or, least of all, in its king that iron will; that indomitable resolution; that readiness to risk everything; to sacrifice everything; and to stop at nothing, which alone might still, perhaps, have saved it. The lack of a great man of action at the head was cruelly felt, but the morale of the nation was also at fault.

In reviewing the causes of this collapse, one should not overlook how signally fortune had turned against the Poles in the preceding two years, how many events on the broader stage of Europe had combined to thwart their hopes and expectations and to produce a situation infinitely unfavorable to them. As ex-

---

[1] So, for instance, Bobrzyński, *Dzieje Polski*, ii, pp. 338 f., Карѣевъ, Паденіе Польши, pp. 25 ff., Костомаровъ, *op. cit.*, ii, p. 119.

[2] Korzon, *op. cit.*, v, pp. 157 ff.

amples, one might cite the fiasco of Prussian policy in 1790, the backdown of the Triple Alliance before Catherine in 1791, the sudden and complete change in the European political constellation that followed, the premature death of the Emperor Leopold, the outbreak of the Revolutionary War at the very time when Catherine most desired to have her hands free, and the unparalleled treachery of Prussia at the moment of the Russian attack on Poland. Few nations, perhaps, have had to conduct their struggle for liberty under such adverse conditions.

The effort made by the Four Years' Diet ended, apparently, in total failure, with the dismemberment of the country and the virtual annihilation of the Polish state. But mere material success or failure is not the highest standard for judging such an effort; there remains the ethical criterion. If the great Powers had annexed the whole of Poland in 1772, the world would have said that the Poles deserved their fate, and, in view of the deathly languor displayed by the nation at that time, it seems probable that the Polish name and Polish nationality would also have perished. Twenty years later, however, a new era had dawned, and Poland fell, not at the moment of her deepest degradation, but just when she was beginning to put forth new life and to show her greatest patriotism and energy. The work of the Four Years' Diet, the lofty character of its leaders, the generous enthusiasms and high hopes of the period, the Constitution of the Third of May, the effort of the Polish army in 1792, and the new struggle for liberty under Kościuszko in 1794 — these things brought at least this inestimable advantage that they furnished the nation with a treasure of spiritual goods upon which it could live and maintain its faith in itself and its future after the loss of its independence. From these tragic but ennobling experiences later generations could convince themselves and the unprejudiced outside world that this nation had not deserved to perish. And so, we think, the Patriots of 1788 deserved well of their country. They did not succeed in saving the Polish state — perhaps no one could have done that; but they did succeed in saving Polish nationality and the spiritual life of their people, which was, after all, more important.

II

Those Polish historians who are wont to trace their country's downfall to the facts of geography are at least right in this respect, that Poland had the unique misfortune of being placed midway between two states, which, having been the last to attain the rank of great Powers and having their territorial foundations only half-built, were throughout the eighteenth century reaching out around them on all sides with a restless, youthful energy, an insatiable voracity, and an indifference to moral scruples, which the older Powers might emulate but could scarcely equal. Poland was not only the weakest state of her size in that age, but she also held the most exposed and dangerous position. While Prussian writers are accustomed to throw the chief responsibility for the Partitions upon Russia, and Russian writers return the compliment in kind, it would seem fairer to divide the honors evenly, for, in our opinion, the Second Partition, like the First, was the result of the common and equal cupidity of both Powers, with Austria playing the part of an interested, and in the end a duped and disappointed, accomplice.

Prussian policy during the period surveyed in this book was essentially one of territorial aggrandizement. The plans, the methods, the immediate objective varied frequently; but, except, perhaps, for Frederick William's projected attack on Austria in 1790, the primary purpose of which was, apparently, to settle the old rivalry between the two German Powers, the great aim — the aim underlying the Hertzberg plan, the alliance with Austria, the crusade against the French Revolution, the Prussian machinations against Poland — was the acquisition of new territories: acquisitions in any quarter — Juliers and Berg, Lusatia, Swedish Pomerania, Courland, Dantzic, Great Poland, or the whole left bank of the Vistula; acquisitions by any means but usually with the minimum of effort, whether by elaborate diplomatic combinations, like Hertzberg's, or by a half-hearted campaign or two, as in the case of the war with France. This aggressive policy was not dictated, of course, by any ideas about ' Prussia's German mission,' or the duty of recovering lands of German nationality. Its basis was simply the conviction that this Prussian Monarchy, which, with its meagre, scattered, and exposed territories, still seemed to be only the skeleton of a state, must take on flesh and bulk, unite its *disjecta membra*, and acquire a defensible frontier.

Well-founded as that conviction might be, it is difficult to overlook the sordidness and blindness of a policy, which saw in the unparalleled upheavals which Europe was then going through, only opportunities for selfish aggrandizement. It is not easy to construct an apology for a king who, in the course of a very short reign, allied himself with almost every state in Europe in turn, and broke faith with almost every one of them. The worst part of Frederick William's record, however, is his desertion of the Poles in 1792 in violation of his solemn engagements, and the initiative which he took in provoking a new partition of the allied state, which had given him no cause of offence whatever.

Apologists have, at any rate, been found even for Prussia's treatment of Poland. One need not, perhaps, pay much attention to such extravagant views as that of Treitschke, who saw in the Constitution of the Third of May only an outburst of the old " mortal hatred against the Germans, the Protestants," which " must be taken by Prussia as a declaration of war "[1] — unless, indeed, Prussia was entitled to consider any attempt on the part of her neighbors to live under decent and orderly conditions as a *casus belli*. The most elaborate vindication of Frederick William's policy is that offered by Heinrich von Sybel, whose argument is substantially as follows.

The alliance treaty of 1790 had been torn up by the Poles themselves, since they had conspired with the Emperor Leopold to introduce their new constitution, without the knowledge and contrary to the wishes of Prussia, and had then passed over more and more openly into the clientèle of Austria, while virtually abandoning their connection with Prussia altogether. Hence " we cannot . . . talk of the breach of an effective treaty in the measures adopted by Prussian policy." Frederick William could, in any case, have defended Poland only if he received the loyal support of Austria. But the latter hastened to " tear asunder the

[1] *Deutsche Geschichte*, i, p. 113.

new bond between the German Powers " through " Leopold's plan of the Polish-Saxon union,"· which Sybel regards as " the cornerstone " of the Emperor's whole political system, and as a plot directed against the most vital interests of Prussia, which was thereby " driven into the arms of Russia." Frederick William's decision in favor of a new partition was then forced upon him by the unparalleled crisis in which he found himself, with Russia, France, and Austria simultaneously announcing offensive plans which ' threatened the whole Continent with the most violent convulsions,' ' called all existing rights and titles of possession in question,' and ' made self-preservation the leading principle of every individual.' The King simply chose the least of evils, the only course which did not lead to evident disaster. He could not have remained neutral in the face of the universal onset of the other Powers; nor could he have allied himself with " the Parisian assassins " in favor of " the Polish slaveholders "; nor could he have thrown himself with all his forces upon the French, while allowing Russia to seize the whole of Poland.[1]

This argument seems to us false in almost every particular, false as a presentation of the course of events and as an interpretation of the motives that determined the King's policy. No evidence whatever has yet been discovered to show that Leopold was consulted in advance as to the introduction of the new Polish constitution. It seems the height of exaggeration to ascribe so important a place in the Emperor's plans to the project for the Saxon-Polish union, or to assert that Prussia was thereby driven into the arms of Russia. Frederick William's decision in favor of a new partition was made before the unparalleled crisis described by Sybel existed — in February or March of 1792 at the latest; and it would be difficult to prove that the various alternatives mentioned above presented themselves to the King's mind at all.[2]

---

[1] The above is based upon ideas that run through the whole of the *Geschichte der Revolutionszeit*, as well as through Sybel's articles in the *Historische Zeitschrift*, x, xii, and xxiii; but especially upon the discussion of the broader aspects of the Second Partition in the work first cited, iii, pp. 224–228.

[2] Sybel's work, which passes as one of the classic histories of the Revolutionary period, bristles with erroneous assertions and judgments regarding Polish affairs. Askenazy, who has pointed out some of them, goes so far as to accuse the German historian of perverting the facts deliberately (*op. cit.*, pp. 130 f.).

The thesis most commonly advanced by German historians is that Prussia's determination to appropriate a part of Poland was a " justifiable act of self-defence " (*eine That gerechter Notwehr*), since the King was placed in a position where he had to decide either to tolerate Russia's exclusive and absolute domination in Poland, or else by a new partition to set bounds to the swelling flood of Muscovite power. " It was a *Machtfrage*." The whole of Poland must not be allowed to fall into Russian hands. Prussia's own safety forbade her to ' permit the Russian garrisons to fix themselves as firmly in Posen and Gnesen, as in Grodno and Warsaw.' [1] — But this view also rests upon an anachronism. It ascribes to the Prussian statesmen of that time ideas which modern historians think they ought to have had, but of which there is no trace in the records. During the early months of 1792 — the time at which the decision in favor of a new partition was taken at Berlin — the King and his ministers were aware that Russia was preparing to recover her old influence in Poland. But did they view the prospect with apprehension ? Not in the least. They believed that Russia was only playing into their hands, for they were at that time firmly convinced that the Empress intended to settle the fate of Poland by a concert of the neighboring Powers, which would restore her preponderant influence, but would also assure to the German Courts a suitable voice, in Polish affairs. The Prussians were not, indeed, disposed to allow Catherine a *sole* and *exclusive* influence in Poland, but they did not believe that such was her aim; and they were quite ready to accord her a *preponderant* influence. In numerous Prussian documents of this time one finds the statement that experience had proved that it was natural and inevitable that Russia should always exercise a far greater authority in Poland than either of the German Powers; and that such a state of things was not only not detrimental to Prussian interests, but infinitely preferable to the situation existing since 1788.[2] It may therefore be asserted that in resolving to provoke a new partition Frederick William was

[1] Cf., e. g., Treitschke, *op. cit.*, i, p. 131; Heigel, *op. cit.*, i, pp. 570–573; Sybel, *op. cit.*, iii, pp. 224–228, and 152, note.

[2] In substantiation of the above, one may cite from among many documents the rescripts to Jacobi of March 1, 17, April 6, 1792 (B.A., *R.* 1, 169); to Lucchesini,

consciously choosing, not the lesser of two evils, but the greater of two advantages. While regarding the restoration of the Russian ascendancy in Poland, not as an imminent and pressing danger, but rather as a positive gain for Prussia, he determined, without any real necessity or compulsion whatever, to exploit the situation still further in order to satisfy his long-repressed covetousness for Polish territory.

It may readily be admitted that Prussia needed to acquire Dantzic, Thorn, and that part of Great Poland which projected so deeply into the side of the Hohenzollern Monarchy. But it was also a Prussian interest of equal, and perhaps even greater, importance that the Republic should be preserved as an effective ' buffer-state,' as a real barrier against the great,' aggressive military Empire in the east. We venture to think that a revived Poland — consolidated and reinvigorated under the Constitution of the Third of May — could never have proved so serious a danger to Prussia as the advance of Russia into the heart of Central Europe to within striking distance of Berlin. At all events, it behooved Prussia to weigh very carefully the advantage of every acquisition in Poland against the perils involved in the aggrandizement of Russia and the necessity of maintaining the existence of the Republic. Frederick the Great appears to have realized this,[1] and so did Hertzberg. Whatever charges may be brought against the latter, it must be said in his favor that he planned to make the needed acquisitions on the east with the minimum of loss to the Republic, and then to assure the permanent integrity of Poland's remaining possessions.[2] But those who came after him were blind to such considerations. In their senseless lust for territory, they demanded far more than they had any need of, thus opening the door to still more inordinate claims on the part of Russia; and to these latter claims they assented without a moment's hesitation, although it was obvious that a

January 25 and April 27 (*ibid., R.* 9, 27); to Goltz, March 22 (*ibid., R.* XI, *Russland,* 133); Schulenburg to Brunswick, May 6 (*ibid., R.* XI, *Frankreich,* 89b.).

[1] Cf. Sybel, *loc. cit.*

[2] Cf. Hertzberg's Memoir in Schmidt's *Zeitschrift,* vii, p. 269; P. Wittichen, *Die polnische Politik Preussens,* pp. 69 f.; Andreae, *Preussische und russische Politik,* p. 27.

partition arranged on so gigantic a scale could mean only the virtual annihilation of Poland. Even German historians admit that Prussia's acquisitions were immeasurably dearly bought.[1] In our opinion, the gain was far outweighed by the disadvantages: the odium inseparable from so signal a breach of treaty obligations; the quarrel with Austria over the indemnities, with its fateful result upon the course of the struggle in the west; the replacement of a weak, quiet, and altogether inoffensive neighbor on the east by a powerful, restless, and aggressive one; and the inclusion within Prussia of a large alien population, which could not be assimilated, and which, had it been permanently retained, would have tended to give Prussia the character of a hybrid, non-national state like Austria. In short, while Prussia obtained by the Second Partition the largest acquisition of territory that she had made down to that time, we think this was nevertheless one of the most short-sighted, disastrous, and morally reprehensible transactions in her history.

III

The majority of the historians who have treated of this period have advanced the thesis that Catherine II disliked partitions; that she would have preferred to rule over the whole of Poland by influence rather than to make territorial acquisitions at its expense, which must be purchased by corresponding concessions to the German Powers; and that the dismemberment of the Republic was forced upon her by Prussia. The Second Partition, like the First, it is said, was a triumph of Prussian policy over Russian. It was, above all, Frederick William's threat to abandon the French war and to turn his attention to the east, coupled with the incorrigibly refractory temper displayed by the Poles and the utter failure of the Confederates of Targowica to fulfil the hopes she had placed in them, which compelled the Empress to agree to a measure which was repugnant to her and contrary to the fundamental aims of her Polish policy.[2] The evidence for this

---

[1] Cf. Häusser, *Deutsche Geschichte*, i, pp. 138, 597.

[2] Among the historians who take this general view of Catherine's aims (and apply it to the Second Partition, in case they treat of that subject at all), one may

view, however, is very inadequate. As far as the Second Partition is concerned, it rests chiefly upon the Empress' delay in the autumn of 1792 in acceding to the demands of Prussia, and then upon her exposition of the motives that had determined her to yield, contained in the original instruction given to Sievers. In our opinion, no such interpretation need be put upon that delay, which can better be explained by Catherine's momentary irritation over the disasters in the west, and her natural desire to affect a certain reluctance about so delicate a transaction; and she was under no necessity, and not at all likely, to disclose her real motives in an official document like the instruction to Sievers, which was not of confidential character and which was obviously intended chiefly to put the best face possible on a very unsavory business. We have already expressed the belief that the Empress' ' opposition ' and ' scruples ' at the time of the First Partition were chiefly a sham, a bit of stage-play for the sake of appearances; and we think it highly probable that her attitude with regard to the Second Partition was very similar.

It is true that no entirely conclusive proof of this can be offered from the documents available, but the indications point strongly in that direction. Beneath the guarded phraseology of the famous rescript to Potemkin of July 18/29, 1791, one can detect Catherine's willingness to accept a new partition if the King of Prussia displayed a covetousness which, in his case, could be assumed with tolerable certainty. One does not find here any signs of a real inclination to resist such a suggestion. We have already noted the astonishing activity of the Russian envoys at Berlin and Vienna in ' provoking ' confidential overtures from those Courts with regard to a partition, and the Empress' discreet but highly significant hints to Prussia on the subject of indemnities, the aim of which was probably to divert the King's ambitions from France to Poland. In April of 1792, at the moment of beginning the intervention in Poland, the Empress' council laid down the principle that in return for the great costs of the

name Sybel, Sorel, Raumer, Janssen, Brückner, Bobrzyński, Kalinka, Askenazy, Smitt, Martens, Solov'ev, and Ilovaĭski. The contrary view is held by only a few writers, among whom one may cite Herrmann, Heigel, Heidrich, Smoleński, and Kostomarov.

enterprise Russia must strive to obtain at least perfect security on the side of Poland for all future time, and that no merely palliative settlement of Polish affairs could be allowed.[1] Coming from a body dominated by Bezborodko, one of the earliest champions of a partition, this dry expression of the protocol gives matter for thought. In the following October Bezborodko, reporting the first definite discussions with Goltz about the Prussian demands, declared joyfully that no opposition was to be expected to " our intention to take the Ukraine," and that he was in favor of allowing the King of Prussia to send his troops into Poland, " since that fits into our plan exactly, and will certainly lead to the quickest dénouement of the affair." [2] When, in addition to all this and to the considerations elsewhere adduced, one recalls how easily Catherine might have averted a partition had she made any genuine effort to do so, how brief and perfunctory her pretended opposition to the arrangement really was, and how little necessity there was for her to give way had she seriously wished to stand out, it is difficult to escape the conclusion that the generally accepted view about her attitude on this question is wrong; that at heart she desired a partition, and from an early date — perhaps from the beginning of her intervention in Poland [3] — secretly intended to bring one about. We cannot agree, therefore, that the Second Partition is to be considered as a triumph of Prussian policy over that of Russia. On the contrary, it seems probable that Russia attained precisely what she had long desired — and that on terms most advantageous to herself — while thrusting the apparent moral responsibility upon Prussia.

If such was the Empress' policy, what were her motives ? It may be doubted whether her conduct was guided, as is sometimes said,[4] by the desire to free the millions of Russian and Orthodox people in Poland and to complete the political unification of the

---

[1] Protocol of March 29 / April 9, Apx. Гос. Сов., i, pp. 906–910.

[2] Note of Bezborodko, of October 26, 1792, Apx. Bop., xiii, p. 275 (here erroneously placed in 1793, and otherwise undated).

[3] That such was her intention appears to be implied in two letters (of Zavadovski and S. R. Vorontsov respectively) published in the Apx. Bop., ix, p. 302, and xii, p. 75.

[4] Cf., e. g., Solov'ev, *op. cit.*, pp. 255 f., 304 f.

Russian race.   It is true that in a few official documents [1] Cath-erine speaks of the liberation of " those of the same faith and blood as ourselves " as one of the advantages incidental to a partition; and she sometimes talked of the necessity of regaining all the lands where the old Russian princes lay buried.[2]   But these sporadic utterances are probably merely phrases intended to justify the Partition, not Catherine's motives.[3]   When she had ' liberated ' her oppressed compatriots from the rule of the Polish state, she did nothing to free them from the far worse rule of the Polish *szlachta*.   Except for an attack on the Uniate Church, she made no effort to assert the Russian character of the annexed region.   Indeed, down to the third quarter of the nineteenth century, the Russian government and Russian society continued to regard that region, not as a fundamentally Russian territory, but as a Polish territory which happened to have a considerable Russian servile population.[4]   The modern conception of the ' rights of nationality ' was so utterly alien to the eighteenth century, Catherine's policy was shaped on such entirely different lines, that it seems incongruous to imagine the Empress as governed by the nationalist impulse, or fired with the ambition to be the unifier of the Russian race.   What she, like her con-temporaries, was vastly more concerned about, was material power, and the glory and profit of making territorial acquisitions. In the various letters that have come down to us in which her ministers and advisers present their ideas about the advantages to be gained by the Partition, one finds a great deal about the strategic improvement of the frontier, and the greater security against Poland and Turkey; most of all, about the mere magni-tude of the acquisition in area and population; but nothing at all about the gain for the cause of Russian national unity.[5]   And doubtless Catherine's views were of the same sort.

[1] E. g., in the rescript to Potemkin of July 18/29, 1791, and the instruction to Sievers.

[2] Храповицкій, Дневникъ, June 4/15, 1793, p. 250.

[3] Cf. Карѣевъ, Паденіе Польши, p. 179.

[4] Пыпинъ, Исторія Русской Этнографіи, iv, pp. 13 ff; Карѣевъ, *op. cit.*, pp. 179 ff.

[5] Zavadovski to S.R. Vorontsov, January 27/February 7, 1793, Markov to S.R. Vorontsov, November 8/19, 1792, January 17/28, 1793, April 18/29, July 27/August

One can therefore accept only with qualifications the plea most commonly put forward by Russian historians in defence of Catherine's policy in the matter of the dismemberments of Poland, and especially of the Second Partition; the plea, namely, that she was only reclaiming what Poland had stolen in the days of Russia's weakness, and continuing the work of the old ' gatherers of the Russian lands.' Kostomarov, for instance, declares that the recovery of the Russian provinces from Poland was the most justifiable of all the territorial acquisitions made in Europe in the eighteenth century, for Catherine was restoring to her Empire what belonged to it in virtue, not of mere dynastic traditions or documents from the archives, but of an age-long, living national tie.[1] It may readily be admitted that the great historic result of her work was the virtual completion of the political unification of the Russian race; but it must be added that that achievement appears to have been only an involuntary and accidental result of her policy.[2] If the provinces in question had never belonged to Russia, and had contained only a solidly Polish population, it can scarcely be imagined that she would have acted any differently.

The material gain accruing to Russia from the Second Partition was immense. Merely in point of size, this was one of the two or three largest acquisitions of territory that any Power has made on the continent of Europe in modern times. From the moral standpoint, there is little to be said for Catherine's conduct. The hypocrisy and the flagrant breach of promises which give so odious an aspect to the affair were well set forth by a Russian statesman of that time, who wrote: " The thing itself is too notoriously unjust, but the perfidious manner in which it was executed, renders it still more shocking. Since we were determined to commit this injustice, we ought to have said frankly that we were robbing Poland to avenge ourselves, because she had tried to make an offensive alliance with the Turks against us; but instead we talked of friendship, we published manifestoes to say that we were seeking only the happiness of Poland, that we wished

7, Apx. Bop., xii, pp. 77 f., xx, pp. 32, 34 ff., 42 ff., 48 ff.; Markov to Razumovski, February 25/March 8, 1793, P.A., XV, 576.

[1] *Op. cit.*, ii, p. 667.　　　　[2] Cf. Карѣевъ, *op. cit.*, pp. 219 f.

to assure to her the integrity of her possessions and the enjoyment of her old government, under which she had flourished with such *éclat* through so many centuries! " [1] It will always be a matter for regret that the assertion of the rights of Russia was not effected without inflicting an even greater wrong upon Poland. And from the standpoint of purely Russian interests, it may perhaps be doubted whether the gains made by the Second Partition out-weighed the resulting disadvantages and dangers, to which the events of the last century and especially of the present time afford striking testimony.

IV

In considering the Polish Question in the late eighteenth century in its broadest aspects, as one of the great international problems of that age, one cannot fail to be impressed with the inefficacy here of certain factors that have served to maintain the existence of other states too weak to defend themselves of their own resources. Holland, Belgium, Switzerland, Portugal, and Turkey have, to a large extent, owed their survival to the fact that one or more of the great Powers were interested in their preservation, and that at times the force of European public opinion has been strong enough to prevent the more unscrupulous forms of international brigandage.

Austria, England, and France, in varying degrees, were interested in the preservation of Poland. Each of them, within the period we have been considering, made some attempt to save the sinking Republic. Pitt's effort in 1791 was, perhaps, the most promising, but it was wrecked, as we have seen, by the blank indifference of the British public to the great questions at issue, and by the firmness and courage of Catherine II. Austria under Leopold II adopted an enlightened policy towards the Polish Question, which, had it been accepted by the other Powers, would, in our opinion, have worked out to the great advantage of all parties concerned. While the Emperor has been accused of conducting the affair with far less energy and determination than its importance deserved,[2] while some historians [3] have even held

---

[1] S. R. Vorontsov to his brother, May 7/18, 1793, Apx. Bop., ix, p. 302.
[2] Cf. Hüffer, *Oestreich und Preussen*, pp. 38 f.   [3] Herrmann and Heigel.

that he was tolerably indifferent about the whole matter, it would seem that he made every effort in behalf of Poland that was compatible with Austria's difficult international position. His policy was condemned to failure by the outbreak of the trouble with France, and by the desertion of Prussia to the side of the Empress. In general, the international situation in the late eighteenth century was extremely unfavorable to Poland. As long as England and France were almost constantly at odds, while Austria and Prussia, according to the *mot* of Joseph II, found their chief business in seeing which should stand higher in the favor of Russia,[1] any effective combined action of the great Powers in defence of the Republic was almost impossible.

As for the deterrent force of public opinion, this was precisely the time when that factor exercised least influence upon the policy of the great Powers, when in most capitals policy was determined by a handful of persons — princes, ministers, favorites, or backstairs intriguers — and when international morality had reached its very lowest ebb. The unprincipled and unscrupulous character of eighteenth century politics is too well known to require description. In one sense, the dismemberments of Poland were nothing exceptional in that age. The history of the century is filled with partitions or projects of partition; there was scarcely a state on the Continent whose dismemberment was not plotted by its neighbors at one time or another during those hundred years. The mania of the monarchs of that day to get as much land as possible — whenever and wherever possible — the conception voiced by Louis XIV that " to aggrandize oneself was the worthiest and most agreeable occupation of a sovereign "[2] afforded an ever-ready motive for partitions. The growing indifference to rights, treaties, promises, or obligations of any kind removed restrictions upon such operations. The doctrine of the balance of power supplied the pretext, for it had been happily discovered that that doctrine, originally invented to assure the existence of the weak states against the strong, might equally well be applied

---

[1] Joseph told Nassau: " Mon métier et celui du roi de Prusse est de travailler a qui sera le mieux avec la Russie." Aragon, *Nassau-Siegen*, p. 282.

[2] Lemontey, *Établissement monarchique de Louis XIV*, p. 369, note.

to combinations of the strong states to destroy the weak, providing the robbers divided the booty evenly among themselves.

But while the dismemberments of Poland fitted in with the whole spirit and tendencies of the politics of that age, there was also something new in them. The First Partition was novel in that this was the first occasion when foreign Powers had dismembered a state without having first gone to war with it or without bloodshed among themselves. If this was taking a long step forward towards making the ' *droit de convenance* ' the sole law in international relations, the Second Partition went even further. In 1793 the partitioning Powers did not even trouble themselves, as they had done in 1772, to invoke some kind of historic titles, drawn from the archives, as at least a formal satisfaction to the public law of Europe. The only excuses which they proffered for their usurpations were: the necessity they were under of exercising a sort of sanitary police over their corner of the Continent to prevent the contagious spread of dangerous ideas — a plea the like of which Europe had not heard, at least since the time of the Wars of Religion; and then their right to ' indemnify ' themselves for their beneficent exertions. If the brazen falseness and cynicism of this were fitted to shock even eighteenth century Europe, the violation by both the partitioning Powers of very recent promises and obligations to the Poles was also more open and shameless than at the time of the First Partition. Hence with right the Second Partition of Poland has always been held up as the supreme manifestation of the tendencies of the ' cabinet policy ' of the eighteenth century; the classic example of the moral degeneracy and rottenness of the old monarchical Europe. One cannot better sum up the moral aspects and not the least of the political consequences of the Partition than in the words of an old writer who declared:

" It was the kings themselves who, on the eve of the insurrection of peoples, taught them that no right existed for them except that of the strongest, and that when they invoked liberty, it was an ignoble sacrilege; they taught them that they were not to be believed even when they spoke of the public tranquillity, and of the respect due to the hereditary power of princes; for these same monarchs who constituted themselves the defenders of monarchy in France, dismembered Poland while appealing to the most anarchical liberty! In short, there was only one law for them, only one principle, that of interest and the glory of their dynasties. The peoples have profited by the lesson." [1]

[1] Laurent, *Études sur l'histoire de l'humanite*, xi, p. 333.

APPENDICES

APPENDIX I

LES deux Cours Impériales par l'article secret de leur Traité d'Alliance ont suffisamment pourvu au cas possible d'une attaque hostile de l'une d'Elles ou de toutes deux ensemble de la part du Roi de Prusse pendant qu'Elles seroient occupées à une guerre avec la Porte Ottomanne. Elles se trouvent également chargées, tant par des engagements contractés entre Elles en particulier que par un Traité solemnel et immédiat avec la République de Pologne de la garantir de ses possessions actuelles. La bonne foy est d'accord avec leur intérêt respectif, pour leur faire respecter religieusement l'obligation qu'Elles se sont imposée à Elles mêmes et pour ne pas souffrir qu'elle soit enfreinte d'aucune autre part. L'Impératrice a déjà manifesté dans plus d'une occasion à Sa Majesté l'Empereur des Romains la fermeté de ses intentions à cet égard. Cependant pour complaire à la sollicitude qu'il a marqué récemment à ce sujet, Sa Majesté Impériale ne balance pas à Lui donner de nouveau l'assurance la plus formelle, que si le Roi de Prusse entreprenoit dans les conjonctures présentes de s'emparer de quelques unes des possessions actuelles de la République de Pologne, Sa Majesté l'Impératrice n'hésiteroit pas un instant de se joindre à Sa Majesté l'Empereur pour faire conjointement à ce Prince les représentations les plus énergiques et les plus capables de le détourner d'un dessein nullement compatible avec la bonne intelligence et la tranquillité entre les voisins, ni avec la religion des Traités; et qu'en cas que ces représentations fussent infructueuses, Sa Majesté l'Impératrice, faisant cause commune avec Sa Majesté l'Empereur, employeroit pour empêcher l'effet d'un tel dessein toutes les forces et tous les moyens que la sûreté de son propre Empire et le besoin d'opposer une défence convenable à son Ennemie actuelle, la Porte Ottomanne, pourroient laisser à sa disposition.

Le Ministère de l'Impératrice, authorisé à être l'interprète des

sentimens et des intentions de Sa Majesté par rapport à la circonstance envisagée ci-dessus, croit avoir parfaitement rempli l'objet
désiré par la Cour Impériale de Vienne, en lui faisant délivrer cet
écrit muni de sa signature.

> Fait à St. Pétersbourg le 10. May (21), 1788.
> Cte. Jean d'Osterman.
> Alexandre, Cte. de Besborodko.
> A. de Marcoff.

APPENDIX II

On Catherine's Attitude towards the Project of a Russo-Polish Alliance

The views of the two chief Polish historians who have treated this
question differ fundamentally here, as on most other questions.
Kalinka declared: "Die Kaiserin ... wünschte entschieden ein Bündniss mit Polen zu schliessen";[1] while Askenazy asserts that the
Empress entered into the alliance project "with deep reluctance,
against her own better judgment," apparently only in order to
satisfy Potemkin.[2] On this point, I incline to the view of Kalinka,
for the following reasons.

(1) The conclusion of a close alliance with Poland was quite in
the traditions of Catherine's policy. Early in her reign, she and Panin
had been very eager for such a connection, especially for the event
of war with the Turks.[3] The reasons which led her to decline
Stanislas' offer during the Crimean crisis have not yet been cleared
up; but they may well have been of purely temporary or accidental
character. From a hitherto unpublished draft of a letter to Potemkin, undated but certainly of 1782–83, it appears that, at the last
Turkish crisis before the one under discussion in the text, the Empress had intended to draw the Poles into active coöperation with
Russia against the Porte, probably by means of a Confederation.[4]
And in discussing the execution of the 'Greek project' with Joseph
in 1782, Catherine spoke of getting Poland to 'enter the lists.'[5]

---

[1] *Der polnische Reichstag*, i, p. 81.

[2] *Przymierze polsko-pruskie*, p. 34.

[3] Чечулинъ, Внѣшняя политика Россіи, *1762–1774*, pp. 263 f.

[4] P. A., X, 53.

[5] September 10/21, 1782: Arneth, *Joseph II und Katharina*, p. 146.

(2) At Kanev, where the plan of alliance was proposed, Catherine allowed Stackelberg and Bezborodko to tell the King that this was a project that particularly pleased her, and one that must certainly be carried out — only carefully and at the right time.[1] Already she indicated that the time she had fixed for realizing it was at the meeting of the next ordinary Diet, then a year and a half in the future. After the Kanev meeting, in all the Russian documents that lie before us, it is assumed as a matter of course that an alliance is to be concluded; and the only question is as to the precise terms.[2]

(3) It is true that Catherine did declare that it was not useful for Poland to become "more active," but she was here condemning, not every alliance with Poland whatsoever, but one that would make the country stronger. It is true that she wrote Potemkin one day that if the Poles showed themselves loyal this time, it would be the first example in their history; but here she was obviously bent on dampening Potemkin's too sanguine hopes about the utility of the alliance, and especially on finding an excuse for preventing him from flooding her army with his Polish friends and creatures. (See his letter and her reply in Solov'ev (Ssolowjoff) *Geschichte des Falles von Polen*, p. 186.) Solov'ev comments quite justly: "Katharina theilte nicht die sanguinischen Hoffnungen Potomkins, der in allen Dingen seiner feurigen Phantasie freien Lauf liess; dennoch wandte sie alle Mittel an, Polen für das Bündniss zu gewinnen."

Finally, Catherine's long delays in attending to the alliance project cannot be adduced as evidence that she disliked and distrusted the plan; for, having from the outset fixed the autumn of 1788 as the time for her action, there was no need to announce her precise intentions much earlier; especially to announce them at Warsaw, where state secrets were very badly kept. In short, in opposition to Askenazy, I should say that Catherine was not dragged into this unfortunate plan by Potemkin, but that she went into it of her own accord, thinking to find in it the best means of keeping Poland in order during the Oriental war.

---

[1] The King to Kiciński: Kalinka, *Ostatnie lata*, ii. pp. 19 ff.

[2] Cf., for instance, the commentary of Bezborodko — doubtless the Empress' mouth-piece here — upon the draft-treaty sent from Warsaw (Русскій Архивъ, 1888, iii, pp. 184 ff.) This undated commentary was written not later than October 6/17, 1787.

APPENDIX III

On Potemkin's Secret Plans

It is well known that Potemkin exercised a stronger and more durable influence over Catherine than any other of her favorites and advisers; that he had a policy of his own, which often conflicted with hers; that he cherished vast, far-reaching personal ambitions, part of which he could not confide even to her. An investigation of those ambitions is of great importance for the study of Russian policy towards Poland in this period; but it is also extremely difficult, for it must be based, for the most part, on the conjectures or rumors as to Potemkin's secret plans of which contemporary writings and diplomatic correspondence are full, on more or less enigmatic passages scattered here and there in confidential letters, and then on what may be inferred from the Prince's own actions. Professor Askenazy, in the brilliant book so often cited here (*Przymierze polsko-pruskie*, pp. 35–41, 199 ff.), has been the first to penetrate deeply into this labyrinth of mysteries and to offer a consistent, acute, and convincing interpretation of Potemkin's secret aims. The following excursus is in substantial agreement with Askenazy's views; but it is also based on the first-hand study of the sources.

From the moment of his rise to power, Potemkin busied himself with plans for acquiring a 'sovereignty' somewhere outside of Russia; this, both because of personal ambition and because it behooved him to provide for his own prospects in case of the Empress' death. If he lived to see Paul or Alexander ascend the throne — both bitterly hostile to him — he could expect no other fate than that of Menšikov or Bühren, unless he were out of reach. His first thought, apparently, was to acquire the duchy of Courland. Catherine not only approved this scheme, but drew up a plan for getting the reigning Duke deposed and putting Potemkin in his place.[1] For some reason, however, she suspended the execution of this plan. Potemkin held to it at least until 1779, but after that abandoned it, whether because he was bought off by the Duke, as rumor had it, or be-

---

[1] See Бильбасовъ, Присоединеніе Курляндіи къ Россіи, in the Рус. Старъ. lxxxiii, ⁱ, pp. 31 ff., especially the rescript to Stackelberg of May 2/13, 1776, in which the Empress announces her intentions.

cause he found Courland too poor an establishment and too near St. Petersburg.[1]

Next, perhaps, or, more probably, contemporaneously with the Courland project, went the plan of gaining the crown of Poland. His acquisition in 1775 of the Polish *indygenat* (a sort of naturalization among the *szlachta*) may have been intended as the first step in this direction. Then from 1776 on, Potemkin appeared as the protector and instigator of the opposition in Poland, the patron of that unholy clique of adventurers, fanatics, and scoundrels who later brought about the Confederation of Targowica and, indirectly, the Second Partition of the Republic. By 1781 it had become the universal conviction at St. Petersburg that the Polish crown was the goal of Potemkin's ambition.[2]

But as the 'Greek project' came more and more to the front, the favorite seems to have transferred his attention to the more glittering project of carving out for himself a new realm around the Black Sea. The Danubian Provinces would serve as the nucleus of this 'Kingdom of Dacia,' but that was not sufficient. Potemkin was accused of wishing to set himself up as a feudal prince, or even as independent sovereign, in 'New Russia,' the Crimea and the adjacent regions already annexed to the Russian Empire, of which he was

---

[1] That Potemkin held to the Courland project as late as 1779 appears from an unpublished letter from Stackelberg to him of January 21/February 1, 1779 (P. A., X, 887). See also the memoirs of his emissary, Karl Heinrich von Heyking, edited by Baron Alfons von Heyking, *Aus Polens und Kurlands letzten Tagen*, pp. 212 ff. Heyking supposes that the Empress did not want the Courland plan to succeed, which would indicate that her distrust of his ambition, so marked later on, began at a very early date. See also Görtz, *Denkwürdigkeiten* i, pp. 123 ff.; Dohm, *Denkwürdigkeiten* ii, Zusätze, xxvi f.; [Helbig], "Potemkin der Taurier," *Minerva*, xxiii, pp. 461 ff.; Seraphim, *Geschichte des Herzogtums Kurland*, 2nd ed., pp. 308 f.

[2] That is the statement of Dohm (ii, Zusätze, xlv ff.), who had it on the authority of Görtz, the Prussian envoy at that time. Cf. also Ségur, *Mémoires*, ii, p. 264; Herrmann, *Russische Geschichte, Ergänzungsband*, p. 107 — where Potemkin's ambitions on the Polish crown are suggested as early as 1775; Castéra, *Histoire de Catherine II*, iii, p. 358. Whether Potemkin ever wholly abandoned the hope of getting the Polish crown may perhaps be doubted. At the very end of his life some of those nearest him surmised that that was still the object of his ambition; see Енгельгардтъ, Записки, pp. 124 f., and in the Memoirs of Stanisław Nałecz Małachowski (Polish), the very interesting but somewhat questionable tale related after his death by Potemkin's favorite niece, the Countess Branicki: "his intention was to win over all the Cossacks, unite with the Polish army, and proclaim himself King of Poland."

governor-general and almost uncontrolled master.[1] However that may be, it is probable that he was much more concerned with the designs on Poland discussed in the text.

The exact extent of his purchases of land in Poland cannot be ascertained at present; but it was undoubtedly enormous. The enterprise began on a large scale about 1781;[2] it was continued with the aid of the Empress, who, for instance, helped him to effect a loan of five million rubles for this purpose in 1787; it went so far that even in 1788 Buchholtz, the Prussian minister at Warsaw, reported that Potemkin had sold all his estates in Russia in order to buy land in Poland, and that this indicated clearly his designs on the country.[3] The statement is substantially true. Askenazy cites a "fragmentary inventory" of Potemkin's property, made out after his death, which would show that he had only 6,000 male peasants in Russia, but over 70,000 in Poland.[4] The latter figure is certainly far too small, however, for from one reliable source it appears that the great estate of Śmila alone contained about 112,000 male 'souls.'[5] At the time of his death the Prince still retained some not very considerable estates in Russia, while his Polish possessions far exceeded in size many a German or Italian state.

These purchases were made in the southeastern palatinates, especially in that of Kiev. That they had a political motive cannot be doubted. Potemkin tried to convince Catherine that it was for the good of the Empire that he should buy up all that corner of Poland which projected into Russian territory and which it was so important for Russia to control. This was to be a veiled form of annexation.[6] Catherine, however, seems presently to have suspected that his real aim was very different and less disinterested; and henceforth she was not so ready to help in these acquisitions.[7] One day the remark escaped her in the presence of her secretary: "From his newly bought

---

[1] See the biography of the Prince in the Рус. Старина, xii, p. 695, xiv, p. 246, Helbig, in *Minerva*, xxiii, p. 228.

[2] Cf. Cobenzl to Joseph, September 12, 1781, *F. R. A.*, II, liii, p. 226.

[3] Report of September 12, B. A., *Fol.* 323.

[4] *Op. cit.*, p. 36.

[5] See the article by Rulikowski on Śmila in the *Słownik geograficzny królestwa polskiego*.

[6] See his letter to the Empress of March 27/April 7, 1788, Сборникъ военно-историческихъ матеріаловъ. Бумаги Князя Григорія Александровича Потемкина-Таврическаго, vi, pp. 252 f.

[7] Cf. her letter to him of January 11/22, 1788, Русская Старина, xvi, p. 446.

lands in Poland Potemkin will, perhaps, make a *tertium quid*, independent of both Russia and Poland."[1] Very similar opinions were generally current at that time. It was supposed, and probably with truth, that as a first step Potemkin wished to have a duchy created for him in the Ukraine, which should be a fief of Poland in the same loose, unreal way as Courland was.[2] At Kanev the Russian ambassador himself told Stanislas Augustus that he had heard that Potemkin desired his great estate at Śmila turned into some kind of a feudal principality.[3] And *de facto* Śmila was such a *status in statu*, with its court, its elaborate military-feudal system, its army of horse and foot.[4]

As to Potemkin's attitude towards the King's plan for an alliance, cf. Stanislas' letters to Kiciński of March 21, March 29, May 8, 1787, in Kalinka, *Ostatnie lata*, ii; Stanislas to Potemkin, May 7, July 16, September 24, October 1, 1787 (P. A., V. 166) and July 14, 1787 (Petrograd Imperial Public Library, Papers of V. S. Popov—these unpublished letters are mainly filled with thanks for Potemkin's efforts to put through the alliance); Брикнеръ, Потемкинъ, pp. 86 ff.; Aragon, *Nassau-Siegen*, pp. 101 ff., 131 ff.; Potemkin's remarks on the King's draft for the alliance treaty, in the Рус. Архивъ, 1888, iii, pp. 184 ff.

The Branicki-Potocki plan for a Confederation in the provinces, the 'national militia,' etc., sent in with a recommendation by Potemkin, probably in January, 1788, is printed in the Рус. Архивъ, 1874, ii, pp. 269–280, and in Kalinka, *Ostatnie lata*, ii, pp. 104–113.

For Potemkin's urgent pleas to conclude matters with the Poles at once, to make use of the magnates, to enlist as many of the Poles as possible in the Russian armies, etc., see his correspondence with Catherine for the first half of 1788 in the Рус. Старина, xvi, and the Сборникъ И. Р. И. О., xxvii. Cf. also Храповицкій, Дневникъ, April 14/25, 1788, pp. 43 f.; Popov to Potemkin, April 14/25, 1788, in the Рус. Арх., 1865, pp. 751 f.; Potemkin to Suvorov, April 29/May 10, 1788, in the Рус. Старина, xiii, pp. 32 f.

On Potemkin's intrigues with the Polish magnates, and the plans for a Confederation which should "restore all the national liberties

---

[1] Храповицкій, Дневникъ, March 16/27, 1787, p. 16.

[2] Cf. the remarks of the Grand Duke Paul, in June, 1787, cited by Bilbasov in the Рус. Стар. lxxxiii, ⁱ, p. 32. Stanislas Augustus worried much over this danger: see Брикнеръ, Потемкинъ, p. 87.

[3] The King to Kiciński, March 21, 1787, Kalinka, *Ostatnie lata*, ii, p. 12.

[4] Cf. the above-cited article in the *Słownik geograficzny*.

without restriction," and perhaps even establish some new kind of oligarchical federalism: cf. the secret memoir of Rzewuski to the Prussian government, November, 1788 (B. A., *Pologne, Fasc.* 1097); Buchholtz's report of November 1 (B. A., *Fol.* 323), and Lucchesini's of December 25, 1788 (B. A., *R.* 9, 27); Zaleski, *Korespondencya krajowa Stanisława Augusta*, pp. 236 ff., 242; Kalinka, *Der polnische Reichstag*, i, pp. 64 ff., 86 f., 105 ff., 113 ff.; Askenazy, *op. cit.*, pp. 37 f.

On Potemkin's efforts to recruit troops in Poland (apart from the forces to be furnished by the magnates), and especially to enlist Cossacks: cf. Арх. Гос. Совѣта, September 25/October 6, 1787; orders to Nerančič, January 25/February 5, 1788, in the Сборникъ воен.-истор. матеріаловъ, vi, pp. 196 f.; Potemkin to Catherine, March 18/29, 1788, *ibid.*, pp. 243 f. Dzieduszycki to Deboli, April 23, 1788 (M. A., Польша, IV, 8), encloses a passport given to a Russian recruiting officer, in Potemkin's name, to enlist troops in the four southeastern palatinates.

On Potemkin's extraordinary interest in Cossacks, his efforts during the winter of 1787–88 to organize a new and very numerous Cossack army, his plan for forming great Cossack settlements along the Polish and Turkish frontiers, etc.: cf. Петровъ, Вторая Турецкая Война, i, pp. 125–129; Stein, *Geschichte des russischen Heeres*, pp. 172 ff.; documents in the Сборникъ воен.-истор. матеріаловъ, vi, *passim;* Арх. Воронцова, xiii, p. 227.

That along with his other projects Potemkin also held in reserve as early as 1788–89 the plan of heading an Orthodox and Cossack rising in the Ukraine is only an hypothesis, but a very probable one. It is quite certain that he later had such a plan (1790); it was universally ascribed to him in Poland during the troubles in the Ukraine in 1789, reported by all the foreign ministers to their courts, and only half denied at St. Petersburg. Cf. Kalinka, *Der polnische Reichstag*, i, pp. 440–443, and Askenazy, *op. cit.*, pp. 38 f.

APPENDIX IV

ON THE CHANGE IN PRUSSIAN POLICY IN THE SUMMER OF 1789

It is only within the last fifteen years that historians have realized the importance of the summer of 1789 as marking a decided turning-point in Prussian policy. For recent discussions of the subject, see:

P. Wittichen, *Die polnische Politik Preussens*, ch. v; F. C. Wittichen, "Die Politik des Grafen Hertzberg," in *Hist. Vjschr.*, ix, pp. 183 ff.; Krauel, *Graf Hertzberg als Minister*, pp. 44 ff.; Luckwaldt, "Zur Vorgeschichte der Konvention von Reichenbach," in *Delbrück-Festschrift*, pp. 232–256; Salomon, *William Pitt*, i[i]., pp. 451 f.; Askenazy, *Przymierze polsko-pruskie*, pp. 55 f. The chief printed sources are the correspondence between Hertzberg and Lucchesini in Dembinski, *op. cit.*, and that of Schlieffen with Hertzberg and Ewart in *Nachricht von einigen Häusern des Geschlechtes der von Schlieffen*, ii, pp. 408 ff.

To Paul Wittichen and Krauel belongs the honor of having first brought to light Hertzberg's proposals for immediate vigorous action that summer. These proposals occupy the central place in Wittichen's defence of Hertzberg, as he finds here the occasion when the minister's much-criticized plan might have been brilliantly executed. Here was the unique opportunity, the neglect of which avenged itself at Reichenbach. Salomon accepts this view, while Krauel argues against it — as I think, with justice. For one may, perhaps, accept the apparently unanimous opinion of the Prussian generals that the army was not ready in September of 1789; and moreover, if one was to go to war, there was no need to begin with such a declaration as Hertzberg proposed, which, without conciliating the enemy, would have alienated every friend. The belligerent Powers would probably have made peace with each other on terms reciprocally much more advantageous than Hertzberg's, and Prussia would have been left isolated and discredited.

Wittichen is responsible for placing in circulation a story which I regard as at best only an unproved hypothesis, and probably an error: the story, namely, of Hertzberg's proposed "Anschlag auf Gross-Polen." He declares that in case the Imperial Courts rejected the Prussian plan of pacification, Hertzberg intended immediately and without further preliminaries to seize a large part, perhaps all, of Great Poland, so that Prussia would thus at once realize the part of the 'plan' that most concerned her, whatever might happen in other quarters. Wittichen thinks that Russia would have offered no opposition to this — at the most, she might have appropriated a few Polish territories herself; Austria would have been terrorized or coerced into submission; as for the Poles, Hertzberg had isolated them so successfully that they must have accepted whatever Prussia dictated. This would, indeed, have been a piece

of treachery and high-handedness seldom paralleled. F. C. Wittichen, Salomon, and Askenazy repeat the tale much as P. Wittichen
has given it.

It is to be noted, however, that none of the texts cited by Wittichen in support of his theory — a few very vague passages from
letters — contain the slightest proof that Great Poland was to be
won by such a violent procedure. There is nothing to show that the
minister did not hold to his old plan of acquiring (a part of) Great
Poland by voluntary cession from the Republic, in return for Galicia
wrested away from Austria.

To the best of my knowledge, we have from Hertzberg's pen only
one fairly concrete account of the military measures recommended
by him that summer. It is contained in his letter to Schlieffen of
October 22, 1789.[1] Here there is no reference to any 'Anschlag auf
Gross-Polen' — an omission which Wittichen attempts to explain
away by all manner of conjectures. Instead there is mention only of
two preliminary military movements, the one on the frontiers of
Galicia, the other on the side of Livonia; and then, in case of a refusal on the part of the Imperial Courts, the invasion of Austrian
territory is to begin.

In Hertzberg's statements regarding a possible war with the Imperial Courts one almost invariably finds him counting on the co-
operation of the Poles. The following passages seem to me significant (August 1, 1789, Hertzberg to Lucchesini): "Je suis d'accord
avec vous sur la nécessité de frapper le grand coup pour nous et pour
nos amis. . . . il me semble . . . qu'il vaudroit mieux, après avoir
reçu notre dernière réponse de Constantinople, que nous offrions
notre plan dilemmatique . . . comme en Hollande, et qu'après le
refus qu'on peut prévoir, nous concertions et exécutions tout de suite
avec nos amis notre grand plan." [2]

(August 22, Hertzberg to the King) . . . "Il me semble que le
cas existeroit toujours de présenter aux deux Cours Impériales sa
[His Majesty's] médiation armée et notre Plan avec le mouvement
de l'armée; . . . en cas qu'il [the plan] ne fût pas accepté par les
deux Cours Impériales, V. M. est sûr de l'alliance de la Porte, de la
Suède et de la Pologne, même avant d'en avoir les actions solemnels
[*sic*]." [3] It would seem hardly probable that even Hertzberg could

[1] Schlieffen, *op. cit.*, pp. 430 ff., reprinted by P. Wittichen, *op. cit.*, pp. 93 ff.
[2] Dembiński, *Documents*, i, p. 403.
[3] B. A., *R.* 9, 27.

have fancied that the Poles would join in the war on Austria, if Prussia began operations by seizing Great Poland.

Summing it up, I think Wittichen's view rests on a mere conjecture, which finds very little support from the sources, and for which anything like a solid proof has not yet been furnished. It is to be noted that Luckwaldt, who has written the most detailed and the most recent account of the events of that summer, makes no mention of any proposed 'Anschlag auf Gross-Polen.'

APPENDIX V

OSTERMANN TO ALOPEUS, MARCH 14/25, 1791 [M. A., Пруссія, VI, 24]

J'ai mis, Monsieur, sous les yeux de l'Impératrice Votre dépêche du 8/19 Févr.[1] Son contenu a été d'autant plus agréable à S. M. I. qu'il est parfaitement conforme aux intentions que Vous avés toujours été chargé d'annoncer en Son nom, tant par les instructions que Vous avés emportées en partant d'ici, que par celles qu'on Vous a fait parvenir ultérieurement durant Votre mission à Berlin. Les unes et les autres expriment constamment le desir et le voeu de S. M. I. de conserver et de maintenir une bonne harmonie imperturbable avec S. M. Prussienne. En effet ce système étant analogue aux intérêts des deux Monarchies et le Roi de Prusse paraissant partager à cet égard la conviction de l'Impératrice, il ne s'agit que de calmer et d'écarter les ombrages et les soupçons qui ont dirigé jusqu'à présent la politique de la Cour de Berlin en sens contraire. Le moyen qu'on Vous a suggéré et dont Vous rendés compte dans la dépêche susmentionnée pour établir et consolider la confiance entre les deux Cours ne repugne en rien à la sincerité des vues de S. M. I. et de Ses dispositions à l'égard de S. M. Prussienne. Elle a assés développées [*sic*] ces dernières dans toute Sa conduite pour ne laisser aucun doute de la facilité avec laquelle Elle se prêtera à tout ce qui pourra effectuer un rapprochement aussi désirable pour les deux Souverains. C'est dans ce sens que nous nous sommes expliqués dernièrement aussi vis-à-vis de la Cour de Dannemark en reponse aux ouvertures qu'elle nous a faites au nom de celle de Berlin relativement aux conjonctures actuelles; et nous avons ordre de Vous autoriser, Monsieur, en cas que cette dernière persiste dans les dispositions qu'on Vous a

[1] For this dispatch, see Dembiński, *Documents*, i, pp. 116–119.

témoignées en dernier lieu, à lui annoncer que l'Impératrice ne fera nulle difficulté de donner les mains à un arrangement provisionel touchant le Traité d'alliance que S. M. Prussienne desire de conclure avec Elle à la suite de notre paix avec la Porte Ottomanne. Vous nous instruirés de la forme que la Cour de Berlin voudra donner à l'acte ou à la convention secrete qu'on pourroit arrêter entre les deux Cours. Nous ne dirons qu'un mot de ce qui doit faire la substance de cette transaction. Elle doit d'abord porter l'engagement mutuel de renouveller après la présente guerre finie les anciennes liaisons entre la Russie et la Prusse sur le même pied où elles ont existées jusqu'à l'année 1788. Ensuite on stipulera en termes propres la promesse positive de la part de S. M. Prussienne, non seulement de ne point s'opposer à ce que l'Impératrice amenât la Porte Ottomanne par tous les moyens possibles à faire la paix aux conditions que S. M. a proposées, à savoir: le renouvellement pur et simple des anciens Traités et transactions antérieures à cette guerre-ci et la cession d'Oczakoff avec son territoire jusqu'au Dniester, de manière que cette rivière serve désormais de frontière entre les deux Empires, mais aussi à employer auprès de la dite Porte Ses représentations et Ses exhortations les plus efficaces et les plus énergiques à fin de la déterminer à accepter ces conditions. . . . Si . . . S. M. Prussienne se détermine à réaliser un accord ou un arrangement analogues au plan que nous venons d'esquisser et qu'Elle Vous fasse connaître Ses intentions définitives là dessus, nous n'attendrons que le rapport que Vous nous en ferés, pour Vous envoyer le projet d'acte ou de convention secrete avec les pleins pouvoirs requis pour le conclure et le signer et le convertir en instrument authentique et revetu de toutes les formalités usitées dans les transactions entre les Souverains.

Le courrier que nous Vous dépêchons, pour mieux cacher sa destination, a ordre de ne s'arrêter auprès de Vous que le tems qu'il lui faudra pour Vous remettre cette dépêche et de passer d'abord à Hambourg, où Mr. de Gross le retiendra une huitaine de jours et Vous le renverra pour chercher les rapports que Vous serés dans le cas de nous transmettre et pour nous les apporter ici. Vous voyés que de cette manière le tems sera épargné autant qu'il est possible et qu'il ne tiendra qu'à la Cour de Berlin d'écarter les extrémités auxquelles les circonstances au grand regret de l'Impératrice et au grand detriment des intérêts respectifs paroissent avoir acheminé les choses.

APPENDIX VI

Notes on Chapter IX

1. On the Origin of Bischoffwerder's Second Mission to Leopold

How far the Emperor was responsible for bringing about this mission is a disputed question. It was asserted in the Prussian envoy's instructions that Leopold had asked to have Bischoffwerder sent to him; and this statement has been very frequently repeated by German historians. Leopold, on the other hand, denied having expressed such a wish;[1] and although this has been declared to be merely a *démenti* for use at St. Petersburg, I am inclined to think the Emperor spoke the truth. If he had really expressed the wish for such a mission, why was it that on Bischoffwerder's arrival his first step was to attempt to persuade the Prussian envoy that he had not done so? Besides, in his report to Grenville of May 15 Elgin said merely: "I even venture to conceive it possible, that should His Prussian Majesty send to the Emperor some confidential person with powers similar to those His Majesty has been pleased to entrust with me (I must add that the Emperor repeatedly mentioned Colonel Bischoffwerder in high terms of approbation), such preliminary stipulations might be immediately signed by us,"[2] . . . The same day Elgin wrote to Ewart at Berlin about the matter, and in the translation of that letter communicated by Ewart to the Prussian ministry the important passage runs: "il m'a paru qu'il Lui [the Emperor] seroit fort agréable qu'une personne de confiance fût envoyée auprès de Lui par Sa Majesté Prussienne avec des pouvoirs semblables aux miens. Sa Majesté Impériale m'a parlé très souvent du Colonel de Bischoffwerder dans les termes de la plus haute Estime et Confiance, qui prouvoient combien Elle désiroit de le revoir."[3] From this it appears that Elgin himself, encouraged by some words of praise for Bischoffwerder on the part of the Emperor, conceived the idea of bringing the 'worthy Colonel' upon the scene in order to help along his own negotiation.

---

[1] "Journal über die Verhandlungen mit Bischoffwerder," Vivenot, i, p. 178.
[2] *F. z. D. G.*, v, p. 251. [3] B. A., *R.* 1, *Conv.* 172.

The question has a certain importance, inasmuch as the Emperor's supposed request has often been taken as a proof of his eagerness in May for an *immediate* alliance with Prussia — an eagerness of which I find no clear signs until about the middle of June, when French affairs suddenly assumed a dangerous aspect.

2. On the Vienna Convention of July 25, 1791

The origin of the much-discussed 'separate article' on Polish affairs may be traced from the following excerpts.

(1) February 21, 1791, Bischoffwerder proposed as one of the articles of the projected alliance: "D'éloigner par des moyens sages et bien concertés l'influence de la Russie en Pologne (comme le foyer d'où la plus part [*sic*] des intrigues de la Cour de Pétersbourg sont parties) sans rechercher néanmoins aucune influence prépondérante en Pologne, ne désirant que le maintien de la constitution actuelle de ce Royaume et un Roi librement élu de la nation polonoise selon leurs Loix sans l'intervention de la Russie.

"(Pour rendre cet Article ostensible on propose de le changer ainsi.) D'éloigner par des moyens sages et bien concertés tout influence prépondérante en Pologne de la part de ses trois voisins, de manière à y maintenir toutefois la constitution actuelle de ce Royaume et un Roy librement élu par la nation polonoise selon leurs loix." [1]

(2) The Austrian 'observation' on this was: "On est prêt d'entrer dans ces vues et l'on est même si persuadé qu'elles sont propres à combiner les véritables interêts des trois Puissances voisines de la Pologne qu'on ne croit pas difficile de consolider ces vues par un nouveau concert entre elles." [2]

(3) July 22, 1791, Bischoffwerder again presented this article in the 'ostensible' form just given, with the additional clauses: "Et pour écarter — après la Révolution qui vient de se faire dans ce Royaume — tout Sujet de jalousie et d'ombrage, les deux Cours sont tombés d'accord: qu'il ne pourra jamais être question d'un mariage entre l'Infante et un Prince des trois Puissances voisines, ni de l'élévation d'un tel Prince dans le cas d'une nouvelle élection au Throne de Pologne." [3]

(4) The final (Austrian) redaction: "Les intérêts et la tranquillité des Puissances voisines de la Pologne rendant infiniment désirable qu'il s'établisse entre Elles un concert propre à éloigner toute

[1] V. A., *Vorträge*, 1791.　　　[2] V. A., *ibid.*　　　[3] V. A., *ibid.*

jalousie ou appréhension de prépondérance, les Cours de Vienne ét de Berlin conviendront et inviteront la Cour de Russie de convenii avec Elles, qu'Elles n'entreprendront rien pour altérer l'intégrité et le maintien de la libre constitution de la Pologne; qu'Elles ne chercheront jamais à placer un Prince de leurs Maisons sur le Trône de Pologne, ni par un mariage avec la Princesse l'Infante, ni dans le cas d'une nouvelle élection, et n'employeront point leur influence pour déterminer le choix de la République dans l'un ou l'autre cas en faveur d'un autre Prince hors d'un concert mutuel entre Elles." [1]

Askenazy [2] finds a contradiction between the recognition of the new constitution implied in the mention of the Infanta and the reference to a possible new election to the throne. He overlooks the fact that the acceptance of the crown by Frederick Augustus was by no means certain, and that in case he refused it, a new election would be necessary even according to the new constitution. I think he is equally in error in asserting that the apparent recognition accorded to the new form of government was belied and reduced to a mere sham by the setting up of a condition impossible of fulfilment, namely the approval of Russia. In the first place, it is nowhere said in the article that Austria and Prussia would submit to a Russian veto on the new constitution; and secondly, they could not know at that time in Vienna that the Empress would never give her consent to the new régime in Poland — in fact, they had reason to think that she would.

The article was certainly not considered at Warsaw as an open sign of Prussia's desertion (as Askenazy regards it): on the contrary, Stanislas Augustus was deeply gratified and encouraged by it. See his letters to Bukaty of August 20, and to the Crown Secretary Rzewuski of August 24, Kalinka, *Ostatnie lata*, ii, pp. 199 ff., and Smoleński, *Ostatni rok sejmu wielkiego*, pp. 240 f.; also de Caché's reports of August 24, 31, September 3, 10 (V. A., *Polen, Berichte*, 1791); Bulgakov's of August 13/24 (M. A., Польша, III, 64).

3. On Bischoffwerder's Attitude towards an Intervention in France

There is no doubt that in signing the Vienna Convention Bischoffwerder went far beyond the instructions given him by the Prussian ministry, but it is not improbable that he may have had further

---

[1] V. A., *Vorträge*, 1791. [2] *Przymierze polsko-pruskie*, pp. 150 ff.

secret orders from the King. This suspicion arises particularly with regard to French affairs. It has been noted in the text that the King was busy in September, 1790, with plans for an intervention in France; in November he promised one of the Count of Artois' agents his aid under certain conditions;[1] in the spring of 1791 there appear to have been further negotiations, in the course of which he stipulated the repayment of his expenses as the condition of his coöperation.[2] These *pourparlers* came to the knowledge of the Prussian ministry only in June, and then only imperfectly, but they were doubtless known to Bischoffwerder. It is also worth notice that some months later Prince Hohenlohe — who as early as September, 1790, was the confidant of his master's views on French affairs — told Fersen that Bischoffwerder on going to Italy had been charged to propose to the Emperor an intervention in France and a scheme for territorial 'indemnities' similar to that which had once been suggested to Reuss.[3] According to Hohenlohe, Leopold rejected the latter idea. Carisien, the Swedish envoy in Berlin, in general a very good observer, also held that one of the chief objects of Bischoffwerder's mission to Italy was to find out the Emperor's views on the state of affairs in France.[4] Insufficient as the evidence is, it is difficult to understand how Bischoffwerder could have entered from the outset with such zeal upon Leopold's proposals for an intervention in France, unless he knew that they corresponded closely to the views of his own sovereign.

APPENDIX VII

On the Austrian Attitude towards the Plan for the Permanent Union of Saxony and Poland

Sybel long maintained that the plan in question was originated by Leopold soon after the revolution of the Third of May, and was proposed by him at that time to Russia.[5] This position Sybel later had to abandon. Herrmann was right in maintaining that the project

---

[1] Schlitter, *Marie Christine*, p. xxii.

[2] Fersen to Taube, April 11, in Klinckowström, *Le Comte de Fersen et la Cour de France*, i, p. 99; instruction to Baron Roll, May 21, B. A., *R.* 1, *Conv.* 172.

[3] Fersen from Prague, September 6, 1791, Klinckowström, *op. cit.*, i, pp. 24 f.

[4] Taube, *Svenska beskickningars berättelser,* p. 85. Cf. also Taube to Fersen, February 6, 1792, Klinckowström, *op. cit.*, ii, p. 165.

[5] See *H. Z.*, x, pp. 418 ff., xii, pp. 280 ff.

originated with the Elector, but wrong in asserting that Leopold never supported it.[1] Beer's account [2] is much more accurate, but fails to notice the real reason for the Emperor's cautious attitude in this matter: the fact that his daughter was married to the prince to whom it was proposed to assure the Polish succession.

Frederick Augustus conceived the plan of the Saxon-Polish personal union as early as June, 1791; [3] it was broached by his minister Gutschmidt to Spielmann at Pillnitz; [4] it seems to have formed one of the topics discussed in a letter from the Elector to the Emperor not long afterwards.[5] At Vienna the plan was immediately approved.[6] While, for the reason mentioned in the text, the point was passed over lightly in the ostensible instructions given to Landriani, Kaunitz added in a secret postscript that this plan was of much importance for Austrian interests, and continued: "Mr. de Landriani ne laissera pas de séconder cet objet autant qu'il pourra sans risquer qu'on nous soupçonne des vues secondaires. Comme au reste l'Electeur tient lui-même très-fortement à la réussite de ce point, il sera plus facile de combiner a cet égard le but essentiel avec les ménagemens délicats auxquels nous sommes astreints." [7] This fear of being suspected of 'vues sécondaires,' which has hitherto been overlooked by historians, is the dominant consideration in the Austrian utterances on this subject.

APPENDIX VIII

ON THE NOTE FROM CATHERINE TO ZUBOV REPORTED BY GOLTZ, FEBRUARY 3, 1792 [8]

This enigmatic episode has been related by all historians of the period, and has given rise to a variety of conjectures. It has been almost universally stated that Goltz actually saw the note in question, but I think that can hardly have been the case, for the envoy nowhere claims to have seen it, and he complains in his report of February 7

---

[1] *F. z. D. G.*, iv, pp. 397 ff.   [2] *H. Z.*, xxvii, pp. 11 ff.

[3] Hartig's report of June 24, V. A., *Sachsen, Berichte*, 1791.

[4] Spielmann to Kaunitz, August 31, Vivenot, i, pp. 239 f.

[5] Cf. the instructions to L. Cobenzl of November 12.

[6] Cf. Schlitter, *Kaunitz, Ph. Cobenzl und Spielmann*, pp. 89 f.

[7] V. A., *F. A.* 62 *A*.

[8] The several dispatches from Goltz cited in this appendix are all to be found in the B. A., *R.* XI, *Russland*, 133.

that he had been unable to learn more of the details of the Russian project, since "*le personnage peureux et borné qui avoit fait la lecture en question*[1] n'a rien su ajouter aux notions déjà communiquées." Cf. the phrase in his report of February 3: "Ce papier n'ayant été lû qu'à la hâte, il a été impossible d'en savoir davantage." The point is not without interest, because it has been so often assumed that the note was written only to be shown to Goltz, and that it was a *ballon d'essai* intended to tempt Prussia out of her reserve.[2]

I think it more probable that this was an ordinary case of a 'leak.' Whitworth, the English envoy, to whom the Russians could have no possible reason for letting out such secrets, had managed to get even fuller information as to these same Russian plans earlier than Goltz, without the latter's knowledge, and apparently through the same channel. If the secret was betrayed in one case, why not in the other?[3]

Whitworth does not speak of a note, but the plan which he reports agrees almost entirely with that described by Goltz. He refrained at first from confiding in his colleague. The latter appears to have broached the subject to him, and to have used his (Whitworth's) knowledge to verify the sources of his own information.

The Russian archives have as yet failed to disclose any documents bearing on this episode. Under such circumstances the incident must remain obscure, but we are certainly not in a position to speak of it, with Häusser, as "a Russian proposition to Prussia for a partition of Poland." All that we can say is that some underling, possibly a servant, in Zubov's household or in the Russian Foreign Office, came to the English and Prussian ministers with an extremely interesting story about the Empress' plans against Poland and her readiness to propose a partition; and that in his conversation with Goltz he claimed that the source of his knowledge was a note from Catherine to Zubov, which he had managed to read. Possibly he was sent to make this revelation by his superiors. More probably he was selling information, genuine or fictitious. The story he told has, in itself, not a single improbable feature. We know, for instance, that at one time there was talk at St. Petersburg of sending Repnin to command the army against Poland.[4] Igelström went

[1] The italics are mine.

[2] Cf., e.g., Häusser, *Deutsche Geschichte*, i, pp. 352 f., and Heidrich, *Preussen im Kampfe gegen die französische Revolution*, pp. 177 f.

[3] Cf. Whitworth's report of January 31, 1792, Herrmann, *Ergänzungsband*, pp. 243 f.   [4] See Сборникъ, xxix, p. 175.

down to take the command in the government of Smolensk just about this time,[1] thus corroborating another detail of the story. It is quite possible, then, that Goltz's informant was truly reporting a genuine note — and vastly important state secrets.

APPENDIX IX

FELIX POTOCKI TO POTEMKIN, MAY 14, 1791 (FROM VIENNA).
[ORIGINAL. M. A., Польша, II, 7][2]

Monseigneur.

Je eu l'honneur de recevoire a Paris la lettre que Votre Altesse a bien voulu m'écrire avant son depart pour Petersbourg, je quitté a l'insant ce pais la pour me rapprocher de vous en attendant ce que S. M. l'Imperatrice voudra bien fair pour la conservation de Notre Republique, mais en arrivant ici je trouvé les nouvelles qu'elle est aneantie ainsi que notre liberté, par le coup que le Roi vient de lui porter, ce Roi que l'Imperatrice a donné à une nation libre n'est plus chef d'unne Republique, il est souverain d'unne Monarchie nouvelle, nous avons perdue notre libertée, nos voisins perdiron bientot la tranquilité, il est donc de lur interet, il est du nôtre, de briser la fatal constitution que le Roi vient de nous imposer, de rétablir la Republique et de lui donner unne forme stable. Tout bon Polonois qui n'est pas seduit par la Cabale Prussienne et Roiale est persuadé que le salut de la Patrie ne peut deja nous venir que de la Russie, sans elle la nation autrefois libre est asservie, le Nombre des Mecontents dans toutes les provinces de la Pologne est grande, mais ils sont intimide, leur courage se relevera si on leur donne de l'appui. Je prend la liberté de joindre ici un projet du Hetman Rzewuski, ce n'est que pour vous fair voir notre bonne volonté, car pour les projets je croi qu'il ne faudra les former qu'après être convenu de la volonté de briser les chaines qu'on vient d'imposer à la Pologne. Pour moi je suis persuadé qu'il est impossible de maintenir la liberté de la Pologne si on laisse la Royauté jointe à la République, un guvernement federative seroit le plus convenable à un pais étendue qui doit servire de bariere entre les plus grandes Monarchies du Monde, les provinces independentes et unies ne pouroient jamais être asservie par un seul, car personne ne pourroit se servir de la force integral de l'état si les provinces ont leur guvernement, leurs

---

[1] Goltz's report of February 17.

[2] I have followed the writer's astonishing spelling and punctuation.

armées, et leurs trésors separes, si leurs interet est necesserement diverses, et si elles ne sont jointes que par l'interet de leur conservation. Je ne sai si je me trompe, mais je croi que ce seroit le moment d'executer ce projet, et la chose se fairé naturelement, si la Russie donnée de l'appui au mecontents, il faudra commencer par unne confederation dans les quatre Palatinats de Volhinie, Podolie, Kiovie et Bracław, qui forme la plus grande Moitié de la force, de la Population, et des revenues de la Pologne, un autre confederation se formeroit en Lituanie et ce deux Confederation etabliroient dans chaque de ces provinces un guvernement civile et militaire, les revenues de l'état serviroient pur solder les troupes de la Province et on formeroit un tribunal pour que la joustice ne soit pas interrompue. Les provinces protesteroient contre le gouvernement et la constitution que le Roi leurs a imposée on jureroient de maintenir la liberté on inviteroient les autres Palatinats a immiter leur exemple, et bientot il seroit suivie, la revolution finiroit par un congres de Provinces Confederes qui prenderoient le nom des Provinces independentes et unies de la Republique de Pologne, on pourroit maime conserver au Roi le titre et les emoluments de sa dignité présente il ne representera pourtant que le president de congres et a sa mort le charge de president ne seroit que pour deux ans.

Voila mes reves mon Prince si on veut les executer ou non il est certain que nous desirons la libertée, et qu'il faut de la tranquilite pour nos voisins. Si Votre Altesse trouvera necessaire que je viens vous voire aiés la bonte de me le dire. Votre Altesse connoit parfaitement l'invariabilité de mes principes le respect et l'admiration dont je suis penetré pour le Souverain qui fait l'ornement de ce siecle, et l'amitié sincère pour votre personne. Mon Prince, votre nom seroit deja immortel, soiés encor le liberateur d'une Nation oprimé pour qu'il soit cherie a jamais.

J'ai l'honneur, etc.

APPENDIX X

BEZBORODKO TO THE EMPRESS, JANUARY 25/FEBRUARY 5, 1792 (FROM JASSY). [M. A., Турцiя, IX, 14]

[Reports his discussions with Potocki and Rzewuski as to a Confederation to be formed in Poland under Russian protection] . . .

Прежде нежели осмѣлюсь я сказать что либо относительно намѣренiя патрiотовъ Польскихъ, дозвольте, всемилостивѣйшая Государыня, изъяснить чистосердечно что главнѣйшая трудность въ томъ предлежить не отъ самихъ Поляковъ, . . . но отъ другихъ дворовъ Польшѣ сосѣдственныхъ. Что касается до Вѣнскаго, хотя настоящія его намѣренія не согласуютъ съ нашими, ибо у него кроется мысль воспользоваться дѣятельности Польши къ тому, чтобъ въ ней пріобрѣсть себѣ союзника одного больше, обуздать короля Прусскаго, и въ случаѣ потребномъ на него обратить сію державу; но когда однажде вѣнскій дворъ увидитъ что Ваше Величество всѣмъ инныя предположенія имѣете, и что оныя тверды и непремѣнны, то онъ конечно не станетъ на пути исполненія ихъ, ибо отнюдь не своиственно чтобъ Императоръ пожертвовалъ союзомъ толь натуральнымъ и толь выгоднымъ, каковъ есть между двумя Императорскими дворами отдаленнымъ видамъ и уваженіямъ, и чтобъ онъ удовольствовался замѣнить оныя связи въ существѣ ничего не значущей, какова у него теперь составлена съ Берлинскимъ дворомъ. Все что ни станетъ онъ дѣлать вопреки намъ будетъ единственно заключаться въ повтореніи совѣтовъ и представленій, на которыя только одна забота будетъ что нибудь отвѣчать, по примѣру какъ и въ войнѣ нашей съ Турками случалось послѣ Рейхенбахской Конвенціи, что обороняясь противу угрозъ и домогательствъ Англіи и Пруссіи должны мы были обороняться и противу робкихъ совѣтовъ Императора, хотя послѣ вопреки симъ совѣтамъ все желаемое одержать предуспѣли. Но съ другой стороны отнюдь себя ласкать не слѣдуетъ, чтобъ въ случаѣ буде берлинскій дворъ приметъ противу насъ силей сторону Короля Польскаго и его единомысленныхъ, призналъ вѣнскій дворъ *casus foederis*, и намъ учинилъ пособіе. Сверхъ того, полагая что число силъ Вашего Императорскаго Величества несравненно превосходитъ таковыхъ Короля Прусскаго, что храбрость войнства вашего ничьей въ свѣтѣ не уступаетъ, — но по утомленію двумя толь тягостными войнами, при истощеніи денежныхъ средствъ, которыя едино чрезъ нѣсколько лѣтъ спокойствія наполнены только быть могутъ, перемѣна Польскаго Правленія не стоитъ будетъ новой тягостной войны, еслибъ онію вмѣстѣ съ Польшей и Пруссіей безъ Австрійскаго пособія производить надобно; а потому и нужнѣе всего самимъ яснымъ образомъ предварительно удостовѣриться въ образѣ прямомъ мыслей берлинскаго кабинета. . . .

А потому смѣю изъяснить мнѣніе мое что при начертаніи плана по дѣламъ Польскимъ прежде приступленія къ исполненію его необходимо надобно снестись съ дворомъ берлинскимъ и весьма искусстнымъ и осторожнымъ образомъ стараться узнать его мысли, и при усмотрѣніи расположенія его пребыть равнодушнымъ, тогдаже твердый дать отвѣтъ Вѣнскому двору. . . . Казалось бы что Берлинскій дворъ съ нѣкоторымъ удовольствіемъ усмотритъ разность мыслей между двумя дворами Императорскими, и по суетности своей направитъ свои старанія съ нами сближиться; но чтоже не сходнаго и въ семъ самомъ сближеніи? Знаю что онъ многія нанесъ вамъ оскорбленія дѣйствовавъ даже и коварно противу пользы и блага Имперіи Вашей . . . но Ваше Величество получили уже всенародное удовлетвореніе соглашеніемъ и тайныхъ и явныхъ враговъ Вашихъ на ваши виды и намѣренія, . . . (The Court of Vienna was about to invite the Empress to accede to its alliance with Prussia.) Я почитаю таковое приступленіе къ союзу другихъ не удобнымъ, но отвергнуть оное явно также не сходно, ибо тогда берлинской дворъ новый поводъ къ вреднымъ его дѣйствіямъ приметъ; вмѣсто того что всего лучше податься на его исканіе и здѣлать союзъ безпосредственнымъ, который ни къ чему бы . . . [*illegible*] кромѣ покоя и гарантіи взаимныхъ владѣній, разумѣя его нынѣшнія владѣнія, а не какіе либо новые захваты. Симъ воспользовались бы мы иа польскія дѣла, остались въ покоѣ послѣ арбитрами между вѣнскимъ и берлинскимъ дворами, и наконецъ по отдохновеніемъ и поправленіемъ разныхъ частей были бы господами рѣшиться на все что намъ нужно и выгодно. Опасность предлежать могла бы со стороны берлинскаго двора по его жадности на пріобрѣтеніе Гданска и Торуна со прочими землями; но и къ сему отнятъ будетъ всякій поводъ когда помянутый дворъ увидитъ что Ваше Императорское Величество единственно намѣрены способствовать возстановленію прежней свободы польской и уничтоженію вредней и опасной для сосѣдей Конституціи безъ всякихъ корыстныхъ видовъ, о которыхъ не можетъ Король Прусскій не чувствовать что въ настоящемъ положеніи дѣлъ, и при развязанныхъ у насъ рукахъ нельзя имъ удовлетворить инако какъ общимъ трехъ сосѣднихъ дворовъ согласіемъ и раздѣлемъ между ними уравнительнымъ. . . .

APPENDIX XI

On Frederick William's Attitude towards the Proposals of Austria and Russia in March, 1792

The rescript to Bischoffwerder rejecting Spielmann's Polish plan is dated March 13, therefore a day after Goltz's dispatches of February 29 arrived in Berlin; but it appears from the rescript to Bischoffwerder of the 14th that that of the 13th was already drawn up before the Russian overtures were known.[1] The King's decision to reject the Austrian plan was, therefore, in no way influenced by the Empress' proposals.

Sybel's statement that Reuss presented Spielmann's memoir on March 10, and was informed on the 13th that Prussia could under no circumstances approve it, is utterly erroneous.[2] The memoir was sent to Berlin only on the 17th and was presented by the Austrian envoy the 22nd.[3]

One cannot possibly agree with the eloquent passage in which Sybel describes the great alternative before which Frederick William was placed by the simultaneous proposals of Austria and Russia, the former inviting him to commit political suicide, the latter offering him prospects of a handsome acquisition; the conflict in the King's breast; the decision determined by the news from Paris of de Lessart's fall, which rendered war with France inevitable and opposition to Catherine impossible. Nor can one subscribe to the conclusion: "Es war . . . nicht das Ergebnis einer lange vorbereiteten Habgier,

---

[1] B. A., *R. 1, Conv.* 172.
[2] Sybel, *Geschichte der Revolutionszeit*, ii, pp. 187, 191.
[3] Reuss' report of the 25th, V. A., *Preussen, Berichte*, 1792.

sondern inmitten eines beispiellosen europäischen Krisis der rasch ergriffene, das kleinste Uebel bezeichnende Ausweg." [1] — Apart from the fact that the Austrian proposals had already been rejected before the Russian ones were known, there is no evidence that Frederick William hesitated a moment about his decision. The news of de Lessart's fall (March 10) could not possibly have reached Berlin by the 13th. Neither then nor for some weeks more did the King know that war with France was inevitable, although he devoutly wished that it were. The determination in favor of a new partition of Poland was not forced upon him by "an unparalleled crisis" (he was doing his best to bring one about), but had already long existed in Frederick William's mind, at least in the form of a pious wish — probably, as Heidrich suggests,[2] ever since the previous August.

APPENDIX XII

DOCUMENTS ILLUSTRATING THE ORIGINS OF THE POLISH-BAVARIAN PROJECT

1. LOUIS COBENZL TO PHILIP COBENZL, MAY 19, 1792. [Private letter. V. A., *Russland, Fasc.* 139]
(Describing Simolin's account of his sojourn in Vienna in March, 1792)

. . . Simolin a dit aussi qu'ayant parlé à Bischofsverder de la future Election de l'Empereur et des pretentions de l'Electeur Palatin à devenir Roi, il lui avoit dit pourquoi ne le feriez Vous pas Roi de Bourgogne, comme la chose avoit été proposée autre fois, à quoi Bischofsverder avoit repondu, si la chose etoit proposée à présent je crois qu'on y consentiroit chez nous.

2. LOUIS COBENZL TO PHILIP COBENZL, JULY 21, 1792. [Official report. V. A., *Russland, Berichte,* 1792]

. . . La reprise de ce Projet [the Bavarian Exchange] a du etre ici d'autant moins inattendue, que je me rapelle avoir entendu dire à Monsieur de Simolin que Bischofsverder lui en avoit parlé, et lui

---

[1] *Geschichte der Revolutionszeit,* ii, pp. 188–191.
[2] *Preussen im Kampfe gegen die französische Revolution,* pp. 181 f.

avoit dit que le Roi son Maître ne seroit pas contraire à l'échange de la Bavière, s'il pouvoit en espérer autant de notre part pour l'Acquisition de Danzic, Thorn et du païs adjacent. . . .

3. ALOPEUS TO OSTERMANN, MAY 8/19, 1792. [M. A., Пруссія, III, 29]

. . . M. de Bischoffwerder m'ayant ecrit de Potsdam de venir le voir à Charlottenbourg où il est arrivé hier avec le Roi, je m'y suis rendu immédiatement après être sorti de la conférence avec le C. de Schoulenbourg. Il s'est répandu en protestations, comme l'avoit fait le Ministre, sur les sentiments d'amitié toute particulière que le Roi son Maître portait à S. M. I. et sur les dispositions relatives aux affaires de Pologne qui en étoient la suite. Il lacha à cette occasion un propos que je crois de mon devoir de ne pas dérober à la connoissance de V. Exc. "Je crois, dit-il, que le vieux Prince Kaunitz a très fort raison, qui prétend que pour écarter une bonne fois tout sujet de discussion entre les voisins de la Pologne, il faudroit la reduire à un objet si insignifiant qu'on put lui laisser la liberté de prendre telle forme que bon lui sembleroit. Ce principe adopté, il seroit facile de s'entendre, et le rôle important de regler cette affaire seroit encore reservé à l'Impératrice. J'en ai parle étant à Vienne et au Comte Razoumovski et à Mr. de Simolin."

M'étant borné à l'écouter tranquillement, je n'y ai rien repondu, et j'ajoute que le Comte de Schoulenbourg n'a jamais articulé le moindre mot à ce sujet.

4. RAZUMOVSKI TO THE EMPRESS, MARCH 11/22, 1792. [M. A., Австрія, III, 52]

Madame.

Les objets importans qui occupent presentement les cabinets des cours les plus en relations avec Votre Majesté Impériale, ont donné lieu à des entretiens et à des developpemens d'idées que je crois devoir porter directement à Sa connaissance.

Le General Bishoffswerder que je connaissais precedement a néanmoins desiré d'être porteur d'une lettre de Mr. Alopeus pour moi. Le concert relatif aux affaires de France a fourni matière à la conversation lorsque le hasard me l'a fait rencontrer, et toujours il m'a fait sentir que les mesures à prendre à l'égard de la Pologne mettraient obstacle à l'activité qu'on aurait à attendre de la Cour de Vienne. Nos entretiens ont été vagues parce que je ne m'y suis livré qu'avec la circonspection que j'ai jugé m'être convenable sous tous les rapports; attentif cependant à ce qu'il me disait, j'ai crû pouvoir hasarder entr'autres idées générales sur la Pologne, un arrangement sortable pour les trois Cours, et propre à porter une atteinte décidée à l'accroissement des forces et de la puissance de cette République. Hier nous étant trouvés à portée de reprendre la même conversation, il me dit qu'il venait de recevoir des nouvelles de Berlin, qui l'instruisaient de la communication qui y avait été faite par ordre de Votre Majesté Impériale touchant les affaires de Pologne, qu'elle était de la même teneur que les depêches qui nous sont parvenues ici dernierement, et que le Roi son Maitre disposé à concourir aux intentions de Votre Majesté Impériale, mais regrettant qu'elles ne fussent pas asses clairement exprimées, avait déja fait solliciter auprès du ministre de Votre Majesté Impériale des explications plus précises. Dans la suite du discours mettant toute finasserie de côté, il revint à l'arrangement dont j'ai fait mention ci dessus, et parlant sans réserve il me dit qu'il le considérait comme le seul moyen d'aller au but commun des trois puissances, tant par rapport à la Pologne que relativement à leurs projets à l'égard de la France. Que si Votre Majesté Impériale voulait s'entendre avec la Cour de Berlin sur un accroissement respectif de possessions en Pologne, on pourrait, comme équivalent, faire revivre en faveur de la Cour de Vienne l'échange tant desiré par feu S. M. l'Empereur Joseph de la Bavière contre les Pays Bas, et en poursuivant le plan projetté à l'égard de la revolution Française, on obtiendrait le double but d'y étouffer la contagion et de ramener les Provinces Belgiques à l'obéissance avant de leur faire changer de domination.

Telle est la substance de ma conversation avec Mr. le General de Bishoffswerder. En me disant qu'il n'avait aucune instruction du Roi son Maître analogue à un pareil projet, il m'a cependant repeté à plusieurs reprises que cette proposition serait accueillie avec satisfaction par Sa Majesté Prussienne et qu'au surplus si elle ne pouvait avoir l'effet desiré, elle resterait ensevelie dans le secret entre le très petit nombre de personnes qui en seraient instruites.

5. Frederick William to Bischoffwerder, March 14, 1792. [B. A., *R. 1, Conv.* 172]

. . . Il paroit que les vues de l'Impératrice touchant la Pologne pourroit amener l'évènement que le Duc de Bronsviq souhaite de voir arriver [1] et dont il parle dans la lettre que je Vous envoié a Dresde, ce qui seroit certainement tres favorable pour cet Etat ainsi que Vous jugés bien que je dois souhaiter que la Cour de Vienne entre dans la meme idée, ce qui est peut etre possible puisque selon toute apparence la Russie restera ferme, la chose etant trop de son propre interet.

APPENDIX XIII

Documents Illustrating the Earliest Discussions between Russia and Prussia Regarding a New Partition

1. Alopeus to Ostermann, May 8/19, 1792. [M. A., Пруссия, III, 29]

. . . Schulenburg said to him: "qu'il alloit écrire au Comte Goltz, qu'il lui revenoit de tous côtés que l'Impératrice avoit pour objet de combiner les affaires de Pologne avec celles de France; qu'il ne comprenoit pas ce que cela voudroit dire, n'en ayant pas la moindre connoissance, et que le Comte de Goltz devoit demander à Votre Excellence des éclaircissements à cet égard."

[The rest of this dispatch, relating to Bischoffwerder's pointed hints about a new partition, is printed in Appendix XII.]

2. Ostermann to Alopeus, June 10/21, 1792. [M.A., Пруссия III, 28]

. . . La franchise avec laquelle Mr. le Comte de Schoulenbourg s'est expliqué avec Vous, Monsieur, sur le dessein de S. M. Prussienne de se faire indemniser par la France des frais que son entreprise doit lui couter, a été envisagée par l'Impératrice comme une nouvelle marque de confiance que le Roy a bien voulu lui donner. S. M. I. ne voit rien que de juste dans une vue aussi naturelle et si son concours y est necessaire, Elle n'attendra pour s'y déterminer que les éclaircissemens ultérieurs sur la nature et le genre d'une indemnité qui très probablement sera aussi reclamée par les autres Puissances qui ont concourru pareillement à l'entreprise. Mais dans cette occasion Elle croit devoir presenter à la méditation et à la considération de S. M. Prussienne, que si la France, déjà ruinée et épuisée par l'anarchie et la desorganisation totale, auxquelles elle est en proye

---

[1] A partition of Poland, cf. p. 238, note 1.

depuis tant d'années, et grevée par la charge des remboursemens qu'elle aura à faire, se voit encore garrotée par une forme de gouvernement et de constitution tellement combinée que les ressources qui lui resteront ne puissent se developper avec l'energie et le ressort indispensablement nécessaires après des secousses aussi violentes et aussi destructives, il ne faudra plus compter ce Royaume pour quelque chose dans la balance générale de l'Europe. Or il paroit essentiel d'examiner dès à présent pour le bien et la tranquillité de celle-ci, à quel point peut influer sur l'un et l'autre l'anéantissement complet d'existence politique d'un Etat aussi considérable que la France. . . .

3. THE PRINCE OF NASSAU TO THE EMPRESS, JUNE 30/JULY 11, 1792. [M. A., *France*, IX, *Princes et Emigrés*, 1792]

Dans une conversation que j'ai eu avec Bischoffwerder [on June 29, N. S.], et pour laquelle il m'a demandé le secret, il m'a assuré que la cour de Vienne ne vouloit autre chose que l'arrangement de la Bavière tel que Votre Majesté Impériale l'avoit proposé autrefois, et que quant à la Prusse l'Empereur étoit convenu de proposer à Votre Majesté Impériale de luy faire ceder par la Pologne les enclaves qui lui conviennent pour arrondir Ses états; que ces arrangemens aiant lieu, il n'en couteroit à la France que quelques morceaux de la Lorraine et de l'Alsace, que la Prusse sentoit bien que . . . la France . . . est un païs si necessaire au maintien de l'Equilibre en Europe.

4. SCHULENBURG TO FREDERICK WILLIAM, JULY 1, 1792. [B. A., R. XI., *Russland*, 133]

[Reporting a conversation with Alopeus] J'ai tâché de le sonder si sa Cour auroit des vues d'acquisition en Pologne, ou si elle se borne simplement au renversement de la Constitution du 3 de Mai. Quoique je ne lui aie pas fait cette question directement, il en a deviné le sens et m'a répondu que l'Impératrice reconnoissoit la justice d'une indemnité parfaite des fraix qu'occasionnoient les affaires de France, et qu'il avoit l'ordre exprès de prier que Votre Majesté voulut communiquer Ses idées comment Elle croyoit que cette indemnité pourroit se procurer. La reponse à cette question sera délicate, mais toujours elle nous rapprochera du but.

5. SCHULENBURG AND ALVENSLEBEN TO FREDERICK WILLIAM, JULY 3, 1792. [B. A., *R.* XI, *Russland,* 133]

[On the subject of 'indemnisation' for the French war] Nous avons la satisfaction d'annoncer à V. M. que non seulement l'Impératrice de Russie la regarde comme juste et naturelle, mais qu'elle promet aussi en cas de besoin d'y concourir en faveur de toutes les Puissances coopérantes . . . Cette ouverture significative est accompagnée de la réflexion que la France étant déjà ruinée et épuisée aujourd'hui, il lui restera difficilement son véritable poids dans la balance générale. L'observation est juste, . . . mais on diroit, Sire, que la Cour de Russie, en plaidant la cause de la France, cherche à détourner l'idée d'un démembrement dont ce Royaume pourroit être menacé, et qu'en offrant sa concurrence pour faciliter les moyens de l'indemnité future, elle veut laisser entrevoir une possibilité de la trouver du côté de la Pologne — le seul où son influence pourroit être employé avec succès. — They mean to draw Alopeus out further "afin de préparer imperceptiblement les esprits aux ouvertures qui vont suivre."

6. ALOPEUS TO OSTERMANN, JUNE 22/JULY 3, 1792. [M. A., Пpyccия, III, 29]

Par le compte que j'ai eu l'honneur de rendre de la conversation du Comte de Schoulenbourg avec le Prince de Nassau, j'ai prévenu en partie les orders de Votre Excellence contenus dans l'Apostille de sa depêche du 10 Juin,[1] mais pour me mettre en etat de les remplir encore plus particulièrement, j'ai saisi le pretexte du besoin de quelque éclaircissement que j'avois demandé au Ministre, et je me suis rendu hier au soir chès lui. Alors j'ai amené insensiblement la conversation à ce qu'il m'importoit d'éclairer. Elle m'a conduit à des résultats, qui à ce que j'ose me flatter, répandront le jour nécessaire sur les vues des Cours de Vienne et de Berlin. Il n'existe pas de concert éventuel entre elles, mais il y a eu naturellement des pourparlers sur le genre des indemnités auxquels elles devroient aspirer. Le remboursement des frais en argent comptant paroissant impossible et ayant même l'inconvénient de grever la France d'une nouvelle masse de dettes, qui la tiendroit garotté et influeroit ainsi sur son existence politique, il a paru au Comte Schoulenbourg que l'Autriche

---

[1] I have been unable to find this apostil.

pourroit faire des acquisitions territoriales sur la France sans que ce Royaume en fut affoibli dans sa valeur politique. La Cour de Vienne n'y trouve d'autre inconvenient que le sentiment de haine et l'odieux dont elle se chargeroit de la part de la plus grande partie de l'Europe; mais dans le fond ce n'est peutêtre que le desir de réaliser son projet de l'échange de la Bavière auquel elle paroit toujours attachée. Ici on n'y trouve plus les mêmes dangers qu'autrefois, pourvû que par de nouvelles acquisitions la balance soit maintenue. L'impossibilité d'en faire sur la France, tant à cause de l'éloignement que par la nécessité de ne pas échancrer ce Royaume comme la Pologne, à laquelle un role subalterne doit être assigné, motive l'idée de chercher les indemnités pour la Prusse en Pologne même. Le Comte de Schoulenbourg m'a assuré de ne pas encore connoître les vues du Roi son Maitre à cet égard; mais il s'est proposé de Lui en parler. La lisière de la Pologne, qui uniroit le Royaume de Prusse à la Silésie, en fait l'objet, et il croit que la Russie pourroit également faire l'acquisition de l'Ukraine Polonoise, à fin de former de ses nouvelles acquisitions sur les Turcs une masse contigue avec ses anciennes possessions. C'est là en gros l'idée que ce Ministre a conçu de la nature et du genre des indemnités. . . .

APPENDIX XIV

On Razumovski's Conversations with Cobenzl of June 30 and July 1, 1792, Regarding the Polish-Bavarian Plan

The chief source for the account given in the text is Razumovski's letter to Bezborodko of July 4, which is supplemented by Ph. Cobenzl's dispatch to L. Cobenzl of September 13 (this latter printed in Vivenot, ii, pp. 202 f.).

With the aid of Razumovski's report I am able to present this incident for the first time, I believe, in its true light. It has long been partially known through the Vice-Chancellor's above-cited dispatch of September, through a few vague references in the Prussian records, and more recently through a brief and very unsatisfactory résumé of the ambassador's report published by Wassiltchikow, *Les Razoumowski*, ii[1], pp. 139 f., and erroneously dated July 23 (instead of June 23/July 4). None of these sources afforded a precise clue as to the date of the incident, or sufficed to show in what relation it stood to the development of the Polish-Bavarian plan. Sybel surmised that these conversations took place in May, just about the time of Schulenburg's first overture to Spielmann; and he conjectured that it was Razumovski who first suggested to the Austrians the idea of reviving the Bavarian Exchange project ("a pregnant hint which was enough to inflame the Vice-Chancellor's mind"), thus leading Spielmann to propose that plan to Schulenburg.[1] Very similar accounts are given in Häusser[2] and Sorel.[3] Heidrich[4] and Heigel[5] are much nearer the truth as to the time and the significance of Razumovski's insinuations to Cobenzl, though Heidrich is certainly wrong in supposing that the ambassador made his suggestions at the impulse of the Austrians.

The text of the Russian ambassador's report follows.

RAZUMOVSKI TO BEZBORODKO, JUNE 23/JULY 4, 1792. "TRÈS SECRET." [M. A., Австрія, III, 54]

Monsieur le Comte.

L'Echange de la Bavière projetté sous le règne de feu l'Empereur Joseph et dont les négociations entamées sous les auspices de Sa Majesté Impériale Notre Souveraine, parvinrent malheureusement a la connaissance du cabinet de Berlin et en furent traversées d'une manière si éclatante, cet échange n'a point cessé d'être, dans le secret du cabinet de Vienne, une maxime d'Etat. J'eus lieu de la soupçonner de bonne source et je mis la plus grande attention à m'en convaincre. La visite que le Roi doit rendre au retour de Francfort à l'Electeur Palatin à Munick a redoublé ma vigilance; enfin, après m'être captivé, j'ose le dire, quelque confiance de la part du ministère d'ici depuis que l'Impératrice ma Souveraine a daigné m'honorer de la sienne en me conférant le poste que j'ai l'honneur de remplir, j'ai voulu m'assurer si le projet en question entrait dans les plans actuels du cabinet autrichien. Dans une conversation familière avec Mr. le Vice-Chancelier Comte de Cobenzl j'ai hasardé de toucher cette corde et ce que j'en ai dit a été fondé sur ma profession de foi à l'égard de cette cour, sur les protestations sincères auxquelles m'au-

[1] *Op. cit.*, ii, pp. 209 f.
[2] *Deutsche Geschichte*, i, p. 358.
[3] *L'Europe et la Révolution française*, ii, pp. 467 f.
[4] *Op. cit.*, p. 225, note 1.
[5] *Deutsche Geschichte*, i, p. 537.

torisent les dispositions loyales et bienveillantes de l'Impératrice envers la Maison d'Autriche, et Son invariable attachement aux principes de notre alliance; que Sa Majesté Impériale prenait par consequent l'interet le plus vif au bien être et à la prospérité solide de la Maison d'Autriche, etc. etc. Nous nous fimes des complimens et cela en resta là.

Le lendemain, Dimanche 20 Juin/1 Juillet, au sortir de l'audience des ambassadeurs chès LL. MM. je trouvais Mr. de Cobenzl: il me prit à part et me dit "Savés vous que notre conversation d'hier m'a roulé sans cesse dans l'esprit. La manière franche et amicale dont nous avons parlé m'a engagé à en faire part au Roi; il vous sait bien bon gré des bons sentimens que vous temoignés. Vous avés penetré notre Secret; nous n'en avons point pour votre cour et vous allés en juger. Nous envisageons la circonstance presante des affaires de l'Europe comme la plus favorable à effectuer l'échange de la Bavierre contre les Pays Bas. Mais avant d'y songer, avant de faire la plus petite demarche, le Roi veut consulter l'Impératrice avec la franchise, la confiance la plus illimitée, et l'intention de Se regler entierement d'après les conseils et les mesures qu'Elle lui suggerera. Le Roi souhaiterait que vous en fissiés l'ouverture; et m'autorise en meme tems à en ecrire à l'Ambassadeur Comte de Cobenzl, le tout sous le plus grand secret, car personne ne s'en doute ici; et le Roi, vous, moi, et Mr. de Spielmann sont et seront les seuls qui en seront instruits. De sorte que si l'Impératrice ne juge point à propos que le projet ait lieu, il sera comme non avenu et restera enseveli entre les personnes qui en sont les depositaires.

L'opposition de la cour de Berlin, a t'il continué, est le plus grand obstacle qui pourrait s'y rencontrer. Sans doute les termes amicals où nous sommes avec elle peuvent nous mettre à l'abri du moins des consequences funestes qui suivirent ce projet sous l'Empereur Joseph, mais ils n'obtiendront [*sic*] surement pas son agrément sans que le Roi de Prusse de son coté fasse une acquisition. Cette acquisition serait comme de raison aux depens de la Pologne, et nomément de Dantzig et Thorn convoités depuis si longtems et dont on ne saurait l'empecher de s'emparer à la premiere circonstance favorable; ce qui même eut été fait deja sous un ministère plus habile. Nous n'hesiterions donc pas d'y souscrire, et quoique par notre echange nous perdrions a peu près 2 millions de revenus, nous ne croirions pas acheter trop cher l'arrondissement et la stabilité de nos possessions.

Tel a été le précis de ce que m'a dit le Comte de Cobenzl. En le quittant j'eus une conversation avec le Baron de Spielmann à peu près de la même teneur. Il me dit au surplus que le Général Bishoffs-verder avec lequel il s'est lié dans les differens voyages qu'il a faits ici, lui avait temoigné dans son dernier sejour très confidement [*sic*] des dispositions très opposées au Système de non agrandissement qu'il professait dans le public et dont on a fait la base du traité de Berlin (ce dont j'ai eu moi même dans le tems des notions positives) et qu'il lui avait touché même quelque chose de conforme à l'objet dont nous nous entretenions presentement. Enfin l'un et l'autre me dirent au nom de leur maitre qu'il considerait la reussite de ce projet comme tenant absolument à la volonté et bonne disposition de l'Im-pératrice et qu'on se conformerait entierement à ce que Sa Majesté Impériale jugerait à propos de decider. Je repondis par les mêmes assurances que ci dessus, mais j'ajoutais que peutêtre dans un ar-rangement pareil faudrait-il avoir egard a des convenances relatives aux interets de Sa Majesté Impériale et que j'y comptais avec la même confiance à laquelle je venais d'inviter le ministère de S. M. Apostolique envers nous. Cette clause ne parut nullement deplaire et apres m'avoir fait les protestations les plus vives des obligations qu'on nous aurait, nous convinmes que j'expedierais un courier et hier au soir on m'envoya le paquet ci joint pour l'Ambassadeur Comte de Cobenzl.

En suppliant V. Exc. de porter cette depêche à la connaissance de Sa Majesté Impériale, j'ose esperer, Monsieur le Comte, de n'être point desapprouvé dans la marche que j'ai suivie. J'avais de fortes presomptions sur l'existence du projet d'echange, jamais moment ne m'a paru plus favorable pour l'effectuer que la Situation actuelle de l'Europe. C'est sous ce point de vue que j'ai cru devoir provo-quer la confidence qui m'en a été faite, et qui soumise entierement au bon plaisir de Sa Majesté Impériale ne saurait porter aucun preju-dice ni à nos interets, ni à nos vues dans la supposition où elles ne seraient point analogues à celles qu'on a ici. . . .

APPENDIX XV

ON THE DATE OF SPIELMANN'S PLAN DISCUSSED ON PAGES 351 f.

This plan was brought to light through the document published in Vivenot, ii, pp. 348–351, and there entitled "Protokoll aufge-nommen zwischen Spielmann und Haugwitz." This document is in the form of an unsigned agreement or convention between the two Courts. It is undated, but it was sent to Vienna along with Spielmann's report of November 6. The question at issue is: when was this plan drawn up and presented to the Prussians?

It should be remarked, in the first place, that the original document does not bear the title 'Protokoll' or any other title. Spielmann refers to it in his report only as a 'plan.' Secondly, while he did not attach a date to it, some one has written on the back of it: "N. B. Dieser höchst wichtige Vortrag muss zwischen dem letzten Bericht des B. Spielmann d. d. x. 15. und der preussischen Verbale Note vom 25. x. redigirt worden [sein]." While one cannot be certain, it is probable that this note was added immediately upon the receipt of the document, and that it indicates the idea then formed at Vienna as to the date of composition of the plan.

The only direct evidence to be obtained from the report of November 6 is the following passage with which that dispatch begins: "Ueber welchen beyderseitigen Entschädigungsplan ich mit Grafen Haugwitz unter Voraussetzung der Allerhöchsten Genehmigung übereingekommen bin, *bevor nach der Hand die ganze Reihe der spätern Unglücksfälle eingetreten ist*,[1] geruhen E. Exc. aus der gehorsamst hier anverwahrten Beylage zu ersehen." Although by no means clear, this passage is enough to refute the statement made by Sybel[2] and Sorel[3] that this 'protocol' represents an agreement reached between Haugwitz and Spielmann after the Note of Merle (October 25) and on the basis of that note. For on this theory, how explain the reference to "the whole series of the later disasters"? How explain the fact that the Note of Merle is not mentioned, and that the principles of the 'protocol' are utterly different from those of the Prussian declaration of October 25? One must do violence to the whole history of the affair to represent a Prussian minister agreeing after the Note of Merle to make his master's occupation in Poland dependent on the conclusion of the Exchange treaty with the Bavarian House. Sybel has evidently given Spielmann's negotiation a quite fictitious dénouement. The "agreement of Merle," of which he speaks, most certainly never took place.

Heidrich has already pointed this out, but I am equally unable to agree with his theory. He declares that the 'protocol' represents an

---

[1] The italics are mine.
[2] *Geschichte der Revolutionszeit*, ii, pp. 362 f.
[3] *L'Europe et la Révolution française*, iii, p. 168.

agreement effected between Spielmann and Haugwitz on the journey westward from Frankfort, or at least before the latter minister's departure from Luxemburg for Verdun (September 26). For this view I can see only two possible grounds: (1) the passage cited above from Spielmann's dispatch of November 6, to which I shall return later; and (2) Haugwitz's letter to Schulenburg of September 30, in which he reports what he has learned of the new Austrian propositions. The sum of what he says is that the Court of Vienna now demands a 'supplement' in Alsace and Lorraine as far as the Moselle; he mentions none of the other provisions of the 'protocol'; he does not hint for a moment that he has already reached a provisional agreement with Spielmann, that a written plan has been presented to him, that he has made any definite proposals as to the Prussian acquisitions.[1] Spielmann, on his side, says in a letter to Cobenzl of September 27: "Mit dem H. Grafen v. Haugwitz habe ich über mein aufhabendes Geschäft ausführlich und umständlich conferiret";[2] and October 15[3] that the King seemed inclined to grant Austria "die Zutheilung anderweitiger reichlicher Surrogate für die Markgrafthümer, worüber ich bereits seit Frankfurt den Grafen von Haugwitz vorläufig bestens zu sondiren und zu stimmen gesucht hatte." — I will readily admit that much of the plan contained in the 'protocol' had been already discussed on the journey from Frankfort; but I do not see any signs whatever that the two ministers had advanced so far that Spielmann could embody their agreement in a written plan, and especially in one like this; and there are many reasons that render it highly improbable that such was the case.

In the first place, consider the initial article about the continuation of the war. Heidrich says, indeed, that at the time of Spielmann's departure from Vienna the Austrians had already grown familiar with the idea that it would take a second campaign to get the terms of peace that they wanted; that they already planned to draw England, Russia, and other Powers into the contest; and that they were inclined to go in for a war of conquest in the grand style. As proof of this he offers only a by no means significant citation from the *Politisches Journal*, pp. 1005 f. When one turns to the Austrian records themselves, one gains quite a different impression: one finds that the great desire at Vienna was to make peace as soon as possi-

---

[1] B. A., *R. XI, Frankreich*, 89 K.

[2] V. A., *Mission in das preussische Hauptquartier de* 1792.

[3] Vivenot, ii, p. 273.

ble. As there is absolutely no reason to suppose that the temper of his Court had changed in the week following Spieimann's departure, one may take, for example, Cobenzl's instructions to the Referendary of September 20,[1] which contain the clearest utterances on this subject. The Vice-Chancellor writes that since nothing lies nearer the Emperor's heart than the speedy termination of the war, this must be one of the objects of Spielmann's special care. He considers further the possibility that the capture of Paris might not end the affair; suggests an armistice and a negotiation for peace during the winter; shows the greatest desire to avoid a "long, ruinous war" at any honorable price. I cannot find here any sign that the Imperial Court had already resolved on a new campaign, on building up a great coalition, or on a grand war of conquest. — Then one should notice the development of Spielmann's ideas on the subject. On September 30 he writes that their main aim must be to get out of this "costly game" (the war) as soon as possible; and hence they ought to offer the French "a very cheap bargain," insisting chiefly that the King of France should be restored to at least a "quasi-freedom."[2] How reconcile this with the great war of conquest, for which, according to Heidrich, Spielmann had just come to an agreement with Haugwitz? Then, on October 4[3] the Referendary has learned of the retreat of the allied armies, and begins to fear "die leider nur zu wahrscheinliche Unvermeidlichkeit einer zweiten Campagne." Finally, on October 15 he has become convinced of the necessity of continuing the war, and exposes at length the reasons that have led him to continue his negotiations *in spite of that fact*. In one place in this report he writes: "Meiner Betrachtung, dass die bisherigen *supposita* durch den unerwarteten Ausgang der Campagne nicht wenig geändert würden, setzt derselbe [Haugwitz] die Ueberzeugung seines Herrn von der absoluten Nothwendigkeit einer zweiten Campagne . . . entgegen."[4] These words are absolute nonsense on the supposition that the two ministers had long been agreed on a plan, the first article of which provided for a second campaign. Unless Spielmann's reports are to be considered a mass of duplicity, one cannot suppose that he had consented to such an article in September — at a time when the allied armies were supposed to be fast approaching Paris. And as for Haugwitz, who in May and again in July had opposed

---

[1] Vivenot, ii, pp. 211–221.
[2] V. A., *Mission in das preussische Hauptquartier*.
[3] Vivenot, ii, pp. 248 f. [4] Vivenot, ii, p. 274.

the war altogether, how can one believe that in September — without any necessity or a shadow of authorization, as far as we can see — he had agreed to a second campaign merely in order to conquer Alsace and Lorraine for Austria?

There is another equally valid reason why this 'protocol' cannot be referred to September. The Emperor had on September 9 approved the ideas of the Conference ministers, who opposed staining the honor of their Court by any active participation in the dismemberment of Poland. Is one to suppose that immediately afterwards Spielmann proposed to Haugwitz the plan for an Austrian occupation of Polish territory — an occupation which might be turned into permanent possession, in case acquisitions failed to be secured elsewhere? On this point, Spielmann speaks quite definitely in his report of November 6. He relates telling Haugwitz (about October 27) that he had had, when he left Vienna, no instructions relative to an Austrian acquisition in Poland; and that it was therefore only in view of the changed circumstances and as his private idea that he had suggested this expedient after his return from Verdun (i.e., after October 12). This seems to me conclusive against Heidrich's theory.

From the dozen similar considerations that might be advanced here, I shall mention but two more. If in September Haugwitz had reached an agreement with Spielmann that could be put into precise written form, why did the King send him back from Consenvoye to receive the Austrian's definite propositions? Or again, how could Haugwitz in September have indicated to Spielmann the exact line of demarcation that his Court desired in Poland? As far as we know, he had received no instructions on that point; his proposals of August had apparently been passed over without an answer; it was only at Consenvoye that the King had drawn on the map the line he meant to claim.

If these reasons seem decisive against placing the 'protocol' in September, it is not hard to show that that document fits in very well with the circumstances of mid-October. In the first place, the passage at the beginning of Spielmann's report of November 6 can be rightly understood, I think, only if one places the emphasis on the word *spätern:* i.e., the plan was drawn up before the *later* disasters set in. For Spielmann proceeds immediately to tell what disasters he is referring to: the retreat from Verdun, which turned into a rout, the total evacuation of French soil, the highly suspicious conduct of the Prussians, the appearance that they were trying to get out of the war and abandon Austria, etc., etc. Now these suspicions appear only in the report of November 6; and they had much to do with inducing Spielmann to change his tactics with the Prussians. In his last preceding report (October 15) he still shows himself convinced of the Prussian loyalty. The change evidently occurred after that. At the end of this report of the 15th, he states that he has decided to go on with the negotiation, and that the plan which he means to proceed by — under reservation of the Emperor's approval — will be sent in later. Then at the very beginning of the next dispatch (November 6), he submits this plan (the 'protocol'), which he has agreed upon with Haugwitz — under reservation of the Emperor's approval — "before the later disasters set in." It is obvious, I think, that October 15 must be taken as the *terminus post quem*.

The *terminus ante quem* can also be determined with fair precision. On October 19 Haugwitz writes to Schulenburg that Spielmann has presented him with a *mémoire* analogous to the principles reported in his letter of September 30.[1] Perhaps the term *mémoire* does not fit very well the document we have been considering; but the word *mémoire* is used rather loosely in the language of this period, and Haugwitz may have chosen it as less suggestive of anything approaching a definite agreement. For several reasons I am convinced that this *mémoire* was really the 'protocol' printed in Vivenot. In the first place, it is not easy to suppose that if Spielmann had presented another document to Haugwitz, he would not have sent it home, or even have mentioned it in his report of November 6. Furthermore, Haugwitz writing to Schulenburg on October 19, immediately after speaking of the *mémoire*, declared that the Court of Vienna seemed more inclined to the continuation of the war (which would appear to be a reference to Article I of Spielmann's plan); and on October 27 he added that the *mémoire* contained the familiar proposition about Alsace-Lorraine as far as the Moselle, the demand for the King's mediation at Zweibrücken, the concession of the line Częstochowa-Rawa-Soldau to Prussia, and a provision about an Austrian occupation, and possibly an Austrian acquisition, in Poland.[1] In short, the *mémoire* described by Haugwitz seems to have contained all the important articles of the 'plan' sent in by Spielmann. Moreover, Haugwitz wrote that he had expressly rejected the proposition about the Austrian occupation in Poland, and Spielmann also reported that this was the only article of his 'plan' to which Haug-

[1] B. A., *R. XI, Frankreich*, 89 *K.*

witz refused to agree. From all this, it seems evident that the *mêmôire* and the 'plan' were one and the same document. The so-called 'pro-tocol' printed in Vivenot represents, then, not an agreement reached after the Note of Merle, nor one dating from late September, but rather the draft of a convention submitted by Spielmann to Haugwitz between the 15th and the 19th of October.

APPENDIX XVI

Documents Illustrating Haugwitz's Final Negotiation at Vienna[1]

1. Haugwitz's Report of December 24, 1792. [B. A., *R*. 1, 170]

En mettant le sceau sur les négociations relativement aux justes indemnités de Ses fraix de guerre dont V. M. a daigné me charger à la Cour d'ici, je crois ne pas devoir tarder de mettre sous les yeux de V. M. les derniers résultats. La reponse à la Note de Merle étant peu satisfaisante, je provoquai la communication de tout ce qu'on feroit passer à la Cour de Russie sur ce sujet. Les termes qu'on employe en s'expliquant vis à vis de l'Impératrice de Russie sur la prise de possession immédiate de V. M. étoient à la verité plus précis, mais la Cour d'ici revenant à une prise de possession interimistique en Pologne de sa part, il sembloit que c'étoit éloigner de fait ce qu'on parut d'ailleurs demander avec sollicitude. . . . Je n'ai cependant pas pû être tranquille, et beaucoup moins pouvois-je me résoudre à quitter Vienne avant que de n'être entièrement rassuré sur le parti definitif auquel se determineroit la Cour de Vienne. En employant donc les moyens, auxquels Votre confiance m'a autorisé, je suis enfin parvenû à vaincre tous les obstacles. Je viens de recevoir l'assurance formelle du Ministère Impérial portant: que S. M. l'Empereur adressera les instances les plus pressantes pour engager l'Impératrice de Russie à consentir à la prise de possession actuelle de V. M. sans y ajouter aucune condition relativement à une prise de possession en Pologne de la part de l'Empereur, en se bornant uniquement à demander que l'Impératrice veuille conjointement avec V. M. *garantir*

---

[1] The chief documents on the Austrian side relating to this negotiation have been published by Vivenot (*Quellen zur deutschen Kaiserpolitik Oesterreichs*, vol. ii), and Haugwitz's reports of December 12 and 19 are printed in Herrmann, *Russische Geschichte, Ergänzungsband*, pp. 308 ff., 314 f.

son consentement à l'échange de la Bavière. Le Ministère de Vienne s'est porté même à motiver le besoin d'une telle prise de possession de la part de V. M. de la façon la plus prononcée, en y ajoutant que l'Empereur étoit intimement persuadé que V. M. étoit disposée a prendre une part vigoureuse à la continuation de la guerre actuelle, mais qu'il étoit également convaincû que l'arrondissement en Pologne et la prise de possession immédiate étoit l'unique moyen de porter V. M. à suivre son inclination à lui porter son secours.

2. RAZUMOVSKI'S REPORT OF JANUARY 21/FEBRUARY 1, 1793. [M. A., Австрія, III, 54]

Le Sieur César . . . ayant entendu parler des préparatifs dans les trouppes de l'Empereur pour entrer en Pologne, a cru devoir s'en expliquer avec Mr. le Comte de Cobenzl. Celui-ci lui a repondu que l'entrée n'aurait point lieu jusqu'à la réception de la réponse de notre Cour au sujet de la garantie conjointe avec celle de Berlin, touchant l'échange de la Bavière et que dans le cas seulement où cette garantie ne serait point accordée. Le Sieur César allarmé de cette réponse est venu s'en ouvrir à moi. Il m'a témoigné avoir ignoré parfaitement la question de la garantie, m'a protesté que ce ne pouvait etre l'intention de son Maitre, et qu'il ne s'en trouvait pas un mot dans les écrits que lui avait laissés à son départ le Comte de Haugwitz. . . . Enfin il m'a soutenu que ces deux points rentraient directement dans le sens de la réponse faite à la note de Merle, réponse qu'il dit avoir été rejetté par le Roi son maitre. Cependant il est hors de doute que le Comte de Haugwitz en a été informé, car il m'en a souvent parlé. Il n'en est pas moins certain que la susdite réponse à la note de Merle n'a point été rendue au Ministère d'ici, que par conséquent elle a été de fait acceptée. Il en resulte donc que le Comte de Haugwitz, pour faciliter les négociations, a mis dans les conférences plus de condescendance que n'en portent ses rapports, et que cette matière qui paraissait entendue entre lui et le Ministère de Vienne pourrait encore être sujet à de nouveaux embarras. Le Sieur César me disant tout cela sous le sceau de la confiance, l'a portée jusqu'à me faire lecture du dernier rapport du Comte de Haugwitz, où . . . il dit que cette Cour ci espere s'assurer du consentement du Roi de Prusse à l'échange de la Bavière; or, ce mot de consentement diffère bien de garantie.

3. HAUGWITZ'S REPORT TO THE KING, MAY 6, 1793. [B. A., *R.* 96, 147 *H*]

. . . Un des principes que la Cour de Vienne a désiré de poser pour base des négociations présentes dès leur origine, c'est celui d'une prétendue *parité d'aggrandissement* qu'elle s'avise de déduire *de l'esprit* de son Alliance avec la Prusse, sans que de son propre aveu il en soit fait mention dans le Traité. . . . J'avoue que dans les premiers tems de ma mission à la Cour Impériale, j'ai entendu produire et reproduire ce principe avec la plus grande assiduité, et que les Ministres avoient le talent de faire valoir comme s'il avoit passé en axiome; mais ils transgressent les loix de la vérité en soutenant "que c'est moi qui l'ai reconnu aux conférences de Luxembourg et de Vienne." Rien de plus faux. Le piège étoit heureusement trop visible. . . . J'ai évité au contraire tout ce qui auroit pû impliquer de ma part le moindre aveu de ce genre, et loin de souscrire aux prétensions d'indemnités que les Ministres Autrichiens m'opposoient pour essayer de contrebalancer celles de ma Cour, je n'ai jamais eu qu'une seule et même façon de répondre à leurs argumens. Je leur objectai "que si l'Autriche croyoit avoir des droits pour être dédommagés des fraix de la guerre, ces titres ne devroient cependant pas être confondus avec ceux de la Prusse. Que l'une étoit partie principale et attaquée; l'autre, partie accessoire et auxiliaire, fesant des sacrifices considérables en faveur d'une cause qui n'est pas la sienne, et pour lesquels elle demande à être indemnisée. Que la Cour de Vienne ayant reconnu l'équité de cette indemnité, la Prusse en se la procurant par son arrondissement en Pologne, n'y retrouve que le recouvrement de ses avances, le fruit d'une coopération dont elle s'est chargée à la requisition de l'Autriche, et de laquelle cette Puissance est obligée de lui tenir compte, tandis que si l'on accorde à celle-ci le droit de réclamer un dédommagement de son côté, ce n'est absolument qu'aux dépends de la France son ennemie qu'elle peut la réaliser."

Tels étoient, Sire, daignez en grace Vous en souvenir, les principes que j'osai Vous soumettre lorsque le 8 Mai de l'année dernière j'eus l'honneur d'entretenir V. M. sur cette matière à Charlottenbourg, et telle étoit ma profession de foi à Vienne, lors même que je n'étois pas encore appelé à discuter rigoureusement cette matière. Mais dès l'instant où je fus autorisé à l'éclaircir de plus près, je l'ai fait sans détour avec une franchise et une précision qui ne pouvoit plus laisser le moindre doute.

(The first occasion for a categorical explanation was at Luxemburg, when he had been charged to announce to Spielmann the terms under which the King would consent to continue the war.) Le Referendaire intime revenant alors à sa thèse favorite de la parité des indemnisations, je saisis l'apropos pour déchirer le voile et pour lui indiquer la différence de nos calculs. Je lui declarai en autant de termes: "que si jamais il pouvoit avoir été question d'établir entre les deux Puissances alliées un Sistème d'égalité dans leur agrandissements futurs, ce Sistème devoit s'entendre uniquement des acquisitions qu'elles seroient à même de faire par des convenances réciproques." (The present case entirely different, etc.).

Je n'en disconviens pas, cette explication acheva de troubler le B. de Spielmann; il me répondit, "que mes principes diamétralement opposés aux siens étoient absolument neufs pour lui et que s'ils devoient prévaloir, il y voyoit *le tombeau de l'Alliance entre les deux Cours.*"

A l'appui de ce que j'avançois, et pour entamer la négociation principale, je remis alors au B. de Spielmann la Note qui avoit été préparée dans le Quartier Général de Merle la veille, 25. Octobre 1792, sous les yeux de V. M. et qui renfermoit les conditions irrévocables qu'Elle venoit de mettre à sa coopération pour la campagne suivante . . . Là dessus j'étalai sur la table du B. de Spielmann l'exemplaire original de la carte de la Pologne sur laquelle, Sire, Vous aviez tracé de main propre dans le camp de Consanvoy la ligne de Vos acquisitions de Czenstochow par Rawa à Soldau. Je lui montrai au doigt cette ligne de démarcation, en lui disant "que telle seroit l'indemnité de V. M. et qu'après en avoir été mise en possession, elle continueroit à l'Empereur pendant la campagne prochaine la même assistance qu'Elle lui avoit accordée dans celle-ci." . . . Il me fallut essuyer pendant trois heures une longue suite de déclamations et de plaintes, dont le retournant fut toujours l'insupportable principe de la parité, et la nécessité de l'adopter invariablement pour base des liaisons subsistantes entre les deux Cours. (He had finally ended the discussion by saying) "Que sans pouvoir remonter au passé, j'étois obligé de m'en tenir à la situation des affaires telle qu'elle se présentoit aujourd'hui. Que la résolution de V. M. et Ses conditions étoient invariables, et que si la possession immédiate de l'arrondissement proposé pouvoit rencontrer les moindres obstacles, la retraite de l'armée Prussienne restoit décidée sans retour." . . .

(At Vienna he had then daily pressed the Austrians for a satisfactory answer, repeating constantly), "que j'entendois par la prise de possession de l'acquisition de V. M. en Pologne *non leur occupation éventuelle ou intérimale, mais leur propriété permanente et leur incorporation complette à la Monarchie Prussienne.*"

A force de renouveller d'heure en heure mes représentations, mes instances, mes déclarations énergiques, et je dirois presque mes comminations, j'eus le bonheur enfin de ramener les deux Ministres du Cabinet à des dispositions plus favorables. . . . Ce fut dans les journées du 21 et 22 Décembre, que s'opéra cet heureux changement; j'obtins le consentement pûr et simple à la prise de possession effective et on laissa de côté les chevilles qui avoient hérissé jusqu'ici l'issue de ma négociation. Les assurances formelles que je reçus de la bouche du Comte Cobenzl et du B. de Spielmann, furent en même tems accompagnées de la promesse positive: "Que S. M. l'Empereur addressera les instances, les plus pressantes," etc. (word for word as in the report of December 24 printed above). . . . La seule restriction qu'on se permit d'ajouter, ce fut: que l'Impératrice de Russie voulut, conjointement avec S. M. le Roi de Prusse, *garantir son consentement à l'échange de la Baviere,* qui me présentoit à la vérité un sens obscur et louche, mais sur laquelle je ne me crus pas obligé, par cette même raison, de faire le difficile, persuadé qu'elle auroit grand besoin d'être déterminé avec plus de clarté dans la suite.

(The 23rd he had had his final audience with the Emperor.) L'Empereur me répondit du ton le plus affectueux, "qu'il étoit bien loin de se permettre le moindre doute sur l'amitié et les sentimens de V. M.; mais qu'il ne pouvoit me cacher une chose qui l'embarrassoit. Vous savez, continua-t-il, que j'ai donné mon consentement à l'aggrandissement du Roi en Pologne; mais puisque S. M. a fait de cette acquisition la condition sine qua non de sa coopération à la guerre, je dois conserver quelques appréhensions que malgré les ordres les plus positifs qui sont adressés au C. de Cobenzl à Pétersbourg, nous ne rencontrions des difficultés pour emporter aussi l'acquiescement de l'Impératrice de Russie." . . . Ainsi finit cette audience mémorable dans laquelle l'Empereur me parla en termes si positifs de *son consentement donné et même de son inquiétude a voir réalisé le plan de V. M.*, sans rappeller une seule de ces clauses restrictives que ses Ministres avoient interjettées auparavant. . . . Il [Cobenzl] poussa même la résignation jusqu'à me dire "qu'il souscrivoit respectueusement aux volontés de son maître convaincu d'ailleurs de la justice de nos prétensions." . . . Dans ces derniers tems de mon séjour à

Vienne j'avois quitté le ton du négociateur pour prendre celui d'un homme *qui veut,* et qui annonce les *volontés* péremptoires de son Maître.

APPENDIX XVII

NOTES OF THE EMPRESS BELONGING TO THE PAPERS OF THE SECRET CONFERENCE OF OCTOBER 29/NOVEMBER 9, 1792.

[P. A., X, 69]

1. Можно бы и то сказать еще Пруссакамъ, что намъ кажется теперь не время начать новые хлопоты когда дѣло идетъ до выручения Нѣмецкой Имперіи и ея цѣлости изъ рукъ Французовъ, кои не токмо завладѣли тремя Курфирствами но и тѣмъ городомъ же гдѣ коронуются Императоры.

2. ¹Правила въ томъ дѣлѣ кажется быть должны отдалить дѣлежъ Польши колико можно.

Послѣ бѣдственной Кампаніи нѣтъ пріобрѣтеній условиться, и мы не вѣдаемъ что дѣлать хотятъ съ нами же ни о чемъ. Тутъ не безъ вѣдома вѣнскаго двора не приступить къ оному дѣлу.

Усилить Прусскаго Короля ни для чего.

Противу честности и обѣщаніи отнюдь ни чево [*sic*] принимать.

NOTE OF THE EMPRESS BELONGING TO THE PAPERS OF THE SECRET CONFERENCE OF NOVEMBER 4/15, 1792.

[P. A., X, 69]

A la manière pressante dont le Comte Goltz a parlé hier, il n'y a qu'à repondre que sans savoir ce que la Cour de Vienne mon Allié repondra et me communiquera je ne saurois rien dire, qu'outre cela il est indispensablement necessaire de savoir quelle sera la conduite de l'Angleterre, que selon nos Avis de Constantinople les intrigues y augmente pour porter le Divan a nous declarer la guerre, qu'on l'a deja porté à faire travailler à un Armement maritime, qu'en conséquence je ne trouve pas que la Prudence permette de commencer de nouveaux embarras tandis surtout que ceux qui existent ne sont pas finis ni que nous puissions en prevoir la fin, étant dans une tres parfaite ignorance sur le plan des hauts Alliés, lequel jusqu'ici a été diamétralement oposé à tout ce que nous avons proposé, et même jusque là que les Princes frères du Roy de France, loin d'être mis en avant, sont chassés de lieu en lieu et prêts à périr de faim et de misère

¹ This note follows immediately upon the preceding in the volume from which it is taken, and in all probability belongs with it.

avec la Noblesse nombreuse qui est restée fidèle à la Cause du Roy qui est reconnue pour celle de tous les Souverains. Que nous n'ajoutons pas foy au bruit general de l'Europe comme si S. M. étoit convenu avec les Rebelles de je ne sai quel arrangement, que nous n'y ajoutons pas foy parce que ces bruits sont injurieux à sa gloire et sa probité.

APPENDIX XVIII

RESCRIPTS OF CATHERINE II. TO SIEVERS WITH REGARD TO THE NEGOTIATIONS AT THE DIET OF GRODNO.

[M. A., Польша, III, 70]

1. MAY 26/JUNE 6, 1793

Après vous avoir annoncé mes intentions en termes ostensibles dans le Rescrit Russe, qui accompagne celui-ci, je ne veux point vous laisser ignorer les motifs particuliers qui m'ont déterminée à faire traiter séparément les objets de cession à faire aux deux Cours Copartageantes d'avec ceux de la nouvelle Constitution et des liaisons politiques et commerciales de la Pologne. . . . Depuis j'ai sçu de differens cotés que les plus sensés d'entre les Polonois sentoient que dans la foiblesse et le néant où leur pays seroit plongé à la suite du nouveau démembrement qu'il vient de subir, il lui seroit difficile ou plutôt impossible de subsister en Corps d'Etat libre et independant. En partant de là, presque tous desireroient assés unanimement de pouvoir suivre la destinée de ceux de leurs compatriotes, qui ont passé sous ma domination. Je ne sçaurois écouter leurs voeux à cet égard sans exciter la jalousie des Puissances voisines et sans leur attirer une foule d'embarras qu'il importe d'éviter dans ce moment. Mais il ne seroit pas impossible d'y suppléer au moyen d'un traité d'alliance et d'union si étroite entre les deux Nations, que sans rendre l'une sujette à l'autre, elles fussent liées inséparablement entre elles. (A somewhat similar plan had been opposed in 1788 by the Court of Berlin.) Quoique les choses soyent changées et par les rapports où je suis avec cette cour et par la position où nous nous trouvons respectivement, il n'en est pas moins certain que si cette question étoit remise sur le tapis dans le tems que nous négocions en commun avec Elle, il en résulteroit de deux choses l'une, ou qu'elle voudroit participer de manière ou d'autre à mes arrangemens avec les Polonois ou qu'elle tacheroit de se procurer encore de nouveaux avantages à leur depens. Ni l'un ni l'autre n'étant ni de ma convenance ni de mes intérêts, j'ai cherché à écarter les Prussiens et à les mettre hors du jeu aussitôt qu'ils auront arrangé et terminé l'article de leurs acquisitions. C'est d'après ces principes que j'ai fait rediger les stipulations du Traité de cession et reglé la marche de la Négociation que je leur ferai proposer et adopter; c'est aussi par cette considération que je n'ai pas voulû que dans votre projet d'acte on fit mention d'aucune transaction éventuelle à l'exception d'un Traité de Commerce pour que la Cour de Berlin ne fit rien de semblable à notre imitation. J'ai laissé à votre choix de proroguer ou de dissoudre la Diette; mais lorsqu'elle se sera rassemblée pour la raison de travailler à l'organisation du gouvernement de la République, ce sera votre affaire de disposer les esprits de manière que la proposition d'un Traité, tel que je viens de le déterminer cy-dessus, me vient d'eux spontanément et comme un accessoire qui n'a été nullement premedité. Je ne mets d'intervale entre la dissolution ou la prorogation et le nouveau rassemblement de la diette que celui de six à huit semaines; car il faut profiter de l'occupation de nos voisins pour arranger solidement et stablement toutes nos affaires avec la République. Malgré la stipulation qui abandonne aux Polonois le soin de l'arrangement futur de leur gouvernement, vous saurés vous ménager les moyens d'y influer indirectement à l'exclusion de votre Collègue Prussien, et sans de bien grands efforts vous continuerés à diriger les esprits dans tous les sens qui conviendront les plus à mes interets.

2. JUNE 23/JULY 4, 1793

. . . Cependant il me paroit qu'il ne sera pas tout à fait superflu de vous retracer aujourd'huy la marche et l'ordre que vous avés à suivre dans la négociation qui vous est confiée et de vous faire part en même tems et dans la plus intime confidence des motifs qui m'ont déterminée à les adopter. Je commencerai par ces derniers.

La Cour de Vienne depuis l'installation de son nouveau Ministère commence à manifester une inquiétude bien plus vive qu'elle ne l'a fait par le passé sur les acquisitions des deux Cours Voisines en Pologne. Après avoir fait d'inutiles tentatives pour en diminuer les portions, elle vient d'avoir recours à moi par des représentations amicales pour m'engager en cas de non-réussite des plans des compensations qui lui étoient assignées dans notre convention avec le Roy de Prusse à lui réserver également en Pologne une part équivalente à celle de chacun de nous deux. Mais en attendant, et à tout évènement Elle me demande à se mettre dès à présent en possession de la Ville de Cracovie et de quelqu' arrondissement de limites du côté de la Gallicie; le tout sous prétexte que cette province sera trop exposée vis à vis des Prussiens après l'occupation qu'ils ont faite de Czenstochova. . . . Cette raison sans doute n'est pas sans poids, mais comme en l'admettant nous risquerions d'un côté d'appauvrir trop la portion restante de la Pologne, et de manquer par là le but que nous proposions de la conserver sur le pied d'un Etat intermédiaire, et que de l'autre en jettant ce nouvel incident au milieu de notre négociation nous ne pourrions que l'embarrasser et la prolonger non sans des inconvéniens majeurs, j'aurois désiré de pouvoir y trouver quelque autre expédient qui put concilier les interets des Autrichiens, sans en venir à une concession de territoire Polonoise vis à vis d'eux, et sans avoir l'air de manquer à nos engagemens vis à vis des Prussiens. Cet expédient le plus naturel seroit celui de faire desister ces derniers de la conservation de Czenstochowa dans la ligne de démarcation qu'ils ont tracée jusqu'ici. Connoissant leur avidité toujours aussi prompte à envahir qu'incapable de se dessaisir de ce qu'ils ont eu une fois en main, il ne seroit pas permis de se flatter d'aucun accommodement à ce sujet, si on venoit à le leur proposer avant que l'arrangement qui nous concerne fut consommé. Mais lorsque celui-ci sera parvenu à toute la maturité, il ne sera peut-être pas impossible à l'aide de l'intervention autrichienne et d'une opposition tant soit peu soutenue de la part des Polonois d'obtenir quelque modification ou relachement sur ce point. . . . En attendant, pour le bien de nos propres affaires, voilà la conduite que vous avés à tenir:

1°. Continués à insister sur la nomination de la delegation pour traiter avec vous et vôtre Collègue Prussien, s'entend avec l'un après l'autre et par conséquent avec vous le premier, sur l'objet de vos declarations respectives. Si pour remporter cette détermination, il vous faudra employer tour à tour les promesses et les menaces, tenés vous sur leur nature à ce qui vous en est prescrit dans vos instructions. Parmi les menaces, si vous les trouvés plus nécessaires qu'autre chose, n'oubliés pas de faire sentir aux nonces de la Diette, que s'ils diffèrent la nomination de la délégation en question, vous avés ordre de rompre la négociation, de vous retirer, et de faire traiter la Pologne en pays ennemi en y levant les contributions et en le livrant à la discrétion des trouppes, . . . et engagés le ministre de Prusse à tenir le même langage.

2°. Dès que de cette manière ou de toute autre vous parviendrés à nouer vôtre négociation, ne perdés pas de tems pour conclurre vôtre Traité et pour disposer les choses de manière qu'aussitôt que nos ratifications vous seront arrivées, elles puissent être échangées contre celles du Roy et de la Diette de Pologne.

3°. Lorsque le tour du ministre Prussien viendra, vous vous établirés naturellement en Conciliateur entre lui et les Polonois. Vous n'y mettrés que le degré d'activité et d'énergie analogue à l'intention cy-dessus annoncée, laissant le champ libre aux objections Polonoises et les appuyant même en tant que de raison et de justice. Il n'y aura non seulement aucun inconvénient, mais beaucoup d'avantage à gagner du tems dans cette seconde négociation.

4°. Laissés les Lithuaniens à eux-mêmes. Accueillés-les, mais ni les conseillés ni les déconseillés. Vous avés fort bien repondu à l'eveque Cossacovsky; mais restés en là, et empechés toute explosion prematurée et par conséquent indiscrette.

3. August 11/22, 1793

. . . Il étoit à prévoir que les différentes mesures mal calculées que les Prussiens ont adoptées au debut même de leur négociation entraveroient la marche de cette affaire par des nouvelles difficultés. . . . Vous êtes très bien entré dans ma façon de penser en posant pour principe de vos explications avec les deux partis que je ne refuserai surement pas mon appui efficace . . . au Roi de Prusse dans tout ce qu'il pourra exiger légitimement de la Pologne en vertu de la Convention conclue entre moi et la Cour de Berlin; mais qu'en même tems je n'employerai jamais la violence et les moyens coercitifs pour forcer les Polonois dans l'état d'abandon et de désolation où ils se trouvent, à recevoir des conditions injustes et onéreuses. (As to the two points which the Poles demanded from Prussia: strict adherence to the line of demarcation indicated by the Convention of St. Petersburg, and certain commercial stipulations in their favor) Je me crois d'autant plus autorisée à insister sur ces deux points auprès du Roi de Prusse que mon exactitude à remplir le premier et ma générosité à l'égard du second peuvent lui servir d'exemple; et puisque les Prussiens et les Polonois s'en rapportent également à ma médiation dans ces différends, je ne pourrai jamais donner mon suffrage que d'après la stricte équité. . . . Il resulte de cet exposé que vous devés soutenir et pousser par tous les moyens qui sont en votre pouvoir, sans cependant user de voyes de fait, la négociation Prussienne appuyée sur les principes developpés cy-dessus, et soutenir en même tems les Polonois dans leurs justes demandes relatives aux deux points en question. Vous devés cependant assurer ces derniers que ma ferme volonté est que le Traité avec le Roi de Prusse se fasse, et que je tiendrai religieusement ma parole à ce dernier. La marche que les Polonois devraient à mon avis adopter dans ce moment-ci, au lieu des clabauderies et des intrigues qui les agitent, devroit être de former en prenant pour base la Déclaration Prussienne du 9 Avril, un contreprojet de Traité dans lequel ils inséreroient toutes les stipulations commerciales qu'ils ont droit d'exiger et les differentes spécifications qui doivent déterminer avec exactitude la demarcation.

Dans ce nouveau Projet de Traité la garantie de la future constitution de la République ne devroit absolument pas avoir lieu, et de quelque manière que les choses aillent, vous aurés soin qu'elle ne s'y trouve pas, ce qui est conséquent au but que je me suis proposé . . . d'écarter désormais les Prussiens de toute influence dans les affaires intérieures de la Pologne. Ce contreprojet communiqué une fois au S^r. Bucholz, la Cour de Prusse, tranquille sur le fond de l'affaire, auroit mauvaise grace de se refuser à des concessions de moindre importance pour elle, et les deux partis se trouveront bientôt d'accord.

4. AUGUST 23/SEPTEMBER 3, 1793

. . . Dans tout ce que vous avez dit et fait en faveur des Polonois, vous avez rempli parfaitement Mes intentions, et la Cour de Prusse, quelque contraire que puissent paroître à ses intérêts la marche que vous avez tenue, ne pourra sans doute s'empêcher de reconnoître les principes de justice et d'humanité qui en ont été la base. Le nouveau Projet de Traité entre la Prusse et la Pologne redigé à la suite des dernières Conférences, Me paroissant réunir en faveur de cette dernière tous les avantages conciliables avec le sacrifice inévitable qu'elle doit faire à la Prusse, Je ne vois plus ce qui pourroit en arrêter la conclusion, et Je vous enjoins expressement de l'accelerer par tous les moyens qui sont en votre pouvoir, evitant toujours la violence et conservant autant qu'il vous sera possible le rôle de conciliateur qui vous a si bien réussi jusqu'à présent. Le prompt achevement de la Négociation Prussien Me tient aujourd'hui d'autant plus à cœur, que Je me suis décidée à n'entamer aucune autre sur les differens objets à regler entre Moi et la Pologne avant que celle-ci ne soit finie.

BIBLIOGRAPHY

THE following list is intended to enumerate the works cited in this book and such other works as the author has found distinctly useful in the preparation of the present volume. Limits of space render it impossible to attempt here an entirely exhaustive bibliography of the immense literature bearing upon the Second Partition and related topics; and such an attempt is scarcely necessary, perhaps, in view of the many admirable bibliographical tools already available for the study of this period, such as Dr. Ludwik Finkel's *Bibliografia historyi polskiej* and Dahlmann-Waitz's *Quellenkunde zur deutschen Geschichte*.

I. ORIGINAL SOURCES

Angeberg, *pseud.* See Chodźko.

Annual Register, The. 1758—. London.

Arneth, Alfred, Ritter von, and Flammermont, Jules. *Correspondance secrète du Comte de Mercy-Argenteau avec l'Empereur Joseph II et le Prince de Kaunitz.* Paris, 1889, 1891. 2 vols.

Arneth, Alfred, Ritter von. "Graf Philipp Cobenzl und seine Memoiren." In *Archiv für österreichische Geschichte,* lxvii (1885), pp. 1–181.

—— "Die Relationen der Botschafter Venedigs über Oesterreich im achtzehnten Jahrhundert." In *Fontes rerum austriacarum,* II, xxii (1863).

—— *Joseph II und Katharina von Russland. Ihr Briefwechsel.* Vienna, 1869.

—— *Joseph II und Leopold von Toskana. Ihr Briefwechsel.* Vienna, 1873. 2 vols.

—— *Marie Antoinette, Joseph II und Leopold II. Ihr Briefwechsel.* Leipsic, etc., 1866.

Auckland, William Eden, Lord. *Journal and Correspondence.* London, 1861–62. 4 vols.

Aulard, A. *Recueil des actes du Comité de Salut Public.* Paris, 1889—. 23 vols. (In the *Collection de Documents inédits sur l'histoire de France, publiés par les soins du Ministère de l'Instruction Publique.*)

Bartoszewicz, K. *Księga pamiątkowa setnej rocznicy ustanowienia konstytucyi 3. maja.* Cracow, 1891. 2 vols.

Beer, Adolf. "Analekten zur Geschichte der Revolutionszeit." In *Historische Zeitschrift,* xxvii (1872), pp. 1–35.

—— *Joseph II, Leopold II und Kaunitz. Ihr Briefwechsel.* Vienna, 1873.

Beer, Adolph, and Fiedler, Joseph von. "Joseph II und Graf Ludwig Cobenzl. Ihr Briefwechsel." In *Fontes rerum austriacarum*, II, liii, liv (1901).

—— *Leopold II, Franz II und Catharina. Ihre Correspondenz.* Vienna, 1874.

Brunner, Sebastian. *Correspondances intimes de l'Empereur Joseph II avec le Comte de Cobenzl et le Prince de Kaunitz.* Mainz, etc., 1871.

Castéra, Jean. *Histoire de Catherine II.* Paris, [1800]. 4 vols.

Casti. See Greppi.

[Chodźko, L.] *Recueil des Traités, Conventions, et Actes diplomatiques concernant la Pologne, 1762–1862, par le Comte d'Angeberg.* Paris, 1862.

[Cobbett, William.] *The Parliamentary History of England from the Earliest Period to the Year 1803.* London, 1806–20. 36 vols.

[Cölln, Frederic von.] *Vertraute Briefe über die Verhältnisse am preussischen Hofe seit dem Tode Friedrichs II.* Amsterdam, etc., 1807–09. 6 vols.

Coxe, William. *Travels into Poland, Russia, Sweden, and Denmark.* Dublin, 1784. 3 vols.

Czartoryski, Adam Jerzy, [Prince]. *Żywot J. U. Niemcewicza.* Posen, etc., 1860.

Czasy Stanisława Augusta Poniatowskiego przez jednego z posłów wielkiego sejmu napisane. Posen, 1867.

Dampmartin, A. H. *Quelques traits de la vie privée de Frédéric-Guillaume II, Roi de Prusse.* Paris, 1811.

Dembiński, Bronisław. *Documents relatifs à l'histoire du deuxième et troisième partage de la Pologne.* Tom. i, 1788–91. Lemberg, 1902.

[Dmochowski, F., Kołłątaj, H., and others.] *Vom Entstehen und Untergange der polnischen Konstitution vom 3. May 1791.* (Translated by S. B. Linde.) Leipsic, 1793. 2 vols.

Dohm, Christian Wilhelm von. *Denkwürdigkeiten meiner Zeit.* Lemgo and Hanover, 1814–19. 5 vols.

Engeström, Lars von. *Minnen och anteckningar.* Stockholm, 1876. 2 vols.

Feuillet de Conches, F. *Louis XVI, Marie Antoinette et Madame Élisabeth. Lettres et documents inédits.* Paris, 1864–73. 6 vols.

France. Ministère des Affaires Étrangères. *Recueil des instructions données aux ambassadeurs et ministres de France. Pologne* (edited by L. Farges). Paris, 1888. 2 vols. *Russie* (edited by A. Rambaud). Paris, 1890. 2 vols.

Frederick II, King of Prussia. *Œuvres.* Berlin, 1846–57. 30 vols. and index.

—— *Politische Correspondenz.* Berlin (vol. xxxv, Weimar), 1879—. 35 vols. published to 1912.

Görtz, Johann Eustach, Graf von. *Historische und politische Denkwürdigkeiten.* Stuttgart and Tübingen, 1827–28. 2 parts.

Great Britain, Historical Manuscripts Commission. *The Manuscripts of J. B. Fortescue, Esq., preserved at Dropmore.* London, 1892–99. 5 vols.

Greppi, E. "Lettere politiche dell' Abate Casti scritte da Vienna nell' anno 1793." In the *Miscellanea di Storia Italiana edita per cura della regia diputazione di storia patria*, xxi (1883). Turin.

Gustavus III, King of Sweden. "Konung Gustafs bref till friherre G. M. Armfelt." In *Historiska Handlingar till trycket befordrade af Kongl. Samfundet för utgifvande af handskrifter rörande Skandinaviens Historia*, xii, no. 3 (1883). Stockholm.

Hansard. See Cobbett.

[Haugwitz, Christian August Heinrich, Graf von.] "Fragment des mémoires inédits du Comte de Haugwitz." In *Minerva, ein Journal historischen und politischen Inhalts, hrsg. von J. W. von Archenholz*, clxxxiv (1837). Jena.

[Helbig, G. A. W. von.] "Potemkin der Taurier. Anecdoten zur Geschichte seines Lebens und seiner Zeit." In *Minerva*, xxii (1797)–xxxvi (1880). Hamburg.

Hertzberg, Ewald Friedrich, Graf von. "Denkschrift über das zwischen Preussen und Polen im Jahre 1790 geschlossene Bündniss." In Schmidt's *Zeitschrift für Geschichtswissenschaft*, vii (1847), pp. 261–71.

—— "Précis de la carrière diplomatique du comte de Hertzberg." *Ibid.*, i (1844), pp. 16–36.

—— *Recueil des déductions, manifestes, déclarations, traités et autres actes et écrits publics, qui ont été rédigés et publiés pour la cour de Prusse par le ministre d'état Comte de Hertzberg depuis l'année 1756 jusqu'à l'année 1790*. Berlin, 1790–95. 3 vols.

Heyking, Alfons, Baron von. *Aus Polens und Kurlands letzten Tagen. Memoiren des Baron Karl Heinrich Heyking (1752–1796)*. Berlin, 1897.

Hurmuzaki, E. de. *Documente privitôre la istoria Românilor*. Bucharest, 1887–1909. 13 vols. and supplement of 3 vols.

Keith, Sir Robert Murray. *Memoirs and Correspondence*. Edited by Mrs. Gillespie Smyth. London, 1849. 2 vols.

Klinckowström, Rudolf, Baron. *Le Comte de Fersen et la Cour de France*. Paris, 1877–78. 2 vols.

Koźmian, Kajetan. *Pamiętniki obejmujące wspomnienia od roku 1780 do roku 1815*. Posen, 1858. 3 vols.

Leeds, Francis, fifth Duke of. *Political Memoranda*. Edited by Oscar Browning. London, 1884. (Camden Society.)

Léouzon le Duc, L. *Correspondance diplomatique du Baron de Staël-Holstein, ambassadeur de Suède en France*. Paris, 1881.

Ligne, Charles Joseph, Prince de. *Mémoires et Mélanges historiques et littéraires*. Paris, 1827–29. 5 vols.

Liske, X. "Zur polnischen Politik Katharina II." In *Historische Zeitschrift*, xxx (1873), pp. 281–304.

Mably, l'Abbé de. *Œuvres*. Paris, l'an III. 15 vols.

Małachowski, Stanisław Nałęcz, Hrabia. *Pamiętniki*. Posen, 1885.

Malmesbury, James Harris, first Earl of. *Diaries and Correspondence*. London, 1845. 4 vols.

Martens, Fedor. *Recueil des Traités et Conventions conclus par la Russie avec les Puissances étrangères*. St. Petersburg, 1874–1909. 15 vols.

Martens, Georg Friedrich von. *Recueil de Traités des Puissances et États de l'Europe depuis 1761 jusqu'à présent*. 2nd ed. Göttingen, 1817–35. 8 vols.

Massenbach, Christian, Freiherr von. *Memoiren zur Geschichte des preussischen Staates unter den Regierungen Friedrich Wilhelms II und Friedrich Wilhelms III.* Amsterdam, 1809. 3 vols.

Masson, C. F. P. *Mémoires secrets sur la Russie et particulièrement sur la fin du règne de Catherine II et celui de Paul I.* Paris, 1800. 2 vols.

Mayno, Edouard, Comte del. *Lettres et dépêches du Marquis de Parelle, premier ministre du Roi de Sardaigne à la cour de Russie (1783–1784) et du Baron de la Turbie (1792–1793).* Rome, 1901.

[Mirabeau, Honoré Gabriel Riquetti, Comte de.] *Histoire secrète de la cour de Berlin.* [n. p.], 1789.

Moniteur, Le (1789–99). Réimpression. Paris, 1840–45. 32 vols.

Mottaz, Eugène. *Stanislas Poniatowski et Maurice Glayre. Correspondance relative aux partages de la Pologne.* Paris, 1897.

[Nesselrode, K., Comte de.] *Lettres et papiers du Chancelier Comte de Nesselrode, 1760–1850.* Paris, 1904–12. 11 vols.

Neumann, Leopold, and Plason, Adolphe de. *Recueil des Traités et Conventions conclus par l'Autriche avec les Puissances étrangères depuis 1763 jusqu'à nos jours.* Leipsic, 1855–1902. 20 vols.

Ogiński, Michel, Comte d'. *Mémoires sur la Pologne et les Polonais, depuis 1788 jusqu'à la fin de 1815.* Paris, 1826–27. 4 vols.

[Pistor, G. K.] *Mémoires sur la révolution de la Pologne trouvés à Berlin.* Paris, 1806.

Politisches Journal. Herausgegeben von einer Gesellschaft von Gelehrten. Hamburg. Jahrgänge 1792, 1793.

Poschinger, Heinrich von. *Also sprach Bismarck.* Vienna, 1910–11. 3 vols.

Prümers, Rodgero. *Das Jahr 1793. Urkunden und Aktenstücke zur Geschichte der Organisation Südpreussens.* Posen, 1895.

Puławski, Fr. "Listy Szczęsnego Potockiego do Katarzyny II a Zubowa." In *Kwartalnik Historyczny*, xvii (1903), pp. 266–76.

Ranke, Leopold von. *Denkwürdigkeiten des Staatskanzlers Fürsten von Hardenberg.* 2nd ed. Leipsic, 1880. 5 vols.

Raynal, G. T. *Histoire philosophique et politique des Établissemens et du Commerce des Européens dans les deux Indes.* Geneva, 1781. 10 vols.

[Schladen, K. F. G. von.] *Mittheilungen aus den nachgelassenen Papieren eines preussischen Diplomaten, herausgegeben von dessen Neffen L. v. L.* Berlin, 1868.

Schlieffen, Martin Ernst von. *Nachricht von einigen Häusern des Geschlechtes der von Schlieffen oder Schlieben.* Berlin, 1830. 2 vols.

Schlitter, Hanns. "Briefe der Erzherzogin Marie Christine, Staathalterin der Niederlande an Leopold II, nebst einer Einleitung zur Geschichte der französischen Politik Leopolds II." In *Fontes rerum austriacarum*, II, xlviii (1896), pp. 1–360.

—— *Kaunitz, Philipp Cobenzl und Spielmann. Ihr Briefwechsel (1779–1792).* Vienna, 1899.

[Schulz, J. C. F.] *Reise eines Liefländers von Riga nach Warschau.* Berlin, 1795–96. 3 Teil.

Ségur, Louis Philippe, Comte de. *Mémoires*. Vols. i–iii of his *Œuvres*, Paris, 1824–27, 33 volumes.

Sienkiewicz, Karol. *Skarbiec historyi polskiej*. Paris, 1839–40. 2 vols.

Spiegel, L. P. J. van de. *Résumé des négociations qui accompagnèrent la révolution des Pays-bas autrichiens, avec des pièces justificatives*. Amsterdam, 1841.

Stanislas Augustus Poniatowski, King of Poland. *Mémoires de Stanislas Auguste et sa Correspondance avec l'Impératrice Catherine II*. Posen, 1862.

—— *Mémoires du roi Stanislas-Auguste Poniatowski*. (Edited by Serge Goriaïnov.) Tom. i. St. Petersburg, 1914.

Staszic, Stanisław. *Uwagi nad życiem Jana Zamojskiego*. Cracow, 1861.

Taube, C. E. B. *Svenska beskickningars berättelser om främmande makter år 1793*. Stockholm, 1893.

Thürheim, A., Graf. *Briefe des Grafen Mercy-Argenteau an den Grafen Louis Starhemberg*. Innsbruck, 1884.

Vivenot, Alfred, Ritter von. *Quellen zur Geschichte der deutschen Kaiserpolitik Oesterreichs während der französischen Revolutionskriege, 1790–1801*. Vienna, 1873–93. 5 vols. (Vols. iii–v, which were edited by H. Zeissberg after Vivenot's death, bear the altered title " Quellen zur Geschichte der Politik Oesterreichs während der französischen Revolutionskriege, 1793–97.")

—— " Thugut und sein politisches System. Urkundliche Beiträge zur Geschichte der deutschen Politik des österreichischen Kaiserhauses während des Krieges gegen die französische Revolution." In *Archiv für österreichische Geschichte*, xlii (1870), pp. 363–489.

—— *Vertrauliche Briefe des Freiherrn von Thugut*. Vienna, 1872. 2 vols.

Vom Entstehen und Untergange der polnischen Konstitution des 3. May 1791. See Dmochowski.

Voss, Sophie Marie, Gräfin von. *Neunundsechzig Jahre am preussischen Hofe. Aus den Erinnerungen der Oberhofmeisterin Sophie Marie, Gräfin von Voss*. 6th ed. Leipsic, 1894.

Wassiltchikow, A. *Les Razoumowski*. Édition française par Alexandre Brückner. Halle, 1893–94. 3 tom. (in 6 vols.).

Wolf, A. *Leopold II und Marie Christine. Ihr Briefwechsel, 1781–1792*. Vienna, 1867.

Wraxall, Sir Nathaniel William. *Memoirs of the Courts of Berlin, Dresden, Warsaw, and Vienna in the Years 1777, 1778, and 1779*. 3rd ed. London, 1806. 2 vols.

Архивъ Государственнаго Совѣта. St. Petersburg, 1869. 2 vols.

Архивъ Князя Воронцова. Moscow, 1876–97. 40 vols.

Гарновскій, Михаилъ. Записки (*1782–1790*). Русская Старина, xv (1876), pp. 9–38, 237–265, 471–499, 687–720; xvi (1876), pp. 1–32, 207–238, 399–440.

Головкинъ, Ѳ. Г., графъ. Записки. Русская Старина, cxxix (1907), pp. 347–372, 669–686.

Державинъ, Г. И. Записки, *1743–1812*. Moscow, 1860.

Екатерина II, Русская Императрица. Бумаги Императрицы Екатерины II хранящіяся въ Государственномъ Архивѣ Министерства Иностранныхъ Дѣлъ. Сборникъ Имп. Рус. Ист. Общ., vii, x, xiii, xxvii, xlii.

—— Дипломатическая переписка Императрицы Екатерины II. *Ibid.*, xlviii, li, lvii, lxvii, lxxxvii, xcvii, cxviii, cxxxv.

—— Императрицы Екатерины II и князя Потемкина подлинная переписка (изъ сборника проф. П. С. Лебедева). Русская Старина, xvi (1876), pp. 33–58, 239–262, 441–478, 517–590; xvii (1876), pp. 21–38, 206–216, 403–426, 635–652.

—— Переписка съ барономъ Мельхіоромъ Гриммомъ. Сборникъ Имп. Рус. Ист. Общ., ɯxxiii, xxxiii, xliv.

—— Переписка съ королемъ Фридрихомъ II. *Ibid.*, xx.

—— Письма и бумаги Императрицы Екатерины II хранящіеся въ Имп. Публ. Библіотекѣ. (Изд. А. Ѳ. Бычкова.) St. Petersburg, 1873.

—— Письма Екатерины II къ графу Стакельбергу, 1773–1793. Русская Старина, iii (1871), pp. 310–325, 474–484, 605–627.

—— Сочиненія Императрицы Екатерины II, на основаніи подлинныхъ рукописей и съ объяснительными примѣчаніями академика А. Н. Пыпина. Изд. Императорской Академіи Наукъ. St. Petersburg, 1901–07. 12 vols.

Енгельгардтъ, Л. Н. Записки, *1766–1836*. Moscow, 1867.

Русская Старина, iii, xv, xvi, xvii, lxxvi, lxxxi, cxxix.

Русскій Архивъ, 1865, 1874[ii], 1876[i, iii], 1878[i–ii], 1888[iii].

Сборникъ военно-историческихъ матеріаловъ. Бумаги князя Григорія Александровича Потемкина-Таврическаго, *1774–1793*. (Изд. Военно-Ученаго Комитета Главного Штаба.) Vols. vi–viii. St. Petersburg, 1893–95.

Сборникъ Императорскаго Русскаго Историческаго Общества. St. Petersburg, 1867—. 144 volumes to 1914. Vols. vii, x, xii, xiii, xviii, xix, xx, xxii, xxiii, xxvi, xxvii, xxix, xxxiii, xxxvii, xlii, xliv, xlvi, xlvii, xlviii, li, lvii, lxvii, lxxii, lxxxvii, xcvii, cix, cxviii, cxxv, cxxxv, cxl, cxli, cxliii.

Храповицкій, А. В. Дневникъ съ 18 января 1782 по 17 сентября 1793 году. Moscow, 1901.

II. Secondary Works

(a) *Works of a More General Character*

Acton, John Edward Dalberg, Lord. *The History of Freedom and Other Essays.* London, 1907.

Andreae, Friedrich. *Preussische und russische Politik in Polen von der taurischen Reise Katharinas II (Januar 1787) bis zur Abwendung Friedrich Wilhelms II von den Hertzbergschen Plänen (August 1789).* Berlin, 1905.

Bain, R. Nisbet. " The Second Partition of Poland." In *English Historical Review*, vi (1891), pp. 331–340.

Beer, Adolf. *Die erste Theilung Polens.* Vienna, 1873. 2 vols. and a volume of documents.

Brougham, Henry, Lord. *Historical and Political Dissertations.* London and Glasgow, 1857. (Vol. viii of his collected *Works*.)

Clapham, J. H. *The Causes of the War of 1792.* Cambridge (Eng.), 1899.

Creux, H. J. *Pitt et Frédéric-Guillaume II. L'Angleterre et la Prusse devant la question d'Orient en 1790*. Paris, 1886.

F. v. S. [not Friedrich von Smitt, as often given]. *Die Theilung Polens in den Jahren 1773, 1793, 1796, und 1815, und der Wiener Kongress im Jahre 1815*. Berlin, 1864.

Ferrand, F.-C. *Histoire des trois démembrements de la Pologne pour faire suite à l'histoire de l'anarchie de Pologne par Rulhière*. Paris, 1820. 3 vols.

Glagau, Hans. *Die französische Legislative und der Ursprung der Revolutionskriege, 1791–1792*. Berlin, 1896.

Häusser, Ludwig. *Deutsche Geschichte vom Tode Friedrichs des Grossen bis zur Gründung des deutschen Bundes*. 3rd ed. Berlin, 1861–63. 4 vols.

Haumant, Émile. *La Guerre du Nord et la Paix d'Oliva, 1655–1660*. Paris, 1893.

Heigel, K. T. *Deutsche Geschichte vom Tode Friedrichs des Grossen bis zur Auflösung des alten Reiches*. Stuttgart, 1899–1911. 2 vols.

Herrmann, Ernst. " Zur Geschichte der Wiener Convention vom 25. Juli 1791 und der östreichisch-preussischen Allianz vom 7. Februar 1792." In *Forschungen zur deutschen Geschichte*, v (1865), pp. 237–290.

Hüffer, Hermann. *Oestreich und Preussen gegenüber der französischen Revolution bis zum Abschluss des Friedens von Campo Formio*. Bonn, 1868. *Ergänzungsband. Die Politik der deutschen Mächte im Revolutionskriege*. Münster, 1869.

Laurent, F. *La politique royale*. Paris, 1865. (Vol. xi of his *Études sur l'histoire de l'humanité*.)

Lenz, Max. " Marie Antoinette im Kampf mit der Revolution." In *Preussische Jahrbücher*, lxxviii (1894), pp. 1–28, 255–311.

Luckwaldt, Friedrich. " Die englisch-preussische Allianz von 1788." In *Forschungen zur brandenburgischen und preussischen Geschichte*, xv (1902), pp. 33–116.

Oncken, Wilhelm. *Das Zeitalter der Revolution, des Kaiserreiches und der Befreiungskriege*. Berlin, 1884–87. 2 vols.

Ranke, Leopold von. *Die deutschen Mächte und der Fürstenbund*. Leipsic, 1871–72. 2 vols.

—— *Ursprung und Beginn der Revolutionskriege, 1791 und 1792*. Leipsic, 1875.

Raumer, Fr. L. von. " Polens Untergang." In *Historisches Taschenbuch*, 1832[iii], pp. 395–537.

Rulhière, Claude de. *Histoire de l'anarchie de Pologne et du démembrement de cette république*. Paris, 1807. 4 vols.

Salisbury, A. T. G. Cecil, Marquess of. *Essays, Foreign Politics*. London, 1905.

Smitt, Frédéric de. *Frédéric II, Catherine et le partage de Pologne*. Paris, 1861.

Smolka, Stanisław. " Stanowisko mocarstw wobec konstytucyi trzeciego maja." In *Przegląd Polski*, 1891[ii], pp. 441–460.

Sorel, Albert. " L'Autriche et le Comité de Salut Public." In *Revue Historique*, xvii (1881), pp. 25–63.

Sorel, Albert. *L'Europe et la Révolution française.* Paris, 1885–1904. 8 vols.
—— *La Question d'Orient au xviiie siècle.* 3rd ed. Paris, 1902.
Sybel, Heinrich von. *Geschichte der Revolutionszeit von 1789 bis 1795.* 4th ed. Stuttgart, 1897–1900. 5 vols.
—— " Polens Untergang und der Revolutionskrieg." In *Historische Zeitschrift,* xxiii (1870), pp. 66–154.
Temperley, H. *Frederic the Great and Kaiser Joseph. An Episode of War and Diplomacy in the Eighteenth Century.* London, 1915.
Tratchevsky, Alexandre. " La France et l'Allemagne sous Louis XVI." In *Revue Historique,* xiv (1880), pp. 241–285; xv, pp. 1–46.
Treitschke, Heinrich von. *Deutsche Geschichte im neunzehnten Jahrhundert.* Leipsic, 1879–94. 5 vols.
Uebersberger, Hans. *Oesterreich und Russland seit dem Ende des fünfzehnten Jahrhunderts.* Vol. i (1488–1605), Vienna and Leipsic, 1906.
Vivenot, Alfred, Ritter von. *Zur Genesis der zweiten Theilung Polens.* Vienna, 1874.
Waliszewski, K. *Polska i Europa w drugiej połowie xviii wieku. Wstęp do historyi ruchu politycznego w tej epoce.* Cracow, 1890.
Wolf, G. *Oesterreich und Preussen, 1780–1790.* Vienna, 1880.
Трачевскій, Александръ. Союзъ князей и нѣмецкая политика Екатерины II, Фридриха II и Іосифа II (*1780–1790*). St. Petersburg, 1877.

(b) *Works Relating More Particularly to Poland*

Askenazy, S. *Die letzte polnische Königswahl.* Göttingen, 1894.
—— *Dwa stulecia, xviii i xix. Badania i przyczynki.* Warsaw, 1910. 2 vols.
—— *Książę Józef Poniatowski, 1763–1813.* Warsaw, 1905.
—— " Materyały i notatki, '1793'." In *Biblioteka Warszawska,* 1900ⁱ, pp. 155–165.
—— *Przymierze polsko-pruskie.* Lemberg, 1900.
Bain, R. Nisbet. *The Last King of Poland.* New York and London, 1909.
Balzer, O. " Państwo polskie w pierwszem siedmdziesięcioleciu xiv i xvi wieku." In *Kwartalnik Historyczny,* xxi (1907), pp. 193–291.
—— " Reformy społeczne i polityczne konstytucyi 3. maja." In *Przegląd Polski,* 1891ⁱⁱ, pp. 222–260, 461–496.
—— " Z powodu nowego zarysu historyi ustroju Polski." In *Kwartalnik Historyczny,* xx (1906), pp. 1–57, 397–441.
Bobrzyński, M. *Dzieje Polski w zarysie.* 3rd ed. Cracow, 1890. 2 vols.
Brüggen, Ernst, Freiherr von der. *Polens Auflösung. Kulturgeschichtliche Skizzen aus den letzten Jahrzehnten der polnischen Selbständigkeit.* Leipsic, 1878.
Cleinow, George. *Die Zukunft Polens.* Leipsic, 1908–14. 2 vols.
Dębicki, Ludwik. *Puławy (1762–1830). Monografia z życia towarzystkiego, politycznego i literackiego na podstawie archiwum ks. Czartoryskich w Krakowie.* Lemberg, 1887–88. 4 vols.
Dembiński, Bronisław. "Mission diplomatique de Félix Oraczewski, résident polonais à Paris pendant la révolution (1791–1792)." In *Bulletin*

International de l'Académie des Sciences de Cracovie. Comptes rendus des séances de l'année 1900, pp. 380–385.

Dembiński, Bronisław. "Piattoli et son rôle pendant la Grande Diète (1788–1792)." In *Bulletin International de l'Académie des Sciences de Cracovie, Classe de Philologie*, etc., *Année 1905*, pp. 53–64.

Dmowski, R. *La Question polonaise.* Traduction du polonais par V. Gasztowtt. Paris, 1909.

Górski, K. *Historya piechoty polskiej.* Cracow, 1893.

Hötzsch, O. "Der Stand der polnischen Verfassungsgeschichte." In *Zeitschrift für osteuropäische Geschichte*, i (1911), pp. 67–83.

—— "Staatenbildung und Verfassungsentwicklung in der Geschichte des germanisch-slavischen Ostens." *Ibid.*, i, pp. 363–412.

Hofman, K. B. *Historya reform politycznych w dawnej Polsce.* 2nd ed. Leipsic, 1869.

Hüppe, Siegfried. *Verfassung der Republik Polen.* Berlin, 1867.

Kadlec, Karel. "Ústavní dějiny Polska podle nových bádání." In *Časopis Musea Královstvi Českého*, lxxxii (1908), pp. 40–66, 241–250, 436–454.

Kalinka, W. *Der vierjährige polnische Reichstag, 1788 bis 1791.* Aus dem Polnischen übersetzte deutsche Originalausgabe. Berlin, 1896–98. 2 vols.

—— *Ostatnie lata panowania Stanisława Augusta.* 2nd ed. Cracow, 1891. 2 vols. (The second contains very valuable documents.)

Klotz, Justine. *L'Œuvre législative de la Diète de 4 Ans.* Paris, 1913.

Konopczyński, Władysław. *Polska w dobie wojny siedmioletniej.* Warsaw, 1908–11. (Forms vols. vii, viii, and xvi of Professor Askenazy's *Monografii w zakresie dziejów nowożytnych.*)

Korzon, T. *Kościuszko.* 2nd ed. Cracow, 1906.

—— "Początki sejmu wielkiego." In *Ateneum*, 1881[1].

—— *Wewnętrzne dzieje Polski za Stanisława Augusta, 1764–1794: badania historyczne ze stanowiska ekonomicznego i administracyjnego.* 2nd ed. Cracow, 1897–98. 6 vols. *Zamknięcie.* Lemberg, 1899.

Kraszewski, J. I. *Polska w czasie trzech rozbiorów.* Warsaw, 1902–03. 3 vols.

Kutrzeba, Stanisław. *Historya ustroju Polski w zarysie. Tom I. Korona.* 3rd ed. Lemberg, 1912.

Leblond, M. A. *La Pologne vivante.* Paris, 1910.

Lehtonen, U. L. *Die polnischen Provinzen Russlands unter Katharina II in den Jahren 1772–1782.* Aus dem finnischen Original übersetzt von Gustav Schmidt. Berlin, 1907.

Lelewel, Joachim. *Histoire de Pologne.* Paris, 1844. 2 vols.

Morawski, T. *Dzieje narodu polskiego.* Posen, 1875–77. 6 vols.

Niewenglowski, D. C. *Les Idées politiques et l'esprit public en Pologne à la fin du xviiie siècle.* Paris, 1901.

Olszewicz, V. "L'Évolution de la constitution polonaise." In *Revue des Sciences Politiques*, 1911, pp. 610–619.

Pamiętnik drugiego zjazdu historyków polskich we Lwowie. Tom I. Referaty. Lemberg, 1890.

Pamiętnik trzeciego zjazdu historyków polskich w Krakowie. Tom I. Referaty. Craćow, 1900.

Pawiński, Adolf. *Rządy sejmikowe w epoce królów elekcyjnych.* Warsaw, 1888. (Forms vol. i of his five-volume work *Dzieje ziemi kujawskiej.*)

—— *Sejmiki ziemskie. Początek ich i rozwój aż do ustalenia się udziału posłów ziemskich w ustawodawstwie sejmu walnego, 1374–1505.* Warsaw, 1895.

Piekosiński, F. " Wiece, sejmiki, sejmy i przywileje ziemskie w Polsce wieków średnich." In *Rozprawy Akademii Umiejętności w Krakowie, Wyd. hist.-fil.,* serya *II.,* xiv (1900), pp. 177–251.

Pilat, Roman. *O literaturze politycznej sejmu czteroletniego.* Cracow, 1872.

Popiel, Paweł. *Powstanie i upadek konstytucyi 3. maja (według dokumentów oryginalnych).* Cracow, 1901.

Prochaska, A. " Geneza i rozwój parlamentaryzmu za pierwszych Jagiellonów." In *Rozpr. Akad. Umiej. w Krakowie, Wyd. hist.-fil.,* serya *II.,* xiii (1899), pp. 1–184.

Rembowski, A. *Konfederacya i rokosz. Porównanie stanowych konstytucyi państw europejskich z ustrojem Rzeczypospolitéj polskiéj.* 2nd ed. Warsaw, 1896.

—— " Reprezentacya stanowa w Polsce." In *Biblioteka Warszawska,* 1893[1], pp. 1–40.

—— " Stany Rzeczypospolitéj polskiéj w znaczeniu prawne-państwowem." *Ibid.,* 1892[iv], pp. 417–441.

—— " Studya nad sejmem Rzeczypospolitéj polskiéj." *Ibid.,* 1893[iii], pp. 288–311.

Roepell, R. *Polen um die Mitte des achtzehnten Jahrhunderts.* Gotha, 1874.

—— " Zur Genesis der Verfassung Polens vom 3. Mai 1791." In *Historische Zeitschrift,* lxvi (1891), pp. 1–52.

Schmitt, Henryk. *Dzieje Polski xviii i xix wieku.* Cracow, 1866–68. 4 vols.

Seraphim, August. *Die Geschichte des Herzogtums Kurland (1561–1795).* 2nd ed. Reval, 1904.

Smoleński, Władysław. *Konfederacya targowicka.* Cracow, 1903.

—— *Ostatni rok sejmu wielkiego.* Cracow, 1897.

—— *Pisma historyczne.* Cracow, 1901. 3 vols.

—— *Przewrót umysłowy w Polsce wieku xviii. Studya historyczne.* Cracow, 1891.

Smolka, S. " Geneza konstytucyi 3. maja." In *Bulletin International de l'Académie des Sciences de Cracovie. Comptes rendus des séances de l'année 1891,* pp. 350–354.

Sokołowski, A. and Inlender, Adolf. *Dzieje Polski illustrowane.* Vienna, 1896–1901. 4 vols.

Solov'ev (German Ssolowjoff), S. *Geschichte des Falles von Polen (nach russischen Quellen).* Uebersetzt von J. Spörer. Gotha, 1865.

Soplica, T. *Wojna polsko-rosyjska 1792 r. Tom I. Kampania koronna.* Cracow, 1906.

Studnicki, Wł. *Sprawa polska.* Posen, 1910.

Sulimierski, F., and others. *Słownik geograficzny królewstwa polskiego i innych krajów słowiańskich.* Warsaw, 1880–1902. 15 tom.

Szujski, Józef. Dzieje Polski. Cracow, 1882–94. 4 vols.

Waliszewski, K. *Potoccy i Czartoryscy. Walka stronnictw i programów politycznych przed upadkiem Rzpltej, 1735–1763.* Cracow, 1887.

Wegner, Leon. *Dzieje dnia trzeciego i piątego maja 1791.* Posen, 1865.

—— *Sejm grodzieński. Ostatni ustęp od 26. sierpnia do 23. września 1793.* Posen, 1866.

Zaleski, Bronisław. "Korespondencya krajowa Stanisława Augusta." In *Rocznik Towarzystwa Historyczno-Literackiego w Paryżu, rok 1870–72,* pp. 147–402.

—— *Żywot Ks. Adama Jerziego Czartoryskiego. Tom I.* Posen, 1881.

Иловайскій, Д. Гродненскій сеймъ 1793 году: послѣдній сеймъ Ржечи-посполитой. Moscow, 1870.

Карѣевъ, Н. Паденіе Польши въ исторической литературѣ. St. Petersburg, 1888.

—— Польскія реформы xviiiвѣка. St. Petersburg, 1890.

—— Историческій очеркъ польскаго сейма. Moscow, 1888.

Костомаровъ, Н. Н. Послѣдніе годы Рѣчи-Посполитой. 3rd ed. St. Petersburg, 1886. 2 vols.

(c) *Works Relating More Particularly to Russia*

Aragon, Louis, Marquis d'. *Un Paladin au xviiie siècle. Le Prince Charles de Nassau-Siegen. D'après sa correspondance originale inédite de 1784 à 1789.* Paris, 1893.

Askenazy, S. "Przyczynek do krytyki depesz M. M. Alopeusza." In *Kwartalnik Historyczny,* xvii (1903), pp. 530–543.

Bilbasov, V. A. *Geschichte Katharina II.* (Uebersetzung aus dem Russischen von M. v. Pezold.) Berlin, 1891–93. 4 parts in 3 vols.

—— *Katharina II Kaiserin von Russland im Urtheile der Weltliteratur.* (Autorisirte Uebersetzung aus dem Russichen, mit einem Vorwort von Dr. Theodor Schiemann.) Berlin, 1897. 2 vols.

Blum, K. L. *Ein russischer Staatsmann. Des Grafen Jakob Johann Sievers Denkwürdigkeiten zur Geschichte Russlands.* Leipsic and Heidelberg, 1857–58. 4 vols.

Brückner, Alexander and Mettig, C. *Geschichte Russlands bis zum Ende des 18. Jahrhunderts.* Gotha, 1896–1913. 2 vols.

Brückner, Alexander. *Katharina II.* Berlin, 1883.

—— "Neue Beiträge zur Geschichte der Regierung Katharina II." In *Historische Zeitschrift,* lviii (1887), pp. 279–309.

Caro, Jakob. *Katharina II von Russland.* Berlin, 1876.

Daudet, Ernest. *Les Bourbons et la Russie pendant la Révolution française.* Paris, 1886.

Dembiński, Bronisław. *Rosya a rewolucya francuska.* Cracow, 1896.

—— "W sprawie krytyki korespondencyi dyplomatycznej." In *Kwartalnik Historyczny,* xviii (1904), pp. 32–46.

Herrmann, Ernst. *Geschichte des russischen Staates.* (Forms vols. iii–vi of the work begun by Philipp Strahl in the series *Geschichte der europäischen Staaten*.) Hamburg and Gotha, 1846–60. *Ergänzungsband. Diplomatische Correspondenz aus der Revolutionszeit*. Gotha, 1867.

Larivière, Charles de. *Catherine II et la Révolution française, d'après de nouveaux documents*. Paris, 1895.

Liske, X. " Beiträge zur Geschichte der Kaniower Zusammenkunft 1787 und ihrer Vorläufer." In *Russische Revue*, iv (1874), pp. 481–508.

—— " Zur Charakteristik Katharina II." In *Historische Zeitschrift*, xxxix (1878), pp. 230–240.

—— " Zur Geschichte der letzten Jahre der Republik Polen." *Ibid.*, xxi (1869), pp. 25–73.

Smitt, Friedrich von. *Suworow und Polens Untergang*. Leipsic, etc., 1858. 2 vols.

Stein, F. von. *Geschichte des russischen Heeres*. Hanover, 1885.

Sybel, Heinrich von. " Katharina II von Russland." In his *Kleine historische Schriften*, i (1869), pp. 147–177. Munich.

Waliszewski, K. *Autour d'un trône. Catherine II de Russie, ses collaborateurs*. Paris, 1894.

—— *Le Roman d'une impératrice. Catherine II de Russie*. Paris, 1893.

Бильбасовъ, В. А. Памяти Императрицы Екатерины II. Русская Старина, lxxxviii (1896), pp. 241–280.

—— Присоединеніе Курляндіи. *Ibid.*, lxxxiii (1895), pp. 3–55.

Брикнеръ, Александръ. Война Россіи съ Швеціей въ 1788–1790 г. St. Petersburg, 1869.

—— Потемкинъ. St. Petersburg, 1891.

Гротъ, Я. К. Екатерина II и Густавъ III. St. Petersburg, 1877.

Григоровичъ, Н. И. Канцлеръ князь Безбородко. Опытъ обработки матеріаловъ для его біографіи. Русскій Архивъ, 1874–77, and Сборникъ Имп. Рус. Ист. Общ., xxvi and xxxix.

Князь Г. А. Потемкинъ-Таврическій. Біографическій очеркъ. Русская Старина, xii (1875), pp. 481–522, 681–700; xiii, pp. 20–40, 159–174; xiv, pp. 217–267.

Князь Платонъ Александровичъ Зубовъ. Историко-біографическій очеркъ. *Ibid.*, xvi (1876), pp. 591–606; xvii, pp. 39–52, 437–462, 690–726.

Петровъ, А. Н. Вторая турецкая война въ царствованіе Императрицы Екатерины II. St. Petersburg, 1880. 2 vols.

Петрушевскій, А. Генералисимусъ кн. Суворовъ. St. Petersburg, 1900.

Пыпинъ, А. Н. Исторія русской этнографіи. St. Petersburg, 1890–92. 4 vols.

Соловьевъ, С. М. Исторія Россіи съ древнѣйшихъ временъ. Изд. Товарищества "Общественная Польза." St. Petersburg, 1893. 6 vols.

Чечулинъ, Н. Д. Внѣшняя политика Россіи въ началѣ царствованія Екатерины II, *1762–1774*. St. Petersburg, 1896.

Щебальскій, П. Русская политика въ Польшѣ до Екатерины II. Moscow, 1864.

(d) Works Relating More Particularly to Prussia

Bailleu, Paul. " Der Ursprung des deutschen Fürstenbundes." In *Historische Zeitschrift*, xli (1879), pp. 410-434.
—— " Graf Hertzberg." *Ibid.*, xlii (1879), pp. 442-490.
—— " Herzog Karl August, Goethe, und die ungarische Königskrone." In *Goethe-Jahrbuch*, xx (1899), pp. 144-152.
—— " König Friedrich Wilhelm II und die Genesis des Friedens von Basel." In *Historische Zeitschrift*, lxxv (1895), pp. 237-275.
—— " Zur Vorgeschichte der Revolutionskriege." *Ibid.*, lxxiv (1895), pp. 259-262.
Bülow, Prince Bernhard von. *Imperial Germany.* London, etc., 1914.
Damus, R. " Die Stadt Danzig gegenüber der Politik Friedrichs des Grossen und Friedrich Wilhelms II." In *Zeitschrift des westpreussischen Geschichtsvereins, Heft xx* (1887).
Droysen, J. G. *Geschichte der preussischen Politik.* Leipsic, 1868-86 (partly in 2nd ed.). 5 parts in 14 vols.
Duncker, M. *Aus der Zeit Friedrich des Grossen und Friedrich Wilhelms III.* Leipsic, 1876.
—— " Friedrich Wilhelm II und Graf Hertzberg." In *Historische Zeitschrift* xxxvii (1877), pp. 1-43.
Flammermont, Jules. *Négociations secrètes de Louis XVI et du baron de Breteuil avec la cour de Berlin, décembre, 1791-juillet, 1792.* Paris. 1885.
Förster, Friedrich. *Friedrich Wilhelm I, König von Preussen.* Potsdam 1834-35. 3 vols.
Heidrich, Kurt. *Preussen im Kampfe gegen die französische Revolution bis zur zweiten Teilung Polens.* Stuttgart and Berlin, 1908.
Hüffer, Hermann. *Die Kabinetsregierung in Preussen und Johann Wilhelm Lombard.* Leipsic, 1891.
Koser, Reinhold. *König Friedrich der Grosse.* Stuttgart and Berlin, 1893-1903. 2 vols.
—— " Aus dem ersten Regierungsjahre Friedrich Wilhelms II." In *Forschungen zur brandenburgischen und preussichen Geschichte*, iv (1891), pp. 593-605.
—— " Die preussische Politik von 1786 bis 1806." In *Deutsche Monatschrift für das gesamte Leben der Gegenwart*, xi (1907), pp. 453-480, 612-637.
Krauel, R. *Graf Hertzberg als Minister Friedrich Wilhelms II.* Berlin, 1899.
—— *Prinz Heinrich von Preussen als Politiker.* Berlin, 1902. (*Quellen und Untersuchungen zur Geschichte des Hauses Hohenzollern*, iv.)
Lehmann, Max. *Friedrich der Grosse und der Ursprung des siebenjährigen Krieges.* Leipsic, 1894.
Luckwaldt, Friedrich. " Zur Vorgeschichte der Konvention von Reichenbach: Englischer Einfluss am Hofe Friedrich Wilhelms II." In *Delbrück-Festschrift* (1908), pp. 232-256.

Naudé, Albert. " Der preussische Staatsschatz unter König Friedrich Wilhelm II und seine Erschöpfung." In *Forschungen zur brandenburgischen und preussischen Geschichte*, v (1892), pp. 203–256.

—— "Die brandenburg-preussische Getreidehandelspolitik von 1713–1806." In Schmoller's *Jahrbuch für Gesetzgebung, Verwaltung und Volkswirtschaft im Deutschen Reiche, N. F.*, xxix[i] (1905), pp. 161–190.

Philippson, Martin. *Geschichte des preussischen Staatswesens vom Tode Friedrichs des Grossen bis zu den Freiheitskriegen.* Leipsic, 1880–82. 2 vols.

Reimann, Eduard. *Neuere Geschichte des preussischen Staates vom Hubertusburger Frieden bis zum Wiener Kongress.* Gotha, 1882–88. 2 vols.

Ritter, Paul. *Die Konvention von Reichenbach (27. Juli 1790).* Berlin, 1898.

Sevin, Ludwig. *Das System der preussischen Geheimpolitik vom August 1790 bis zum Mai 1791.* Berlin, 1903.

Süssheim, Karl. *Preussens Politik in Ansbach-Bayreuth 1791 bis 1806.* Berlin, 1902.

Unzer, Adolf. *Hertzbergs Anteil an den preussisch-österreichischen Verhandlungen, 1778–79.* Frankfort, 1890.

Volz, G. B. " Prinz Heinrich von Preussen und die preussische Politik vor der ersten Teilung Polens." In *Forschungen zur brandenburgischen und preussischen Geschichte*, xviii (1905), pp. 151–201.

—— " Friedrich der Grosse und die erste Teilung Polens." *Ibid.*, xxiii (1910), pp. 71–143, 225 f.

Welschinger, Henri. *La Mission secrète de Mirabeau à Berlin (1786–1787).* Paris, 1900.

Wittichen, F. C. " Die Politik des Grafen Hertzberg, 1785–90." In *Historische Vierteljahrschrift*, ix (1906), pp. 174–204.

—— *Preussen und England in der europäischen Politik, 1785–1788.* Heidelberg, 1902.

—— " Zur Vorgeschichte der Revolutionskriege." In *Forschungen zur brandenburgischen und preussischen Geschichte*, xvii (1904), pp. 253–262.

Wittichen, Paul. *Die polnische Politik Preussens 1788–90.* Göttingen, 1899.

(e) *Works Relating More Particularly to Austria*

Beer, Adolf. *Die orientalische Politik Oesterreichs seit 1774.* Prague, etc., 1883.

Genelin, Placid. *Leopolds II äussere Politik.* Programm, Trieste, 1883.

Herrmann, Ernst. " Die polnische Politik Kaiser Leopolds II." In *Forschungen zur deutschen Geschichte*, iv (1864), pp. 385–438.

[Hormayr, Joseph von.] *Lebensbilder aus dem Befreiungskriege. Ernst Friedrich Graf von Münster.* 2nd ed. Jena, 1845. 3 vols.

Kalinka, W. " Polityka dworu austryackiego w sprawie konstytucyi 3. maja." In *Przegląd Polski*, 1873[i].

Krones, Franz. *Ungarn unter Maria Theresia und Joseph II, 1740–1790.* Graz, 1871.

Langwerth von Simmern, Baron Heinrich. *Oesterreich und das deutsche Reich im Kampfe mit der französischen Revolution.* Berlin, 1880. 2 vols.

Sybel, Heinrich von. "Kaiser Leopold II. Gegen Ernst Herrmann."
In *Historische Zeitschrift*, x (1863), pp. 387–432.
—— "Noch einmal über Leopold II gegen E. Herrmann." *Ibid.*, xii (1864),
pp. 260–283.
Wolf, A. *Oesterreich unter Maria Theresia, Josef II und Leopold II.* Berlin, 1883.
Wolfsgruber, Cölestin. *Franz I, Kaiser von Oesterreich.* Vienna and Leipsic, 1899. 2 vols.
Zeissberg, Heinrich von. *Erzherzog Carl von Oesterreich.* Vienna and Leipsic, 1895.
—— "Erzherzog Carl von Oesterreich und Prinz Hohenlohe-Kirchberg.
Ein Beitrag zur Geschichte des Feldzuges in die Champagne." In
Archiv für österreichische Geschichte, lxxiii (1888), pp. 1–77.

(f) Works Relating More Particularly to Other States

Askenazy, S. "Upadek Polski a Francya." In *Biblioteka Warszawska*,
1913[i], pp. 1–35, 209–262.
Aulard, A. *Études et leçons sur la Révolution française.* Paris, 1893—.
7 vols. (to 1913).
Baehrendtz, F. J. "Om Sveriges förhållande till Ryssland under Konung
Gustaf IV Adolfs förmyndarstyrelse." In *Historiskt Bibliotek utgifvet af Carl Silfverstolpe*, vii (1880), pp. 251–286, 507–530.
Barral Montferrat, Dominique, Marquis de. *Dix Ans de paix armée entre
la France et l'Angleterre, 1783–1793.* Ier tome. Paris, 1893.
(No more published.)
Baumgarten, Hermann. *Geschichte Spaniens zur Zeit der französischen
Revolution.* Berlin, 1861.
Blok, P. J. *Geschiedenis van het Nederlandsche Volk.* Groningen, 1892–1908.
8 vols.
Boethius, S. J. "Gustaf IV Adolfs förmyndareregering och Franska Revolutionen." In *Historisk Tidskrift*, 1888, pp. 95–130, 177–230.
Chuquet, A. *La Campagne de l'Argonne* (1792). Paris, 1886.
Flassan, G. R., Comte de. *Histoire générale et raisonnée de la diplomatie
française.* 2nd ed. Paris, 1811. 7 vols.
Flathe, Theodor. *Die Verhandlungen über die dem Kurfürsten Friedrich
August III von Sachsen angebotene Thronfolge in Polen und der sächsische Geheime Legationsrath von Essen.* Meissen, 1870.
—— "Die Verhandlungen über Sachsens Neutralität, 1790." In *Archiv
für sächsische Geschichte*, ix (1871), pp. 165–192.
Geffroy, Auguste. *Gustave III et la Cour de France.* Paris, 1867. 2 vols.
Goetz-Bernstein, Hans Alfred. *La Diplomatie de la Gironde.* Paris,
1912.
Grosjean, Georges. "La Mission de Sémonville à Constantinople." In
La Révolution Française, xii (1887), pp. 888–921.
Handelsman, M. "La Constitution polonaise du 3 mai 1791 et l'opinion
française." *Ibid.*, lviii (1910), pp. 411–434.
Holm, Edvard. *Danmark-Norges udenrigske historie under den Franske*

Revolution og Napoleons krige fra 1791 til 1807. Copenhagen, 1875. 2 vols.

Jorga, Néculai. *Geschichte des osmanischen Reiches.* Gotha, 1908–13. 5 vols.

Lecky, W. E. H. *A History of England in the Eighteenth Century.* London, 1878–90. 8 vols.

Lemontey, Pierre-Édouard. *Essai sur l'établissement monarchique de Louis XIV.* Paris, 1818.

Marichalar, Amalio, Marqués de Montesa, and Manrique, Cayetano. *Historia de la legislacion y recitaciones del derecho civil de España.* Madrid, 1861–72. 9 vols.

Muriel, Andrés. *Historia de Carlos IV.* Madrid, 1893–94. 6 vols. (*Memorial Histórico Español*, vols. xxix–xxxiv.)

Odhner, C. T. " Gustaf III och Katarina efter freden i Wärälä." In *Svenska Akademiens Handlingar ifrån år 1886*, ix (1894), pp. 145–208.

Pella y Forgas, Joseph. *Llibertats y antich govern de Catalunya.* Barcelona, 1905.

Pétiet, René. *Gustave IV Adolphe et la Révolution française: Relations diplomatiques de la France et de la Suède de 1792 à 1810, d'après des documents d'archives inédits.* Paris, 1914.

Pingaud, Léonce. *Choiseul-Gouffier. La France en Orient sous Louis XVI.* Paris, 1887.

Pölitz, K. H. L. *Die Regierung Friedrich Augusts, Königs von Sachsen.* Leipsic, 1830. 2 vols.

Rose, J. Holland. *William Pitt and National Revival.* London, 1911.

—— *William Pitt and the Great War.* London, 1911.

Salomon, Felix. *Das politische System des jüngeren Pitt und die zweite Teilung Polens.* Berlin, 1895.

—— *William Pitt der Jüngere.* Erster Band. Leipsic, etc., 1906.

[Schinkel, B. von.] *Minnen ur Sveriges nyare historia.* (Samlade af B. von Schinkel, författade och utgifne af C. W. Bergman.) Stockholm, 1855–81. 12 vols. *Bihang.* (Utgifvet af S. J. Boethius.) 1880–83. 3 vols.

Schrepfer, Rudolf. *Pfalzbayerns Politik im Revolutionszeitalter von 1789–1793.* Nuremberg, 1903.

Stanhope, Philip Henry Stanhope, fifth Earl of. *Life of William Pitt.* London, 1861–62. 4 vols.

Wahrenberg, C. F. I. " Bidrag till historien om Konung Gustaf III⁵ sednaste regeringsår." In *Tidskrift för Litteratur, utgifven af C. F. Bergstedt*, 1851, pp. 321–365.

Zinkeisen, J. W. *Geschichte des osmanischen Reiches in Europa.* Gotha, 1840–63. 7 vols.

INDEX

INDEX